paradigms
and promises

paradigms and promises

New Approaches
to Educational
Administration

William Foster

PROMETHEUS BOOKS

Buffalo, New York 14215

Published 1986 by Prometheus Books
700 East Amherst Street, Buffalo, New York 14215

Library of Congress Cataloging-in-Publication Data

Foster, William, 1945-
    Paradigms and promises.

    (Frontiers of education)
    Bibliography: p.
    Includes index.
    1. School management and organization.
2. Universities and colleges—Administration.
3. Organizational change. 4. Organizational
effectiveness. I. Title. II. Series.
LB2805.F62   1986   371.2   86-18749
ISBN 0-87975-351-X
ISBN 0-87975-366-8 (pbk.)

Printed in the United States of America

Frontiers of Education

Series Editor: Philip G. Altbach

Other titles in the series:

Higher Education in American Society
edited by Philip G. Altbach and Robert O. Berdahl

Excellence in Education
edited by Philip G. Altbach, Gail P. Kelly, and Lois Weis

The American University:
Problems, Prospects, and Trends
edited by Jan H. Blits

Contents

Introduction

In recent times the twin fields of organizational theory and administrative theory have become unsettled. The scientific rigor of each has been questioned, and the ability of each to meaningfully contribute to the understanding of human affairs has been disputed. Indeed, the current tendency in organizational and administrative theory is to turn away from the technical and technological emphases so characteristic of the management and organizational sciences, in favor of the development of a culturally relevant approach that builds on two irreducible features of human life: culture and politics.

The science of administration, as developed in this century, demonstrates an insensitivity to culture and politics. Instead, the science of administration attempts to abstract from something called "administrative behavior" sets of regularities, predictions, and lawlike statements that crush any more subtle distinctions about the nature of organization and administration. The science of administration, and much of organizational theory, has really been a science of management: how managers can set in motion certain technical procedures that result in the satisfactory performance and increased motivation of employees. A short examination of the topics of almost any introductory text in educational administration would bear this out; culture, politics, morals, and ethics receive, at best, scant attention.

This is hardly adequate for an administration that sees or-

9

ganizations as both social and moral orders—social institutions that constrain and influence our lives as almost nothing else does. For example, the school as a social institution has tremendous impact on an individual's life. School is more than simply a class to attend or a degree to attain; rather it is a living statement of culture and of values that forms a part of the consciousness of every social member. The administration of education is perhaps one of society's most central concerns; yet when administrative programs neglect social analysis, they neglect the possibility of choosing a more attractive future. This text intends to present the reflective administrative student with a set of issues, concerns, and problems that have been sorely neglected in standard fare.

Orthodox accounts of administrative theory systematically exclude a body of scholarship because it does not suscribe to a positivistic way of viewing the universe. This scholarship is critical in its efforts, examining the basic assumptions of administrative theory and linking it to the practice that evolves. We present here, then, just such a critically informed theory of administration, one that attempts to link administrative practice to social and cultural issues. Its foundational assumption is that administration, particularly educational administration, involves the alignment of people in an educative and transformative fashion. In addition to controlling the empire through controlling the budget, administration makes a statement of values and possibilities. An administrator must deal with technical issues, of course, but these can be learned adequately and possibly more effectively on the job, through hands-on experience, working with other administrators, and attending in-service sessions. The meat of the administrator's work is not the technical aspect of management; rather, it involves the establishment of a community and a culture within an organization and the development of an organization's self-reflective ability to analyze its purpose and goals.

As might be apparent, this books adopts a perspective informed by a critical social theory. We view administration and education in the context of wider social arrangements and attempt to reflectively comment on the relationships that obtain between these elements. How does administration contribute to the type of society we have? In what ways does it impede or enhance our cultural ideals and values? These are the difficult

Just what the Catholic schools should do

questions, yet if they are never asked (and too often they are not), our administration and our patterns of education will remain in the same rut that has led to a crisis of confidence in education and schooling.

Such a crisis manifests itself in a number of ways, but none is more poignant than the everyday erosion in the self-image of teachers and administrators. When various commission reports, studies of schooling, and proposals for reform appear in an unrelenting wave, they cannot but help undermine confidence. These reports and studies point to the alarming inadequacies of our educational system, from elementary grades through university preparation. They cite the number of drop-outs, the misuse of time, the weakened curriculum, and the decline in revered test scores. While these studies are critical, they are also strangely unreflective, with an underlying reluctance to explore the causes of school failure or to put the school experience into the context of larger social relations. Often, spending more time in school is equated with getting better results, but this type of thinking ignores the fact that schooling and administration occur in a wider context, one that needs its own critical analysis. Calling for excellence without concurrently analyzing social conditions is simply blowing in the wind.

A prime concern, then, of this presentation is the critical analysis of both administration and education that is a basic ingredient for reform. A critical analysis, in turn, is premised on an understanding of the relationship of theory to practice. Educational and other administrators are distinguished by their commitment to practice: it is what they live and breathe. Many claim that they have an innate reluctance to deal with theory; for theory, after all, is only theory. The argument that what we study in a university setting has only the remotest relevance to what we do has some truth: many times what we study is but a sterile reflection of the real world. Yet, it can be noted that all practice derives from theory, whether that theory is intuitively developed over the course of a career or more formally developed through courses of study.

In this text, we do not use the word "theory" as it is defined in administrative texts or in research classes, that is, as a formalistic set of propositions that, when verified, produces laws of behavior. This definition assumes that verifiable laws of human behavior are possible. This text argues that such an assumption is an unthinking translation of physical science to human action. Human action occurs in a historical context that is ever being formed anew; given this context, laws that predict human behavior can only be so trivial as not to warrant mention. Another assumption—that theory exists in some kind of atemporal sphere, untouched by human action or emotion—must also be questioned, because not only does theory inform practice, but practice must inform theory. Each exists in a dialectical relationship to the other. What we do must affect how we think. In turn, practice— all practice—derives from some kind of theory about how the world operates. Thus, we use theory to mean a way of seeing, a perspective on the world, a means for putting together the disparate events of our life in a meaningful fashion. When we refer to practice, we mean the activities and actions of our theoretician, what he does to give form to ideas. The relationship is ongoing and dependent, in the sense that one presupposes and demands the other. What we do depends on how we see, and how we see depends on what we have done.

Theory

Practice

Thus, theory *is* important: in our usage it provides a way of seeing. More importantly, administrators who have more ways of seeing—more theories—accessible to them also have more available options and choices for practical action. By providing alternative theories we provide alternative perspectives and ways of seeing. In doing this, we provide the possibility of a more reflective practice, one that combines theoretical insights with practical action.

This text presents much theory in its selection of different ways of seeing. Its readers are expected to be professors and students of administration and education, and those simply interested in the philosophy and sociology of administration and organization. The theories cover Marxist and neo-Marxist perspectives, as well as more orthodox approaches to educational, administrative, and organizational analysis. In a sense, the text can be read in two ways: a presentation of traditional ideas in the field of administration (largely, but not exclusively, educational administration), and a critical appraisal of those ideas.

This text is premised on a dialectical concept: that human affairs are not entirely predictable; that discourse and analysis are inevitable and desirable; that there is no *one* best system;

that we are in a constant state of evolution and change. Critical analysis, as pursued in each chapter, is an essential part of our human development. There are competing theories and competing practices, and it is our role as administrators, individuals of action, to sort among them in order to come up with strategies and courses of action that do justice to our values and beliefs. A critical theory is necessary: it encourages us to view events in historical perspective, to doubt the validity of received truth (at least in how we manage our human affairs), and to contine our search for more adequate solutions to our problems. Critical theory, as used here, means just that. No solution is presented, only the suggestion that the effort is worth the energy. No recipe for action is given, only the idea that action is needed and valued. No formula is proffered, only the clue that change occurs through reflective consideration of ideas. All theories, all constructs, all practices are open to critical reflection. No one individual, no one school of thought is privy to the secrets of the universe. Orthodox administrative theory, as this is developed through a positivistic and functionalistic analysis, receives heavy criticism in this text; this does not mean, however, that neo-Marxist and other schools of thought are immune: they, too, make assumptions and have world views that need a critical response.

Thus, the material presented to the administrator and the student of administration in this volume is intended to challenge and to question. It attempts to motivate the aspiring administrator and the established student of administration in education to reconsider, for a moment, cherished assumptions and ways of thinking. It is designed, finally, to give a larger social context to the idea of administration; indeed, to say that if we are in control of organizations, particularly those significant and meaningful organizations designed to educate our youth, then we should consider the broader, major questions of a society that is located in a particular time and a particular space. We are historically situated and what we do, even in the smallest space and time, does have significance.

James March, a well-respected, innovative, and thoughtful organizational theorist and educator, has observed that "Any effort to improve American education by changing its organization or administration must begin with skepticism. Changing education by changing educational administration is like changing the

March

course of the Mississippi by spitting into the Allegheny" (1978, 219). We are not exactly out to prove him wrong; we do suggest that the various and varied models of administration so far available have been premised on assumptions that would indeed prove him right. Models of change in organizations have been premised on rationalistic fantasies of how change occurs: set up a planning committee, develop strategies, convince gatekeepers, and implement the change. This has not worked, largely because change does not occur in such a planned and rational fashion. Culture, symbols, rituals, and even political statements are all a part of the change process. Leadership occupies a similar theoretical vacuum: leadership is treated as the management of small groups— the manager's implementation of strategies designed to improve group cohesion or group productivity. But this is not leadership; in reality it is the attempt to disguise managerial functions under the rubric of leadership, in the hope that workers will acquiesce to managerial directives. Leadership, we hope to show, is a much broader phenomenon. Organizational theories suffer the same fate, and these also need to be explored. Thus March's dictum is accurate in one sense: if we continue to view educational organizations in the standard way and refuse to place them within the context of the demands of a critical and social theory, our attempts to change them will indeed be like spitting into the Allegheny. We believe that administrators and students of education *can* generally make a difference, perhaps a slight one, but a difference nonetheless. But they can only make this difference by adopting different ways of seeing; clearly, the orthodox perspective of educational administration is deficient.

This text will attempt to demonstrate that the orthodox vision lacks certain crucial aspects. It provides us a certain, positivistic way of viewing school organizations as ahistorical constructs, givens in the social world, and subject to our presumably informed analysis. This theory neglects how each school can differ from the others, yet all can still, in some way, promulgate social values. *Whose* values do these schools distribute? Secondly, the orthodox perspective provides a particular model for administrative action, a model based, essentially, in business practice. While this may not be bad per se, it does raise some questions about the nature of the educational enterprise. In our society, business is oriented toward achieving a profit; what is the orientation of

Administration is leadership. It is Communication of possibilities. it is a way of communicating a view... and an empowerment of others.

education? In this text, we will claim that educational systems are fundamentally different, and that the type of managerial practices reserved for business enterprises are inadequate for what educators hope to accomplish. Yet much of educational administration depends entirely on a management and business model for its legitimation. Again, an examination of the literature in the field will show that private, profit-oriented firms, and the theory of such firms, provide much, if not all, the rationale for educational administration. We hope to provide an alternative that makes as much, if not more, sense to the administrator.

Finally, orthodox theory denigrates much of the leadership potential of administration. Administration is leadership. It is the communication of possibilities. In this sense, much of orthodox theory removes administration's ability to demand change, to revise the current way of doing things, to consider varied and different ways of approaching the same subject. Leadership, in our formulation, is not simply management: rather, it is a way of communicating a vision and an empowerment of others. Leadership lies not in the position *given*, but in the position *taken*.

In this text we hope to acquaint the administrative student with a different way of thinking about education and its administration and to suggest that administration as a field of study has come of age. The maturity of the field, however, requires its reconstruction as a moral science and as a critical science. To this end, this text contains two parts. The first part (chapters 1, 2, 3, 4, and 5) provides the foundations of a critical approach, examining the strengths and weaknesses of orthodox theory and providing an alternative conception based in critical social theory. It concludes with an analysis of the relationship of schooling to cultural reproduction, emphasizing the usefulness of this knowledge to administrative performance. The second part (chapters 6, 7, 8, and 9) examines some major topics in administration: organizations, leadership, and change. It provides both a conventional and a critical review of these topics. The last chapter proposes some strategies for administrative action that might help to implement the concerns of the entire text.

Thanks and acknowledgments are now in order. Part of this work was supported by a faculty research grant from the University of San Diego. I owe my appreciation to Dean Edward DeRoche for his support. I conducted the research for the chapter on leadership while I was writing a monograph on the same subject at Deakin University in Australia. My thanks to Richard Bates, a friend and source of many of the ideas in this text, John Smyth, and other members of the faculty at Deakin for their intellectual stimulation and personal support. I also wish to thank my colleague Joseph Rost for his critical help, and my colleagues and mentors Bruce Cooper and Steven Selden for their encouragement over the years. Phil Altbach provided the initial impetus to start this project; I was lucky to have him pushing and prodding until it was completed. Sincere thanks to Barbara Konie Bergstrom, who provided detailed editing of the text. She is a remarkable wordsmith who provided the coherence the text initially lacked. Finally, let me dedicate the text to my family: my mother, brother, Kit, Paul, Christine, and James.

1

Administration as a Moral Science

Partly for the purpose of defense and partly for the purpose of gain-
ing status the leaders in administration claimed the label "scientific"
for their accounting procedures. They were not equipped through
their training to ask or answer the really basic questions in educa-
tion. But they were energetic, capable men and they rushed into the
vacuum that existed and built an empire of professional courses on a
foundation of sand.

—Raymond E. Callahan, 1962.

What should a student of school administration study? Traditionally, there has been only one answer: practicing and future
administrators should study educational administration in order
to learn the scientific basis for decision making and to understand the scientific research that underlies proper administration.
Universities train future administrators with texts that stress the
scientific research done on administrative behavior, review various studies of teacher and student performance, and provide a
few techniques for accomplishing educational goals. Such approaches instill a reverence for the scientific method, but an un-
fortunate disregard for any humanistic and critical development
of the art of administration.

  This text takes a different approach: we essentially suggest
that administrators in educational settings are critical humanists.

humanist

They are humanists because they appreciate the usual and unusual events of our lives and engage in an effort to develop, challenge, and liberate human souls. They are critical because they

critical

are educators and are therefore not satisfied with the status quo;
rather, they hope to change individuals for the better and to improve social conditions for all. This text tries to build on this
heritage of practicing administrators by offering a new model of
educational administration based in a critical humanist tradition.
A scientific model of administration, to the degree that this depends on a positivist model of science, comes under attack here
because we feel that it inadequately considers the many social,
cultural, and educational issues in our society. We will consider
some radical evaluations of schooling sympathetically because
they offer a different perspective that might be of considerable
value to the administrator. We intend to provide the new school
administrator with a set of diverse and critical perspectives that
will help him or her to become a critical humanist.

Traditional locus of ed. ad.

Educational administration has been located within the social
sciences, as a subdivision of such disciplines as psychology, sociology, and, to a lesser extent, economics and political science.
Psychology, for example, added to the conceptual base of administration by addressing such issues as job satisfaction, motivation, climate, and leadership. Sociology contributed to the field by
referring to the concepts of roles and systems. This symbiotic
relationship with the social sciences was in turn guided by the
search for a "grand theory" of administration: a theoretical
framework that would explain and predict administrative behavior. Administrative scholars in this century have made an overriding effort to develop predictive laws of administrative and
organizational behavior; attempts to develop such theories of behavior continue today, though without much success.

Critical theory of locus of ed. adm

What happens to the field of educational administration when
the grand theory does not materialize? When the basic assumptions and frameworks of the major parent disciplines are themselves challenged? Then the study of educational administration
takes a completely new course and locates administration in
philosophy and history, as well as in the revised versions of the
traditional disciplines. This text explores this new approach, with
a particular emphasis on what it might mean for the practical
lives of individuals in a practical profession.

Administration, Hodgkinson (1978) reminds us, is "philosophy-in-action." This might be an unusual observation to make. Many administrators consider themselves somewhat removed from philosophical musings; they are concerned with the world of action, of doing, of maintaining a somewhat orderly system involving communications with superiors and subordinates, negotiations, and conflict. Yet this is the point exactly: philosophy involves a set of beliefs about how the world is structured, and administrators, knowingly or not, put those beliefs into practice. Whenever an administrator writes a memorandum or lifts a telephone, he or she acts on an underlying philosophy of administration, developed over time through experience and training. Reflection on the underlying assumptions and philosophy provides self-understanding and that, in turn, may provide a better administration.

ADMINISTRATION IN CONTEXT: THE LIBERAL-DEMOCRATIC STATE

Such reflection on the basic philosophies in administration depends on an appreciation of the nature of schools and the state. Effective administration is grounded in an understanding of some basic principles and problems of schools in our society. We wish to introduce some of these here in order to build a case for the viability of alternative perspectives on the administration of education. Schools are formal institutions, institutions that exist for a purpose. The purpose can be conceived of in short- or long-range terms. In the short range, schools (and administration) serve to educate a particular historical group in subject matter considered essential for success in the social world. That is, the administrator is concerned with running an organization where the instruction of identifiable groups of students occurs. In the long run the staff of a public school engages in the perpetuation of a way of life, and possibly in the improvement of that way of life, for the countless individuals who go through the system. Because of this, it is important for the administrator to be aware of the foundations of *this* historical system and of the role of the school in maintaining it.

Western-style democracies are liberal societies. They represent *political liberalism*

Strike

a tradition of liberal thought that can be traced back to the decline of medieval society and the emergence of English and continental scholarship. All modern Western states are essentially founded on a model of political liberalism. Strike, a contemporary liberal philosopher, outlines the central concerns and foundations of a liberal ideology:

> 1. Liberals assume that knowledge is a function of experience, not authority, and that individuals have the competence and duty to be rationally autonomous. 2. Liberals assume that there are limits on social authority and that there is a private sphere of beliefs and conduct over which the individual should exercise autonomy. 3. Liberals assume that social privilege and authority are neither natural nor inheritable. Social position must be earned and authority must be justified. (Strike 1982, 3)

Liberal ideology is thus concerned with some concepts basic to our society: individualism, rationality, equality, and privacy. Clearly, both liberal and conservative political preferences are but variants of a general theory of liberalism in the state.

Liberal ideology and practical problems

The analysis of the liberal state is important for educational and other administrators because it raises some fundamental dilemmas about schooling and the state in our time. For example, a liberal philosophy would support a democratic form of government wherein the authority of the governors rests on the consent of the governed; yet modern states have become increasingly bureaucratic in their administration, with authority deriving from expertise. A liberal philosophy would support an individualistic rationality that makes choices on the best evidence. This, however, tends to erode such social institutions as the church and the family that base choices on tradition. A liberal philosophy would support the equality of all, yet private ownership of property leads to a system of economic inequality. A liberal philosophy would support the concept of private values, yet private values cannot be taught within a public system. These are just a few of the dilemmas that lie at the heart of administering any public system in modern times, and they are reflected to one degree or another in the surface maladies that affect schools. A critique of liberal philosophy can be useful for educational administrators who recognize that the major institutional role of schools is bedeviled with problems and contradictions. This critique would, for example, point to and dispute the rationalistic and individualistic assumptions in liberal philosophy. Social relations, it might be argued, are located within economic relations, and economic relations are class based in a liberal and capitalistic society. Schooling merely serves to perpetuate the inherent dilemmas, rather than resolve them. These arguments will be considered in some detail later; for now, it is important to recognize that there are a number of conflicting perceptions about schools and the personnel in them.

The educational administrator can therefore see that many contemporary issues and problems of schooling in our society are not simply specific to one or another generation, but have their source in some fundamental contradictions and issues inherent to the system. In a way, schools are caught between the demands of the political and the economic systems. Administrators must face this reality. A new and revitalized educational administration, like its counterpart in the "new" public administration, accepts the basic social dilemmas and then starts from a value position to develop institutions that are more just and fair. A theory of administration developed outside of an articulated context is of little value in helping schools to achieve purpose; a theory of administration, therefore, must be situated within a larger, embracive theory of schools in society.

Such a theory, we will suggest, must be both critical *and* supportive of liberal tenets. Such liberal values must be supported to the degree that they allow for individual freedom and political representation, but criticized to the degree that they prevent equality of opportunity and lack of mobility.

Strike (1982) provides a sophisticated defense of liberalism and its relation to education. Strike suggests that *"The central public function of schooling in a liberal state is the democratic distribution of rationality"* (1982, 12, italics in original). By rationality Strike means the idea of the *reasonable* citizen, one who acts according to collectively derived rules and norms and who can be convinced by evidence. Yet Strike finds that public schools in a liberal state cannot reproduce communal values:

> Public schools cannot be united by a shared commitment to a shared set of private values. They fail therefore to generate communities in

which pedagogical relations are characterized by trust and intimacy. This state of affairs generates a society in which student values are formed more by peers than by adults and erodes the schools' capacity to transmit even those liberal values which are clearly public. (Strike 1982, 253)

In Strike's analysis the theory of liberalism requires that equality be granted for various value systems (freedom of expression) and that such a theory be reproduced through a system of common schools. However, such schools would themselves violate the theory if they adopted a private system of values, even while knowing that "the transmission of private values is necessary for genuine education to occur" (1982, 87). In this view, public schools are in a bind: private values, such as religious values, are important to the determination and preservation of culture, yet under a doctrine of fairness and liberal equality schools cannot communicate them. The cultural relevance of the school is undermined by the principles of liberalism.

This argument provides a reasonable alternative to neo-Marxist thought on the subject. Strike's work explores how a public school can provide equality of opportunity to children, so that they may have equal access to the structures of success in this country, without continuing to contribute to the reproduction of classes that have unequal opportunities by virtue of parents' economic and social position. He believes it cannot be done without restructuring public education to develop small, community-oriented schools and ensuring the viability of private schools. However, this very argument again illustrates the problem of liberal thought in contention with a highly bureaucratized society that divorces administration and teaching from the development of culturally relevant value systems.

Public schooling is not a neutral endeavor that can only promulgate public values: in its theory of administration and in its theory of teaching, it reflects the demands of the wider society. Strike's fair and concerned presentation essentially neglects the ways in which a liberal and capitalistic society provides rules of operation that result in de-individualized, vocationalistic institutions. As Strike does show, the empiricist and positivist program that underlies the theory of modern pedagogy undermines any humanistic and rational effort; in a similar vein, empiricist and

positivistic theories of administration fail to question the structure of administration and its relation to liberal and democratic
values. Strike's failure to develop the relationship between economic and bureaucratic structures and schooling is ultimately
liberal thought's failure to deal effectively with systemic inconsistencies. Thus, we need to examine in detail an alternative
critical approach to schooling and its administration.

DEVELOPING A MORAL SCIENCE

Such a project is not unique to education. Dissatisfied with
current orthodoxies, the social sciences in general have attempted
to inject a critical spirit into social inquiry. The liberal solution,
depending on scientific research, has been found wanting. Sociology in particular has met challenges from new perspectives,
many continental in origin and often inspired by neo-Marxist
thought. In anthropology, Dell Hymes (1973) and others suggested that anthropology must be "re-invented." Political science,
long dependent on a systems model for studying political behavior, found itself becoming concerned with attempting to understand human actions rather than merely predicting them. Benjamin (1982) suggested that history become the foundation of the
social sciences, while Moon (1982) claimed that political study
must first and foremost concern itself with freedom. Organizational theory has also been radically changed, as Perrow (1979)
has observed. Public administration, educational administration's
ally, underwent a similar transformation resulting in a "new public administration," a discipline concerned with justice and equity
rather than efficiency and economy (see Bellone, 1980). In short,
all of the social science disciplines and their spin-offs were, to one
degree or another, affected by a dramatic conceptual shift.

This shift provides a different way of looking at both social
science and administration. Social science, in the new perspective,
is *always* tied to "ought" questions. The very nature of the
questions we ask presupposes a "should-it-be-this-way" question.
Values are part of the nature of social science. In social science,
the very act of studying the subject may change the subject. One
is hard pressed to study things as they "are." In a discipline such
as administration, and in social science generally, the object is

Administration is
—a purposive activity
— not generic but dependent on the
nature of the institution

24   Paradigms and Promises

not to describe, but to understand and to improve. Thus, research must have its origins in practice, yet be critical of it in an attempt to change current conditions. Administration is a *purposive* activity: it is designed to achieve the purposes of the institution. Not all institutions have similar purposes; therefore, administration is *not* generic but dependent on the nature of the institution. In *educational* institutions, the function of administration is to be *educative,* while in profit-seeking institutions, the function of administration is to realize a profit. This radical concept disagrees with a century of administrative theory.

Dissatisfaction with current administrative approaches for examining social life stems from administration's inability to deal with questions of value and morality and its inability to fulfill its promises. For example, Griffiths (1983, 208) criticizes orthodox theories because they "ignore the presence of unions and fail to account for the scarcity of women and minorities in top administrative positions." Ericson and Ellett ask "Why has educational research had so few real implications for educational policy?" (1982, 497) and answer that an empiricist research program, modeled on the natural sciences, fails to address issues of understanding and interpretation. This failure precludes researchers from reaching a genuine understanding of the human condition. It is time, they argue, to treat educational research as a moral science (1982, 511). The science of administration can also be a moral one, a critically moral one.

The term "moral" is being used here in its cultural, professional, and ethical sense, not in a spiritual or religious sense. The moral side of administration has to do with the larger context of what it means to be human. The context of administration requires that an administrative science be reconstructed as a moral science. An administrative science *can* be empirical, but it also must incorporate hermeneutic (the science of interpreting and understanding others) and critical dimensions. Social science has increasingly recognized that it must be informed by moral questions: the paradigm of natural science does not apply when dealing with human issues. As a moral science, the science of administration is concerned with the resolution of moral dilemmas. A critical and a literary model of administration helps to provide us with the necessary context and understanding wherein such dilemmas can be wisely resolved.

Language of dilemmas

The language of dilemmas

The language of dilemmas is taken from Ann and Harold Berlak (1981) who developed this concept for the act of teaching. Teaching, like administration, involves the resolution and possible transformation of dilemmas. The Berlaks (1981, chap. 7) suggest that all teachers face three areas of dilemmas: control, curriculum, and societal. Control dilemmas involve the resolution of classroom management and control issues, particularly the issue of who is in charge and to what degree. Control dilemmas center *Control dilemmas* on four questions: (1) Do you treat the child as a student, focusing narrowly on cognitive goals, or as a whole person, focusing more broadly on intellectual, aesthetic, social, and physical dimensions? (2) Who controls classroom time? In some classrooms, children are given latitude in scheduling their activities; in others, class activities follow a strict and mandatory schedule. (3) Who controls operations or what goes on in the classroom? (4) Who controls the standards and defines success and failure?

Similar dilemmas occur in the curricular domain and relate to *Curric. dilem.* whether the curriculum is considered as received, public knowledge—the kind found through studying textbooks—or whether it is considered private, individualized knowledge, of the type achieved through discoveries and experiments. These curricular difficulties also depend on whether one conceives of the child as a client or as an individual. A client receives professional services generated from a body of knowledge, whereas the individual receives personal services generated from his or her particular needs and context.

A final set of dilemmas has to do with what children bring to *Societal* school and how they are to be treated once there. One concerns the distribution of teacher resources: should all children be given equal resources (time, attention, etc.)? should one focus more resources on the less talented, in order to bring them up to standards, or on the more talented, in order for them to reach their full potential? The same question arises in regard to the distribution of justice. Should classroom rules be applied uniformly without regard to the differing circumstances of each child, or should family background, economic factors, and other sociological influences be considered? Should a teacher stress a common culture or ethnic differences and subculture consciousness?

Much of teaching involves resolving such dilemmas by making a variety of decisions throughout the school day. Such decisions can be made, however, in a reflective or an unreflective manner. An unreflective manner means simply teaching as one was taught, without giving consideration to available alternatives. A reflective approach "involves an examination, from the widest possible range of perspectives, of *present patterns* of resolution, *alternative possibilities*, the *consequences* of present and alternative patterns, the *origins* of present patterns and of proposals for alternatives" (A. and H. Berlak 1981, 237). Thus, reflective teaching suggests that dilemmas need not be simply resolved but can be *transformed* so that a higher level of teaching expertise is reached.

This same logic can be applied to administration. Administration involves the resolution of various dilemmas, that is, the making of moral decisions. One set of dilemmas involves control: how much participation can teachers have in the administration of the school? how much participation can parents and students have? who evaluates and for what purpose? is the role of administration collegial or authority centered? The area of the curriculum brings up similar problems: is the school oriented to basic skills, advanced skills, social skills? should the curricula be teacher made or nationally distributed? should student evaluation be based on teacher assessment or standardized tests? Finally, an additional set of dilemmas pertains to the idea of schooling in society. Should the schools be oriented to ameliorate the so-called deficits that some students bring with them, or should they see different cultures and groups as strengths? Should schools be seen as agents of change, oriented to the creation of a more just society, or as socializers that adapt the young to the current social structure?

These significant questions have plagued social philosophers for generations, but they are not abstract questions: *they are continually being answered in the day-to-day activity of teaching and administration.* Often, these questions are being answered unreflectively. If administrators could look at these dilemmas in reflective terms, which means to engage in the critical evaluation of self, role, and institution, then perhaps the dilemmas could not just be resolved through everyday action, but could indeed be transformed. Administrative leadership, then, leads to transformative action and this, indeed, is what *leadership* is all about. Transformative action entails making decisions in a moral context. The context of schooling is a complex fabric woven from the threads of individual lives—teachers, students, parents, and citizens—the threads of group values and culture, and the social threads of politics and economics. Administrative decisions are moral decisions and, as such, must recognize the weave of the fabric. We must reject the idea of a positivistic science and begin to think in terms of administration as a moral science. What has passed for social science and administrative science is now suspect.

Scholars, indeed, now use the terms "postpositivistic" and "postempiricist" science. Haan even suggests that:

> Because social scientists' claims of value neutrality are no longer tenable . . . and because many moral ideas that social scientists inadvertently use can withstand neither public scrutiny nor professional debate, social science faces a crisis of legitimation. This difficulty might be alleviated if social scientists were to examine their moral bases, work to construct a theory based on wide consensus, and then come to use moral theory reflectively and openly. (Haan 1983, 218)

Educational research has felt this moral revolution as well. Soltis's demand (1984, 9) that "research in education broadly conceived must be empirical, interpretive, normative, and critical" is evidence of educational scholars' growing awareness that the claims of positive science in education can be shown to be far from convincing.

Some scholars in educational administration have shown an awareness of and receptivity to the new ideas. Culbertson (1983, 20-21), for example, has noted that "we are more keenly aware than previously that individuals and groups *do* intervene incessantly to change and shape ongoing activities in which they participate and that this condition causes us to be more skeptical about the discovery and validation of universal laws." Sergiovanni (1984, 275) further suggests that "Mainstream thought continues the tradition of building a science of administration closely tied to the social science disciplines and aligned with the principles of logical positivism. . . . But significant branches in the stream of scholarly argument in administration are becoming apparent." He goes on to mention renewed interest in "normative science" and "interpretive science."

Clearly a number of scholars in the social sciences and in the educational disciplines are both concerned about the basic paradigm within which their "normal" science operates and intrigued by the possibilities offered by alternative conceptions. This suggests that the social sciences need to consider their moral aspects: the necessary empirical work must be balanced by interpretive and critical understandings, for it is these that distinguish the human sciences from the natural sciences. In other words, administrative theory can be informed by a reflective and critical model. It can look, on the one hand, to literature and a literary model as a way for understanding the context of actions and the moral issues involved; on the other hand, it can use a critical model to draw the connections between administrative action and social values.

NEW MODELS FOR ADMINISTRATION

Allison (1983, 12) suggests that "it is only through the development of critical literature that any field can coordinate its progress toward producing valid knowledge about things of interest." With a few exceptions, educational administration has remained devoid of a critical literature because the field's basic faith in the scientific method for solving social problems had made it reluctant as a whole to engage in critical dialogue. Looking to literature and literary criticism as a model for understanding the context of administration may be helpful to our own notions about this field of inquiry. If we turn away from scientific models of administration and look at literary models, we may widen our perspective on different ways of considering administration. This allows us to be both formative and critical. Northrop Frye, the distinguished literary critic, addresses the role of criticism in literature:

> Criticism will always have two aspects, one turned toward the structure of literature and one turned toward the other cultural phenomena that form the social environment of literature. Together, they balance each other: when one is worked on to the exclusion of the other, the critical perspective goes out of focus. If criticism is in proper balance, the tendency of critics to move from critical to larger social issues becomes more intelligible. (Frye 1973, 25)

This is true with educational administration as well: a critical literature prevents the field from turning inward to its own self-concerns; it suggests the need for considering the wider social context within which administration operates. Administration, in turn, becomes less concerned with the promulgation of systems of control as with the development and reproduction of community and cultural systems. If educational administration is by its nature more allied to the critical disciplines than the scientific ones, then the need for a critical literacy is apparent.

A school administrator should look to a literary, rather than scientific, model to guide his or her work in part because literature deals with human events, with tragedy and comedy. It provides a point of view, and an unfolding of human history. It shows how individuals relate to each other, how they love and cheat, are both evil and virtuous. Administrators have the school as their text, and society, the context. Understanding the school can be seen as the equivalent of understanding a work of literature: it is multi-faceted, complex, and tells a story. How the story is written depends on the characters involved. The administrator is not the author, for this text is jointly conceived, but he or she may be the critic. As a literary critic, the administrator reflects on the coherence of the text, on its significance, on the development of both plot and characters. The administrator can then provide a commentary on these guided by his or her own sense of moral rightness, much in the same fashion that literary critics comment on the morality of the text they review. The administrator as literary critic, if we can carry this metaphor further, looks at the moral atmosphere of the institution, at its cultural expressions, and at its contextualism. This indeed is an appropriate metaphor for many of the ways administrators already behave. What needs to be added is the wider social context in which administration itself occurs, a context that provides opportunities for moral decisions. The analysis of this wider context should be what administrative theory is all about. If theory doesn't serve, inform, and change our moral and critical practice, it is of no help.

We need to stand administrative theory on its head: rather than individualistic theories of schooling, we need cultural and literary ones; rather than an instrumental and bureaucratic rationality, we need a communicative rationality; rather than a decontextualized system, we need one that establishes context;

30   Paradigms and Promises

and rather than a positivistic and behavioristic vocabulary, we need one that can encompass various aspects of our life.

A new three-tiered model is needed for administrative study. One tier involves the empirical study of organization and administration through descriptions of perceived reality and economic and political structures. Such data help us understand social organization and social divisions. A second tier involves understanding individual constructions and interpretations of reality. Social reality is mutually created; finding meaning in events requires inquiry and understanding. The administrative student must be in a position to ask not only "what?" but also "what is the meaning?" A literary model treats every situation uniquely, every story personally. Like individual works of fiction, each social situation builds a plot, presents a set of characters, and then asks the participant to enter this world and validate it as real. The administrator who works from a literary model realizes that he or she must "read" the situation to be effective.

The third tier suggests that description and understanding are not enough; they certainly provide information and insight, but they do not address movement and change. The third tier, then, is critical inquiry, a reflective process that includes dialogue oriented toward achieving true democratic participation by all members of the community. In this sense, our model of administrative theory aims at human freedoms. The description and interpretation of organization and administration (the first and second tiers) are firmly tied to the critical examination of social issues. Such a critical examination provides an overall vision and a sense of purpose not achieved by simply looking at the current situation; indeed, the very idea of administrative leadership implies that one has the ability to reflect on the present situation, critique it, and develop an alternative that mobilizes others. Sergiovanni (1984, 278) refers to this when he says that "Improving the social order gives educational administration a normative quality which must of necessity become an important part of inquiry, analysis, and practice. In short, educational administration is a science of designing courses of action aimed at changing existing situations into preferred ones."

A consensual, critical, and communicative foundation for administration implies a democratic, rather than a bureaucratic emphasis in administrative studies. As Bates (1983, 39) has ob-

Bates' four issues

served: "In my view, there are at least four issues that must be taken account of in constructing an *educational* theory of administration and an appropriate institutional structure for the management of knowledge. These are the democratisation of social relations, the democratisation of knowledge, the democratisation of communication, and the democratisation of cultural concerns."

Bates argues that the dominant bureaucratic/systems-theory emphases in administrative study bypass the need to develop an educationally and politically relevant administrative practice and theory. If educational administration is to remain true to its educational commitment, then it must indeed begin to consider the implications a democratic political theory carries for both schooling and its administration. An administrative theory must be concerned with how schooling may solidify social relations based on different economic classes. It must also examine the distribution of knowledge within schooling, in order to determine if such distribution carries a strong relationship to class membership. It needs to address the issue of unilateral communication between administration and other organizational members, with the understanding that participatory democracy is founded on free expression. Finally, an administrative theory must become concerned with the formation and revitalization of culture within schools, a culture that promotes a democratic and uncoerced form of governance. An administrative theory that begins to incorporate these concerns becomes not a legitimization of systems of control modeled on the private appropriation of labor and capital, but a truly educative and democratic attempt to rationalize institutions and celebrate individual freedoms.

Educational administration must involve organizational members themselves in the construction and analysis of the established organizational structure. If we accept the proposition that organizations are fundamentally "social constructions of reality" (Berger and Luckmann 1971; Greenfield 1985), then one role of administration can be not only to control those structures but also to demystify them. Mystification means that the organization takes on a life of its own; it is no longer a historical entity created by individuals, but rather a "thing" that exists outside of human actions. The organization that has become objectified and solid in the minds of the members requires a critical analysis of its structure in order to project possible changes that make the

Dialectics — ability to see in every position its opposite

Dialectics as used here

organization a more humane and equitable place. The demystification of structure requires the analysis of both content and
definitions.

It follows from these decidedly moral concerns that administration must be informed by critique—the ability to reflect dialectically on the conditions of existence and the structures of power.
Dialectics as it is used here means the ability to see in every
proposition its opposite; for example, that we have schooling implies that perhaps not having schooling is another and still to be
examined alternative. We propose that administration, particularly *educational* administration, is concerned with empowerment. One provides power not only through education as it is
normally defined, but also through access to decision-forming
arenas and through an analysis of one's own place in the hierarchy. This empowerment requires the development of a critical
approach to administration in order to balance the tensions that
arise from the twin needs of controlling structure and liberating
individuals. This proposition is radical in its design. Administrators are often thought of as ones who have power, not those
who share or give it; but power can be achieved through giving it
away. This paradoxical conclusion might suggest that an administrator, in the role of literary critic, looks for examples of powerlessness and tries to empower students, parents, and individual
teachers who are without it.

Administration, thus, can be seen as a moral science that
must use all possible modes of inquiry to understand both itself
and the reality of schooling. Organizational theory, reproduction
theory, change theory, and critical theory all make the new administrator face the dilemmas of administration in moral terms.

A moral science means no easy answers, no prescriptions to
follow, and no recipes, scientific or otherwise, to guide behavior.
In addressing social science generally, Hirschman (1983, 31), a
distinguished economist, tells us that "Morality is not something
like pollution abatement that can be secured by slightly modifying the design of a policy proposal. Rather, it belongs in the
center of our work; and it can get there only if the social scientists
are morally alive and make themselves vulnerable to moral concerns—then they will produce morally significant works, consciously or otherwise."

When administration is considered as a moral science, administrators must deal with moral dilemmas. Each decision carries moral, rather than just technical implications. This realization distinguishes the administrator from the technocrat. *Each administrative decision carries with it a restructuring of a human life;* this is why administration at its heart is the resolution of moral dilemmas. The new administrator will operate from a set of values that stresses not only research in the field but also understanding and critical inquiry.

Educational administration is concerned with enpowerment
— tensions that arrive from
... twin ~~concerns~~ needs of controlling structure and liberating individuals
... power can be achieved by giving it away

2

Critical Reflections on the History of Administrative Theory

Administrative theorists in this century had an overriding concern for purging administration of any nonscientific dimensions. Administration as a field depended on a theoretical framework informed largely by a version of science derived from the tenets of logical positivism, a philosophical movement in the earlier part of this century. Logical positivism asserted that only scientific knowledge, which was verifiable in principle, was true knowledge and could be expressed in logical, and therefore true, form. This, of course, removed a good deal of human affairs from the realm of truth; values, ethics, and morality would simply become matters of assertion or preference. To its credit logical positivism aimed at eliminating mystic and metaphysical thought that concealed the structure of human relationships. At the same time though, it disallowed any scrutiny of questions of human values, declaring these to be scientifically meaningless and thus illegitimate concerns for consideration. In this way of thinking, value statements are incapable of scientific proof; therefore, they do not have any meaning within a scientific system. The only system that could provide true, verifiable knowledge was science.

Administrative theory was built on this foundation, and it remains the dominant way of approaching administration even today. Over the years our institutions have built a structure of

36   Paradigms and Promises

administrative training programs that has uncritically accepted the assumptions about people and ideas generated by logical positivism. As a result, practicing administrators are divorced from theoretical reflection on the most vital and dynamic parts of their field—the moral, ethical, and value dimensions. The skills one associates with administration are themselves based in such evaluative approaches to the world. Strong empirical work should be valued, but within a context established by an understanding of the nature of the social and educational system of which we are a part. Administration is not just a technical skill: it is a way of ordering the world according to a set of values and beliefs. Administration exists within various contexts: the managerial context, concerned with the running of the organization; the political context, concerned with the distribution and acquisition of resources; the leadership context, concerned with the development and change of the institution and of the people within it; and the social and cultural context, concerned with the nature of administration and the institution within our social and cultural systems. This last context has frequently been neglected in administrative studies in education, yet it is crucial for a proper understanding of the administrative task.

THE DEVELOPMENT OF THEORY

An appreciation of these various contexts of administration requires that we first understand the historical and current status of theory in the field, and that we develop a critique of the current orthodoxies. Current educational administration has been informed by a variety of ideas taken from psychology, sociology, and management literature. These ideas and their theoretical implications for educational administration will be assessed here, with particular focus placed on those theories that have had a major influence on the *administration* of schools, as opposed to the *organization* of schooling. Since knowledge of the history of the field is essential for the reflective administrator's understanding of the present situation, we will present the historical development of the field of administration and management, culminating in the movement toward a scientific theory of administrative behavior in schools.

Scientific Management

Frederick Winslow Taylor, whose ideas gained currency in the early part of this century, can be considered to be the father of scientific management, an influential body of concepts that continues to structure the field of administration. Scientific management, also known as Taylorism, attempted to lay aside the intuitive, artistic method of administration and to substitute in its place a science of management informed by hard data and real facts. Science, time, motion, and efficiency hallmarked this approach. Taylor contributed a good deal to the field of industrial engineering, but his ideas on management soon extended to other areas.

Taylor claimed that every job has one best way of being accomplished, and Taylorism involved finding the best way. It depended on the rigorous and often tedious use of the stopwatch to determine the most efficient motions for increasing production. The role of management in this case lay in researching the most efficient way of doing tasks and then providing the most minute and detailed training so that workers had no latitude in their methods of performing their chores. This, in turn, would lead to the most efficient production schedule and the most efficient use of worker time: the increased efficiency would lead to higher production, more profits, and consequently, the argument went, higher salaries for workers (Taylor, 1947). In essence, Taylorism was a mechanistic system designed to standardize the workplace. It received an understandably hostile reaction from labor leaders but was quickly accepted, if never really implemented, by the business community.

Taylorism revolved around certain principles, each designed to improve workplace efficiency. For example, Taylor suggested that scientific management rested on thirteen major principles. Callahan (1962, 28-34) condenses them into five major elements:

- Time and motion study—discovering the specific time and body motions needed to accomplish a particular job.
- The standardization of the job—developing a particular routine that every worker could follow.
- The setting of particular tasks to be itemized, accomplished, and recorded during the day.

• The development of "functional foremanship"—training foremen to understand and to effectively supervise their workers' daily tasks.

• The addition of a planning department to analyze the jobs in the organization and develop them in conformity to the principles of scientific management.

Braverman (1974) shows how Taylorism remains the foundation for much of modern management theory and practice. He maintains that Taylorism took the *craft* knowledge possessed by each worker, systematized it by breaking it down into component parts, and then made control over the parts the prerogative of management, resulting in the "deskilling" of the individual laborer. What labor once owned—the skills, techniques, and knowledge needed for a craft—became a management possession, and labor's only role is to produce at management direction.

Taylorism had significant influence in education. Franklin Bobbitt, a professor of educational administration at the University of Chicago, and Ellwood Cubberley, dean of education at Stanford University and widely published in educational administration, both enthusiastically endorsed the widespread application of Taylor's principles to education. In their view, running an educational system was much like running a business organization: certain parallels could be drawn between workers and teachers, products and students, administrators and managers; therefore, strong scientific management could benefit the schools as much as it did Bethlehem Steel. Cubberley found that:

> By means of standards and units of the type now being evolved and tested out it is even now possible for a superintendent of schools to make a survey of his school system which will be indicative of its points of strength and weakness, and to learn from the results better methods and procedures. In time it will be possible for any school system to maintain a continuous survey of all the different phases of its work, through tests made by its corps of efficiency experts, and to detect weak points in its work almost as soon as they appear. (Cubberley 1916, 325)

Bobbitt had a similar approach to education, with a particular concern for the development of curriculum. He believed that school administration ought to be concerned with what the "products" of the system needed in later life. To this end business and community leaders would be surveyed to identify a detailed list of skills, and administration would then design specific objectives for teaching these skills. Bobbitt had a wide-ranging respect for the influence of science on education:

> The technique of scientific method is at present being developed for every important aspect of education. Experimental laboratories and schools are discovering accurate methods of measuring and evaluating different types of educational processes. Bureaus of educational measurement are discovering scientific methods of analyzing results, of diagnosing specific situations, and of prescribing remedies. Scientific method is being applied to the fields of budget-making, child-accounting, systems of grading and promotion, etc. (Bobbitt 1924, 41)

These educators, and dozens of others who wrote in the period between 1910 and 1930, had significant impact on the field through training future administrators, publishing books and articles, and addressing a variety of conventions and meetings. In sum,

> The new professors of educational administration gave the stamp of university approval to elitist assumptions about who constituted good school board members and to the corporate model of school organization. They tried to develop "scientific" ways of measuring inputs and outputs in school systems as a tool of management, and to elaborate ways in which the school might rationalize its structure and curriculum to fit new industrial and social conditions. (Tyack 1974, 136)

The perspective of these educators still has strong influence in the field and has colored much of the research occurring in education and educational administration. By the 1930s, however, this approach had been modified.

The Human Relations Movement

This usual, but perhaps inaccurate, title applies to a theoretical perspective generated by a series of research projects that began in the late 1920s at the Hawthorne plant of the Western Electric ✳

Company. This research originally intended to extend Taylor's work by investigating industrial conditions that led to increased production. The initial studies concerned the level of illumination provided for workers: in one experiment, lighting was held at constant levels for one group and decreased in level for the other group. The researchers found that production increased in both the experimental and control groups despite the variations in lighting levels. In further studies designed to explain this anomaly, the Harvard researchers Mayo and Roethlisberger manipulated work conditions of their experimental group to see just what caused the increase in production. While observing six women at their tasks, the researchers added rest periods, increased and decreased their length, and otherwise altered the women's working environment. The researchers found that none of their manipulations of the work environment, including a return to the original working conditions, seemed to affect production. The researchers finally concluded that the very fact of being the subject of attention by researchers, coupled with the type of social relations that emerged among the test group, had influenced the output of the group.

The Hawthorne studies concluded that the patterns of *social* relations in a work setting are of major, if not prime, importance. The final study of the Bank Wiring Room indicated that peer interactions controlled worker output. For example, if a piece-rate system was in force, the workers would establish norms that regulated the output of each individual, so that no one person could outproduce others to the extent that management would become dissatisfied with the average output. Thus the idea of informal group and informal leadership structures entered the social sciences. These concepts have remained influential within the literature and consistently popular with management. Some sociologists have discussed how management has at times used these concepts as tools to manipulate workers through managerial attempts to control informal structures.

The Hawthorne studies have received criticism for their findings, their methodology, and for the purposes they have served (see Carey, 1967). In a sense, social psychologists have "adopted" the studies as a basis for the development of various psychologically based interventions in the workplace. The Hawthorne research essentially put the Taylorism movement into perspective by arguing that a simple economic approach to work was inadequate, even misguided, in terms of human psychology. Further, the model adopted by the Hawthorne researchers presented an early version of social-systems theory that influenced a major focus of later research (Burrell and Morgan 1979, develop this argument). This line of research saw workers in the workplace as exemplars of equilibrium and disequilibrium within a system composed of many factors: as various conditions within the workplace (social conditions, physical conditions, family considerations, etc.) influenced the worker, productivity would increase or decrease. This seems to be a mere cause-and-effect relationship, but in reality the causal conditions would be much more complex. Several interactions occurred simultaneously, and the Hawthorne studies attempted to discover some of them. It is now commonplace to read studies of worker performance, job satisfaction, quality of life in the workplace, worker participation in decision making, and leadership, all of which trace their lineage back to the Hawthorne studies.

The human relations work provided a necessary antithesis to the formalism of scientific management. The human relations movement stressed the importance of informal organization and the type of cultural system that emerges among the organization's members. Moreover, it pointed to the importance of the human factor in organizations and thereby reacted against the mechanistic notions of Taylorism.

At the same time, though, the human relations movement provided management with a set of concepts that simply served as another tool to control workers. As Etzioni (1964, 40) says, "Implicit in many Human Relations writings is the suggestion that the task of the social scientist is to show management how to engage in the art of social engineering to the benefit of all concerned." That is, the human relations studies developed powerful concepts for management: if one could control the informal organization (in terms of attitudes, leadership, and so on), then one could essentially control the peer network that set the norms of production, absenteeism, quality, and so on. The workers' legitimate demands in terms of production, pay, and other factors were never emphasized; the stress lay in investigating how a firm's productivity could be increased without any additional costs to management.

Despite its managerial bias, the human relations movement has significantly influenced administrative theory. While human relations remain a major theme in organizational development and organizational change, it could reasonably be argued that the human relations movement and the contemporary focus on administrative decision making have progressively and systematically reinforced Taylorism's basic accomplishment: the concentration of control in the hands of management. Contemporary models continue the Tayloristic distinction between manual and mental labor: some of us do physical work; others tell us what physical work to do.

CONTEMPORARY SOCIAL SCIENCE ACCOUNTS

Chester Barnard

The earlier schools of Taylorism and human relations emphasized improving workplace conditions in order to improve productivity. Later theories showed much more concern for the "scientific" study of administration and how administrators behaved in an organizational context.

Chester Barnard might be considered the nexus between the two efforts. His book *The Functions of the Executive,* first published in 1938, remains one of the dominant influences in organizational literature. Barnard had the foresight to examine the total organization as a complex system made up of interdependent parts. His contributions became an integral part of much of the later organizational theory generated by scholars in academia.

Barnard, an executive for Bell Telephone in New Jersey, gave serious thought to his profession and provided a distinctly contemporary approach to understanding administration and organization. He attended to both the organizational and the human elements in the system, as his definition of organization reflects: "An organization comes into being when (1) there are persons able to communicate with each other (2) who are willing to contribute action (3) to accomplish a common purpose. The elements of an organization are therefore (1) communication; (2) willingness to serve; and (3) common purpose" (Barnard 1968, 82). Thus, Barnard developed some of the generative ideas expanded on by later administrative theorists.

Many of Barnard's observations on administration are now quite popular. For example, he suggested that administration's primary role lies in developing a cooperative system through establishing moral leadership in the organization. In many ways, Barnard's work contains the seeds of the current emphasis on organizational culture. He saw organizational leaders as responsible for creating a culture of mutual effort and cooperation—a radical departure from Taylorism and its emphasis on reward and punishment.

However, Barnard's theory of the organization did not lack problems; in particular, he held a questionable theory of authority and social relations within the firm. Barnard stated that authority lay in the subordinates' willingness to accept and comply with orders: "whether an order has authority or not lies with the persons to whom it is addressed, and does not reside in 'persons of authority' or those who issue these orders" (1968, 163). This implies that all action within the organization is voluntary, that a subordinate can indeed exercise a degree of free will in deciding whether to accept an order or not. It ignores the reprisals available to the superior if, in fact, the subordinate refuses to comply with an order. These retributions change the situation rather dramatically. Barnard saw the organization as a real system of cooperative elements, each doing its job and equally contributing to organizational effectiveness. The reality of organizations— their conflicts, bargaining, and politics—seems much different.

Herbert Simon

Herbert Simon, a Nobel laureate in economics, might be considered the first modern student of an administrative science. Although indebted to Barnard's earlier work, Simon's *Administrative Behavior* (1965, first published in 1945) gained renown for its critique of previous work on administration and for its development of a behaviorally based, scientific description of organization. Some earlier theorists of management had developed principles for running an organization that included such commonly accepted ideas as "Administrative efficiency is increased by a specialization of the task among the group"; "Administrative efficiency is increased by arranging the members of the group in a determinate hierarchy of authority"; and "Administrative efficiency is increased by limiting the span of control at any point in the hierarchy to a small number" (Simon 1965, 20-21). In his critique, Simon lambasted these "principles of administration," as he labeled them, particularly the work of Gulick and Urwick (1937). By taking each principle and showing its counterexample, Simon established himself as a major force in what he considered to be the "reconstruction" of administrative theory. His major contribution lay in relocating the theory of administration from an analysis of external structures such as chains of authority and spans of control, to the examination of the internal, cognitive decision-making processes of administrators. As he says, "The difficulty has arisen from treating as 'principles of administration' what are really only criteria for describing and diagnosing administrative situations. . . . In the design of administrative organizations, as in their operation, over-all efficiency must be the guiding criterion" (Simon 1965, 35-36).

This becomes the subject of much of his work. Building on Barnard's distinction between efficiency—using resources wisely—and effectiveness—achieving organizational goals—Simon develops a sociologically and psychologically informed emphasis on organizational performance that stresses, first, the limited ability of individual members to make fully rational decisions; and second, the wider ability and necessity for the organization to set the value conditions and structures for individual decision making. Thus, individuals can only make rational decisions within the bounds of the organization's intents and goals; such decisions are to be judged by the organizational principle of efficiency: getting the most benefit for the least effort.

In his endeavor, Simon established the tenor for future generations of administrative and organizational scholars. He emphasized a science of administration based in the behavioral sciences and "opened a whole new vista of administration theory" (Etzioni 1964, 30). By pointing out that the organization consisted not only of task conduct—that is, employees doing whatever jobs they are supposed to be doing—but also of decision making, by superiors not directly engaged in production who make decisions about production, Simon added a new dimension to theorizing about organizations. In his theorizing about rationality, Simon again added to organizational analysis: he believed that decision makers did not opt for the best decision, but, because they were

Logical positivism holds that ethical standards are devoid of "meaning", i.e. they cannot be proven scientifically

cognitively limited to the alternatives that could be processed, *Satisficed* "satisfied" for the best decision under the particular circumstances. This concept became important in both psychology and organizational theory.

Simon's contributions, however, should be put into perspective. While he was brilliant within the particular framework he *Simon - logical positivist* used to address organizations and administration, the very framework itself can be disputed. Simon might be considered to be one of the very few who consciously articulated a philosophical position upon which to base his administrative pronouncements; he used the philosophy of logical positivism. This philosophy holds that ethical statements are devoid of meaningful content, "meaningful" in the sense of verifiable or provable. The only statements that can be proven are those that are either logically true or those that correspond with empirical documentation. Science is therefore only concerned with recording the facts, not with deciding questions of value or ethics. Having adopted this position, Simon concluded that a science of administration could have no ethical content but must be concerned with factual statements only; as he says (Simon 1965, 253), "There is no place for ethical assertions in the body of a science," a proposition that will be challenged in the remainder of this text.

Simon, in essence, set the stage for the contemporary approach to administrative studies. His remarkable influence on the field might be summarized in these statements:

- Administration can be a science equivalent to any natural science.
- An administrative science is based in logical positivism.
- An administrative science is value free and objective. *
- An administrative science is concerned with the study of correct decisions and the process of making correct decisions.
- For an administrative science, rationality is defined as the selection of means toward achieving ends.
- The ends to be achieved are not a matter of concern for the administrative scientist, but are set by policy-making bodies.

These assertions suggest that administrators must not let values influence their decisions, that administration can be reduced to a set of technical propositions, and that administration is only concerned with maintaining efficiency. We must disagree with each.

Current Approaches

Contem. adm. ed. theory [handwritten margin note]

Contemporary educational administration theory might be seen as a composite of Taylorism, human relations, and modern social science perspectives. In the 1950s, the nature of theory in educational administration became the topic for extended discussion that continues to date. In essence, the debate revolved around the question of developing a science of educational administration along the lines proposed by Simon.

From the 1930s to the 1970s, theories of educational administration took essentially opposite directions. One theory had practical concerns that developed out of school situations: these were hoped to be amenable to the type of scientific analysis proposed by Taylor and his educational popularizers. This effort emphasized the collection of data that attempted to rationalize the practice of administration so that schools could be more effectively managed. The mountains of collected data yielded inconclusive results. The National Education Association's (NEA) *Eleventh Yearbook* (1933) claimed that research in education had yet to solve some of the basic issues and suggested some topics for investigation that seem painfully familiar:

1. Are present college entrance requirements valid?

2. How can secondary school curriculums be revised to meet the needs of the youth of America?

3. How do the technics of adult education differ from those of elementary education?

4. Can attitudes be measured?

5. Can teaching ability be predicted?

6. When, if ever, is vocational guidance effective?

7. To what extent should the school attempt to modify the influence of the home on the child?

8. When can vocational training be given most profitably? Can schools offer such training effectively? (NEA 1933, 311)

By the late 1950s, however, the second thrust became evident. The research in educational administration became less oriented to solving the day-to-day problems of the system than to accumulating data that would lead to the development of explanative theories of administration. Simon was important to this shift of emphasis. In addition, the more general milieu was affected by technical developments in the Western world, the successes registered by the "hard" theoretical fields, and the dominance of logical positivism as the preferred justification for social science. The new scholars of educational administration walked into this intellectual atmosphere as individuals influenced by new ideas from administrative scientists, psychologists, and sociologists. Their work gave rise to the "theory movement" in educational administration, a movement dedicated to building a legitimate science founded on axiomatic laws.

A number of major universities, many funded by the Kellogg Foundation, sought to take the lead in developing a science of educational administration. These institutions provided a nurturing haven for theorists like Jacob Getzels, Andrew Halpin, and Daniel Griffiths, all leaders who called for the removal of now-discredited precepts or principles of administration and the development of an adequate disciplinary foundation. The theory movement remains the primary focus of today's professors of educational administration. (Textbooks in the field bear this out: see, e.g., Silver 1983; Hoy and Miskel 1982.) Knezevich, for example, comments on developing a science of administration:

> Educational administration may never attain the tightly structured theories characteristic of the "hard" sciences such as physics; human behavior may be clouded by emotions and is influenced by far more antecedents and stimuli than the behavior of electrons or other inanimate objects. Nonetheless, it is possible to establish on at least a probabilistic basis a set of functional relations between antecedents and consequences in human behavior in organizations or elsewhere. This approach enables a reduction in, even if it does not eliminate, the margin of error in administrative decisions. (Knezevich 1984, 135)

Although Knezevich grants that a science of administration may never become a social physics, his gracious allowance does not reduce the effect of his argument. Emotions, which we would normally think of as distinguishing us in some way from rocks, crabs, and electrons, only "cloud" the issues; presumably, if we could get rid of this emotional overlay we could probe the real depths of administrative behavior. This behavioristic and positivistic analysis of what a science of administration is all about is not isolated to a few thinkers; it is symptomatic of the field at large.

To their credit, the early professors of educational administration challenged the profession by providing what were then stimulating new ideas, and critiqued it by showing the inadequacy of what passed for research and theory. The grand design for developing a theory never materialized though, largely because it had a flawed vision of the social sciences. Culbertson has summarized the core ideas at the foundation of the theory movement:

Core ideas of theory movement

1. Statements about what administrators and organizations ought to do cannot be encompassed in science or theory.

2. Scientific theories treat phenomena as they are.

3. Effective research has its origins in theory and is guided by theory.

4. Hypothetico-deductive systems are the best exemplars of theory.

5. The use of the social sciences is essential in theory development and training.

6. Administration is best viewed as a generic concept applicable to all types of organization. (Culbertson 1983, 15)

science of administration

These scholars noted that administration as a discipline needed to move from the "how do I manage a school board?" type of question to more abstract and generalizable concerns. The science of administration, as opposed to its practice, described what administration *is*, not what it ought or should be—much like biology describes what a clam is, not how to eat it. The scientist must also to some extent divorce theory from practice, because practice is localized in the specific situation, while theory is abstract and generalizable to all relevant situations. Therefore, theory is best derived by starting from hypotheses and validating them, largely through quantified research, rather than starting from the reality and developing situational understandings. To do this, the educational administrative theorist must turn to the disciplines of psychology, sociology, and, to some degree, economics. Finally, this argument asserted that administration is a generic field that can be studied across disciplines.

Halpin's work provides an example of the best of the theory movement, even though Halpin at times made an uneasy alliance with his own theory. Halpin, whose 1966 book *Theory and Research in Administration* exemplified the development of the new theory, began the first part of his work by identifying a "paradigm" to guide research into educational administration. The paradigm has all the required dimensions of the new movement: it looks at (1) the organizational task, (2) the *behavior* of the leader, (3) the variables linked to the behavior, and (4) the criteria of effectiveness (1966, 42-43). Halpin (1966, 44) sets these standards for research: "1. It is desirable to confine our inquiry to concepts that have definable referents in *behavior* or in the *products of behavior*. 2. It is important to discriminate between *descriptions* of behavior and *evaluations* of behavior." Halpin thus generously conforms to the criteria for this new social science of administrative behavior, examining what it is that administrators do, not what they ought to do and the behavioral dimensions of their work situation.

In the second half of this quite remarkable book, however, Halpin departs from the positivist approach to research by suggesting that school administrators should indeed have training in the arts and humanities. Citing a wide variety of literary works, Halpin demonstrates his real concern for what administrators should do. Halpin shows his own humanity in an eloquent passage on a particular problem encountered by the advocates of the theory movement:

> Here I shall perform the *coup de grace* which I suppose will alienate me from the camps of both superintendents and scientists. In reiteration of my leitmotif I suggest that if we are to learn how to observe —how to see what is "out there"—we had better avail our-

selves of a rich heritage which superintendents and scientists alike have studiously ignored: the heritage of the humanities. For what else is the function of the poet, the playwright, and the novelist than to examine and describe the perplexing enigma of the human condition? Who other than the creative artist is better equipped to describe man "in the round"? But the man of letters has been discredited by the market place. To such extent that we as educators have adopted the standards of the market place we, too, have discredited him. The voices of the market place have pleaded for increased technical specialization, and the universities have responded with all the determination of an ambitious salesman eager to give the customer precisely what he wants. (Halpin 1966, 296)

Halpin shows us in brief the basic flaw of the theory movement: even a complex design based in an even more complex philosophy could not in the end come to grips with the realities of human existence. The formalistic cages of logical positivism could not capture such realities, nor were they suited for the quantified methodology of the social sciences in general. In abstracting and then attempting to develop the equivalent of a social physics, the theory movement failed to ask why, what, and who.

By the 1970s, the theory movement had gathered a number of critics even within its own ranks. Griffiths, in 1979, wrote about the "intellectual turmoil" in the field. Halpin (1970) talked about the "fumbled torch" in developing administrative theory. Erickson (1979) called for a new paradigm that would reconceptualize administrative theory. Others had equally vociferous criticisms. This outcry was not limited to educational administration: it affected social science in general.

The reaction against the theory movement had its origin in several factors, one, certainly, the abstractness and even sterility of the theory itself. It failed to answer some of the central dilemmas of administration; indeed, it hardly addressed *education* at all. Because of this failure, scholars turned to more pragmatic concerns in studying administration and education and looked, for example, at the politics of education, sex, and racial equity within schools and the economics of schooling. In addition, Kuhn's 1967 book, *The Structure of Scientific Revolutions,* had a tremendous impact on the social sciences. Although devoted to a study of the nature of knowledge acquisition in the natural sciences, Kuhn's research suggested that science is governed by paradigms shared by a community of researchers. His argument found a sympathetic ear among the social scientists who for years had considered differing perspectives on the nature of social reality to be the norm. When applied to administration, Kuhn's ideas suggested that the search for a unified theory of administration, predictive and value free, was in vain. Certain scholars within the field began to articulate clear and well-stated alternative positions to the dominance of positivistic science. As a result, contemporary students of administration can now recognize diverse perspectives and numerous paradigms for examining administrative theory.

Basic flaw of theory movement:
Could not come to grips with the
basic reality of human existence
  Theory movement failed to ask
     why
     what
     who

Paradigm - a pattern or example
Gram — a list of the inflected forms
of a word
(Gk - pattern)

3

Paradigms and Promises:
Re-Viewing Administrative Theories

Our only hope for the rationalization of the power structure lies in conditions that favor political power for thought developing through dialogue. The redeeming power of reflection cannot be supplanted by the extension of technically exploitable knowledge.
—Jurgen Habermas, 1970.

The history of thought in educational administration outlined in the last chapter culminated in the theory movement of the 1950s and 1960s. This movement attempted to put educational administration on a footing as sound as that of psychology or economics by developing theoretical constructs that could be tested in the world of organizations. The grand theory, however, was never found: whenever one aspect of schooling and administration seemed a likely basis, further investigation pointed to another feature. The very idea of developing a continuum between natural scientific theory and social science theory has proven false. A science of administration will need to incorporate more than an objective accumulation of facts before it can begin to help us understand organizations and change them for the better. We have begun to realize that our conceptions of science, of schools, and of organizations are governed by the language we use to

53

discuss them, that is, by our paradigms and our metaphors. These provide frames, perspectives, and ways of organizing our reality. This chapter explores these concepts and suggests that we could use several frames or perspectives to examine schools and their administration.

PARADIGMS AND METAPHORS

Kuhn (1967) has argued that science is governed by paradigms or frameworks and ways of seeing. The paradigm, in effect, defines what are researchable questions and acceptable answers; it provides the boundaries for investigation into the area of concern. In the orthodox paradigm for natural science, scientists would be trained in accepted methods, read orthodox textbooks, and gradually accumulate knowledge. Thus, for example, when Newton conceived of the universe as a system that operated somewhat like a clock, he enabled other scientists to develop laws that could accurately predict the phenomena of a clocklike system, within the limits of that paradigm. When continuing research probes the limits of such a paradigm's explanatory power however, unanswered questions arise. Heretics begin to doubt the validity of the entire paradigm. At that point, for Kuhn (1967), a scientific revolution occurs and the paradigm shifts, as it did when Einsteinian relativity theories supplanted Newtonian mechanics. Significantly, the paradigm shift involves what amounts to a conversion process, a process of "seeing the light."

These views fundamentally challenge the illusion that science progresses gradually, accumulating facts and developing knowledge. Some philosophers of science go even further. Feyerabend (1978, 306) claims that the distinction between science and other pursuits of knowledge "is not only artificial but also detrimental to the advancement of knowledge. If we want to understand nature, if we want to master our physical surroundings, then we must use *all* ideas, *all* methods, and not just a small selection of them." Further, the idea of "science" becomes ideological and separated from what it is that scientists do:

> Scientists do not solve problems because they possess a magic wand—methodology, or a theory of rationality—but because they have

studied a problem for a long time, because they know the situation fairly well, because they are not too dumb . . . and because the excesses of one scientific school are almost always balanced by the excesses of some other school. (Besides, scientists only rarely solve their problems, they make lots of mistakes, and many of their solutions are quite useless.) Basically there is hardly any difference between the process that leads to the announcement of a new scientific law and the process preceding passage of a new law in society. (Feyerabend 1978, 302)

Many would argue that Feyerabend's views are extreme but they do suggest that the scientific enterprise is a complex and human one; that objective knowledge of natural phenomena is often gained through subjective exploration and shifts in ways of seeing the universe.

Such views on paradigms and paradigm shifts have been applied with vengeance to social science. The paradigm concept has helped in classifying different ways of seeing both organizational and administrative realities. In educational administration in particular, a debate has emerged regarding which paradigm is right and which is wrong. This indicates a change in the way the field views itself. The sociology of organizations and administrative theorizing now have a number of different paradigms available for viewing social realities. The paradigm one adopts largely depends on one's training and experience. The very concept of paradigm raises our awareness to more than one dominant way of seeing things.

For example, Burrell and Morgan (1979) have suggested that organizational sociology has four major paradigms for viewing organizations; these account for most of the research done in social theory, organizational studies, and educational administration. A short review of these four paradigms will be useful in understanding the dominant tensions that affect the field.

The first, the functionalist paradigm, embraces the assumptions that the social world is objective, real, and concrete; that scientists standing, as it were, outside of this world can record and accumulate facts about it. In this paradigm all things have a function, all serve some ultimate interest. Thus, schools are functional for social systems insofar as they prepare youngsters for the outside world. Functionalism does not challenge the social order; rather it assumes that things are right as they are: the scientist merely has to find the underlying regularities that guide social structures. Most of the research done in educational administration and organizational theory can be labeled functionalist in character. It is particularly acritical in nature; it treats organizations as concrete realities outside of the individual lives of those persons within them and it takes a fairly optimistic view of theory's ability to restructure organization. Most texts in educational administration present the functionalist paradigm in systems theory, role theory, and other avenues of exploration that treat the organization as a given reality, one that neither needs nor deserves any critical analysis.

A second paradigm has to do with interpretive modes of inquiry. The organization is considered to be a social construct: rather than being an objective reality, the organization is an idea shared by others. In this paradigm individuals *are* the reality; shared and consensual sense making guides behavior, and a large part of our organizational lives involves constructing and interpreting meanings. The methodology used in the interpretive perspective involves questioning those "natural" structures and events, probing how we as individuals come to understand one another. Social organization in this view is constructed after the fact; we engage with each other in activities and events and then describe that engagement in terms of rational conduct. Of major concern here is how the involved actors themselves engage in the construction of meaning systems. In this, the paradigm departs from the concept of the scientist as an objective and neutral observer of social facts. Instead, the paradigm suggests that science itself is composed of common-sense practices that result in social constructions. The proper role of the observer, then, lies in trying to understand the common-sense notions and the underlying assumptions that form the basis for human interaction (Giddens 1976, 52-53).

A third paradigm, radical humanism, shares much in common with the interpretive paradigm. It eschews functionalist and positivistic approaches to analyzing social data, but it extends the interpretive paradigm by maintaining that socially created structures also serve material interests. Structures are not created *de novo;* they have a historical reality that has resulted in differences in power, differences that have led to forms of domination by some over others. In this paradigm, individuals certainly create their own worlds, but those worlds assume a historical structure in which arenas of power, and thus domination, become a major factor. Individuals do not just construct their own realities in consort with others; they do so in the context of historically determined social structures that constrict free consciousness and serve the interests of only some individuals. The radical humanists, therefore, look to an examination of forms and expressions of power, and have the end goal of creating more equitable and just social structures.

Burrell and Morgan label the fourth paradigm "radical structuralism." This paradigm shares certain assumptions with the functionalist paradigm, particularly that social structures are somehow "out there" and open to investigation. It departs from functionalism in its claim that such structures arise out of material interests and become dominating forces. Rather than seeing society as ordered and harmonious, radical structuralists see it as the concrete expression of conflicting interests. Much of the work using this paradigm has a Marxist nature that aims at the analysis of inequalities generated by capitalistic systems.

Tracing the development of these four paradigms is an effective way to introduce some major differences between various sociological theories of organization. However, these paradigms have the same weakness as all taxonomies: by collecting a wide and diverse body of literature into rigidly defined groups, they lose much of the flavor of the individual pieces. In addition, by presenting four ways of seeing, they themselves form a way of seeing. The underlying assumption is that one could rationally evaluate each paradigm and then choose one compatible to one's own views. However, this is probably mistaken: in strict usage a paradigm is as much a set of blinders as it is a lens. Objectively, no one paradigm is as good as any other, yet each is subjectively better; the adoption of a particular paradigm depends on one's emotional commitment, training, and experiences. A paradigm "shifts" through insight, discovery, and conversion, not through rational and neutral evaluation and selection.

A paradigm also governs the dominant metaphors in a field of study (Morgan 1980). A comparision of metaphoric constructs can further delineate the differences between these systems of thought. According to Morgan (1980), in this century the meta-

Metaphor of functionalism

phors of machine and organism have dominated the functionalist paradigm of organizations. This way of seeing organization, or social structures generally, examines it mechanistically: different parts of the organization work together in some type of relationship to each other, and the whole functions to produce or do something. The other dominant metaphor governing functionalism, the metaphor of the organism, often appears in many forms of academic discourse. This metaphor sees the social structure as a system that changes and responds to environmental influences. Again, parts make up the whole, and the whole is treated as a functional unit having an independent life. In recent years, such terms as "loosely-coupled systems" (Weick 1976) and "organized anarchies" (March and Olsen 1976) have modified these dominant metaphors, though the basic metaphoric reference remains. These newer orientations do serve, however, to "demythologize" (Benson 1983) the fantasy of organizations as rational, goal-seeking units that act according to principles of mechanics or biology.

Metaphor of language game

Morgan (1980, 615) also discusses two other metaphors that illustrate different paradigms. The first, the metaphor of a "language game," suggests an interpretive paradigm. Drawn from the work of the philosopher Wittgenstein, a language game implies that what we do is what we say: that different types of activities are characterized by different "languages" and that these, like games, have their own rules. Thus, understanding the language is crucial to interpreting the world. The social construction of reality in this case is a construction through language; the associated metaphors involve "construction," "building," "frames," and so on (see Hanson 1985). Morgan chooses the metaphor of the psychic prison to characterize the radical humanist paradigm. This metaphor brings to mind the idea of being trapped in a reality not fully of our own making, of being unwittingly socialized into a particular social structure and believing that such a structure is natural and inevitable. Why social structures are this way and who benefits from this construction are questions that are rarely asked.

The concept of paradigm, and the related one of metaphor, has challenged the dominance of positivistic thinking so characteristic of American social science. Indeed, the line of positivistic and behavioristic thinking from Taylor through Simon and contemporary theorists has been as much a product of language as it is

of empirical research. The paradigm used to conceive of administration and the metaphors developed to talk about it have pro-
foundly influenced how administrators think of schooling. The
functionalist paradigm that has governed research and theory in
administration is now being confronted from both the interpretive
and critical stances. Educational administrators need to not only
be familiar with the concept of paradigm, but also to know which
particular paradigms govern thought in their field. At this point
there are three major paradigms or frames that influence educational administration theoreticians.

THREE FRAMES FOR ADMINISTRATION

Functionalism

Tries to impose an order and "cleanness" on things

Current debate in administrative theory in education centers
around three different approaches to the study and practice of
administration: the functionalist perspective, the phenomenological alternative, and the critical model. Functionalism in administration is represented by what might be called orthodox or mainstream theory. Taking its legacy from Taylorism, human relations, and systems theory, the research within this frame tends to
be positivistic, objectivistic, and supposedly neutral. The majority
of the theoretical and research-based work done in educational
administration reflects a functionalist frame of mind. Griffiths,
for example, reviews certain prominent researchers in educational
administration and finds, "Both the past and present researchers
can be said to be working within structural functionalist theory.
Aside from being less rigorous at present, there is really little
difference between the two sets in the nature of the theory they
espouse" (1983, 217). In general, mainstream theorists in educational administration espouse quantitative research that explores
categories of behavior derived from structural-functional analyses
of school organizations. The literature is rife with studies of
communication patterns, role structures, school climate, motivation patterns, and so on. All of these studies assume that organizations are concrete entities populated by role players and that
systematic study of these entities will yield reliable and predictable knowledge. Science, not philosophy, governs in the hope that

a critical mass of empirical studies will eventually result in the accumulation of a verified, or at least not falsified, body of knowledge that will rationalize practice: "When theory is based on systems that are logical, rational, explicit, and quantitative, practice will be similarly rational" (Hoy and Miskel 1982, 28). The prevalent assumption is that current practice is clouded by values and emotions and is simply more or less nonrational. Practitioners need a science of administration based in functionalism to rescue them from their own humanity. While this assessment of functionalism in administration is harsh, a number of the leading scholars in the field, challenged by alternative viewpoints, are indeed rethinking their positions. Sometimes this results in paradigm shifts; at other times, in vigorous defenses of functionalist methods. Two alternative approaches have generated much controversy in the field: a phenomenological approach and a perspective grounded in critical theory. Both provide new frames for educational administrators and theoreticians.

The Subjectivist Position

In 1974 Greenfield gave an address in Bristol, England, that had repercussions for over a decade. Greenfield took issue with the prevailing conception of organization and administration; in particular, he focused on researchers' and scholars' tendency to objectify the concept of organization. As Greenfield tells us, organizations are not objectively real phenomena; they are constructs, the products of individual agreement. In other words, they are socially constructed. If this is the case, then organizations are not "given" to us in the sense that material objects might be given. They cannot be studied in the same way that material objects might be studied. Organizations are human creations, the products of human will; therefore, their study should be concerned with human intention, existence, and history. Greenfield believes that organizations are "subjective understandings that people choose to live by—thereby making them real only through their own will and effort" (Greenfield 1984, 3). He clarifies his position:

> The dominant theory in educational administration assumes a real world, independent of the observer, in which organizations *do* exist —as solidly, clearly, and unavoidably as trees, tigers and Truth. But

as Wittgenstein and a long line of subjectivist philosophers point out, what the observer sees is dependent upon who sees it. In this sense, organizations are reflections of self rather than objective, external entities to which self must be adjusted. The failure of contemporary theory in educational administration is due in substantial measure to its insistence upon objectifying and reifying the organization. The cost of this error is that all the contributions that individuals make to organizations as unique, independent, wilful, erratic, and fallible human beings are lost to the theory. (Greenfield 1984, 17)

Greenfield expresses a subjectivist view of educational and organizational realities: that "organizations are inside people and are defined completely by them as they work out ideas in their heads through their actions in the practical world" (Greenfield 1983, 1). The points made in his development of "an anarchistic theory of organization" (1982) merit attention because of their challenging nature. Greenfield summarizes his major propositions about organization and administration. First, he maintains, it is the individual who acts; organizations cannot act because they do not exist in the common definition of this term. Organizations are not organisms with a life of their own; rather, they are constructs. Second, Greenfield posits that "we live in separate realities. What is true for one person is not for another" (1982, 5). Each individual, then, perceives the organization differently, and rationality lies in the eye of the beholder. What the superintendent sees is conditioned by a number of factors different from those affecting how the student perceives the organization; what is rational for one may be irrational for the other. Third, the understanding of an organization depends on the understanding of individual intention—why individuals act as they do. Individual motivations are diverse, yet how can we understand administration without understanding why individuals act as they do? In addition, we need an understanding of individual values, a topic that functionalist theory neglects by creating a dichotomy between objective facts and subjective values. Yet it is the value dimension of our lives that makes events and organizations meaningful. Our search for facts is conditioned by the development of systems of logic and rationality in Western thought; yet such systems of thought are themselves fraught with paradox: they have internal consistency, but accepting their basic validity requires the equivalent of a leap of faith, a leap made from outside the system itself. The acceptance of a logical or rational proposition ultimately depends on a belief in the veracity of the system in question. For Greenfield language is crucial, "Language is power" (1982, 8). How we define categories, events, and people can make the difference between whether they are treated favorably or repressively. Language constructs structure.

Greenfield's thesis has profound implications for the study of educational administration and for the preparation of administrators. Two extreme preparatory models suggest themselves. The administrator-as-scientist, schooled in the scientific method and concerned with quantifiable results, applies the findings of social science research as best he or she can, and brings progress to the school by performing all other required scientific or pseudoscientific activities. The administrator-as-humanist, trained in the arts and sciences and experienced in the ways of the world, brings feeling and intuition to the profession. Orthodox theory endorses the scientist model, but the humanist model may offer a more accurate description of the effective administrator. Indeed, Greenfield argues (1982, 7) that history and law are the appropriate disciplines for training administrators because these disciplines recognize both the failings and accomplishments of individuals and provide a perspective on the course of events that guide our lives.

Gronn (1983; 1984) also writes from an interpretivist perspective, though with a different emphasis. He too challenges the dominant framework by investigating the uses of language in structuring administrative work. For Gronn, the talk *is* the work: the work of principals in schools, for example, is largely conversational work. Principals spend a high percentage of their time engaged in dialogue; the dialogue itself provides a means of controlling the milieu of schools. Research into administration thus requires linguistic analysis of work situations and the reconstruction of history and conversation. The history of the individual administrator (biography) is important because it provides a context for understanding the intentions and meanings that occur; linguistic analysis of dialogue is important insofar as it demonstrates the subjective understanding of life in schools as this is indicated through language (Gronn 1984). The two principles of talk and history that underlie Gronn's approach to administration radically depart from the scientific, managerial approach so characteristic of the literature. Gronn looks at administrators as human actors cast into particular jobs that require them to interact with other such actors in order to establish common understandings about what it is that they do, and to find means for controlling and managing the particular environment in which they interact.

In summary, these subjectivist interpretations show that individuals make up the social network, and that individuals together form the various constructions that we label organizations. The subjectivist interpretation of organizations asserts that only individuals make reality, and that our common way of considering organizations is largely a fabrication. The subjectivist position therefore rejects the functionalism that considers the organization as an objective unit unto itself. By extension, the subjectivist administrator would value the actions, biographies, and language of the individuals in the organization; the functionalist administrator would be much more concerned with the functioning of the organization as a whole. Greenfield, with his emphasis on how organizations are composed of individuals who value and think, and Gronn, with his emphasis on how such organizations are characterized by language usage and language games, characterize major differences between the orthodox and functionalist approach to organizational theory and the interpretive alternative.

The Critical Frame

Orthodox administrative theory has also been challenged by perspectives informed by the critical work of social thinkers from Britain, Germany, and France. When applied to schools and administration, this work has been labeled a critical theory of educational administration. It can be discussed in terms of theoretical reflections and practical implications.

The theoretical base involves a critique of positivism and the related ideas of fact-value separation and value neutrality in administration, a critique of modern rationality as it is embodied in administrative principles, and a focus on the ideas of power and liberation as concerns for administration. The fact-value distinction arises out of the positivist assertion that only facts constitute legitimate scientific knowledge. Scientific knowledge, in this view, is that which can be reduced to "true" statements, statements that correspond to mathematical logic. Because values do not lend themselves to this kind of reduction, they lie outside the ken of science and are meaningless for the scientist. A science of administration based on these principles cannot consider the value dimension except as it is recorded as a series of facts, e.g., a percentage of the population believes in X. The administrator's role then is not to make a right or good or wise decision (values), but to make an efficient decision (facts) that achieves some goal set by others. Critical theory in administration argues that, first, this presents a too-constricted view of the scientific enterprise, and, second, that the fact-value dichotomy is artificial and false. Facts are identified as facts only through our values; in making any kind of decision, the administrator is advancing someone's values. Every decision about what "is" the case is also a statement about what "ought" to be the case. A decision to close a school, for example, may be an expression of the hard-headed fact that the school system needs to save resources, but it is also a statement of values and of priorities: *this* school ought to be closed because no other option is as viable.

Because of the practice of treating administration as only a means to achieve predetermined ends, critical theory has a further concern. Instrumental rationality means that rationality is largely considered a function of means-ends chains: an action is rational if it achieves some end. Rational actions are therefore instrumental, but if all actions are treated this way, what becomes of the search for the ends themselves? Formal or substantive rationality is concerned with searching for desired, valued, ends of a substantive and political nature. In administrative thought in particular, and in society in general, the substantive questions are not questions at all—they are givens. Citizens have limited input into how the system is conducted, in terms of such issues as distribution of wealth and the development of policy. Administration serves as a means for implementing policies established by elite decision-makers and demanded by technological imperatives, rather than as a guide for involving all citizens in the democratic determination of ends.

In administrative theory, rationality becomes a property of organizations and organizational systems rather than of individuals. Rationality is only considered in its instrumental sense, as a means for achieving ends. Since individuals do not have the capacity to consider *all* alternative means for achieving those ends (in Simon 1965, they are "boundedly rational"), they are not fully rational. The organization, which comprises groups of individuals, is rational because it can draw on the rationalities of many individuals. Each alone is limited, but when organized these individuals complement each other; thus the organization as a unit is more rational than any given individual in it. This delegation of rationality to the organization is uncomfortable for a critical theory of administration. It displaces responsibility for rational action from the individual to the organization, thereby the person loses the ability to make decisions concerning ends and means.

We can see from this discussion that organizational or societal ends or goals are of major importance to the development of a critical frame. What ends are to be pursued, whom they benefit and whom they harm, and how they contribute to a social vision are crucial questions in this approach. This means a commitment to the idea of *praxis*. An administrative and other social theory must go beyond mere analysis of institutional structures to show how theory can inform action, and action can lead to justice. Praxis, though, is not just given: it is dialectical in that it is continually and critically challenged, reformulated, and challenged again. Thus a critical theory can also be a practical theory.

Communicative practices are another concern for a critical theory. Rational and free discourse hallmarks a democratic society, but authoritarian and bureaucratic structures often impede such expression. Lines of authority and unequal status differentials serve to restrict communication and to distort issues of a public nature. Finally, cultural concerns also become part of a critical frame on administration. School organizations have cultures, and cultures include shared sagas, myths, rituals, and symbols. Cultures also serve to rationalize and legitimize administrative actions and thus can transmit a hierarchy of power and domination within the school. Administrators from a critical frame will be particularly sensitive to this issue. The critical theory of administration is based largely on the work of the Frankfurt school, which will be considered in another chapter. For administrators, this perspective parallels what was earlier discussed as the radical humanist approach. Although basically sympathetic to the interpretive approach of Greenfield and others, it attempts to go further by analyzing how constructed social structures themselves become seen as real and so solidify the way power is distributed in a society. Such a theory is concerned with analysis and education: exposing so-called objective conditions and helping to show future possibilities.

The three frameworks of functionalism, interpretive theory, and critical theory offer different ways of conceptualizing organization and administration. One aims at discovering regularities leading to prediction and lawlike regularization of administration; another looks at how meanings are created and choices imposed. A critical theory has a threefold purpose: to develop empirically based, nonpositivistic studies of organization and administration; to engage in the interpretation of meaning; and to evaluate the potential of social structure to empower or disempower the individuals within them. These three are termed the empirical, hermeneutic, and emancipatory interests of a critical theory.

Threefold purpose of critical theory

CRITICAL THEORY IN ORGANIZATIONAL CONTEXTS

The role of criticism in education and in the arts has a distinguished history, one carried further by American thinkers such as Dewey, and European philosophers such as Kant, Hegel, Marx, and others. However, in science influenced by logical positivism, the role of critique is muted and does not take place within the structure of the inquiring system. Positive science aims at the progressive accumulation of facts and solution of puzzles from within a received paradigm. Social science, though, does more than build a data base; it offers a series of possibilities that are by nature critical reflections on history. By focusing on what is, the social sciences and literature indicate what could be; by indicating what could be, these disciplines offer at least a nascent critique of what is. But the critique remains unfocused and fixated at this level unless a critical theory is consciously addressed within the structure of theory itself. A critical theory is thus conscious self-reflection in Dewey's sense, but more than this, it is also structured reflection on economic and cultural conditions and the ideologies that support them. Administrators can look to a critical and reflective theory because it enables them to better understand the hierarchical and bureaucratic situation of their employment, because it helps in understanding how theory itself helps to determine how we look at things, and because it helps in understanding how technical and bureaucratic forms of life come to dominate the institutions that we would hope to be responsive and adaptable. In this sense, a critically informed theory is not only moral decision making but also an analysis of the entire context of complex organizations.

The structure of modern organizations including the school encourages the development of a critical and moral theory of administration. In modern organizations hierarchy is very important. The development of hierarchy in turn results in the concentration of control over the means of production (what is produced by the organization) by a few (i.e., administrators and managers). In addition, "In hierarchical organizations (or in a bureaucratized society) it is not only the means of economic production that become concentrated, but also the means of theoretical reflection" (Brown 1978, 376). A variety of rules are "sedimented" (Clegg 1981) in the workplace and serve to legitimate the existing system of concentrated control and to structure the boundaries or frames of individuals in the organization. These sedimented rules have to do with the way individuals interact with each other in the organization: for example, who can talk to whom and about what in the organization, and how the work is conducted. Such rules project "the way it is" and are given, if not necessarily accepted, atheoretically. Leadership in the hierarchy increasingly requires conformity to the established theoretical structure. An administrative theory that projects a critical dimension adopts the constructed nature of social structures as a major assumption. The constructed nature of reality means that sedimented rules are not dictated by nature or history, but are man-made conventions that serve somebody's interests. This means that such structures, while deep and meaningful, are not "natural" and could be changed if the agents acting in those structures freely communicated about change. Such agents, though, need to be informed by a theory of action that helps to expose concentrations of control and enables the agents to discuss rational alternatives. An administration serious about the notion of participatory democracy will be able to review and bring to discussion the subconscious rules that guide behavior within the organization.

Further, pseudoscientific theories of management and of administration serve to legitimate and structure the subject they themselves are studying. There is a dialectical relationship between the development of theory, its promulgation by intellectuals, and the structure of practice. Astley and Van de Ven (1983, 269) note that "organization theory not only reflects organizational reality, it also produces that reality. . . . Like other social sciences, it helps to structure its own subject matter. By giving accounts of organizational phenomena, theory helps to give objectivity to the practices to which it refers."

A positivist theory of organizations thus yields a positivist practice of organizational behavior, while a critical theory may well yield a critical practice. As Argyris (1973, 266) has noted, social science theory tends to become both normative and coercive; it provides the theoretical rationale for those practices aimed at consolidating the concentrations of power. Intellectuals formulate theory that in turn is used to structure the institution in particular ways (Clegg and Dunkerly 1977, Gramsci 1971). As intellectuals study administration, for example, they develop theories of administrative behavior that attempt to reflect actual practices within schools; however, the practices themselves begin to conform to their theoretical analysis because the theoreticians have status and power. This is a circular process: the scholar proposes that Theory X operates in schools; the administrator takes this prescriptively and changes his or her behavior to conform to Theory X; the scholar then researches the institution and "discovers" Theory X at work. In this fashion, intellectuals help to create certain social structures out of the universe of alternatives.

Theory in a positivistic sense provides an "image" of organization, one that may be far removed from its complex reality. Theory provides metaphors and images of schools and, in so doing, helps to structure schools along these lines. Allison (1983, 16) finds that "The literature is so riddled with the 'school as . . .' construction that the metaphor has become the message. Rarely does one encounter a nonmetaphorized reference to schools as independent and discrete phenomena." Thus, schools are bureaucratic, open systems, and so on. These formulations are deep and impressive, but each provides a certain way of conceptualizing the school and thereby a way of structuring its reality according to a particular, theoretically conceived framework. Insofar as these images pretend to display the school in its totality, they become acritical. When these images of schools provide us with information and ways of thinking, they are useful to our understanding of what this organization is like; insofar as these images prescribe ways of being for an organization, they become dominating ideologies. Thus, a student who studies administrative theory and discovers that "leadership style" is both important and situational might return to his or her organization with a preconceived notion of what leadership "really" is and begin to implement a particular style that misses the whole point of being a leader. Only a critical awareness of the limits of theory can avoid this.

A critical theory also becomes necessary to put the issues of concentration and hierarchy into perspectives. A critical perspective enables administrative theory to become a moral science in that it can reflect back on the conditions of its own formation. Without this perspective, theory becomes positive, and in so doing, "colonizes the life world" (Habermas 1984), a phrase indicating the increasing spillover of bureaucratic principles into the spheres of morality and art and a consequent "loss of meaning" in cultural systems. Schools are institutionalized mechanisms of cultural and symbolic reproduction, social integration, and personality development; to the degree that a school administration attempts to bureaucratize and rationalize these cultural areas, the symbolic universe becomes unable to create meaningful systems. In such cases there is a resulting disenchantment with education and culture: "the disenchanted world is stripped of all ethical meaning; it is devalued and objectified as the material and setting for purposive-rational pursuit of interests" (McCarthy 1984, xvii). Schools become arenas for the competitive accumulation of skills that will be useful in achieving material and technological dominance: a sorry picture for an educational institution designed to further civilization.

A theory of administration can contribute to the bureaucratization of the lifeworld (a term denoting cultural formations and "normal" practices) by insisting that the educational community conform to standards of efficiency, accountability, and predictability normally required only of technical and scientific enterprises. There is, then, a spillover from such demands into the area of cultural formation. As a result the middle- and under-classes are subject to rationalistic demands that subvert their own roles in the democratic state. If theory defines educational communities as "systems" with universal characteristics and without any individually distinguishing features, then universal standards will be applied to schools without regard for the unique characteristics of a cultural community. That is, the "lifeworld" of an individual system is projected into a standardized reification of systems in general. In this context, forms of social and cultural production—particular forms of life—are assimilated into a unitary cultural system that denies the unique experiences and perspectives of specific cultural communities.

By and large, educators and educational administrators are idealistic. However, we live in an era of expanding technology that provides us with both increasing comfort and increasing danger; we engage with the world through various forms of work, some of which satisfy and some of which alienate; we shop, work, and play in a social environment in which some people simply have more than others. What does administrative theory, in its scientific bent, have to say to these real-world conditions? Not a great deal. Yet we, as teachers or administrators, are engaged in a profession whose purpose *is* to make a difference. The joy of being an administrator or a teacher is to recognize and understand that each life makes a difference.

Administrative theory from Taylor on cannot deal with this. It looks at the routine and the normal. This attitude might be fine for an organization that produces universal and standard products; it is inappropriate to educational administration that confronts plurality, exceptions, and differences. A critical theory of administration is necessary because a critical theory requires us to reflect on what we do and how what we do affects all who encounter us. A critical theory seeks the moral base of decisions and the effects of those particular decisions on the youngsters in our charge. It asks how our organization impedes the learning and progress of students. It asks how we, as individuals, can make a difference.

A positivistic and functionalist science of administration dismisses these types of questions. The practice of administration, dependent only on data-gathering strategies, ignores them. If such questions are important, and we hope that they are, the alternative is to reconceptualize and to reconstruct the field of educational administration so that it can critically evaluate both its theory and practice.

4

Foundations for Critical Analysis
in Administration

INTRODUCTION

We have briefly looked at three frameworks for conceptualizing administrative activity—the functionalist, phenomenological, and critical ones. In this chapter, we need to explore in more depth the rationale behind the critical approach to administration, to sketch out its foundations, and to show how aspects of these three frameworks can be integrated in a critical approach. These will be examined as they are pertinent to the development of a critical framework for educational administration and will serve to provide a context for later chapters.

Critical theorists are scholars who have approached social analysis in an investigative and critical manner and who have conducted investigations of social structure from perspectives originating in a modified Marxian analysis. The dominant approach to critical theory finds its assumptions and arguments located in and responsive to the work of the Frankfurt school, a group of diverse German thinkers, many of whom emigrated to the United States during the Second World War. The Frankfurt school is known for its commentaries on science, culture, rationality, and social and economic systems. Although inspired by Marx, the Frankfurt school attempted a broad-scale investigation

Critical theory

of modern society that rethought economic analyses and, moreover, contributed to sociological and psychoanalytic theory. Critical theory, however, might also be used in a more general sense to discuss those concepts that do not presume to give a positive and unilateral definition of history and society, but to hold them up to inspection. Critical theory, then, questions the framework of the way we organize our lives or the way our lives are organized for us. It probes foundational assumptions that are normally taken for granted and seen as natural outgrowths of historical process. A critical theory locates human relationships in structural variables, particularly those of class and power, without, however, compromising the possibility for change. Thus, a critical theory examines sources of social domination and repression, but with the caveat that since we ultimately make our worlds, we can ultimately change them. Finally, a critical theory is committed to values; its critique is largely oriented toward how created social structures impede the attainment of such values as democracy and freedom.

Critical theory of administration

A critical theory of *administration,* by its nature, would seem to be a strange creature indeed. Critical theory, by definition, critiques and examines; it holds up the systems we believe in and are somewhat attached to and says "consider this more fully." Administration, though, or so we are led to believe, is associated with running an organization efficiently and effectively, without regard to ultimate ends or consequences. Administrators carry out policy directives and establish a sound organizational structure, a structure that in the terms of critical theory may be deficient. Critical theory and administration, then, seem at opposite ends of the room, and certainly never destined to dance together.

This objection to a critical theory of administration can be overcome on several fronts. First, this view of administration is a legacy of positivistic social science. It assumes that, for example, ends and means, facts and values, can easily be separated: we give the administrator the means and the facts and leave the values and ends to those who know better. Administration, though, is basically concerned with values and with ends; otherwise, why would we choose this profession? Certainly not to simply be a vehicle carrying others' ideas; if anything, our current thinking about the profession suggests that the administrator establishes the type and clarity of vision and purpose crucial to the organization. This administrator is not necessarily the chief executive or the superintendent; the administrator at the firing line is just as much (if not more so) responsible for providing a sense of purpose. This, second, is related to the idea of leadership. Administrators can, and perhaps must, be leaders. Leadership, as we hope to demonstrate, is concerned with the very questions raised by the critical theorists. Leadership is not a holding company for the school organization; rather, it is oriented toward change and toward the realization of wants, needs, and values. Thus, the administrative leader is also a critical theoretician, because he or she is not satisfied with the status quo and has a sense of direction and an often-compelling purpose. The administrative leader is imbued with a sense of value, of what is important and what is not. In this way, the administrator can utilize the ideas of critical theory to inform his or her role in the organization, to embark on a course of practical action, and to work toward attaining an organization that is both productive and liberating. This, at its heart, must be the purpose of a critical theory; it is *not* oriented toward either a return to the past or a destruction of the present. It is oriented toward the possibilities of the future, a future in which all can participate equally. We can now review some of the dominant themes that appear in the work of critical theorists, recognizing that it is only possible here to summarize those ideas in critical theory most pertinent to administrative concerns.

Deetz and Kersten provide an organizing framework for examining the contributions of the critical theory school. Critical theory has three tasks: understanding, critique, and education. Further,

Three tasks of critical theory

> Understanding requires descriptions of the social reality in the organization and the forces that form, deform, sustain, and change that reality. Critique focuses on examining the legitimacy of consensus and reason-giving activities in an organization and the forces bearing on them. Education develops the capacity of organizational members to engage in self-formation through participation in organizational practices and decision making that are free and unrestrained. (Deetz and Kersten 1983, 148)

These three themes, understanding, critique, and education, are indeed at the heart of both a critical theory of society *and* a critical theory of administration. The positivist-functionalist approach to social study is rejected; in its place we put self-inquiring systems of thought.

CRITICAL THEORY AND THE SEARCH FOR MEANING

Understanding in this context is related to the objective and subjective search for meaning, and refers to the methods of research and inquiry used to gain an understanding of nature, an understanding of man, and an understanding of man in nature. In this respect, Habermas (1971) posits three "cognitive interests" as anthropologically given: first, technical interest, oriented to establishing control of nature and to gathering objective knowledge; second, historical-hermeneutic interest, oriented toward the interpretation and understanding of human nature and history; finally, emancipatory interest, aimed at realizing conditions of freedom. These interests arise from three fundamental aspects of the human condition: labor, communication, and power (1971, 313). All social groupings engage in these forms of life: labor or work is the production of things, from crops to airplanes; communication is the shared development of meaning structures; power is the expression of political relationships.

The technical interest is expressed through the technical control of man over nature through work and labor. The historical-hermeneutic interest is expressed in communication, developing common understandings of our histories and of ourselves. This interest, fundamental to social groupings, involves the need to establish norms, morals, and relevance. There is also a fundamental interest in freedom and in the channeling of power. This is expressed through a critical theory that reflects back on our self-understanding to expose asymmetrical relations of power. There is, in other words, a motive toward justice in human conduct.

Our research efforts, then, will take the form outlined by cognitive interests. On one hand, the search for quantitative and objective knowledge about nature and man is represented in modern society by the natural sciences that, in theory, objectify the phenomena of study in order to develop predictive laws of behavior. This model of science has, of course, been applied to the study of social behavior. Critical theory has no argument with the quantitative and empirical studies of social behavior; only when these are seen as the *only* ways of gaining information are they called into question.

Social action occurs in a historical context and is pregnant with subjectively created and shared meanings. Hermeneutics addresses these meanings by understanding texts in the context of the historical time in which they were developed. This concept, applied to understanding man in nature, looks at meanings (text) in the context of history and tradition. For example, this approach would be concerned with how a group of students establishes a culture in the context of the school; with what the idea of "school" means to these students; and with the analysis of their intersubjective interpretations of the organization. This is not the same as collecting social facts through surveys and questionnaires; it involves the penetration of meaning structures through interpretive and qualitative analysis, and is concerned with how meanings are constructed in a social milieu.

Both objective and subjective knowledge are important; they complement each other and presuppose each other (Apel 1967, 23). Even the hard natural sciences require a complementary relationship between the objective, laboratory-developed data *and* the community of scientists that intersubjectively interprets the data. These concepts provide a complementary analysis of man over nature and man in nature. They address both labor and communication, but they only address relationships of power in descriptive terms. A critical theory is needed to look to the relationship of technical and historical-hermeneutics interests in the context of the development of equitable power structures. Giddens (1976, 161) observes that "every cognitive and moral order is at the same time a system of power, involving a 'horizon of legitimacy'" and, because of this, its ability to free or oppress human beings remains moot.

CRITICAL THEORY AS SOCIAL CRITICISM

The Franklin school most fully develops this agenda of critique, paying particular attention to the development of modernity and its effects on the individual and the state. Critique in this vein has been largely negative, exposing areas of system domination over individual consciousness. A list of topical areas is beyond our intentions here, but we will offer a short review of the areas of rationality, positivism, legitimation, and culture. The significance of this critique for the administrator lies in the fact that social structures are never perfectly formed, but reflect levels of labor, communication, and power that may be unequally distributed, yet may also be open to change if subject to critical analysis and administrative action.

Rationality has been a dominant concern of critical theorists in this century, and a prime concern of organizational and administrative theorists. The organization as a rational, goal-seeking entity has been the dominant conception of mainstream scholars; this, in turn, has depended on a particular view of individual rationality as, essentially, instrumental and goal driven. Critical theorists, however, have argued with this. For example, Horkheimer (1974, first published in 1947) wrote of the *Eclipse of Reason*, claiming that there was a difference in what he labeled subjective and objective reason. This differentiation between reason, not one normally found in current discussions of this subject, was fundamental to the arguments of the critical theorists. Essentially, the difference of concern here was that between instrumental reason and reason located in an "objective" moral sphere. Prior to the Enlightenment, rationality adhered to an objective and moral system of thought. As Horkheimer explains:

> Great philosophical systems, such as those of Plato and Aristotle, scholasticism, and German idealism were founded on an objective theory of reason. It aimed at evolving a comprehensive system, or hierarchy, of all beings, including man and his aims. The degree of reasonableness of a man's life could be determined according to its harmony with this totality. Its objective structure, and not just man and his purposes, was to be the measuring rod for individual thoughts and actions. (Horkheimer 1974, 4)

What was reasonable in this schema was what corresponded to an objective system of God and nature, and of man's striving to achieve the just state and the right society. In a sense objective reason stood outside individual capacities; indeed, such capacities were to be measured against such reason. By the time of the Enlightenment and its emphasis on human progress through science, reason came to be conceived of in more instrumental terms:

communicative interaction

as the subjective calculation of means in order to achieve ends. Thus, when one talks of rational action in organizations, one means those efforts designed to achieve goals; this is instrumental reason, formalized and abstracted. It has little to do with the provision of meaning or the illumination of ends. Questions concerning the good life and the just society are not necessarily irrational but they are arational; in this context, they reflect tastes and preferences rather than serious efforts at democratic consensus. Each "lifestyle" is as good as every other, and standards are relative to what patterns of consumption they set. Habermas (1970) has addressed these questions and has updated Horkheimer's concerns. He does this by distinguishing between purposive-rational action, similar to instrumental or subjective reason in Horkheimer, and communicative interaction, similar to objective rationality. Note, however, that he bases these concepts in action: how individuals act in social groupings according to some theory of rational behavior.

Habermas has argued that forms of action reflecting work and communication (the technical and historical-hermeneutic interests) were traditionally embedded. Purposive-rational action, which reflects the technical interest, was embedded in communicative interaction, which reflects the historical-hermeneutic interest. Technical control depended on and was embedded in the communicative formulation of goals and ends in whose service the technology was harnessed. Communicative interaction was aimed at establishing community, which included consensual norms and values that guided action in a society. Here the traditional themes deal with "justice and freedom, violence and oppression, happiness and gratification, poverty, illness, and death" (Habermas 1970, 96). Labor based on purposive, means-ends action is placed within the context of these other themes.

However, with the progress of science, the destruction of systems based on magic and myth, and the rise of capitalism, purposive or instrumental rationality becomes decontextualized from communicative interaction. Giddens, for example, tells us: *Giddens*

The process of the expansion of technical rationality is accompanied by two other phenomena: the "disenchantment" of the world, and the concomitant replacement of mystical or religious norms by abstract "rational-legal" imperatives. ... On the one hand, religion

magic, mysticism, become inevitably squeezed out of the organisation of human conduct in the major institutional spheres of our society; on the other hand, the predominant forms of social protest
become utopian, futile outbursts against the imperatives of rational-
isation, and themselves assume a "mystical" character. (Giddens
1973, 275)

Societies now based on technological progress and positivist
science become dominated by the need to produce, for the particular economy is fueled by technology and consumerism and the
private appropriation of wealth. Purposive-rational systems of
action take on a life and logic of their own, and means-end rationality, reflected in decision-rules, strategic planning, and problem-solving techniques, becomes the source of legitimation for the
political system:

> The property order change(s) from a *political relation* to a *production*
> *relation,* because it legitimates itself through the rationality of the
> market, the ideology of exchange society, and no longer through a
> legitimate power structure. It is now the political system that is
> justified in terms of the legitimate relations of production. ... The
> institutional framework of society is only mediately political and
> immediately economic. (Habermas 1970, 97)

In other words, the social system becomes driven by the economy and by administrative decisions designed to accommodate
technical progress and capital accumulation. A new stage in rationality is reached, a stage of technocratic decision making using
an instrumental or purposive rationality. The technocratic strategies, though, must ultimately clash with the norms and values
of tradition. A technocratic administration tries to depoliticize
these, but finds that instrumental rationality cannot re-create
meanings or culture, which lie at the level of communicative interaction. Whereas previously such systems of purposive-rational
action depended on communicative interaction for their formation, they are let loose and set up a division in life between, for
example, organizational realities and family structures. Politics,
which was once concerned with the practical—that is, the realm
of practical life aimed at improving the human condition—now
becomes concerned with the technical—that is, the realm of efficient decision making aimed at keeping the system on course.

The practical and the technical are no longer distinguished, and politics, rather than being open to communicative discussion, is designed by decision makers to become a science. But political science leaves out of its arenas the expressions of individuals; these are seen only as aggregate votes that affirm or disaffirm policy decisions rather than having any input into the character of the decisions themselves.

administration based on purposive-rational conception

An administration based on a purposive-rational conception of action becomes an administration of means and forecloses discussion of ultimate goals and values. The science of administration, to the extent that it is based on a positivistic methodology that does not incorporate qualitative understandings, furthers the goals of a technocratic administration. Positivism is a subject of concern for both administration and critical theory and relates closely to the distinction between purposive-rational action and communicative interaction.

positivism

Positivism, as a systematic formula for the conduct of investigation, denies the meaningfulness of value and ethical systems. This, in turn, enhances a purposive rationality by stressing the gathering of objective facts and the neglect of meanings. Through positivism, social structures become mystified and naturalized; by using positivist methods to abstract the characteristics of a society in one given epoch, all history is considered to reflect the same set of circumstances and causations. This reduces human history to the history of one set of events, those that the positivist researcher investigates. By producing data and predictions for that set of events, the researcher in turn sets the course for future events by limiting our understanding of the possibilities. As Sewart (1980, 325) claims, "the positivist attitude" means that "the intersubjective constitution of the meaning of social action is identical to an object in the natural world."

Positivism, though, has paradoxical results. The positivist view of science, for example, maintains the separation of facts from values, relegating values to the category of preference. It also separates theory from practice by claiming that theory can be verified only logically and never verified through practice. Held discusses the result of this orientation:

> In the name of value-freedom, a certain value-orientation is championed to the exclusion of all others. In the name of a separation

between theory and practice, a particular form of practice is sanctioned. Seemingly passive, contemplative reason masks an underlying level of committed reason. Not being open to rational investigation and solution, practical questions become the province of the private individual and in the end can be justified only by reference to a
decision or a commitment of belief or faith. By confining rational decision procedures to those utilized by the natural sciences, positivists
reduce ethics to decisionism and close off ultimate principles and
values from the possibility of rational justification. (Held 1980, 170)

If positivism claims that values and ethics are nonmeaningful
in the scientific sense and merely social preferences, how can
such issues be established in an objective sense and not simply as
desires or wants? This question has been asked for centuries; its
traditional resolution has been through objective systems of faith
and religion, or dialectical systems of political action. In the ancient systems, the role of politics "was continuous with ethics, the
doctrine of the good and just life. As such it referred to the sphere
of human action, *praxis*, and was directed to achieving and maintaining an order of virtuous conduct among the citizens of the
polis" (McCarthy 1978, 2). In systems of faith, reasonable behavior was that which led to the leading of the good and virtuous life,
characterized by the cardinal virtues of faith, hope, and charity.

This emphasis in politics, an orientation to the good and the
just, remained through Adam Smith, who envisioned the scientific study of politics as contributing to practical advice for the
legislator, with the resulting growth in the wealth of the whole
(Paul 1979). Smith's successors, though, increasingly saw a dis-
continuity between the study of politics and its application to
practice. Paul (1979, 121) finds that "Senior and Mill divided political economy into a science and an art . . . with the science
having nothing definitive to say to the political artist, the legislator." By the latter part of the nineteenth century, this dichoto-
mization was accomplished; economics had become based on
mathematical models and was used, in turn, to predict political
behavior. The idea of politics as the search for the just state was
no longer a tenable position; instead, politics became the narrower
attempt to find political regularities and to predict political behavior. Logical positivism, developed in the 1920s but with a legacy going back through Comte, became the philosophical justification for the scientization of politics. Political study in educa-

tional administration, of course, followed these developments. Theories of political economy in schools, for example, must be evaluated "according to how well they predict or explain behavior, not according to how well they correspond to humanistic notions of the complexity of human and of social behavior" (Boyd and Crowson 1981, 322). Issues of a valuative nature are of little or no consequence here; what matters are the facts and the predictions, not rightness or justness.

Indeed, in the modern models of politics, the moral dimensions are simply not appropriate subjects for discussion because they do not lend themselves to deductive inquiry or objective scrutiny. But there may in fact be a way to ground the discussion of ends in ways that are not simply preferential. Habermas, with his theory of communicative competence, provides a way for the grounding of values and politics.

In what way can we justify a search for basic norms, such as truth and justice, without resorting to mere statements of preference or imposed systems of belief? The search for these values has to be grounded somewhere other than in preferences if they are to be considered of any universal significance. This significance involves "a universalistic morality embedded in a system of participatory democracy, providing the opportunity for discursive will-formation" (Held 1980, 295). This simply means that all individuals can express their desires without constraint and can come to an agreement about actions to be taken. Habermas (1975; 1979) grounds this search for norms in language itself. Our very language makes certain "claims" on us. It asks that we be comprehensible: the language we speak must be mutually understandable to each speaker; the content must be true insofar as it refers to mutually accessible material. It must be truthful in that the recipient can acknowledge the presumed validity of what is said. It must be rightful insofar as both speaker and hearer can agree that they are engaging in a conversation that has a given context (Habermas 1979, 4-5). In summary, truth, rightness, truthfulness, and comprehensibility are "validity claims" that speakers make on each other. Truth addresses the objective world of facts where speakers can come to a conclusion based on empirical evidence agreed to by a community. Rightness refers to social relationships where individuals assert their mutual, socially sanctioned interaction through speech; that it is right to engage in discourse as members of a society and culture. Truthfulness addresses the subjective reality of the individual who, in speaking is asserting a demand that his or her statements be given credence. Finally, in speaking and using language, we are also claiming that what is being said is comprehensible and understandable (Habermas 1979, 68).

These rules for communicative interaction suggest that in every conversation we engage in establishing norms of conduct; every conversation involves our saying things that have a context, that have a presumed truthfulness, that have reference to shared values and norms, and that are expressed in a language that we both understand. These rules underlie all and any language. More than this, though, such rules underlie the search for a universally applicable theory of norms, one whose possibility is denied by positive science. If norms of truth, truthfulness, comprehensibility, and rightness are embodied in the structure of language itself, then it is not such a far claim to say that these norms form a basic part of human conduct. If that is so, a critical theory can be founded on the search for social systems that embody such norms. For Habermas, the linguistic rules correspond to social norms of truth, justice, and equality, and it is on these that a critical theory can secure its foundation. Our language usage is premised on our implicit assertions that truth, no matter its violation, is a basic norm informing language interactions. Similarly, we are claiming that what we say has a right to be heard; linguistically we claim a certain equality of expression. Both of these claims further the idea of justice, that the various language claims must be evaluated on the basis of just criteria, those of truth, rightness, and truthfulness. Thus, a critical theory of administration, or any critical theory of society, can be legitimated not on an idealistic conception of the good, but on a foundation built in the very structure of human interaction. Language itself, in Habermas's formulation, serves as the prototype for norms of justice, equality, and so on. These in turn lead to a demand for a participatory democracy, since language is available to all and contains the seeds for equal political interactions. Because language is a basic aspect of our humanity and is representative of all social conditions, it stands in *ideal* form as the prototype of democratic participation.

Language, however, can become distorted. In this context,

this means that communication is articulated through and in organizational structures that themselves reflect power relationships. This, in turn, can result in communication that is constrained by power differentials, even to the degree of creating ideologies that govern language usage. Thus, a further role of critical theory is analysis of false forms of consciousness that contribute to the distortion of communication. A model for this is psychoanalysis, wherein with the help of a therapist the patient can be taken inward, as it were, to see how he or she has developed repressive structures that have prevented the realization of the true relationships that have affected personal history.

Schroyer (1973, 166) has suggested that Habermas's concern with language represents "a purely formalistic concept" that needs to be grounded in analyses of political and economic differences. Bernstein (1976, 224) also asks "under what conditions will agents who have a clear understanding of their historical situation be motivated to overcome distorted communication and strive toward an ideal form of community life?" These comments suggest the idealistic nature of Habermas's thesis; still, a distinction needs to be made between the idealized conditions for pure speech and the latent structure of norms within speech. If we accept Habermas's arguments, this structure of norms justifies a rejection of a positivist stance that relegates the normative dimension to the area of preference. The structure allows solid footing for an approach that accepts norms and values as basic components of any system or theory of social life.

Habermas's formulation of the notion of an ideal speech situation could be thought of as an attempt to restore rationality to the domain of communicative interaction and to subordinate the instrumental dimensions. But this project is not accomplished either through a call for the past or through an idealized version of the future. Rather, much of his work is located in an analysis of present systems of interaction, including an analysis of the material structure of social systems. While communicative interaction and the ideal speech situation emphasize the analysis of basic human conditions for establishing norms of participation and democracy, the analysis now turns toward an examination of actual historical structures that tend to distort the ideal conditions.

How modern systems legitimate themselves is a major feature of Habermas's thought, and one most pertinent to students of administration. In modern societies, the political system, traditionally thought of in terms of the search for a just and equitable society, becomes tied to the economic system. In a liberal state, the political system asserts equality of all: liberal theory states that each of us has the right to vote, the right to free expression, and equal protection under the laws. The political system is tied to the concept of equality of representation. However, this cannot be carried over to the economic system, where inequality of wealth is legitimated as necessary. If the relations of production can be shown to invalidate any theory of just exchange, as Marxian analysis of liberal capitalism claims, than the ideology supportive of the political sphere is threatened. This, in Habermas's view, can lead to a legitimation crisis for liberal capitalism. The response to this is to necessitate the intervention of the state in order to regulate the economy. In this new historical phase, advanced capitalism, the state actively intervenes in the economy to establish an equilibrium of sorts. The need for legitimation remains unchanged, but the structure for legitimation has fundamentally altered: it is no longer tied to political models but to economic ones. The state must come up with an alternate source of legitimacy. The rise of the welfare state, the implementation of compulsory schooling (with its progressive ideology), and the growing linkages between science, technology, and state administration have all been offered as possible and interdependent avenues for establishing legitimation.

Legitimation, in this analysis, is tied to the twin concepts of rationality and motivation. Rationality in the sense of purposive-rational action suggests that citizens can reasonably expect the government to engage in rational planning activities that will result in increasing wealth and consumption. To the degree that the state administration cannot rationally engage in long-range planning for economic growth (partly because of its inability to control economic fluctuations), the possibility for a rationality crisis (Habermas 1975, 61) remains. Essentially, a rationality deficit means that although expectations are raised in regard to achieving material ends, these expectations cannot be satisfied for the society at large. A rationality crisis occurs when our instrumental expectations of economic fulfilment outstrip the state's ability to satisfy these expectations on the basis of political criteria, e.g., in an equitable manner. For example, different interest groups may lobby the state for different and incompatible policies that may not be in the interests of society as a whole. The society, in other words, has instrumental expectations for a continued rise in the standard of living, but the state can only satisfy certain powerful interests. Thus its ability to rationally plan the economy is called into question.

This relates to a motivation deficit as well. If purposive rationality is dominant and decontextualized from communicative interaction, what other than instrumental objectives will motivate the populace? Further, are instrumental objectives enough? Motivation, for Habermas, can be examined in two ways: first, as the residue of precapitalist religious values and, second, as the utilitarian values of an instrumental society. The first has been eroded by the increasing secularization and technologization of society. Thus, the motive for success and achievement spurred by the realization that success is rewarded in the afterlife or that success demonstrates salvation is eroded by an increasingly secular society that suggests that rewards are given now, and in proportion to the amount of private effort expended. In one example, the motive for success in schools is often not contingent on the need to demonstrate a command of sectarian knowledge, or on some belief that it shows one's knowledge. Rather, it is predicated on instrumental concerns: preparation for college and preparation for career. Habermas (1975) claims that once such religious and social values are eroded, they cannot be replaced by state administrative action. These motivations occur through communicative interaction; they represent a substantive rationality, in error as it might be, that sees the world in a certain way and then designs motivational systems to encourage the young to perpetuate such a world. A state administration geared toward an instrumental notion of life could not re-create these motives in its youth. Even a school system designed to socialize children suffers from this same fate, partly because it adopts an achievement mentality predicated on instrumental success.

Even the second source of motives, an instrumental and utilitarian desire for achievement, is also being eroded: "People lose faith in the market as a fair distributor of scarce values (as the state's very intervention raises issues of distribution and as the increasing level of education provides aspirations and expectations that cannot be coordinated with occupational opportunity, etc.)" (Held 1980, 293). Thus, instrumental motives do not find universal success because, for example, it is clear that achievement in school does not automatically lead to accumulation of wealth.

The combination of possible rationality deficits and possible motivational deficits leads, in this analysis, to a possible legitimation crisis. Legitimation is the state's right to be recognized as worthy (Habermas 1979, 178) and as receiving loyalty. A legitimation crisis challenges these two suppositions by questioning the state's right to rule. In Habermas's analysis, if a rationality deficit develops and a motivation deficit then becomes apparent, a legitimation crisis is possible. In essence the people question government's ability to equitably satisfy those basic wants and needs in a sense determined by previous government action and by the progression of an instrumental rationality. An administration oriented simply towards means and not towards consideration of ends contributes to such a crisis. It steers the existing system according to economic and other dictates without considering cultural and social issues. For example, a school system bases its legitimation with the public on its instrumental capacity: it promises its public that its alumni will be certified for college or jobs, but graduates classes with a high proportion of dropouts, poor exam scores, and minimal competence. The administration might be concerned with bureaucratic imperatives without fully considering how its actions and promises are routinely regarded by its constituency. A legitimation crisis, then, is a crisis in the erosion of authority, a questioning whether the system of governance can continue to steer the course. This can occur at the local as well as the national level and is related to changes in motivation and in rationality. Habermas discusses the possibility of a legitimation crisis in these terms:

> A legitimation deficit means that it is not possible by administrative means to maintain or establish effective normative structures to the extent required. During the course of capitalist development, the political system shifts its boundaries not only into the economic system but also into the socio-cultural system. While organizational rationality spreads, cultural traditions are undermined and weakened. The residue of tradition must, however, escape the administrative grasp, for traditions important for legitimation cannot be regenerated administratively. (Habermas 1975, 47)

analytic scheme based on possibilities and tendencies rather than on predictions

There is a dual tension between the economic system that depends on the private appropriation of wealth and the political system that depends on the public display of equality. If the economic system is threatened, thereby threatening the state's legitimacy, the state administration cannot re-create the legitimacy needed by the political system because such legitimacy is founded on consensual norms that themselves have been eroded by instrumental rationality. At the same time, the political system whose legitimacy is being threatened is given increasing scrutiny, and the question of rule by elites could be raised.

Habermas's ideas suggest an analytic scheme based in possibilities and tendencies rather than in prediction. If we accept these possibilities, we can see that there is room for, indeed demand for, a critical theory of society concerned with analyzing the context of purposive-rational action and that of communicative interaction, with the idea of coming to terms with a practical way of organizing our lives so that all are given both equal economic and political chances. A critical theory is emancipatory in the sense that it attempts to find a practical way of changing social structures to ensure liberation. A critical theory is aimed, therefore, at finding conditions of emancipation, as well as realizing the full potential of democracy.

The search for such conditions, in addition to the analyses of rationality, communication, and legitimation, also involves analysis of modern culture. The argument put forth largely by the earlier members of the Frankfurt school is that purposive rationality or instrumental reason has undermined the role of critique and reflection in culture. As culture itself succumbs to the demands of instrumental rationality, it becomes a "culture industry," a means for instant gratification. As Giroux (1983, 20) points out, the term "industry" used in relation to culture "pointed not only to a concentration of political and economic groups who reproduced and legitimated the dominant belief and value system, it also referred to the mechanisms of rationalization and standardization as they permeated everyday life." This analysis attempts to show how in modern society culture becomes amusement and loses its critical turn: "The man with leisure has to accept what the culture manufacturers offer him" (Horkheimer and Adorno 1972, 123). Their analysis of the film industry carries these sentiments further:

culture becomes equated with amusement

> Real life is becoming indistinguishable from the movies. The sound film, far surpassing the theater of illusion, leaves no room for imagination or reflection on the part of the audience, who is unable to respond within the structure of the film, yet deviate from its precise detail without losing the thread of the story; hence the film forces its victims to equate it directly with reality. . . . sustained thought is out of the question if the spectator is not to miss the relentless rush of facts. Even though the effort required for his response is semi-automatic, no scope is left for the imagination. (Horkheimer and Adorno 1972, 125)

Popular culture imprisons the imagination and the power of reflection through repeated and graphic assaults that stress themes of consumption and pleasure. In our day, the television news becomes the thirty-minute encapsulation of the sensational and the absurd. Best sellers are judged by their mass appeal that, translated, means their gratuitous levels of sex and violence, or for the more refined, their ability to provide instant diets, instant management, and instant therapy. Sustained analysis becomes the province of intellectuals, a province socially defined through credentialing even though critique occurs informally at all levels. Such critique must struggle to survive against the odds established by a culture industry geared not to the production of works designed for intricate discussion, but for the introduction of the new and the current in a cycle of profit accumulation. The culture industry represents a particular refinement of capitalism and modernity: it takes what was a spontaneous, original, and sustained effort and turns it into a commodity whose consumption feeds back into production values and interests. Such an industry affects the process of education, itself founded on different principles, in subtle and perhaps undetermined ways. Education cannot provide the immediate and sensual gratification the culture industry demands. This produces a very real conflict in those who must interact with both systems of thought daily.

SUMMARY

This brief overview of generations of work in the area of critical theory has focused on Habermas because of his seminal contribution to the analysis of modern states. In general, it can be said

Critical theory is based first and foremost in a critical analysis of the capitalistic system

that critical theory is based, first and foremost, in a critical analysis of the capitalistic system. Capitalism, as a form of economic interaction, takes the labor power of individuals and converts it into surplus capital by paying salaries that, taken together, hardly represent the profits accumulated from the corporate enterprises for the few lucky owners. Modern states, in this analysis, have compensated for such inequities through state welfare programs, designed to provide those social benefits lacking in a strictly capitalistic system. This, combined with modern advertising, consumption and increasing standards of living, and the culture industry, serves to legitimate the entire system, despite the inequities in wealth it produces.

Members of a society also have an interest in freedom from inequities, as minority groups in North America in particular have demonstrated. Unrealized ideological promises of equality, freedom, and so on, lead to a crisis in legitimation for the modern state. If the state operates according to principles of instrumental rationality and says, in effect, that promises of success will be fulfilled, but the effort meets unexpected obstacles, then the system's rationality will be politicized and questioned. In addition, motivational issues that depend on traditional-religious formulations and belief in modern rationality also become suspect; they fail to arouse the basic desire for success characteristic of previous eras, when workers in the system could have absolute faith in the system's ability to reward hard work.

For administrators and those interested in schools in general, this body of thought provides one means of analysis of modern society. It is not without its problems, certainly; at the same time, it respects and upholds the concept of the *democratic* formation of social structures. Such critical theory aims to understand, critique, and educate. This could appropriately describe the status of the role of the modern administrator. Certainly the position involves developing understandings of the various people and positions involved in running a school. It also involves a critical appraisal of the extant reality of schooling: perhaps not critical in the sense that has been discussed here, but still critical of policies and regulations that are perceived to stand in the way of proper school performance. Finally, the educative dimension is of particular importance in the development of a system that prepares individuals for both democratic participation and occupational involvement.

Thus, while administrators could be seen to participate *on a general level* in the concerns of critical theory, knowledge of critical theory itself could provide a level of participation that would raise administration to the arena of practical action or praxis. By this we mean an administration particularly oriented to the idea of change, change accomplished through a critical and educative dimension. Such practical action is one informed by theory, a theory of how society works and not simply an acritical theory of how to manage within a set of given circumstances. If the choice were given, most administrators would opt for a self-reflective and critical analysis of schooling and administration oriented toward providing a more just and equitable situation for all. Indeed, most administrators strive for this, but do so while bound within the constraints of a positivist methodology and a positivist theory and without regard to the critical analysis of both economic and political social conditions. Critical theory provides a way for considering these larger questions. While it does not give us rules to manage, neither does orthodox social science, whose rules and procedures are probably of less help to the administrator in practice. Critical theory provides an attitude, a way of conceptualizing reality, and a way of addressing social change through individually formulated actions. It does not prescribe; it does not determine; rather, it attempts to educate, and in so educating attempts to introduce us to our surroundings and how they consciously or unconsciously influence us. For the administrator, then, such knowledge is not aimed toward providing rules for action, or developed for controlling students and teachers or others involved in the mutual determination of the educational enterprise. Rather, it is aimed at freeing our basic socialized conceptions of what education means and what social structures mean; in so doing it allows us to be individuals.

What critical theory and its proponents prod us to do, in the final analysis, is to raise legitimate questions about social structure: the questions of class, power, and culture. Obviously, these questions are rather quickly glossed over in orthodox theory, if they are addressed at all. Yet from a critical theorist's perspective they remain significant. In addressing class critical theory raises the question of the appropriation and distribution of resources in society. The particularly sticky issue here is whether the conditions of wealth are reproduced; in other words, is one advantaged in this society by one's parents' position, or do all have equal opportunities for success? A good deal of research suggests that heritage is a major and significant determinant of later achievement and success. Power is another related issue. Is power achieved through participation in elite networks, as some would claim, or is it meritocratically distributed, as liberal theory would have it? Finally, culture needs to be considered. Have we developed a technocratic culture that denies the individuality of its members, or does culture still allow for different and varied forms of expression? These questions underlie the research and scholarship that look at a fundamental issue in Western societies: how is the culture and the system of economic stratification produced through schools and schooling? Such a question is fundamental for administrators concerned with the ultimate equalization of schools in society.

A basic concern for educational administrators should be how schooling contributes to the development of students

5

The Radical Reconstruction
of Schooling

INTRODUCTION

One of the failures of contemporary theory in educational administration is its reluctance to deal with concerns that are truly
educational. Much of administrative theory is borrowed from business management and theories of the firm. As an examination of
much of the dominant work in administration will show, educational concerns such as the role of students, the work of teachers,
and the nature of the curriculum get only passing reference if
they are mentioned at all. Yet a basic concern for educational
administrators should be how schooling contributes to the development of students: what does it do to students and for students?
If administration is to be truly *educational,* then it must be concerned with educational issues, in particular, who succeeds in
school and who does not.

Willard Waller (1932), a sociologist in the early 1930s, was
among the first to study the relationships that occur among staff
and students in schools. He aptly described student subcultures
and the conflict that inevitably occurs when students are forced
into a regimen that totally engulfs them. Contemporary theorists
who have been concerned with both the nature and effects of
schools have continued this approach. The most trenchant anal-

93

Administration is concerned not just with managing an organization, but with making moral decisions that lead to a more just society.

ysis of these questions has been done by scholars in a radical tradition (radical in the sense of getting to the basic issues). A primary question here is how do schools contribute to the reproduction of social strata? This is an important issue for administrators if we maintain that administration is concerned not just with managing an organization, but with making moral decisions that lead to the realization of a just society. Administrators should be leaders, and as leaders they must be prepared to ask hard questions about the nature of the institution being led. The radical scholars have raised such questions. How are society and culture reproduced through schooling? Why are the sons and daughters in the underclass apt to be fathers and mothers of underclass children too? How is a culture of sexism and violence perpetuated? Why can't schools break the cycle of class reproduction? These and other questions lie at the heart of the radical reconstruction of schooling. *The central issue for administration is the maintenance of legitimacy of schools.* When, however, it can be shown that, in a society committed to liberal political values such as equality of opportunity, social classes reproduce themselves, high proportions of minority students drop out of school, and effective schools are largely those that draw from a population whose values reflect school values, then the legitimacy of administration is in question. However, there is no conspiracy by teachers or administrators to force children out of school or to ignore the needs of ethnic and racial minorities. For the most part, schools are populated by caring and concerned people. The paradox of how schools are committed to equality while they simultaneously underserve certain segments of the population is to some degree resolved by an analysis of theories of social and cultural production and reproduction.

CORRESPONDENCE THEORY — *Schools and economic order*

Bowles and Gintis (1976) have addressed the relationship between schooling and the social and economic order through a theory that suggests that schools correspond to the needs of the economic order. In their view, the social relationships that occur in educational settings between, for example, administrators, teachers, and students duplicate the hierarchy of the workplace, i.e., manager, foreman, worker; further, schools serve largely to inculcate the norms, values, and habits the economic system needs for efficient productivity (1976, 13). A capitalist society, in this view, is largely driven by forces of production. Such forces of production require a work force acceptant of its position and trained in the virtues of punctuality, obedience, and industry. As they say (1976, 151), the school system "works to justify economic inequality and to produce a labor force whose capacities, credentials, and consciousness are dictated in substantial measure by the requirements of profitable employment in the capitalist economy." Schools reproduce inequalities because those very inequalities are needed in a hierarchically divided economic system.

That there are structural similarities between educational and work organizations is worth noting; it is another step though, as Cohen and Rosenberg (1977) have pointed out, to say that schools function to reproduce such inequalities. The argument becomes too mechanical and functionalist; it imputes a rationality to social structure that probably is not there. Giroux's response is to the point:

> Lacking a thought-out theory of consciousness or ideology, Bowles and Gintis grossly ignore what is taught in schools as well as how classroom knowledge is either mediated through the culture of schools or given meaning by the teachers and students. They provide no conceptual roots to unravel how knowledge is *both* consumed and produced in the school setting. (Giroux 1981, 7)

A more adequate approach would be to look at how school structures are culturally reproduced by human agents.

THEORETICAL MODELS OF STRUCTURE

Giddens, an English sociologist, has written at length on the problems of structure and reproduction. His analysis is at a macro level, looking at the question of how human beings establish structures and still interpretively construct reality. Gidden's work is a useful introduction to an overview of reproduction theory.

Giddens's central concern is explaining how social life is both created by actors yet also controls them. For Giddens social life is a "set of *reproduced practices*" that may be examined:

> First, from the point of view of their constitution as a series of *acts,* "brought of" by actors; second, as constituting forms of *interaction,* involving the communication of meaning; and third, as constituting *structures* which pertain to "collectivities" or "social communities." (Giddens 1976, 104)

These three elements are related in a dialectical tension: acts inform interactions that yield structures; the structures may not be either "wholly intended or wholly comprehended" (1976, 102). Structures have a certain duality: they are both created by interactions and are also the context for interactions. Giddens calls the reproduction and transformation of structures "structuration," and it takes place in the contexts of space and time (Giddens 1979).

In relation to educational institutions, then, the structure is not simply given to agents (actors). The agents take an active role in creating structure through interactions, but the interactions themselves are conditioned by past and present structures. This process of structuration reflects relations of power in which some agents attempt to get other agents to accept their definitions of the situation. In schools this process is reflected in a teacher's attempt to provide structure to a classroom through giving rules of interaction. Students are expected to "buy into" these rules and, if they do, a structure is formed. This structure, though, must be continually reshored every day as different agents test the different boundaries and versions of reality. Of course, the boundaries and versions are set by the more powerful over the less powerful.

What if students do not "buy into" such structures? Papagiannis, Bickel, and Fuller (1983) have looked at the issue of school dropouts from a perspective informed by Giddens's work. They show, first, that the idea of "dropout" is a socially created category; it is not a problem that resides in the individual alone. As they say:

> Dropping out and other failures of schooling are not due to genetic deficiencies, cultural deprivation, or use of pernicious social ascription procedures by racist teachers. Instead, school failure is viewed

as a socially organized "accomplishment" involving both teachers and students in the culturally sanctioned allocation of social roles. (Papagiannis et al. 1983, 371)

But they go on to say that this accomplishment takes place in the context of a structure that is established in the context of different classes. Such different class relations are visible in the schoolroom, and contribute to different interpretations of how schoolrooms should be structured. Papagiannis et al., for example, report on research that finds:

In schools where social class differences were sharp and easy to typify, teachers grouped students through unself-conscious reference to commonsensically related physical and familial factors. These included manner of dress, personal grooming, body odor, social workers' reports on the intactness and economic self-sufficiency of the family, and so on. Teachers then used this same information as an interpretive resource in unreflectively making *different* evaluations of the same behavior for students with *different* characteristics. As a result, the same interactive tactic, such as taking verbal initiative, was reinforced for some students but discouraged for others. (Papagiannis et al. 1983, 375)

Given these kinds of reactions, Papagiannis and his colleagues report that dropping out is a very *rational* decision on the part of youngsters. In Giddens's terms, they "see through" the structuration process and reject it: *"All social actors, no matter how lowly, have some degree of penetration of the social forms which oppress them"* (Giddens 1979, 72). Such youngsters do not necessarily engage in a form of consciously rational assessment of their situation, though some obviously do, but many "read" the conditions of structure and conclude that other social situations would be more beneficial to them, despite any long-run effects.

In what way then does a particular structure that represents dominant groups such as the upper and middle classes in society occur in schools? Bourdieu and Passeron (1977) attempt to answer this with their analyses of how schools reproduce culture. Bourdieu talks of "cultural capital" as analogous to economic capital: the more one has, the wealthier one is, at least in terms of dominant systems of cultural interaction. Cultural capital, however, is that which the dominant group in society controls, and "Just as our dominant economic institutions are structured to favour those who already possess economic capital, so our educational institutions are structured to favour those who already possess cultural capital" (Harker 1984, 118). The ability of schools to respond more effectively to middle- and upper-income groups is based largely on the fact that these groups possess the cultural capital that schools endorse as natural. To succeed in school, a member of an out-group must acquire the necessary cultural capital—in Bourdieu's terms, acquire a new "habitus," which refers to those cultural practices that incline an individual to behave in a culturally specific manner (Bourdieu 1979). The habitus is that group of actions, refinements, language, and behavior represented and reproduced in a given cultural setting. The habitus is seen in the practices and behavior of a child born wealthy and a child born poor, though each habitus will likely reflect a different cultural tradition. The habitus is achieved through socialization practices that interact with general social conditions. It will be different for each child and each generation. However, the school reflects the culture of the dominant group: the tastes, preferences, language, and so on, of the powerful group is used in schools; those who come to school without this habitus must either leave, be rejected, or learn a new habitus. In Bourdieu's terms, this does "symbolic violence" to members of other cultural formations. Agents come to schools, each with his or her own cultural background, which itself is changing according to different circumstances. The underclasses, though, have the deck stacked against them because the habitus they have is not valued currency within the school. It is not valued because it does not reflect the culture of the dominant group. At the same time, the school presents the dominant cultural legacy as natural and legitimate: "The particular economic and cultural practices inherent within an organisation or society which eventuate from the operation of the habitus appear 'normal' and 'natural'" (Watkins 1985, 18). Bourdieu thus takes a culturally specific approach to analyzing reproduction of class in school situations. Societies, in his view, contain a number of different cultural groups, each of which reproduces itself in new generations. Each individual develops a habitus, the expression of a familial culture within the habits, attitudes, and practices of the individual person. Schools as social institutions are geared toward the reproduction of the habitus displayed in the dominant, powerful social culture. Other cultures are symbolically violated within the school because they do not represent the means for "making it," for success and achievement as they are defined by the dominant group. The school attempts to provide an opportunity for the student to acquire the "proper" habitus, those learnings that will be valued and appreciated by the members of the dominant classes. Even when it cannot, it must "inculcate recognition of the legitimacy of this [dominant] culture and of those who have the means of appropriating it. Symbolic domination accompanies and redoubles economic domination" (Bourdieu and Boltanski 1978, 217).

A MARXIST ANALYSIS

Some of these issues re-appear in Sharp's analysis of schools (1980). Part of her analysis begins: "It is not the consciousness of men that determines their existence, but their social existence that determines their consciousness" (Marx 1970, 20; quoted in Sharp 1980, 87). Sharp adopts Gramsci's (1971) idea of hegemony, in somewhat the same way that Bourdieu talks of habitus, to explain how school knowledge and structure are reflective of the dominant classes. Hegemony, a term taken from the Italian HEGEMONY Marxist Gramsci, refers to "a set of assumptions, theories, practical activities, a world view through which the ruling class exerts its dominance. Its function is to reproduce on the ideological plain the conditions for class rule and the continuation of the social relations of production" (Sharp 1980, 102). Hegemony, however, is not given but continually established. The result is the establishment of social attitudes that unquestioningly accept things as they are: for example, it is a natural condition that there should be more educational options for the rich than for the poor—this is the way the world works, indeed, is the way the world should work.

Sharp asks how hegemony is reproduced in schools. This passage from Sharp illustrates dimensions of a hidden curriculum that tends to structure relationships:

> Within the classroom, pupils are engaged in processes which legitimate and in the last analysis reinforce the concept of the teacher as

> *the* pivotal authority, having the power to structure the pupil's day, define what is to count as knowledge, regulate the patterns of inter-action through exercising control over classroom norms and regulations, as well as over the allocation of rewards and punishment through the grading and classification system. Within these overall constraints, however democratic or permissive the teacher, pupils carry on their educational "work" individually rather than collectively and are encouraged for their diligence, social conformity and deference to the teacher's authority. (Sharp 1980, 124)

This structure of authority is itself reproduced at the school and district level, with authority being centralized and rewards closely controlled. In both the classroom and the wider sphere, what counts as knowledge is also controlled. Eggleston (1977) has described curricular knowledge as being either received or reflexive. Received knowledge is that knowledge packaged in textbooks and workbooks and publicly accessible. It is handed down to students as the proper and unquestioned reality, even when the community that originates such knowledge is itself in confusion and disarray. The reflexive perspective, on the other hand, suggests "that important parts of the definition, distribution and evaluation of curriculum knowledge are the consequences of human choices and that important sociological consequences flow from such choices" (Eggleston 1977, 54). This means that curricular knowledge is constructed by somebody for some purpose: what is taught is a function of who wants what taught. Curriculum writers, for example, can interpret history or mathematics to their liking. The reflexive perspective suggests that they do so in ways that can be culturally and historically biased; the received perspective would suggest that they simply portray the true set of facts. Schools usually, and particularly at the lower levels, present a received version of curricular knowledge that tends to glorify both history and science.

Sharp's analysis, then, considers why the working classes—presumably a substantial portion of the population and the most affected by unequal distributions of wealth—continue to accept a received curriculum and definitions of knowledge imposed upon them by a ruling class. Liberal theory, as discussed in the first chapter, is considered inadequate. Sharp writes that in liberal theory, "the school is seen to be the site of a cultural clash where the working-class pupil, who has previously been exposed to different cognitive assumptions, values, accents, or language, is sub-ordinated to a middle-class culture via middle-class teachers im-posing their own conception of the good and the true on their pupils who have been differently socialized" (1980, 132). In her analysis, culture clash is not the dominant motif of schooling. The concern to make schools relevant to the needs of different cultural groups is entirely misplaced: the differences between classes arise not just from cultural artifacts but from differences within the material base, between rich and poor. "What happens in schools," she writes (1980, 133), "is not the imposition of a middle-class culture on other groups whose own culture is quite alien, but a process of further ideological incorporation of the subordinate classes." Thus, it is not a particular cultural variant that is being expressed so much as it is the idea of the right way of doing things. Working- and under-class children are not expected to *become* middle class; they are expected to subscribe to the notion that there *should be* different groups in a society, some meant to produce and others to control. This ideology is made even more effective by its contention that there is a possibility of movement, from the producers or workers to the managers or controllers—a possibility, indeed, but one open on only an extremely selective basis.

Finally, Sharp notes that:

> A Marxist analysis of the ideological role of schooling does not therefore imply a model of the school pupil as an over-socialized, completely ideologized responder to forces beyond his control. Schools also, it needs to be emphasized, produce and reproduce dis-tinctive patterns of opposition which mediate their ability ideolog-ically to incorporate successfully all those who pass through them.

This, therefore, is no simple model of domination, whereby those who have openly oppress those who have not. Rather, it is a model where those who have look to the ones who do not and say, "It's there for the taking if only you'll try." Hegemony is a matter of beliefs, values, and hope that the system is right, and that it is you who are wrong, or incapable, or not smart enough.

Anyon (1981) is concerned with the empirical justification of the theoretical arguments put forth by Sharp and others. Anyon studied five schools "in contrasting social-class settings—in what I call working-class, middle-class, affluent-professional, and executive-elite communities" (1981, 119). In the working-class school, she found that school knowledge "was not so much bodies of ideas or connected generalizations, as fragmented *facts* and *behaviors*. Teachers spoke of knowledge as 'the basics' and indicated that by this they meant behavior skills such as how to multiply and divide, how to syllabify, how to sound out words and write sentences, and how to follow directions" (1981, 120). In interviews, these same fifth-grade students talked about their inability to go to college and their limited opportunities even while speaking of "the United States as 'the best place in the world'" (1981, 121). In the affluent-professional school, things are somewhat different. Anyon tells us that "School knowledge in the fifth grades in this affluent professional school was more abundant, difficult, analytical, and conceptual than knowledge in the working-class school. It also, in contradistinction to the working-class school, involved frequent attempts to engage the children in inquiry and in solving problems conceived by themselves" (1981, 124). It is clear from Anyon's work that certain differences exist between schools reflecting different social classes. Even magnet and alternative schools, as any administrator who has worked with them knows, embrace such differences. While Anyon enters into a programmatic definition of what should be done in terms of politicizing youngsters, her work is valuable in that it exposes different *empirical* realities in schools made up of students from different *class* backgrounds.

THREE STUDIES ON SCHOOLING

An Australian study is of value in developing some of the ideas given above. This research study examined the differences between comprehensive secondary schools (public) and independent schools (private) in Australian society, a society probably more similar to United States society in terms of class division than it is to its Commonwealth sister, Britain. This study by Connell et al. (1982) is exemplary in its research methods and findings. It goes beyond the mechanistic views of working-class versus ruling-class differences and instead explores more sophisticated conceptions of class differences and schooling's effect on them. Their study addresses the idea of ruling class; many protest this notion because it inspires visions of kingly domination, but this is not what it means. A somewhat lengthy quote gives meaning to the concept:

> Mrs. Middleton, for example, is married to a man who is the managing director of a firm employing several thousand people and making a significant contribution to Australian industrial production and export; who is on the boards of a number of other companies; a leader in various industry organizations; and influential in a large welfare organization and in the shaping of welfare policy in his state. When asked how she would describe her social position, Mrs. Middleton defined it as "not of the establishment." Nor is it only people like Mrs. Middleton who do not see social relationships in terms of class or power. When we have given talks to parents and teachers about our research, our use of the term "ruling class" has given offence, raised eyebrows, and caused confusion.
>
> Mrs. Middleton thinks of her husband as "not of the establishment," and we think of him as a member of the ruling class. (Connell et al. 1982, 144)

Mr. Middleton is a member of a ruling class because he is in a network of similarly situated people whose activities result in the "regeneration of a general set of relations of power and privilege" (1982, 145). Thus, the idea of the ruling class does not pertain to an appointed group, but rather to a group who through family ties, individual successes, and certain opportunities find themselves exerting more influence on the conduct of the society as a whole than other individuals not similarly located. The juxtaposition is between ruling class and working class: those who are in neither category are labeled middle class in this study. Again, class is not a fixed concept; rather it pertains to what resources individuals have and how they use them.

The study used what we might call "long interviews," in-depth interviews of students, their parents, teachers, and principals, all designed to get to the heart of the experience of being a student in a particular school. The interviews focused on two groups: "the families of people doing manual or semi-manual work on the one hand; and of managers, businessmen, and professionals on the other" (1982, 30).

In these interviews, the researchers were required to redefine their notions of class, as being not a particular location but rather an approach to one's resources. As they say, "Classes are not abstract categories but real-life groupings, which, like heavily-travelled roads, are constantly under construction: getting organized, divided, broken down, remade" (1982, 33). Clearly, in this study class is a real and intransigent feature of life in a modern and capitalistic society, whether the occupants choose to label it as such or not. However, it is not a location so much as it is a way of thought; the researchers interviewed families that were separated in terms of class, in which, for example, the wife came from the ruling class and the husband from the working class. Their relationships with social institutions differed approximately on these same dimensions.

In their interviews with the families, it became clear that the relationship of different classes—working or professional—to the schools was of quite a different order. Schools, in their analysis, reproduce class distinctions, but not in a simple or forthright manner. Both public schools and private schools attempt to educate, but the definitions of education and the attempts to realize education depend on particular interpretations, interpretations that denigrate the working-class experience of reality. The interesting point here is the difference between public schools that serve the working classes, and private schools that serve the ruling classes:

> Our basic argument is that there is a fundamental difference here between working-class and ruling-class education. We summarize it in this formula: the ruling class and its schools are articulated mainly *through a market,* while the working class and its schools are articulated mainly *through a bureaucracy.* (Connell et al. 1982, 133)

This distinction between bureaucratic and market strategies to schooling helps to differentiate what was not previously clear: public schools operate under a bureaucratic principle that requires them to be responsive to state constraints, and thereby to be less responsive to parental demands; private schools operate under a market principle wherein parents and their children can choose and, in choosing, exert some control over who is hired and what occurs. This makes a fundamental difference in the way the two approaches to education are organized. This is not to say that private schools are completely constrained by parental choice.

Many, indeed, are so selective that it is difficult for even the best student to enter; still, they are responsive because they depend on reputation and desirability.

This puts a greater responsibility on the public school. The working-class parents in this study had a tremendous respect for the benefits of education, perhaps because, growing up in or after the depression, they saw education and school "as a way of putting a *floor* beneath their kids' future economic circumstances" (1982, 141). In the ruling classes, the same motivation was apparent, but here it was linked to the prevention of downward mobility, to maintaining the type of privileged existence the parents know.

Schooling, thus, is well respected by the working class as well as by the more privileged classes, but it still serves to reproduce class divisions through disarranging working class knowledge: "The things that working-class people confidently and securely know are pushed aside or devalued as not being proper, socially-recognized knowledge" (1982, 169). In Sharp's terms, this is surely hegemony, the substitution of one set of practices and ideas for another. What the schools do, in this analysis, is to negate dissent; intellectual life, in other words, is formed around the principle of dissent. Universities in which teacher and administrator training occur are, or should be, hotbeds of dissenting and questioning viewpoints, for this is the foundation of a university. Intellectual life depends upon critique and the emergence of different viewpoints, but in both elementary and secondary schools, this viewpoint, the concept of dissent, is not only neglected but also actively repressed. This becomes a contradiction in the schooling of the young. While dissent should be encouraged by the life of the mind, it is not. In some circumstances, this leads to resistance to school authority, to resistance to those in control. This resistance "is pitted *against* the bearers of knowledge. It becomes anti-intellectual, and, partly for that reason, open to commercial exploitation" (1982, 172). An entire industry springs up to service the needs of adolescents, from punk rockers to surfers.

A final note about this study concerns its findings regarding gender relations. The school's role in the process of forming constructions of masculinity and femininity is probably secondary to the family but of significance nevertheless. Adolescents work out patterns of current and historical relations between the sexes within the context of an organization that stresses, for example, athletics for boys and subordinate activities (e.g., cheerleading) for girls, and a social structure, the family, traditionally based on notions of patriarchy. Given the changing roles of men and women in society, adolescents have to work out the often-conflicting definitions of what it means to be male or female, and must do so in an organizational structure that itself provides conflicting messages. Here gender and class interact: the resolutions of a working-class boy are different from those of a working-class girl, and those of a ruling-class boy, from a ruling-class girl.

Willis's *Learning to Labour* (1977), a study of English school boys, has undoubtedly been the most influential of the reproductive genre. Like the Australian study discussed above, it goes beyond a simple thesis that schools ideologically reproduce class divisions: it shows that schools offer opportunities that could eliminate class distinctions if taken, but such opportunities are rejected because of class distinctions. Willis's account examines this paradoxical conclusion.

This book examines how the working class (understood as involving manual and often repetitive labor; no "career" as we would normally think of it) perpetuates itself despite what liberals would label the opportunities afforded for advancement. We could predict, for example, that individuals would take unchallenging, repetitive labor if their skills prevented them from progressing into more middle-class occupations in a technological society. Dropouts, push-outs, and a generation growing up in a world where early contribution to family coffers was expected might conform to this model. But what of contemporary youth, who cannot wait until they reach the age to leave school, who reject the opportunities for advancement offered, who, despite their knowledge of "the importance of an education," still decide to pursue what are essentially dead-end occupations?

In the normal way of thinking, such individuals simply do not make it because they fall at the lower end of the spectrum in terms of intelligence, talent, and motivation. Willis objects to this:

> I want to suggest that "failed" working class kids do not simply take up the falling curve of work where the least successful middle class, or the most successful working class kids, leave off. Instead of as-

suming a continuous shallowing line of ability in the occupational/ class structure we must conceive of radical breaks represented by the interface of cultural forms. We shall be looking at the way in which the working class cultural pattern of "failure" is quite different and discontinuous from the other patterns. (Willis 1977, 1)

It is not a matter of the working class being caught in a filter that allows the best to progress, as a deficit theory might have it, but of the conflict of various cultural patterns. Willis examined this ethnographically by studying "twelve non-academic working class lads" (1977, 4) as they progressed through school. The progress of these "lads" through the school system is a fascinating exploration of the cultural and idiosyncratic patterns of the individual who resists authority or resents the teacher's ability to control a situation. Consider this: "During class teaching a mouthed imaginary dialogue counterpoints the formal instruction: 'No, I don't understand, you cunt'; 'What you on about, twit?'; 'Not fucking likely'; 'Can I go home now please?'" (Willis 1977, 13). Such is the expression of opposition, perhaps one not altogether restricted to the British Isles. The "lads" in this study were counterposed to those who abided by the system, the ones the "lads" called the "ear'oles," a term apparently taken from their propensity to listen to and not oppose the teacher's views. These boys were, in the school's view, the good ones, the ones who struggled to conform and to succeed. The story of the "lads" is a story of nonconformity, of resistance, and of subversion of the school's intentions for them. Clothes, smoking, and sex are dominant concerns of the "lads." Work also dominates: a job means money for clothes, smoking, and sex despite its effects on school. The part-time work puts money in the pocket and in hard times helps the family budget. Work does something more—it serves to introduce these boys into the "real world" and to strengthen their conclusion that schooling produces very little of substance, and certainly not anything that allows for a good date or extra spending cash.

The good date, that is, their relationships with girls, finds "Their most nuanced and complex attitudes" (1977, 43). Uppermost are tales of conquest: of male sexual ability versus female desire. In this culture, gender differences are reinforced. At the same time, the "girlfriend" relationship represents a serious affair: the girlfriend is not just another "lay"; rather, she is a possible spouse who, in those terms, must be pure and virginal.

How do girls resolve this? Willis finds that:

> The resolution amongst working class girls of the contradiction between being sexually desirable but not sexually experienced leads to behaviour which strengthens "the lads" sense of superiority. This resolution takes the form of romanticism readily fed by teenage magazines. It turns upon the "crush," and sublimation of sexual feeling into talk, rumours and message-sending within the protective circle of the informal female group. (Willis 1977, 45)

For the boys, this "romanticism is tolerated with a knowing masculinity, which privately feels it knows much more about the world" (Willis 1977, 45). The lads' culture of gender relations is matched by their views on race and violence. In fact, racism and violence form a major part of their orientation to the world. Racism and violence relate to the gender issues, reflecting a culture that requires proof of masculinity, of control over a hostile world, of the ability to establish one's own rules.

The "lads" come to reject the offerings of the school and to resist the efforts made to incorporate them into the dominant culture. This resistance is not an individualized or localized effort; indeed, it cannot be understood at all in those terms but must be understood in the context of class differences. One might claim that the institutional form, school, represents the language, theory, and practice of a dominant class; it rejects the language, theory, and practice of the working class. Not to resist school, in this sense, is to reject one's class position, a rejection of one's culture, family, and aspirations. The acceptance of one's class position is the acceptance of a life of routine and economic hardship, a life made palatable in some instances by the idealization of sex and violence; yet the working class "lads" freely choose— they look forward to—the opportunity to get out of school and to join the "real" world of manual labor and reject the artificial world of mental labor. This freedom of choice leads to entrapment (Willis 1977, 120). Why does this occur?

Willis (1977, Part II) advances the concepts of penetration and limitation as explanatory tools for understanding this reproductive process. Penetrations occur at the cultural level, the level of shared group awareness, and enable the group as group to penetrate or expose the contradictions and inconsistencies in the social structure. For the working class, these occurred in three ways. One was a type of rational assessment of the costs and benefits of subscribing to school ways. Conforming to school requirements and obtaining the school-granted qualifications provided opportunities for the future indeed, but only by requiring sacrifices in the present, particularly the sacrifice of immediate gratification (1977, 126). To get scholastic qualifications and to perhaps join the middle class requires sacrifice of immediate gratification.

Second, Willis analyzes the availability of work itself. If prestigious occupations are largely limited to those with the language, culture, and contacts of the ruling class, and if whatever is left falls to whomever regardless of their qualifications, then the problem of becoming overskilled for unskilled positions arises. School diplomas do not just certify acquired knowledge in a meritocratic fashion; they legitimate a particular class whose rules of success are acquired in the family, not in the school. Willis observes:

A few [of the working class] can make it. The class can never follow. It is through a good number trying, however, that the class structure is legitimated. The middle class enjoys its privilege not by virtue of inheritance or birth, but by virtue of an apparently proven greater competence and merit. The refusal to compete, implicit in the counter-school culture, is therefore in this sense a radical act: it refuses to collude in its own educational suppression. (Willis 1977, 128)

Willis's third assessment has to do with the cultural understanding of the different logics that pertain between individual and group success. The class as a whole understands that there is no social mobility; individual successes may be attained by conforming to school processes, but never the movement of the entire class because this would mean, by definition, the emergence of a classless society. Capitalism however, and again by definition, is a class-based society, requiring that some be the workers who give labor power and others the entrepreneurs who use the labor power. The cultural recognition of this allows members of this culture to focus their creative energies elsewhere (Willis 1977, 130).

If there is such an understanding of these processes at the cultural level of the working class, why do they not reject the system in its entirety, become, in a sense, a political movement? Because, in Willis's argument, these penetrations are only partial and limited: "Cultural penetrations are repressed, disorganised and prevented from reaching their full potential or a political articulation by deep, basic and disorienting divisions" (1977, 145). The most significant division pertains to the interaction of gender and the distinction between mental and manual labor.

In the first place, the essential unity of mental and manual labor is divided: the school as a system makes this division in terms of its categories of academics and vocationalism, theory and practice. School knowledge, valued knowledge, is academic. In other words, a choice is forced between mental pursuits *or* academic pursuits. The key point for the working class examined in this study is that manual labor is "associated with the social superiority of masculinity, and mental labour with the social inferiority of femininity" (Willis 1977, 148). For the lads, manual labor becomes a way of asserting their social superiority, their sense of control, and it is for this reason that the penetration becomes limited. The sense of superiority gained from gender discrimination finally makes acceptable the inferior status accorded by social category of manual to mental labor. In the "lads'" culture mental labor is effeminate. It requires no characteristic masculine skills, no sense of physical exertion, and to be masculine, in the sense here defined, is to be real and in control.

The lads' story, then, is one of contradictions and inconsistencies. The institution, school, is no coercive bearer of domination. It indeed provides a way out and a transformational possibility for members of the working class, but it does so on its own terms, terms located within the dominant class-based milieu. Such terms are rejected for the cited reasons. The working-class youth see their future within the general structure of a class society; while they collectively penetrate that structure to some degree, they also accept those features that assure them some measure of control. "Capitalist freedoms," says Willis (1977, 175), "are potentially real freedoms and capitalism takes the wager, which is the essence of reproduction, that the freedoms will be used for self-damnation." This is a complex picture of how political potential becomes muted through the accumulated process of schooling.

Gordon (1984, 111), in her review of Willis's work, has noted that "primary schools are noticeable for a concern for multiculturalism and tolerance for diverse styles of behaviour. As one moves up the education ladder, however, knowledge of the codes and practices of the dominant culture become increasingly presupposed." As one moves up the ladder, the ability to penetrate the dominant ideology, and the corresponding limitations, also becomes increasingly real. The picture is complex because it is not just schools, or family, or work opportunities, or culture: rather it is how these interrelate to each other, how they help to form and structure the others.

Ogbu provides a third approach to understanding how schools relate to children and youth. While his work comes out of the orthodox anthropological tradition, it shares a number of interesting continuities with ideas developed previously. Ogbu (1978; 1981; 1982), an African anthropologist trained in the United States, was primarily concerned with the study of the black mi-- nority in American society. He focused his research on the black population in Stockton, California. Ogbu's work examines why certain minority groups in this country have a consistent pattern of failure in schools, while other minority groups, such as Orientals, have a pattern of reversed failure, that is, an initial failure that has been significantly overcome. Ogbu argues that these patterns of failure cannot be properly understood without focusing on the relationship of the groups to the wider social structure and the history of oppression of such groups. Many such studies of failure look to classroom processes, suggesting that there are cultural discontinuities between middle-class school culture and the culture brought to school by minorities. However, this explanation fails to consider the origin and continuation of such cultural differences. They may be perpetuated in a classroom situation through teacher and students having different cultural biases and expectations, but this does not suggest why these differences exist, and why they continue to exist despite intensive "remediation" efforts.

Ogbu endorses what he labels a "multilevel approach" (1981, 14) that looks not only at the process of classroom interaction, but also at the role of the family, the neighborhood, and the political-economic system. He enters the two categories of "taxpayer," normally the middle and upper classes, and "nontaxpayers," the less affluent. To be a taxpayer, a person "must live in a neighborhood that does not have many welfare recipients, especially recipients of aid to families with dependent children, or AFDC; the person should be middle class or 'working class'; and, preferably, he or she should be white" (1981, 19). Taxpayers, the white middle-class majority, view the system of education as one that provides equal opportunities, where even the poorest can move up into respectable occupations should they give it the effort. For the nontaxpayers, the largely black communities, this beneficent view of the educational process is belied by what they consider the realities of the system. One reality is that of job ceiling: no matter what credentials are accumulated within the community, there will always be a limit on the jobs available for members of the community. Ogbu states (1981, 16): "Adopting a historical stance, as he or she should, the ethnographer may find that traditionally *blacks have not been permitted to compete freely as individuals for any jobs they wanted and for which they had the educational qualifications and ability*—a phenomenon we have designated as a *job ceiling.*" The job ceiling helps determine reactions to school because, while parents hope that their children can get high-paying positions, an informal consensus perceives opportunities as limited. This, in turn, leads to what the majority community labeled "survival strategies." The strategies ranged from political activism within the black community, oriented toward achieving better life chances, to hustling, pimping, and other exploitative activities. Survival strategies require "knowledge, attitudes, and skills that are not wholly compatible with those required for white middle-class type of classroom learning and teaching" (Ogbu 1981, 22).

Thus in this analysis the blacks in Stockton, and presumably in other communities, are a *castelike minority.* In respect of their history of oppression and their current situation of struggle, they represent more of a caste than a class. Ogbu offers a definition:

> Castelike minorities are distinguished from immigrant and other types of minorities in that (1) they have been incorporated into the society rather involuntarily and permanently, (2) they face a job and status ceiling, and (3) they tend to formulate their economic and social problems in terms of collective institutional discrimination, which they perceive as more than temporary. Examples of castelike minorities in the United States include blacks, Indians, Chicanos, and Puerto Ricans. Blacks were brought here as slaves more than

400 years ago and after emancipation relegated to lower-caste status; Indians were the original owners of the land who suffered military defeat and were removed to reservations almost from the beginning of American society; Chicanos were conquered in the Mexico-American War during the first half of the nineteenth century and were then relegated to subordinate status, a status that was extended to other Mexicans who have since immigrated from Mexico; Puerto Ricans were annexed as a colonial people in 1898. All four minority groups have felt the effects of their subordination for generations. (Ogbu 1982, 299)

Such castelike minorities often define their culture in distinction to the majority culture; black culture is "that behavior which is *not* white. In general, black culture is defined in *opposition* to white culture" (Ogbu 1982, 299). There is in fact a good deal of mistrust of the dominant culture, not altogether misplaced. Something akin to double jeopardy is involved: the white taxpayers see the black minority population as in need of "special" services through the school system, without considering the occupational structure, while the nontaxpayers see the educational system as an expression of the closed choices of the white occupational structure.

SUMMARY

The ideas contained in this chapter are particularly challenging for the administrator. They are abstract and incriminate the very system that we are charged with managing. Administrators can make a difference. While most of the concepts included here suggest that only massive political change can be effective, there is still the possibility of small efforts in individual locations. Such efforts must politicize teachers and staff and make them aware of these conditions.

There are four main ideas of administrative importance in this chapter. The first, the idea of class, is an uncomfortable idea for most of us because we think of ours as a classless society, one in which Horatio Alger stories are the norm and not the exception. Class seems such a fixed concept, like a peculiar kind of congenital wart. But the studies here show that class is a concept that defines one's appropriation of resources, one's position in a society. Thus, the ideas of a ruling class and a working class are not so farfetched: some individuals control resources and others don't; one set appears to give the "rules" and the other to accept them. The ruling class, in brief, makes the rules by which others organize their lives. A society like the United States has quite a complex class structure that is somewhat open, yet nevertheless conforms somewhat to a class ideology. Blacks and other minorities are actively sought for management, administrative, and other important positions, and this is a certain sign of mobility between classes. But the idea of mobility itself expresses the concept that one class must be brought up to the standards of another, and that therefore the other members of the basic class are locked into position. Success is dependent on rejection of class, and such success is limited to only a few.

Second, the material considered here relocates failure from individual pathology to systemic properties. School failure, in these analyses, is more than just a lack of effort or lack of ability. Rather, the lack of effort, when present, must be put into a context that includes a number of other interacting factors, including notions of culture, economic realities, and historical systems of oppression.

Third, these analyses refute the once-popular social science construct of "cultural deficit." Its logic maintained that minority students did not do well as a group in schools because they lacked language skills and the values and attitudes necessary for school success. For these groups to succeed, the argument went, schools had to intervene at earlier and earlier ages, remediating language and other deficits by teaching "standard" English and other skills. Studies such as have been presented here have shown the cultural deficit model to be completely without foundation. Linguists, for example, have shown that the black English of urban poor is as logical and as complex as its standard counterpart, and probably more direct (Labov 1970). Similarly, it is clear that the minority groups considered put as high a premium on education as any other group, but the lived realities of their situation intervene in such a way as to make alternative passages more viable.

The final advantage in considering such studies concerns the currently popular notion of instructional leadership, this being a newly found role for school administrators. The studies here suggest that instructional leadership may be no more than a resurrection of deficit models and, indeed, if it means tightening control and implementing strict disciplinary policies, may have an effect opposite to what was intended. The message for administrators might be that leadership in the school setting involves attempts at social change, and not the stabilization of the system in place. Administrators who are leaders can have an effect in at least two ways: they can educate staff and others about the realities of the situation as discussed here, and work at the transformation of the school in the context of larger social transformations.

An administration informed by a literary model will turn to studies such as these for an understanding of student groups in schools, particularly an understanding of the unacceptably high drop-out rates (sometimes approaching 50 percent) of youngsters in poor, urban areas. An administration informed by critical theory, again, will be able to place this understanding within the context of social structures driven by inequalities of power and money.

6

Critical Perspectives
on Organizational Theory

The modern, complex organization plays a consistent and vital part in the lives of most individuals. Usually twelve to sixteen years of each person's life are spent in the particular organizational form of school. Because schooling is so pervasive and has such a strong impact on us, administrators of schools should develop a ready view about the theory of organization, both to develop deeper understanding and to see the organization as a man-made institution amenable to change.

Organizational theory should be distinguished from administrative theory. Organizational theory largely deals with what organizations are, how they are structured, and how they fit into the environment. Administrative theory, on the other hand, deals with how organizations are—or should be—run and so with issues of control and management. Of course, the two types of theory have close and obvious links, but for analytical purposes we need to maintain this distinction. To identify the theories of administration and management and theories of organization hampers the development of a general organizational theory and indicates its current managerial bias.

Administration has three essential sources for theory: consultants to management, managers themselves, and behavioral scientists concerned with how administration works. Taylor epitomizes industrial and managerial consultants concerned with showing management the "one best way" for running the organization. Barnard represents the executives who attempt to derive their own theory of organization. Simon exemplifies behavioral scientists who seek a final and predictive set of laws about administrative behavior. Each group espouses not just a theory of administration, but also has a theory of organization built into its framework. This chapter will consider the implicit and explicit frameworks guiding the study of organizations.

A GUIDING FRAMEWORK

Burrell and Morgan (1979) conceptualize organizational theory using four governing paradigms: functionalism, the interpretive paradigm, radical humanism, and radical structuralism. Most of traditional Western organizational theory can undoubtedly be classed under the functionalist paradigm. Most of it shares functionalism's assumptions. Organizations are seen as objective, real entities that can be analyzed by organizational researchers who, in turn, can isolate facts about the organization that will lead to predictions about organizational performance. The organizational world is stable, predictable, manageable. Functionalism is expressed in organizational theory and administrative theory by the view that organizations are composed of parts, each of which can be rationally managed in order to make the whole a more productive unit. The various wholes, taken together, form the functional social system.

The organization itself is but another social fact that can be dissected and reassembled. We are, of course, simplifying this complex area, but for general purposes much of traditional organizational theory has rested on basic assumptions about organizations. Contemporary approaches have modified aspects of the functionalist paradigm, but it is hardly fair to claim that functionalism is no longer the guiding force behind organizational theory. At the same time, there is a growing diversity of opinion regarding what organizations are and how they should be studied. The interpretive framework, for example, is no longer easily dismissed and might be considered a major force behind modern critiques of functionalist positions. In fact, contemporary accounts of organizations seem to blur the boundaries between paradigms, so that any position must take various others into account, indicating the relativity involved in studying organizations. While previous functionalist accounts aimed at finding the absolute dimensions of organization, there is now a recognition that no one account captures the essential reality. To examine this body of literature and to show how there are a number of ways of considering organizational theory, we will examine a theory of organizational structure, bureaucracy, and look at the development of systems approaches in their various dimensions. Contemporary theory will then be considered, as well as critical approaches to organizational theory.

BUREAUCRACY

It has rightly been noted that modern organization theory is largely a footnote to Weber, the German sociologist who wrote about the development of modern bureaucracy around the turn of the century. Weber made significant contributions in three areas: his analysis of bureaucratic organizations, his analysis of forms of authority, and his concern with the impact of bureaucratic forms. Weber's approach to organization has largely been linked with what most texts label a "classical" approach, in the sense that it has served as the foundation for most of the later studies. The classical approach, as well as a number of more contemporary efforts, is concerned with the issue of structure. What structures do certain types of organizations take and why do they adopt those structures? Weber certainly was concerned with this, but his wide appeal stems from his concern with how structure relates to broader social questions linked to the economy and politics of the modern state.

Weber asked, in what ways are modern organizations different from feudal ways of organizing? He found that modern organizations are structured according to bureaucratic principles that are geared to the values of efficiency and production, both the underpinnings of the industrial state. Bureaucracy for Weber (1946) differed from traditional forms of organizing in these ways: fixed rules govern the division of labor; a hierarchy of office within the bureaucracy allows certain officers to legitimately control others; written documents form the basis for management; employees are chosen on the basis of competence rather than favoritism; fixed salaries are paid to employees; employees, particularly managers, do not "own" their positions—they can be fired for incompetence; and relations between employees are based on technical performance.

For us, such observations appear commonplace, but Weber's genius lay in identifying them and separating them from the patriarchal structure previously common. Thus, Weber could contrast a feudal-type system, where promotion and effectiveness were based on principles of loyalty, nepotism, and individual adjudication, with principles of bureaucracy. Bureaucratic principles in effect removed the person from the office; rather than depending on good will or family relationships, bureaucracy mandates that competence is the overriding factor for success. A fixed salary and written rules bolster competence. Bureaucracy serves to increase efficiency: only the most competent are progressively rewarded, so they operate in an atmosphere that rewards technical perfection. Bureaucracy has a double edge: although it depersonalizes individuals by looking to their performance only, it offers individuals protection. Fixed salaries, rewards based on competence, and rules of procedure protect the individual from arbitrary and unjust authority. In a bureaucracy, individuals have recourse (grievance) on the basis of the very rules that might serve to depersonalize them.

The bureaucracy has, for obvious reasons, been likened to a machine; indeed it presents a very mechanical picture of organizations where efficiency governs and relationships are highly impersonal. It should be noted though that Weber spoke in terms of ideal or pure types. This image of the bureaucracy as a machine was the model or ideal upon which modern forms of organizing were based; that the real organization may not correspond to the ideal type in all of its ways does not disturb the power of Weber's analysis.

Weber also considered the foundational principles of bureaucracy by comparing them to previous epochs. Unlike feudal kingdoms, bureaucracies are organized along the lines of rational-legal action. Weber raised the question of why people obey. In an organization such as a school, why do directives from the superintendent's office carry force? Is it because it is customary to obey such directives, because the personality of the superintendent is so overpowering that people want to obey, or because individuals have a contract, part of which stipulates obedience? Weber's analysis identified three sources for authority.

Traditional authority stems from custom and tradition. Such authority is community based and requires the presence of consensual value structures that undergird the normal "way of doing things." Another source of authority for Weber was charisma, an individual's ability to command obedience through his or her own personal leadership. Weber's final source was rational-legal authority that commands obedience on the basis of formal laws and contracts between parties that satisfy certain ends. Bureaucracy is founded on this last source of authority: obedience is achieved in a bureaucracy through a series of rules and regulations based on contract law. They are followed because abiding by them results in a salary or other reward desired by the individual.

Thus rationality in a bureaucracy can be considered purposive; a rational action links a means to an end. Purposive rationality differs from substantive rationality, which uses traditionally accepted ends to guide action. This distinction forms the basis for Weber's analysis of the impact of bureaucracy on human life, his third contribution to organizational sociology. Discussions of bureaucracy often neglect Weber's contribution to this third area, variously portraying him as either a neutral scientist of natural phenomena or a proponent of bureaucratic organization. In reality, however, Weber was particularly concerned with the effect of bureaucracy on the individual, because he saw it becoming an "iron cage" that would imprison the modern individual.

As purposive rationality supplanted more traditional forms of rationality, it released the individual from the tyranny of superstition and myth and allowed him or her to "set ends for himself autonomously and to realize these ends by the mobilization of means in a way appropriate for achieving them" (Lenhardt 1980, 5). This rationality could be liberating; it could allow the individual to order his or her life according to the rational consideration of ends to be achieved. However, in Weberian analysis the needs of the economic system (capitalism) fuel the development of institutions that promote economy and efficiency. Bureaucracy separates workers from their products, so they work not so much for the end product but for the salary involved. As a result individual choice becomes subjugated to institutional demands. The possibility of rational action free of constraint is lost; institutional rationality dominates and the average citizen regresses to a *belief* in the ends established by the institution and the bureaucracy. The individual, no longer a free agent making rational choices, succumbs to an encompassing bureaucratic rationality. Thus, Weber exposes the paradox of the modern state: it frees individuals from the constraints of tradition and custom and gives them the opportunity for self-determination; yet, the development of industry and technology makes individuals dependent on the organization and driven by its needs. Individuals become trapped in the iron cage because they expect and are expected to serve the interests of the organization first and foremost.

Bureaucracy is a double-edged sword. It provides an efficient way of organizing production or services; it also provides some guarantees to the employees in terms of salary, performance, and so on. At the same time, it seems to use employees for its own ends, but this, perhaps, is not fully accurate. Perrow (1979), like Weber, notes that organizations are tools in the hands of their masters and that the top of the bureaucratic structure is never bureaucratized. That is, someone makes the rules: the top echelon of the bureaucratic pyramid has more input in establishing rules than the middle and lower echelons. Bureaucracy provides a means for certain of the institution's owners to efficiently dominate others in pursuit of their own ends.

Weber certainly looked at the structural elements of organization in his analysis of bureaucracy. In so doing, he embraced a critical spirit, as other classic writers did not. Weber embraced a synoptic view: he was concerned not only with the formation of bureaucracy but also with its relationship to capitalism, classes, and economics. His scope was enormous, though organizational theory remembers him chiefly for his analyses of bureaucuracy.

SYSTEMS APPROACHES

A second major approach to organizational theory, the systems perspective, has both a technological emphasis and a psychological one. It tends to incorporate much of Weber's thought on bureaucracy, but while Weber focused on the role of organizations in human affairs, the systems perspective stresses the role of human affairs in organizations. The systems perspective also derives from the work of Taylor and other managerially oriented writers.

Foundation for the Systems Perspective

General systems theory was developed by von Bertalanffy (1950) in the early part of the century to examine the relationship between an organism and its environment. Systems theorists attempt to distinguish between open and closed systems. In a closed system there is no interaction between the system and the environment; it is static and in a state of equilibrium. An open system, however, interacts with the environment and is dynamic and changing. For von Bertalanffy, the premier example of an open system is a biological organism such as an amoeba. The organism must interact in some fashion with its environment. When it does so, the organism displays systemic characteristics that include: the input and transformation of energy; homeostasis—the organism attempts to maintain a steady state in response to environmental demands; differentiation, in which different parts serve specialized functions; negative entropy or the idea that the system must change and grow in order to survive; and equifinality, the property enabling a system to achieve a final state without going through all the previous stages of evolutionary development—for example, a newborn, granting evolution, does not have to first be a fish, a reptile, an ape, and so on (Katz and Kahn 1966).

Systems theory has found a ready and appreciative audience among organizational theorists. The distinction between closed and open systems is often used to distinguish between so-called classical organizational thought (Taylor, Weber) and more contemporary approaches. Scott (1978), for example, classifies such theorists as Weber, Mayo, and Barnard as closed-system thinkers. Later thinkers are seen as being open system because they consider the environment's impact, even though the notion of environment remains somewhat fuzzy. Systems theory has taken on an almost moral quality in much of organizational thought, so that it becomes increasingly difficult to attempt to conceptualize organizations apart from a systems perspective. A systems approach to organizational analysis is the dominant framework, yet one that is not entirely successful for reasons to be developed later. For now, however, we can state that the transition from organism to organization results in reifying the organization, treating it as a thing or as an organism itself. As a result these conceptions lose any theory of action: what people *do* is secondary to how the system functions. In the end we lose sight of the organization as a constructed endeavor that reflects human intention and action.

SOCIAL SYSTEMS THEORY:
SOCIAL PSYCHOLOGY AND ORGANIZATION

Mayo and his colleagues developed a social systems perspective on organizations by looking at the Western Electric plants (Burrell and Morgan 1979). In an elementary fashion they focused on the workers' relationship to the internal and external organizational environment, concentrating on worker interactions in the context of the organization, and thereby departing from the scientific management emphasis on fitting the worker into the managerial structure. Barnard (1968) carried these concepts further, developing an image of the organization as a cooperative system where workers and managers labored together in meeting the needs of the mother organization. (See chap. 1, pp. 42–43.) Mayo's and Barnard's ideas had a major impact on the later social system theorists who modified and expanded their concepts. Mayo and his associates have stressed the role of the informal organization and of the peer networks that arise within the organizational structure, and how these serve to modify the formal structural arrangements designed for efficient production.

Currently, social system theorists in this vein approach organizations from the perspective of worker involvement in the organization, focusing largely on how to achieve more participative structures in the organizational workplace. This open-systems perspective takes into account outside influences on worker motivation. It fairly clearly represents a social-psychological approach to the individual in the workplace.

The simplest and among the most influential model in this approach has been that developed by McGregor in *The Human Side of Enterprise* (1960). McGregor contrasted two models of man with different implications for techniques used to control workers: Theory X suggested that people were inherently lazy, unwilling to work hard, and shunned responsibility; and Theory Y implied that people love work, are conscientious about their performance, and normally look for increasing responsibility. Management, in turn, could treat workers in a Theory-X fashion, adopting the principles of scientific management, or in a Theory-Y fashion, treating workers as responsible individuals. These opposing models, while simple in conception, have had an amazing effect on organizational theory. Organizational theorists have adopted Theory Y as a humanistic alternative for structuring organizations, although it originated as a managerial tool.

A variant of McGregor's model is the Theory-Z concept proposed by Ouchi (1981). Ouchi updates the Theory X-Theory Y dichotomy by suggesting that heralded Japanese management practices (Theory J) can be found in certain American organizations (Theory Z), and that more companies can and should move to a Theory-Z mode of operation. Theory Z involves developing a managerial philosophy, implementing holistic relationships, involving the union in decision making, and so on. Bureaucracy in this approach becomes a straw man and the source of corporate evil. Unfortunately, Ouchi neglects bureaucracy's positive effects in Western democracies, such as the built-in protections for worker rights, fair treatment, and equal opportunities for appointment and advancement. Perhaps more damning an assessment is that Theory Z is but a culturally modified version of an idealized Japanese business practice. To some extent, cultural differences such as the limited role of women in the Japanese work force are indeed recognized, but the economic and political backdrop for Japanese management is neglected. Unlike Japan (Cole 1982) there is a large pool of reserve labor in the United States. In a sense, Japanese management must court workers to recruit them for an extended period. Also, political differences, particularly protectionist trade policies, affect Japanese management. Theory Z fails in much the same way Theory X and Y did: they all idealize and simplify a complex network of interactions. Nevertheless, the best-selling status of this work testifies to its influence, at least in the short run.

These approaches to human relations certainly represent an advance over the mechanistic ideas of Taylorism, but they still have a managerial bias. They attempt to *incorporate* workers into the organizational structure by using scientific methods to determine worker satisfaction. Perhaps these scientific experiments make workers more susceptible to managerial intervention.

Social Systems Theory: The Technical School

The open-system concept can also cover theories that deal more with the organization as an entity, rather than with the relationships that occur within them. These approaches emphasize how the organization's structure, however it is conceived, contributes to differences between organizations, and further, how the environment impacts on these organizations. The major aspects of structure examined include size and organizational technology (the particular process for converting raw products into finished ones). The size of the organization did not seem to contribute to other structural differences; as Perrow (1979, 161) has noted, "[Size] has not proved to have much of an analytic cutting edge, nor has geographic location, age, or physical resources." Technology, the study of the productive processes, was of more interest.

The technology of the organization interested theorists looking at the structural side of organizations, particularly the development of rules, operating procedures, and lines of authority. They wanted to learn how the social dimension of organizations could be most efficiently coordinated with the technological dimension. Lawrence and Lorsch (1967) noted that organizations were structurally required to differentiate roles and labor and, at the same time, to integrate the different parts into a functioning whole. This was done through the rules and the roles, which depended, to some extent, on the nature of the technology in the organization.

The technology of the organization (we will later consider whether schools have a "technology") was said to relate to organizational structure: routine technologies such as the assembly line develop routine, i.e., bureaucratic, organizations, while innovative technologies lead to personalized and nonbureaucratic organizations. This body of research into the relationship between the production process (the technology) and the social structure (the interpersonal relationships) used the term "socio-technical systems" to refer to organizational designs based on the inter-relationship of the type of productive process (originally, coal mining) and the type of hierarchy in place (such as work teams instead of individuals).

The emphasis on technology resulted in the development of the contingency theory, a concept that has broadened in recent years. Burns and Stalker (1961), Lawrence and Lorsch (1967), and Thompson (1967) addressed the contingency approach in various ways, and contingency theory has become a dominant intellectual force in respect to organizations in recent times. In essence, contingency theory says that there is no determinant relationship between such organizational variables as size, technology, and the social structure of the organization, but that the structure of each depends on environmental pressures and the products of the firm. According to contingency theory, there is no "one best way" to manage an organization; rather, management is contingent not only on the organization's products but also on major environmental forces such as the nature of the market and the nature of the political environment at that particular time. Therefore in certain situations, a rigid and bureaucratic management may be appropriate; in others, a looser, more relaxed approach might be necessary.

Contingency theory is probably the most dominant current approach to organizations. It has the advantage of relating the "right" organizational structure to the type of environment with which the organization interacts. In so-called turbulent environments, an organization must be responsive, with management keyed to changes that may be occurring outside; in a placid environment a management concerned with internal consistency might be more appropriate. Thus, a company producing goods that remain in fairly stable demand no matter what crises occur in the political world requires one type of organizing principle; companies that react violently to slight shifts in the political winds require others.

In the final analysis, the relativity of contingency theory is intellectually unsatisfying. A perspective grounded in traditional organizational thought faces the overwhelming temptation to find *the* analysis of organizations. Since traditional organizational theory fundamentally assumes that universal laws can be derived to explain organizational phenomena, contingency theory is only a middle step on the way to achieving ever-increasing accuracy of description. Contingency theory "reverts to the old dichotomies, putting the new wine into the same old bottles" (Perrow 1979, 165). It relies on the distinction between bureaucratic and human-relations models for describing the organization and offers a "new" approach to organizational management that vacillates between the bureaucratic and human-relations approaches depending on environmental stability or turbulence. Finally, the contingency approach makes certain assumptions about the nature of organizations, tending to see them as real entities subject to managerial discretion and somehow separate from the environment. All these constructs are open to challenge.

CONTEMPORARY APPROACHES: PROCESS AS METAPHOR

Scott (1978) has suggested that a number of contemporary approaches to organizations can be classed as "social models" that extend the Western Electric studies by using an open-systems context. However, many of the contemporary approaches do not radically depart from systems theory overall, and most keep the traditional analyses more or less intact within their own models. Yet they use new metaphors that make a striking contribution to a somewhat dull literature. These models concentrate on the process of organization, rather than on a technology or a structure, and present the process through unusual metaphors that attempt to discover a parallel between our ways of organizing and our ways of seeing. Interestingly, many of these approaches originated with respect to educational organizations, perhaps because the technology of teaching is not particularly well defined. Overall, these approaches that feature the social aspects of organization over its technical or rational aspects might be seen as reactions to the formalism of previous models. In this sense, they attempt to demystify organizational theory, removing from theory its esoteric concepts of structure, goals, and organizational rationality and replacing them with the idea of actors. For example, Weick's notion of loose coupling builds on his previous concept of "enactment" in the organization (Weick 1979; 1976). Enactment is a largely psychological process of creating and defining the organization and its environment. It involves the process of identifying and selecting those parts of the world that are important and can be dealt with. The world is not given, as it is in a rational model of organization, but created. Thus, members of a health system enact an organizational world quite different from the organizational world enacted by members of a record company or an automobile corporation. Members in each organization must select and attune themselves to different aspects of the total environment in which they find themselves. As Weick (1979, 27) says, "People free-associate, introspect, rifle through piles of images, and play percentages that they'll find something that captures a portion of organizational reality everyone else has missed." Enactment and a corresponding mutual creation of reality form a large part of loosely coupled systems. In enacting an environment individuals create subtly *different* realities, and differences arise on how things are connected and organized.

Loose Coupling

Although the idea of "looseness" has appeared in the literature before (e.g., Bidwell 1965), Weick's concept of loose coupling (1976) struck a sympathetic chord among organizational theorists when it appeared. Dissatisfied with systems theory's inability to account for the tremendous diversity in organizational function, Weick developed the idea of a loose coupling between organizational subsystems. In systems theory generally, what happens in one subsystem should by definition affect the other subsystems—they are interrelated parts of a whole. However, in education particularly, what happens in the classroom is often only indirectly conditioned by changes in the superintendent's behavior; thus, Weick concludes, these subsystems may be only loosely connected.

Weick opens his description of loosely coupled systems by presenting the following analogy:

Imagine that you're either the referee, coach, player, or spectator at an unconventional soccer match: the field for the game is round; there are several goals scattered haphazardly around the circular field; people can enter and leave the game whenever they want to; they can throw balls in whenever they want; they can say "that's my goal" whenever they want to, as many times as they want to, and for as many goals as they want to; the entire game takes place on a sloped field; and the game is played as if it makes sense. . . .

If you now substitute in that example principals for referees, teachers for coaches, students for players, parents for spectators, and schooling for soccer, you have an equally unconventional depiction of school organizations. (Weick 1976, 541, citing March, personal communication)

This picture of schooling, then, begins with the premise that rationality itself, and the rational-legal framework for analyzing organizations, is in reality merely a set of conventions we have adopted, and that organizations contain more "realities" than we are normally aware of. However, because we are used to thinking of organizations in tidy, rational ways, Weick maintains we have failed to see such other realities as loose coupling. As in the soccer game, loose coupling refers to the way the elements (subsystems) in the organization are connected, perhaps only haphazardly and with no clear or even rational purpose. Thus, to use one of Weick's examples, the counselor may be only loosely coupled to the principal. Each has a certain degree of autonomy, and each may affect the other in only the most general of ways; yet they are bound together in a certain fashion.

Loose coupling gives organizations a number of functional advantages. For example, it allows a certain amount of organizational stability because changing events can be restricted to only one part of the system. A crisis in the classroom generally does not involve the central office. Loose coupling also allows for successful local adaptations without changing the entire organization. It also might allow the organizational actor more control over events in a limited universe: with little firmly connecting the actors in the hierarchy, each can proceed more or less in his or her own fashion, thus each has more freedom and self-control. While loose coupling has other advantages for an organization, under certain circumstances these advantages might become disadvantages. Each feature of loose coupling that ensures the organization's survival today might, in the long run, be maladaptive for the same organization.

While loose coupling expands our conception of organizations as systems, it remains essentially bound to the overall systems viewpoint and cannot escape from critiques of that perspective. Loose coupling is striking only insofar as we accept the idea of organizations as systems modeled on organisms. Weick modifies the progression of thought here. Systems theory starts with the basic organism as a system and then proceeds in a hierarchical fashion to more and more complex systems that culminate in the social organization. Weick still favors the hierarchical approach from simple to more complex systems, raising the question whether social systems are only more complex variants of organic systems. To suggest that they are may be too reductionist and may fail to address the unique nature of social systems.

The Institutional Approach

Some organizational theorists have also focused on the school in particular as an organization. A leading view, the institutional school of thought, conceives of the school as not just another organization, but as a social institution. An institution differs from other organizations insofar as it commands public respect and scrutiny and serves some major social purpose. "The process of institutionalization," Perrow (1979, 186) tells us, "is the process of organic growth, wherein the organization adapts to the strivings of internal groups and the values of the external society." The major question of this approach concerns how schools as institutions respond to social demands. Meyer and Rowan (1977; 1978) propose that schools as institutions are characterized by an uncertain technology—the technology of the classroom is not well understood and is idiosyncratic. The manufacturer can control the mechanics and pace of production, but schools cannot regulate the transmission and retention of knowledge. The evaluation of teachers is, therefore, largely ceremonial. While it is almost impossible to control what happens in a classroom, control can be exerted in the choice of teachers; thus, public education becomes highly credentialed through state agencies. Schools can be thought of as "loosely coupled" in part because the administration is oriented outward, toward ensuring continued public support and accreditation, rather than inward, toward controlling the instructional process. What happens in the school itself is based on what Meyer and Rowan (1978) label the "logic of confidence." Since there are little or no formal procedures governing activity within the schools, we presume that individuals in the schools are actually doing what they are supposed to be doing. Much of the work of schools attempts to reinforce this logic of confidence through rituals and rites of classification and evaluation.

This view of schools recognizes that what schools "produce" (i.e., the graduates) varies enormously in talent, knowledge, and ability. To evaluate each graduate in terms of competence would in many cases undermine confidence in schools; therefore, the schools turn to a ritual certification of their graduates. The schools and the public alike assume that this certification guarantees some certain level of competence on the part of the graduate, so in this way, schools serve as a personnel sorter for society. For employment purposes it makes little difference where one went to high school; what matters is that one completed high school. Schools thus certify competence for employers, without making any individual determination of ability.

Although this approach is refreshing because it links schooling to the wider social system, it does not deal with some basic issues in schooling, particularly the political and economic role of the school in society.

Garbage Cans and Anarchies

Another approach to organizations, initially applied to university settings but now in more general currency, is March and Olsen's (1976) concept of organizations as organized anarchies characterized by garbage-can processes of decision making. Like Weick, March and Olsen reject the view of the organization as a tidy, rational endeavor. The organizations they study are more anarchic. Events are not and cannot be fully planned; they happen anyway as often as not and their final outcome is largely predicated on chance. Thus, organizations cannot be fully managed in the sense of establishing systematic methods of control; rather, the organization can only be nudged here and there, while prayers are offered for a desirable outcome.

The ambiguity at the heart of organized anarchy stems from different conceptions of rationality. In Herbert Simon's early work (1965) he proposed that a truly rational organization would be one peopled with individuals who could clearly evaluate all alternatives available for reaching a particular goal and then select the most efficient and effective one. Simon observed that people are limited in this respect: fully rational decisions are beyond the bounds of human rationality. Individuals satisfice: they take the alternative that seems best at the time. March and Simon (1958) extend this observation by showing that how people satisfice in the organization—that is, make decisions and choose alternatives—is largely controlled by the premises that are established in the organization. Such normally unwritten rules and procedures govern individual conduct and set the stage for organizational performances. Therefore, individual decisions are made in the context of the established premises. Part of the premises in the organization would be related to the organizational goals that help to define the purpose of the organization; but in an organization where the goals are ill defined or defined in only the most general way, the premises are ambiguous and limited as guides to action. By showing the relationship of decision making to rational behavior, March and Olsen (1976) conclude that in those organizations having little agreement on specific goals, a garbage-can process of decision making and organized anarchy characterized by ambiguity exist. Such an organization is observed among structures such as universities, where there is little or no agreement on the technology (i.e., what to teach or how to teach) and the hierarchy is weak (administration fails to control faculty decision-making powers).

This garbage-can model of decision making suggests the following: problems arise within the organizational structure and standard solutions are applied, but the problems are not often amenable to any given solution; thus, solutions and problems are dumped into the organization's figurative "garbage can," where planned solutions attach to inappropriate problems and problems find unusual solutions. Chance encounters often determine what happens, and major events are related to but minor causes.

The garbage-can process has three major features: unclear technology, contested goals, and fluid participation. To borrow the business-school example, in an organization that produces widgets for mass consumption, the technology of widget production is undoubtedly well known: one must follow certain procedures, manipulate certain raw material in certain ways to get a bunch of widgets. Fortunately, this is not the case in organizations devoted to less clear processes. In a university, one wishes to develop the mind, to provide skills, and so on, but exactly how to do this in a standardized way is not clear. The technology is ambiguous. The same argument applies to goals and preferences. University presidents can wax eloquent on the mission of their university, but specific programmatic proposals must satisfy a number of vested interests and contentious debates often ensue. Finally, the decision-making process is characterized by fluid participation. Not everyone in the organization shows the same degree of interest in an issue; participants come and go.

Weiner's (1976) study of a desegregation case in San Francisco illustrates this well. He found that a committee set up to provide recommendations on the process of desegregating the schools was characterized by the fluid participation of those most affected. The committee's issues and agenda were largely controlled by members who could attend meetings on a regular basis and develop some expertise about the issues. The committee members who could afford the time to do this were largely white, middle- and upper-class women who were not employed on a regular basis. The minority representatives had to work and could not devote the time needed to control the committee's agenda.

The intriguing concepts developed by March, Olsen, Cohen, and others help us to understand in some fashion the happenings in an educational setting. To some extent, however, the idea of anarchy has probably been oversold. Schools and other organizations are characterized by certain regularities: events are scheduled, people have and keep appointments, and paychecks are normally delivered. Further, when Cohen and March (1974) attempt to develop rules for leadership in an organized anarchy (for example, they suggest that college presidents devote time to the issues, reconstruct the organizational history, allow the opposition a voice, and use other, somewhat Machiavellian tactics), they almost contradict their first set of premises. Rules and their application are characteristic of rational approaches to organization; the bureaucracy, in fact, could be defined as people bounded by sets of rules. Eventually, even organized anarchy is forced to recognize the institution's underlying bureaucratic structure that operates according to the dictates of politics and economics.

The Organization as Culture

Recently, the idea of organizational culture has swept the management field. This body of literature looks at organizations as cultures and radically departs from the previous scientific and behavioral emphasis found in management and organizational literature. The concept of organizational cultures comes in part from the failure of other, normal managerial approaches to organizations, and in part from the 1980s' emphases on the Americanized version of Japanese successes in establishing organizational cultures. This important approach to culture in no way replicates traditional, anthropological studies of organizational culture; rather, it more or less assumes that organizations have cultures and then proceeds to give advice to managers on how such cultures might be developed to increase productivity and performance.

Such popular books as *In Search of Excellence* (Peters and Waterman 1982) and *Corporate Cultures* (Deal and Kennedy 1982) focus on the culture as a manipulable aspect of the organization. This approach to organizations focuses on how a particular organization establishes its culture through central features like symbols, rituals, sagas, and myths. The argument here is that corporations and other organizations establish a culture, whether they want to or not. This culture can contribute to organizational goals or not; but more importantly for many of these writers, managers can manipulate the culture so that it is both innovative and productive at the same time.

The idea of a culture in the organization is a major and applauded departure from the behavioral and scientistic view of previous managerial approaches. It draws attention to the fact that whenever people gather together, they engage in a form of communication that results in the establishment of shared ways of addressing the world. Rituals, symbols, and metaphors are used to enable individuals bounded by an organizational space to interact and share their common experience. This is universal: classrooms, corporations, and nations have a culture, with some more intricate than others.

The literature goes further than this; not only do we study culture but we are also encouraged to manipulate it. The popular literature tells us that managers must analyze the particular culture in their organization, understand the symbols and metaphors in use, and then engage in a program of change designed to produce a new culture where dominant symbols and metaphors can be altered to reflect the particular reality the manager happens to envision. This is a very muted view of culture. We cannot analyze culture from armchair comfort; nor can we change it through progressive rational strategies. Culture is the lived and experienced collection of beliefs that are not really amenable to rationalistic intervention by managers.

Def. of culture

Leaders can change a culture, but not by following particular programs of intervention. Instead, they change a culture through their own enactments of the aspects of culture they value. Thus culture is not an intellectual exercise, but an intuitive expression of one's own beliefs that are formed through parental training, formal schooling, and informal experiences.

As an expression of organizational theory, this cultural approach is lacking in several respects. Granted, it is a step above usual managerial theories of how to manage the firm. At the same time, however, it takes a curiously manipulative approach to managing culture. Deal and Kennedy (1982, 19) say, "We hope to instill in our readers a new law of business life: In Culture There is Strength," presuming that managers are not *part* of a culture and can indeed manipulate an organization's culture from some outside, higher plane. These works clearly indicate that there are "good" managers and, presumably, "bad" managers. The good manager gets the culture to conform to his or her way of envisioning reality. The bad manager, apparently, has simply not jumped into the anthropological literature and surfaced with arcane terms to apply to what were formerly common features of the work organization. Quite clearly, a manager's ability to label coffee breaks as rituals hardly results in a cultural analysis of the organization. This literature also neglects the basic political and structural aspects of organizations. At this time, it is more of a strategic approach for managers than a legitimate approach to understanding organizations. When this perspective adopts a commitment to values basic to the larger social culture and adapts these to the needs of corporate organizations, then perhaps this approach will become fully respected.

Culture based management

Political Approaches

Neglected in the usual approaches to organizational theorizing are the political dimensions in the organization: how the organization is pulled together or rent apart by politics. The political model tends to incorporate notions of culture and loose coupling, although it directly focuses on such processes as collective negotiating in the firm, the development of coalitions and interest groups, and contests for organizational supremacy and control. It developed as a conscious alternative to the rational, goal-seeking model of organizational behavior. As Pfeffer and Salancik observe:

> Because of conflicting demands, imperfect information, contests for control, and the loose couplings between organizations and environments, rational actions and rational designs are by definition virtually impossible. Imbedded in all definitions of rationality is the idea of goal attainment, but if there are multiple and conflicting goals, how can we define rationality? We want to suggest that organizational design is itself a process filled with contradictions and dilemmas. (Pfeffer and Salancik 1983, 105)

In this model, the twin themes of influence and control are dominant and management is less a process of establishing routine procedure and cultures than an ongoing process of negotiating over the allocation of valued resources. However, power in the organization can be institutionalized within individuals and offices, and organizational rules can be established that govern the uses of power. This contributes to structure, yet the structure is not set in time. There are self-interested individuals in the organization who ally to further common interests, thereby threatening power structures. Political analysis of the organization occurs, both at the micro level (Bacharach and Lawler 1980) and at the macro level.

Zald's analysis of organizations as political economies has suggested that over time organizations develop "constitutions," the "fundamental normative structure. . . . a set of agreements and understandings which define the limits and goals of the group (collectively) as well as the responsibilities and rights of participants standing in different relations to it" (Zald 1970, 225). The constitution sets the framework for internal and external organizational interactions with the environment. Actors in the organization negotiate within the limits of the constitution over politics (power) and economy (resources). The distribution of power, the particular reward structures, and the rules for executive succession can all be subject to contestation and negotiation. In a school district, for example, the constitution reflects the formal, state-approved charter of the system as well as the informal rules, regulations, and norms of the area.

This organizational structure does not reflect a rational, goal-seeking entity, as some systems theories would suggest, but rather a collection of actors who more or less share a mutual purpose and orientation. Yet within this structure differences arise over the distribution of power (between teachers and students, teachers and administrators, administrators and other administrators) and rewards. Individuals collectively (e.g., teacher associations) negotiate to change the allocation of rewards and the distribution of power, to rewrite, in some small way, the provisions of the constitution.

Such ways of looking at organizations have been appropriately labeled theories of the middle range (Bacharach and Mitchell 1981). They do not focus on the macro aspects of organization, particularly the relation of the organization to larger environmental and social factors, as Weber's and structuralist theories do. Nor do they focus on micro processes such as individual enactments in the organization, as Weick and others do. Rather, they attempt to look at the organization as a collection of actors engaged in organizationally relevant behavior—political maneuvering and collective action. Both micro and macro aspects inform this model, but they do not receive primary attention. Groups make up the organization, groups involved in rewriting, to whatever extent they may, the historically developed constitution of the organization.

For the administrator and the theorist, all three levels of analysis are proper: organizations are made up of individuals and of collectivities, and both exist in a social context. A critical approach to organizational theory attempts to recognize all three levels and to evaluate the meanings given in each.

CRITICAL REVIEWS OF ORGANIZATIONAL THEORY

The New Science

Ramos (1981) has proposed a "new science of organizations" that essentially suggests that currently formulated organizational theory is based exclusively on market organizations, those engaged in the production, distribution, and sale of goods. He suggests that other organizational forms are possible, and claims that organizational theory is naive because it fails to recognize alternate ways of organizing that meet the diverse needs of a society. Current organizational theory and current organizations are marketcentric: they center on the demands of the marketplace and perpetuate an instrumental reasoning that spills over into all other aspects of life.

Ramos's (1981, 104-105) charges against organizational theory are paraphrased here:

- The market organization is geared to the demands of the economy; it is largely instrumental. Organizational theory sees this instrumentality as characteristic of all human behavior, even though the market organization is only a fairly recent development in world societies.

- Organizational theory adopts a perspective that human behavior is instrumental, then fails to account for the dynamic of human interaction and interpersonal relations; if these are mentioned at all, they are mentioned in the context of how the organization can use such interactions to further its own goals.

- In the market society, the concepts of "labor" and "work" are freely and inaccurately interchanged: labor is selling of personal productive power because of the structure of the economic system, while work is the freely given expenditure of effort in order the achieve personal satisfaction. In a market society, alienated from the social system. Leisure time becomes equated with time when labor is not required, rather than in its previous sense, time to engage in "the most serious endeavors" (Ramos 1981, 113).

Ramos' new approach called economic para- paradigm

In Ramos's view we have developed societies that are passionately devoted to production and consumption; these features override any other value in modern life and result in populations of dissatisfied, unhappy, rebellious, and disenfranchised individuals. It also results in an ever-increasing alienation of society from nature; the problems of impending environmental disaster and megascale war illustrate how a market system geared to its own internal dynamics cannot predict the consequences of those same dynamics. An organizational theory that both reifies and legitimates such marketcentric forms of organization obviously contributes to the problem.

Ramos's solution involves rethinking organizational theory, so that it can intellectually justify a "multicentric" society. A multicentric society has many organizational forms, and the marketplace is only one of them. In Ramos's new approach, labeled the "para-economic paradigm," the market or the economy is only one aspect of total life. Ramos says:

> The para-economic paradigm assumes that the market is an enclave within a multicentric social reality where there are discontinuities of several sorts, multiple substantive criteria of personal life, and a variety of designs of interpersonal relations. Second, in this social reality the individual is only incidentally a utility maximizer; basically he strives for ordering his existence according to his needs for personal actualization. Third, the individual with access to alternative social spaces is not compelled to total conformity to the market price system. He is granted opportunities to "work" or even "beat" the market system, creating and participating in a variety of social settings which differ one from the other in nature (Ramos 1981, 123)

Ramos envisions a society of alternative social spaces that allows one to contribute in a variety of ways and makes personal growth and satisfaction a prime consideration. In this vision the individual has value. A reconstructed organizational theory would develop and test ideas for achieving such a society, for making it both productive and satisfying, and for finding new organizational forms. Many of Ramos's arguments find their parallel in the work of Strike, considered earlier. For example, Ramos considers the necessity for a multicentric society that allows for different and alternative lifestyles and, presumably, different values. Strike, in turn, argues that a single, publicly supported organizational system cannot re-create the alternative private

Dialectical approach studies contra-
dictions and the process of resolving
contradictions

value systems upon which this society was founded and in which it believes. Like Ramos, Strike would endorse smaller, diverse organizations where alternatives can be expressed. Ramos's macro orientation to organizations does provide us with critical insights.

A Dialectical Approach to Organizations

Ramos's vision of organizations is essentially an optimistic one; the flavor of his ideas is that a multicentric society, geared to individuals, is indeed possible if we take the opportunity to re-think what it is we are all about. While his analysis is trenchant, it places too much faith in voluntaristic and individualistic critiques of social forces and too little in analyses of historically located objective and material structures. A recent group of organizational analysts takes a dialectical approach to the study of historically located organizations, using the logical analysis of thesis and antithesis that leads to synthesis.

A dialectical approach to organizational analysis is best understood in comparison with its orthodox cousin. The scientific study of organization presumes that objective knowledge about the organization can eventually be obtained through scientific research, that verified and replicable knowledge can be gathered by studying the elements. The dialectical approach suggests that the elements of social life each contain their own contradiction; the dialectical approach studies the contradictions and the processes of resolving contradictions. Scientific knowledge in the social sciences depends on the use of metaphor, but each metaphor contains its own contradiction (every statement contains its opposite). Thus, in Taylorism the organization is a machine; but, we now realize at least the possibility that the organization is *not* a machine: organizational study involves recognizing and analyzing the contradiction involved in being a machine and being not-a-machine. Dialectical thinking involves seeing the "not" in place of "is."

The dialectical approach involves analyses of various aspects of organization, in particular, the analysis of contradictory theorizing about organizations. In a seminal article Benson (1977a) proposed some principles for the dialectical analysis of organizations. First, an organization is always in the process of changing,

Benson

but the process of change occurs within an established structure. Organizations have a built-in tension between structure and process, and organizational analysts study how this tension is continually resolved. Second, Benson discusses "totality," that organizations simultaneously exist as individual, independent entities (the primary focus of orthodox organizational theory) and as parts of the whole social network of other organizations and institutions. Another task for organizational analysis is determining how this tension between parts and wholes is dialectically resolved. Benson's third principle is one of contradiction, that the social fabric of organization is rife with "ruptures, inconsistencies and incompatibilities" (Benson 1977a, 3) and that these are a proper object of attention. As organizational contradictions are identified and studied and as theories about organizations are modified, new arrangements emerge that are also subject to contradiction. This embodies Benson's fourth and last principle, praxis or the ability to find alternative practices that embody mutually held values and goals; again, these alternatives are themselves open to dialectical analysis.

PUTTING IT ALL TOGETHER

Astley and Van de Ven (1983) use part of Benson's framework to analyze the major debates in organizational theory. Their analysis provides a valuable dialectical perspective on how we look at organizations. They provide a synoptic overview of the major strands of organizational theory and then ask dialectically oriented questions that give us the flavor of the prevalent issues:

1. Are organizations functionally rational, technically constrained systems, or are they socially constructed, subjectively meaningful embodiments of individual action?
2. Are changes in organizational forms explained by internal adaptation or by environmental selection?
3. Is organizational life determined by intractable environmental constraints, or is it actively created through strategic managerial choices?
4. Is the environment to be viewed as a simple aggregation of organizations governed by external economic forces, or

as an integrated collectivity of organizations governed by its own internal social and political forces?

5. Is organizational behavior principally concerned with individual or collective action?

6. Are organizations neutral technical instruments engineered to achieve goals, or are they institutionalized manifestations of the vested interests and power structure of the wider society? (1983, 245)

These questions summarize the major debates in organizational theory. Up to now, organizational theory has been examined from several different approaches, each having certain value for the administrator. These include perspectives based on structure, such as bureaucracy and parts of systems theory; on psychology and enactment, such as garbage cans, loose coupling, and organized anarchies; on politics and collective action; and on culture and symbology. Such varying views of organization are bewildering for theorist and practitioner alike. How can they be put together in some organized fashion that still incorporates the concerns of the critical theoreticians? We can explore two possible methods, one taken from a conventional approach and one from a more critical approach.

Bolman and Deal (1984) have suggested that our ways of viewing organizations can be likened to "frames" or ways of seeing. Organizational theory has four major frames: the structural, which ranges from Taylor and Weber to the contingency and technological approaches; the human resource frame, which represents the human relations school through Theory Z and beyond; the political frame, which addresses coalitions, power, and status; and the symbolic frame, which incorporates the cultural approach with loose coupling, anarchies, and so on, and treats the organization in a dramaturgical manner. Each frame provides a way of viewing the organization and, from its perspective, a way of problem solving within the organization. Therefore, some problems *are* structural and using a structural frame is appropriate, while others may be political, symbolic, and so forth. Bolman and Deal suggest that managers adopt the strategy of "reframing," the process of "switching across frames to generate new insights and options" (1984, 240). Reframing requires looking at a situation or problem and analyzing it through all four different lenses to come to an integrative approach that reflects multiple realities. For these authors, situations or problems can be "critically reframed" by asking what each frame ignores and contributes when applied to the situation. As they claim:

> Each recasting of the problem immediately suggests new questions to ask and new options for action. For any given situation, one or two of the frames may be much more useful than the others. But deliberate and critical reframing can be a powerful way to break out of our "psychic prisons"—the automatic assumptions that limit what we see, how we think, and what we do. (Bolman and Deal 1984, 245)

Critical reframing may indeed be a useful way for integrating a diverse set of literature, although it still accepts the organization as somewhat isolated from historical and social events. Morgan (1980) has previously used the metaphor of "psychic prisons" to describe how the language and metaphors we use in talking about organization capture us, so that we lose the critical ability to relate the organization to historical structures of hierarchy and domination. Reframing allows us to consider competing perceptions of organization, but it does not allow us to question the idea of organization itself.

A second way of attacking the contradictions in organizational theory is to use a perspective generated by Ranson, Hinings, and Greenwood (1980). They address the question of how socially created organizations can still exhibit structure. While Bolman and Deal take a fairly atemporal and ahistorical approach to this question, Ranson et al. approach it in a historical fashion. For these authors, organizational structures are both shaped by and shape individual actors: through time they are "constituted and constitutive" (1980, 3). Ranson et al. divide their argument into three dialectically interrelated concerns: provinces of meaning, dependencies of power, and contextual constraints. These both contribute to and change structure.

Provinces of meaning involve the creation and re-creation of meanings by organizational actors. These "interpretive schemes" allow us to attach meaning to events; further, they allow us to place ourselves within a received scheme, which we can accept or contest. The received scheme is determined by the dependencies of power. The organizational structure, continually re-created by provinces of meaning, reflects power and status differentials be-

MEANING
POWER
CONSTRAINT

tween organizational members. Power "is the capacity to determine 'outcomes' within and for an organization, a capacity grounded in a differential access to material and structural resources" (1980, 7). Thus, interpretive meanings do not occur out of context; the context is the organizationally validated internal and external distribution of resources.

Ranson and his colleagues suggest that an emphasis on the creation of meanings and the establishment of interpretive schemes can be overdone; indeed, broad social, physical, and economic constraints prevent the creation of reality from scratch, as it were. Other "contextual constraints" arise from organizational characteristics such as size and technology and environmental characteristics such as the market. The three concepts of meanings, power, and constraints interact and occur in a *temporal* framework. On a day-to-day basis, the meanings generated by organizational actors become foremost; over a longer period, attention turns to the enduring structures of the organization in its environment. As Ranson et al. say:

> Thus, we would expect actors and transactional patterns to be determinate in the uncertain day-to-day experience of organizations; emergent regularities and constraints of size, technology, and environment to become apparent in the medium term; and an order of meaning, value, and belief to be sedimented in the long-term structuring of organizations and their contexts. (Ranson et al. 1980, 14)

TIME

By introducing the neglected but important variable of time, these authors are able to incorporate into organizational analysis the previously unconnected perspectives of phenomenology, politics, and structure. Most of the previously discussed theories of organization could be placed somewhere within the temporal continuum that Ranson et al. draw. Organizations are structured creations.

The work of Bolman and Deal and Ranson, Hinings, and Greenwood could arguably be said to incorporate a dialectical as well as a critical framework. They are critical to the extent that they analyze and critique other ways of looking at organizations; they are dialectical insofar as they contrast perspectives and see that the positive notions of one find their negation in what is not said.

In essence, the dialectical approach centers on Benson's (1977b) four major analytical problems in organizational theory: action, power, level, and process. The problem of action relates to how organizational phenomena and structures are reproduced through the actions of given individuals within the organization, and how these actions contribute to the development of a collective identity and reality. Power raises problematic questions: Who has it? How does it become unequally distributed within the organization? How do power relationships function as mechanisms of social control? The level of analysis is also important. While traditional approaches to organizational study have focused on the individual organization as the unit of anaysis, we should also look at micro-processes to discover how individuals construct their own realities, and macro-processes to understand the relationships between organizations in a society. Finally, process itself is relevant. Traditional studies have focused on the organization as if it existed in a time warp. A processual analysis would attempt to look at the organization over time, and to analyze the processes of change and innovation to see how they occur in relation to other changes in the social system. The administrator, then, can look at the organization not only through a variety of frames, but also in a dialectical manner, moving between individuals and structure and relating them to wider or perhaps more constricting perceptions of the nature of organizations. This gives us a new way of conceptualizing schools and school systems: freed from a static systems model, our new model recognizes organizations as human constructs that become concretized over time but still remain open to change by human intervention.

7

Organizational Change

There could be nothing more paradoxical in historical terms than this change: man, at the beginning of the industrial age, when in reality he did not possess the means for a world in which the table was set for all who wanted to eat, when he lived in a world in which there were economic reasons for slavery, war, and exploitation, in which man only sensed the possibilities of his new science and of its application to technique and to production— nevertheless man at the beginning of modern development was full of hope. Four hundred years later, when all these hopes are realizable, when man can produce enough for everybody, when war has become unnecessary because technical progress can give any country more wealth than can territorial conquest, when this globe is in the process of becoming as unified as a continent was four hundred years ago, at the very moment when man is on the verge of realizing his hope, he begins to lose it.

—Erich Fromm, 1961.

Organizational change is big business. Corporations, volunteer agencies, state, federal, and local governments, welfare agencies, schools, and other assorted groups spend considerable sums of money on programs and materials offering advice on how to change. This national pastime involves uncounted numbers of consultants, each with his or her own approach (often his or her quick fix) and models of how to go about adapting organizations to a changing environment.

147

As a category of social action, organizational change largely falls within a functionalist perspective about organizations. The organization is seen as an entity in its own right, one that can be manipulated in some degree to effect change in either the structures or the patterns of interaction within the organization. Change occurs *within* an organization, but not many of these analyses recommend change *of* an organization. The organization continues to exist as an entity in the context of a given sociocultural system whose existence and purpose are never subject to attention. For many modern strategists change is planned change, not historical evolution.

Goodman and associates (1982), however, categorize organizational change along two dimensions: planned change and adaptation. Adaptation brings an evolutionary perspective to how certain organizations survive and others fail over a particular stretch of time. The dominant model of adaptation here, the population-ecology perspective, suggests that certain organizations adapt to their particular environmental niches better than other organizations; and consequently the adapting organizations will be the ones that last (Aldrich 1979). This model takes a long-term, evolutionary view of change that in effect applies a Darwinian perspective to organizations. It suggests that organizations follow a three-step process: variation, in which the organization differentiates itself in a random fashion; selection, in which those characteristics appropriate for the particular environment are selected; and retention, in which the organization maintains and reinforces characteristics suitable to a particular environment. In this model of evolutionary change the organization is more or less considered an organism that is affected by its environment in much the same manner as an organism might be.

This model, while challenging, has its drawbacks for the student of change. It is an essentially unfalsifiable, circular argument: organizations that fail, fail because they do not adapt to the environment; those that succeed do so because they did adapt. No external criterion validates these assertions; rather, they are taken as self-evident. Also, this model suffers from the same weaknesses as evolutionary theory itself. Modern arguments suggest that Darwin's theory may be subject to modification, for example, that major changes can occur quite quickly and dramatically after long periods of dormancy. An alternative conception of organizational change argues that it is managers in organizations who make decisions that affect the life of the organization. Child (1972), in his "strategic choice" model, and Chandler (1977), in his historical account of General Motors, provide persuasive arguments that managerial decision making indeed influences the evolution of the organization. Managers make strategic choices that cause the organization to adapt or not to adapt to environmental demands. Another response to this evolutionary approach is that it is framed in such long time periods that it becomes irrelevant to discussions about how to change organizations. Even if it is true that over the course of history certain organizations will adapt to their enviroment better than others, this still does not preclude the need to consider organizational change within our life spans.

Planned change and those interventionist strategies designed to effect a transformation of the organization are our major emphasis here. Organizations and the people in them are constantly changing. Every day brings different problems and different re-

FIGURE 1
MODELS OF CHANGE

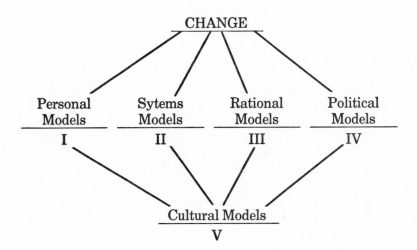

sponses: how can individuals intervene in the processes of change to produce a new or at least a different kind of organization?

At least five models of change address the major conceptualizations about change in organizations: the personal-therapeutic model, the systems-organic model, the rational-managerial model, the political-economic model, and the symbolic-cultural model of change (see fig. 1).

Each of these models attempts to define an aspect of reality as *the* context for organizational change. Of course, in capturing only a slice of reality, each model is incomplete; those dimensions important to other models are not considered. Organizational change can be likened to a large layer cake: the cake comprises a number of ingredients held together by some inexplicable chemistry. Various layers represent the various aspects of change: one layer represents rational behavior and rational attempts to effect change in the organization; another layer represents the political environment of the organization; a third, the personal and emotional make-up of the organization, and so on. The whole cake is covered by, and held together through, an icing consisting of symbols, metaphors, and culture. Each of these approaches to change will be considered individually, but these models are separated here for analytical purposes only. In reality, change programs and processes of change borrow to some degree from each of the models.

THE RATIONAL-MANAGERIAL APPROACH

This rational-managerial strategy for change assumes that the organization is populated by rational actors; that such actors will be swayed by evidence concerning the need for change; and that such change can be accomplished through a strategy or program that is largely sequential and dependent on data.

Large-scale efforts to change organizations that are based on the accumulation of data and are dependent on management initiative could be considered to fall into this model. It encompasses, for example, the research and development laboratories in education that gathered data on the improvement of educational processes to convince school districts to change their way of organizing instruction. It also encompasses the broad projects of the 1960s and 1970s that required school districts to devise elaborate programs to effect change in the system in exchange for federal funding. These were all very rational, very systematic approaches to the change process. Havelock (1973) provides a rational approach to organizational change by using a "change agent" in his six-step model. In brief, Havelock's "change agent" relies on the following procedure:

Stage 1—Enter into the organization: recognize its clients, leaders, and gatekeepers and its position in regard to its environment.

Stage 2—Make a diagnosis: identify the organization's problems and the opportunities; determine its goals and the amount of support behind them.

Stage 3—Discover the available resources: learn who are experts and who are innovators.

Stage 4—Choose a solution: after diagnosing the problem and identifying the resources, find a solution through research, brainstorming, and testing possible alternatives.

Stage 5—Build acceptance for the chosen solution: communicate the solution to other actors; identify and work around the resisters.

Stage 6—Stabilize the innovation and build in a capacity for self-renewal.

(Taken from Havelock 1973)

In its time this was heady stuff. A change agent, usually an external consultant, could enter the organization and use data-gathering devices (such as "authentic feedback," force-field analyses, needs surveys, and so on) to identify organizational problems, research possible alternatives, and then choose solutions, thereby providing methods for organizational renewal. A rational expert provided a rational solution, much as a mechanic would diagnose and repair or replace a misfiring carburetor.

Yet despite the support of federal programs and massive amounts of federal funding, this approach to change never accomplished its promises. As Baldridge and Deal comment:

> Much literature of the preceding two decades written on organiza-
> tional change focused on planned, rational change. . . . These ap-
> proaches shared a rational, "planning-can-work" philosophy, and
> overlaid on that philosophy was a social science "planning and
> evaluation" model. But those rationalistic approaches to change
> have worn thin, battered by the winds of environmental, political,
> and economic trends. (Baldridge and Deal 1983, x)

The reason for the failure of many of the attempts at planned,
rational change, or at least its failure to achieve its promised
goals, lies in the realities discussed in other models of change.
While organizations and their members are rational at times,
they are certainly not the mechanically rational individuals that
this approach presumes.

THE PERSONAL-THERAPEUTIC MODEL

Another model that has wide currency in the change literature is
a personal-therapeutic approach. Technically this is not a model
of *organizational* change; yet this approach appears frequently
enough in the literature of organizational change to warrant its
discussion here. This model of change rests on the major assumption that change must begin on the individual and interpersonal level. Meaningful organizational change can only result
from change generated in individuals. Since the organization is
made up of individuals, each acting according to some role or
script, to change the organization first requires that the individuals themselves are changed in some significant fashion. This
model includes such topics of concern as self-concept, personality,
integration, conflict management, communication processes,
trust development, personality fixations, values clarification, and
so on. Indeed, many of these topics have traditionally appeared
under the rubric of organizational development, but because organizational development has itself changed so much over the
last decade, it will be considered under another heading. In organizational terms, the personal-therapeutic model is reflected in
the National Training Laboratory work in the 1960s, in managerial encounter groups, and in other organizational efforts to
clear personal barriers that prevent clear and open communication
in the firm.

The classic example of the personal-therapeutic model is Lewin's work (1951) on change. He isolated three stages in the change process: unfreezing, changing, and refreezing, and Schein (1969) elaborates on them. Unfreezing, Schein says (1969), assumes that significant behavior, beliefs, attitudes, and so on, are organized by one's self-image. In Goffman's (1967) language, this results in a "presentation of self" to others in various contexts. The presentation can differ depending on the context, so one's self-image in the home may substantially differ from that operative at work. Unfreezing may occur when the self-image is "disconfirmed" by any of a number of processes: for example, when it becomes clear that how you think about yourself radically differs from how others perceive you, or when your "reality" is not everyone else's reality.

This process of disconfirmation leads to a situation in which change is possible. Basic assumptions and beliefs may be re-examined, and new information about the situation accepted. This, in turn, can lead to "cognitive redefinition," redefining the ego based on identification with a particular or generalized other. The practice of brainwashing (Schein 1969) is an extreme example of this process. Here, the captor attempts to disconfirm the previous beliefs of the prisoner, to convince him or her that what seems yellow is really red. The prisoner, his self-image shaken, begins to identify with the captor and to redefine the essence of the situation. In a more benign model husbands and wives make adjustments in marriage to develop a mutual redefinition of and accommodation to their situation. In an organizational situation, for example, a new principal, superintendent, or any individual possessing some degree of authority may redefine the context in new ways and thereby create some "cognitive dissonance" (Festinger 1957) that requires other organizational actors to re-view their values and beliefs in the revised context.

The last part of this model, refreezing, involves stabilizing and practicing the new image within the various situations in which other individuals will either confirm or disconfirm it, thus leading back to the first stage of the personal-therapeutic model.

In a fascinating application of this model Alderfer (1982; Alderfer and Smith 1982), who would normally consider himself an organizational development theorist, has applied a number of personal-therapeutic concepts to race relations in organizations.

Aware of racial prejudice in this country, Alderfer became particularly concerned about the ways that prejudice against blacks becomes manifest in organizations. He essentially finds that while many white males in organizations can express sympathy and concern for blacks facing prejudice in organizations, they nevertheless lack any real awareness of the concept of racial identity. They have little concept of what it means to be "white," largely because for them being white is normal, the status quo. It is being the dominant and dominating group in society. Alderfer is *not* concerned with eliciting sympathy from whites in typical liberal fashion. He attempts to get white males in particular to come to terms with what it means to be a white male in twentieth-century America: to in fact understand that they are a part of a racial group that has a history of oppressing others. Alderfer uses a therapeutic model in his work. He helps groups of white males recognize their racial identity and become aware of their responsibility (admittedly, often accompanied by guilt) to people of color.

THE ORGANIC-SYSTEMS MODEL

The two major assumptions made in this model are both encompassed by the model's description. The organic aspect assumes that organizations are similar to organisms—they grow, develop, change, and die. The systems aspect assumes that organizations are systems composed of interrelated and interdependent subsystems. These twin assumptions have led to the largest movement to implement change in organizations: organizational development. Organizational development has a varied history, a competing number of definitions, and widespread disagreement over what it *really* is. Over the years its emphasis has shifted from a preoccupation with personal issues, such as how well individuals communicate, to more structural issues.

Essentially, organizational development has both a conceptual framework and a set of strategies aimed at making organizations self-correcting and self-renewing. Organizational members learn productive ways of dealing with organizational problems, of interacting with each other, and of developing confidence in their individual and group skills. Usually, organizational development involves an outside consultant whose stated role is not to impose solutions, but to train actors in the knowledge and skills needed to overcome a variety of problems.

This model addresses itself to both cognitive and affective change; however, it attempts to go beyond the personal and the individual level characteristic of the personal-therapeutic approach. For example, it stresses training in interpersonal skills, consultation with work groups rather than individuals, and interventions into both structural and normative areas.

Organizational development looks at three levels of activity in the organization: the interpersonal, the subsystem, and the organization-as-a-whole. Its ultimate goal is adaptability, the organization's ability to effectively respond to changing conditions in its environment. Schmuck and his colleagues (1977) have suggested four standards that measure adaptability: *problem solving*—the ability to recognize and mobilize to solve problems as they develop; *resources*—the ability to maintain a variety of resources that can be used as situations warrant; *responsiveness*—the ability to quickly communicate throughout the organization information about environmental changes that affect individual subsystems and require action; and *assessment*—the ability to determine whether an organization is meeting its goals.

The organizational development consultant helps the organization incorporate these standards into its structure. The consultant examines and clarifies communication paths, uncovers and then works with conflict within and among the subsystems, improves meeting procedures, collaborates on solutions to identified problems, and assesses change strategies (Schmuck et al. 1977). Organizational development is similar in concept to a rational-managerial approach; indeed, it might be thought of as a combination of the aspects of a rational-managerial approach and a personal-therapeutic model. However, organizational development emphasizes process, while the rational-managerial approach stresses programs or products, and organizational development has an organizational systems perspective, while the personal-therapeutic approach has an individual orientation. Thus, organizational development, sometimes labeled as organizational renewal, deals with both the human processes in organizations (norms, values, communication styles) and the non-human processes (technology, structure, policies, and procedures)

(Lippitt 1982). In recent years it has devalued the interpersonal aspects of the organization to focus more on the structural aspects, partly in an effort to achieve some tangible result that justifies its interventionist program.

Organizational learning, a term developed by Argyris and Schön (1978), is closely related to organizational development but is distinctive in its own right. Argyris and his colleagues are more concerned with how organizations learn—in much the same way that humans learn—than with how organizations change. Argyris's concepts might be considered one step ahead of much of the work that occurs under the organic-systems framework. The concept of organizational learning does not depend on rationalistic models of change but views change as a learning process. It offers a significantly more complex and sophisticated view of human systems that incorporates psychological, sociological, linguistic, and cultural dimensions and examines the process of organizing. Argyris starts by asserting that there is a basic difference between what we say and what we do, and that we are unaware of the difference. He labels what we say as the "espoused theory-of-action," that is, how we cognitively interpret our behavior and action to ourselves and to others. How we act is labeled our "theory-in-use," that is, our actual behavior as it is observed by others. Thus, an individual might say and truly believe that he or she acts primarily for the good of others, but nevertheless continue to act in a manner interpreted as self-serving by others. This failure to link thought and deed leads to a variety of errors.

Error correction in this model generally occurs in two ways that both use feedback loops. Argyris distinguishes between single- and double-feedback loops. A single loop identifies an error and then loops back to correct it, in somewhat the same way as one might relight a candle that went out in the middle of dinner. A double loop corrects the immediate error but then loops back again to correct the source of the error: one not only relights the candle but also rises to close the window.

The possibilities of single- or double-loop learning suggest that two models of action are possible. Model I behavior represents actions that are single loop in nature; errors are identified and corrected, but the basic source of those errors—what Argyris and Schön (1978) label the governing variables—remains untouched. These governing variables can be considered to be social norms that direct our behavior, such as the need to be rational, to be competitive, to be unemotional, and to not express negative feelings. In our society, for example, the typical child is expected to be "nice" to adults; if a boy, to be strong; if a girl, sweet; yet the child must also win and succeed. These norms are primary inhibitory loops that prevent double-loop learning from occurring; these basic norms, in turn, are reinforced by secondary inhibitory loops, those occasional situations in which group dynamics reinforce the individual conclusions about social norms, for example, in informal, after-class discussions where students reinforce each other about not disagreeing with the teacher. When this Model I behavior is lifted to the organizational level, it becomes, in Argyris's terminology, Model O-I, and reflects the same essentials just mentioned.

Model II is the model of action that reflects double-loop learning. Here, the governing variables themselves are exposed and examined to result in what Argyris labels "discussing the undiscussable." Not only are the errors open to inspection, but the underlying norms that promote such errors are also available for consideration. Inconsistencies that develop through the inherent conflict between what we think we do and what others see us as doing are opened up and surfaced for analysis. For example, a class that takes pride in cooperative learning and mutual goals might discuss its existent competitive reward structure. Argyris (1982) finds that most people aspire to Model II behavior: they believe that there should be trust in organizations, that communication should be open, that one should freely express one's feelings and thoughts, that sacrifice has a place in human affairs. However, most people also have enormous difficulty in incorporating Model II behavior into their own behavioral repertoire, *and* they fail to recognize that they have this difficulty.

Argyris's concern, therefore—and his link to organizational development—is enabling organizations to exhibit Model II behavior, at that level designated Model O-II. In working with top management, Argyris has found that many clients can in fact learn Model II behavior in laboratory-type settings but revert to Model I behavior when re-placed in the organization. This finding implies that our "undiscussable" norms are deeply entrenched, and that organizational development programs such as his, while well founded, make naive assumptions about human action. Argyris might contend that proper training and support could lead executives to develop Model II theories-in-use that would in turn affect the actions of the rest of the organization. In any case Argyris's concerns do show us the potential of the organic-systems approach when it is informed by humanistic issues and when it goes beyond the laboratory strategies used to make executives feel comfortable only with each other.

THE POLITICAL-ECONOMIC MODEL

Another way of thinking about change in organizations has had an increasing influence in recent years. The political-economic model looks at the effects of politics and economics as models for change and the virtues of comprehensiveness, economy, and reasonableness. It encompasses much organizational reality within its scope, yet is parsimonious in its use of select concepts. It recognizes the political and economic activity of organizational members: they are not simply passive recipients of change sent down from above, but are actively concerned with power and reward.

The political approach stands out particularly when compared to structuralist approaches to organizations that see organizations as bureaucratic structures that can be measured in terms of size, technology, differentiation of roles, and so on. The structuralist approach neglected the way individual members of organizations actively create and change their organizational reality. Partly in reaction to this structuralist emphasis, theorists created such concepts as garbage-can models of decision making, loose coupling, and others applicable to features of organizational life. These, however, seem to neglect the question of how organizational structures emerge and stabilize over a period of time, and how organizations change—sometimes on a daily basis— while still maintaining their identity. A political-economic model looks at organizational change and accounts for both structure (bureaucracy) and process (organized anarchy).

The political-economic model of organizational change has several distinguishing characteristics. First, it sees the organization as a political system that has real and symbolic resources. Real resources are those tangible and relatively permanent resources the organization controls, from salary to pencils. Symbolic resources are the relatively intangible and often-changing resources such as status, power, and prestige. Second, this model postulates that the organization has political actors, each having his or her own self-interest at stake. Third, coalitions form within the organization and develop collective strategies for achieving mutual control of certain resources. The relationship between the historical structure and norms of the organization (who controls what; who should control what) affects the development of coalitions: the organization's historical structure and norms influence the objectives of coalitions, and the coalitions, in turn, influence the evolution of the norms and structure in a dynamic relationship. Finally, the organization exists within a political environment where conflict is an integral and even desirable component.

Zald (1970) has made a valuable contribution to this literature by developing a categorization of the political economy that includes the following: economic factors, political factors, internal and external dimensions. This combination provides a fairly comprehensive account of how the political economy can affect the organization. Both the external environment and the internal environment have political and economic aspects. The political factors affecting the external environment are its legislative bodies, executive offices, the courts, political parties and interest groups, the media, competitors, and interested citizens. In addition, the external environment has economic controls such as technological factors, labor supplies, consumer demand, market viability, and so on. Both the political and economic external constraints have an impact on how the organization adapts to its circumstances. The external factors help to determine whether the organization has a market and the technology and labor required to meet the demands of that market.

The political and economic dimensions also occur within the organization. The internal economic factors include accounting and reporting rules; pay, promotion, and tenure requirements; the budgetary process; merit systems and other economic rewards or inducements. Internal political aspects include distribution of power and authority, the nature of the hierarchy, coalitions, recruitment patterns, and the organization's constitution. The constitution, the unwritten code of conduct for people in the organization, comprises the norms, values, myths, and so on, that govern individual behavior. While one may not know what the organization's constitution allows, what it forbids becomes very clear: newcomers to the organization are quickly socialized into the meanings and fabric of organizational life.

Change in the organization occurs through the manipulation of economic and political processes. This model would contend that it is not process interventions or rational strategies or even personal change that changes organizations. Rather, the manipulation of rewards, changes in supply and demand, and the development of interest groups have the most profound effect on organizational life. The political process, of course, depends on coalitions, negotiations, and bargaining; thus change occurs through these very processes.

SYMBOLIC AND CULTURAL ASPECTS

The literature on organizational theory and change has increasingly recognized that symbols, metaphors, and other aspects of an organization's culture have a broad and often controlling impact. This position suggests that changes in the metaphors will result in changes in the organization. Confused or conflicting symbols result in a confused and conflict-ridden organization.

Deal and Wiske (1983) contribute to this view of the organization by examining how different metaphors control different views of organizational reality. In the rational-technical view the controlling metaphor is the factory, and the emphasis is on goal achievement. In the political view the metaphor used is the jungle, and the emphasis is on power. In the symbolic view the temple provides the metaphor, with the emphasis on the various myths, rituals, and ceremonies that coalesce the organization into a collective unity. As we saw in the last chapter, other authors (Bolman and Deal 1984; Deal and Kennedy 1982) have pursued this "cultural" approach to organizational analysis and its prospects for change. They maintain an effective organization functions through the combination of interactive and widely accepted myths, symbols, and rituals; change, therefore, is accomplished through change in these areas.

This interest in organizational culture has two major foundations, cultural anthropology and phenomenology. Anthropologists have long studied and classified native cultures, looking at such features as kinship systems, rites and rituals, symbols and taboos. Phenomenology, particularly as derived from Husserl through Schutz, considers how meanings are established, largely through face-to-face encounters in day-to-day interaction. A community shares meanings through the development of symbols, both overt (for example, the text of a book) or covert (for example, reading "between-the-lines" for intentions).

A culture uses rituals as a systematic and repeatable way of conveying and confirming common symbols, as Turner (1972) has observed. Turner, among the first contemporary scholars to look at cultural aspects of industry, suggests that several types of rituals are observable in modern organizations. Rites of passage may occur when individuals enter the organization and have to "learn the ropes" or are promoted, transferred, or otherwise physically moved about, in or out of the organization. Schools rely on graduation ceremonies to certify in a ritualistic way that something has occurred in four years: that education has taken place and that the staff has successfully performed its duties. Second, rites of sameness or difference reinforce status differentials or similarities with certain rituals (who sits where at lunch, what clothes are traditionally worn by what groups). Third, rituals concern the management of time, a practice universal in other organizations but particularly noticeable in schools. Turner cites punching the time clock as an example that not only symbolizes the cultural virtue of punctuality, but also reinforces the status of those organizational members not required to punch in. Finally, rituals of performance become important, especially when there is no clear connection between the work and its outcome. In schools, because there is no particularly clear connection between what a given teacher does and how a student achieves, rituals of performance take on significance.

Sarason's work (1979) shows how the "culture of the school" interacts with well-intentioned but often futile efforts to change the institution. Sarason starts with an interesting position. He asks, what if we were Martian observers, come to earth for a brief period of time? What would we see if we looked at schools? Would we wonder why the institution is open for five days and then closed for two? Would we inquire into the ways the rooms are arranged, or ask why there is one adult for numerous children? For Sarason these and other questions indicate that schools contain regularities that often escape us because they are part of the fabric of the organization. Such regularities are both programmatic and behavioral: they regulate what we do as well as the programs that we embrace. The regularities are held in place by the glue of culture: the rituals, symbols, and so on, that give meaning to our daily quest for glory. Sarason concludes that because we have such a systematic expression of culture in the school, schools are exceedingly hard to change. Change requires, at least, an understanding and modification of the regularities that affect not only our in-school behavior, but also our expectations about how we are supposed to behave in this given system.

In summary, symbols, rituals, and the like, are expressions that help us to recognize the social world in which we live. We gain an understanding of and appreciation for our particular culture only by comparing it with other cultures; we recognize our sameness, in a sense, only through recognizing difference. The idea of culture becomes a means for thinking about how a social grouping becomes cohesive and develops similar values and world views. On a smaller scale, not only do societies have culture, but organizations do also. Indeed, any human assemblage that persists over some time forms a culture. It could be argued that this latter conception of culture is weak because the "culture" that might emerge in an organization is fragmented, place-bound, and hardly representative of the deep concept that anthropologists use; yet it does help us to understand a number of realities that occur in organizations and, in particular, to differentiate between different organizations and institutions. Whether we can "use" such a construct to promote change is problematic. For example, understanding the norms, mores, and relationships that govern our behavior in an institution does not necessarily mean that we can step outside of those same governing rules to cause change.

MODELS OF CHANGE: EVALUATION

No one model of change explains how or why organizations change. The layer-cake analogy mentioned earlier might capture the reality of change and organizational change more fully than any one model. Organizations and institutions are complex and planned change in them is equally so. Experience has shown that the rational, top-down approach has not worked to the extent envisioned. The Rand Studies (Berman and McLaughlin 1978) indicated that planned change was really a process of mutual adaptation by both the funders and the fundees. Farrar et al. (1980) find that such planned change really is what they call a "lawn party": some guests come for the food, some for the conversation, some have been coerced into coming, and some don't know why they came. Planned change in this view is more a process of continuing evolution and development, as the "guests" get to know each other and each other's expectations and abilities.

In a similar way, organizational development has not had the effect originally envisioned. The literature has disputed the ideas that, for example, an outside consultant is needed over a long period of time, and that people resist change. Organizational development, in fact, seems to be a coat of many colors, with little agreement on how to really define it (see Fullan, Miles, and Taylor 1980).

The other models—personal-therapeutic, political-economic, cultural-symbolic—hold up better because they correspond more accurately to what we know of how people and organizations change. Of course, these models reflect the traditional disciplines of psychology, politics, and anthropology in their analysis of change processes and thereby "academize" the change process. Although each model alone cannot account for the contributions of the others, all make their essential contributions. The political-economic model, for example, considers the issue of "constitutions" in the organization and reflects a normative, and therefore cultural, consensus, yet it does not explore this in depth. Each model could nest within the other: symbolic-cultural concerns could be considered part of the political-economic environment; yet the politics and economics of a group could be seen as only an aspect of its overall culture. Depending on one's level of analysis, the same holds true for the personal-therapeutic model.

Change, then, is a complex factor for educational administrators and other school people. It is best considered as a multilayered and interactive set of elements, not all of which need to be considered simultaneously.

CRITICAL PERSPECTIVES ON CHANGE

It is imperative that the school administrator has a critical regard for the idea of change itself. If not frequently considered, the idea of change can overwhelm: reports from national commissions, funding possibilities from state and federal agencies, statements by state superintendents—all ask or demand change on the part of individuals whose major interest lies in providing a meaningful experience for youngsters under their care. But who and what needs to change?

One might apply a critical perspective on change to the language of change. Much of it sees the organization almost as a monolith that exists outside of and apart from the individuals who compose it. We have seen previously that this can be disputed. The organization is made up of people, each of whom helps to construct a particular social reality that, in turn, is objectified. Change should therefore be aimed not at *the* organization but at the people in it. Further, in much of what we hear, change is considered to be something designed and accomplished. Through this linguistic trick the language of change persuades us that change is mechanical, like changing an air filter or changing the oil. But unless we are dealing with physical, mechanical objects, change is a process, one that has no ending but keeps unfolding. Change in this model can be much like the way a child matures: perhaps one doesn't see the hour-to-hour or day-to-day growth, but after a six-month absence, changes are noticeable. The language of change can be deceitful, for it tells us that if we do "X," then "Y" will happen. But, there is more to change than causality: we all change and develop continually. Organizations are no different.

Change can also be disguised as motion. Popkewitz (1982; Popkewitz and Tabachnick 1981) argues that two central paradigms have guided modern change efforts, the center-to-periphery approach and a problem-solving model. Both, he claims, ignore the idea of fundamental change. The center-to-periphery approach, as Farrar et al. (1980) have discussed it, involves a central agency, such as the federal government, developing and then relaying to the "periphery" various models and plans for change. The problem-solving approach involves the activity of various agents who define problems in the system and then adopt solutions for them. Both of these approaches share various features, according to Popkewitz. They both look to experts to provide analyses and, perhaps, solutions; they maintain faith in scientific attempts to find answers to community problems; and they refuse to consider fundamental inconsistencies in the very structure of the system itself. Thus change becomes only motion: the deep structural changes that might be necessary to revalidate an educational system are glossed over and only surface changes are proposed. There is a lot of movement and a lot of activity, but no real change:

> But this movement and activity takes-for-granted the structure by focusing on the "system" as an entity in and of itself. The neutrality does not question the goals of the system. The focus upon the system as a separate entity removes questions about how institutional norms and beliefs filter into and intervene in the daily life of the system. (Popkewitz 1982, 30)

To address change perspectives that take greater systemic properties into account and that do not presume the entire system to be fixed requires adopting a critical perspective on the change process. Oakes and Sirotnik (and see Sirotnik 1984 and Oakes and Sirotnik 1986) find that:

> Taking an acritical stance, we usually think of schools as neutral, non-political places that go about their business of educating children as well as they can. We assume they are eager for new practices that will enable them "to do better." . . . Little attention has been given to the examination of the values and beliefs on which school practice rests. (Oakes and Sirotnik 1983, 3)

Yet, they claim that it is these unconsidered beliefs that form the basis for how schools are organized and conducted. Change efforts, then, should be oriented toward critical inquiry. Oakes and Sirotnik use a three-part paradigm involving three modes of inquiry: empirical, aimed at gathering the "facts" of the situation through such objective means as survey research and quasi-experimental methods; interpretive or hermeneutic, aimed at probing the meanings and understandings actors give to events; and critical, aimed at exposing and analyzing conditions that lead to the suppression of the human spirit.

This framework can be implemented through the use of "collaborators" who work with school staff in developing a reflective and critical process of inquiry. Oakes and Sirotnik (1983) adopt a strategy taken from Freire's (1970) work in South America that involves relinquishing power games, "relinquishing ritualistic and symbolic authority games" (Oakes and Sirotnik 1983, 27), and "problematization," making a "problem" out of what would normally be considered unproblematic. In a school, for example, teachers and administrators could ask why certain groups have certain powers, why administration controls certain resources, why a particular schedule is in force, and so on. This problematization allows the participants to develop a reflective consciousness about prevailing conditions and so develop alternatives. "Change"—essentially, devising a plan or strategy that changes practice in some meaningful way—does not purport to solve a problem. Rather, it suggests a continuing and ongoing trial of different ways of organizing reality that is itself subject to the process of problematization or critical inquiry.

and

empirical modes, requires collaborators who are familiar with the process (outside consultants or teachers or administrators in the school itself). Nevertheless, attempting to engage a school body in this self-reflective approach to change has its difficulties.

> There are two major obstacles facing a collaborator attempting to "tune in" to a school that has indicated some interest in an improvement project—obtaining a genuine invitation to participate *with* the people there in a fundamental change effort and breaking through the "culture of silence" in order to begin to determine with them what the crucial problems they face are. Because these two obstacles are so closely intertwined, overcoming them is particularly difficult. Establishing rapport at administrative levels and securing support (or, at least approval) for collaborative change efforts, is usually a prerequisite. (Oakes and Sirotnik 1983, 31)

Tuning in and breaking through: these are the two major aspects of bringing about meaningful change. Once these are accomplished, the possibilities for action are heightened. Action here refers to more than the adoption of technically oriented strategies, such as criterion-referenced instead of norm-referenced tests, for improving the school environment. While such strategies may indeed be useful, the heart of critical inquiry involves developing an organization populated by a *community of scholars* who can engage in continuing and unrepressed communication about existent school conditions and possibilities for change. Such a community does not look at change efforts as additive, adding to the structure that is already there, but as transformative, changing and transforming the basic structures that have been established. In this sense this approach to change in the school is critical.

Here, then, we approach the idea of change as praxis, that is, as practical action aimed at clarifying and resolving social conditions. Praxis must be thought of as practical action, informed by theory, that attempts to change various conditions. Practical action in the context of the school involves our critical appreciation of current realities and our critical attempts to evaluate and change these realities in the light of our knowledge about social structures. This is to say in part that change in the schools cannot be divorced from change in the larger social arenas, and that change in one presupposes change in the other. Administrators certainly deal in such arenas all the time.

The major effort for change can be aimed at developing truly representative systems of participation in the school and democratic ways of realizing organization. Change in the rational model is oriented toward new products and ways of organizing reality through programs such as Headstart and, more recently, developing effective schools. Such endeavors fail to get at the basic rationale of change efforts: to develop a *process* wherein individuals can rationally attempt to communicate wants and needs without distortion and be instrumental in the participatory development of an educational institution.

In one respect, then, change involves a raising of consciousness about possibilities by penetrating the dominating ideas or total ideologies and analyzing the possible forms of life. This orientation, while political and cultural, is also critical, because it suggests that we attempt to cut through the "natural," taken-for-granted status quo to explore new arrangements. This particularly challenging task asks us to question the given structures and divisions: those between teachers and administrators and students, for example. It also asks that we momentarily suspend our heritage and history, particularly as they have determined our current structures.

In the final analysis, a critical perspective on change requires a synoptic overview of change in society. Informed by cultural studies relating to the reproduction of classes within schools, by organizational theories that stress the enactment and reproduction of organizations, and by a critical theory that locates organizational structures in the wider nexus of political and economic relations, the change theorist will have to carefully consider how the institution can be changed. Change involves more than the development of rationalistic programs and more than attempts at altering the particular culture of the school. Change in a meaningful sense will, by its nature, have to include the analysis of the institution within the wider society. This indeed is what praxis is all about; it is concerned with making theory meaningful at the level of practical action, and with showing how individuals caught in the tensions of everyday organizations can re-create their particular universes in a fashion that accomplishes what they want. Given the failure of various well-financed, rational strategies of change, it is not hard to conclude that organizational change needs to involve political action. Administrators are certainly politically adept, but here we ask them to channel that adeptness to create social change. Political action is the attempt—your attempt and ours—to achieve ends that are not just instrumental, but that achieve more equitable conditions for all school people when they are realized. This effort means engaging in leadership within the school, a leadership oriented toward the concept of social change.

8

Leadership

Never has the human occasion been piled so high with awful difficulty.

—Robert Tucker, 1981.

Administration, Hodgkinson (1983) has observed, is leadership. Educational administration involves, among other things, the presentation of values and images of the proper way; this, in turn, entails leadership. Yet the concept of leadership often receives poor treatment from scholars and educators alike. Often, it is mistaken for the ability to manage small groups in accomplishing tasks; at other times, as a means for improving production. We shall argue that both views adopt a fundamentally mistaken approach to leadership insofar as they identify leadership with aspects of management, as they focus on task accomplishment, and as they neglect to deal with followers' needs and requirements. The construct of leadership needs to be dismantled and rebuilt to be useful and helpful.

THE PROBLEM WITH LEADERSHIP RESEARCH

We all know the term "leadership" from experience: we learned it in elementary school, envied it in high school, and perhaps even

169

practiced it in college. Yet such a common term seems to defy definition, particularly a scientifically rigorous one, although many have tried to encapsulate it. Their definitions, though, have been limited largely by the disciplinary affiliation of the definers. Hersey and Blanchard define leadership this way:

> Leadership is the process of influencing *the activities of an individ-* *ual or a group in efforts toward goal achievement in a given situa-* *tion.* . . . the leadership process is a function of the *leader,* the *fol-* *lower,* and other situational variables)—L = f (1,f, s). (Hersey and Blanchard 1972, 68, italics in original)

This definition is widely shared (e.g., Owens 1981; Fiedler 1967; Blake and Mouton 1975) and is the basis for a number of training programs (situational leadership, nine-by-nine grids, and so on). Under examination, however, it hardly gets to the point of what we normally consider to be leadership. Not all leadership is clearly motivated toward the achievement of a specific goal, and perhaps not all leadership takes place in proximate physical situations; certainly, not all leadership can be reduced to the simplicity of a formula. The definition provides only an empty abstraction that neglects the crucial dimensions of culture, politics, and power.

What are other ways of defining or studying leadership? Bennis (1959, 259) observed that "the concept of leadership eludes us or turns up in another form to taunt us again with its slipperiness and complexity." Stodgill (1974, vii) found that "The endless accumulation of empirical data has not produced an integrated understanding of leadership." Miner (1975, 5) gave up: "The heresy I propose is that the concept of leadership itself has outlived its usefulness." Burns (1978, 2) observed that "Leadership as a concept has dissolved into small and discrete meanings. . . . A superabundance of facts about leaders far outruns theories of leadership." Dubin (1979, 227) finds that "By focusing on leaders' interpersonal relations with followers we have simply chosen a relatively trivial dimension." Jago (1982, 315) finds that "Although behavioral scientists have granted few topical areas greater research attention, the results of these efforts remain a bewildering melange for even the most serious student of organizations." McCall (1976, 142) observes that "After forty years of accumulation, our mountain of evidence about leadership seems to offer few clear-cut facts. Most of the relative certainties deal with things that are *not* true, reflecting a tendency to hone our understanding of leadership by inadvertently finding out what it is not." Perrow has the last word:

> The research on leadership has left us with the clear view that things are far more complicated and "contingent" than we initially believed, and that, in fact, they are so complicated and contingent that it may not be worth our while to spin out more and more qualifications. (Perrow 1979, 107)

For those looking at the phenomenon of leadership through scientific lenses, the study has dead-ended. The scientific, largely sociopsychological approach has toppled under its own weight. These gloomy assessments of the leadership construct require that we examine two questions: What kind of leadership research has led to these evaluations? What can a reconsideration of the foundations and purpose of leadership reveal?

LEADERSHIP RESEARCH: THE PSYCHOLOGICAL MODEL

Jago (1982) has identified four major perspectives on leadership; we will add one further perspective. These all fall under the broad domain of a psychological model, here taken to mean a concentration on the individual and the social group. Jago's first perspective dealt with traits such as intelligence, confidence, ability to communicate, and so on, that leaders supposedly possessed. This trait approach to leadership research never proved especially fruitful: one could continue to list particular traits only to find that some leaders did not possess some of the traits. The trait approach was not generalizable. In his review of leadership research Stodgill (1948; reprinted in Bass 1981, 68) essentially killed the trait approach with his finding that "leadership is not a matter of passive status nor of the mere possession of some combination of traits."

Researchers abandoned the trait theory and turned toward a study of leader "behaviors." Starting in the mid-1940s, studies at a midwestern university identified two factors supposedly associated with leadership behavior. These were "consideration," whether the leader was people-centered and concerned with the personal problems of the group, and "initiation of structure," whether the leader was task-centered and concerned with goal achievement. Four quadrants were possible, each representing a range from low to high. Thus, leaders could be high on task, low on consideration; they could be high on consideration, low on task; they could be low on both consideration and task; or, the preferred condition, they could be high on both dimensions. These studies spawned numerous training programs designed to raise both task and consideration behavior; but, as Jago (1982, 320) observes, "Managers can indeed be trained to behave in ways characteristic of high consideration and high initiating structure but the expected pay-offs from such training are not necessarily realized."

This and other theories considered in this section distinctly failed to distinguish between management and leadership. They are considered to be synonymous terms: this is an error in both definition and conceptualization. If leadership were to be taken seriously in these theories, then they would have to acknowledge the fact that leadership, by definition, does not exist in isolation, without followers. By ignoring the followers' own cultural and normative world, by focusing only on management prerogatives, these theories certainly cannot be expected to have much pay-off.

The two-factor model's inability to predict leadership led to a third perspective in the mid-1960s: Fiedler's (1967) "contingency" model of leadership, the most widely researched and most widely criticized framework for leadership study (Bass 1981, 341). Fiedler assumes that individuals have a particular leadership "style," and further, that the leader's effectiveness in a given situation will depend on the "match" between his or her style and the relationship between the leader and the group, the nature of the task, and the type of authority the leader commands. The style to be used is contingent on whether the relationships between the leader and group are poor or good, whether the task is structured or unstructured, and whether the leader commands a position of high or low authority. In Fiedler's work, the interaction between these various combinations yields eight possibilities or "octants." According to his theory, where leader-member relations were good, where the task was structured, and where there was strong position power, the most effective leadership would come from a task-oriented individual. The same would be true if all these conditions were reversed; a task-oriented leader would still be appropriate. Only if the conditions were mixed would one need a consideration-oriented leader. Thus in Fiedler's model of leadership one needs to imagine a line broken into eight segments; leadership effectiveness will vary depending on which segment one is located and whether one leaned toward structure or process (task or consideration).

Fiedler's answer to leadership, then, was to insert the "right" individual into the existing organizational condition. If the right individual were not available, then the condition should be changed to match the characteristics of those currently in power. This is the "leader match concept" that Fiedler et al. (1976) have developed.

This contingency theory and the leader-match concept are not fully accepted constructs in the field and the subject of considerable dispute, despite their popularity with educational training agencies and intermediate units. The empirical findings cast some doubt on the whole approach. Hosking and Schriesheim (1978, 500) find that "In fact, when the relevant studies are critically examined, and a distinction drawn between those that constitute adequate tests of the model and those that do not, the results are far from encouraging." In their review of Fiedler, Chemers, and Maher's book on leadership effectiveness (1976), these same authors conclude:

> Despite the publisher's claims that the [contingency] model and leader match have been "thoroughly validated," this is clearly nonsense. Given the severe problems noted . . . such a claim would almost be amusing, if it were not for the fact that some leaders may be injured by the application of leader match. (Hosking and Schriesheim 1978, 504)

Hunt (1984b) labels the fourth development in leadership research second-generation contingency theories such as path-goal theory and the Vroom/Yetton model of decision making. Path-goal theory (House 1971) suggests that the function of the leader lies in the clarification of what particular organizational paths lead to goals valued by subordinates. The leader helps followers achieve such goals by showing them the appropriate directions to take. Leadership, however, is contingent on the nature of followers (their skill level, maturity, and so on) and on the nature of the work setting (type of task to be accomplished, clarity of the procedures to be used). The leader adjusts his or her style to the needs of the situation in order to increase motivation and clarify paths. (Fiedler would argue that leader style is basically fixed rather than adjustable.) The research results from examining path-goal theory have been mixed (Bass 1981, 446-47; Jago 1982, 326).

The other model cited by second-generation contingency theorists is the Vroom/Yetton approach (1973). This model presents leaders with a decision tree to help them make the "best" decisions under certain circumstances. Vroom and Yetton identify five possible decision styles that range from leader-only decisions to group-only decisions, with variations of these in between. The particular style chosen depends on one's response to several questions, such as whether the group will have to carry out the decision or whether there is a time requirement for making a decision. The answers to these questions lead one along a decision tree to identify a particular decision-making style for that decision. This model has also received some critical review, particularly with respect to its practice of using managers' self-reports to test its success and its inability to determine whether managers say the same thing that their subordinates observed them doing (Field 1979).

The fifth perspective on leadership might be considered a third-generation approach. Here, we find later efforts to understand leadership that still treat leadership as essentially a psychological and small-group phenomenon. The theories here include attribution theory, reinforcement theory, exchange theory, and the multiple influence model of leadership.

Attribution theory does not ask what leadership *is* but how we *attribute* leadership to certain individuals. As Hunt (1984b, 37) mentions, "To find the meaning of the term *leadership* one must study the way in which the label is used, when it is used, and how individuals develop assumptions about the nature of leadership." Leadership in this approach is less concerned with the behaviors of leaders than with the process leaders and subordinates use to create a particular reality in which an act labeled "leadership" occurs. While this approach to leadership is a fairly new and interesting one, it tends to become a vicious cycle with no exit. This variant of the realist/nominalist debate—do these concepts such as leadership really exist, or are they useful, agreed-upon fictions—is essentially unresolvable.

Reinforcement theory views leadership behavioristically, seeing it as simply the reinforcement of behaviors on the part of leaders and the concomitant reinforcement of leadership by subordinates. This model, however, violates everything we know about cognitive psychology and how people learn. The more interesting exchange theory model explains leadership as a result of mutual exchanges between the leader and his/her followers. The leader provides followers with psychic and material rewards in exchange for their support and loyalty; the leader also gives the group task direction and a feeling of satisfaction and accomplishment. The group, in turn, provides the leader with a sense of power and control. As long as there is a mutual exchange of rewards, the leadership process proceeds undisturbed; however, when the exchange becomes asymmetrical—for example, if the leader fails to adequately clarify the task to be accomplished—then the process breaks down and a search for new leadership begins. Graen and Cashman (1975) have modified this model somewhat to examine what they label the vertical dyad linkage theory. Here, the focus is on the individual exchange relationships between the leader and an individual subordinate (thus, vertical and dyadic). This theory predicts that in an organization vertical dyadic relationships result in the differential allocation of rewards, such as status, power, and so on, to an "in-group" upon which the leader relies to control the organization.

The final model examined in this section is Hunt's (1984a; 1984b) multiple influence model of leadership. This model

> assumes that an organization's environment, its context for action (size and technology), and its structure (all macrovariables), as well as conditions within work units in the organization (microvariables), affect the role of a manager. These conditions do this first by influencing a manager's leader behavior. Second, they serve as contingencies that combine with leader behavior to affect work unit performance and satisfaction-related outcomes such as satisfaction, organizational commitment, involvement with the job, absenteeism, and esprit de corps. (Hunt 1984b, 32).

This seems to say that because an organization has multiple contexts to consider, managers can exert multiple influences over those particular contexts, as well as be influenced by those contexts. In this model "discretionary" leadership (Hunt 1984b, 33) means that managers engage in behavior that makes the reward system clearer. The manager provides more concise directions that show employees the movement and direction of the enterprise. This approach differs from the former contingency approaches primarily because it considers factors other than just the work group, in particular, the macro-oriented organizational environment. Of course, as more and more variables that affect the organization and its management are taken into account, the theory becomes more complex and less relevant for understanding particular behaviors in given situations.

In summary, the major charge that might be leveled against these various theories of leadership is that they do not address leadership at all. They are essentially various theories on how to manage the firm. These models of leadership are really concerned with management rituals designed to enhance organizational supremacy. The prime concern in many of these theories is getting workers and worker groups to produce more effectively or more efficiently. The second- and third-generation theories seem to associate leadership with management *in the organization,* thereby ignoring other forms of leadership that occur in extraorganizational contexts. Leadership and management are conflated; one is identified with the other. Path-goal theory, the multiple-influence model, exchange theory, etc., are most concerned with how managers in organizations get employees to follow their directions and to subscribe to their viewpoints. They use different approaches but certainly have a common theme: the managers are the leaders.

THE POLITICAL MODEL OF LEADERSHIP

This managerial model of leadership is belied by more political theories of leadership that do not place leadership solely in the context of business organizations or the military. Here, we look at leadership in more abstract terms that are not tied to the desiderata of a particular enterprise. Indeed, in these political representations, followers exert as powerful an influence on leaders as leaders exert upon followers, a perspective not normally found in the theories previously considered. Further, these approaches take into account the most dynamic aspect of leadership, that of politics. Leadership is not seen as merely effective management; leadership is more the playing out of the political process in terms satisfactory to both leaders and followers.

Selznick's work *Leadership in Administration* (1957) is a classic in this genre. For Selznick, the leader is not just the manager; the leader is concerned with "critical" (as opposed to routine) decisions in the institution. Critical decisions involve the definition of purpose, not simply linking means to the ends desired, or developing a harmonious team through human-relations types of activities. Rather, the leader engages in activities that provide meaning: "The institutional leader . . . *is primarily an expert in the promotion and protection of values."* (Selznick 1957, 28, italics in original). From this, Selznick develops three propositions concerning leadership: leadership occurs in a social situation; leadership is not the same as holding an office or making decisions; and leadership is dispensable.

The first proposition tells us that leadership involves interactions that occur within a social situation; however Selznick does *not* consider leadership "situational." He notes that "it does not follow that the *nature* of leadership varies with each social situation" (1957, 23). We are again coming to this conclusion some thirty years later. The second proposition tells us that leadership is not to be confused with official position or with the exercise of authority. Unfortunately, we habitually consider those in charge as the leaders of the organization. This rather narrow definition of leadership confuses the authority of office with the broader notion of leadership. In other words, leadership can occur outside of any particular organizational context. Selznick's third proposition states that leadership is not always needed; indeed, some social processes within organizations neither demand nor need leadership. Kerr and Jermier (1983) express the flavor of Selznick's idea in their notion of "substitutes" for leadership: for example, a professional staff well versed in the intricacies of their jobs simply do not need someone else to inspire them because they have the demands of the jobs internalized. Selznick's propositions form the basis of much of the leadership research that has followed. Indeed, current emphases in leadership theory return to some degree to the attributes Selznick discussed in his seminal volume.

Burns, another original thinker, has done much to re-orient our notions on leadership. Burns (1978, 12) sees leadership "as a special form of power" and power as the utilization of resources in order to achieve valued goals and ends. He does not interpret power in any mechanical sense, nor does he consider it coercive. As Burns (1978, 11) says, "the most powerful influences consist of deeply human relationships in which two or more persons *engage* with one another." Power need not be power "over": it could be power "to." Burns defines leadership this way:

> *Leadership over human beings is exercised when persons with certain motives and purposes mobilize, in competition or conflict with others, institutional, political, psychological, and other resources so as to arouse, engage, and satisfy the motives of followers.* (Burns 1978, 18, italics in original)

Here Burns is saying, first, leadership is practiced over people, not over people-as-objects. Second, it is purposive, oriented toward a goal, a vision, a possibility. Third, leadership is political. It involves competition and conflict, because we all have different visions of the possible and resources to achieve visions are limited. Finally, leadership does not exist in isolation, apart from followers' own motives, ideas, and wants. Leadership is "inseparable from followers' needs and goals" (1978, 19). Followers interact dynamically with leaders; at times followers are leaders and leaders are followers.

Burns makes a major contribution by proposing two types of leadership: *transactional* and *transformational*. Transactional leadership involves the exchange of valued goods, such as the type of "exchange" a politician might make when he or she caters to the electorate in order to receive votes. Transactional leaders may appear in most social situations—from small groups to national politics—where leadership is exercised. This type of leadership investigates the motives and needs of followers and then designs a program that suits both the needs of the followers as well as the needs of the leader. In transactional leadership the leader appeals to the motives of the followers and attempts to satisfy them in some way. The transactional leader enables the followers to reach those particular individual, group, or national goals that are considered important.

The transformational leader, however, does not just attempt to meet the goals of followers, but tries in fact to transform them, to raise them to a different and higher level. The leader in effect challenges the followers to meet goals that the followers, and sometimes the leader, never even dreamed about. The transforming leader is, in Burns's words (1978, 455), "moral but not moralistic. Leaders engage with followers, but from higher levels of morality; in the enmeshing of goals and values both leaders and followers are raised to more principled levels of judgment. . . . Much of this kind of elevating leadership asks *from* followers rather than merely promising them goods." The leader's task in this regard is essentially "consciousness-raising on a wide plane" (1978, 43). We have all experienced this type of leadership—in books, in politics, or in our everyday affairs. Through it, we learn new ideas, new values, and new ideals. In fact, we are often overtaken by this kind of leadership: it presents those unfamiliar ideals and expectations that we still identify with and hope to make our own.

Tucker (1981) provides a critique of Burns's work by observing that Burns makes an essentially incorrect distinction between leadership and power wielding. Burns would consider a Stalin or a Hitler to be power wielders, not leaders; Tucker would respond that these individuals indeed exerted leadership over people— after all, they had many followers. Tucker also suggests that Burns misses the key point of what leaders *do,* how they function as leaders. Tucker sees leadership as politics and politics as leadership. Politics, in his view, is the active direction of a community, whether local, regional, or national. Dictators can be leaders because they direct a political community. Tucker also addresses what leaders do:

> First, leadership has a diagnostic function. Leaders are expected to define the situation authoritatively for the group. Second, they must prescribe a course of group action, or of action on the group's behalf, that will meet the situation as defined. . . . Third, leadership has a mobilizing function. . . . we may describe these functions as diagnostic, policy formulating, and policy implementing. (Tucker 1981, 18-19)

Tucker relates the prime components of leadership to policy formulation and development: developing a course of action for the group. This approach is somewhat more conservative than Burns's; it neglects the transformative nature of leadership and, further, makes a firm distinction between diagnosis, formulation, and implementation. Often, these steps do not appear in any kind of straightforward fashion: policy formulation takes place before any adequate diagnosis; implementation changes the formulation; and so on.

Bennis (1983) gives us another study of leadership that has an interesting reconception of the traditional managerial approach to leadership. Bennis (1984, 66) finds that the leaders and executives he studied seemed to have these qualities: vision, a direction and view of the future; communication and alignment, the ability to share the vision and bring others into its service; persistence, consistency, and focus, maintaining the vision and directing activities toward its accomplishment; empowerment, creating an organization where individuals can accomplish things; and finally, organizational learning, the ability to learn from errors. These factors allow an organization to develop what Bennis labels as "transformative power." Bennis's summary of the meaning of transformative power provides insight into recent ways of studying leadership:

> In sum, the transformative power of leadership stems less from ingeniously crafted organizational structures, carefully constructed management designs and controls, elegantly rationalized planning formats, or skillfully articulated leadership tactics. *Rather, it is the ability of the leader to reach the souls of others in a fashion which raises human consciousness, builds meanings, and inspires human intent that is the source of power.* Within transformative leadership, therefore, it is vision, purposes, beliefs, and other aspects of organizational culture that are of prime importance. (Bennis 1984, 70, italics added)

While Burns and Tucker stress the leader as an individual, Selznick and Bennis look at the leader in the context of the institution or the organizational culture. However, their conceptions have a number of features in common. Leadership is seen as an interactive process between the leader and his followers, rather than an individual's manipulation of a group. The process itself is largely political in nature in that it deals with both the exchange and distribution of valued resources and the definition of the appropriate order or the right way. The symbolic nature of leadership is stressed; the symbols provide vision and power.

The symbolic dimensions of leadership might be seen to expand on the political models in significant ways. The cultural format would see the leader as being a symbol of what is true and good within the institution. In this framework a leader operates at a distance, communicating a particular meaning to members of the organization through various message systems, press releases, and public acknowledgment of his or her accomplishments—sometimes embellished by an active imagination—without necessarily engaging in face-to-face interactions. The symbolic processes that leaders use also include the construction and reconstruction of sagas, myths, and stories, the enactment of rituals, and the more general developments of a universe that attributes meaning and causation to leadership acts. As Pfeffer (1983, 486) says, "Leaders serve as symbols for representing personal causation of social events." The leader in this instance stands in such a role because he or she can give meaning to an otherwise empty universe. Like a general who can rally troops to an uncertain fate in service to a "cause," such leaders provide a vision of both the necessary and the sacred. These studies make a major advance over the thinking that defines leadership as a subset of management and as merely the process of motivating subordinates to accomplish tasks.

A CRITICAL MODEL OF LEADERSHIP

While the politically informed models of leadership are superior in their formulation, they make the mistake of seeing leadership as a property inherent to individuals rather than as an act performed within a social context. They see leadership in voluntaristic terms, abstracted from the structural—i.e., economic and political—features of the particular society or organization.

These theories often posit that leadership flows from an individual in a position of power, that the leader has an idea or a vision, and that the leader's communicated ideal changes followers in some way. Leadership becomes attached to the individual. A more adequate conception, found to some degree in Burns, is that individuals engage in leader acts at various times in their lives. Then they are leaders, but at other times they may be followers. Thus, leaders and followers are not categories with exclusive membership; followers will be leaders and leaders followers. Leadership is based in a shared culture and does not result from position or power. Yet, with the development of modern society and the rise of hierarchical organizational forms, leadership becomes associated with position and power. The leadership concept, once broad based and open to all, now has only limited application. In modern societies, we tend to see leadership as being intimately related to particular social positions rather than as emergent in community and group actions. Rosen tells us that:

> The watershed of complex society has been the development of systems of caste, class, bureaucratic, and sexual stratification unknown or muted in simple systems. Paralleling this, the development of leadership systems is equally clear: leadership systems have tended to become increasingly closed, ascribed, and power based. (Rosen 1984, 43)

Thus, we can see that the idea of leadership needs to be critically evaluated. While we can agree with Burns's and Tucker's notions on leadership, we have to consider how the concept has become so closely identified with the social system within which it is used, an aspect of leadership the political approach does not fully appreciate. Even the idea of transformative power and the vision that it sparks neglect a predominant dimension of modern social relations: whose vision is it? Perhaps we can rescue the idea of leadership by developing a critical model of leadership.

What is the value of adopting a critical framework for leadership? Grob discusses the meaning of the critical spirit:

> In pointing to the critical spirit as the ground of all leadership, my intent has been to argue that without that willingness to examine one's life, alleged leaders in any and all areas of human endeavor must, of necessity, become identified with their purposes, purposes which inevitably congeal into fixed doctrines or dogma. In short, potential leaders *without this ground* find themselves in the service of fixed ideas or causes, and thus agents of the use of power in their behalf. *No longer nourished by a wellspring of critical process at its*

center, leadership "dries up" and becomes, finally, the mere wielding of power on behalf of static ideals. (Grob 1984, 270, italics in original)

At issue here is the idea that leadership in some fashion involves the pursuit of goals, but that this will be only a static pursuit if the goals themselves are not continually challenged and analyzed. Leadership requires critical reflection and analysis; it is not so much a science as a way of directing and reflecting upon human action.

Power and the lack of power can be either uplifting or crippling. It uplifts when one has a sense of power with others and over situations; it cripples when one does not. Kanter's work (1977) documents how power is a major factor in organizational feelings of success and leadership. Part of her work analyzes power in corporations and shows how the modern bureaucratic organization tends to distribute power unequally; in so doing it creates centers of power and powerlessness. She argues that what is sometimes seen as a preference for male managers is really a preference for managers who have power. Historically, it is men who have had the most power in organizations. The powerless manager, lacking a base for authority, accentuates the rules and engages in close and nitpicking supervision. The powerful manager, in contrast, shares power with peers and subordinates, mentors individuals, and engages in a form of corporate entrepreneurship that as often disregards the hard and fast rules as it obeys them. As she says:

> "Power" in organizations ... is synonymous with autonomy and freedom of action. The powerful can afford to risk more, and they can afford to allow others their freedom. The bureaucratic machinery of modern organizations means that there are rather few people who are really powerful. Power has become a scarce resource that most people feel they lack. Although the scramble for political advantage still distinguishes relative degrees of power, the organization places severe limits on everyone's freedom of action. The powerful get more, but they still share some of the mentality of powerlessness. (Kanter 1977, 195)

Power must be a dominant concern of leadership: the modern organization, with its rules and hierarchies, develops a technological mentality that limits autonomy and freedom of action and shackles vision and the critical spirit. Leaders who have vision and spirit can share power. In so doing they release the very human potential of the agents in the organization.

Leadership also involves the examination and demystification of those structures within which leadership occurs. Organizations and modern social structures are in fact created by us; they do not occur historically determined. We can sometimes control the type of organization that we want to have, but we often do not realize this. One aspect of leadership is communicating to others that the particular situation, the particular organizational form, is made by us and can be changed by us. Berger and Luckmann (1967, 134) have addressed this nicely: "It is essential to keep pushing questions about the historically available conceptualizations of reality from the abstract 'What?' to the sociologically concrete 'Says who?'" Demystification is simply that. Because we take for granted the way things are, they indeed become "mystic" in the sense that they are beyond normal discourse and reason; they become essences that are not subject to any kind of human action. However, organizations and other human constructs are indeed of our own making: leadership shows us how we can change them.

Changing these man-made constructs requires that battles be fought. The advertising industry, the political industry, and various other industries attempt to convince us that their biased visions reflect the realities of our world. We seem to be continually bombarded with messages about the importance of being young, being in charge, being handsome or pretty, being appropriate subjects for industrial speculation. These messages often use distorted language (Ramos, 1981) that attempts to persuade us to accept its bias despite the inadequacy of its message. Ramos (1981) addresses the idea of "cognitive politics," the "conscious or unconscious use of distorted language, the intent of which is to induce people to interpret reality in terms that reward the direct and/or indirect agents of such distortion" (Ramos 1981, 76). Numerous examples of this appear in both government and corporate life. Edelman (1977) has discussed how linguistic labeling often serves to mystify the root problems. For example, poverty in this country has its root source in economics, but rather than dealing with this openly, we have evolved a complex set of labels and programs that in effect see poverty as a problem of the poor, not as a problem of the economic system. We have evolved social work agencies, counseling agencies, "wars" on poverty, and the like, all of which divert our attention from the basic cause of poverty to focus on how the poor can be "treated." As Edelman (1977, 27) says, "If economic institutions functioned without unemployment, poorly paid work, degrading work, or inadequate industrial pension and health programs, there would be manifestly very little poverty." In schools we see something of the same phenomenon. Those children who need our help the most are linguistically labeled as "deviant," beginning a vicious cycle that has no winners. This is a characteristic of distorted language: the relationship between the activity and the outcome is masked.

Leadership involves the probing of language structures and the unmasking of distortions. In this sense we can say that leadership must be critically educative: it can not only look at the conditions in which we live, but it also must decide how to change them.

Brian Fay, a social philosopher, has argued that the role of social scientists is to educate (1975; 1977). In offering his educative model, Fay rejects the traditional, positivistic account of social science that requires we develop laws that explain and predict human behavior. He finds this technical model wanting insofar as it fails to account for the role the actors play in structuring their lives and in changing those structures. Fay says:

> According to this educative conception, the function of the social scientist is not to provide knowledge of quasi-causal laws to a policy scientist who will determine which social conditions are to be manipulated in order to effect a particular goal, but rather *to enlighten the social actors so that, coming to see themselves and their social situation in a new way, they themselves can decide to alter the conditions which they find repressive.* In other words, the social scientist tries to "raise the consciousness" of the actors whose situation he is studying. (Fay 1975, 103, italics in original)

Fay has addressed his comments to social scientists, but one could suggest that they are just as applicable to our conceptions of leadership. Leadership is not manipulating a group in order to achieve a preset goal; rather, it is empowering individuals in order to evaluate what goals are important and what conditions are helpful. The educative use of leadership results in the empower-ment of followers. The leader here is truly concerned with the development of followers, with the realization of followers' poten-tial to become leaders themselves. Kegan and Lahey nicely address this aspect of leadership:

> But people do not *grow* by having their realities only confirmed. They grow by having them challenged as well, and being supported and listened to, rather than defend against, that challenge. We de-fined *leadership* as the exercise of authority. But a person whose way of being in the world—in a family, at work, or as a citizen—amounts to the exercise of authority *on behalf of facilitating the de-velopment* of those around him or her, is the person who can truly be called a leader. (Kegan and Lahey 1984, 226, italics in original)

It should be becoming clear that a critical model of leadership that exposes linguistic distortions, empowers followers, and de-velops potential is largely conditioned on language. Indeed, Pon-dy (1978, 95) suggests that leadership *is* a "language game" in which those actors who can "make sense of things" and mean-ingfully communicate that sense are the leaders. Leadership con-fronts dual tasks, one positive and one negative, when using lan-guage. The positive task is in fact to make sense of things and to communicate that sense. For an administrator, this means both making sense of the educational environment *and* developing a sense of purpose. Schooling can be as varied as the individual philosphies of education it encompasses; without the joint involve-ment of both administrator and the teacher, sense making can be chaotic and confusing. The negative side of leadership has to do with the analysis and critique of inhibiting structures in the school. Most schools, for example, are arranged hierarchically, and this particular structure is taken as a given. The hierarchical arrangement is reinforced through such procedures as annual evaluations and the allocation of space and the allotment of time. A leader could expose how the hierarchy hinders undistorted com-munication, how "better ideas" become stifled because of formal constraints, and how democratic participation (necessary for a leadership that is not just power wielding) suffers because of bu-reaucracy. Leadership's goal is reaching a standard of rational discourse in which all arguments can be heard without regard to the class or status of the respondent.

This dissolves the traditional hierarchical ranking between the leader as an office holder (position-power) and the led. It suggests that hierarchical ranking—being titled "principal" or "superintendent"—has nothing to do with leadership. More often than not, the position holder is smply an organizational manager who ensures that organizational goals are accomplished more or less on schedule, but this is not leadership. As we have defined it above, leadership can spring from anywhere; it is not a quality that comes with an office or with a person. Rather, it derives from the context and ideas of individuals who influence each other. Thus, a principal may at times be a leader and at other times, a follower. A teacher may be a leader, and the principal a follower. Leadership is an act bounded in space and time; it is an act that enables others and allows them, in turn, to become enablers.

At its heart, leadership—the search for democratic and rational participation in social events—is political. It is a political act to educate people; it is a political act to demystify structures and penetrate "normal" conditions; it is a political act to argue for participation in decision making. Leadership involves the careful interplay of knowledge and action: knowledge of organizations and action on behalf of undistorted communication. In this respect we all can exercise leadership.

Zaleznik addresses leadership and demonstrates how leaders are those who do not just accept given conditions in their activities:

> Leaders tend to be twice-born personalities, people who feel separate from their environment, including other people. They may work in organizations, but they never belong to them. Their sense of who they are does not depend upon memberships, work roles, or other social indicators of identity. What seems to follow from this idea about separateness is some theoretical basis for explaining why certain individuals search out opportunities for change. The methods of bringing about change may be technological, political, or ideological, but the object is the same: to profoundly alter human, economic, and political relationships. (Zaleznik 19, 133)

This is the essence of leadership: the desire and attempt to change the human condition. It is a political *and* courageous act to attempt to empower followers. As we have tried to show, leadership does not reside in systems of management, in grids or formulas. Leadership is conscious of conditions and conscious of change. Its twin concerns of empowerment and transformation focus on the same goals as the spirit underlying critical theory—to release us from our prisons of ideology and to give vision. Empowerment shares power by modifying those hierarchical structures that set up false distinctions among their members: empowerment enables unrestrained discourse. Transformation communicates message and symbol to show us possibilities far beyond our current achievements: it provides a vision, a vision of a just and equal social order. Leadership is the process of transforming and empowering.

9

Praxis: Action Working with Theory

In this text, we have tried to redefine the limits of administrative action. We have consciously espoused a position that suggests that administration must at its heart be informed by critical models oriented toward social justice and individual freedom. This is not just "nice"; it determines our entire way of life and the purpose of our most important social institution, education. Most current administrative theories are models of control; they are incapable of addressing the questions that make administration a *worthy* discipline. As models of control, certain of their assumptions are inconsistent with the principal premise of a democratic society: the ability of each individual to contribute to the formation of a rational consensus on how institutions should be governed. It is not control that is in question, but rather the source of that control. Control freely conferred through democratic consensus differs from control achieved through physical coercion, technical superiority, or scientific knowledge. In this endeavor we have looked at various ways of examining theories of administration in schools. After briefly reviewing them, we will examine some ways in which administration can make a critical difference in schooling.

THE SCIENTIFIC STUDY OF ADMINISTRATION

Administrative studies have been greatly influenced by scientific and managerial perspectives based in the notion that a "true" science of human behavior could be developed. From Taylorism through contemporary accounts, the dominant theme has been that if enough effort were put into investigation, we would eventually formulate valid laws of administrative behavior. Taylor's vision of scientific management was not just historically influential; his conception of how to manage an organization remains a staple of modern lore, as it did in generations past. Taylorism and its focus on the collection of information and techniques for management provide a perspective and a way of seeing that, left uncorrected, result in the bifurcation of the organization into the rulers and the ruled.

The scientific emphasis on management continued with much more sophistication throughout the century. The scientific management movement led to a variety of functionalist approaches to organizational study and the study of administration that culminated in the theory movement in educational administration.

Some elements of functionalist thought remain pertinent to administration theory, but it is necessary to provide a critical context for such thought. Many studies of schooling with a functionalist framework are highly original and useful but need a critical context. This context requires a foundation in critical social theory, an analysis of the production and reproduction of culture, and an orientation to leadership and change. A critical administration works with both teachers and students to attain just causes and brings visionary approaches to the construction of enfranchising institutions. A critical administration involves political action on many fronts. Connell and his colleagues make the point well.

> Education has fundamental connections with the idea of human emancipation, though it is constantly in danger of being captured for other interests. In a society disfigured by class exploitation, sexual and racial oppression, and its chronic danger of war and environmental destruction, the only education worth the name is one that forms people capable of taking part in their own liberation. The business of the school is not propaganda; it is equipping people with

the knowledge and skills and concepts relevant to remaking a dangerous and disordered world. In the most basic sense, the process of education and the process of liberation are the same. They are aspects of the painful growth of the human species' collective wisdom and self-control. (Connell et al. 1982, 208)

The administrator, the teacher, and the student of administration and schooling work not to reproduce a given social world, but to remove the limits set by it. To achieve this task theory must become practical, must inform our methods of dealing with the world and influence our ways of framing our condition. Administrators and students of administration can utilize theory in their actions with others by using it to work with others. This means reflecting on the purpose and foundations of critical administration and then putting the models of leadership and change to work.

WORKING WITH TEACHERS

The craft of teaching has become susceptible to the Taylorization of instruction, the increasing tendency to divorce instructional knowledge from its source in the instructor. This deskilling of the profession occurs through the development of standardized curricula with little or no relevance for the tapestry of local conditions; through mandated competencies that disregard the professional knowledge of the teacher; through behaviorally oriented objectives that reduce teacher autonomy; and through countless other devices designed to somehow scientize the profession.

A critical administration that takes its educative role seriously can help to insulate the professional teacher from this deskilling tendency by educating teachers about the nature of the task and by empowering the teachers themselves. Empowerment can occur in a number of ways; one might be the institutionalization of a critical inquiry process in school through the use of a reflective, clinical supervision. Clinical supervision could develop critical and reflective capabilities among schoolpeople. "Clinical supervision, as a form of collaborative action," Smyth (1984, 426) observes, "is posited as a more robust conceptualization of what it might mean for teachers to become actively involved in the reflexive process of analyzing and theorizing about their own teaching, its social antecedents, and possible consequences."

While many models of clinical supervision are socially and politically naive, they at least provide the promise of a means for reflective dialogue between teachers and administrators. The crucial stipulation must be made that supervision applied here *is* dialogue, and not control; in this sense, administrators themselves must be supervised. Unfortunately, humanistically oriented administrators have regarded clinical supervision as only a set of techniques whose implementation will result in the improvement of instruction. They have paid little attention to the possibly radical implications of focusing on teacher-administrative cooperation in action designed for solving dilemmas. The techniques of clinical supervision are but a secondary focus, if even necessary. Neither stages nor steps should receive the prime attention, only efforts to understand and to change.

Supervision, a term denoting "to watch over," normally implies the close control of a work situation by someone with power greater than the person performing the particular role. Clinical supervision intends to remedy this discrepancy of power in the occupational situation by attempting to make the supervisor more of a helpmate and constructive critic than overlord. Kanter's work (1977) shows the wisdom of this method. She concluded that the more power a supervisor had, the more power he or she would be willing to share. Close supervision often resulted from an insecurity about personal power that expressed itself in demonstrations of who "the boss" really was. Supervision based on the principles of power sharing is simply a more effective way to run an organization. Supervision, administration, and other organizational roles can become more effective through the development and use of ideas founded in a critical approach.

A critical educational administration tries to liberate teachers and administrators from the preconceptions that lock them into socially unproductive relationships. This indeed is the very idea of education itself. The Berlaks see the following as a possible role of the school administrator.

Heads [administrators] may see their primary role as educator: to raise questions about preferences of the community and of teachers, which are normally taken for granted, and to assist a search for alternatives; in other words, to encourage critical inquiry. Heads who take this view see themselves as first among equals, their special leadership responsibilities flowing from their experience as teachers, their (presumed) ability to initiate and sustain critical inquiry, and the delegation of authority from the public to insure the coordination and coherence of the educational programs internal to the school and throughout the schooling sequence. (A. and H. Berlak 1982, 248)

Administrators who see their responsibility in this way engage in dialogue and dialectics with their staff. Dilemmas inherent to instruction and to running a school are isolated and described. Patterns of resolution, both current ones and their alternatives, are discussed. Historical determinations and biographies are surfaced. Practical action is then presented and accepted, action that may result in the transformation of the dilemma and the achievement of a new plane of challenge. This is a revolutionary role for administrators. Rather than attempting to apply the dogma of received social science theory—by adopting, for example, a leadership "style" designed to get maximum productivity from the robotic worker—this model encourages us as administrators to *engage* those with whom we work in a quiet transformation of our situation. This can be accomplished through relinquishing authoritarian roles and seriously considering leadership and leadership implications. The administrator-as-leader puts things into context. In so doing he or she transforms the goals and visions of co-workers. Administrators face a dominant problem in the constant struggle to create an organization where personnel are bureaucratically aligned; the leadership of an organization, however, transforms this problem by transforming personnel attitudes through creating a meaning-full system.

WORKING WITH STUDENTS

A critical approach to administration must grapple with the nature of schooling in this society. Formal education as we practice it is more than the articulation of systems of knowledge; it is also the often-unconscious creation of structures of personal and social meaning. Schooling enslaves while it frees: it produces and reproduces society and culture, but it also opens up avenues of liberation and of protest. Schooling helps in the re-creation of hegemony by giving the current moral order legitimacy.

Administrators concerned with change, with the actual creation of opportunities for all, can look to their school as an opportunity for implementing the critical, empirical, and hermeneutic dimensions that critical theory demands. Empirical studies of school regularities are needed. Drop-out rates, tracking patterns, discipline patterns, instructional and curricular content, internal social systems, and so on, must be scrutinized and in turn, be fleshed out with meaning. What do the particular patterns mean to different participants in the school process—students, teachers, parents, and others? Taking a critical turn, how do such patterns contribute to the reproduction of a given social structure? This approach is neither mechanical nor easy, but it will awaken the sensibilities of the school community.

However, such information is only a starting point for the development of praxis with students. A next step entails the exploration of consciousness with students to develop the limits and possibilities of political action, an understanding of community, and an empathy for how environments themselves help perpetuate powerlessness for students. In some instances schools can be a refuge for a dominated and oppressed individual or group within a community.

The administrator as educator attempts to explore with students the historical circumstances of their conditions, whether it involves social comfort or societal oppression. Each group needs to know the dilemmas and contradictions a society faces in working out the concrete sets of relationships that characterize it. Each group needs to realize that its particular birthright, including race and gender, means differing social responses and differing opportunities to the group as a whole.

This process largely politicizes the school and the students, but in such a way that they become historically informed and sociologically aware. This theory of education returns to Dewey, who believed that the virtues of democracy and the sins of oppression are best learned through their practical analysis in an informed context. This process often means conflict and danger for students, teachers, and administrators; in becoming aware of the limits society imposes on certain groups, the path to removing those limits becomes more tempting and the established power structure more confining. Leadership accepts the risk and conflict, and channels this creative energy into socially useful patterns.

Historically, political leaders have frequently asked us to make sacrifices for the sake of developing better circumstances, and to engage in conflict to meet or protect some of our cherished ideals. Our literature on school administrators rarely discusses this dimension of leadership; administrators are portrayed in less than glowing terms, as mere bureaucrats. Yet many administrators do ask for sacrifices, do make transformations, and do empower. They take risks and deal with conflicts. Administration needs more stories about these types of adminstrators to give us, as a profession, the confidence we need to raise questions of a critical nature that, despite their risks, may ultimately lead to the formation of a more proper educational organization.

WORKING WITH THE COMMUNITY

A long, mythical tradition maintains that schooling is a local function. In fact, local school boards and administrators often respond more to state and federal mandates than they do to local ones. Working with the community can be a rewarding and dramatic application of a critical social theory, and a demanding demonstration of its educative potential. Parents involved through site councils, parent and teacher associations, and advisory groups provide a constant source of insight and change; yet this resource is often neglected, establishing a consequent division between home and school. A critical administration can undertake both the representation and transformation of community values. The school has many communities within its context. Each offers a source of opportunity for working for social change. The school could serve as a site for working out the contradictions of the wider society in miniature form. Schools establish distinctions between working and ruling classes, contribute to gender-specific roles, and deintellectualize certain parts of the curriculum (vocational versus academic preparation)—the community must deal with all these subjects. Such concerns raise the consciousness of the community and shift the responsibility for dropping out from the individual student to the context of student-school relationships. Indeed, a foundation for critical administrative theory is the consensual development and sharing of relationships of power. This must certainly include the community within the structure of the school organization. Often school problems are considered problems of the community only: school failures have little to do with school structure but result from the specific make-up of the community. Problems of the systems are shunted off to other areas rather than being dealt with as problems of the total school-in-community. Discipline in schools, to take one example, is neither a school problem per se nor simply a problem of "troubled kids" in a troubled community. Instead, it is a problem of schools *and* community that often results from students' attempts to resolve personal and social issues of a much wider scope within the concrete and safe world of the educational institution.

A critical theory provides administrators a way of working with the community in productive and participatory endeavors. It attempts to bridge the we-they gap that currently divides much of administrative practice from community input. This requires more than good intentions from administrators or teachers; it requires the re-structuring of organizations.

WORKING WITH CULTURE

Working with students, staff, and community is working with culture. Burlingame (1984, 298), for example, notes that "The cultural perspective highlights that most in society will see the school as a powerful agent for inculcating important tribal stories." In this perspective, the school is a place to tell and re-tell the various stories that provide a mythology of performance. These stories, however, sometimes conflict, and which stories eventually dominate depends to some extent on the artfulness of the teller. A school culture could be thought of "as an anthology of competing stories" (Burlingame 1984 305) and the administrator has the dual role of storyteller and listener. This role can be critical for staff, students, and community because the stories not only re-create the past but also open up the future. However, such story-telling needs to take a point of view grounded in the critical analysis of school culture and policy. Too often the idea of school culture means an established and dominant viewpoint for inducing others to accept a particular ideology that benefits only some. This limits culture to instrumentality, a tool for use, rather than substantiality, an expression of values and norms. Working with culture means working with given values and norms that are grounded in some way. Our norms and values can be grounded in universal attributes of language, particularly truth, freedom, and justice, but often these are used in ways that discriminate and oppress. Ideas promoted in the name of truth may result in error. A culture of school must engage in frequent dialectical analysis to prevent one particular way of viewing things from overriding the rightful expression of other perspectives.

School culture is based on shared rituals, myths, ceremonies, and so on, but beyond these more surface aspects, the culture is shared through common values as expressed through the surface elements. What should these values attempt to attain? Basic values relate to expressions we use everyday—truth, justice, democracy, freedom, and others—but are often neglected in our organization. In a culture, these values aren't simply given—they are continually achieved through struggle, conflict, and risk. A school culture that encourages such values encourages struggle, conflict and risk.

WORKING WITH ORGANIZATION

In an era when American industry has become more and more concerned with organizational democracy and worker participation, the schooling organization has remained essentially unchanged since the 1800s. This society must reconsider its methods of organizing schools. The current fashion creates a school organization with a structure similar to those typical of early industrial organization; yet a school's purpose fundamentally differs from that of industry.

Whyte and Blasi (1982, 137) have identified three possible models for organizing in our society: authoritarian, bargaining, and community democracy. The authoritarian model reflects the kind of organizational structure we have seen with Taylorism and very bureaucratic structures. It represents a top-down approach to administration, where workers are completely disenfranchised from decision-making ability. Control of work lies outside the control of workers: they simply perform to management specifications. In the second model, workers, reacting to the restraints of the authoritarian model, form collective associations to protect their interests. Unionization and its inherent conflict between worker and manager are characteristic of this model that basically reflects the organizational reality found within school districts. Collective bargaining agreements structure the personal and interpersonal relationships of school people, whether classified or certified. The written agreement determines the conduct of the organization's business, and a defensive atmosphere often prevails. Although this bargaining model represents an advance over the authoritarian, it nevertheless leads to the stagnation of the organization. The union becomes self-serving, its purpose the increasing accumulation of benefits that will legitimate its continued existence. Administration, in turn, becomes reactive and bemoans its lack of authority and the excessive demands placed on it.

These two models, *particularly in education,* create an organizational system that sets people against each other to create two classes of employees, those with power and those trying to get it. The organization's educational nature becomes secondary to struggles for control. As was historicaly true, teaching becomes a skill performed according to the demands of an external agency such as administration. Administration becomes a skill designed to standardize the role of teachers. This self-defeating behavior isolates teaching and administration from their educative purpose. They become enmeshed in playing out roles, as certainly scripted for them as for any actor on a stage. Escaping from this confining situation indeed requires a new form of organization.

The third model proposed is that of community democracy. In industry, this often takes the form of worker ownership, where worker councils and workers themselves have input and control over managerial decisions. This is not joint management in the sense that everyone runs the company; rather, it is delegated management. This model recognizes that decisions have to be made and authority exercised, because not everyone is as capable or motivated as others. However, in terms of policy directives and avenues for the firm's future growth, all have some say: for example, representatives of elected worker councils might sit on the board of directors to control and oversee managerial direction.

Consider this model for education. What if teachers were given input into decision making and were allowed to control not only classrooms but also organizations? What if various constituents—teachers, minority groups, other community members, administrators—were allowed access to the school board so they, rather than a small group of wealthy elected representatives, made the decisions? What if teachers ran a school collectively, with the administration, within limits, serving their needs? This potentially radical reformulation of our school system has been tried elsewhere with success. This success suggests that the bureaucratically and hierarchically structured way of running our schools is simply one of many alternatives. Further, if we are serious about our leadership roles and the values of our democratic society, some of these participatory modes should at least be given a chance.

Sirianni (1984) has sanely suggested that perhaps our society needs a plurality of organizational forms. In some cases a bureaucratic structure might be necessary, but bureaucracy is not necessarily a universal solution. This is particularly relevant to schools. In essence we have a national system of education: a school in Wyoming is likely to have a structure similar to any in the country. Such schools can hardly be responsive to local needs and desires. Liberation is a valued term for education; pluralism of both instruction and organization should be equally important. A plurality of organizational structures would allow us, as critical administrators, to experiment with various ways of realizing democracy within the school. Sirianni concludes his essay by observing:

> No structural or organizational design could ever fully predict or predetermine how people would utilize and modify structures to their own purposes. But we can continue to think through the problems of organizing democracy and equality only by abandoning the search for the singular ideal. Instead, we must develop a perspective that is simultaneously global and systemic in its conception of social relationships; it must be as pluralistic as the people who would inhabit our organizations and the aspirations they would bring with them. (Sirianni 1984, 500-501)

Achieving these types of organizations is no mean task. It requires that we as administrators be willing to talk and communicate and to consider political action that leads to the restructuring of those institutions under our control. It requires our reconceptualization of what administration is all about—whether it can accommodate alternative ways of seeing or whether it is oriented solely to a managerial role. Our optimistic theory of administration assumes that both current and future administrators in education are basically committed to the values of a democratic society, but see those values more often neglected than preserved. While they may look for a way of realizing those values within the constraints of the given system, here that system itself is not given at all. Experimentation with different ways of organizing schools can begin with one district trying these new ideas in just one school. The system is constructed by us and through us; it can change through various forms of our leadership.

SUMMARY

Working with students, teachers, community, culture, and organization is basically praxis oriented toward sharing power, leadership, and effecting change. The material in this text has been designed to facilitate this form of praxis by assuming that the administrator in education is concerned with the issues of justice and equity and with the making of wise decisions, not necessarily popular ones.

To this end, we have looked at various models of administration, from the positivistic to the critical, at the foundations of a critical theory, at the issue of production and reproduction of culture, and at issues of organization, leadership, and change.

Administration, as we have suggested, can be informed by a moral and literary model. A literary model suggests that we might better understand administration if we looked at schools as texts being written, rather than as social structures needing scientific delineation and definition. A text being written is in a continual process of transformation; it changes according to local characters, circumstances, and cultures. Like a novel, whose form is universal but whose content is individual, a school represents a given purpose accomplished through many narratives.

However, a novel is incomplete without critique. Literary criticism weaves a thread of history into the fabric of literary events; it compares and contrasts a particular literature with its counterparts and so builds an awareness of history, action, and character. In somewhat the same way, an administration that is critical compares and contrasts the given situation with that of the possible and the desired. A literary model sees the history of administration and organization as a variety of texts being written, each of which encapsulates a different feature of leadership and change.

What is included in each text becomes an aspect of historical awareness. In our current historical situation we can and need to become aware of the reproductive and productive ways that schools create visions of both the past and the future in each generation. Visions of the past reproduce class and gender relationships; visions of the future modify historical relationships by innovative educational practices. A critical examination that adopts leadership as its frame helps to reformulate visions, enabling a more equitable future for new generations.

Administration can be instrumental in bringing about practical change, but such change requires detailed and hard study, commitment, and the practice of leadership. Further, it requires dedication to political action and a frame of mind that both *believes* and *critically reflects*. The school *leader* puts critical theory to work—through reflection, understanding, and education.

References

Alderfer, C. P. 1982. "Problems of Changing White Males' Behavior and Beliefs Concerning Race Relations." In *Change in Organizations,* edited by P. Goodman et al., 122-65. San Francisco: Jossey-Bass.

Alderfer, C. P., and K. K. Smith. 1982. "Studying Intergroup Relations Embedded in Organizations." *Administrative Science Quarterly* 27:35-65.

Aldrich, H. E. 1979. *Organizations and Environments.* Englewood Cliffs, N.J.: Prentice-Hall.

Allison, D. J. 1983. "Toward an Improved Understanding of the Organizational Nature of Schools." *Educational Administration Quarterly* 19(4):7-34.

Andrews, K. R. 1968. "Introduction" In *The Functions of the Executive,* by C. Barnard. Cambridge, Mass.: Harvard University Press.

Anyon, J. 1981. "Elementary Schooling and Distinctions of Social Class." *Interchange* 12(2-3):118-32.

Apel, K.-O. 1967. *Analytic Philosophy of Language and the Geisteswissenschaften.* Dordrecht, Holland: D. Reidel.

Argyris, C. 1973. "Some Limits of Rational Man Organization Theory." *Public Administration Review* 33:253-67.

Argyris, C. 1982. "How Learning and Reasoning Processes Affect Organizational Change." In *Change in Organizations,* edited by Goodman et al., 47-86. San Francisco: Jossey-Bass.

Argyris, C., and D. Schön. 1978. *Organizational Learning: A Theory of Action Perspective.* Reading, Mass.: Addison-Wesley.

Astley, W. G., and A. H. Van de Ven. 1983. "Central Perspectives and Debates in Organization Theory." *Administrative Science Quarterly* 28:245-73.

Bacharach, S. B., and E. J. Lawler. 1980. *Power and Politics in Organizations.* San Francisco: Jossey-Bass.

Bacharach, S. B., and S. M. Mitchell. 1981. "Toward a Dialogue in the Middle Range." *Educational Administration Quarterly* 17(3):1-14.

Baldridge, J. V., and T. Deal, eds. 1983. *The Dynamics of Organizational Change in Education.* Berkeley: McCutchan.

Barnard, C. [1938] 1968. *The Functions of the Executive.* Cambridge, Mass.: Harvard University Press.

Bass, B. 1981. *Stodgill's Handbook of Leadership.* New York: The Free Press.

Bates, R. 1983. *Educational Administration and the Management of Knowledge.* ESA Monograph 841. Victoria, Australia: Deakin University Press.

Bellone, C. J., ed. 1980. *Organization Theory and the New Public Administration.* Boston: Allyn and Bacon.

Benjamin, R. 1982. "The Historical Nature of Social-Scientific Knowledge: The Case of Comparative Political Inquiry." In *Strategies of Political Inquiry,* edited by E. Ostrom, 69-98. Beverly Hills, Calif.: Sage.

Bennis, W. G. 1959. "Leadership Theory and Administrative Behavior: The Problem of Authority." *Administrative Science Quarterly* 4:259-301.

———. 1983. *The Chief.* New York: William Morrow.

———. 1984. "Transformative Power and Leadership." In *Leader-*

ship and Organizational Culture, edited by T. J. Sergiovanni and J. E. Corbally. Urbana, Ill.: University of Illinois Press.

Benson, J. K. 1977a. "Organizations: A Dialectical View." *Administrative Science Quarterly* 22:1-21.

———. 1977b. "Innovation and Crisis in Organizational Analysis." In *Organizational Analysis: Critique and Innovation,* edited by J. K. Benson. Beverly Hills, Calif.: Sage.

———. 1983. "Paradigm and Praxis in Organizational Analysis." In *Research in Organizational Behavior,* edited by L. L. Cummings and B. M. Staw, vol. 6, 33-56. Greenwich, Conn.: JAI Press.

Berger, P., and T. Luckmann. 1967. *The Social Construction of Reality: A Treatise in the Sociology of Knowledge.* Garden City, N.Y.: Doubleday Anchor.

Berlak, A., and H. Berlak. 1981. *Dilemmas of Schooling: Teaching and Social Change.* New York: Methuen.

Berman, P., and M. W. McLaughlin. 1978. *Federal Programs Supporting Educational Change.* Vol. 8, *Implementing and Sustaining Innovation.* Santa Monica, Calif.: Rand Corporation.

Bernstein, R. J. 1976. *The Restructuring of Social and Political Theory.* New York: Harcourt, Brace and Jovanovich.

Bidwell, C. E. 1965. "The School as a Formal Organization." In *Handbook of Organizations,* edited by J. March, 974-1022. Chicago: Rand McNally.

Blake, R. R., and J. S. Mouton. 1964. *The Managerial Grid.* Houston, Tex.: Gulf Publishing Co.

Bobbitt, F. 1924. *How to Make a Curriculum.* Boston: Houghton-Mifflin.

Bolman, L. G., and T. E. Deal. 1984. *Modern Approaches to Understanding and Managing Organizations.* San Francisco: Jossey-Bass.

Bourdieu, P., 1979. *Algeria 1960: The Disenchantment of the World, the Sense of Honour, the Kabyle House or the World Reversed.* Cambridge, England: Cambridge University Press.

Bourdieu, P., and J.-C. Passeron. 1977. *Reproduction in Education, Society, and Culture.* Beverly Hills, Calif.: Sage.

Bourdieu, P., L. Boltanski, and M. de Saint Martin. 1978. "Changes in Social Structure and Changes in the Demand for Education." In *Contemporary Europe: Social Structures and Culture Patterns,* edited by S. Giner and M. S. Archer. London: Routledge & Kegan Paul.

Bowles, S., and H. Gintis. 1976. *Schooling in Capitalist America.* New York: Basic Books.

Boyd, W. L., and R. L. Crowson. 1981. "The Changing Conception and Practice of Public School Administration." In *Review of Research in Education,* edited by D. Berliner, 9:311-73. Washington, D.C.: American Educational Research Association.

Braverman, H. 1974. *Labor and Monopoly Capital.* New York: Monthly Review Books.

Brown, R. H. 1978. "Bureaucracy as Praxis: Toward a Political Phenomenology of Formal Organizations." *Administrative Science Quarterly* 23:365-82.

Burlingame, M. 1984. "Practical Implications of the Cultural Perspective." In *Leadership and Organizational Culture,* edited by T. J. Sergiovanni and J. E. Corbally. Urbana, Ill.: University of Illinois Press.

Burns, J. 1978. *Leadership.* New York: Harper and Row.

Burns, T., and G. M. Stalker. 1961. *The Management of Innovation.* London: Tavistock.

Burrell, G., and G. Morgan. 1979. *Sociological Paradigms and Organisation Analysis.* Exeter, N.H.: Heinemann.

Callahan, R. 1962. *Education and the Cult of Efficiency.* Chicago: University of Chicago Press.

Carey, A. 1967. "The Hawthorne Studies: A Radical Criticism." *American Sociological Review* 32(3):403-16.

Carlson, R. 1965. "Barriers to Change in Public Schools." In *Change Processes in the Public Schools,* edited by R. Carlson et al. Eugene, Ore.: University of Oregon, Center for the Advanced Study of Educational Administration.

Chandler, A. D. 1977. *The Visible Hand: The Managerial Revolution in American Business.* Cambridge, Mass.: Harvard University Press, Belknap Press.

Child, J. 1972. "Organizational Structure, Environment, and Performance: The Role of Strategic Choice." *Sociology* 6:1-22.

Clegg, S. 1981. "Organization and Control." *Administrative Science Quarterly* 26:545-62.

Clegg, S., and D. Dunkerly. 1977. *Critical Issues in Organisations.* London: Routledge & Kegan Paul.

Cohen, D., and B. Rosenberg. 1977. "Functions and Fantasies: Understanding Schools in Capitalist America." *History of Education Quarterly* 17(2):113-37.

Cohen, M. D., and J. G. March. 1974. *Leadership and Ambiguity: The American College President.* New York: McGraw-Hill.

Cole, R. 1982. "Diffusion of Participatory Work Structures in Japan, Sweden, and the United States." In *Change in Organizations,* edited by P. Goodman et al., 166-225. San Francisco: Jossey-Bass.

Connell, R. W., D. J. Ashenden, S. Kessler, and G. W. Dowsett. 1982. *Making the Difference: Schools, Families, and Social Division.* Sydney: George Allen & Unwin.

Cubberley, E. 1916. *Public School Administration.* Boston: Houghton-Mifflin.

Culbertson, J. 1983. "Theory in Educational Administration: Echoes from Critical Thinkers." *Educational Researcher* 12(10):15-22.

Deal, T. E., and A. Kennedy. 1982. *Corporate Cultures: The Rites and Rituals of Corporate Life.* Reading, Mass.: Addison-Wesley.

Deal, T. E., and M. S. Wiske. 1983. "Planning, Plotting and Playing in Education's Era of Decline." In *The Dynamics of Organizational Change in Education,* edited by J. V. Baldridge and T. E. Deal, 451-72. Berkeley: McCutchan.

Deetz, S. A., and A. Kersten. 1983. "Critical Models of Interpretive Research." In *Communication and Organizations: An Interpretive Approach,* edited by L. L. Putnam and M. E. Pacanowsky. Beverly Hills, Calif.: Sage.

Dubin, R. 1979. "Metaphors of Leadership: An Overview." In *Crosscurrents in Leadership,* edited by J. G. Hunt and L. L. Larson, 225-38. Carbondale, Ill.: Southern Illinois University Press.

Edelman, M. 1977. *Political Language: Words That Succeed and Policies That Fail.* New York: Academic Press.

Eggleston, J. 1977. *The Sociology of the School Curriculum.* London: Routledge & Kegan Paul.

Ericson, D. P., and F. S. Ellett, Jr. 1982. "Interpretation, Understanding, and Educational Research." *Teachers College Record* 84(4):497-513.

Erikson, D. 1979. "Research on Educational Administration: The State of the Art." *Educational Researcher* 8:9-14.

Etzioni, A. 1964. *Modern Organizations.* Englewood Cliffs, N.J.: Prentice-Hall.

Farrar, E., J. DeSanctis, and D. Cohen. 1980. "The Lawn Party: The Evolution of Federal Programs in Local Settings." *Teachers College Record* 82(1):77-100.

Fay, B. 1975. *Social Theory and Political Practice.* London: George Allen & Unwin.

———. 1977. "How People Change Themselves: The Relationship Between Critical Theory and I to Audience." In *Political Theory and Praxis: New Perspectives,* edited by T. Ball. Minneapolis: University of Minnesota Press.

Festinger, L. 1957. *A Theory of Cognitive Dissonance.* Evanston, Ill.: Row, Peterson.

Feyerabend, P. 1978. *Against Method: An Outline of An Anarchistic Theory of Knowledge.* Wiltshire, England: Verso Press.

Fiedler, F. 1967. *A Theory of Leadership Effectiveness.* New York: McGraw-Hill.

Fiedler, F., M. M. Chemers, and L. Maher. 1976. *Improving Leadership Effectiveness: The Leader Match Concept.* New York: John Wiley.

Field, R. H. G. 1979. "A Critique of the Vroom-Yetton Contingency Model of Leadership Behavior." *Academy of Management Review* 4:249-57.

Freire, P. 1970. *Pedagogy of the Oppressed.* New York: Continuum.

Fromm, E. 1961. "Afterword." In *1984,* by G. Orwell, 259-60. New York: New American Library.

Frye, N. 1973. *The Critical Path.* Bloomington, Ind.: Indiana University Press.

Fullan, M., M. Miles, and G. Taylor. 1980. "Organization Development in Schools: The State of the Art." *Review of Educational Research* 50(1):121-84.

Giddens, A. 1973. *The Class Structure of the Advanced Societies.* New York: Harper and Row.

————. 1976. *New Rules of Sociological Method: A Positive Critique of Interpretive Sociologies.* New York: Basic Books.

————. 1979. *Central Problems in Social Theory: Action, Structure, and Contradictions in Social Analysis.* Berkeley and Los Angeles: University of California Press.

Giroux, H. 1981. "Hegemony, Resistance, and the Paradox of Educational Reform." *Interchange* 12(2-3):3-26.

————. 1983. *Critical Theory and Educational Practice.* ESA Monograph 841. Victoria, Australia: Deakin University Press.

Goffman, E. 1959. *The Presentation of Self in Everyday Life.* New York: Doubleday Anchor.

Goodman, P. et al. 1982. *Change in Organizations.* San Francisco: Jossey-Bass.

Gordon, L. 1984. "Paul Willis—Education, Cultural Production and Social Reproduction." *British Journal of Sociology of Education* 5(2):105-16.

Graen, G., and J. F. Cashman. 1975. "A Role Making Model of Leadership in Formal Organizations: A Developmental Approach." In *Leadership Frontiers,* edited by J. G. Hunt and L. L. Larson. Kent, Ohio: Kent State University Press.

Gramsci, A. 1971. *Selections from Prison Notebooks.* Edited and translated by Q. Hoare and G. Smith. New York: International Publishers.

Greenfield, T. B. 1982. "Against Group Mind: An Anarchistic Theory of Organization." *McGill Journal of Education,* 17(1):3-11.

———. 1983. "Environment as Subjective Reality." Paper presented at the Annual Meeting of the American Educational Research Association, Montreal.

———. 1984. "Theories of Educational Organization: A Critical Perspective." Manuscript prepared for the *International Encyclopedia of Education: Research and Studies.* Ontario: Ontario Institute for Studies in Education.

———. 1985. "Theories of Educational Organization: A Critical Perspective." *International Encyclopedia of Education: Research and Studies.* Oxford: Pergamon Press.

Griffiths, D. E. 1979. "Intellectual Turmoil in Educational Administration." *Educational Administration Quarterly* 15(3):43-65.

———. 1983. "Evolution in Research and Theory: A Study of Prominent Researchers." *Educational Administration Quarterly* 19(3):201-21.

Grob, L. 1984. "Leadership: The Socratic Model." In *Leadership: Multidisciplinary Perspectives,* edited by B. Kellerman, 263-80. Englewood Cliffs, N.J.: Prentice-Hall.

Gronn, P. 1983. "Accomplishing the Doing of School Administration: Talk as the Work." *Administrative Science Quarterly* 28.

———. 1984. "'I Have a Solution . . .': Administrative Power in a School Meeting." *Educational Administration Quarterly* 20(2):65-92.

Gulick, L., and L. Urwick, eds. 1937. *Papers on the Science of Administration.* New York: Institute for Public Administration, Columbia University.

Haan, N. 1983. "An Interactional Morality of Everyday Life." In *Social Science as Moral Inquiry,* edited by N. Haan, R. N. Bellah, P. Rabinow, and W. M. Sullivan, 218-50. New York: Columbia University Press.

Habermas, J. 1970. *Towards a Rational Society.* Translated by J. J. Shapiro. Boston: Beacon Press.

———. 1971. *Knowledge and Human Interests.* Translated by J. J. Shapiro. Boston: Beacon Press.

———. 1975. *Legitimation Crisis.* Translated by T. McCarthy. Boston: Beacon Press.

———. 1979. *Communication and the Evolution of Society.* Translated by T. McCarthy. Boston: Beacon Press.

———. 1984. *The Theory of Communicative Action: Reason and the Rationalization of Society.* Vol. 1, translated by T. McCarthy. Boston: Beacon Press.

Halpin, A. W. 1966. *Theory and Research in Administration.* New York: The Macmillan Company.

———. 1970. "Administrative Theory: The Fumbled Torch." In *Issues in American Education,* edited by A. M. Kroll. New York· Oxford.

Hanson, M. 1984. "Explorations of Mixed Metaphors in Educational Administration Research." *Issues in Education* 2(3):167-85.

Harker, R. K. 1984. "On Reproduction, Habitus, and Education." *British Journal of Sociology of Education* 5(2):117-28.

Havelock, R. G. 1973. *The Change Agent's Guide to Innovation in Education.* Englewood Cliffs, N.J.: Educational Technology Publications.

Held, D. 1980. *Introduction to Critical Theory.* Berkeley and Los Angeles: University of California Press.

Hersey, P., and K. H. Blanchard. 1972. *Management of Organizational Behavior.* 2d ed. Englewood Cliffs, N.J.: Prentice-Hall.

Hirschman, A. O. 1983. "Morality and the Social Sciences: A Durable Tension." In *Social Science as Moral Inquiry,* edited by N. Haan, R. N. Bellah, P. Rabinow, and W. M. Sullivan, 21-32. New York: Columbia University Press.

Hodgkinson, C. 1978. *Towards a Philosophy of Administration.* Oxford: Basil Blackwell.

———. 1983. *The Philosophy of Leadership.* Oxford: Basil Blackwell.

Horkheimer, M. [1947] 1974. *Eclipse of Reason.* Reprint. New York: Seabury Press.

Horkheimer, M., and T. W. Adorno. 1972. *Dialectic of Enlightenment.* New York: Seabury Press.

Hosking, D., and C. A. Schriesheim. 1978. "Review of *Improving Leadership Effectiveness: The Leader Match Concept,* by F. Fiedler, M. M. Chemers, and L. Maher." *Administrative Science Quarterly* 23:496-505.

House, R. J. 1971. "A Path-Goal Theory of Leader Effectiveness." *Administrative Science Quarterly* 16:321-38.

Hoy, W. K., and C. G. Miskel. 1982. *Educational Administration: Theory, Research, and Practice.* 2d ed. New York: Random House.

Hunt, G. 1984a. "Organizational Leadership: The Contingency Paradigm and Its Challenges." In *Leadership: Multidisciplinary Perspectives,* edited by B. Kellerman, 113-38. Englewood Cliffs, N.J.: Prentice-Hall.

———. 1984b. *Leadership and Management Behavior.* Module No. 13-2536. Chicago: Science Research Associates.

Hymes, D. 1974. *Reinventing Anthropology.* New York: Random House Vintage Books.

Jago, A. G. 1982. "Leadership: Perspectives in Theory and Research." *Management Science* 28:315-36.

Kanter, R. 1977. *Men and Women of the Corporation.* New York: Basic Books.

Katz, D., and R. L. Kahn. 1966. *The Social Psychology of Organizations.* New York: John Wiley.

Kegan, R., and L. L. Lahey. 1984. "Adult Leadership and Adult Development: A Constructionist View." In *Leadership: Multidisciplinary Perspectives,* edited by B. Kellerman, 199-230. Englewood Cliffs, N.J.: Prentice-Hall.

Kerr, S., and J. M. Jermier. 1983. "Substitutes for Leadership: Their Meaning and Measurement." In *Leadership and Social Change,* edited by W. R. Lassey and M. Sashkin, 59-73. 3d ed. San Diego: University Associates.

Knezevich, S. J. 1984. *Administration of Public Education: A Sourcebook for the Leadership and Management of Educational Institutions.* 4th ed. New York: Harper and Row.

Kuhn, T. 1970. *The Structure of Scientific Revolutions.* 2d ed. Chicago: The University of Chicago Press.

Labov, W. 1970. "The Logic of Nonstandard English." In *Language and Poverty,* edited by F. Williams. Chicago: Markham.

Lawrence, P. R., and J. W. Lorsch. 1967. *Organization and Environment.* Cambridge, Mass.: Harvard University Press.

Lenhardt, G. 1980. *On Legal Authority, Crisis of Legitimacy and Schooling in the Writings of Max Weber,* translated by R. Meyer. Institute for Research on Educational Finance and Governance Program Report No. 80-B19. Stanford, Calif.: Stanford University.

Lewin, F. 1951. *Field Theory in Social Science.* New York: Harper.

Lippitt, G. L. 1982. *Organizational Renewal: A Holistic Approach to Organization Development.* 2d ed. Englewood Cliffs, N.J.: Prentice-Hall.

McCall, W., Jr. 1976. "Leadership Research: Choosing Gods and Devils on the Run." *Journal of Occupational Psychology* 49:139-53.

McCarthy, T. 1978. *The Critical Theory of Jurgen Habermas.* Cambridge, Mass.: The MIT Press.

———. 1984. "Translator's Introduction." In *The Theory of Communicative Action: Reason and the Rationalization of Society,* by J. Habermas. Vol. 1. Boston: Beacon Press.

McGregor, D. 1960. *The Human Side of Enterprise.* New York: McGraw-Hill.

March, J. G., and H. A. Simon. 1958. *Organizations.* New York: John Wiley.

March, J. G., and J. P. Olsen. 1976. *Ambiguity and Choice in Organizations.* Bergen, Norway: Universitetsforlaget.

Marx, K. 1970. *A Contribution to the Critique of Political Economy.* Moscow, USSR: Progress Publishers.

Meyer, J. W., and B. Rowan. 1977. "Institutionalized Organizations: Formal Structure as Myth and Ceremony." *American Journal of Sociology* 83:440-63.

————. 1978. "The Structure of Educational Organizations." In *Organizations and Environments,* edited by M. Meyer et al. San Francisco: Jossey-Bass.

Miner, J. B. 1975. "The Uncertain Future of the Leadership Concept: An Overview." In *Leadership Frontiers,* edited by J. G. Hunt and L. L. Larson. Kent, Ohio: Kent State University Press.

Moon, J. D. 1982. "Interpretation, Theory and Human Emancipation." In *Strategies of Political Inquiry,* edited by E. Ostrom, 149-78. Beverly Hills, Calif.: Sage.

Morgan, G. 1980. "Paradigms, Metaphors, and Puzzle Solving in Organization Theory." *Administrative Science Quarterly* 25:605-22.

National Education Association. 1933. *Educational Leadership: Progress and Possibilities.* Eleventh Yearbook. Washington, D.C.: National Education Association.

Oakes, J., and K. Sirotnik. 1983. "An Immodest Proposal: From Critical Theory to Critical Practice for School Renewal." Paper presented at the annual meeting of the American Educational Research Association, Montreal, Canada.

Ogbu, J. 1978. *Minority Education and Caste: The American System in Cross-Cultural Perspective.* New York: Academic Press.

————. 1981. "School Ethnography: A Multilevel Approach." *Anthropology and Education Quarterly* 12(1):3-29.

————. 1982. "Cultural Discontinuities and Schooling." *Anthropology and Education Quarterly* 13(4):290-307.

Ouchi, W. G. 1981. *Theory Z: How American Business Can Meet the Japanese Challenge.* Reading, Mass.: Addison-Wesley.

Owens, R. 1981. *Organizational Behavior in Education.* 2d ed. Englewood Cliffs, N.J.: Prentice-Hall.

Papagianiss, G. J., R. N. Bickel, and R. H. Fuller. 1983. "The Social Creation of School Dropouts: Accomplishing the Reproduction of an Underclass." *Youth & Society* 14(3):363-92.

Paul, E. F. 1979. *Moral Revolution and Economic Science.* Westport, Conn.: Greenwood Press.

Perrow, C. 1979. *Complex Organizations: A Critical Essay.* 2d ed. Glenview, Ill.: Scott-Foresman.

Peters, T. J., and R. H. Waterman. *In Search of Excellence.* New York: Harper & Row.

Pfeffer, J. 1983. "The Ambiguity of Leadership." In *Perspectives on Behavior in Organizations,* edited by J. R. Hackman, E. E. Lawler, and L. W. Porter, 486-92. New York: McGraw-Hill.

Pfeffer, J., and G. R. Salancik. 1983. "Organization Design: The Case for a Coalitional Model of Organizations." In *Perspectives on Behavior in Organizations,* edited by J. R. Hackman, E. E. Lawler, and L. W. Porter, 102-11. New York: McGraw-Hill.

Pondy, L. R. 1978. "Leadership Is a Language Game." In *Leadership: Where Else Can We Go?* edited by M. W. McCall and M. M. Lombardi. Durham, N.C.: Duke University Press.

Popkewitz, T. 1982. "Motion as Education Change: The Misuse and Irrelevancy of Two Research Paradigms." Paper presented at the annual meeting of the American Educational Research Association, New York, N.Y.

Popkewitz, T., and B. Tabachnik, eds. 1981. *The Study of Schooling: Field Based Methodologies in Educational Research and Evaluation.* New York: Praeger.

Ramos, A. G. 1981. *The New Science of Organizations: A Reconceptualization of the Wealth of Nations.* Toronto: University of Toronto Press.

Ranson, S., B. Hinings, and R. Greenwood. "The Structuring of Organizational Structures." *Administrative Science Quarterly* 25:1-17.

Rosen, D. M. 1984. "Leadership in World Cultures." In *Leadership: Multidisciplinary Perspectives,* edited by B. Kellerman, 39-62. Englewood Cliffs, N.J.: Prentice-Hall.

Sarason, S. B. 1982. *The Culture of the School and the Problem of Change.* 2d ed. Boston: Allyn and Bacon.

Schein, E. H. 1969. "The Mechanisms of Change." In *The Planning of Change,* edited by W. Bennis, K. Benne, and R. Chin. 2d ed. New York: Holt, Rinehart & Winston.

Schmuck, R. A., P. J. Runkel, J. H. Arends, and R. I. Arends. 1977. *The Second Handbook of Organization Development in Schools.* Eugene, Ore.: University of Oregon, Center for Educational Policy and Management.

Schroyer, T. 1973. *The Critique of Domination.* New York: George Brazillier.

Scott, W. R. 1978. "Theoretical Perspectives." In *Environments and Organizations,* edited by M. W. Meyer et al., 21-28. San Francisco: Jossey-Bass.

Selznick, P. 1957. *Leadership in Administration.* New York: Harper & Row.

Sergiovanni, T. J. 1984. "Developing a Relevant Theory of Administration." In *Leadership and Organizational Culture: New Perspectives on Administrative Theory and Practice,* edited by T. J. Sergiovanni and J. E. Corbally, 275-92. Urbana, Ill.: University of Illinois Press.

Sewart, J. 1980. "Jurgen Habermas's Reconstruction of Critical Theory." In *Current Perspectives in Social History,* vol. 1, 323-56. Greenwich, Conn.: JAI Press.

Sharp, R. 1980. *Knowledge, Ideology and the Politics of Schooling: Towards a Marxist Analysis of Education.* London: Routledge & Kegan Paul.

Silver, P. 1983. *Educational Administration: Theoretical Perspectives on Practice and Research.* New York: Harper and Row.

Simon, H. [1947] 1965. *Administrative Behavior: A Study of the Decision-Making Processes in Administrative Organization.* 2d ed. New York: The Free Press.

Sirianni, C. 1984. "Participation, Opportunity, and Equality: Toward a Pluralist Organizational Model." In *Critical Studies in in Organization and Bureaucracy,* edited by F. Fischer and C. Sirianni, 482-503. Philadelphia: Temple University Press.

Sirotnik, K. 1983. "What You See Is What You Get—Consistency, Persistency and Mediocrity in Classrooms." *Harvard Educational Review* 53(1).

Sirotnik, K., and J. Oakes, eds. 1986. *Critical Perspectives on the Organization and Improvement of Schooling.* Boston: Kluwer-Nijhoff.

Smyth, J. 1984. "Toward a 'Critical Consciousness' in the Instructional Supervision of Experienced Teachers." *Curriculum Inquiry* 14(4):425-36.

Soltis, J. F. 1984. "On the Nature of Educational Research." *Educational Researcher* 13(10):5-10.

Stodgill, R. M. 1948. "Personal Factors Associated with Leadership: A Survey of the Literature." *Journal of Psychology* 25:35-71.

———. 1974. *Handbook of Leadership: A Survey of Theory and Research.* New York: The Free Press.

Strike, K. A. 1982. *Educational Policy and the Just Society.* Urbana, Ill.: University of Illinois Press.

Taylor, F. W. 1947. *Scientific Management.* New York: Harper Bros.

Thompson, J. 1967. *Organizations in Action.* New York: McGraw-Hill.

Tucker, R. C. 1981. *Politics as Leadership.* Columbia, Mo.: University of Missouri Press.

Turner, B. A. 1972. *Exploring the Industrial Subculture.* New York: Herder and Herder.

Tyack, D. B. 1974. *The One Best System: A History of American Urban Education.* Cambridge, Mass.: Harvard University Press.

Von Bertalanffy, L. 1950. "The Theory of Open Systems in Physics and Biology." *Science* 3.

Vroom, V., and P. W. Yetton. 1973. *Leadership and Decision-Making.* New York: John Wiley.

Waller, W. 1932. *The Sociology of Teaching.* New York: Wiley.

Watkins, P. 1985. *Agency and Structure: Dialectics in the Administration of Education.* ESA Monograph 844. Victoria, Australia: Deakin University Press.

Weber, M. 1947. *The Theory of Social and Economic Organization.* Edited and translated by A. M. Henderson and T. Parsons. New York: Oxford University Press.

Weick, K. 1976. "Educational Organizations as Loosely Coupled Systems." *Administrative Science Quarterly* 21(1):1-19.

———. 1979. *The Social Psychology of Organizing.* 2d ed. Reading, Mass.: Addison-Wesley.

Weiner, S. 1976. "Participation, Deadlines, and Choice." In *The Dynamics of Organizational Change in Education,* edited by J. V. Baldridge and T. Deal, 278-305. Berkeley: McCutchan.

Whyte, W. F., and J. R. Blasi. 1982. "Worker Ownership, Participation, and Control: Toward a Theoretical Model." *Policy Sciences,* no. 14:137-63. Reprinted in *Critical Studies in Organization and Bureaucracy,* edited by F. Fischer and C. Sirianni, 377-405. Philadelphia: Temple University Press.

Willis, P. E. 1977. *Learning to Labour: How Working Class Kids Get Working Class Jobs.* Hampshire, England: Gower Press.

Zald, M. 1970. "Political Economy: A Framework for Comparative Analysis." In *Power in Organizations,* edited by M. Zald, 221-61. Nashville, Tenn.: Vanderbilt University Press.

Zaleznik, A. 1977. "Managers and Leaders: Are They Different?" *Harvard Business Review* 55(3):67-68.

The Southern Version
of
Cursor Mundi

Volume I

ÉTUDES MÉDIÉVALES DE L'UNIVERSITÉ D'OTTAWA
OTTAWA MEDIAEVAL TEXTS AND STUDIES

The Southern Version of *Cursor Mundi*

**Volume I
Edited by
Sarah M. Horrall**

General Editor
Sarah M. Horrall

The University of Ottawa Press
Ottawa, Canada
1978

TABLE OF CONTENTS

ACKNOWLEDGEMENTS

I should like to thank first of all those teachers who aroused my interest in biblical paraphrases and encouraged me at various stages in my study: J. D. Pheiffer of Trinity College, Dublin, L. M. Eldredge of the University of Ottawa, and especially A. P. Campbell of the University of Ottawa whose love for *Cursor Mundi* encouraged me to take on this work.

I must also thank the staffs of various libraries for their constant help: in Canada, the University of Ottawa Library and especially their Inter-Library Loans Department, and in England the staffs of the British Library, the Bodleian Library, and the Library of Trinity College, Cambridge. I must also thank those people at the College of Arms in London who went to unusual trouble to give me access to their manuscript.

For permission to publish manuscripts in their possession I thank the Corporation of the Kings Heralds and Pursuivant of Arms and in particular for the good offices of Dr. Conrad Swan, Ph. D., M. A., F. S. A., York Herald of Arms; the Master and Fellows of Trinity College, Cambridge; and the Bodleian Library, Oxford.

Special thanks go to Margaret Rejhon, who spent long hours of labour in deciphering my handwriting and typing the manuscript.

The research for this book was made possible first by doctoral fellowships from the Canada Council, and then by a research grant from the same organization.

The book has been published with the help of a grant from the Canadian Federation for the Humanities, using funds provided by the Social Science and Humanities Research Council of Canada.

Introduction

The *Cursor Mundi* is a verse history of the world, based on scripture, telling the story of mankind from Creation until Doomsday. The poem, which is almost 24,000 lines long in some versions, was written by an unknown poet in the north of England about 1300. Although the original composition has not survived, it was copied many times over the next 150 years, and is now extant in nine manuscripts.[1]

The poem is the best and most comprehensive of its kind in Middle English. Most Middle English biblical paraphrases base themselves on a very few sources, usually relying heavily on the *Historia Scholastica* of Petrus Comestor. The *CM* poet, on the contrary, has shown a wide knowledge of the traditional motifs of biblical exegesis, and he draws on an unusual variety of French, Latin and English sources. The poem which he produced is a well-proportioned compilation of pre-existing material translated into serviceable Middle English verse.

The only modern edition of the work appeared between 1874 and 1893, when Richard Morris and several colleagues published a transcription of five manuscripts of the *CM,* four of which were in northern or north Midland dialects. The transcriptions were accompanied by a sketchy, inaccurate critical apparatus which is now completely out of date. However, because Morris' work is the only edition of the whole poem available, most generalizations about the *CM* are based on it, and on the conclusions suggested by his critical apparatus. A new edition of the poem, with thorough analysis of the poet's sources, ideas and techniques, has long been needed.

Since Morris' version appeared, many more of the sources used by the *CM* poet have come to light. Comparison with these sources confirms Morris's finding that MS C,[2] a northern version,

---

[1] MS McGill Univ. 142, listed as a tenth MS of *CM* in BROWN, *Index*, 2153, is in fact part of a version of the *Southern Assumption*. See Michael G. SERGENT, "The McGill University Fragment of the Southern Assumption", *Mediaeval Studies*, XXXVI (1974), 186-98.

[2] See below, p. ff., for an explanation of the MSS sigla.

is the extant MS which is closest to the poem actually written by the mediaeval poet. Morris stopped there, however, considering that all other MSS, though perhaps dialectally interesting, were simply less perfect copies of the poet's original. Because the southern MSS (HTLB) differed most from MS C, Morris and his collaborators considered them to be merely hopelessly corrupt copies of the original poem, worthless for establishing the text of the original.

The present edition is based on entirely different assumptions. At some time in the late fourteenth century, someone in the south central Midlands came across a copy of the *CM* in a MS something like the extant MS G. The MS, or perhaps MSS, which he found, contrary to Morris' assumption, did preserve several original readings which are lost in each of the northern versions. Systematically this person revised the poem he found in the MS or MSS, changing phonology, morphology, rhymes, vocabulary and ideas, and completely revising the ending of the poem. As a result, southern England acquired not a corrupt copy of a northern poem, but a new poem, substantially changed in language and scope from its original.[3]

Southern audiences seem to have appreciated the revisor's efforts. The new version of the poem was copied at least four times, in formats ranging from parchment volumes with decorated initials, to large paper compilations of romances, adventures, and works of moral improvement. One of these is known to have belonged to a nun at the Bridgittine double monastery of Syon, just outside London. As late as 1442, the scribe of MS B was so aware of the *CM* as a living poem that he again modified the work, revising many lines and substituting extracts from another poem for some parts of the *CM,* exactly as the scribe of MS C had done 100 years before him.[4]

The text of the northern versions of the *CM* has long been available in Morris' edition, which was reprinted in 1961-6. For the first time, the present volume makes the southern translation of the work, including the highly interesting Bedford MS (MS B), equally available for consideration by scholars. The *CM* is here printed from a little known MS in a south Midland dialect (College of Arms Arundel LVII), with variants from three more, two of which have never been printed before (MSS Trinity College, Cambridge R.3.8; Bodleian Laud Misc. 416; British Library Additional 36983). The present volume contains approximately one third of the southern version of the poem. The rest will appear in two further volumes,

---

[3] Cf. Rolf KAISER, *Zur Geographie,* whose work documents some of these processes of revision.
[4] See, e.g., Carleton BROWN, "*CM* and the Southern Passion".

the last one containing a discussion of the authorship, place and date of composition, MS relations, etc.

The present volume constantly invites the reader to compare the readings of the southern version of *CM* with those of the northern MSS as printed by Morris. In order that these comparisons be as accurate as possible, each volume will contain a list of corrections to Morris' transcriptions of the northern MSS.

Each volume of this edition will also contain extensive explanatory notes. These are designed first of all to explain the *CM* itself. They deal first with the poet's sources, how he combines them or shifts from one to another while composing his own work. They also show how his original conception, most often preserved in MS C, changes as the poem is copied, revised, and copied again. However, the notes also attempt to place the *CM* in the context of similar literature in Old and Middle English, Old French, Latin, Hebrew and to some extent Celtic. This study of analogues to the *CM* enables the editor to determine in each instance whether the poet is using a commonplace of biblical exegesis, or a motif rare in Middle English but common in Old French biblical paraphrases, or an idea so rarely found in extant works that the *CM* poet's use of it remains a mystery. These notes should help to illuminate not only the *CM* itself, but also the large body of biblical literature in several mediaeval languages which has been relatively little studied of late. In this biblical literature, the *CM* occupies a unique place, because of its length, its scope, and its author's broad and eclectic knowledge of the traditions of exegesis in his time.

THE MANUSCRIPTS

H Arundel LVII[5] College of Arms, London

Vellum, 175 fols., approximately $12\frac{1}{2} \times 8\frac{1}{2}$ inches, usually in double columns[6] of forty lines each. Fols. 1-132 contain the *CM*.[7]

---

[5] See William Henry BLACK, *Catalogue of the Arundel Manuscripts in the Library of the College of Arms* (London, 1829), pp. 101-3 ; Hupe, *CM*, p. 68*.

[6] In MSS GHTLB the passion story, 11.14934-17110, is copied in single columns of long lines.

[7] Fols. 133-75 contain a copy of the *Pricke of Conscience*, imperfect at beginning and end. Cf. Richard MORRIS, ed., *The Pricke of Conscience*.

Collation:[8] flyleaf

a[8]   with a[i] missing fols. 1-7
b[8]   fols. 8-15
c[8]   with c[i] missing   fols. 16-22
d[8]   with d[viii] missing   fols. 23-9
e[8]   with e[i] missing   fols. 30-6
f[8]-i[8]   fol. 37-68
j[8]   with j[v] missing   fols. 69-75
k[8]-o[8]   fols. 76-115
p[8]   with p[viii] missing   fols. 116-22
q[8]   with q[i-iii] missing   fols. 123-7
r[6]   with r[i] missing   fols. 128-32
s[8]   with s[i-v] missing   fols. 133-5
t[8]-x[8]   fols. 136-75
y missing; perhaps contained 10 fols.
to accommodate the remainder of *Pricke of Conscience.*

Handwriting: A clear, regular bastard hand. y and þ are always distinguished, u and n only sometimes. Initials, etc. are decorated in red and blue.

Date: About 1400?

History: The MS was probably copied at or near Lichfield.[9] Although it is kept with the Arundel MSS at the College of Arms, it was not part of the original bequest of the Duke of Norfolk.[10]

Previous editions: Morris, *CM,* printed a few lines of the MS, chiefly 11.153-270, pp. 1657-63, and 11.17853-18028, pp. 1024-32.

T   Trinity College, Cambridge R.3.8[11]

Vellum, 144 leaves, approximately 12¼ × 8¼ inches, usually in double columns[12] of 40 lines each.

Contains only *CM.*

Collation: a[8]-r[8]   r[vii-viii] blank.

---

[8]   The collation printed by MORRIS, *CM,* p. 1663, contains a number of errors. The MS itself has pencilled signatures in a modern hand, but these err at fol. 128 and thereafter.
[9]   DAREAU and MCINTOSH, "A Dialect Word", p. 21.
[10]   See BLACK's *Catalogue,* p. [99].
[11]   See Montague Rhodes JAMES, *The Western Manuscripts in the Library of Trinity College Cambridge,* II (Cambridge, 1901); HUPE, *CM,* pp. 67*-8*.
[12]   See note 6 above.

Handwriting: A clearly written bastard hand. þ and y are distinguished and so often are u and n. Large initials are decorated
in red and blue. There are frequent marginal notes in 16th and
17th century hands, mainly summarizing the content of the
poem.

Date: About 1400?

History: McIntosh believes this MS was copied at Lichfield by a
scribe who is responsible for several other extant MSS.[13]
Various names in later hands appear at the end of the MS,
which was given to Trinity College by George Willner.

Previous editions: Printed in full by Morris, *CM*.

L   Laud Misc. 416[14] Bodleian Library

Paper, 289 leaves approximately $12 \times 8^{1}/_{2}$ inches.

The *CM* occupies fols. 65r-181v[15] usually in double columns[16] of
about 46 lines each.

Collation:[17]   a   fols. 1-8   The original folio numbers in Roman
numerals indicate that 36 fols. are missing from the beginning.
b^{12}-d^{12} fols. 9-44
e^{12} fols. 45-55 e^{ix} is partly torn out.
f^{12} fols. 56-64   with f^{x-xii} missing.
g^{12} fol. 65 with g^{i-xi} missing.
h^{16}-k^{16} fols. 66-129
l^{16} fols. 130-43   with l^{ii} and l^{xv}, conjugate leaves, missing.
The bottom half of fol. 141 is also gone.
m^{16} fols. 144-59
n^{16} fols. 160-71   with n^{iii-iv} and n^{ix-x} missing.

---

[13]   McINTOSH, "A New Approach", pp. 6-7; DAREAU and McINTOSH, A
Dialect Word", p. 26 n. 5.
[14]   See H. O. COXE, *Catalogi Codicum Manuscriptorum Bibliothecae Bod-
leianae Partis Secundae* (Oxford, 1858), p. 306; HUPE, *CM*, pp. 68*-9*.
[15]   The MS also contained: unknown material on the missing first 13 fols.;
Peter Idley's Instructions, lacking about 1900 lines, on 23 fols. at beginning and
otherwise imperfect, fols. 1-64v (*Index* 1540); Vegetius in prose, fols. 182r-226v
(*Index* 3185); LYDGATE's *Siege of Thebes,* fols. 227r-254r (*Index* 3928); LYDGATE
and BURGH's *Secrees of Old Philisoffres,* fols. 255r-287v (*Index* 935); CHAUCER's
Parlement of Foules, fols. 288r-9v, imperfect at end (*Index* 3412).
[16]   See note 6 above.
[17]   Determined by original numbering of folios, catchwords and watermarks.
The latter indicate that fols. 66-226 are on different paper from the rest of the MS.
These fols. contain the entire *CM*, except for its table of contents, and the prose
Vegetius.

o^{10} fols. 172-81
p^{12} fols. 182-92   with p^{ix} missing.
q^{12}-r^{12} fols. 193-216
s^{12} fols. 217-26   with s^{xi-xii} missing.
t^{12} fols. 227-38
u^{16} fols. 239-54
v^{12} fols. 255-65   with v^{xii} missing.
w^{12} fols. 266-76   with w^{i} missing.
x^{12} fols. 277-87   with x^{xii} missing.
y   only fols. 288-9 remain. Approximately 8 fols. would be required to complete the *Parlement of Foules*.

Binding: The covers are wooden and the back is leather. The MS formerly had clasps, which are now broken. MSS Laud Misc. 503 and 512 have similar bindings.

Handwriting: A neat bastard hand. þ and y and u and n are clearly distinguished. Final n and r sometimes end in a flourish.

Date: 1459, from an inscription on fol. 226 v:
"Scrip*tus* Rhodo *per* Joh*anne*m Newton die 25 Octobris 1459".

History: Belonged to the Bridgettine Abbey at Syon, just outside London.[18] On the back flyleaf is the name Syster Anne Colvylle. Archbishop Laud's name appears on fol. 1.

Previous editions: Morris, *CM*, printed 11.1-270, pp. 1651-62. He also printed 11.9325-11614, 11.16227-18512, and various smaller sections to fill in gaps in MS F. Brandl and Zippel print 11.10647-10782 and 11177-11276.

B   MS Additional 36983[19] British Library

Paper, 305 leaves, approximately 11 × 8½ inches. The *CM* occupies fols. 1-174,[20] usually copied in double columns[21] of 31 lines each.

---

[18]   See KER, *Medieval Libraries*.
[19]   See *Catalogue of Additions to the Manuscripts in the British Museum in the Years MDCCCC-MDCCCCV* (London, 1907); HUPE, *CM*, p. 68*.
[20]   However, *CM* 11.14916-17288 are replaced, on fols. 118r-127v, by 11.1-1140 of the *Meditations on the Supper of Our Lord*; see the edition by J. M. COWPER (London, 1875), EETS OS 60. *CM* 11.22005-23898 are replaced, on fols. 159r ff. by 11.4085-6407 of the *Pricke of Conscience*. Cf. the edition by R. Morris.
The MS also contains: CHAUCER's ABC Hymn to the Blessed Virgin, fols. 175r-178v (*Index* 239); *The Three Kings of Cologne* in prose, fols. 179r-215v; the rhyming *Titus and Vespasian*, fols. 216r-254v (*Index* 1881); "Michael III" from the *SEL.*, fols. 255r-261v (*Index* 3453); CHAUCER's *Truth*, vol. 262 r (*Index* 809); LYDGATE's "A knyght that is hardy as a lyon", fol. 262r-263r (*Index* 55); "The ABC of Aristotle", fols. 263r-v (*Index* 471); a single stanza in praise of Mary, fol. 263v (*Index* 4091); "The Legend of Ipotis", fols. 264r-268r (*Index* 220); *Speculum Gy de*

The first 174 fols. are numbered in Roman numerals in the upper right hand corner.

Collation:[22]   a   indeterminate, fols. 1-16. Probably a^{16}, with a^{ix} missing and an extra leaf added after a^{xvi}.

b^{16}-j^{16} fols. 17-160

k^{18}-l^{18} fols. 161-96

m   indeterminate; fols. 197-215. Sewing and watermarks suggest m^{20}, with m^{xx} missing.

n^{14} fols. 216-29

o^{18} fols. 230-47

p^{16} fols. 248-63

q   indeterminate; fols. 264-80. Sewing and watermarks suggest q^{16} with a leaf added at the end.

r   indeterminate; fols. 281-92. Probably r^{12}, but r^i and r^{xii} are not conjugate.

The rest of the gatherings cannot be determined. Modern pencil numbering says s^3 and t^{10}. Three more fols. are required after fol. 305 to complete the "Life of St. Dorothy".

Handwriting: A vernacular hand, with many tags and tails, especially on final letters. þ and y are distinguished but u and n are not. Many words are separated by dots or by fine vertical strokes.

Date: Fol. 215v bears the date Jan. 1, 1442.

History: The MS came to the British Museum from the Bedford Public Library.

Previous editions: Morris, *CM,* printed 11.1-270 and the colophon in his edition, pp. 1651-62.

C   Cotton Vespasian A iii[23] British Library

Vellum, 163 leaves, approximately $8^{7}/_{8} \times 6^{1}/_{2}$ inches, in double columns containing about 46 lines per col.

Warewyke, fols. 268r-275r (*Index* 1101); William LYCHEFELDE's "Complaint of God", fols. 275r-279v (*Index* 2714); "Passio Sancti Erasmi", fols. 279v-280v, imperfect at end (*Index* 173); "The Abbey of the Holy Ghost", fols 281r-285v; "The Charter of the Abbey of the Holy Ghost", fols. 285v-297v; "The Myrrour of Mankind", fols. 298r-305r (*Index* 1259); Osbert BOKENHAM's "Life of St. Dorothy", fol. 305v, imperfect at end (*Index* 3936).

    21   See note 6 above.

    22   Determined by original numbering of folios 1-174, catchwords, watermarks and sewing. There is also a pencilled signature in the upper left corner of the first folio of most of the gatherings. This was presumably done when the MS received its modern binding. The watermark throughout is very similar to Briquet 2784-5.

    23   See *A Catalogue of the MSS in the Cottonian Library Deposited in the British Museum* (London, 1802); HUPE, *CM,* pp. 63*-5*; LAMBERTS, *Dialect,* p. 7.

Contains only *CM*.

Collation:[24] fol. 1 a flyleaf
a[12]-g[12] fols. 2-85
h, fols. 86-101, originally had fourteen leaves, with sewing visible after fol. 92. Fols. 96 and 97 have been pasted on to stubs.
i[12] with i[i] missing fols. 102-112
j[12]-l[12] fols. 113-48
m[15] fols. 149-63

Handwriting: Wright calls the first hand in the MS "a round heavy characteristic 14th-century hand."[25] þ and y are not distinguished, nor are u and n. A second hand appears on fol. 92r and continues until 8 lines down on fol. 93v col. 1. Much of the material in this hand is unique to MS C. The first hand resumes until halfway down fol. 95v col. 2. The second hand then carries on until the end of fol. 98v. This second hand is a much more cursive bastard. It does differentiate between u and n, but still fails to distinguish þ and y. A third hand has made occasional corrections in the MS.

The MS is decorated with occasional red capitals and with a few marginal sketches, such as that of Noah's ark on fol. 12v. These are labelled in the same handwriting as the text.

The lines which appear in Morris' text as headings in heavy type are actually running headlines in the MS. Several more have been cropped after fol. 28.

Date: About 1340.[26]

Previous studies: This MS has had more attention than any other because it represents the original poem more closely than any of the other complete MSS extant. It was edited in full by Morris, *CM,* and extracts have often been printed. Several studies of the MS have also been done. Wright reproduces part of fol. 123v in facsimile.[27]

---

[24]   Several pages have been copied in the wrong order. They must be read as follows: 2r 3r 2v 3v; 131r 132r 131v 132v.
[25]   C.E. WRIGHT, *English Vernacular Hands*, p. 11.
[26]   *Ibid.*
[27]   MORRIS and SKEAT, *Specimens of Early English*, II 11.11373-11796; ZUPITZA, *Ubungsbuch*, 11.19603-19732; EMERSON, *A ME Reader*, 11.1-270; SAMPSON, *Cambridge Book of Prose and Verse*, 11.7439-7592; BRANDL and ZIPPEL, *Mittelenglische Sprach-*, 11.10647-10782, 11177-11276; DICKENS and WILSON, *Early ME Texts*, 11.1-38; BROWN, *Religious Lyrics of the XIVth Century*, 11.25403-25486, 25487-25618; BENNETT and SMITHERS, *Early ME Verse and Prose*, 11.1-100, 1237-1432. Work on this MS alone is by BROWN, "*CM* and the Southern Passion"; LAMBERTS, *Dialect of CM*; SNOUFFER, *Verbal Syntax of CM*. The facsimile is in C.E. WRIGHT, *English Vernacular Hands*, Sample 11.

F Fairfax 14[28] Bodleian Library

Vellum, 125 leaves, approximately $10\tfrac{1}{4} \times 6\tfrac{1}{2}$ inches in double columns of 48 lines per col. Contains only *CM*, to which is appended a version of the *Distichs* of Cato.

Collation: fols. 1-3 consist of one flyleaf and 2 fols. of table of contents.
> a[12]-d[12] fols. 4-51. The pricking of gathering d was done with an awl.
> e[12] missing. This would have contained 11.9325-11614.
> f[12] This is incorrectly bound. f[i-xi] are fols. 53-63. f[xii] is fol. 52.
> g[12] fols. 64-75
> h[12] missing. This would have contained 11.16227-18512.
> i[12] fols. 76-85 i[iii] and its conjugate i[x] are missing.
> j[12]-l[12] fols. 86-121
> m fols. 122-5 An indeterminate number of fols. is missing from the beginning of this gathering.[29]

Handwriting: A neat bastard hand. y is clearly distinguished from þ, but u and n are not.

Date: Late fourteenth century?

History: The MS is connected with Lancaster.
> A colophon on fol. 123v says: "Stokynbrig scripsit istum librum willo keruour de lancs". Fols. 1 and 3v contain scribbled accounts related to that county.[30]

Previous editions: Printed in full by Morris, *CM*. Furnivall also printed 11.304-78 of the *Distichs* of Cato from this MS.[31]

> See FAUSBØLL, *A Study*.

G Göttingen University theol. 107 r[32]

I have examined this MS only on microfilm.

---

[28] See Falconer MADAN and H.H.E. CRASTER, *A Summary Catalogue of Western Manuscripts in the Bodleian Library at Oxford* (Oxford, 1937), II ii, pp. 777-8; HUPE, *CM*, pp. 66*-7*.

[29] The gathering probably contained 14 leaves. The Table of Contents in this MS indicates that it would have contained the same material as MS C. C's 1648 further lines would have filled about $8\tfrac{1}{2}$ fols. in F. No other copy of this version of the *Distichs* of Cato exists (BROWN's *Index* 169 is in error here). Comparison with the Latin version of the *Distichs* printed by Boas and the French version edited by Furnivall, *Minor Poems*, suggests that no more than 13 cols. are missing from the Fairfax poem, and probably rather less. Thus gathering m would have been composed of $8\tfrac{1}{2}$ fols. of *CM*, about 3 fols. of Cato (missing) and 2 fols. of Cato (extant).

[30] See also MOORE, MEECH and WHITEHALL, *ME Dialect Characteristics*, p. 2.

[31] FURNIVALL, "How Cato was a Paynym"; cf. WHITING, "Notes on the Fragmentary Fairfax Version".

[32] See *Die Handschriften in Göttingen*. II *Universitäts-Bibliothek* (Berlin, 1893), p. 353; HUPE, *CM*, pp. 65*-66*.

Vellum, 169 fols., approximately 27 × 18 cms., usually in double columns[33] with about 36 lines each. Contains only *CM*, but the table of contents shows that it would have ended with "Saint Patrick's Purgatory".[34]

Collation:[35] a^{12}-f^{12} fols. 1-72

g^{14} fols. 73-86

h^{12}-m^{12} fols. 87-158

n^{12} fols. 159-69 with n^{ii} missing.

> G's Table of Contents indicates that the MS would have contained approximately the same material as C. This would have required another 25 leaves, plus more to accommodate "Saint Patrick's Purgatory". Probably at least three gatherings are lost at the end of the MS.

Handwriting: A neat vernacular hand. þ and y are not always distinguished, nor are u and n.

Date: Second half of the fourteenth century?

History: A colophon on fol. 114v gives the name of the man who had the MS made: "Iohn of lindbergh".[36] On the flyleaf is a book-plate of C. T. Sullow, with a note that he purchased the MS at auction in Hanover, June 14, 1786.

Previous editions: Morris, *CM,* prints the MS in full. Brown also prints the "Song of the Five Joys", 11.25619-25683.[37]

E Edinburgh Royal College of Physicians[38]

I have seen this MS only on microfilm.

Vellum, 50 leaves plus several fragments, in double columns containing approximately 40 lines per col.

Collation: This is impossible to determine, as the leaves are now pasted on to modern paper. The pages are incorrectly bound. *CM,* 11.18989-22417 appears on fols. 37r-50v. *CM,* 11.22418-24968 appears on fols. 1r-15v, although one fol., containing 11.24520-24968, is missing. Four leaves are lost between fols. 43 and 44, and two are lost between fols. 45 and 46.

---

[33] See note 6 above.
[34] See Morris, *CM,* V, p. 4a.
[35] Based solely on catchwords.
[36] See Morris, *CM,* p. 979.
[37] See Brown, *Rel. Lyrics of the XIVth Century,* 31.
[38] See John Small, *Engl. Met. Homs.,* xi-xxii; Hupe, pp. 62*-3*.

Handwriting: The MS is in three different 14th century vernacular hands. Hand 1 (fols. 1-15) distinguishes þ and y, but not u and n. Hand 2 (fols. 16-36) is somewhat smaller. Although u and n are not distinguished, y is frequently dotted to distinguish it from þ. Hand 3 is the largest and least neat in appearance. u and n are sometimes distinguished here.

Date: Late 14th century?

History: The MS was bequeathed to the Library of the Royal College of Physicians in 1741 by Dr. John Drummond, its president from 1722-1727.

Previous editions: A short extract is printed in John Small, *English Metrical Homilies*, and 11. 19603-19732 in Zupitza, *Übungsbuch*. The MS appears in full in Morris, *CM*, pp. 1587-1616, 1237-51, 1616-37, 1367-1429. The MS was studied by Hörning, *Die Schreibung der Hs.E des CM*.

Add. MS Additional 31042[39] British Library

Paper, 183 fols., counting 2 flyleaves at each end, approximately $10^3/4 \times 8$ inches. The *CM* fragments,[40] 11.10630-14914 and 17111-17188, are found on fols. 3r-32v. These are in double columns of 34-42 lines per col.

Collation: This is impossible to determine finally, as the individual leaves are now pasted on to modern paper. However, the

---

[39] See *Catalogue of Additions to the MSS in the British Museum in the Years 1876-1881* (London, 1882), pp. 148-51; H.L.D. WARD, *Catalogue of Romances in the Department of Manuscripts in the British Museum* I (1883; rpt. London, 1961), pp. 928-54; K. BRUNNER, "Hs Brit. Mus. Additional 31042", *Archiv* CXXXII (1914), 316-27; Dieter MEHL, *The Middle English Romances of the Thirteenth and Fourteenth Centuries* (London, 1968), p. 260.

[40] The MS also contains: *The Northern Passion*, fols. 33r-50r (*Index* 1907); the alliterative *Seige of Jerusalem*, imperfect, fols. 50r-66r (*Index* 1583); *The Sege of Melayne*, imperfect, fols. 66v-79v (*Index* 234); a hymn to the Virgin, lacking its first stanza, fols. 80r-81v (*Index* 2168); *Roland and Otuel*, fols. 82r-94r (*Index* 1996); LYDGATE's "Complaint þat Crist maketh of his Passioun", fols. 94r-96r (*Index* 2081); verses on the kings of England by Lydgate, imperfect at end, fol. 96 (*Index* 3632); LYDGATE's *Dietary*, imperfect at beginning, fol. 97 (*Index* 824); a four-line song, fol. 97v (*Index* 3778); *The Quatrefoil of Love*, fols. 98r-101v (*Index* 1453); a short rhymed prayer, fol. 101v (*Index* 1051); a translation of Psalm 51, imperfect at end, fol. 102 (*Index* 990); LYDGATE's *Interpretacio Misse*, imperfect at beginning, fols. 103r-110v (*Index* 4246); "The Rose of Ryse", fol. 110v (*Index* 3457); the rhymed *Three Kings of Cologne*, imperfect at beginning, fols. 111r-119v (*Index* *31; Supplement to *Index* *854.3); stanzaic "Prouerbis of Salamon", fols. 120r-122r (*Index* 3861); "Merci Passith Riȝtwisnes", fols. 122v-123r (*Index* 560); "Do Merci bifore thi Judement", fol. 123 (*Index* 3533); "Mercy Passes all Things", fol. 123v-124v (*Index* 583); *Richard Coer de Lion*, imperfect, fols. 125r-163v (*Index* 1979); Apocryphal History of the Infancy, fols. 163v-168v (*Index* 250); *Parlement of the Thre Ages*, fols. 169r-176v (*Index* 1556); *Wynnere and Wastoure*, imperfect at end, fols. 176v-181v (*Index* 3137).

evidence of catchwords, watermarks,[41] and the comparison
with other copies of the same texts suggests the following:

fols. 1-2 flyleaves of vellum from a 15th century breviary.

a   indeterminate, fols. 3-8. Watermarks suggest at least a[10].
Watermark A.

b[24]   fols. 9-32. Watermark A. This ends the *CM* portion of
the MS.

c[22]   fols. 33-53 with c[xxii] missing.[42] Watermark B.

d[20]   fols. 54-73. Fols. 54-60 and 67-73 have watermark C,
fols. 61-6 have watermark D.

Fols. 74-124 indeterminate. Fols. 74-9 have watermark E,
with at least one leaf lost after fol. 77 and at least one
after fol. 79.[43] Fols. 80-90 have watermark F. Fols. 95-102
have watermark E with a leaf missing after fol. 96 and
another after fol. 102[44]. Fols. 104-119 have watermark G
with two unnumbered stubs visible after fol. 110. Fols. 121-4
have watermark E.

e   indeterminate but possibly e[22], fols. 125-44, with one leaf
added after e[xxii]. Three fols. are missing after fol. 143.[45]
Watermark H.

f[24]   fols. 145-68. Watermark I.

g   indeterminate, fols. 169-81. Watermark I. Watermarks
suggest that five leaves are missing at the end of *Wynnere
and Wastoure*.

fols. 182-3   flyleaves as at beginning.

Handwriting: The handwriting is more cursive here than in any of
the other *CM* MSS.

Date: Mid-flfteenth century.

History: The MS was copied by Robert Thornton, who also copied
Lincoln Cathedral Library MS A i 17. Thornton's signature
appears on fols. 50r col. 2 and 66r. He probably came from
East Newton near Pickering in Yorkshire.[46] Unlike the
Lincoln Cathedral MS, this one seems to have left the Thorn-

---

[41]   Nine different watermarks appear in the MS: A-a bull; B-rather like
Briquet 15203-4, 15206; C-a wagon; D-somewhat like Briquet 4399; E-a long thin
spear shape; F-a round mass; G-somewhat like Briquet 11632; H-very like Briquet
3868; I-somewhat like Briquet 4642 and 4644.

[42]   Cf. E. KÖLBING and M. DAY, ed., *The Siege of Jerusalem* (1932; rpt.
Oxford, 1971), EETS OS 188, 11.289-374; WARD, *Catalogue*, p. 928.

[43]   Cf. S. J. HERRTAGE, *The English Charlemagne Romances* II (London,
1880), p. 44; WARD, *Catalogue*, pp. 953-4.

[44]   Cf. BROWN, *Index*, 3632, 990.

[45]   Cf. E. BRUNNER, *Der Mittelenglische Versroman über Richard Löwen-
herz* (Vienna, 1913), p. 251; WARD, *Catalogue*, pp. 945, 947.

[46]   See M. S. OGDEN, *The "Liber de Diversis Medicinis"*, rev. rpt. (London,
1969), EETS OS 207, pp. x-xvii.

ton family's possession before the middle of the 16th century. Offord has suggested that the John Nettleton whose name appears in a 16th century hand on fols. 49r and 139v is the same man whose name appears in 1565 in a list of people who owned MSS.[47] The MS apparently found its way to America and was purchased by the British Museum through J. Pearson on July 12, 1879.

Previous editions: This MS has never been printed. See STERN, "London Thornton"; HORRALL, "London Thorton".

SELECTION OF A BASE TEXT

The base text for this edition has been selected for reasons both scholarly and pragmatic. The northern versions of *CM* have long been available in Morris' text. His transcriptions are reasonably accurate and could easily be made more so by a list of corrected readings such as appears at the end of the present volume. However, the MSS of the southern version of *CM* have been rather poorly served because of the attitude to them shown by Morris and his collaborators.[48] The only southern MS which Morris printed, T, is an excellent one, but its choice was probably dictated largely by its availability and completeness. MS L, while it is a reasonably good text, shows several omissions and misunderstandings as against HT, and would be unsuitable for use as a base. MS B is an extremely interesting version of *CM* which has been virtually unknown until now. The scribe has taken considerable liberty with the phrasing of his exemplar, and has eventually interpolated large sections of a different poem into the *CM*. MS B is obviously unsuitable as a base text, but it deserves to be much better known. Hence the very full apparatus of variants, largely from MS B, which appears in this edition.

MS H, which was finally chosen as a base text for the present edition, contains a text which is very slightly better than MS T's. Unfortunately MS H is missing several leaves, but in the present

---

[47] See M. Y. OFFORD, ed., *The Parlement of the Thre Ages* (London, 1959), EETS OS 246, p. xii; cf. C. E. WRIGHT, "The Dispersal of the Libraries in the Sixteenth Century" in WORMALD and WRIGHT, *The English Library*, pp. 157-8 and 173 nn. 24-5.

[48] See above, p. XI.

edition these are supplied from MS T. MS H has also been less readily available for use by scholars because of its location in the College of Arms.

STRUCTURE OF THE POEM

The *CM* may be roughly divided into the following sections:[49]

I — Chronological History

(a) Prologue   11.1-270
(b) 1st age: Creation to Noah, 11.271-1626
(c) 2nd age: Noah's Flood to the building of Babel 11.1627-2314
(d) 3rd age: Abraham to the death of Saul 11.2315-7860
(e) 4th age: David to the Babylonian captivity 11.7861-9228
(f) 5th age: birth and early life of the Virgin and Christ 11.9229-12751
(g) 6th age: Baptism of Christ to the finding of the Cross 11.12752-21846
(h) 7th age: Doomsday 11.21847-23908

II — Short Poems

(i) Prayer to the Blessed Virgin 11.23909-23944
(j) Sorrows of Mary 11.23945-24658
(k) Apostrophe to St. John 11.24659-24730
(l) Festival of the Conception of the Virgin 11.24731-24970

III — Additional Poems

(m) Exposition of the Creed 11.24971-25102
(n) Exposition of the Pater Noster 11.25103-25402
(o) Prayer to the Trinity 11.25403-25486
(p) Prayer for the Hours of the Passion (Matins of the Cross) 11.25487-25618
(q) Song on the Five Joys of Our Lady 11.25619-25683

---

[49] These divisions are based on Morris, *CM*. V, pp. vii-ix.

(r) Book of Penance (Prologue and three parts) 11.25684-29547

(s) Cato's *Morals* Morris, *CM,* pp. 1669-1674

The *CM* exists in three different forms:

(A) The oldest appears to have contained only Sections I and II above, ending with item (1). This is the poem described in the prologue, 11.131-222. The only extant MS which might have had this shape is MS E, which ends at 1.24968. Unfortunately this MS survives only as a fragment, beginning at 1.18989. No one can now say whether or not the MS originally contained a full text of the *CM* in a form exactly as described in the prologue.

(B) The second form of the *CM* is found in three northern MSS. These are the MSS which contain Morris' so-called "additions":

MS C contains items a-n, p, o and r.
MS F contains items a-p, r and s
MS G would have contained items a-r[50]

(C) The southern version, MSS HTLB, contains only the material of chronological history, ending after the account of Doomsday, although the prologue in these MSS retains 11.217-20, which state that the poem will deal with items (j) and (l).

EDITORIAL PRINCIPLES

This edition is intended to be a copy of MS H, with only obvious scribal blunders corrected on the basis of the other MSS. Leaves which are missing in MS H are printed from MS T. Abbreviations are expanded in italics, and headings and decorated capitals appear in bold face type. The first letter of every line of the poem is capitalized in this edition, although the scribe occasionally forgot to do so in the MS. Otherwise the scribe's own capitalizations are allowed to stand. The spacing of words is made to conform, as much as possible, to modern practice. Any other changes in the text are enclosed in square brackets and the MS reading is recorded in the variants.

---

[50] See MS G's Table of Contents in Morris, *CM,* V, pp. 1a-4a.

The variants are not designed to include differences of dialect or spelling. Only differences in words or phrases, or in word order are included. Rules for transcription of the variants are much the same as for the text itself, except that square brackets which appear in the text are not repeated in the variant. Also, because the capitalization in MS B is so erratic, I have capitalized in that MS only in accord with modern practice. The form for each variant is as follows: the word or phrase as it appears in my transcription of MS H, followed by a square bracket, then the variant readings for that word as they appear in the other MSS, in the order TLB. Different variants of the same word are separated by semi-colons; the whole is followed by a period.

Appendix A is a list of corrections to Morris' transcriptions. In these, the reading from the printed text is followed by a square bracket, the initial representing the MS, and the correct reading of the MS itself. Emendations to Morris' text, printed in square brackets in his edition, are allowed to stand without comment if they are purely conjectural. However, if the letters were originally written by the scribe but have since become illegible through blots, holes, etc., I enclose them in pointed brackets in the MS reading. Thus if Morris' transcription of MS C reads "b[ad]" and no note appears in Appendix A, then the MS reads simply "b". If Appendix A, however, has "b[ad]]C b ⟨ad⟩", then the scribe originally wrote "bad", but the "ad" has since become illegible.

References to other works in the Explanatory Notes and in the Introduction are either by abbreviation or by author and short title. An explanation of abbreviations used precedes the Explanatory Notes. Full information about other works will be found in the Bibliography. Transcriptions in the notes from unpublished MSS consulted on microfilm follow the same rules as all other transcriptions except that no emendations at all are attempted.

To produce the text and variants, I worked originally on microfilms of the MSS. I have since carefully compared my transcriptions of the microfilms with the MSS themselves, except for MSS G and E, which I have seen only on film.

This edition retains the line numbering used in Morris' text. This numbering is often unsatisfactory, for Morris sometimes numbered spurious lines, and at other times printed in parallel columns lines which were not in fact the same. However, I must make frequent references to the northern MSS for comparison with this edition, and a dual system of line numbers proved impossibly cumbersome.

This edition is based on certain assumptions about the relationship among the various MSS of the poem. I can accept none of the previously published MSS stemma, for reasons which will be fully discussed and justified in Volume III. Therefore my own assumptions must be outlined here.

MS C is clearly the extant MS which is closest to the *CM* poet's original version, although it contains many corruptions. In the notes, I assume that MS C's reading is closest to the original French or Latin, unless I state otherwise. The southern version of the poem, represented by MSS HTLB, is derived from a MS similar to G, though not G itself. To produce the southern version, this MS, in a North Midland dialect, was systematically revised and translated.

Introduction to This Volume

SOURCES

It is not possible to document in a short space the *CM* poet's indebtedness to each of his sources. When composing his poem, he apparently sat with several books open before him, choosing lines from each one to be combined in his own narrative.

The major sources, aside from the text of the Vulgate, which the poet has used for the Old Testament section of his work are:

(1) the *Elucidarium* of Honorius Augustodunensis[51]

(2) an anonymous Old French poetic paraphrase of the books of *Genesis* and *Exodus* to which was added a poem on the history of the wood of Christ's cross[52]

(3) the Old French *Bible* of Herman de Valenciennes[53]

(4) the *Historia Scholastica* of Petrus Comestor[54]

---

[51] *Elucid.* Yves LEFÈVRE, *L'Elucidarium et les lucidaires* (Paris, 1954). This poem was much translated but the *CM* poet seems to have used the Latin text. This source was first pointed out by KALUZA, "Zu den Quellen", pp. 451-2.

[52] *Trad. anon.* MS BN fr. 763 fols. 211r-272. This is not the MS which the *CM* poet used, but it is the closest of the extant copies to the version which the poet must have known. Another partial copy exists in MS Montpellier, B. municipale, 437, and the poem is also combined with Herman de Valenciennes' *Bible* in MS Arsenal 3516. A. S. NAPIER, *Rood Tree*, pp. xxiiiff, first pointed out that the *CM* version of the cross wood story came from this source. No one has previously noticed the *CM*'s indebtedness to this version of *Genesis,* however.

[53] *Bible.* Herman de VALENCIENNES, *La Bible von Herman de Valenciennes* II, ed. Otto Moldenhauer (Griefswald, 1914), and extract in Earl BARTSCH, *Chrestomathie de l'ancien français*, 10th ed. (Leipzig, 1910), pp. 71-6. The first volume of the Griefswald edition has apparently never been published. For the early section of the work, therefore, I have consulted a microfilm of University of Chicago MS H.27. B.6.12. The *CM* poet's debt to Herman is discussed by Lois BORLAND, *The Cursor Mundi,* and "Herman's *Bible*", and by Philip BUEHLER, "The *Cursor Mundi*".

[54] *Hist. Schol., PL* CXCVIII 1053ff. This was first mentioned as a source by Haenisch, "Inquiry into the Sources of the *Cursor Mundi*" in MORRIS, ed., *CM,* EETS OS 99, pp. 1*-56*.

(5)   the Latin *Legende* version of the story of the Cross Wood[55]

(6)   Honorius Augustodunensis' *De Imagine Mundi* [56]

The poet here and there interjects a few lines from additional sources. These borrowings are very brief and may have come to the *CM* poet through an intermediate source not yet discovered.

(1)   Hugh of St. Victor's *Adnotationes Elucidatoriae in Pentateuchon* [57]

(2)   the *Revelations* of the pseudo-Methodius [58]

(3)   the *Chateau d'amour* of Robert Grosseteste [59]

(4)   the *Etymologiarum* of Isidore of Seville [60]

(5)   the *Speculum Ecclesiae* of Honorius Augustodunensis [61]

---

[55] *Legende.* The Latin *Legende* has been printed by W. MEYER, "Die Geschichte des Kreuzholzes vor Christus"; SUCHIER, *Denkmäler*; C. HORSTMANN, "Nachträge zu den Legenden", pp. 465-70; LAZAR, "La Légende de l'Arbre de Paradis"; Betty HILL, "The Fifteenth-Century Prose Legend". I quote from Lazar's text, which is closer to the version which the *CM* poet used than any of the others.

[56] *DIM, PL* CLXXII 165ff. This was first pointed out by KALUZA, "Zu den Quellen", p. 452.

[57] See below, n. to 11.359-72 *et passim.*

[58] See below, n. to 11.1465-6 *et passim.*

[59] See below, n. to 11.701-10.

[60] See below, n. to 11.2091ff.

[61] See below, n. to 11.5745-50, 6909-10.

Text of
the Southern Version
of Cursor Mundi

Here bigynneþ þe boke of storyes
Þat men callen cursor mundi

Men ȝernen iestes for to here
And romaunce rede in dyuerse manere
Of Alisaunder þe conqueroure
Of Iulius cesar þe emperoure
Of gre[c]e & troye þe longe strif   5
Þere mony mon lost his lif
Of bruyt þat barounbolde of honde
Furste conqueroure of engelonde
Of kyng Arthour þat was so riche
Was noon in his tyme him liche   10
Of wondris þat his knyȝtes felle
And auntres duden men herde telle
As Wawayn kay & oþere ful abul
For to kepe þe rounde tabul
How kyng charles & rouland fauȝt   15
Wiþ Sarazines nolde þei [be] sauȝt
Of tristram & of Isoude þe swete
How þei wiþ loue firste gan mete
Of kyng Ion and of Isombras
Of Idoyne & of amadas   20
Storyes of dyuerse þinges
Of princes prelatis & of kynges

1-152   *missing in* H. *Here printed from* T. *Heading om* B. þat men callen]callid L.
1   ȝernen]lykyn L.
5   grece]greke T. þe]*om* B. longe]strong LB.
6   mony mon]many a man L.
8   Furste]The first L.
10   Was]*om* B. him]so L; was him B.
11   his]among his L. þat his knyȝtes felle]hill king heye B.
12   men herde]as men here L.
13   kay]and Gay B. ful]*om* B.
14   For to kepe]Which that kept L.
16   be]*om* T. sauȝt]cawght L.
20   *second* of]*om* B.
21   Storyes]Of storis B.
22   princes]prynce B.

Mony songes of dyu*er*se ryme
As englisshe frensshe & latyne
To rede & here mony are prest   25
Of þinges þ*a*t hem likeþ best
Þe wise mon wol of wisdome here
Þe fool him draweþ to foly nere
Þe wronge to here riȝt is looþ
And pride wiþ buxo*m*nes is wrooþ   30
Of chastite þe lecchoure haþ lite
Charite aȝeyn wraþþe wol flite
But bi þe fruyte may men ofte se
Of what vertu is vche a tre
And vche fruyt þ*a*t men may fynde   35
He haþ from þe rote his kynde
Of good pire com gode þerus
Werse tre wers fruyt berus
Þ*a*t i saye þus of þis tre
Bitokeneþ mon boþe þe & me   40
Þis fruyt bitokeneþ alle oure dedes
Boþe gode & euel who so riȝte redes
Oure dedes fro oure herte take rote
Wheþ*er* þei turne to bale or bote
For bi þ*a*t þing mon draweþ tille   45
Men may him knowe for good or ille
Ensau*m*pel herby to hem I sey
Þ*a*t rage in her riot al wey
In ryot & in rigolage
Spende mony her ȝouþe & her age   50

---

23   of]& B.
24   As]In B.
25   are]is L.
27   here]lere B.
29   riȝt]þe right L.
32   charite...wol]And wraþ agens charite B.
33   But]And L. may men]men may B.
34   vche a] þe B.
35   vche] euery L.
37   pire]pyrthe L; pery B. com]comeþ B.
38   *first* Werse]A wers L; þe wers B.
     second wers] þe wers B.
39   þ*a*t...saye]Whan I speke L.
40   Bitokeneþ] Hyt bytokenyþ L.
44   turne]com B.
45   mon]men B.
46   Men]Then L; Mon B.
47   In sapil to hem I may say B.
48   rage]regneþ B. riot]reame B.
50   Spende mony]Many spend L. ȝouþe...her]ȝounge B.

For now is he holden nouȝt in shouris
But he con loue paramouris
Þat foles lif þat vanite
Him likeþ now noon oþere gle
Hit is but fantom for to say   55
Today hit is tomorwe away
Wiþ chaunce of deþ or chaunge of hert
Þat softe bigan endeþ ful smert
For whenne þou wenest hit trewest to be
Þou shalt from hit or hit from þe   60
He þat weneþ stiffest to stonde
War him his fal is nexte at honde
Whenne he so soone doun is brouȝt
Whider to wende woot he nouȝt
But to whom his loue haþ him led   65
To take suche mede shal he be sted
For þere shal mede wiþouten let
Be sett to him for dew dett
Þerfore blesse we þat paramoure
Þat in oure nede doþ vs socoure   70
Þat saueþ vs in erþe fro synne
And heuen blisse helpeþ to wynne
For þouȝe I sumtyme be vntrewe
Hir loue is euer I liche newe
Hir loue is euer trewe and lele   75
Ful swete hit is to monnes hele
Suche oþere in erþe is founden none
For she is modir & mayden alone
Modir & mayden neuer þe les
Þerfore of hir toke ihesu flesshe   80
Who þat loueþ trewely þis lemmon
He shal haue loue þat neuer is woon

---

51   shouris]storijs B.
52   con]om B.
53   foles]folye B.
54   Him likeþ]Ther is lykyd L.
55   fantom]fantasy LB. for to]y you L.
56   tomorwe]tomorn B.
57   chaunge]chaunce B.
59   To]om B.
62   at]to B.
64   Whider]Wheþer L.
72   heuen...helpeþ]makiþ vs þe blis B.
73   þouȝe] yf B. I]þou L.
77   Oþere] onoþer B. founden] om B.
80   þerfore] om B. toke] take þerfor B.
81   line om L. Who þat]Scho so B. trewely] welle B.
82   line om L. loue] þe loue B. is woon] schall whan B.

For in þis lif she faileþ neuer
And in þat oþer lasteþ euer
Of suchon shulde ʒe matere take   85
ʒe crafty þat con rymes make

Of hir to make boþe geest & songe
And preise hir swete son amonge
What bote is hit to sett trauaile
On þing þat no þing may availe   90
Þat is but fantom of þis Werd
As we ynowʒe han seen & herd
Materes fynde we may in dede
Rymes of hir to make & rede
Who so wol of hir fairnes spelle   95
Fynde he may ynouʒe to telle
Of hir goodnesse of hir trouþhede
Fynde men may aboute to sprede
Of treuþe of loue of charite
Was neuer hir make ne neuer shal be   100
Lady she is of peples alle
Meke & mylde wiþouten galle
Next to nedeful to calle on
And reiseþ euer þe synful mon
Ihesu made þat mayden swete   106
Alle oure bales for to bete   105
Herby men may her helpe wel knowe
She preyeþ for synful heʒe & lowe
Whoso doþ hir worshepe may be bolde
She wol him ʒelde an hundride folde   110
In hir worshepe bigynne wolde I

---

83   For] And L.
84   And] And I B. þat oþer] the todir L.
85   shulde] schul B.
86   ʒe] þe LB. crafty] craftis B.
90   On]Of B. no...may] wille noght L.
91   fantom] fantasy L; fantosijs B. Werd]worlde here B.
92   As...herd] As yt is yn many boke rold L. As] And B. herd]here B.
93   fynde...may] may we fynd B.
97   *line om* L. of] & B. trouþhede] trewhede B.
98   *line om* L. men] he B.
99   *third* of] & LB.
100   ne]nor L.
101   peples] peple B.
103   *first* to] and L. *second* to] þat here B.
105-6 *transposed in* TLB. bete] lete L.
107   Herby] *om* L. may] may sone L. wel]*om* L.
108   preyeþ] prayit B.
109   Whoso] Who L. bolde] told B.
111   wolde] wille L.

A werke þat shulde be lastyngely
For to do men knowe hir kyn
þat muche worshepe dud vs wyn
Sum maner þing is good to knawe   115
Þat done was in þe olde lawe
Bitwixe þe olde lawe & þe newe
How crist vs bote bigan to brewe
I shal ȝou shewe bi myn entent
Soþely of hir testament   120
Al þis world ar þis book blynne
Wiþ cristis helpe I shal ouer rynne
And telle sum geste principale
For al may no man haue in tale
But no werk wel laste may   125
Wiþoute good grounde to laste ay
Þerfore þis werke I wol founde
On a selcouþ studfaste grounde
Þat is þe holy trinite
Þat al is made of his bounte   130
Furst at himself I sett my merk
And aftir to telle of his hond werk
Of þe aungels þat firste felle
And siþ I wol of adam telle
Of his ospringe and of Noe   135
And sumwhat of his sones þre
Of Abraham & als of ysaac
Þat holy weren wiþouten lac
Siþen shal I telle ȝou newe
Of Iacob & of Esaue   140
Siþen shul ȝe here hit tolde
How Ioseph was bouȝte & solde
Of þe iewes & of Moises
Þat god his folke to lede him chees
How god bigan þe lawe him ȝyue   145
Whiche þe iewes shulde in lyue

---

114   þat] And þat B.
118   vs...bigan] began our bote B.
120   Soþely] Trewly B.
123   sum geste] of þe B.
128   selcouþ] ful B.
130   is] om B.
134   siþ...adam] deþ of adam I wille B.
137   als] om B.
139   newe] now B.
141   hit] om B.
144   him] he B.
145   þe...him] hym þe law to B.

Of saul þe kyng & of dauy
How he fauȝte aȝeyn goly
And siþþe of salomon þe wise
How he was crafti iustise   150
How crist cam þourȝe prophecie
His owne folk for to bye
Siþþe hit shal be rad ȝow þanne   fol. lr col. 1
Of ioachym and of seynt anne
Of mary also hir douȝter mylde   155
How sheo was born & bare hir chylde
How sheo was bore whenne & whare
How sheo hym to þe tempel bare
Of þo kynges þat hym souȝte
That þre presentes to him brouȝte   160
How þat heroude kyng wiþ wrong
For crystes sake slowȝe children ȝong
How þat ihesu to egipte fledde
And how he was þennes ledde
And þere shul ȝee here many [a] dede   165
Þat ihesu dide in his childehede
Siþen of þe baptiste Ion
Þat baptized ihesu in flum iurdon
How ihesu aftir his fastynge longe
Was temptide wiþ þe spirit of wronge   170
Siþen of iones baptizyng
And how hym heuedede heroude þe kinge
How þat ihesu crist hymselue
Chees to hym apostles twelue
And openly bigan to preche   175
And alle þat seke were to leche

---

152   for] aȝene B.
153   MS H *begins*.
154   *second* of] *om* B.
155-6 *transposed in* B.
156   bare] born L.
157   whenne] & whan B.
158   hym] hir chyld B.
159   Of þo] And of þe B.
160   That] And B. to] þey B.
161   þat...kyng] þe kyng heraud B.
162   For] Forth B.
165   a] *om* H.
167   Siþen] And seþ B. þe] *om* B.
168   þat] How he B. ihesu] crist B.
170   of]*om* B.
172   And] *Om* B. heuedede]byhedid L.
175   bigan] gan B.
176   þat]þe B. were] for B.

And dide myracles mony & ryfe
Wherfore þe iewes bigon to stryfe
Siþþe how god of his myȝte
Turned watir into wyn riȝte   180
Of fyue þousande men þat he
Wiþ fyue looues fedde & fisshes þre
Of a man shal we þen fynde
Pat god ȝaf siȝte & borne was blynde
And of þe spousebriche of o wommon   185
Pat þe iewes demed to stoon
How he heled a man vnfere
Pat seck was eyȝte & twenty ȝere
How mary maudelene wiþ grete
Coom to wasshe oure lordes fete   190
Of hir and of martha also
Pat bisy was aboute cryst þoo
Of lazar þat deede lay vndir stoon   fol 1r col. 2
How he was reised in flesshe & boon
How iewes ihesu ofte bisette   195
And for his prechyng also him þrette
How þei pyned hym on þe rode   198
And how þei shedde his blessed blode   197
And ȝif god wole þenne shal I telle
How he siþþen harrewede helle   200
How iewes wiþ her greete vnskille
Wende his vprysynge to stille
How he vproos & siþen vpstay
Mony a man hit herde & say
How þat he of myȝtes moost   205

---

178   bigon] gan B.
180   into] to B.
181   Of] How B.
182   Wiþ...fedde] Fede with v loues B. þre]þe B.
186   stoon]stond B.
187   he] om B. vnfere] in feere L; þat was vnfer B.
188   twenty] þrety B.
191   Of...of] How sche and B.
192   þat...was] Wer bessy B.
193   vndir] in B.
194   in] om B.
195   iewes] þe Iewis LB. ihesu ofte] oft Ihesu B.
196   And] om B.
197-8 transposed in MSS HTLB. blessed] preshious L.
198   pyned] naylid L; payned B.
199   I telle] stelle B.
200   he siþþen] þat gode B. harrewede] heryed B.
201   iewes] þe Iewes B. her] om B.
202   vprysynge] resurection B.

Sende to erþe þe holy goost
Touchynge þe apostles of her feest
How þei endede meest and leest
How oure lady endede and ȝolde
Hir semely soule hit shal be tolde   210
How þe holy cros was kidde
Longe aftir þat hit was hidde
Of antecristes coome þat shal be kene
And of þe dredeful dayes fiftene
Þat shul come bifore þe domes day   215
Siþen of þe doom wole I say
Þen of oure ladyes mournyng mode
Whenne hir sone henge on rode
Þe laste resoun þat I shal spelle
Of hir concepcioun wole I telle   220
Þese are þe materes red on rowe
Þat in þis book wole I showe
Shortly rennynge on þis dede
For mony þer aren for to spede
Nedeful me þinke hit were to man   225
To knowe hymself how he bigan
How he bigan in world to brede
How his osprynge bigan to sprede
Boþe of þe firste and of þe la[st]e
In what course þis world is paste   230
Aftir holy chirches astate
Þis ilke book is translate
Into englisshe tonge to rede   fol. lv col. 1

---

206   erþe] þe erþe B.
207   apostles] postilles B.
208   How] And how B.
212   þat] *om* B.
213   coome] comyng L.
215   bifore] tofore TL; afore B. þe] *om* LB.
218   hir sone] Ih*e*su B. henge] hang B. on] on þe T; vpon þe B.
219   shal] wille B.
220   hir] þe B.
221   are] ben B. red on rowe] good & trew L; rede & row B.
222   wole I] I wille B.
224   mony...aren] þ*er* be mane þere B.
225   þinke] þinkit B.
227   brede] dred B.
228   bigan] gan B.
229   la[st]e *There is a hole in* MS H *where the missing letters should be.*
230   In] How & B. þis] þe L.
231   astate] state B.
232   book] *om* B.
233   tonge] for B.

For þe loue of englisshe lede
For comune folke of engelonde   235
Shulde þe better hit vndirstonde   236
Þat speche þat moost vs may spede   243
Moost to speke hit were greet nede
Selden hit is for any chaunce   ,245
Englisshe tonge preched in fraunce
ȝyue we vche londe his langage
þenne do we noon outrage
To lewed men englisshe I spelle
Þat vndirstondeþ what I con telle   250
And to hem speke I alþer moost
Þat ledeþ her lyues in pryde & boost
And spenden her lyues in treuandise
And myȝte amenden in mony wyse   254
Wo shal hem be her lyf so spende   257
Þat fynde þerof no fruyt at þe ende   258
Now of þis prolouge wole we blynne   265
In crystes nome oure book bygynne
Cours of þis world men shul hit calle
For almeest hit reherseþ alle
Take we oure bigynnynge þan
At hym þat al þis world bigan   270

Hereþ now of þe trynite dere
And of þe makyng of þis world here
Alle men owe þat lord to drede   271
Þat made man to haue mede
Þat euer was & euer shal be

---

234   þe] *om* B. of] of þe B
235   comune] þe comon B.
236   þe] it B. hit] *om* B.
237-42   *omitted in* MSS HTLB.
243   moost vs] vs most B.
245   hit] *om* B. any] an B.
246   preched in] praysed & B.
247   ȝyue we] ȝif we ȝif B.
249   I] to B.
253   And] That L. lyues] lyf L. treuandise] tyrandyse L.
255-6   *missing in* MSS HTLB.
257   Wo] He wo B. so] to L.
258   þe] *om* LB.
259-64   *missing in* MSS HTLB.
265   we] I B.
267   Cours] þe cours B. þis] þe B.
268   almeest...reherseþ] nerehand it is rehersid B.
270   At] Of LB.
270b   of þe] *om* B.

Wiþouten ende in trynite
He þat lorde boþe god an man   275
Al maner þing of hym bigan
Pouȝe he bigan al oþere þinge
Hymself hadde neuer bigynnynge
Of hym coom al in hym is al
Al holdeþ he vp from doun fal   280
He h[ol]deþ heuen & erþe stidefaste
Wiþouten hym may no þing laste
Þis lord þat is so mychel of myȝte
Purueyed al into his siȝte
And þat he ordeyned wiþ his witt   285 fol. lv col. 2
He multeplied and governeþ hit
Þerfore he is þe trynite
Þat is o god & persones þre
And ȝif þow wenest hit may not be
Byholde þe sonne þenne maist þou se   290
In þe sonne þat shynes clere
Is o þing & þre seere
A body rounde hoot and liȝte
Þese þre we fynde at a siȝte
Þese þinges þre wiþ noon art   295
Mow not be fro oþere depart
For ȝif þou take þe liȝte away
Þe erþe haþ no sonne parfay
And ȝif þe heete away be goon
Sonne forsoþe hastou noon   300
But vche maner man wel woote
Þe kynde of sonne is to be hoote
Þe sonnes body þat I neuene
Bitokeneþ þe fadir god of heuene
And bi þe liȝte þat lastynge is   305
Hit is þe sone kynge of blis
And bi þe hete vndirstonde hit so

---

275   He þat] Of that L; þat ilke B.
276   maner] *om* B.
280   Al...vp] He holdeth vp all B.
281   h[ol]deþ. *There is a hole in MS* H *where the missing letters should be.*
282   hym] ende T.
284   into] to L.
286   multeplied] multyplyeth B. governeþ] govuernyd L.
289   wenest] trow L. hit] þat B.
295   þinges þre] þre þinges B.
296   not] none B., be] *om* TL. depart] be depart T; parte B.
301   vche maner] euery B.
303   neuene] neueyne L.
304   þe...god] god þe fadyr B.

Þe holy goost comeþ of hem two
And fadir is he calde forþi
For he is welle þat neuer is dry   310
And ouer þis hymself wrouȝte
Alle þinges whenne þei were nouȝte
His sone is wisdome þat al þing wate
For al þe world he halt in state
Al þing he halt from mysfare   315
Þat þei not turne to sorwe & care
Þe holy [goost] is þe godhede
Þat ȝyueþ lyf to alle we rede   318
Þis lord þat I bifore of seide   323
Firste in his witt he al purueyde
His werkes he dooþ as sotele wriȝte   325
And siþen he reiseþ hit in siȝte
Forþi is god as seiþ scripture
Non elder þen is creature
Elder of tyme nys not he   fol. 2r col. 1
But elles more in dignite   330
Þis wriȝte þat I speke of here
Is prynce ouer al wiþouten pere
For oþere wriȝtes mot tymber take
But he hymself con tymber make
For of hymself he took þe euene   335
Þat he made wiþ boþe erþe & heuene
But we shul vndirstonde
Þat he wrouȝte not al his werke wit honde
But seide wiþ worde & also soone

---

310 For] om B. first is]ys þe B. second is] shalle L:
312 þinges] thyng L.
313 is] his L.
314 halt] holdeth B.
315 þing] þinges T. halt] holdeth B.
316 not] ne L.
317 goost] om H.
323 bifore] ere B; seide] red L.
324 he] om B.
325 as] as a L.
326 hit] all B.
327 as] om B.
329 nys] is TB.
331-2   reversed in B.
332 Is] He ys B. ouer] of B.
333 mot] most B.
334 But] And L., con] gan B.
335 þe] om B.
337 shul] shull alle well B.
338 þat] om L. his] om T. his werke] om B. honde] his honde TB.

Al his biddynge hit was doone   340
Smartlyere þen ȝe may wynke
Or any mannes herte may þinke
And as clerkes saye þat are wyse
He wrouȝte hit not bi partyse
But he þat made al þinge of nouȝt   345
Al þe world togider he wrouȝt
To be set in lengþe and brede
Þe mater firste þerof I rede
Þat is þe elementes to say
Þat firste shaples togider lay   350
He delt hem ful in sixe dayes
In parties as þe scripture sayes
Þe elementes firste in dayes þre
Pre þinges wiþinne hem þer be
Þese elementes þat al þing byndes   355
Foure þer ben as clerkes fyndes
Þe lowest hit is watir and erþe
Þe þridde is eyr and fuyr þe ferþe
And we seye þat he þus bigan
As austyn seiþ þat holy man   360
As we in his bookes fynde
Firste he wrouȝte aungel kynde
Þe world and tyme þese þinges þre
Byfore alle oþere þing made he
Þe world I calle in myne ententes   365
Þe matere of foure elementes
Þat ȝit was þenne of fourme vnshapen
Wherof was siþþe partyes taken
Al shaples was hit not forþy   fol. 2r col. 2
For hit of shappe had sum party   370

---

342   any...herte] manys hert any tyme B.
347   be set] bysette L.
348   firste þerof] þerof fyrst B.
351   in] *om* B.
352   parties] scripture B. scripture] party B.
353   firste] *om* B.
354   hem] *om* L. þer]*om* B.
355   þese] þe TB.
356   Foure] Foure þinges B. þer] they L.
357   hit] *om* L. hit is] bene þe B. and] & þe B.
358   is] þe B. and] the LB., *second* þe] is L.
360   As] And L. þat] þe B.
365   in] be B.
366   of] of þe B.
368   was siþþe] siþ was T; were siþ B.
369   shaples] chapels B.

But perfore shaples hit was how
For hit hadde not as hit haþ now
He wrouȝte vpon þe oþere day
Þe firmamente þat is to say
Þe sky wiþ sterres grete & smalle   375
Wiþ watir shynynge as cristalle
Þat is on hyȝe and þat is vndir
In þis he souned al to wondir
Þe þridde day god dide bi grace
Þe wattres drawe into a place   380
And bad a drye place shulde be
Þe wattres alle he calde þe see
Þe drye he calde erþe þat kynge
And bad hit grisyng fruyt forþ brynge
Al þing to be waxinge þere   385
And in hemself her seed to bere
Þe ferþe he bad and was done
Boþe were made sonne and moone
Eyþer wiþ his dyuerse liȝte
To parte þe day fro þe nyȝte   390
In tokenynge of tydes to stonde
Dayes and ȝeres boþe dwellonde
And þe sterres greete and smale
Þat we may se wiþouten talle
In þe hyȝest element of alle   395
Þereynne fuyre haþ his stalle
Þe fifte day he failed nouȝte
Of watir foul & fysshe he wrouȝte
Þe fisshe to watir as we fynde
Þe foules he toke to the wynde   400
Alle goynge beestes þe sixte day
And adam als he made of clay
He was laste made as lordyng
To be maister ouer al þing
In a dale he wrouȝte adame   405

---

371   shaples] schapels B.
373   oþere] todyr B.
375   sterres] þe sterris L.
377   þat is] In þis B.
380   a] one B.
381   And] He B.
384   grisyng] cresyng L; grayþe & B.
387   bad and] made þat B.
397   fifte] first L; fourþe B.
400   foules] foule LB.
402   als] om B.
405   wrouȝte] made B.

Þat ebron hette in ebreu name
Þese sixe dayes he wrouȝte his wille
Þe seuenþe of werke he helde him stille
He vs ȝaf ensaumpel þore   fol. 2v col. 1
Þat we shulde holde hit euermore   410

Þe firste werke as ȝe herde neuen
God wrouȝ[t]e þe angels of heuen
And sette hem in his hyȝe pales
Wiþouten pryde to ben in pees
For þis peleys was so ryche   415
As myȝty kyng noon oþer lyche
He ordeyned hym two creatures
To serue hym þere wiþ honures
Þat shulde a hool noumber be
Many a þousande to telle and se   420
Þe whiche tale no wey shulde be more
And nedeful bihoued hit wore
Þis noumbrary he ordeyned þon
Shulde be boþe of aungel & mon
For he wolde be þat kyng of crafte   426
Worsheped wiþ two maner shafte   425
Þe ton wiþ aungel þat is goostly
And als wiþ mannes body
Of aungels wolde he serued be
Þat ordres shulde ha þryes þre   430
He chees to hym þat lorde hende
Þat man þe ordre shulde be tende
But þe aungels he wrouȝte formast
Ouer alle he made her pouste past
Þei were boþe faire and wyse   435

---

406   ebreu] ebrews B.
409   ȝaf ensaumpel] ensample ȝafe B.
410   we] he L.
411   werke] weke B. ȝe] we B.
412   wrouȝte] wrouȝe H.
421   tale] in tale L. no wey] *om* L; ne was B.
422   bihoued] byhove L; behoueth B.
423   noumbrary] nombyr L; nombre þat B.
425-6   *reversed in* MSS HTLB.
425   shafte] of shap L.
427   þe ton] That oon LB. aungel] aungelys B. þat is] *om* L.
428   And with man þat bodyly B.
430   þryes] þes B.
432   þat] Than L. man þe] mannys B. tende] þe tende B.
433   aungels] aungell B.
434   her] hys B.
435   faire] few L.

Somme of lasse somme of more prise
He ȝaf on most to knowe & fele
ȝif þat he couþe haue born hym wele
And sette hym beste in his halle
As prynce & syre of oþere alle   440
And for he was so wondir liȝt
Lucifer to name he hiȝt
And whenne he hadde perceyued þis
Þat he was ouer alle oþer in blis
Alas caytif he knewe nouȝt   445
Þat god himseluen hadde hym wrouȝt
Ful sorweful sawe he þat tyde
Aȝeynes god he toke a pryde
Liȝtly he lette of alle his fere   fol. 2v col. 2
To god hymself wolde he be pere   450
Not pere alone but myche moore
For vndir hym he wolde alle wore
And he hymself her commaundour
Who herde euer of siche traytour
Þat he þat not hadde but of hym   455
Aȝeyn his lorde shul[d] waxe so grym
He seide sette my sete I shal
Aȝeynes hym þat is beste of al
In þe norþ syde shal sitte my sete
Seruyse of me shal he noon gete   460
Why shulde I hym seruyse ȝelde
Al shal be at myn owne welde
But he was marred of his wille
Ful soone he fonde hit ful grille
For lenger þen he þouȝte þat pryde   465
In heuen myȝte he not abyde
For in þat court þat is so clene

436   *second* somme] and som B.
440   syre...oþere] lorde above hem B.
441   And] *om* B.
444   ouer... oþer] hyest B.
446   hadde hym] hym had B.
447   sawe] synnyd L.
449   Liȝtly] Lytill L; Wlyghtly B.
450   wolde he] he wold L.
451   Not] No B.
453   her] þere B
454   siche] suche a L. Who...siche] And he hymselfe þere B.
456   shuld] shul H.
459   sitte] y sett B.
462   Al] I T.
466   not abyde] no lenger byde B.

No filþe may dwelle ne be sene
Seynt mychael for her aller riȝt
Roos aȝeyn hym to fiȝte　　　　　　　　　　　　470
Aȝeyn hym ȝaf he batel grym
Out of þat court caste he hym
Lucifer firste doun he brouȝt
And siþþe þat wiþ hym held ouȝt
And scoured þat court of hem so clene　　　　475
Þat siþþe her stide was þere not sene
Þis was þe fende þat formeste felle
For hys pryde from heuen to helle
For þenne his name chaunged was
Fro lucifere to sathanas　　　　　　　　　　480
Fro ful hyȝe he fel ful lawe
Þat of his lorde wolde stonde noon awe
Wiþoute koueryng of his soore
For mercy geteþ he neuer more
For god owe not ȝif hym mercy　　　　　　　485
Þat þeraftir wolde not cry
And þus he loste þat hyȝe tour
Þere was he not fully an hour
For soone aftir þat he was made　　　　fol. 3r col. 1
He fel wiþouten lenger abade　　　　　　　490
Þe oþere aungels þat fel hym wiþ
Whiche forsoke goddes griþ
Aftir þe wille þei to hym bore
Fel þei to helle lasse and moore
Somme in þe erþe somme in þe lifte　　　　495

468　　ne] no B.
469　　aller] ansuerde B.
470　　aȝeyn] aȝenst B.
471　　Aȝeyn]Aȝens B.
472　　þat] the L. caste he] þay caste B.
473　　firste doun] doune fyrst B.
474　　siþþe] alle þo L.
475　　scoured] made B.
476　　þat] *om* B. her] his L; in þat B. not] non B.
479　　For] And B.
481　　ful] *om* T.
482　　wolde...awe] he wille not know L.
483　　Wiþoute...his] And for þat grete trespas & L. koueryng] gouernyng B.
484　　For] *om* L. geteþ] gete B.
485　　owe...hym] wolde ȝeve hym no B.
486　　wolde] wille LB.
489　　þat] *om* B.
490　　wiþouten] & no L. abade] bad B.
492　　Whiche] þe which B.
493　　Aftir...þei] And as many as good wille L. þei to] þat þay B.
495　　erþe] ayre B. lifte] erþ left B.

Þere þei dryȝe ful harde drifte
Her peyne þei bere on hem ay
And so shul do to domes day
But þo þat lesten wiþouten wyte
Were confermed þere as tyte   500
Þei may neuer assente to ille
No moore þen euel may do good wille
Þe noumber þat out of heuen felle
No tonge in erþe hit con telle
Ny fro þe trone of þat blis   505
How fer into helle hit is
But bede seiþ fro erþe to heuen
Is seuen þousande ȝeer & hundrides seuen
By iournees whoso go hit may
Fourty myle eueryche a day   510

Of bodily substaunce for to wite
Monnes soule Þat is hite
As I ȝow telle þe kyng of craft   511
Wolde be worsheped with two shaft
Boþe wiþ aungel & wiþ mon
Adam perfore made was þon
Þe tende order to fulfille   515
Þat lucifer hade made to spille
Of erþe only was adam nouȝt
But of foure elementes wrouȝt
Of watir his body is flesshe laire
His heer of fuyr his honde of ayre   520
His heed wiþynne haþ yȝen tweyn   523
Þe sky haþ sonne & moone certeyn

---

496   dryȝe] abide L.
497   peyne] paynes B.
498   do] *om* T. do to] do til TL; into B.
499   lesten] lefte TLB. wyte] witt B.
500   confermed] conformyd B. þere as] tho as L; also B.
502   good] goddis B.
504   con] may L.
505-6   *om* B.
508   ys vijᶜ vij Mˡ seventen & vij B.
509   whoso] who B.
510   a] *om* TL.
511   telle] tolde TL; say B.
512   Wolde] Wille L. shaft] shap L.
514   Adam þerfore] þerfore adam B.
516   lucifer] lucifel T. to] *om* TL.
517   was adam] Adam was B.
519   is] hys B.
520   heer] hete B. *second* his...of] þe breþe of þe B.

And as me*n*nes yȝen are sette to siȝt   525
So serueþ sonne & moone of liȝt
Maister sterres are þer seuene
Seuen holes haþ ma*n*nes heed euene
Whiche ȝif þ*o*u wolt þe biþinke   fol. 3r col. 2
Þow mayst hem fynde wiþ litel swy*n*ke   530
Þis wynde þ*a*t we men drawen ofte
Bitokeneþ wynde þ*a*t bloweþ olofte
Whiche is þonder & leityng led
As onde wiþ host in brest is breed
Into þe see al watir synkeþ   535
And mo*n*nes womb al licoures dry*n*keþ
His feet hym bereþ vp fro fal
Also þe erþe vpholdeþ al
Thonder fyre ȝyueþ mon his siȝte
Thonder eyer of heryng myȝte   540
Þis wondur wynde hym ȝyueþ onde
Þe erþe makeþ hym fele & fonde
Þe hardenes þat men han in boones
Hit comeþ of þe kynde of stoones
On erþe as groweþ tres and gres   545
So nayle & here of mannes flesshe
Wiþ beestes dou*m*be man haþ fele
Of þing hym likeþ euel or wele
Of þese þinges I haue herd seide
Was adames body togider leide   550

---

525   And] *om* B. me*n*nes] manys B.
526   sonne...moone] þe mone & sun B.
527   are] ben B.
528   Seuen] And vij B.
531   we] *om* B.
532   olofte] on lofte T; of lofte B.
533-4   *om in* L.
534   brest is] brestiþ B.
535   watir] watyrs B.
536   And] So B. womb] body B. licoures] watyrs B.
537   bereþ] beren T.
538   Also] Ryght so B. vpholdeþ] bereþ vp B.
539   mon] a man B.
540   eyer] oþer T; of eyre B.
541   hym] yt L.
543   þe] That B. in] of LB.
544   Hit] *om* L. kynde of] kyndest B.
545   On] Of B. as] þere B.
546   nayle] nayles B.
547   Wiþ] Of L. man] a man B. haþ] of L.
548   wele] ille L.
549   herd] here B.
550   adames] manys B.

For þese resouns þat ȝe haue herde
Man is calde þe lesse werde
// But resoun ȝitt herde ȝe nouȝte
Wherof mannes soule is wrouȝte
Of goostly liȝte men seye hit is   555
Þat god haþ made to his likenes
As preent of seel in wexe þrest
Þerynne he haþ his likenes fest
He haþ hit wrouȝte as frend & fere
No þing to hym is so dere   560
His godhede is in trynite
Þe soule haþ propur þinges þre
Menyng & þat of þinges to se
Þat is and was and euer shal be
Vndirstondynge haþ hit riȝte   565
Of þinges seyn and oute of siȝte
Wisdome also hit haþ in wille
Þe goode to do and leue þe ille
Alle þe myȝtes þat may be   fol. 3v col. 1
Wonen in þe hooly trynite   570
Alle vertues haþ a soule I wis
Þat oute of synne clensed is
And as god þat is in oon & þre
Wiþ no manere creature may be
Vndirgropede ne ouergone   575
But he ouertakeþ euerychone
So þe soule wiþouten wene
To al þing hit is vnsene
Þouȝe hit of al þinge haue siȝt
To se a soule no man haþ myȝt   580

---

551   þese resouns] þis reson B.
552   lesse werde] last werk L.
555   goostly] þe holygoste B.
556   to] in L.
557   seel] wex B. wexe] seale B.
559   &] or L.
561   is] om B.
563   of þinges] ys of þing B.
565   hit] he B.
566   þinges] þing B. oute] nought B.
567   also hit] he B. in] all att B.
569   þe myȝtes] thynggis L.
571   vertues] uvrtours L. a] þe B.
573   þat] om LB.
574   Wiþ] May L. may] om L.
576   After 1.576,B adds a line: þough it of all þing haue be sene.
577   wiþouten] is as I B.
579   þouȝe] Thoght L; ȝef B. þinge] þingis T. haue] haþe B.

Now haue I shewed ȝow þus hider
How two þinges holden man togider
Þe soule is goostly þing to telle
Þe body hit is flesshe and felle
Adam was made of mannes elde   585
As he myȝte hymseluen welde
As austyn seiþ þat lyeþ nouȝte
And wiþouten paradys wrouȝte
Here now ȝe resoun of his name
Why he was calde adame   590
In þis name are foure lettres leide
Þat of þe foure ȝates be seide
As eest. west. norþe. & souþe   594
So myche is adam for to mouþe   593
And þow maist aske wiþouten blame
Why god hym ȝaf so greet a name
For soþe þat is liȝte to rede
Hit tokeneþ adam & his sede
Ouer al þe world shul be sprade
And þerof to be lorde made   600
And as oure lord hadde heuen in honde
So shulde man be lorde of londe
Þerfore he ȝaf hym to bigynne
A lufsome londe to dwellen ynne
A lond of lyf ioyes and delys   605
Whiche men callen paradys
Into þat lond þat swete place
Was adam brouȝte whenne he made wase
He ȝaf hit hym as heritage   fol. 3v col. 2
To ȝelde þerfore no knowlage   610
But to holde hit wel vnbroken
A forbode bitwene hem spoken
But for þat he helde hit nouȝt

585   mannes elde] manne non so eld L.
586   As] Wele L.
587-8   *om in* L.
589   now] mow TL.
590   calde] clepid L.
599   þe world] *om* L. shul] shulde TL.
600   to] schall B. made] I made B.
601   hadde] hath B.
605   delys] delices T.
607   þat] the L.
609   hit...as] hym þere it to B.
610   no] non B.
611   vnbroken] & blythen L.
612   A] And L. forbode] forewarde B.

He made vs alle in bale be brouȝt
In care he brouȝte vs & in sore   615
As I shal telle ȝow forþermore

Of [þe] astate þe world was ynne
Byfore þe tyme of adames synne
Whanne adam was made also soone
In paradise he was done
Þe beestes boþe he & sheo
Adams siȝte were brouȝte to   620
Fisshe in watir & foule to fliȝte
Al was brouȝte in adam siȝte
Alle were brouȝte to serue adame
For þat he shulde ȝyue hem name
Þis kyng þat con his craftes kepe   625
Slyly he made adame to slepe
Out of his syde as seiþ þe booke
Wiþouten sore a ribbe he toke
Of þat ribbe he made a womman
To adam þat was firste his on   630
Whenne sheo to adam was brouȝte
Virago hir name he wrouȝte
Þerfore hette sheo virago
For of þe man made was sho
Naked were þei boþe tweyn   635
Ashamed were þei nouȝt certeyn
God hem blessed & bad hem brede
And multeplye wiþ her in sede
Adam he seide how þinkeþ þe
In þis place is feire to be   640
Þis is a stede of weleful wone
Of ioye and blisse wanteþ hit none
Here lasteþ lyf wiþouten ende

---

615 &] all & B. &...sore] lesse & mor L.
616a þe] *om* H. astate] state B.
619 beestes boþe] besteþ beþ B.
621 in] and L. to] in B.
626 to] *om* B.
627 as] so B.
628 sore] gref L.
629 Of...ribbe] Adam þerof B.
630 To fore adam was alle alone L.
632 he] was B. wrouȝte] tought L.
634 þe] a B.
638 in] *om* L.
641 weleful] weleþful TB.
642 Of] On L. and] no B. wanteþ] lakkeþ B.

Here is no þing to amende
Here is blis þat lasteþ ay   645
Neuer nyȝt bot euer is day
Is no man wiþ herte to þenke   fol. 4r col. 1
Ne clerke þat may wryte wiþ enke
Þe mychel ioye þat hem is lent
Þat done here my commaundement   650
Of trees and fruyt here is good wone
Alle shul þei be þyne but one
Of hem alle þi wille to do
But þat o tre come ȝe not to
Þat stondeþ amyddes paradyse   655
For ȝif ȝe do ȝe be not wise
Þis tre haue I done in friþþe
For I wole haue hit to my griþþe
ȝif ȝe hit touche to ȝow seye yȝe
On doubel deþ shul ȝe dyȝe   660
Beþ war and takeþ good entent
Brekeþ not þis commaunement
Herby may we alle se
Þat he hem ȝaf a wille fre
Þe good to do and leue þe ille   665
Boþe be put in her fre wille
Wit and wisdome he hem ȝaue
Miȝte and fairhede for to haue
Of al erþe made adam kynge
To lasten wiþouten endynge   670
Among hem euermore hele
Telle we sumwhat of his wele
Ar he brake þat god forbade
In mychel blisse was he bistade
Of his wyf so faire and fre   675

---

645   blis] lyȝt B.
646   Neuer] Here ys neuyr B. is] *om* LB.
647   Is] Ther is LB. to] may B.
648   clerke þat] no man B.
651   and] of L.
652   þei] *om* LB.
653   hem] them L. þi] ȝoure B.
654   o tre] one B. ȝe] þe L.
655   amyddes] amaide in L.
656   For] And L.
660   shul ȝe] ȝe schall B.
664   a] *om* L.
666   be] he TL. fre] *om* B.
669   made] he made L.
673   forbade] hym bade B.
674   was he] he was B. bistade] stad TL.

Þat myche myrþe was on to se
Þese beestes coom hym alle aboute
As to her lord hym to loute
Foule in fliȝte fisshe on sonde
Alle bowed hym to foot & honde   680
At his wille þei ȝeode & cam
As he hadde ben makere of ham
Þese beestes were so meke in dole
Wiþouten hirtynge þei ȝeode hole
Among þe wolues lay þe shepe   685
Safly myȝte þei togider slepe
Þe hound harmed not þe hare   fol. 4r col. 2
Ne no beest souȝte oþere to forfare
By þe deer þat now is wilde
As lomb lay þe leoun mylde   690
Þe gryp also bysyde þe bere
No beest wolde to oþere dere
Þe scorpioun forbare his tonge
Fro beestes þat he lay amonge
Al maner þing in dyuerse wyse   695
ȝalde to Adam her seruyse
Þe nedder þo was not bitter
For he was euer wys & witter
For as we rede in booke meest
He was more wys þan any beest   700
Þe sonne was þat tyme we say
Seuen siþe briȝtere þan now a day
Þe mone was þat tyme also briȝt
As sonne now on dayes liȝt
Holde no mon þis for no foly   705
Þe prophete seiþ þus ysay

---

677   þese] That L.
678   hym] þay gan B.
679   in fliȝte] and B. on] on þe B.
680   hym to] to hym B. foot] fete B.
684   hirtynge] hurt L.
686   myȝte þei togider] to gadyr myght þay B.
687   hound] houndys B.
688   no beest] none B. forfare] fare L.
689   þat] as L.
690   lomb] a lambe L. mylde] wyld L.
692   No] None B. to] do L; þo B.
694   Fro] For B.
696   ȝalde] ȝeldyd B.
697   þo was] was þe B.
700   more wys] wyser LB.
704   now] ys now B. dayes] the day LB.
705   second no] om B.

Alle þinges as we may se
Hyȝe or lowe in world þat be
Þei were of gretter strengþe & myȝt
Bifore þat adam dide vnriȝt   710
//To adam soone was sent a sonde
Þat souȝte hym selly for to fonde
Whenne sathan sey þat he was chosen
To haue þe blis þat he hadde losen
Sory he was þat false file   715
And þouȝte man to bigyle
He þouȝte þo ioyes for to stynte
Þat god to mankynde hadde mynte
Aȝeyn god he wexe so grille
His hondewerke he þouȝte to spille   720
And trowed wiþ his greet enuy
Of god to wynne þe maystry
Now man is sett bitwene two
On eiþer syde he haþ a foo
Bitwene Sathan and his wyf   725
Adam is sette in mychel stryf
Boþe were þei on adame   fol. 4v col. 1
For to brynge hym into blame
Boþe þei ben on o party
To ouercome man wiþ tricchery   730
Þe wyly fend hym helde on hyȝe
Hym geyned not com adam nyȝe
Namely in his owne shap
To spede he hoped ha non hap
Þerfore a messangere he sende   735
By whom beste to spede he wende
Þenne he chees a litel beest

---

707   Alle þinges]As alle thyng L. as]þat B.
708   or] and LB.
710   Bifore] Afore B.
712   souȝte] thoght L.
714   hadde] haþe B.
715   file] vyle L.
716   to] for to B.
717   þo] þe TLB. ioyes] Iewis L.
719   Aȝeyn] Ayens B.
721   wiþ] thorog LB.
728   into] to L.
729   on] of L.
730   wiþ tricchery] witterly B.
732   geyned] gayne B. com] to come L.
733   Namely] And namely B.
734   spede] speke B. ha] to haue B. non] no TL.

Whiche is not vnwylyeest
Þe nedder þat is of siche a shaft 740
Moost of queyntyse & of craft
Queyntly tauȝte he hym þe gynne
At þe wyf to bygynne
And þourȝe þe wyf to wynne þe man
Þenne gooþ þis neddre & not blan 745
In his slow satan þenne was
Wondur is he entred in þat plas
But of his sufferaunce he hym lete
Þat beest wiste how þat bale to bete
For mon he made þat he mouȝte 750
Synne or leue as hym good þouȝte
And by skile of his owne dede
Shulde be merked þenne his mede
To bowe and lyue wiþouten ende
Or elles to dyȝe and to woo wende

How adam brake goddes commaundement
Wherfore kynde of man was shent
Adam wandride in þat wele 755
In myche myrþe ioye & hele
When adam was fro eue a þrawe
Þe nedder nyȝe to hir gon drawe
And seide womman telle me why
Þat ȝe ete not al comynly 760
In paradise of eueryche tre
She seide sertes so nowe do we
Of alle trees but of one

---

738 Whiche] Why L. vnwylyeest] þe vnwyliest L.
739 shaft] shap L. nedder] addyr B.
741 gynne] Iynne L.
742 þe] hys B.
744 þis neddre] þe adder B.
745 satan þenne] þan satan L; Sathan B.
746 Wondur] Wonderly LB. is he] om L.
748 first þat] The L. second þat] hys B.
752 þenne his] þat ys B.
753 bowe] bye B. lyue] loue B.
754 to woo] wo to L.
754a goddes] þe L.
754b kynde] þe kynde B.
755 wele] well B.
756 hele] wele B.
757 a þrawe] ydraw L.
758 nedder] addyr B.
761 line om B.
762 followed by Bote onely of þis one tre B.

Þat is outtake to vs alone
Oure lord in forbode haþ hit leide   765 fol. 4v col. 2
Wost þow þe why: nay sheo seide
But sheo seide ȝif we come þer nyȝe
On doubel deeþ shul we dyȝe
Þis o tre shulde himseluen haue
And alle þe oþere to vs he ȝaue   770
And trowest þow þat hit so be
As he ȝow seide sheo seide ȝe
Nay seide he wiþ greet tresoun
But þerynne liþ suche resoun
But for he wolde not ȝe were   775
Paryngal to hym nor pere
Þe soþe fro ȝow wole I not hyde
He woot wel þat what tyme or tyde
Þat ȝe hadde eten of þat tre
As goddes shulde ȝe boþe be   780
To knowe boþe good and ille
ȝe shulde be lordes at ȝoure wille
Of hit ȝe ete so rede I ȝow
And ȝe shul fynde hit for ȝoure prow
Þis hetyng was þat tyme ful mykel   785
But hit was ful false and fikel
Soone so sheo þis fruyt bihelde
Sheo ȝerned hit to haue in welde
Sheo let not for drede nor blame
But took and ete & ȝaf adame   790
What bote is longe þis tale to drawe
Þei ete hit boþe in litel þrawe

---

764   to...alone] of euerychone B.
765   hit] vs B.
766   Wost þow] Wotyst L. þe] neuer B.
768   shul we] we schull B.
769   shulde] schall B.
770   oþere] todyr B.
772   ȝow] the L.
773   wiþ greet] withoute B.
775   wolde not] nold L. ȝe] þat ye ne L; þat he B.
776   Paryngal] Egall L. to] wiþ B. nor] ner no L; no B.
777   fro] for B.
779   hadde eten] ete B. þat] þis B.
780   goddes] god is so L. shulde] schall B.
782   shulde] schull B.
786   hit] his T. ful] þat tyme B.
787   Soone so] So sone as B.
788   ȝerned] lykyd L.
789   nor] ne L.
791   bote...to] is it bot lenger B.
792   hit] of yt L; om B. in] in a L; a B.

Al for nouȝte þei ete hit boþe
Wherfore oure lord god was wroþe
For þat ilke appeles bitte   795
Her sones teeþ eggen ȝitte
And so shal do til domes day
Here aȝeyn may no man say
Whenne eyþer sawe oþer naked
For shame þei stoode boþe & quaked   800
Þenne þei sey þat bare þei were
In welþe and ioye þat were clad ere
Þei hullud hem I telle hit þe
Wiþ leues of a fige tre
Whenne þe fend þus hadde hem nome   805 fol. 5r col. 1
Wel he wende ha god ouercome
And seide wiþynne his sory þouȝt
I haue made hym worche for nouȝt
His heuen shal he haue his one
Of adam part geteþ he none   810
To brynge into þat heritage
Þat I have lost bi myn outrage
He lyȝed fals þeef for why
ȝitt hadde god of adam mercy
Þat he were lost god wolde nouȝt   815
For he wiþ tricchery was souȝt
Þe fend was wel moore to blame
Þat so falsely gyled adame
God wiste þe fend had adam blent
ȝitt wolde he not þat he were shent   820
But pouȝe he wolde· ȝyue adam grace
First shulde he byȝe dere þat trespace

---

796   eggen] akyn L; eggyd B. ȝitte] tyte B.
797   do] om B. til] tell L.
798   Here] þer B.
800   boþe] om L.
801   sey] seid L. bare] boþe L.
802   welþe] wele B.
803   I] as I B. hit] om B.
805   þus hadde] had þus L.
806   ha god] god to L; he had god B.
809   his one] allone B.
812   lost] left L. bi] þorough B.
813   fals þeef] falsly B.
814   of] on L.
815   god wolde] þat wold god B.
818   gyled] begyled B.
821   pouȝe] thoght L; ȝef B.
822   shulde he] he schall B. þat] hys B.

Of Þe astate Þe world was Inne
Aftir Þe tyme of adames synne
Als fast as þei had done þat synne
Oure wo bigan to bigynne
Al maner blis fro hem was went   825
For þei brake þat commaundement
Soone bigan he vengeaunce kyþe
As lord þat firste was meke & bliþe
Al bigan to stire and stryf
Aȝeyn adam and eue his wyf   830
Bytwene hemself roos stryf also
Þe strenger beest þe weyker slo
Vchone of oþere to make his pray
As we may se now vche day
Fro þat tyme firste coom deþ to man   835
And þat tyme al oure wo bigan
Þese wronges þat ben of euel wrake
Þere bigynnynge dide þei take
Synne and sake shame & stryf
Þat now ouer al þe world is ryfe   840
Mercy lord strong wickedhede
Made adam do so foule a dede
Hymself hadde lost & al his kyn   fol. 5r col. 2
But oure lord hadd raunsoumde hym
On suche a wise as he hadde þouȝt   845
Byfore er he þe worlde wrouȝt
But þat was not done al for nede
But þourȝe his owne nobelhede
For ȝif he hadde wolde he myȝte man
Wel better ha made þen he was þan   850

822a astate] state B.
822b þe] *om* TL.
824   wo bigan] lorde wraþ gan B.
828   As] þat B.
830   Aȝeyn] Aȝens B.
831   roos] wex B.
832   slo] dud slo T; to slo B.
834   day] a day B.
835   Fro] For L. firste ... deþ] com deþe fyrst B.
838   þei] ther L.
842   so] þat B. a] *om* B.
843   hadde] he had B.
844   But] But sythyn L. hadd] *om* L.
845   he] *om* L.
846   he] *om* B. wrouȝt] was wrought B.
848   þourȝe] for B. nobelhede] noble dede L.
850   þen] þat B.

Wiþ flesshe þerfore he coom in place
And filled þis world of his grace
His grace hit was & noon oþere
Þat he wolde bicome oure broþere
Wiþ þe fend þerfore he fauȝte   855
And wiþ his fadir he made vs sauȝte
//Leue we now of þis spelle
Of oure story furþere to telle
Whenne adam sey he had mysdone
He wente to hyde hym also soone   860
He wende to hyde hym among þe trees
Fro his siȝte þat al sees
Al for nouȝte hym hidde adame
Oure lord hym called by his name
Lord he seide Whenne I þe herde   865
For I sawe þat I mysferde
I and my wyf wente vs to hyde
Shame vs pouȝte þe to abyde
For oure bodyes al bare were
Adam he seide so tolde I þe ere   870
I þe tolde meest and leest
What hit was to breke my heest
But now is þis appel eten
And my biddyng is forȝeten
And þat þou hast þus done þis mys   875
Þiseluen is to wite I wis
Lorde he seide of þis gilt here
Is sheo to wyte þat is my fere
Þat þow me ȝaf my wyf to be
For principally sheo beede hit me   880
Sheo bede hit me wiþouten blynne
Sheo haþ me fyled wiþ her synne
Al þis may sheo not ȝeynsey   fol. 5v col. 1
Sheo owe to bere þe gilte awey
Ihesu seide to hir anoon   885

---

851   in] to B.
852   filled] hilled T.
856   he] om B.
858   Of oure] And of þis B. furþere] forþe L.
860   also] full B.
861   wende] went B.
866   For] om L.
870   þe] om B.
875   þus] om LB.
879   þat] And þat B.
882   fyled] foulyd B. her] þis B.
885   Ihesu] God L; Oure lorde B.

Why dudest þou þis dede wommon
Sheo seide þe worme me drowe þertille
Þat I haue done aȝeyn þi wille
To þat worm of wraþþe & wrake
Oure lord þenne þus he spake   890
Þow worme þou shalt acursede be
Moore þen any oþere beest to se
For on þi wombe þow shalt slyde   894
Moore þen any oþer beest in tyde   893
Fro þis day forþ shal hate be   895
Forsoþe bitwene womman and þe   896
Erþe shal be þi mete for nede   898
Bytwene [þin] and wommannes sede   897
Womman to stynge awaite þou shal
And pyn heed ȝitt tobreke sheo shal   900
Þouȝe þou in hete euer wolde be sted
In colde shal euere be þi bed
And þou wommon for þis dere
In sorwe shalt þou þi childer bere
Þow shalt be slayn wiþ double dede   905
Harde hit is for to rede
Þow shalt be vndir mannes heeste
To hem be buxome meest & leste
Þow shalt haue euer þi heed hid   910
Þi shame shal not be vnkid   909
And ȝitt þat þow now hast mysgoon
Hit shal be [b]et bi a wommon
Of synneles man made I þe
In womman shal ȝitt my wonyng be
But hit shal not be ȝitte so nyȝe   915
To keuer my loos firste mot I hyȝe

---

887   me drowe] drofe me B.
889   þat] thou L; þe B.
890   he] to hym B.
893-4   *reversed in* MSS GHTLB.
894   slyde] glyde B.
895   forþ] foreward B. hate] þou hatid L; yt B.
896   and] *om* L.
897-8   *reversed in* MSS GHTLB.
897   þin] *om* H; þe B.
900   ȝitt tobreke] tobreke ȝit T; ȝett breke B. ȝitt] *om* L.
904   shalt þou] þou shalt L.
906   to] þy B.
909-10   *reversed in* MSS HTLB.
911   now ... mysgoon] hast now mysdone B.
912   be] *om* L. bet] et H; holpe B.
915   be ȝitte] ȝitt be T; ȝet be it B.
916   keuer] rekevir L. mot] mon L.

And þou man þat haast vndirtaken
Þi wyues rede and myne forsaken
Noþing shalt þou þerwiþ wynne
Þe world is cursed of þi synne   920
In erþe shalt þow swete & swynke
Wynne þat þou shalt ete & drynke
Alle þe dayes of þyn elde   fol. 5v col. 2
Breres and þornes hit shal þe ȝelde
Þerof shalt þou ete gresses sere   925
Þow shalt bye þi breed ful dere
Til þow turne aȝeyn & quake
To þat erþe þow were of take
For þou art now but pouder pleyne
To pouder shalt þow turne aȝeyne   930
He turnede þenne his wyfes name
And Eue fro þenne hir cald adame
Eue sheo hette fro þat day
Þat modir of many is to say
God made hem þo curteles of hyde   935
Þerwiþ her flesshe for to shryde
Lo he seide Adam how
Likeþ þe þis dede now
I made euel and good to ȝow knowen
But ȝee were soone ouerþrowen   940
ȝe trespassed at þe tre of lyf
Þerfore ȝe ben in woo and stryf
He put hem out of þat plase
Into þe world þere þei made wase
Adam dere hit shal be bouȝte   945
Til hit be bet þat þou hast wrouȝte
Take þi wyf in þi honde
Leue ȝee shul þis lufsum londe
Into þe wrecched world to be

---

917   And] And take B.
922   Wynne] To wyn B. &] or L.
924   hit…ȝelde] schall be þy telde B.
925   shalt þou] schaltow B.
927   &] in T.
930   shalt þow] þow schalt B.
931   þenne]þo B.
932   hir] om B.
935   þo] þenne TLB.
936   shryde] hyde B.
939   ȝow knowen] ȝour knowing B.
940   ouerþrowen] ouer trowing B.
944   þei] he B.
946   Til] To B. bet] bote L.

Þi lyf shal þinke longe to þe   950
Longe peyne þere shalt þou dryȝe
And siþþen on doubel deeþ to dyȝe
ȝe shul be flemed fro my face
Til þat I ȝow sende my grace
Þe oyle of mercy ȝee mote abyde   955
I hete to sende hit ȝow sum tyde
Alas seide adam woo is me
Þat I trowed not lorde to þe
Lorde my lyf is me ful looþ   960
Þat I euere made þe wrooþ   959
I woot but þe I haue no frende
Tel me er I fro þe wende
What manere and wiþ wha[t] þinge   fol. 6r col. 1
May I gete þi sauȝtelynge
Adam he seide wel seystou now   965
Herkene I wole telle þe how
Amonge þine oþere werkes hende
Of þi wynnyng ȝyue me þe tende
Of al þi fruyt holde partyes nyne
And I wole þat þe tenþe be myne   970
Lord he seide þou ȝyuest al
Why shulde þi part be so smal
Þe haluendeel or parte þe þridde
We wole þe ȝyue ȝif þow bidde   974
Þenne was he put out almeste naked   989
Into þe londe þere he was maked   990
Þerynne he led a longe lyf
And gate childeren bi his wyf
Out is he put adam þe wrecched
Fro paradyse fully flecched

---

951   þere] yet L. shalt þou] þou schalt B.
952   siþþen] aftyr B.
954   ȝow...my] sende þe oyle of B.
956   hete to] schall B.
958   trowed...þe] schall not þy face se B.
962   er] now or B.
963   *first* What] On what B. *second* what] whaþ H.
966   I] & I B.
967   þine...werkes] þi werkys oþer B.
969   þi] þe B.
970   And] For B. þat] *om* B.
972   shulde] schall B.
973   parte] *om* B.
975-88   *not in* MSS GHTLB.
990   þere] þat B.
993   he] *om* B.
994   fully] fouly T; foule e L. flecched] flyghtid L; flitted B.

A wal of fyre þer is aboute 995
May noon come yn þat is þeroute
An aungel haþ þe ȝate to gete
Wiþ swerde in honde of myche hete
//To telle man wiþ þi lore
What lond is paradise and whore 1000
Siþþe we here þerof spelle
Good hit were for to telle
Paradys hit is a pryue place
Ful of myrþe and of solace
Þe louelyest of alle londes 1005
Towarde þe eest in erþe hit stondes
Londe of lyf of roo and reste
Wiþ blisse and bote broiden beste
Þere euer is day and neuer nyȝte
And al aboute ful of liȝte 1010
Mony vertues þere is sene
Þe herbes euer ylyche grene
Mony oþere blisses elles
Floures þat ful swete smelles
Trees of fruyt of dyuerse mete 1015
Þat dyuerse vertues han to ete
Þat ȝif man ete oþer while of oon fol. 6r col. 2
Hunger shal he neuer haue noon
ȝif he ete of anoþere tree
Fursty shal he neuer be 1020
Þe þridde whoso eteþ moore or les
Shal he neuer haue werynes
Of oon who so eteþ at þe laste
In oon elde shal he euer be faste
Sekenes shal he neuer noon dryȝe 1025
Ne neuer shal his body dyȝe

---

996   þeroute] withoute B.
997   gete] kepe B.
1002   for] þerof B.
1003   hit] om B.
1004   myrþe] might L.
1005   þe] om B.
1007   second of] & B.
1010   ful of] is euer B.
1011   is] be B.
1013   Mony] And many B. blisses] blys B.
1015-1140   missing in MS B (leaf lost).
1020   Fursty] Thurst L.
1021   whoso] who TLB.
1022   werynes] wrethnes L.
1023   so]om L.

Hit is an orcharde of delyces
Wiþ all swetenes of dyuerse spices
Who so dwelleþ þere him þar not longe
Her soun is softe & swete of songe   1030
Soun of foules þat þere syngeþ
I mydde þat londe a welle spryngeþ
Þat renneþ oute of foure stremes
Passynge into dyuerse remes
Þese stremes þat þus þere bygynne   1035
Þourȝe mony oþere londes þei rynne
Þe firste is tigre wiþouten lees
Þen iules pigre and eufratees
Þei bringe stoones fro paradis
So preciouse nowhere founden is   1040
Þis paradis is sette so hye
Miȝte neuer flode come þer nye
Hit was free of noeus floode
Þat al þis world ones ouerȝode

How caym þe cursed wiþ wowe
Abel his broþer slowe
Now adam is in erþe bistad   1045
Wiþ gras & leeues is he clad
Soore he swanke & eue his wyf
Vpon þe erþe to wynne her lyf
Wiþ myche swynke was þat þei wan
Þe firste þei were to sawe bigan   1050
Þe firste childe þat euer sheo bare
Was caym cursed ful of care
And aftir hym I wole ȝow telle
A blessed childe hiȝte abelle
Þis abel was a blessed blode   1055 fol. 6v col. 1
And caym was þe fendes fode
Was neuer worse of modir born
Þerfore was he aftir forlorn
Þis abel was an herde of fee
Blessed and holy man was he   1060

1028   of dyuerse] and of L.
1029   þar] dare L.
1030   Her] His L.
1031   Soun] The note L.
1032   spryngeþ] ther spryngyþ L.
1044a   þe] *om* TL. wowe] vow L.
1050   to sawe] þat sowe L.
1055   blessed] blesfull L.
1057   modir] body L.

Riʒtwis he was goddes frende
And trewely ʒaf to him his tende
For his offerynge was riʒtwise
God payed was of his sacrifise
For caym ʒaf his wiþ euel wille   1065
Oure lord loked not þertille
For þis tiþe þat þei delt   1068
Caym þat I tofore of melt   1067
To his broþere yre bare
Alas þat he bouʒte sare   1070
Aʒeyn abel he roos in stryf
Wiþ murþ[r]e brouʒte hym of his lyf
Wiþ a cheke boon of an asse
Men seyn abel slayn wasse
Whenne caym hadde his broþer sloon   1075
He wolde haue hidde his cors anoon
But preued was soone his sory pride
Þat body myʒte he no weye hyde
For vndir erþe myʒte hit not reste
Þe cley vp þe body keste   1080
His broþer deeþ he wende stille
But myʒte he not þe body hille
Þerfore men say ʒit to þis tyde
Is noone þat longe murþer may hyde
// Whenne he hadde done þis deolful dede   1085
To his fadir hoom he ʒede
Whenne his fadir yʒe on him kast
A sikyng of his hert out brast
For mystrowynge hadde he soone
Þat he sum wickede dede hadde done   1090
For by his chere he say hym wrooþ
So loked he euer breme and looþ
Sone he seide to me þow tel
Where hastou done þi broþer abel
He vnswered wordes were vnmylde   1095 fol. 6v col. 2
Whenne was I kepere of þi chylde

1067-8   *reversed in* MSS GHTLB.
1067   tofore] byfore L.
1068   þei] he L.
1072   murþre]murþe H.
1077   preued] þurveid L.
1078   þat] So that L.
1088   of] out of L. out] *om* L.
1091   say] made L.
1092   breme] grym L.
1095   wordes were] wiþ wordis L.

Tiþinge of hym con I telle noon
To brenne his tiþe he bigon
Vpon þe felde his fadir went
To seche abel wiþ his entent   1100
Þe fadir and þe modir boþe
To blame caym were ful loþe
Til þat þei þe soþe hadde seene
Of þing þei wiste not but bi weene
Hem þou3te kynde hym wolde forbede   1105
To haue done so cursed a dede
His dede hadde euer ben hid
Ne hadde ihesu hymself hit kid
Hit to hide my3te he nou3t
For ihesu þat al wrou3t   1110
He þat firste flemed adam
For þat appel þat he nam
He nolde not hymself feyne
But caymes dede fully atteyne
And he wole þat men bye þe outrage   1115
Þat murþereþ so his owne ymage
He wende to haue scaped wiþ al
For any mannes clepe or cal
But þenne coom oure makere
To speke wiþ þat traytour þere   1120
Of þat morth and þat tresoun
He dide þat traytour to aresoun
// Caym where is þi broþer abelle
Certes he seide I con not telle
Aske his fadir where he be   1125
For he was not bitake to me
God seide telle me & not layne
Whi hastou þi broþer slayne
His blood on erþe shedde hit is
And aftir wreche cryeþ I wis   1130
Hit leueþ not wreche to crye

1098   brenne] greme L.
1102   were] þey wer L.
1103   þat] *om* L.
1107   ben] by L.
1108   Ne hadde] Nadde T; Ne L. ihesu] God T. kid] had kyd L.
1110   ihesu] god T.
1114   atteyne] taynt L.
1116   murþereþ] murdrid L.
1121   morth] murdour L.
1122   þat] anon þat L. to aresoun] reson L.
1128   hastou] hast þou L.
1131   wreche] thy wreche L.

For to shewe þi felonye
For þi synful werke to se
Erþe þow shalt now cursed be
Þat so resceyued þi broþer blode   1135 fol. 7r col. 1
Wiþ pyne hit shal þe ȝelde þi fode
For þi mychel felonye
Þis whete shal waxe cockul hye
In stide of þyn oþere seede
Þe shal not growe but þorn & wede   1140
For þyne euele wrecched hede
Þow shal euer lede þi lyf in nede
Þi dredeful dede haþ no make
Of alle dedes hit is out take
Sikerly I telle þe here   1145
Þow shalt hit bye ful selly dere
For þouȝe I wolde forȝyue hit þe
Hit is not worþi forȝyuen to be
To what cuntre so þow wende
Shalt þou no man fynde þi frende   1150
Among what folke þat þou abide
Þow and þyne be knowen shal wyde
Wiþ alle shal þou be knowen vile
Where þow wendes in exile
My hondewerke þus eguþ me   1155
Þat I shal take vengeaunce on þe
For how shulde any erþely flesshe
Dwelle wiþ þe in sikernes
Whenne felowshepe & broþerhede
Myȝte þe not kepe from foul dede   1160
// Caym say his synne was knowed
And þat þe erþe hadde hit showed
He wiste aȝeynseyinge was noon

1132   For] And for L.
1134   Erþe] *om* L.
1135   resceyued]distroied L.
1138   cockul] cokyld L.
1139   þyn] *om* L.
1140   þe...wede] To þe ne shall grow corne ne whete L.
1142   euer] *om* B. in] eu*er* in B.
1147   þouȝe] ȝef B.
1149   cuntre] court L.
1150   Shalt þou] Schaltow B.
1153   shal þou] schaltow B. knowen] holden TLB.
1154   Where] Whereso B. in] by L.
1155   eguþ] ought B.
1156   I...on] vengance schall I take of B.
1161   his] þis B. knowed] coude B.
1163   was] was þ*er* B.

Oure lord he vnswered sone þon
Lord he seide nowe se I wele   1165
My synne haþ sette me in vnsele
I am ouertake wiþ siche tresoun
I am not worþi to haue pardoun
I shal be flemed for my synne
Vnkouþe londe to dwelle wiþynne   1170
In vnkouþe londe shal ende my wo
Whenne þei me fynde þei wol me slo
So fer I woot I shal be flede
God wolde nowe I were dede
Nay seide oure lord beþ hit not so   1175 fol. 7r col. 2
Al þat þe seeþ shal not þe slo
But I shal sette on þe my merke
Alle shul hit se to rede as clerke
Shal noon be so bolde þe to sloo
But þi falsede to wite hem fro   1180
In token of þi lastynge penaunce
Þe shal be lent a long meschaunce

Whenne adam abelles body fonde
For sorwe a fote myȝt he not stonde
To bury þei his body bere   1185
Adam and eue wiþouten fere
Þis is þe mon men sayn was born
Boþe his fadir & modir biforn
He hadde his eldermodir maydenhede
And at his buryinge al maner lede   1190
A hundride wynter fro þis stryf
Adam þenne forbare his wyf
For sorwe of abel þat was slayn
Til counfort was sende him aȝayn
Bode word cam hym fro heuene   1195

1164   he] *om* B. sone] *om* L.
1166   sette] let L.
1169   for] fro LB.
1170   Vnkouþe] Vnkond T. wiþynne] Inne TB.
1171   shal] schall I B.
1174   God wolde] Wolde god B. I] þat I B.
1175   beþ...not] yt shalle not be L.
1176   þe seeþ] the seith L; þou seyst B. not þe] þe not B.
1178   to] & B. clerke] a clerk L.
1185   þei] *om* B. bere] did bere L; þay it beere B.
1189   eldermodir] elder B.
1190   *line om* B.
1191   fro] aft*er* L; for B.
1194   Til] To B.
1195   Bode] A L; Gode B. hym] to hym LB.

And bade hym by an auₙgels steuene
Þat he shulde wiþ his wyf mete
For oure lorde hadde ordeyned ȝete
A childe to ryse in his osprynge
Þat many shulde out of bale brynge   1200
He þat shulde saue þe folke fro synne
Shulde not be borne of caymes kynne
//Heraftir was born an holy childe
Seeth þat was boþe meke & mylde
Of whom cryst hymseluen caam   1205
Ful fer to telle fro firste adam
Þis childe was goddes frende
And trewely ȝaf to hym his tende
He ȝaf hym al þat hym byhoued
His breþer as hymself he loued   1210
Eue þouȝte herof ful feire
Þat god wolde sende hem siche an heire
For abel was hem woo Inowȝe
Þat caym so his broþere slowȝe
Of adam telleþ þis story   1215 fol. 7v col. 1
Þat he sones hadde þritty
And douȝteres also fele to telle
Wiþouten caym and abelle
Þe sister was ȝyuen to þe broþer
Þe lawe þenne myȝte be noon oþere   1220
So wolde god hit moste nede
To do oure kynde for to sprede
Vnsely kaym þat was in hate
Wiþ god and man at foul debate
Nouþer he ne his ospringe   1225

1196   an] *om* L.
1198   hadde] hath LB. ȝete] yt LB.
1199   ryse] rayse B.
1203   Heraftir] Thereafter L.
1206   fro firste] of B.
1207   childe] Ilke chyld B.
1208   And trewely] þat tendyrly B. to] *om* B.
1210   hymself] him T.
1211   herof] þerof B.
1213   was hem] were they L; was her B.
1214   þat] Which þat B. so] *om* B. his broþere] hym felonsly L.
1216   sones hadde] had sonys B.
1217   also] as B.
1220   þenne] ȝafe it B.
1221   hit moste] at þat tyme was L.
1222   kynde] kynrede B.
1224   at foul] full att B.
1225   ne] ner L; nor B.

Loued oure lord no maner þinge
For þei hym greued in her dedes
He hem forsoke in alle her nedes
To do þe euele myche þei souȝte
Awe of hym stode þei nouȝte   1230
Þat bouȝte þei aftir wyf & chylde
Wiþ watir were þei drenched wylde
As ȝee shul here how hit bifel
Of noe floode whenne I shal tel
For alle were euele & noone gode   1235
Þei drenched alle in noeus flode

Of adam endynge telle wolle I
And of þe oyle of mercy
Adam past nyne hundride ȝere
No wonder þei he wex vnfere
Al forwrouȝte wiþ his spade
Of his lyf he wex al mate   1240
Vpon his spade his breste he leyde
To seeth his son þus he seyde
Sone he seide þow moste go
To paradyse þat I coom fro
To cherubyn þat ȝate warde   1245
Þat kepeþ þo ȝates swyþe harde
Seeth seide to his fadir þere
How stondeþ hit fadir and where
I shal þe telle he seyde to sey
How þow shalt take þe riȝte wey   1250
Towarde þe eest ende of þe ȝonder vale
A grene way fynde þow shale
In þat wey shaltou fynde and se   fol. 7v col. 2
Þe steppes of þi modir and me
Forwelewed in þat gres grene   1255

1229   þe] *om* B. euele myche] the worste alle L. souȝte] þought B.
1230   stode] had LB.
1234   shal] *om* B.
1235   alle were] þay were all B.
1236   noeus] þe B.
1238   þei] yef B. wex] were B.
1239   Al forwrouȝte] And euyr wroght B.
1240   No wondyr þough he were made B. mate] made T.
1245   þat] the L.
1246   þo] the LB.
1249   he seyde] þe soþe B. sey] seeth L.
1250   How] *om* L. take...wey] hold ovir this heth L.
1251   þe] *om* L. vale] wall B.
1253   shaltou] shalt þou L. fynde and] *om* B.
1255   Forwelewed] Forstopyn L; forwelkyd B.

Þat euer siþen haþ ben sene
Þere we comen goynge as vnwyse
Whenne we were put fro paradyse
Into þis ilke wrecchede slade
Þere myself firste was made   1260
For þe greetnes of oure synne
Miȝte siþen no gras growe þerynne
Þat same wole þe lede þi gate
Fro heþen to paradise ȝate
He seide fadir say me þi wille   1265
What shal I saye þe aungel tille
Þow shalt hym seye I am vnwelde
For longe lyued and am in elde
And so in stryf and sorwe stad
Þat forwery I waxe al mad   1270
Þow him pray som worde me sende
Whenne I shal fro þis worlde wende
Anoþer ernede shal þer be
Þat he me sende worde bi þe
Wheþer I shal haue hit ouȝte in hyȝe   1275
Þat me was hette þe oyle of mercyȝe
Whenne I was dryuen fro paradis
And leste hit by my foly nys
Aȝeyn þe wille of god I wrouȝte
Sumdel I haue hit bouȝte   1280
My sorwe haþ euer siþen ben newe
Now were hit tyme on me to rew
// Seeth wente forþ wiþouten nay
To paradyse þat same day
He fonde þe steppes hym to wyse   1285

1257   comen] were L. as] boþe L.
1259   ilke] selfe B.
1260   myself] I myselfe B.
1262   siþen] Seth B.
1263   þi] om B.
1264   heþen] hennes TLB.
1265   fadir] aftyr B.
1268   lyued] lying B. and am] am I T.
1269   And so] Also B. sorwe stad] sebyll state B.
1270   waxe al] am nye L.
1272   þis] þe B.
1274   worde]some worde B.
1275   Wheþer] Wher TLB.
1278   And...by] þat I loste for B.
1279   Aȝeyn] Aȝens B.
1281   euer...newe] ben euer seþe to now B.
1282   hit] om B. on] of B.
1284   þat] þe TB.

Til he come to paradyse
Whenne he þerof hadde a siȝte
He was aferde of þat liȝte
So greet liȝte he say þere
A brennynge fyre he wende hit were   1290
He blessid hym as his fadir bad
And wente forþ & was not drad
Þe aungel at þe ȝate he fond   fol. 8r col. 1
He asked him of his erond
Seeth set tale on ende   1295
And tolde whi he was sende
He tolde him of his fadir care
And of his elde & of his fare
But sende him worde whenne he shal dyȝe
Lenger to lyue may he not dryȝe   1300
And whenne god hadde hym diȝte
Þe oyle of mercy þat was hiȝt
Whene cherubyn his ernde herde
Mekely he hym vnswerde
To ȝonder ȝate þou go & loute   1305
Þi hede wiþynne þi body wiþoute
And tente to þingis wiþ al þi myȝte
Þat shul be shewed to þi siȝte
Whenne seeth a whyle had loked In
He say so mychel wele & wyn   1310
In erþe is no tunge may telle
Of flouris fruyt & swete smelle
Of ioye & blis so mony a þinge
Amydde þe londe he say a sprynge
Of a welle of honoure   1315
Fro hir renne stremes foure
Fison. gison. tigre & eufrate

1286   Til] To B.
1290   A] *om* B.
1292   drad] adrad B.
1294   He] And B.
1295   Seeth] þo Seþe B. tale] the tale LB.
1296   tolde] tolde hym B. sende] þeder sent B.
1297   fadir] *om* L.
1299   But sende] Send þou L. But...worde] Gode worde sende hym B.
1301   god] þat god B.
1302   þat] which L.
1305   ȝonder] þe yondyr B. ȝate] yerd L.
1308   þi] þe be B.
1312   fruyt] of froyte B. &] *om* B. smelle] of smell B.
1316   Fro] Of B. hir] yt L. renne] ronne L; springeþ B.
1317   gison] Eyson L.

Alle erþe þese witen erly & late
Ouer þat welle þen loked he
And say þere stonde a mychel tre   1320
Wiþ braunches fele no bark þat bere
Was þer no lyf in hem þere
Seeth bigan to þenke whyȝe
Þat þis tre bicoom so dryȝe
And on þe steppes þouȝte he þon   1325
Þat dryed were for synne of mon
Þat ilke skil dude hym to mynne
Þe tre was dryȝe for adam synne
He coom þo to þat aungel shene
And tolde hym þat he hadde sene   1330
Whenne he hadde hym þus toold
He bad hym efte goo & biholde
2 He loked in efte & stood þeroute   fol. 8r col. 2
And say þingis þat made him doute
Þis tre þat I of eer seyde   1335
A nedder hit hadde aboute bileyde
Cherubyn þe aungel briȝte
Bad hym go se þe þridde siȝte
3 Him þouȝte þenne þat he seiȝe   1340
Þis forseyd tre rauȝte ful heiȝe   1339
Vnto þe sky rauȝt þe top
A newe born chylde lay in þe crop
Bounden wiþ his swaþelynge bonde

1318   erþe þese] thise' erþe L; þis B. witen] weten TL; wenten B.
1319   þen] þo B.
1321   braunches fele] braunche Ifillyd B. fele] sele L. þat] yt L.
1322   lyf] lefe B.
1323   þenke] marvayle L.
1324   þis] that B. bicoom] was B.
1326   for] þorough B.
1327-8 *reversed in* MS B
1327   skil] tre B.
1328   þe] þat ilke B. adam] his fadirs L.
1329   þat] þe B.
1330   þat] what B.
1331   hym þus] þus him T.
1332   efte] ofte B.
1333   in efte] ofte B. þeroute] withoute B.
1334   And] He B.
1335   þis] The L. of eer] eer of TL; before of B.
1337   þe] þat B.
1339-40 *reversed in* MSS FGHTLB
1339   rauȝte] rawft L; reche B.
1341   Vnto] To B. rauȝt...top] rechyd yt vp B.
1343   swaþelynge bonde] swadelbonde B.

Þere þouȝte him hit lay squelonde
He was aferde whenne he hit siȝe   1345
And to þe rote he caste his yȝe
Him þouȝte hit rauȝte fro erþe to helle
Þere he say his broþer abelle
In his soule he say þat siȝte
Þat kaym slowȝe forwaryed wiȝte   1350
He wente aȝeyn for to shawe
To cherubyn al þat he sawe
Cherubyn wiþ chere mylde
Bigan to telle him of þat chylde
Þat chylde he seide wiþouten wene   1355
Is goddis sone þat þou hast sene
Þi fadir synne now wepeþ he
He shal hit clense þe tyme shal be
Whenne þe plente shal come of tyme
Þis is þe oyle was hiȝte to hyme   1360
To hym & to his progenye
Wiþ pite he shal hem shewe mercye
Whenne seeþ had vndirstonden wel
Þe aungelis seying euer a del
His leue he took of cherubyn   1365
And þre curnels he ȝaf to hym
Whiche of þat tre he nam
Þat his fadir eet of adam
Þi fadir he seide þou shalt say
Þat he shal dyȝe þis þridde day   1370
Aftir þou be comen hym to
Loke þat þou seye to hym so
But þou shalt take þe pepenes þre   fol. 8v col. 1

1344   squelonde] wepond L; cryande B.
1346   And to] Vnto L; To B. rote] rete B.
1347   hit] he L.
1350   forwaryed] þat weryd B.
1355   wene] wone L.
1358   þe tyme] somtyme B.
1359   of] to B.
1360   was] þat was B. to] om B.
1362   hem] om B.
1364   euer a del] euerydele B.
1366   ȝaf to] toke of L.
1367   Whiche] þe which B.
1369   þi] To þy LB. he seide] om B.
1370   þis] þe TB.
1371   Aftir] Afftyr þat B.
1372   to] om B.
1373   þe pepenes] þes kernellys B.

Þat I took of þe appul tre
And putte vndir his tunge roote 1375
To mony men þei shul be boote
Þei ben cidur. cypres & palme fyne
To mony þei shul be medicyne
Þe fadir bi cidur shal þou take
Hit shal be tre wiþouten make 1380
Of cipres bi þat swete sauoure
Bitokeneþ þat swete sauyoure
Þe myche swetnes is þe sone
Þe palme to fruite hit is wone
Mony cornels of o tre moost 1385
Gode ʒiftis of þe holy goost
// Seeth was of his erned fayn
And soone come to his fadir aʒayn
Sone he seide hast þou sped ouʒt
Hast þou any mercy brouʒt 1390
Sir cherubyn þat auŋgel
Þat porter is þe greteþ wel
And seiþ þe world shal nyʒe han ende
Ar þe oyle may to þe wende
Pourʒ birþe of a blissed childe 1395
Þat shal þe world fro shame shylde
For þi deeþ he bad me say
Hit shal be þis day þridde day
Adam herof was glad ful blyue
So glad was he neuer er his lyue 1400
Whenne he herde to lyue no more

1375   putte] putt yt B.
1376   men þei] a man it B. shul] shuld L. be] do B.
1377   cidur] sydrys B.
1379   þe] Thy L. bi] this L ; be þe B.
1381   Of] The L ; Of þe B. bi þat] which is L ; be þe B. sauoure] of savour L.
1382   þat] oure TB. swete] om B.
1383   is] is in L.
1384   to...is] bytokenyþ without L.
1385   Mony] Thise L. of...tre] lest & L.
1386   Gode...of] Come from L.
1389   hast þou] hastow B.
1390   Hast þou] Hastow B.
1392   is] om L. þe greteþ] he gretyþ þe B.
1393   nyʒe] neuere B. han] om L.
1394   Ar] Ar he T. wende] sende T.
1395   birþe] the byrth LB.
1397   For] And of B.
1398   Hit shal] þu schulde B. shal] shalbe L. first day] om B.
1399   herof was] was þo B. ful] and B.
1400   er] in L ; er in B.

Þo he lowȝe but neuere ore
And þus to god gan he cryȝe
Lord Inowȝe mon lyued haue iȝe
Þou take my soule out of my flesshe   1405
And do hit where þi wille is
For of þis world he was ful mad
Þat neuer o day þerynne was glad
Nyne hundride ȝeer & more ȝare
He luyed here in sorwe and kare   1410
Leuer hym were to ben in helle
Þen lenger in þis worlde to dwelle
Adam as him was tolde biforne   fol. 8v col. 2
Dyȝed on þe þridde morne
Grauen he was bi seeth þon   1415
In þe vale of ebron
Þe curnels were put vndir his tunge
Of hem roos þre ȝeerdis ȝonge
And soone an ellen hyȝe þei wore
Þenne stode þei stille & wexe no more   1420
Mony a ȝeer yliche grene
Holynesse in hem was sene
Stille stoode þo ȝerdes þre
Fro adames tyme to noe
Fro noe tyme & fro þe flood   1425
To Abraham hooly & good
Fro Abraham ȝitt stille stood þay
Til moyses þat ȝaf þe lay
Euer stood þei stille in oon
Wiþouten waxinge oþer woon   1430
Nomore of þe ȝerde[s] now
But of a story I shal telle ȝow
Adam lyued nyne hyndride ȝere

1402   but] and L. ore] tofore L.
1404   mon] *om* L; now B. iȝe] ye T.
1405   þou] *om* B.
1407   he was] was he B. ful mad] right sad L.
1410   sorwe and] mochell B.
1415   þon] his son L.
1417   þe] Thise L.
1418   Of hem] þerof B. þre] þe TB; thise L. ȝeerdis] treis L.
1419   an] *om* B.
1422   was] were B.
1423   þo] þe B.
1427   Abraham] Adam L.
1428   Til] Telle L; To B. þat] *om* L; tyme þat B.
1431   þe] þo T; thise L. ȝerdes] ȝerde H.
1432   a] þe B.

And þritty wynter also in fere
Whenne he was deed soone anoon   1435
His soule was to helle goon
And alle þat diȝed fro þis to þon
Þat Ihesu diȝed god and mon
Hem myȝte helpe noon holyhede
But þei to helle muste nede   1440
He myȝte þinke þe stide stronge
Þat in þat place was so longe
Foure þousande ȝeer in þat woo
Thre hundride ȝeer also
So longe fro Adam was to telle   1445
Til oure lorde harwede helle   1446

Þe genealogy of adam olde
Of seeth and caym shal be tolde
Seeth spoused his sister delbora þo   1449
Oure lord bad hit shulde be so   1450
He gat a sone of hir enos
A man þat was of mychel loos
For he was þe firste man   fol. 9r col. 1
Þat cry on goddes name bigan
Nyne hundride ȝeer seuene & fyue   1455
So longe lastede seeth his lyue
Enos his sone lyued by dene
Nyne hundride ȝeer & fyue I wene
Caym his sone his lyf he led
Nyne hundride ȝeer as hit is red   1460
Eyȝte hundride ȝeer lyued malalyel
And fyue & twenty ȝeer to tel
Nyne hyndride ȝeer & sixe iareth
Þat was þe fifte kyn fro seeth

1434   wynter] om B.
1437   diȝed...to] euyr dyed B.
1438   þat] To B. god] bothe god L.
1439   noon] no T.
1440   þei] all B. muste] þo most B.
1441   He] Hym B. þinke] thyng L. stide] stound L.
1444   Thre] Sex B. also] & foure also B.
1446   Til]telle L; Or B.
1447 & 1448   only in C.
1449   delbora] dellora L.
1451   of...enos] as goddis wil was L; þat hight Enes B.
1454   þat] To L. on] or B.
1456   lastede ... his] lastyþ Seethis L. his] on B.
1461   malalyel] maladiel T, corrected from original malaliel
1463   ȝeer] om B.
1464   fifte] fyrst B. fro] of B.

Of iareth elde þe fourty and   1465
Was passed ouer þe firste þousand
Enok his sone wiþouten pere
Lyued in erþe þre hundride ȝeere
He was þe firste þat letturre fond
And wroot summe bookes wiþ his hond   1470
To paradise was he take þon
And þere he lyueþ in flesshe & boon
He comeþ tofore domes day
To fiȝte for þe cristen lay
Wiþ antecryst he shall fiȝte   1475
For to were þe cristen riȝte
He & his felowe · Elye
Antecryst shal do hem dye
And wiþ her rysyng fro deþe to lyue
Þei shul felle þat false stryue   1480
Adam as þe story sayes
Dyed in þis Enok dayes
Of Enok coom matussale
Lyued neuer man so longe as he
Til nyne hundride ȝeer was goon   1485
And seuenty failed hit but oon
Lameth his sone his elde to neuene
Seuen hundride ȝeer seuenty & seuen
Of lameth coom his sone Noe
In whoos tyme þe flood gan be   1490
Þe formast world Adam bigan
Þerof lameþ þe laste man
Hit lasted wel a þousande ȝeere   fol. 9r col. 2
Sixe hundride to & sixty sere
But er þat oþer world bigynne   1495
Speke we more of kaymes kynne

1465   Of] *om* B. elde] *om* L. þe] de B.
1470   And] He B. summe] *om* L. bookes] boke B.
1471   was he] he was B.
1472   in] *with* B.
1473   comeþ] come B. tofore] byfore LB.
1476   þe cristen]crystys B.
1480   þat] þe B. stryue] styve L.
1482   þis] *om* B.
1485   Til] To B.
1486   seuenty] xvij L; seventene B.
1488   seuenty] sexty B.
1491   formast] forþermast B.
1492   þerof lameþ] And lameþ was B.
1494   to] & two B.
1495   þat] þe TLB.

// Whenne caym hadde don þat cursid dede
Þat he was waryed alle we rede
He fledde away fro oþere men
Into a stide þat hiȝte Eden   1500
To him was spoused calmana
As was to seeth delbora
Soone a sone of hir gat he
Þat enos het as a cite
Of þat ilke name he took   1505
We fynde no terme of him in book
Þere woned caym wiþ his brood
Þe firste cite bifore þe flood
Of enos coom malalyel
And of him coom matussalel   1510
Lameth þre sones had wiþ mayne
Iobal . cabal . tubaltaine
Þis lameth het lameth blynde
Kaym he slouȝe bi chaunce we fynde
In þe flood was he fordone   1515
Iobal þen was his eldest sone
He was firste herde & fe delt wiþ
Tubaltayne þe formast smyth
Tobal her broþer firste vndirfong
Musyk þat is þe soun of song   1520
Organes harpe & oþere glew
He drouȝe hem out of musyk new
A sistur hadde þo breþeren tweyne
Noema was called certeyne
She was þe formast webbe in kynde   1525
Þat men of þat crafte fynde
Hir fadir was þe firste on lyue
Þat bigan to double wyue
Þei þat þese wondir werkes wrouȝt

1498   waryed] warnyd L. alle] as B.
1513-4   *are copied after* 1. 1516 *in* B.
1513   blynde] þe blynd L.
1516   þen] *om* B.
1517   He] Iobal B. fe] feir L; *om* B.
1519   *om* B. vndirfong] vnderstond L.
1521   Organes] Orgone B.
1522   hem] *om* B.
1523   þo] the L.
1525   formast] fyrst B. webbe] *om* L; weuer B. in] of B.
1526   fynde] dud fynde T.
1527   on lyue] Alyue L.
1528   to double] doble to B.
1529   þese] this L.

Hit ran hem wel þat tyme in pouȝt   1530
Þat þis worlde shulde come to ende
Wiþ watir dreynt or fyre brende
Two pilers þei made of tyel þat on   fol. 9v col. 1
Þat oþer was of marbul stoon
Þese craftes alle þat þei dide so   1535
Þei put hem in þese pileres two
Þe stoon aȝeyn þe watir to laste
Þe tiel aȝeyn þe fire not braste
Þei wolde þat whoso aftir coom
Shulde be wissed bi her wisdoom   1540
Þerfore let god hym lyue so longe
Þat þei myȝte seke & vndirstonde
Þe kynde of þingis þat were derne
Cours of sunne moone & sterne
Whiche cours may noon al lere   1545
Pouȝe he lyued an hundride ȝere
Whenne so mony ȝeer is past oute
Þe mychel spire is ronnen aboute
In so long tyme is not to leyne
Þe planetes are alle went aȝeyne   1550
Of her firste makyng into þe state
As clerkes now wel woot þate   1552

How mannes synne þat I of mene
Corrupted al þis world bidene
Whenne iareth þat ȝe herde me neuen   1553
Had elde of hundride winter & seuen
Mikel malis was firste in mon   1555
But neuer tofore as was þon
In adames tyme was woo ynouȝe

1530   wel...tyme] þan full well B.
1531   þis worlde] þe werk B.
1533   tyel] yron L. þat] was B.
1534   þat oþer] The todir LB.
1536   pileres] piles B.
1538   tiel] yron L.
1541   let god] god lete B.
1545   noon al] no man B.
1546   þouȝe] Yf þat B
1548   ronnen] turnyd B.
1550   alle went] went alle TLB.
1551   her] þe B.
1552   As] þat T.
1552b   Corrupted] Corrupte TB; Coruptyth L. þis] þe B.
1553   neuen] of neuen B.
1554   hundride] an hundred B.
1556   neuer] none B. tofore] bifore T. was] it was B.

But þenne was þere more wouȝe
Namely among kaymes kynne
Þat delited hem but in synne   1560
Hem þouȝte al wel þat was her wille
Þat þei drouȝe euere hem tille
On alle þinge was more her þouȝt
Pen on god þat hem wrouȝte
So blynde þei wexe in her siȝt   1565
Þat couþe þei do no maner riȝt
Euer þei ȝaf her lyf to lust
Þat shende her soulis al to dust
Wymmen as we hit fynde   1568a
Wente togider aȝeyne kynde   1568b
And men also þe same wyse   1568c fol. 9v col. 2
As þe deuele wolde deuyse   1568d
Of soþfastenes as seiþ þe sawe   1569
Þei left euer þe good lawe   1570
Þe lawe of sooþnes ny of kynde   1571
Wolden þei no tyme fynde   1572
Al wexe wicked & in stryf   1573
Þe broþer took þe oþeres wyf   1574
Her kursednes was not vnkid   1575
Þe lawe of kynde þei so fordid   1576
Þe shame & synne þat þere was oute   1579
To telle were sumdel doute   1580
Þe fende wende fully wiþ þis   1581
Þat al mankynde shulde han ben his   1582

1558   more wouȝe] wo mow L.
1560   þat] Which L. delited] delyte B.
1562   þat...hem] To god ner grace drew þey nevir L.
1563   On...her] Of worldly thyng was alle their L.
1564   þen] & no þyng L.
1566   couþe þei] they cowde L. maner] man B.
1568   þat] And B.
1568a   hit] om L.
1568b   aȝeyne] aȝeynes TLB.
1568c   þe] in þe B.
1570   left] loste B.
1571   ny] & L.
1572   Wolden] Nold L. no] neuyr no B.
1574   oþeres] broþers B.
1575   was] nas L. vnkid] vnkynde B.
1576   þei] om L. so] om B.
1577-8   om in FHTLB.
1579   &] of L. þere was] þey wer L.
1580   To] for to B. were sumdel] all wer grete L.
1582   shulde han] had B.

So ferforþly þat god not myȝte   1585
Brynge man into state of riȝte
Into þe astate þat he had tynt
But god al oþerewyse mynt
His owne hondiwerke so soone
Wolde he not hit were fordone   1590
Þerfore in forme of iuggement
A newe vengeaunce on hem he sent
His foos to brynge alle of lyue
And clense þe world of synne ryue
Bi his grace to ȝyue hem gritth   1595
Þat he monkynde shulde restore wiþ
Whenne he bihelde þe foly stronge
God þat biden hade so longe
Þouȝe he were wrooþ no wonder nas
Þis worde he seide anoon in plas   1600
Þis was þe worde he seide þanne
Me reweþ þat I made manne
But alle þat þis word here & sene
Woot not what hit is to mene
Þis word was a prophecye   1605
Þat was seyd for his mercye
Of þe reuþe he siþþe kidde
Whenne he himself to pyne didde
For his chosen on rode tre
What was his reuþe may we se   1610
By þis word þat þere was seide   fol. 10r col. 1
His mercy was bifore purueide
To poo þat were on his party

1583-4   *om* HTLB
1585   ferforþly] ferforþ TL; ferþerly B. not] ne LB
1586   state] þe state B.
1587   astate] state B. tynt] mynde L.
1588   God to vs was more kynde L.
1591   in...of] as sonne & B.
1592   A] þe B. on] vpon B. he] *om* B.
1593   foos] sone B. of] from L; on B.
1594   synne] synnys B.
1595   Bi] Wiþ B. gritth] graþ B.
1598   God...hade] þat he had abedyn B.
1599   þouȝe] ȝef B. nas] it nas B.
1600   þis...seide] To this world a seid L.
1601   he] þat he B.
1603   here] herde B. &] or L.
1604   not] *om* T; now B.
1607   he siþþe]hymself L.
1608   himself] for vs L. pyne] deth meke B.
1610   What] þat B. may we] now mow ȝe B.

For to brynge hem myȝtily
As his owne his kyndam tille   1615
His enemyes alle for to spille
Aȝeynes hem was so wrooþ
And bi his riȝt hond swoor an ooþ
Þat þei shulde alle haue shenful dede
Saue þe goode wolde he rede   1620
Þouȝe alle þe foolis were forlorn
Þe goode shulde be forborn
As hit at noe flood bifelle
Wherof I shal siþen telle
But firste a tre of noe kynne   1625
I shal here sette ar I bigynne

Here bigynneþ of noe lede
Þe secounde world for to sede
Fyue hundrid ȝeere had noe   1627
Whenne he had geten sones þre
Þe first was sem . cam þat oþer
And Iapheth hette þe þridde broþer   1630
God spak vnto Noe þan
Þus his resoun he bigan
Noe he seide I telle þe
A! þis world bytrayeþ me
Þei han lefte me & my lawe   1635
Of me stonde þei noon awe
Al is forȝeten þat fraunchise
Þat I ȝaf man in paradise
Þe erþe wiþ synne is foule shent
Al riȝtwisnesse away is went   1640
Foule lustis & wicked hede

1615   second his] om LB.
1617   was] þat were B. wrooþ] wroght L.
1618   an] his B.
1619   shulde] schull B. shenful] shemful T; in word & L.
1620   Euyr lastyng ioy þat to god did rede L.
1621   þouȝe] Yf B. þe foolis] othir L.
1624   siþen] ȝow B.
1625-6   om L.
1626b   sede] rede B.
1627   Fyue] Nyne B.
1629   þat oþer] þe toþer T.
1630   And] om B.
1631   vnto] to B.
1636   þei] hem B.
1638   man] hem B.
1639   wiþ synne] within B.

Han fuyled þis world in lengþe & brede
No man her synne may say ne seke
Þerof to heuen recheþ þe smeke
Couetise lecchery and pryde   1645
Haþ spred þis world on euery syde
Alle are þei worþi to wite
Of woo is noon founden quyte
But I shal hem laye ful lawe   fol. 10r col. 2
Þat set so lytil of myn awe   1650
Wreche to take hit is to done
I shal hem drenche in watir soone
Alle hem but þi wyf and þe
Þi sones & her wyues pre
ȝe eiȝte for ȝoure leute   1655
Alone I haue grantide gre
Wiþ þyn ospringe I haue mynt
Restore þe folk þat shal be tynt
Fro þe moost to þe leest
Shal nouþer haue lyf foule ne beest   1660
But er þat I my vengeaunce take
I wol þat þou a vessel make
Sir telle me wherof hit shal be
Hit shal be made of square tre
A shippe must þou nedis diȝte   1665
Þi self shal be þe mayster wriȝt
I shal þe telle how brood & long
Of what mesure & how strong
Whenne þe tymbur is festende wel
Wynde þe sidis eueryche a del   1670
Bynde hit firste wiþ balke & bonde

1642   fuyled] fyllid LB. in] of B.
1643   say] se L. ne] no TB; nor L.
1644   þerof] þat vp B.
1646   on] in L. euery] eche a LB.
1647   are þei] þay ar B.
1648   Of...founden] þere ys none of alle B.
1649   hem laye] ley hem B.
1653   but] saf L.
1655   ȝe] To you L. ȝe eiȝte] And ȝe B.
1656   I...gre] sauyd schull ȝe be B.
1657   I haue] haue I B.
1658   Restore] To restore L. folk] folde B.
1660   nouþer] none B.
1664   square] quarry L.
1665   A...þou] An arke þow most B.
1667   &] how B.
1670   Wynde] Bynde L. a] om LB.
1671   balke] bak B.

And wynde hit siþþen wiþ good wonde
Wiþ picke loke hit be not þinne
Plastre hit wel wiþoute & ynne
Seuen score ellen longe & tene   1675
Þries eyȝte on wyde on heiȝte fiftene
Fiftene on heiȝt is þe entent
Fro grounde to þe tabulment
Hit shal be made wiþ stages sere
Vchone for dyuerse manere   1680
Þou shalt byneþen on þat oon syde
Make a dore wiþ mesure wyde
A sperying wyndowe als on hyȝe
Loke þi werke be not vnslye
An hous þerynne to drynke & ete   1685
Wardrope þat þou not forȝete
Of alle manere beestis take þe tweyne
To wone þere wiþ her makes certeyne
Of vche beest þat is wrouȝt   fol. 10v col. 1
Foule ne worme forȝete ȝe nouȝt   1690
In þe oue[r]mast stage shal þou be
Foules nexte vndir þe
Siþen alþer nexte honde
Meke bestis þei shul vndirstonde
Þo þat are tame & mylde   1695
And vndir hem þenne þe wilde
Also þat þou make a boure
To kepe wiþynne þi wardestoure
In þe boþum shal be no stalle
For al her filþe shal þerynne falle   1700

1674   Plastre...wel] Plateyd B. ynne] *with* in B.
1675   ellen longe] ȝerdys B.
1676   *first* on] yt L; of B. *second* on] of B.
1677   on] of B.
1678   grounde] þe grounde B.
1680   vchone for] Eche on B.
1681   þat oon] þe tone B.
1683   als] all B.
1685   An] And H.
1686   þat] loke B.
1688   her] hys B. makes] make LB.
1690   ȝe] þou L.
1691   ouermast] ouemast H.
1692   nexte] and next L.
1693   alþer nexte] alleþer next þy L; aftyr next B.
1694   þei] *om* L.
1696   þenne] þat B.
1698   wiþynne] in B. wardestoure] warn stoure B.
1699   no] a LB.

Hit shal be mychel wiþouten pere
In makying sixe siþe twenty ȝere
So longe tyme I haue hem lent
Þat wol come to amendement
And if any wol tente to þe   1705
Þat þei þerynne may saued be
Whenne þou hast wel þi tymber layd
And hit is to þi wille payde
Þou & þi wyf shul firste yn te
Þi sones & her wyues þre   1710
Also þat ȝe take ȝow wiþ
Foule & beest þat shal haue griþ
Þe meke togider two & two
Þe wylde by hemself also
Of vchone take þou tweyne In   1715
To holden vp her owne kyn
Be wel war for any swynke
Þat þou ne wante mete ne drynke
Do now wel I leue þe
But I come efte þe to se   1720
If I se þou worches riȝt
I shal holde þat I þe hiȝt
Now woot noe what to do
And hewe tymbur þat fel þerto
He ȝaf wriȝtis her mesure   1725
And hymself dude his cure
Þei wrouȝte faste in dyuerse place
Himself fastened boþe bonde & lace
But euermore as he wrouȝte   fol. 10v col. 2
Folke to preche forȝat he nouȝte   1730

1702   siþe] tymes B.
1705   wol] þer wyll B. tente] tend L.
1707   wel] *om* B.
1709   firste yn] þerin B. yn te] entre L.
1711   ȝe] þou L; ȝow B. ȝow] þe L.
1712   &] *om* B.
1715   tweyne] two B.
1716   her] he T.
1718   ne wante] want not B.
1719   leue] byd B.
1721   þou] the L. riȝt] A right LB.
1722   þe] haue B.
1724   hewe] hewid þe L; how B.
1725   her] his L.
1726   dude] and L.
1727   dyuerse] euery B.
1728   bonde] reme B. lace] brace B.
1730   forȝat] forȝet B.

To warne hem of goddis wreche
How god had wiþ hym a speche
He hit tolde to many man
Wherfore he þat shipp bigan
Wiþ skorn alle hym vnswered   1735
And seide why is þis cherle fered
Þei seide greet wondir hem pouȝte
Why he was so ferde for nouȝte
He were þei seide worþ to be s[h]ent
Þat of his wordes toke tent   1740
Whenne noe say þis trauail tynt
Of his prechyng þenne he stynt
Hit is but foly to ȝyue counsel to
To hem pat wol but foly do
Þerfore he lefte þat cursede lede   1745
And went & dude his owne dede
More wiþ hem he greued nouȝt
Til he had his ship wrouȝt
He was glad whenne hit was made
Riȝt as god bifore hym bade   1750
Whenne he hadde do[ne] þe commaundement
He bode not but þe iugement
Þat god of myȝte wolde worche his wille
As he bifore seide hym tille
Þen cam god at tyme his   1755
To Noe for to speke of þis
Whenne he hadde wiþ him spoken
Hymself þe dore soone hadde stoken
Þe wyndowe was wiþ siche a gyn
Hit myȝte open & spere wiþyn   1760

1731   of] in B. wreche] wirche B.
1733   man]A man LB.
1735   alle hym] þey all B.
1736   fered] aferde B.
1738   so ferde] aferde B.
1739   þei seide] om B. worþ] worþy B. shent] sent H.
1740   of] to B. tent] entent LB.
1741   þis] his TLB:
1745   þat] his B.
1747   he] him T.
1750   hym] om B.
1751-2 reversed in B.
1751   done] do H.
1752   but þe] bote ne B.
1753   of myȝte] almyghty B.
1755   at] whan B. his] was B.
1757   he] god B. him] Noye B.
1758   hadde] haþe B.

Whenne þis was done þer was no bide
Stormes roos on euery syde
Sunne & moone þe liȝt can hyde
Hit merked ouer al þis world wyde
Þe reyn fel doun so wondir faste   1765
Þe welles wexe þe bankes braste
Þe see to ryse þe erþe to cleeue
Þe spryngis alle oute to dreue
Leytynge fel wiþ þondir and reyn   fol. 11r col. 1
Þe erþe quook and dened aȝeyn   1770
Sunne and moone lost her liȝt
Al þe world turned to nyȝt
Þat sorwe to se was greet awe
Þe buyldyngis fel boþe hyȝe & lawe
Þe watir wex ouer þe pleynes   1775
Þe beestes ran to mounteynes
Men & wymmen ran hem wiþ
Wel þei hoped to haue had griþ
Al for nouȝte þei wente afote
Whenne þei þere cam hit was no bote   1780
Þe foulis flotered þo on hyȝe
And fel whenne þei myȝte not dryȝe
For nouȝte fled beest & man
Al to late þei hit bigan
In þat watir soone þe[i] swam   1785
Syde bi syde wolf & man

1761   þer] þo L
1762   Stormes] þe stormys B. euery] ilke a B.
1763   þe] her B. can] gan TLB.
1764   merked] markenyd L; derkyd B. al þis] þe B.
1765   fel] come B.
1767   *first* to] gan L. cleeue] cleft T; claf L.
1768   oute ... dreue] abowte draf L.
1770   dened] dyvid L.
1771   lost] yt lost L.
1773   þat] Than L.
1774   buyldyngis] boudlynggis L.
1775   ouer] on B.
1776   mounteynes] þe mountains L.
1778   Wel...to] þey wende well þere B.
1779   afote] on fote L.
1780   Whenne...cam] Alle for nought B. no] non B.
1781   flotered þo] flakeryd B.
1782   not] not lenger L. dryȝe] flye B.
1783   beest] boþe beste B.
1784   hit] *om* B.
1785   soone] þo B. þei] þe H; þere B.
1786   wolf] beste L.

Þe lyoun swam bisyde þe hert
Dide no beest to oþere smert
Þe sparhauke bi þe sterlynge
Þei tentede oþere no maner þinge   1790
Þes ladyes tent not þo to pride
Þei swam bi her knaues syde
For lordshipe was þere no stryf
Was no man gelous of his wyf
Oþere to helpe was noon so slye   1795
Alle þei drenched by & bye
Alle þei drenched euerychone
Was noon fro deþ myȝte gone
For her synnes wepte þei þan
Allas to late þei bigan   1800
Þenne desired þo caytifs badde
Þat þei hadde ben by noe ladde
But þouȝe þat noe was in quert
He was [not] al in ese of hert
Þe wynde hym ledde on þat flood   1805
He nuste whide[r]warde he ȝood
Heuen & erþe he flet bytwene
He nuste where his ship wolde bene   1808
Þei were ful ferde of her lyues   1810 fol. 11r col. 2
Þat was wiþ hym m[e]n & wyues   1809
But þe lord ful of myȝt
To Noe bifore her lyues hiȝt
Noe þo wiste wiþouten wene
Þe folk was al deed bidene
Wiþ soor wepynge he hem ment   1815
And turned to god al his tent

1788   no...to] none of hem B. to] *om* L.
1789   *om* B.
1790   *om* B.
1791   þes] The L; þis B. tent] tented T.
1794   no man] none þere B.
1795   slye] schy B.
1797   þei] were LB.
1798   noon] none þere B.
1801   þo] þe B
1802   hadde...ladde] ne hadde done att Noyes rad B.
1804   not] *om* H. in] at B. of] in B.
1805   ledde] drofe B. þat] the LB.
1806   whiderwarde] whidewarde H; neuyr whedyr B.
1808   nuste] nyst neuer B. wolde] shuld L. bene] lene L.
1809   was] were B. wiþ hym] *with* In B. men] mon H; boþe þe men L.
1814   folk] folde B. was] were TB. al] þo L.
1816   tent] entent LB.

He fyned neuer nyȝte nor day
For þo caitifs for to pray
For monkynde as seiþ þe boke
But durste he neuer wiþ yȝe vp loke   1820
He preyed to god for her sake
No vengeaunce on þo soulis to take
As was taken in þat whyle
On her bodyes þat were so vile
Siþ þei were perisshed so reuly   1825
On her soulis to haue mercy
So had þei hade wiþouten faile
Hadde þei done noes counsaile
Whenne þei forsook his prechyng
And took his speche to scornyng   1830
But now þei fynde hit þerfore
Þat wolde not leue on Noe lore
For whil þat god ȝaf hem grace
Þei were not ferde of his manace
//Þis reyn reyned euer on one   1835
Til fourty dayes were agone
Þe heȝest hil þat was owhore
Þe flood ouer passed seuen ellen & more
Þer was no creature on lyue
Þe grounde myȝte reche ne ryue   1840
But hit were fisshe þat flet on sonde
Miȝte no þing on grounde stonde
On þat streem þe ship gan ryde
Þo wawes beten on euery syde

1817 fyned] faynyd L; blan B. nor] ne B.
1819 monkynde as] manhode B.
1820 he] they L.
1822 on...soulis] on þo foulis L; of hem B.
1824 On her] Of their L. bodyes] goodys B.
1825 perisshed] dede B.
1828 noes] by noies LB.
1830 to] in B.
1832 wolde] nold L. leue] lere L; lyfe B.
1833 whil] why B.
1834 ferde] a ferde B.
1836 Til] To B. agone] come & goon L; all gone B.
1837 owhore] thare L.
1838 passed] passeþ B.
1839 no] non LB.
1840 þe] þat þe B. ne] no B.
1842 on] on þe B.
1843 streem] flode B.
1844 þo] þe TLB. beten] went B. euery] eche a B.

Þe stormes straked wiþ þe wynde   1845
Þe wawes to bete biforn & bihynde
Noe & his euere loked doun
To drenche wende þei hadde be boun
But be we truste wiþouten stryf   fol. 11v col. 1
Þei weren wery of her lyf   1850
Til seuen siþes twenty dayes were gon
Þe flood stood stille euer in oon
Aboute fyue moneþes hit stoode
Wiþouten fallyng þat fers floode
Ofte þei wende her ship wolde ha ryue   1855
Wiþ wynde or wawe or dynt of clyue
But ʒitt is good kyng of blis
To helpe euer whenne his wille is
Whenne þis vengeaun [ce] þus was wrouʒt
Oure lorde þenne on noe þouʒte   1860
And bigan to haue pite
Of him his ship and his meyne
Þat myʒty kyng soone I wis
Turned her bale into blis
Aʒeyn he made þe wattres go   1865
Into þe places þat þei coom fro
Þe erþe wex bare er þei wende
Þe ship on londe bigan to lende
On ermonye hit gon stonde
A heʒe hil in holy londe   1870

1845   stormes] stremys L.
1846   to] om LB. bete] bote T.
1847   euere] wyf L.
1848   wende...hadde] they had went L. wende] when B.
1849   we] þow B. truste] stille L; tryst B.
1850   þei] Alle they L.
1851   Til] To B.
1852   in] at B.
1855-6   *reversed in* B.
1855   Ofte] Owghtyn L. her] þe B. wolde] shuld LB. ha] om B. ryue] revyn L.
1856   clyue] chyn L.
1857   good] god L; lorde B.
1859   þis] his T. vengeaunce] vengeaun H.
1862   his ship] om B. *second* his] on hys B.
1863   soone] is sone B.
1864   Turned] Turne L. her] his L.
After 1, 1864, MS B *repeats* 1. 1858: To help euyr when his will is.
1865   þe] om B. go] to go B.
1866   places þat] place þere B.
1867   er...wende] of þe wynd L.
1870   A] And B. heʒe hil] hille hie L; heigh ys B. holy] þe holy L.

Þe sunne bigan þo hir to kyþe
Noe wex þenne ful bliþe
And seyde to his sones þre
Childre he seide what rede ȝee
How shul [w]e of þis watir wit   1875
If þat hit be fallen ȝit
By a foule þei seide wite may we
If þe erþe bare be
To shippe wol he come no more   1880
If he fynde bare erþe þore   1879
His wyndowe opened þo noe
And lete a rauen out fle
He souȝte vp & doun þere
A stide to sitte vpon sumwhere
Vpon þe watir þere he fond   1885
A drenched beest þere fletond
Of þat flesshe was he so fayn
To shippe coom he not aȝayn
Þerfore þe messangere men saye   fol. 11v col. 2
Þat dwelleþ longe in his iournay   1890
He may be calde wiþ resoun clere
Oon of þe rauenes messangere
And whenne Noe perceyued was
Of þe reauenes deseit in plas
He let out a dowfe & took hir fliȝt   1895
And fonde no place vpon to liȝt
She coom aȝeyn wiþouten blyn
Noe roos vp & let hir In
Siþen abood he seuene dayes

1871   bigan] he gan L. þo hir] for L. hir to] to clere B.
1872   Noe] And Noye B.
1875   shul we] shulde H.
1877   þei] he L; *om* B. seide] *om* B.
1879   erþe] ere L; þore] ȝore B.
1881   His] þis B. oþened þo] than opynnyd L.
1884   A] *om* L.
1887   þat] þe B.
1888   not] no more B.
1889   men] þei T.
1893   Noe] þat Noye B.
1894   deseit] dissert L. in] & B.
1895   out] oute do B. &...fliȝt] in plight B.
1896   And] He B. no] a B. vpon] wheron B.
MS B *inserts an extra line here:* Noye ros vp withouten blyn.
1897   coom aȝeyn] founde non place B.
1899   abood he] aboute B.

Aftir þat þe bibel sayes 1900
He sent þe dowfe anoþer siþe
She wente forþ & was ful bliþe
Soone she coom & dwelt nouȝte
An olyue braunche in mouþe brouȝte
Þenne was Noe wel I knawe 1905
Þat þe flood hit was wiþdrawe
But ȝit bood he seuen dayes in rest
For fere lest any damming brest
Siþ he made hem alle out dryue
Foule & beest man & wyue 1910
Þese beestis were ful glad in moode
Whenne þei hadde her kyndely foode
Oure lord dide hem soone to sprede
Wiþinne her owne kynde to brede
Þenne bad god vnto noe 1915
To leue þe ship wiþ his meyne
A tweluemoneþ was go bi þis
Bi þat same day I wis
Þat day tweluemoneþ þat he ȝeode In
He hit left more ny myn 1920
As perus maior þe gode clerk
Telleþ of hym in his werke
To him þenne coom oure lord hende
And seide Noe leue frende
Þou & pi sones wiþ her wyues 1925
I haue saued alle ȝoure lyues
ȝow ȝitt haue I forborn
Þat in my vengeaunce be not lorn
To ȝow ȝitt þat I haue let lyue fol. 12r col. 1
My brode benesoun I ȝow ȝyue 1930

1901 sent] sende T; lete out L.
1904 mouþe] his mouþe B.
1906 hit] *om* B.
1908 lest...brest] the daungir lengger lest L. damming] dam myght B.
1911 þese] The L.
1913 sprede] spede B.
1914 Wiþinne] In B.
1919 þat] *om* L. ȝeode In] yedyn L.
1920 ny myn] þan Myne B.
1921 As] And B.
1923 þenne coom] come þo B.
1924 leue] my leue B.
1925 þou] þe B. sones] sonne L. wiþ her] & ȝoure B.
1927 *om* B.
1928 lorn] lorde B.
1929 þat...let] haue I lent B.

I wol þat of þi osprynge brede
Al maner nacioun and lede
Vche þing on his wyse
I wol þei do þe seruyse
Noe was of his blessyng bliþe   1935
And lete reyse an auter swyþe
He ȝeode to worshepe god as wyse
Þeron made he sacrifise
Oure lord god al weldyng
Him liked wel her offeryng   1940
He seide Noe for no chaunce
Shal I not take siche vengeaunce
Fro me dounward man drouȝe his [þ]ouȝt
Now are þei fully doun ybrouȝt
And if þou worche aftir my lore   1945
Þou shalt fare wel þerfore
To gode þewes þou þe ȝyue
Loue wel trouþe whil þou lyue
For þat ȝe biforn han sene
Vche man lyue trewely bidene   1950
If þou wolt trowe on my rede
Fle falshede & þefte as dede
Whoso of flesshe wol haue her fode
Loke þei kaste awey þe blode
Alle þat wol trewely holde her lede   1955
Blood to ete I hem forbede
Of beest wiþ clouen foot in two
Wiþ chowyng quode ȝe ete also
I warne ȝow now alle bidene

1934   þei] þat þey B.
1936   reyse] om L. swyþe] make swyþe L.
1937   ȝeode] went B.
1938   made he] he made his B.
1939   weldyng] wyllyng L.
1940   Him] om L. offeryng] ospryng L.
1942   not] om B.
1943   Fro] For B. man] men B. drouȝe] take L. his] her B. þouȝt]ȝouȝt H.
1944   are] or L. ybrouȝt] be broght L; brought B.
1947   To] Go L. þewes þou] ȝeftys ȝow B.
1948   lyue]leve L.
1950   Vche] That L. lyue] þat levyþ L. bidene] & clene B.
1951   þou] he L; ȝe B. wolt] wille LB.
1952   falshede] falsnes B. þefte...dede] oþer mysdede L.
1953   flesshe] þe flesch B. her] þe LB.
1955   wol trewely] truly will L.
1956   Blood] Bold L.
1957   in] on L.
1958   also] no mo L.

Ete of no beest of kynde vnclene   1960
O no maner worm þat is made
Ne foule þat reueþ his lyflade
Also ʒe ete of no flesshe ellis
Þat in slowʒe & erþe dwelles
Siche fisshe & flesshe of boþe I say   1965
Loke ʒe caste þe body away
To þe and þyne I bidde also
Be noon so bolde oþer to slo
For whoso sleeþ mon or wyf   fol. 12r col. 2
Þer is no raunsoum but lyf for lyf   1970
I made man aftir myn owne ymage
I wol noon oþer do outrage
Euel ow no mon to do to oþere
But vche to be oþers broþere
A couenande now I hete þe   1975
Þou shalt fro nowe my reynbowe se
Whil þou may se my bowe wiþoute
Of siche a flood þar þe not doute
If man mysdooþ on oþere wyse
On hem I shal sette my Iustise   1980
Þat shal ben at þe day of Ire
Whenne I shal come to deme wiþ fyre
Wiþ trewe werkis loke ʒe dele
As ʒe wol loue ʒoure soule hele
And ʒeldeþ to ʒoure creatour   1985
Þe tenþe part of ʒoure labour

1960   Ete] Ne ete L; ʒe ete B. no] om L.
1962   Ne] No B. þat reueþ] with raven þat haþe B.
1963   Also] Alle L. ete] ne ete L. no] om L.
1964   &] or LB.
1966   ʒe] þat ʒe B.
1967   þyne] to þyne B. I bidde] om B.
1968   Be] Be þe B.
1972   wol] wold L. noon...do] þat none do oþer B.
1973   first to] om T. second to] om LB.
1974   to be] be to B. oþers] oþere TLB.
1975   A] One B. couenande] comaundment LB. now...hete] ʒef I to B. hete]hete
        to TL.
1976   my] þe L.
1977   bowe wiþoute] raynebowe oute B.
1978   a...þe] vengaunce þe þare B. þar] dar L.
1979   mysdooþ] myssey B. wyse] I wys B.
1980   I shal] schall I B.
1981   þe] þat T.
1982   shal]om B.
1984   ʒoure] þe T.
1985   And] om B. ʒeldeþ] ʒelde þe B.

Gode men I wol þat ȝe se
Bytwene Adam and Noe
Þe tyme was euer Iliche grene
Þat no reynbowe þere was sene   1990
And þei no reyn on erþe felle
Plente on erþe myȝte men telle
Ne þurt no mon ete flesshe þat tyde
Til hit made mannes pride
Now is for synne & pryd of man   1995
Þe erþe feblere þen hit was þan
Fro þe watir þat hit so wesshe
Þerfore man not now ete flesshe
And feblere mannes state now is
Þen hit was þenne forsoþe I wis   2000
Whenn Noe left þe ship alone
He hadde six hundride ȝeer & one
Þe elleuenþe wyntur was witterly
Þeraftir as telleþ vs metody
Whenne þe world was goonde   2005
In elde of þe þridde þousonde
Noe þe trewe wiþouten synne
A newe lyflode he dide bigynne
A newe lyflode went þei to be   fol. 12v col. 1
Himself and his sones þre   2010
Moost to tilþe he ȝaf hym þan   2013
To flitte breres he bygan
So longe flittyng to hem he souȝt   2015
Þat vynetrees he hem wrouȝte

1988   Bytwene] Betwyx B.
1989   euer Iliche] eueryliche T; evir liche L.
1990   þere...sene] was I sene B.
1991   þei] ȝef B.
1992   on] of B.
1993   þurt] durst LB.
1995   for] þe B.
1996   þe] In LB.
1997   Fro] For L. hit] is B. wesshe] wysshe L; wech B.
1998   man mot] Men mow B.
2000   forsoþe I wis]forsoþenes B.
2003   wyntur] ȝere B. was] was after L; afftyr B.
2004   vs] om B. metody] þe story L.
2009   A] To TLB. þei] þe T. to] om TLB.
2010   Himself] Noye B.
2011-2   *om in* HTLB.
2013   tilþe] tyle B.
2014   he] they L.
2015   longe] longh B.
2016   vynetrees] wynetrees T. he] they L.

A day bifel he was forswonken
And vnwarres of wyn dronken
Þouȝe he himself firste hit wrouȝt
Þerfore þe wyn spared him nouȝt   2020
Dronke he lay & slept by his one
Þere þe sunne vpon hym shone
Naked on þat lyme lay he
Þat men þinke moost shame to se
His mydelest sone was cald cam   2025
Bihelde & say his fadris shame
He kidde he was vnkynde ynouȝe
To scorne he his fadir louȝe
To his broþer Iapheth seide he
Broþer come now hider and se   2030
What is þat seide Iapheth broþer
Þi fadir slepeþ seide þat oþer
He lyþ here come se þou shalle
Naked vpon his lymmes alle
Broþer he seide þou seist folye   2035
And þat I trowe þou wolt abye
If þou of þi fadir make despit
Þou beest of his blessyng quyt
His ȝonger broþer was ful wo
For þe elder wrouȝte so   2040
A mantel fro his necke he toke
And ȝeode bacwarde as seiþ þe boke
He & his elder broþere seem
Blessedest of þat barnetem
Til þei coom þere her fadir lay   2045

2018   wyn] þe wyne B.
2020   him] he LB
2021   He lay aslepe hymselfe alone B.
2023   on] of B.
2025   His] þe B. was] men B.
2026   Bihelde] Behynde B.
2027   He kidde] Vnkyd L. vnkynde] & vnkynd L.
2030   now] om B.
2031   Iapheth] his B.
2032   þi] My B. þat oþer] þe toþer TB.
2034   vpon] on B.
2036   And] om B.
2038   beest] art L; schalt be B.
2039   His] þe B.
2041   fro] of B.
2042   as] so B.
2043   elder] eldest TLB.
2044   Blessid they were of þe kyng of hevyn L.
2045   Til] To B.

Þerwiþ hym couered þay
Herby may we vndirstonde
Was no breech foundide þo in londe
Noe wiþ þis mantel awoke
His sones scorne he vndirtoke   2050
His malisoun on hym he leyde   fol. 12v col. 2
And siþ to him þenne he seide
Cam wiþouten any doute
Vndir þi breþeren þou shalt loute
Vndir hem to be as þral   2055
Þou and þyn ospring al
Þe oþere two for her couerynge
Noe ȝaf his brood blessynge
To seem & lapheth þenne seide he
Now shal hit al forȝyuen be   2060
Lathþe & wrappe or any pliȝt
If ȝe aȝeyn me han done vnriȝt
Of ȝow shal þe ospringe sprede
Þat shal ouer al haue lordehede
Blessed shal be ȝoure tabernacle   2065
Ful of myrþe & of myracle
And god hit grante þat hit be so
Þat al þis world be ȝouris two
To cam he seide foule feloun
Þou hast þe kynde of þat natioun   2070
Of caym curside moost of oþere
Þat wiþ tresoun slouȝe his broþere
Do þe swithe out of my siȝt
Þou art & shalt be cursed wiȝt
By me owe þou not to dwelle   2075
I drede þi wonynge be in helle
Fle fro me þou waryed þing

2046   þerwiþ] With þe mantell B.
2048   Was] þere was B. foundide] fond L; *om* B.
2049   awoke] woke B.
2052   to] vnto B. þenne] þus L; *om* B.
2059   To] Go B. þenne] þo T.
2060   hit] *om* L.
2061   &] or LB. wrappe] vnryght B.
2062   aȝeyn me] *om* B. done] done any B.
2063   sprede] breede B.
2064   ouer] of B.
2067   be so] so be L.
2068   be...two] yours ij° be L. two] also B.
2069   foule] þow foule B.
2074   & shalt be] a full B.
2075   By] With L.

Now shul we parte for þi skornyng
Awey he fledde he and his
Oure lordis enemyes þei were. I wis   2080

Noe þe graciouse & þe gode
Lyued fourty ȝeer aftir þe flode
Nyne hundride ȝeer & ten siþe fyue
So longe lastede Noes lyue
For his trewe lyf to neuene   2085
He sitteþ now wiþ god in heuene
His sones þat I biforn of melt
Al þis world bitwyxe hem delt
To seem asye . to cam aufryk
To iapheth europe þat wilful wyk   2090
Alle þese [þre] were ful ryche   fol. 13r col. 1
But seem part was noon oþere lyche
For þe world was as we here
Dalt in þre partyes sere
In þre partyes pryncipal   2095
But þei were not paringal
For asye is wiþouten hope
As myche as aufryk & europe
Asye is þe þridde in dole
And is þe haluendel ȝitt al hole   2100
Hit is þe best for þeryn is
Þe holy londe and heþenis
Wiþ preciouse stoonis spices of prys
In þat lond stondeþ paradys
Inde and peris . and arabye   2105
Babilone . Iuda and sulie
And mony oþere dyuerse cuntre

2079   first he] þay B. second he] boþe he B.
2081   second þe] om B.
2083   Nyne] Sevyn B. siþe] and B.
2085   lyf] love L.
2086   sitteþ] is L.
2087   sones] socour L. melt] tolde B.
2088   bitwyxe] bytwene LB.
2089   asye...aufryk] he gaf Asie / To Cam he gaf Aufryke L.
2090   europe...wyk] he gaf Europe L. wilful] wikkyd B.
2091   þre] om H. ryche] riche to grope L.
2092   was noon] nas not L.
2093   was] om T. we] ȝe B.
2096   not] om L.
2100   ȝitt] om B.
2105   first and] om B.
2106   sulie] Surry B.
2107   dyuerse] om B. cuntre] contreyes B.

Þerynne is babilone þe moost cite
// Aufrik is þat oþer partye
Bifore þat wasse called libie   2110
Mony a cuntre þerinne es
And hoge citees more and les
Þerynne is cartage a cite stronge
And oþer many also amonge
Þe myche londe of ethiopye   2115
Ienile . mortaygne & indie
Þat lond is moost into þe souþ
Þere þat blo men are ful couþ
// Þe þridde party is not best
Hit is moost into þe west   2120
Al on þis syde þe grickisshe see
Hadde Iapheth to his lyuere
Hit hette Europe where moost today
Abideþ of þe cristen lay
Þerynne is Roome þe heed cite   2125
Abouen alle þat owe to be
And mony anoþer riche kyndom
Þat I to telle haue no toom
Of þese þre bigan to sprede
Þe world to fille on lengþe & brede   2130
Of hem roos mony men   fol. 13r col. 2
Of dyuerse kyndes sixe siþe ten
Knyȝt & þral and fre man

2109   þat oþer] þe todyr B. partye] partete B.
2110   Bifore þat]þat somtyme B.
2112   hoge] grete B.
2113   is] *om* T. al] þat B.
2114   many also] al so many TB. amonge] one B.
2115   þe] A B. of] is B. ethiopye] Echophe B.
2116   mortaygne] nartayrn L; mortelage B.
2117   þat] This L.
2118   þere] Where B.
2119   party] part T; pte B.
2121   syde] side is L; halfe B. grickisshe] grekys L; grete B.
2122   Iapheth]Iaphell B. to] vnto L; all B.
2123   moost] *om* B. today] in fay L.
2124   of] most of B.
2125   þe] þat B.
2126   owe] it ought B.
2127   riche] right L.
2128   I] it B. haue] haue I B.
2129   Of] On B.
2130   to fille on] full of B.
2131   roos] aros B.
2132   sixe siþe] sexty & B.
2133   Knyȝt] Lorde B. &] *om* L. þral] kyng B. fre] bonde B.

Of þese þre briþeren bigan
Of sem fre mon of iapheth knyȝt   2135
Þral of cam waryed wiȝte   2136

Bigynne we nowe to telle of sem
And siþen of his barnteem
Sem was trewe in goddes lore   2139
He lyued seuen hundride ȝeer & more   2140
Þis ilke sem wa[s] cald sedek þo
Siþen melchisadech also
Oure swete lady as we fynde
Coom out of þis same kynde
Of salem preest & kyng he was   2145
Þat now het ierusalem in plas
Þe firste he was of oþere born
Þat wiþ wyn and breed of corn
Made sacrifise to god so trewe
In tokenyng of þe lawes newe   2150
Þis sem lyued I rede of here
Til ysaac was of seuenty ȝere
Sem hadde fyue sones fre
Of oon to speke is good to me
Þat is of hym of whoos sede   2155
He was born þat bett oure nede
Arphaxat lyued wiþouten were
Þre hundride & eiȝte & þritty ȝere
Foure hundride ȝeer his son caynan
And eiȝte & þritty fro he bigan   2160

2134   briþeren] fyrst B.
2135   mon] men B.
2136   þral] And þralle B. waryed] þat weryed B.
2137-8 *om* FGHTLB
2141   was] wal H.
2142   melchisadech] mylchysathek L.
2144   þis] þe LB. kynde] *om* L.
2147   of] of alle L. of oþere] þat was B. born] byforn L.
2148   wiþ...and] dyd make B. and] *om* L. of] & L.
2149   to...so] so to god B.
2150   tokenyng] fygure B. þe] þo T. lawes]lawe B.
2152   seuenty]seuenten B.
2153   sones] sonne L.
2155   of hym] *om* B.
2156   He...born] Was borne he B. þat...oure] our bote at L.
2157   Arphaxat] Arfayat B.
2158   Þre...þritty]CCC and xxxviij L. þritty] twenty B.
2159   *line om* B.
2160   *line om* B. eiȝte...þritty] xxxviij L.

Foure hundride ȝeer his sone sale
And also þritty ȝeer and þre
Foure hundride ȝeer his sone heber
Wiþ foure & fourty sett to þer
// Phaleth his sone witterly   2165
Two hundride ȝeer nyne & þritty
Ragan his sone þat was
Twelue score ȝeer saue oon las
Two hundride ȝeer serut his sone
And þritty was his lyf in wone   2170
Foure score & eiȝte nachor had lyue   2172 fol. 13v col. 1
Thare his sone two hundride & fyue   2173
Þat oþer elde endeþ in thare   2175
Whiche bigan at good noe
Þat tyme was þis world so ȝonge
Þat alle me[n] spak wiþ o tonge
Þat is ebrew for to say
Þat iewes speke ȝitt to þis daye   2180
// Iapheth hadde him sones seuene
A party synful for to neuene
Gomor . madan . Gena . Magog
Tubal . Tiras . and mosog
Þis gomor hadde sones þre   2185
Togoriens . riphat . Asine
Gena had foure oon cethim
Elisa tharsis . and dothahim

2161   sale] Saule L.
2162   ȝeer] *om* B. *The scribe wrote* þretty ȝere, *corrected* ȝere *to* þre, *and added a superscript* t.
2163   ȝeer] *om* T.
2164   foure & fourty] x liiij L.
2165   Phaleth] Fabeþe B.
2166   nyne & þritty]and xxxix L; & Nyne & fourty B.
2168   saue] *om* B.
2169   ȝeer] *om* B.
2170   was] ȝere B. in wone]yronne L; was done B.
2171-4   *condensed to* 2 11.*in* HTLB.
2172   & eiȝte] ȝere B. lyue] in lyve L.
2175   þat oþer] þe toþer TLB
2176   noe] noy are L.
2178   men] me H.
2179   þat is] And that was L.
2180   to] into B.
2181   him] *om* B.
2183   Gena] Gyna B.
2185   þis] *om* B.
2186   Asine] & Asine L.
2187   oon] oon was L.

To eillondis þes þei drow
Of hem sprong foly ynow   2190
Cam foure sones had hym
Chus phut canan & mephaim
Of chus saba & ielula
Sabatha regma sagabata
Of chus bicam nembrot also   2195
Þat in his tyme dide myche woo
For he was proud fers & felle
Of hym now wol I telle

Þis nembrot wiþ his foule pride
He wende to worche wondrs wyde   2200
Fer aboute men bar his name
Miche he couþe of synne & shame
Of babiloyne kyng stif in stour
And also wrongful emperour
Robber & monqueller greet   2205
Al he lyued wiþ euel bygeet
Was þer noon þat woned him by
Þat myȝte of him gete mercy
Ouer al he went wiþ greet outrage
Þat tyme was þere but o langage   2210
Ebreu þe firste þat adam spak
Fro eest he brouȝt an euel pak
Into þe felde of semare   fol. 13v col. 2
Sixty werkemen þei ware
To dwelle wiþ nembroth þei coom   2215
And tooke a counsel amonges hem
A foly counsel took þei soone

2189   To eillandis] ille landys B. þes] all thise L ; *om* B. þei] *om* L.
2190   foly ynow] folys newe B.
2192   & mephaim] nepthalim B.
2193   saba] come Sala L.
2194   regma] regina L.
2195   chus] this Chus L.
2196   dide] was B.
2199   wiþ] wis T.
2200   worche] haue wrought B.
2202   he couþe] couþe he B.
2204   And] *om* B.
2208   þat...him] Of hym þat myght B.
2209   Ouer] On B.
2210   was þere] þere was B.
2212   brouȝt] wrought B.
2214   þei] þere B.
2216   a] *om* B.

To werre vpon þe sunne & moone
Here witt was ful of felony   2220
Þerfore a foly counsel seide I   2219
Of her pryde couþe no mon telle
In sennare þei toke to dwelle
Nembrot hem seide on þis wyse
Me þinkeþ sires þei were vnwyse
Oure eldres þat biforn vs were   2225
Whenne þei couþe fynde in no manere
For to kepe hem fro þat flood
Þat dreynt þe world and ouerȝood
I rede we bigynne a newe labour
Do we wel & make a tour   2230
Wiþ squyre & scanteloun so euene
Þat hit may reche heiȝer þen heuen
God shul we conquere wiþ fiȝt
Aȝeyn vs shal he haue no myȝt
Or at þe leest holde hym stille   2235
And lette vs not to do oure wille
Þat euer whenne we haue chesoun
Frely may clymbe vp and doun
Þese foolis soone gedered hom
Wiþ greet enuye þis werk bigon   2240
Two & sixti fadome brade
Was þe groundewal þat þei made
Whenne þei hadde made þe grounde
Þe werk þei reisede in a stounde
Wiþ tyel & teer wiþouten stoon   2245
Oþer morter was þer noon

2218   werre] we B.
2219-20   *reversed in* GHTLB.
2219   seide] say B.
2223   hem] *om* B.
2225   vs] *om* B.
2227   þat] þe B.
2228   dreynt] dryvyþ L. ouerȝood] evir yode L.
2232   heiȝer þen] to B.
2233   shul we conquere] shalbe conquerid L.
2234   Aȝeyn] Aȝens B.
2236   And] þat he B.
2237   chesoun] encheson B.
2238   may] to L. clymbe] come B.
2239   soone] þo B. hom] sone B.
2243   made...grounde] þe gronde made B.
2244   reisede] reryd B.
2245   wiþouten] & B.
2246   Oþer] For oþer L.

Wiþ corde & plum þei wente so hyȝe
Þe hete of sunne myȝte þei not dryȝe
Wiþ horses & wiþ camel hyde   2250
Þei hiled hem heete to abyde   2249
Þei seide wheþer god be wrooþ or blyþe
His estres wol we se swyþe
Now we ben þus fer warre   fol. 14r col. 1
Oure wille may he not forbarre
//But grete god þat is so hende   2255
A curteys vengeaunce can he sende
Þei þat outrage on hym souȝte
Lymme no lyf he refte hem nouȝte
But so he menged her mood
Þat noon oþere vndirstood   2260
Of siche speche as he wolde say
Her tongis dyuersed fro þat day
For shame vchone þat werk forsoke
And went away as seiþ þe booke
Þerfore hit hette babiloyne   2265
Þat shent þing is wiþouten asoyne
Þere were alle þe speches part
Of dyuerse londis to dyuerse art
First was but oon & no moo
Now are þer spechis sixty & two   2270
Þis tour was selly made on hiȝt
Fyue þousande steppes stood vpriȝt
Also eiȝte score & fourty þerto
Þus made þese foolis hem to do

2247   þei wente] went þay B.
2248   sunne] þe sonne LB.
2249-50   *reversed in* GHTLB
2250   horses] horse TB.
2252   estres] craft L. His...wol] It heyghteþ well B. swyþe] & swiþe B.
2253   þus...warre] so hie & farre L.
2255   grete] þe gode B.
2256   can] gon LB.
2258   Lymme] Lyfe B. no] ne TLB.lyf] lyme B. refte hem]left hym L.
2260   noon] none of hem B.
2261   Of] With B.
2262   Her] þe B.
2264   as] so B.
2265   hit] *om* B.
2266   is] *om* B. asoyne] sone B.
2268   londis to] reamys & B.
2270   Now]And now B. spechis] *om* B.
2271   selly] sone L.
2273   fourty] foure TL; *om* B. þerto] two B.

Ten myle compas al aboute 2275
Þat story telleþ out of doute 2276
At þis werke was not sem 2279
Ne noone of his barnteem 2280
Þerfore ebreu her speche han þay
Þat iewis holden to þis day
// Þis nembrot was þe firste kyng
Þat fonde in maumete mystrowing
Longe he regnede in þat londe 2285
In maumetrye first feiþ he fonde
Þat he bigan lasteþ ȝete
Sarazines wol hit not lete
Aftir his fadir þat was dede
A vigur was maad by his rede 2290
He commaundide alle men
As god þei shulde þat þing ken
What for loue & what for doute
Alle hit worsheped to loute
Þis euydense byhelde oþere 2295 fol. 14r col. 2
Þat summe for fadir & als for broþere
For frendes dede þat was hem dere
Ymages þei made of metalles sere
Bi hem þis lawe was þo bigunne
Soone was hit ouer al runne 2300
For frendes deeþ ouer al þe londe
Siche mysbileue vp þei fonde
Fendes crepte þo ymagis wiþynne
And ladde folted men to synne

2275   compas] þe compas B.
2276   þat] þe B. out of] withouten doute B.
2277-8   *om in* FGHTLB.
2281   ebreu her] her ebrew L; þe Ebrew B.
2284   in maumete] in mament L; Mamatry B.
2288   lete] forȝete B.
2289   his] þat his B. þat] *om* B.
2291   alle] to all B.
2292   þing] Image B.
2294   to] & B.
2296   þat] *om* B. als] som LB. broþere] modir L.
2297   dede] dethe B. was] were T.
2298   þei] *om* B. metalles sere] metall clere B.
2299   þo] *om* B.
2300   was hit] yt was B.
2301   deeþ] doþe B.
2302   mysbileue]nys beleue B.
2303   þo] þe B.
2304   folted men] many folys B.

Thre sones had thare oon abram   2305
Also nacor and aram
Thre sones had nacor þe lele
Vs and bus and batuele
Of vs coom Iob of bus balam
Of batuel rebecka & laban   2310
Of aram a sone wiþ douȝtris þre
Melcha . loth & dame sare fre   2312

Of þe þridde elde is now to telle
Who so wole a stounde dwelle
Of Abraham now wol we drawe   2315
Þat roote is of þe *cri*sten lawe
I say þerfore he is þe roote
For of hym sprong oure alþer boote
Þat boote þat brouȝte vs into myrþe
Þourȝe þe hooly maydenes birþe   2320
Of hym & his kyn shul we rede
Þat wondirly bigan to brede
Oure lady wex out of his sede
We pray hir for hir maydenhede
Þat we may of þis story say   2325
Hir to worshepe hir sone to pay
Abraham þat we here of neuen
Was wel loued wiþ god of heuen
Trewe he was euer in dede
Ful of feiþ & of holyhede   2330
He and his good wyf sare
Ful of chastite þei ware
Two douȝteres had aram his broþ*er*

2305   *om* L. Thre...oon] Thare þre sones had B.
2306   *om* L. nacor] machore B.
2307   nacor] matore B.
2308   *first* and] *om* B.
2309   balam] labam B.
2312   &] *om* B. fre] þe fre B.
2313-4   *om* FGHTLB.
2314a   elde] age B.
2314b   *Followed by* Of abraham B.
2316   þe *cri*sten] crystys B.
2317   I] *om* B.
2319   *first* þat] And þat B. *second* þat] *om* B. into] alle in B.
2321   his] of his B.
2324   hir] here B.
2327   here] *om* B.
2328   loued] belouyd L. wiþ] of LB. of] in L.
2330   Ful of] Of full B. *second* of] *om* TLB

He spoused þat oon nachor þat oþer
For bi þe lawe þat þei lyued ynne   2335 fol. 14v col. 1
Men shulde not spouse but in her kynne
He was boþe meke and hende
Oure lorde him made his pryue frende
He loued soþfastenesse & riȝte
Þerfore oure lord to him hiȝte   2340
A childe to brede of his ospringe
Þat al of þraldam shulde bringe
And þer shulde also of his seede
So myche puple aftir breede
Þat no man myȝte þe somme neuen   2345
Moore þen þe sterres of heuen
Ne þenne þe grauels in þe see
So multiplyinge shulde þei be
He leued þis wiþ herte stabel   2350
Þis biheste myȝte be no fabel   2349
As he leued so he fonde
Oure lorde helde him trewe couenonde
But longe he ladde him wiþ delay
To more þe mede of his fay
//Of sixty ȝeer he was & fyue   2355
Whenne his fadir was faren of lyue
For him he was in mournyng þouȝt
Til oure lord him counfort brouȝt
And seide to hym wiþ a sown
Abraham loke þou make þe bown   2360
Þou þi catel and þi meyne
Out of þis londe þat ȝe fle

2334   Þat oon] þe toon TLB. nachor] & Nacor B. þat oþer] þe toþer TLB
2335   þat þei] þey þat B. ynne] þen B.
2336   Men] þey B. spouse] wedde B. her] his B.
2338   him made] made hym B.
2340   to him] hym be B.
2341   brede] bryng B.
2343   also] aftyr B.
2344   aftir] of B.
2347   om B. in] of L.
2348   shulde] schull B.
2351   leued] beleuyd B.
2352   him] his B.
2353   wiþ] in B.
2354   fay] paye B.
2356   of] on L.
2357   þouȝt] broght B.
2358   Til] To B. brouȝt] þought B.
2361   þou] Wiþ B.
2362   ȝe] þow B.

ʒe shul wende to a bettur londe
To loth þi broþer sone in honde
To canaan ʒe mosten drawe   2365
A lond þat I shal ʒow shawe
Þou leue aram þe londe of ire
Of canaan to be lorde and syre
Þider to wende be not ferde
Þere shal be þi kyndely erde   2370
Alle þat wonen þer aboute
To þe shul be vndirloute
Þere shal þi name reysed be
And alle þe heires þat comen of þe
I shal hem blisse þat þe wol blisse   2375 fol. 14v col. 2
My blissyng shul þe oþere mysse
// Abraham went & wiþ him loth
Meyne & catel wel I woot
He coom & dwelled he and þei
Bisyde sichen in a valey   2380
But þere felons folk þei fond
Þat myche waasted of þat lond
Als soone as þei þider cam
God him shewed to abraham
And seide abraham þis is þe land   2385
Þat þou & þyne shul haue weldand
Abraham of trouþe so trewe
By bethel reised an auter newe
He worsheped god kyng of blis
And he him blessed & alle his   2390
Abraham turned him into þe souþ
To se þat londe þouʒt vnkouþ
In pees he wende hit haue in wolde
As oure lord hadde hym tolde
But soone whenne he had þe lond   2395
An hunger fel I vndirstonde

2365   ʒe] ʒow B.
2369   ferde] aferde B.
2372   To...be] Schall be to þe B.
2374   þe] þo] TL.
2375   blisse] blylys B.
2376   oþere] neuyr B.
2381   felons] felowis L.
2385   þe] þy B.
2388   By bethel] Besely B.
2391   him into] to B.
2392   þouʒt] he thoght L; hym þought B.
2393   wolde] hold L.
2394   hadde...tolde] hym had I tolde B.

Her corn wanted on vche syde
Hard hit was hem to abyde
Abraham to selle fond no sede
To egipte wende most he nede   2400
Sare his wyf wiþ hym to lede
Hade þei no corn hem wiþ to fede
And as þei þidurwarde went
Þis forwarde made þei þere present
//Lemmon he seide soore I me drede   2405
Now we go bi þis vncouþ lede
For þou art feir whenne þei þe se
Wiþ myȝte þei wol þe take fro me
Seye þou þerfore to oon & oþer
Þat þou art my sistir & I þi broþer   2410
Elles þe folk whenne þei þe se
Wol me sle for loue of þe
Sir she seide hit shal be do
Þenne coom þei þat cuntre to
Whenne þat folk had hir sene   2415 fol. 15r col. 1
Alle speke of hir she was so shene
And so hir preysed to þe kynge
Þat he made hir to hym brynge
But god hir kepte þat was hir wiþ
And saued hir so in his griþ   2420
Þat myȝte no man wiþ leccherye
Hir body touche wiþ vilenye
Þe kyng was ferd for goddes gram
And delyuered hir to Abraham
And seide why mades þou vs in were   2425
To calle þi wyf þi sister dere
Take hir here and brouke hir wel
Of þyn wol I neuer a del

2399   selle fond] tylle fonde he B.
2401   Sare] Bare L. wiþ] *om* L. to] gan B.
2402   Hade] Nad L. hem] hym L.
2404   made... present] þey made verament B.
2410   þat] *om* TLB.
2412   loue] þe loue B.
2414   þat] þe B.
2415   þat] þe B.
2416   speke] spake B.
2418   made hir] hir made TLB.
2419   wiþ] wight L.
2420   so]*om* B. his] þat B.
2421   myȝte...man] no man myght B.
2426   To calle] And callyd B. dere] *om* B.

But leuer me is of myn þou haue
Gold and siluer he hym ȝaue   2430
And commaundide þourȝe his lond
Men shulde him plese & haue in hond
And whenne he wolde no lenger lende
Þat he most frely hamwarde wende
And alle þe godis he wiþ him led   2435
To lette him streitly he forbed
Abraham went home & his wif sare
He loued hir bet þen he dide are
For worshepe þat she made him wynne
And she vnsouȝt sakles of synne   2440
Into betel þei coom anoon
Þere he firste sett his auter stoon
Bitwene him & his neuew loth
Beestaile þei hade ynouȝe I woot
To commune pasture þei took þe lond   2445
Þat þere lay nexte her hond
But whenne her stoor bigan to brede
Her pasture þo wex al nede
Þerfore her herdis stroof for hit
Her beestis nedis most þei flit   2450
Fro þat folk þei were among
Þat dide her stoor myche wrong
Þe nabethens þat lodly lede
Ful of wronge & wickedhede
Þei myȝt wiþ hem haue no rest   2455 fol. 15r col. 2
Þei most part to seke her best
Abraham seide wiþ wordis hende
Loth my neuew and my frende
Þis lond is wyde þat we are ynne
God vs helpe hit to wynne   2460

2429   But] om B.
2431   commaundide] comaunde B.
2436   He] þe kyng B.
2438   first he] And B. bet] bettur TB.
2440   And] ȝett B. vnsouȝt] was B.
2442   firste sett] sett fyrst B.
2446   her]to her B.
2448   þo wex]wex þo B.
2450   nedis] nede TL. nedis...þei] most þey nedys B.
2451   Fro] For TB.
2452   þat] þey B.
2455   wiþ] for B.
2458   and my] my gode B.
2460   wynne] twyn B.

Of þis cuntre þat is so wyde
Þou chese to wone on sum syde
Wheþer þou chese on riȝt or left
I wol take þat þou hast left
Loth loked toward flum iurdan   2465
A dale he chees to hym þan
A lussom lond & fair cuntre
Þe flum ran þourȝe fair to se
Þe lond of gomor þerby lys
Þat þenne was lyk to paradys   2470
Þat tyme ar hit had done þe sake
Til god þeron vengeaunce can take
Þat lond to wone In loth þouȝt beste
Abraham chees toward þe eest
Þe lond of sodom bar greet blame   2475
For hit was in a wickede fame
Þei synned so foule among hom
Þat boþe hem cursed god and mon
Abraham last & his þan
Bisyde þe lond of canaan   2480
Vndir þe foot of mount mambre
Þere he chees to sette his se
Þat ilke stide hett chebron
A wondur wynsum stide in won
He made an auter in þat stide   2485
And sacrifise þeron he dide
Þat oure lord shulde on him mynne
And make him worshepe to wynne
His tabernacle he sette þer sone
God lete myracle for hym done   2490
// In þat lond was a werre strong
And hit lastede sum del long
Foure kynges werred vpon fyue

2462   wone] one B.
2463   on] *om* B.
2464   take] ches B.
2465   toward...iurdan] to sodam B.
2466   A dale] þat valley B.
2468   flum] flode B. þourȝe] þoroght B.
2472   Til] þat B. can] gon LB
2473   wone] wynne LB.In] *om* B.
2474   toward] into B. eest] west B.
2476   a] *om* B.
2478   boþe] god L; *om* B. god...mon] boþe þe men & women L.
2479   last...his] by left hym L; lefth & ys B.
2484   wynsum] wynfull B.
2490   for] þere for B.

Þe fyue aȝeyn þe foure to stryue
Þei smoot togider neuer þe latur   2495 fol. 15v col. 1
In a dale bisyde a watur
So long þei hew on helm & shelde
Þat foure of fyue wan þe felde
Þe fyue ȝaf bak to wynne away
And fellen into a putt of clay   2500
Þere fel þei doun al in swowe
And her enemyes þere hem slowe
Siþ þei took to wynne þat lond
Al þat þei bifore hem fond
Loth þei tok and led hem wiþ   2505
Was noon þei wolde graunte griþ
Þei helde hores was þe lond
For þei hadde þe ouer hond
Hard helde þei loth þat day
A mon vnneþe myȝte passe away   2510
To come to Abraham for to telle
Of lothis chaunce how hit felle
Abraham was ful euel likonde
Whenne he herde þis typonde
He dide to geder togider his men   2515
Þre hundride eiȝte seruauntis & ten
And pryuely he made hem byde
Til aȝeyn þe euentyde
And þo he brouȝte hem to a pas
Men calde þere þen themas   2520
Þere he delt his folk in two
Þat þe oþere shulde, not skape hem fro
Þese kyngis hadde of no mon doute

2494   aȝeyn] aȝens B. to] gan B.
2495   smoot] fought B.
2497   helm] hem B.
2498   þat] þe B. fyue wan] þe fyue had B.
2501   al] *om* B. swowe] a slouȝe B.
2506   þei] þat þey B.
2507   was þe] þat was her B.
2510   A mon] *om* B. passe] any scape B.
2511   for] *om* B.
2512   felle] bifelle TB.
2513   was] *om* T.
2514   þis] þat B.
2515   togider] to hym L.
2516   eiȝte] & eyght B. &] *om* B.
2519   And þo] þan B. pas] pas *altered to* plas L; place B.
2520   calde] calle B. þere þen] yt there L.
2523   þese] þe T.

Her folk þei scatered al aboute
Abraham þat was in trouþe strong   2525
Heþen men he mett among
Fro hem he delyuered loth
Wiþ al þat catel vche grot
Slayn were þo knyȝtis þat nyȝt
Þourȝe þe grace of god almyȝt   2530
Þe folk of sodom were ful fayn
Whenne abraham was comen aȝayn
Þei sawe her frendis hool & sounde
And wiste her foos brouȝte to grounde
Melchisedech wiþ wille glade   2535 fol. 15v col. 2
Offeryng of wyn and breed made
Þat of ierusalemes londe
Was kyng & prest & hade in honde
Trewe he was wyse and hende
Of her conqueste took þe tende   2540
Abraham his benesoun ȝaf he
And bad alle to hym tentynge be
Of pray wolde abraham nouȝte haue
But vche man his owne ȝaue
Miche was þe loue word þon   2545
Þat Abraham gat of mony mon
Þei seide hit was he in siȝt
Oure lord in him wolde holde his hiȝt
// Abraham went hoom & wiþ him ledde
His folk & whenne he was in bedde   2550
In sleep he herde oure lordis steuen
Soþely to him spak in sweuen

2524   Her] His B. þei] he B.
2525   trouþe] þe crowþe B.
2526   Heþen men] Herdmen B. among] hem among B.
2528   þat] þe TB. vche] euery B.
2529   þo] that L. knyȝtis] kyngis B. þat nyȝt] with myȝt L.
2530   almyȝt] by nyȝt L.
2531   were] was TLB.
2534   foos] foe men B.
2536   of] with L.
2541   benesoun] blessyng B.
2542   alle...hym] hem all B.
2543   pray] þe pray B.
2544   man] a man L. ȝaue] he ȝafe B.
2546   mon] a man LB.
2548   Oure] þat oure B. in...holde] wold holde in hym B.
2550   folk] flocke TL.
2551   oure] ourer B.
2552   in sweuen] full evyn B.

And seide Abraham þar þe not drede
I shal þe helpe in al þi nede
Þat I haue þe in dede hiȝte   2555
To wynne þou shal not faile myȝte
Lord he seide how may þis be
What is þi wille to ȝyue to me
Þou wost wel childe haue I noone
But my seruauntis sone alone   2560
Þat serueþ me eliazar
Myn heire wolde I þat he war
Siþ þou me ȝaf noon oþer barn
Nay seide god I shal þe warn
Þat he þyn heire shal not be   2565
But a seede þat comeþ of þe
Abraham he seide come heroute
Byholde þe sky al aboute
Þe childer þat of þe shul brede
No more shal þou con hem rede   2570
Þen sterres in sky or sond in see
To knowe hit shal ful selcouþe be
Be trust in þis þat I þe hiȝt
Þe hit to reue shal noon haue myȝt
Abraham þis word forȝaat nouȝt   2575
Oure lord to serue was al his pouȝt
Þenne made Abraham his sacrifise   fol. 17r col. 1
As god him tolde on what wyse
Whenne þis was don & al purueide
A voys þenne þourȝe a cloude seide   2580
Þat þer aftir a wel longe while
In egipte shulde his sede exile

2553   þar] dar L.
2554   helpe] kepe B.
2555   I haue þe]þe haue B.
2556   shal] om B.
2558   is] as B. ȝyue] wynne L. second to] om B.
2563   Siþ] Syn L.
2567   heroute] þeroute T; oute B.
2568   sky al] fyrmament B.
2569   þe childer] þat chylde B.
2570   shal þou] schaltow B.
2571   first in] or T; on L; of þe B. second in] by þe B.
2572   selcouþe] felcouþe L; couþe B.
2573   Be] But L; om B. in þis] well to me B. þe] have B.
2574   þe…reue] To reue þe B. noon] no man B.
2575-2734   a leaf missing in H. Text is from T.
2575   þis] for þis B. forȝaat] þat B.
2580   þenne] om B.
2581   þer aftir] aftyrwarde B. wel] om B.

In þraldome foure hundride ȝere
But þei shulde aftir bye hit dere
Þei shulde hem holde in þat þrong   2585
But wroken on hem shulde be þat wrong
Þenne shulde þe seed of abraham
Aȝeyn com to her londe þan
In pees her heritage to holde
As tofore was hett & tolde   2590
Sare was childeles ȝitt wiþ þis
Þat myche þeraftir ȝerned I wis
She serued hir þis womman
Þat Agar hett Egipcian
She seide to Abraham priuely   2595
Þou seest no childer bere may I
And siþen I may bere no barn
Agar my womman I þe warn
Bi þe shal ligge if þou wol so
For I am bareyn me is wo   2600
If any childe of hir were þine
I wolde holde hit as for myne
Sare as she bifore had seid
Bi hir hosbonde agar leid
Agar was wiþ childe in hy   2605
And liȝtly let of hir lady
To Abraham dam sare saide
Þat wenche þat I bi þe layde
For she is wiþ childe bi þe
Greet spit she leteþ bi me   2610
Abraham hir sone vnswerde
Chastise hir þou hast þe ȝerde
So chastised sare hir þat day
Þat she was fayn to fle away
But in hir fliȝte as she ȝode   2615
An aungel coom biforn hir stode

2586   be þat] þay be B.
2590   tofore...tolde] I before have Itolde B. hett &] yt L.
2591   wiþ þis] Iwys B.
2592   ȝerned] longid L.
2596   childer] chylde B.
2601   hir] hers B.
2605   in] on B.
2606   liȝtly] lighter B. let] light L. lady] body L.
2608   *first* þat] þe B.
2609   For] *om* B. bi] wiþ L.
2610   Greet] And grete B. leteþ bi] haþe of B.
2613   sare hir] her Sare B.
2616   biforn] & byfor L; & afore B.

In wildernes bi a welle   fol. 17r col. 2
Þus gan he to hir spelle
He seide Agar whennes comes þou
And whodirwarde woltou go now   2620
Fro my lady she seide I go
For me she doþ mychel wo
Þe aungel seide wende aȝeyn
Hir to serue þou be feyn
Wende aȝeyn I saye for þi   2625
Of þi seed ȝitt shal multepli
Muchel folke and I þe warn
Þou art wiþ a knave barn
Þou calle him Ismael Agare
God wol couer þe of þi care   2630
He shal be fers & cruel boþe
Aȝein alle ledes wondir wroþe
Aȝein him alle. aȝein alle he
A wondir wiȝte mon shal he be
Agar hoom to hir lady went   2635
And serued hir wiþ good entent
Soone aftir for to telle
She was liȝter of ismaelle
Whenne he was born abraham had þon
Foure skore & six ȝere ouer gon   2640
Of þis childe he was as bliþe
As his fadir were brouȝt to lyue
Whenne he was fyue skore ȝere & nyne
God spak to him a litil tyme
Abraham he seide for me þou go   2645
I shal go for þe also
Multeplie þi seed I shal

2619   whennes] when L. comes þou] comstow B.
2620   go] om B.
2622   me...doþ] sche dothe me so B.
2625   I saye] he sayde B.
2626   ȝitt shal] schall ȝett B.
2628   þou] þat þou B. knave] om B.
2632   Aȝein] Aȝens B. wondir wroþe] he schal be loþe B.
2633   second aȝein...he] meyen schall be B.
2634   shal he] he schal B.
2638   liȝter] L has lighter, changed to lightyd.
2640   skore] score ȝere B. ȝere ... gon] Igone B.
2641   þis] his B.
2642   were] was B. to] of B.
2643   fyue] foure B. ȝere] om B.
2644   tyme] steuyn B.

He louted & þanked him of al
Þenne dud oure lord to eche his name
And seide þou hettest now abrahame   2650
Abraham hastou ȝore be calde
Þat name no lenger shaltou halde
Þi name is þus myche to rede
As fadir of mony folke in dede
And if þou holde my techyng   2655
Of þe shal com prince & kyng
Þat shul welde al þis cuntre   fol. 17v col. 1
As I bifore haue hette to þe
Þat þou hast had in knowleche
Þine as heritage shul hit reche   2660
Al þe kyndome of þis lond
To haue & holden in her hond
But now I wol a couenant new
Of þe & þine be holden trew
An holy token for to ken   2665
To parte ȝou from opere men
Holdeþ forwarde on þis wise
ȝoure knaue childre ȝe circumcise
Þe eiȝteþe day fro þei be born
Þis is to say þat þei be shorn   2670
On þat ilke lymme wher wiþ
Þei be knowe fro wymmen kiþ
Loke ȝe do as I say þe
As ȝoure soulis shul saued be
Who so is not so. þei may be bolde   2675

2648   of] with B.
2649   dud] seyde B. eche] change L.
2650   now] no mor L.
2651   ȝore] long B.
2652   no...shaltou] schaltow no more B.
2653   þus] as B.
2654   mony] mochell B.
2657   shul] þou B. al] *om* B.
2658   to] *om* B.
2662   hond] lond L.
2663   now] non L. a] of L. couenant]comenaunt B.
2664   trew] vntrew L. *The* vn *is superscript with a caret, in the same hand.*
2666   ȝou] þe B.
2669   eiȝteþe] viij L.
2670   þis] þat B.
2671   On] Of B. ilke] *om* B. wherwiþ] þat þey war with B.
2672   þei] *om* B.
2673   ȝe] þou B.
2675   *first* so] *om* L. þei] he B. be bolde] byhold L.

Þei shul not of my folke be tolde
Þou & þi childer hit shul bigynne
And al þat woneþ þi hous wiþynne
Loke fro þe be done away
Þe mon þat wol not holde his lay   2680
For þe werke of circumcisyng
Bereþ greet bitokenyng
Ne þi wif þat hette sare
Fro now shal she hett so no mare
Hir name shal be eched so   2685
Bi hir shal mychel good be do
Suche a son she shal þe bere
Þat shal be kyng & caysere
He shal serue me to queme
Þe lawe ful wel shal he ȝeme   2690
Þis couenaunt was faste wiþ þis
Oure lord went to heuen blis
// Abraham toke his men in sauȝt
And dud as god him hadde tauȝt
Him self & ismael he share   2695
And siþen alle his þat men ware
Of pritty ȝeer fro he was born   fol. 17v col. 2
Was Ismael when he was shorn
His fadir nynty & nyne þat day
Þei vndirtoke þis newe lay   2700
Wherby þei are kud & knowen
Þo folke þat of her kynde are drawen
// Whenne hit was hoot vpon a tide

2676   þei] þat B.
2677   hit shul] schall it B.
2678   woneþ] comeþ B.
2679   fro] þat fro B.
2680   þe mon] All men B. his] þis B.
2682   greet bitokenyng] a grete tokenyng B.
2683   Ne] Now B.
2684   Fro] om B.
2685   eched] changid L.
2688   þat] He B.
2690   þe] þis B. he] be B.
2691   couenaunt] comaundement B.
2693   toke] anon L. in sauȝt] sawght L.
2694   him hadde] had hym B.
2695   ismael] Israell L.
2696   siþen] om L. his...men] that his men L; þe men þat his B.
2697   fro] that L.
2701   Wherby] Wheþer L. are] be B. &] or L.
2702   þo] The LB. are] wer LB
2703   hit] Abraham B. vpon...tide] on a day B.

Abraham sat his hous bi syde
Biside þe dale of mount mambre   2705
He loked him fro & þenne say he
Toward him com childre þre
In likenes of god in trinite
But as oon he honoured þo
As o god & no mo   2710
Þe trinite say he bi þat siȝt
And gestened hem wiþ him þat nyȝt
Furst himself her feet wesshe
And siþ hem fed wiþ calues flesshe
Butter & breed þei eet also   2715
Þei asked sare where is sho
Abraham seide ȝondir wiþynne
Oure lord seide I wol þou mynne
At myn ȝeyncome bi my lif
A son shal haue sara þi wyf   2720
Sare wiþynne þere she sat
Herde þis word & lowȝe þerat
And seide on scorne wher we shal
Bicom aȝeyn to childer smal
For elde she wende to bere no barn   2725
But no þing she þouȝt may warn
But þat he may his wille do
Bi þat he com aȝeyn vs to
Þou shalt haue childe in litil while
Þar þe not for scorne smyle   2730
She seide for soþe smyle I nouȝt
And if [she] dude hit hir forþouȝt
Aftir þis rest vp roos þei
And abraham led him inwey

2707   childre] þe chyldyrn B.
2708   god in] þe B.
2711   say...þat] se hym be B.
2712   And] þey B. gestened] gestid L. hem] *om* B.
2713   wesshe] he wysch B.
2716   asked...sho] askyr *after* Sare tho L.
2718   þou] þe L. for sorow sche may no chylde wyn B.
2719   ȝeyncome] yencomyng L. bi...lif] *without* stryf L.
2723   on] in B.
2724   to] *om* B.
2725   wende to] thoght myȝt L.
2730   þar...for] þou nede not in L. smyle] to smyle L.
2731   She...soþe]For sothe she seid L.
2732   And] *om* L. she] *om* T. dude...hir] so did she yt L.
2733   rest] sone B.
2734   inwey] þe waye B.

Oure lord loked to sodomam   2735 fol. 16r col. 1
And þus saide to Abraham
Abraham he seide fro þe
Wol I not hele my pryuete
Þou and þyne are me so dere
Þat I wol ȝe my counsel here   2740
Of sodom haue I herde þe cry
Þe stinche recheþ to þe sky
Þe world is wors þen men neuen
Þe reeche recheþ into heuen
To se wol I myseluen go   2745
Of þat cry if hit be so
Þere wol I take vengeaunce strong
Þerto shal hit not be long
// Lord seide Abraham þyn are
Shalt þou þyne owne so forfare   2750
Hit semeþ not to be þi wille
For þe wicked þe goode to spille
Þi riȝtwisnes wol not so
For þe wicked þe gode to slo   2754
If þou þere fynde fyue siþe ten   2757
Fourty or þritty trewe men
Twenty or ellis twyes fyue
Shul alle þerfore haue her lyue   2760
Þus seide oure lorde but þere was noon
Trewe founde but loth aloon
Oure lord went forþ þon
Abraham to his hous hoom
At oon euentyde two aungels coom   2765
To lothus hous into sodom
Þei fond loth sittyng bi þe ȝate
To hem he roos fro þere he sate

2735   *Text again from* H. sodomam] Sodam B.
2738   hele] hyde B.
2741   cry]sey L
2742   *missing in* L.
2744   reeche] smoke B.
2746   Of] And of L. Of þat] To se þe B.
2750   Shalt þou] Schaltow B. so] folk B.
2753   þi] þe B. wol ... so] þe gode to se B.
2755-6   *om in* MSS FGHTLB
2757   siþe] or B.
2758   Fourty] þretty B. þritty]Fourty gode B.
2761   þus] ȝus T; þis B.
2763   forþ] his wey B.
2764   hoom] wan B.
2765   At] And B.

He preyed hem in goddis name
To gestne wiþ him & come home   2770
As for þat nyȝte & þei seide nay
But in þat strete dwelle wolde þay
But loth to his hous hem ledde
Wiþ siche as he had hem fedde
But er þei to bedde were boun   2775
Folke gedered out of þe toun
Foule felouns wiþ wicked entent   fol. 16r col. 2
Aboute lothis hous þei went
ȝong & olde childe and man
Hem þouȝte late þei þider wan   2780
On loth þei cryed þe hous aboute
And bad he shulde sende hem oute
Þe gestes hym cam by nyȝte tale
For soþe þei seide knowe hem we shale
Her sory synne on hem þei souȝte   2785
To haue done hit if þei myȝt
But loth er þey were warre
Fast þe dores con he barre
ȝerne on hem he cryed mercy
Þat þei shulde leue her foly   2790
He seide I haue here douȝteres two
Take and do ȝoure wille wiþ þo
My gestis lete ȝe lye in pees
For goddis loue wiþoute males
Þe more loth on hem souȝt   2795
Þe more þei preesed & ceesed nouȝt
Al his preyere myȝte not avayle
Nadde ben goddes good counsaile

2769   He] And B.
2770   gestne] gest B. & come] þay went B.
2771   As] *om* B. &] but L; *om* B.
2772   strete] stede B.
2775   *missing in* B.
2776   *An extra line follows* 2776 *in* B: To loteys house þey made hem boun.
2777   wicked] gode B.
2779-80   *om* B.
2780   wan] cam L.
2782   he] þey B.
2783   þe] Thy L. hym] that LB
2785   Her] hir L.
2786   To] For to B. if] yf þat L.
2787   er] or þat B.
2788   þe] his L. con] gon TLB. he] to B.
2795   loth] þat lote B. on] upon B.
2797   preyere] prayers B.
2798   Nadde] Ne had LB.

Þat made þo synful folk so mad
Þei niste where þei were bistad 2800
Oure lord made hem so blynde
Þat dore ne hous couþe þei not fynde
Her owne witt wiste þei nouȝt
Wheþen þei coom ny what þei souȝt
To loth spak on aungel þen 2805
& seide hast þou here any men
Sone or douȝter þat þou owe
To þe longynge hyȝe or lowe
Lede hem swyþe out of þis toun
Er þat hit be sonken doun 2810
Loth went & to his frendes spake
Þeroute Þei shulden his douȝtren take
Ryse vp he seide & fle ȝe soone
Þis cite today shal be fordone
Al þat loth myȝte to hem say 2815
Hem þouȝte hit was not but play
But erlyer men myȝte see fol. 16v col. 1
Þe aungels bad loth to flee
Þei seide [fle] wiþ þi meyne
Lest ȝe be lost wiþ þis cite 2820
Whenne þei seȝe loth be lettonde
Þei hym took by þe honde
His wyf and his douȝteres two
Þat myȝte vp loke þer was no mo
Whonne þei were fro þe doute 2825
And brouȝte feire þe toun wiþoute
Bi þen be goon þe liȝt of day
Þei bad hem holde forþ her way

2799 þo] om B.
2800 niste] wist neuere B.
2801 hem] them L.
2802 couþe] cowde L. not] non LB.
2803 wiste þei] ne wyst L.
2804 Wheþen] When LB. what] whedyr B. souȝt] þoght B.
2806 men] man B.
2807 þou] to þe L.
2812 þeroute] þat oute B. þei] þat TL.
2813 ȝe] you L.
2816 was not] nas no þyng L. play] a play B.
2817 erlyer] anon L; erly or þat B. see]her & se L.
2818 aungels] aungell B.
2819 þei] He B. fle] om H.
2820 ȝe] þou L
2821 be] om L. lettonde] flyttand LB.
2825 fro] fer fro B.
2827 Bi...begoon] Began þan B. begoon þe] by come ther L.

And but þei wolde forfaren be
To loke bihynde hem forbede he   2830
No dwellynge here þat ȝe make
Til ȝe þe ȝonder felde to take
Lest ȝe be take þese among
And slayn al for her wrong
// Lorde seide loth wiþ leue of þe   2835
In litil segor wolde I be
Þou haste þenne þider ȝare
For I do nouȝt til þou come þare
Bityme þat þe sunne ras
Strong cry in þat toun was   2840
Oure lord let reyne on hem anoon
Fro þe skye fuyr & brymstoon
Sodom & gomor wiþ al þe lond
Þat aboute hem lay nyȝehond
Of alle þo wonyngis þat þer was   2845
Is nouþer lafte tre ny gras
Ny no þing of þat lond vnsunke
Siche as þei breu þo þei drunke
Lothis wyf þis cry herde
And longed to se how þei ferde   2850
Wondris fayn wolde she fynde
And as she loked hir bihynde
A stoon she stondeþ bi þe way
And so shal do til domes day
As a salt stoon men seen hir stonde   2855
Þat beestis likken of þat londe
And ones in þe wike to say   fol. 16v col. 2
Is she clene likked away

2832   Til] To B. to] haue L; *om* B.
2834   her] their L.
2835   leue] þe leue B.
2836   In] Att B.
2837   haste] haste þe LB.
2838   til] to B.
2840   þat toun] þo tounnes T; þe cete B.
2842   þe skye] hevyn B.
2843   &] *om* B.
2845   þo] the LB.
2846   nouþer] þere non B.
2847   þat] þis B.
2848   *first* þei] þe B. þo] *om* L; suche B.
2849   þis] their L.
2854   do] stond L; *om* B. til] to B.
2855   seen] se B.
2856   likken] lykkyd B. *second* þat] þe B.

And siþ þei fynde hir on þe morne
Hool as she was biforne   2860
Þere fyue citees were wont to be
Is nouȝt now but stynkand see
Þat semeþ as lake of helle
No lyuyng þing may þerynne dwelle
If any fisshe þerynne be gon   2865
By ledyng of þe flum iurdon
Þe lyf is soone fordo wiþ stynke
Fro hit into þat watir synke
Men fyndeþ lumpes on þe sand
Of teer no fyner in þat land   2870
Þere stondeþ euer wondirly
A cloude þerfro vp to þe sky
If þou a brond þerynne wolt caste
Þe fire hit holdeþ þere stidfaste
Þourȝe brennyng of þat brymston   2875
Wherof þere is myche won
Þerby groweþ sum appel tre
Wiþ apples selcouþe feir to se
Whenne þei in honde are like a bal
To pouder þourȝe þat stynke þei fal   2880
Alle cristen men I rede ȝe take
Ensaumple bi þis wooful wrake
Þat al for lecchery done was
Þe foulest þat euer coom on plas
Þat hit was wicked was wel sene   2885
Bi þat wreche þat was so kene
Hoot & stynkynge is þat lake

2859   hir] his T.
2861   þere] þere þo TL; þer þe B.
2862   stynkand] a stynkyng B.
2863   lake of] blak as L; þe lak of B.
2864   þing] þin T.
2867   soone fordo] done sone B.
2868   Fro] Whan B. þat] þe B. synke] doth synke B.
2869   on] of B. þe] that L.
2870   no] non LB. þat] þe B.
2872   þerfro] evyn B.
2873   brond] rod B.
2877   sum] an LB.
2878   selcouþe] right L; þat ben B.
2879   are] be B.
2880   pouder] þondyr B. þat] þe B. þei]om B.
2882   bi] of B.
2884   on] in LB.
2885   second was] it was B.
2887   is] was B.

Fuyr & brymstone was þe wrake
Out of kynde her synne was done
Þerfore her kynde lost was soone   2890
Fleeþ þat synne al þis werde
For þis wreche þat ȝe haue herde
God forbede ȝe do þat synne
Þat ȝee in helle þerfore brynne
But if ȝe nede synne shal do   2895
Þe synne of kynde holde ȝou to
Þe kyndely synne wiþ wommon   fol. 17r col. 1
But sib ne spoused take ȝe noon
So fer ȝoure synne folweþ nouȝt
To forgete him þat ȝow wrouȝt   2900
Mony men for ouerwele
Hymself couþe nouþer se ne fele
Til þei synke into þat pit
Þat no man may hem þen flit
So dide þese wrecches of ioye tome   2905
Þei douted not goddis dome
Her welþe made hem oon & alle
In synne and sorwe for to falle
Þen coom a doom in hastite
To hem þat longe had spared be   2910
So shal dyȝe wiþouten ende
Þat in tyme wol not amende
// Loth ȝe herde telle of eer
Into þe felde he drouȝe for feer
In a caue he hidde him þo   2915

2889   her] þat B.
2890   lost was] was lost L.
2892   þis] þe B. ȝe] I L. herde] told L.
2894   in...þerfore] þerfore in hell B.
2895   synne shal] þe syn to B.
2896   to] vnto L.
2899   folweþ] ȝe folow B.
2900   wrouȝt] haþe bowght L.
2902   couþe nouþer] can not B. ne] so L; no B.
2903   Til] To B. þat] þe B.
2904   þen] þennes TB.
2905   tome] torne B.
2907   welþe] wreþ B.
2909   a doom] Iugement L. in hastite] of chastyte B.
2910   had spared] spared had B.
2911   dyȝe] do B.
2913   ȝe] þat ȝe B.
2914   þe] a B. for feer] forþe ere L.
2915   hidde him] hym hyd B.

He and his douȝteres & no mo
Abraham went on þe morne
To þat stide þere he was biforne
Had of oure lord taken his leue
And say þat soore gan hym greue   2920
Towarde þe cites loked he
A sorweful siȝte hit was to se
He sawe þat cuntre al bydene
Þat so fair biforne had bene
Wiþ sparcle & smeke couered abouen   2925
As hit were a brennyng ouen
For hit was goddes riȝtwis wreke
Þer aȝeyn durste he not speke
// Loth hym helde þe caue wiþynne
Himself & his douȝteres twynne   2930
But her fadir þat þei þere sawe
Þei wende alle men were don of dawe
Þourȝe þat ilke woful wrake
Þe elder to þe ȝonger spake
Sister in pryuete to þe I say   2935
Þou seest þis folk is al away
But loth oure fadir & we two   fol. 17r col. 2
Alyue is now lefte no mo
I leue monkynde fordone be
But hit be stored by me & þe   2940
Þis world is brouȝte to ende me þink
ȝyue we oure fadir ynouȝe of drynk

2916   &...mo] two B.
2918   þat] þe B. þere] þat B.
2919   Had] þere he had B. taken] take B.
2921   þe] þo TL.
2923   þat] þe B.
2924   so...biforne] before so fayre B.
2925   sparcle] sparcles TB.
2926   a brennyng] brennyng of an B.
2927   goddes riȝtwis] rightwes godis B.
2929   hym helde] hymselffe B.
2930   twynne] tweyne LB.
2931   þere]om B. her]þayre B.
2932   wende] wyst L. don...dawe] ouerþraw L; doun a dawe B.
2933   þourȝe] To B.
2935   in...þe] to þe In priuite B.
2936   folk] worlde B.
2937   loth] om B.
2938   Alyue] On lyfe B. is now] now is TLB.
2939   fordone] schall stroyed B.
2940   me & þe] þe & me B.
2941   brouȝte] brode B.
2942   ȝyue] ȝef B. ynouȝe] ȝif Inough B.

Whenne he is dronken witturly
In bed we shul go lye hym by
For myʒte we any barnes brede   2945
Me þinke þe world þerof had nede
As þei had spoke so þei wrouʒt
Þe fadir his owne dede wiste nouʒt
He wist not whenne he bi hem lay
But boþe wiþ childe soone were þay   2950
Amon & moab were geten so
Bitwixe loth & his douʒteris two
Of hem coom so wickede lede
Þat nouþer drouʒe to worþi dede
To a stide þat het damas   2955
Þiderwarde her wonynge was
Of mony men þat were gode
Þei refte catel & shedde blode
// Abraham siked in hert ful soore
Fro þen he wolde þat he wore   2960
To a cuntre cadades he flit
Abimalech was lord of hit
His sistur he calde sara his wyf
Þat for hir shulde ryse no stryf
He dredde þe folk ful of pryde   2965
Whil he lyued hem bysyde
But hard hit is to kepe I wis
Þing þat vche man wolde were his
And namely siche a þing
As is desired of greet lordyng   2970
Abimalech fined nouʒt

2944   go] *om* B.
2945   For...we] ʒef we myght B.
2946   þe...þerof] therof þe world L.
2950   boþe] sone B. soone] boþe B.
2952   Bitwixe] Betwene B.
2953   so] þe B.
2954   þat nouþer] They ne L. nouþer drouʒe] neuyr doght B.
2956   her] he T.
2959   siked] siʒhed LB. in...ful] wondyr B. ful] *om* T.
2960   þen] þens B.
2961   cadades] hight cadadas B.
2962   Abimalech] Amalech B.
2965   þe] of þe B.
2966   Whil] When B.
2967   kepe] speke B.
2968   þing] Of þing B.
2969   namely] many B. a þing] þingys B.
2970   As]*om* B. lordyng]lordyngis B.
2971   Abimalech]Amalech B. fined]faynyd L.

Til sarra was tofore him brouȝt
But god on nyȝt coom to þe kyng
In sleep & seide þis tokenyng
Wolt þou kyng short þi lyf   2975
Þou hast anoþer mannes wyf
Lord he seide wolt þou me sloo   fol. 17v col. 1
Þat wist not þat hit was so
Þei tolde boþe to oon and oþer
She was his sister he hir broþer   2980
And also lord wel woost þou
She is clene as she was ar now
I woot he seide be ȝee clene
Hit were not so had I not bene
Fro touche of hir I saued þe   2985
Þat þou shuldes not synne in me
ȝelde hir to hir husbonde wiȝt
He is a prophete holy and riȝt
And if þou do any oþer rede
Þou and þyne alle shul be dede   2990
// Vp roos þe kyng anoon bi nyȝt
And calde his men into his siȝt
Of his warnyng he hem tolde
Þei were aferde boþe ȝonge & olde
He dide to calle abraham soone   2995
And seide why hast þou þus done
What haue I done aȝeyn þi like
Þat þus woldes me biswyke
Sir he seide I me biþouȝte
Þat goddes awe dred ȝe nouȝt   3000
ȝoure harm wende I so best to fle

2972 Til]To B. tofore]before B.
2973 But] om B. on] at L; be B.
2975 þou] þy B. þi] þe B.
2977 wolt þou me] wiltow one B.
2978 þat] I B.
2980 he] & he TB.
2981 woost þou] wostow B.
2982 She] þat sche B.
2983 be] ȝitt be TLB.
2984 so...not] yf I so nere had B.
2985 Fro touche] For cause B.
2987 wiȝt] here B.
2989 do] done L.
2991 þe] þat B. bi nyȝt] ryght B.
2993 his] þis TL.
2996 hast þou] hastow B.
2998 þus] þou B. biswyke] vngolyke L.
3001 wende...so] I wende B.

And seide she shulde my sister be
To abraham þo ȝaf þe kyng
In worship mony a ryche þing
And made hym moost to hym priue   3005
Toke him to welde al þat cuntre

Bi þis coom sara to þe tyde
Of birþe myȝt she no lenger abide
Þen was yssac hir sone born
Þat was longe bihet biforn   3010
And circumcised þe eiȝteþe day
Aftir þe custom of þat lay
Þe name of Issac is to say
A mon þat tokeneþ ioye & play
And for þe burþe of yssac   3015
Greet ioye dide his frendes make
Þat wondir childe ful of hap   fol. 17v col. 2
Whenne he was wened fro þe pap
His fadir slouȝe sheep & neet
And made a feest to frendes greet   3020
Mete and drynk he ȝaf hem alle
Þat wolde come to his halle
Isaac was ȝongur þen Ismael
On a day bitidde and fel
Þat þese breþere pleyed same   3025
Sara bihelde & þouȝte no game
She seide Abraham þat bastard
Do him away he haue no part
Wiþ my sone of oure heritage
Or elles þou doost greet outrage   3030
I wol whatsoeuer men say
His modir & he be done away

3004   a] *om* B.
3005   *first* hym] hem L. to] *with* B.
3006   cuntre] conty L.
3008   abide] byde LB.
3010   biforn] toforn TL.
3012   þat] þe B.
3019   sheep] bothe schepe B.
3020   greet] gete L.
3022   to] into B.
3023   þen] that L.
3024   On] And on B. bitidde...fel] yt befyll B.
3025   breþere] chyldyrn B. pleyed] pley in L; pleyed in B.
3028   haue] hathe B.
3029   oure] *om* B.
3030   þou doost] dostow B.

Abraham þis took to herte
And þ ouȝte hir wordis ful smerte
Herfore he was in heuy þ ouȝte 3035
Til oon aungel him worde brouȝte
Abraham he seide þinke not ille
Þou most do þi wyues wille
Of þi mayden & hir barn
Hir biddyng shal þou not warn 3040
For ysaac shal bere þe name
Of þi seed sir abrahame
Of ysmael out of spousage
Shal mony come kene & sauage
On þe morne whenne hit was day 3045
Boþe were þei done away
Out of þat hous was put agar
Hir sone on hir bak she bar
Watir & breed wiþouten more
She tok hir wiþ & wept ful soore 3050
Now gooþ þat wrecche wille of wone
In wildernesse wandrynge alone
Her breed wanted her watir is goon
Hope of her lyues hadde þei noon
By a welle vndir a tre 3055
Þe childe she leyde & gon to fle
For sorwe she myȝte not þeron seen fol. 18r col. 1
But wayted whenne hit deed shulde ben
And whil she mened þus hir mood
Coumfort coom hir sone good 3060
An aungel coom & seide agare
What dost þou why makes þou care

3033   to] at B.
3034   ful] were full B.
3035   Herfore] þerfore B.
3036   oon] þe B.
3038   do] nedys do B.
3040   shal þou] schaltow B.
3043   out...spousage] and hys lynage B.
3044   sauage] sage L.
3045   morne] morwe T.
3047   þat] þe B.
3051   wille] wele L. of wone] alone B.
3052   alone] in wone B.
3053   second her] he T.
3054   Hope] om L. her] om B. hadde] hope had L.
3056   fle] sle L.
3059   And whil] I wylle L. mened] mevid L; mengyd B.
3060   hir sone] to her B.
3062   dost þou] dostou TB. makes þou] makestow B.

God haþ herde þi childes cry
Rys & take hit vp forþi
Lede hym ʒonder & haue in mynde   3065
A welle þere þou shalt fynde
And a tre wiþ fruyt ful goode
For þe and þi childes fode
Here shal þou wiþ him wone
And foster forþ here þi sone   3070
She dide þe childe drink of þe welle
In þat wildernes gon þei dwelle
Longe dwelled þei so þoore
Til ismael was waxen more
And elynge lyf þere þei ledde   3075
In wildernes were þei fedde
Whenne he to mon waxen was
Archer was he beste in plas
Whenne he hadde good elde kipt
He spousid a wyf of egipt   3080
And woned þere as wilde man
In þat desert þat hett pharan
// Þis abraham was of longe abode
And also of ful clene lyflode
Oure lord hym ʒaf his lawe to hede   3085
And made hym patriarke in dede
He seide Abraham I shal þe ʒyue
Þe lawe þat þou owe in to lyue
Lord he seide myself and myne
At þi wille al is þyne   3090
I and my wyf are þyne owen
Þat are we wel aknowen

3064   Rys] Aryse B.
3066   þere...shalt] schaltow þere B.
3069   shal þou] schaltow B.
3070   foster] bryng B. here] so B.
3072   In þat] And in þe B.
3073   Longe] So long þey B. þei so] *om* B.
3074   Til] To B. ismael] Isaell L.
3075   An elynge] A long L.
3078   Archer] An Archer L.
3080   spousid] weddyd B. of] *om* T; in B.
3081   And] He B. wilde] a wyld L.
3082   hett] high L.
3083   of longe] long of B.
3084   of] a L. ful] *om* B.
3085   hym ʒaf] ʒafe hym B. hede] rede L; lede B.
3088   in] men B. lyue] leve LB.
3089   Lord] Sare B. self] lyfe B.
3092   þat] And þat B.

Þi biddyng wol we do ful fayn
Shul we do neuer þer aȝayn
What shal I do lord þou me telle 3095
Þou shalt go in to þat felle
Þere shal þou fynde my messanger   fol. 18r col. 2
Of erþe make þou an auter
Boþe of þi corn & of þi fee
Þere shal þou afferynge make to me 3100
Gladly lord as þou hast seide
Soone was abraham purueide
Of crop of korn and oþer catel
To god his tiþe ȝaf he wel
Hit brent reche ros vp ful euen 3105
Þe smel was swete & souȝte to heuen
In þat tyme þat I of mene
Þe folk was good þe world was clene
So good beþ hit neuer I wis
So myche of welþe so myche of blis 3110
Þouȝe man myȝte neuer so myche welde
So faste hit draweþ to doun helde
To wrecched dome al is went
To lerne god ȝyue fewe entent
Þe childe bereþ now þe witt away 3115
Foly is gomen nowaday 3116

Of ysaac now wole we neuen
Þat loued was wiþ god of heuen
Hereþ of god al weldonde 3117
How he asayed his trewe seruonde
Wel loued abraham ysaac

3094 aȝayn] aȝay T.
3095 þou] ȝow B.
3096 felle] selle B.
3097 shal þou] þou schalt B.
3099 *This line appears in* MS B *after line* 3101.
3101 as...seide] þo seyde he B.
     B *inserts 2 lines here*: As þou haste seyde so schall it be *and* 1.3099.
3103 and] of B.
3105 brent] brenne B. reche] þe reche L; riche B.
3107 of] *om* B.
3108 folk] worlde B. good] Clene B. world...clene] folke gode B.
3109 beþ] beyth L. beþ hit] schall it be B.
3112 helde] elde B.
3113 wrecched] wrech B.
3114 lerne]louyn B. fewe entent] þey no tent B.
3115 now...witt] wiþ þe L. *The* wiþ *is inserted above the line with a caret.*
3116 gomen] comyn L; gomiyn B. nowaday] now all day B.
3116b of] in L.

His sely sone wiþouten lak   3120
He tauȝte him firste god to drede
And so to leue al wickedhede
He bigan to loue hym so
Þat myȝte he no whyle him forgo
Oure lord wolde as myȝty kyng   3125
Asaye abraham wiþ sum þing
To abraham oure lord spak
And seide where is þi sone ysaac
Al at þi wille þenne lord seide he
I wol þat þou offere him to me   3130
Gladly lord þou me him ȝaue
Good skil hit is þat þou him haue
To oure lord he was so trewe
Þat myȝte no pite make him rewe
But he had leuer his childe spille   3135 fol. 18v col. 1
Þen do aȝeyn his lordes wille
Þis childe was bihet mony a ȝere
Ar he were sent sough[t] wiþ preyere
Abraham wende wiþouten wene
Þat he shulde his heire haue bene   3140
Now is he asked on þis wyse
To god to make of sacrifise
Þouȝe hit were grisly and grille
He laft not oure lordis wille
But asked him wiþouten abyde   3145
How he him shulde sacrifise þat tyde
And he to telle þo bigon
ȝondir hyȝe hille vpon
Shal þou brenne þi sone for me
Gladly lord þenne seide he   3150
Now shul ȝe here how hit wasse
Þe childe he caste vpon an asse
And took wiþ him knaves two
But þei ne wiste whider to go

3120   His] A B.
3122   wickedhede] wrechydhede B.
3129   þenne] *om* B.
3134   þat] That þer L; þer B. pite] bete B.
3136   aȝeyn...lordes] aȝens goddys B.
3137   a] *om* B.
3138   sought] sough H. sought wiþ] þorouȝ B.
3143   þouȝe] ȝef þat B. grisly and] fule B.
3146   him] *om* B. sacrifise] sacryfy hym B.
3152   caste] did cast L.
3153   And] He B.
3154   But] Boþe L. ne wiste] nuste TLB. whider] wheþer LB.

Þat feld he welke dayes þre   3155
To seche þe stide þere he wolde be
Whenne he coom þere as he tiȝt
Of þe asse þe childe dude he liȝt
Toke him wiþ him no mon more
His meyne he bad abyde him þore   3160
His counsel wolde he no mon say
Why he þat childe brouȝte þat way
Swerd ne fyr forȝat he nouȝt
ȝong Isaac a fagot brouȝte
Sir he seide where shal we take   3165
Þat beest oure sacrifise to make
Siþ we wiþ vs brouȝte noon
God he seide shal sende vs oon
Wiþ þis he stood þe childe nyȝe
And drowȝe his swerd pryuelye   3170
Þat þe childe were not war
Er he had done þat char
He lifte his hond him to smyte
But goddis aungel coom ful tite
Ar he myȝte ȝyue þe dynt   3175 fol. 18v col. 2
His swerde bihynde him he hynt
And bad him þere bisyde him take
A sheep his sacrifise to make
He loked bisyde him in þe þornes
And say hit longe by þe hornes   3180
Þe angel helde stille þe swerd
And saide of coumfort siche a word
Abraham holde stille þin arm
To þi sone þou do no harm

3155   feld...welke]folowyd hym B. welke] went L.
3156   stide] place B. he wolde] yt schuld B.
3157   ashe] he had B.
3158   *second* þe...he] he dyd doune B.
3159   Toke] He toke B. him] he L; *om* B. no mon] meyne no B.
3160   him] *om* B.
3165   Sir] fadyr B.
3166   sacrifise] ofryng for B.
3170   pryuelye] full preuely B.
3171   were] was L.
3172   That he wold a made þat far L.
3176   His] þe B.
3177   bisyde him] besydes B.
3178   sheep] ram B. to] wiþ to B.
3179   bisyde] besydes B.
3180   longe] honge TL.
3184   no] none B.

Oure lord forbedeþ him to slo   3185
Þi dere sone þat þou louest so
Þou louest hym more wiþouten wene
Þen þi sone þat is now sene
Wel louest þou hym and drede
Wel shal he quyte þi mede   3190
ȝe shul his blessyng haue for why
Myche he shal ȝow multiply
For loue of þi faiþful fay
Shal vche lede come to þi lay
God haþ today þe visited so   3195
Þi dede shal neuer of mynde go
Þi buxomnes al folk shal fynde
Þat shul be bred of þi kynde
Of þis lettyng he was ful glad
And dude as þe aungel him bad   3200
Þe sheep he sacrifised & brent
And siþen homwarde he went
Þe fadir gon þe sone forbede
To any man to telle þis dede
Fadir he seide be ful bolde   3205
For me beþ hit neuer tolde
Þei went aȝeyn to bersabe
Þere þei had lefte her meyne
//Sara had six score ȝeer & seuen þo
And dyȝed wiþouten childer mo   3210
Þen ysaac no moo she bare
And abraham for hir had kare
In ebron biried hir abraham
Þere firste was buried olde Adam

3185   him] þe hym L; þou hym B. to] *om* B.
3187   wiþouten wene] þat is now sen B.
3188   þat...sene] *with*outen wene B.
3189   louest þou] louestou T; þou louest B. and] in L.
3190   shal...þi] þou hast quit hym hys B.
3194   lede] chill B.
3195   to day] þis day B. visited] visit B.
3196   þi] þis B. of] fro L.
3197   al] þe B.
3198   be bred] come B.
3200   þe] *om* B. him] *om* B.
3202   homwarde he] he homewarde B.
3203   gon...sone]þe son gan B.
3205   ful] ȝou B.
3206   beþ] shalle LB. tolde] be told LB.
3210   And] When sche B.
3213   ebron] Ebrew L.
3214   þere] þat B.

Abraham willed in his lyue
Þat ysaac had wedded a wyue
And wolde she were if hit myʒt be
Of his kynde & his cuntre
Men shulde hir seche in þat land
Þere his frendes were weldand   3220
A seriaunt sone commandide he
Þat moost knew of his pryuete
Þat euer had ben at his fyndyng
Fro he was a chylde ʒing
Vpon his kne he dide him swere   3225
Þat he shulde trewe erned bere
And þat he shulde ʒyue hool entent
To fulfille his commaundement
Frend he seide wende in hye
Vnto mesopothanye   3230
Þere þou woot oure frendes wone
To seke a wyf to my sone
And if she may be founden lele
Brynge hir hoom wiþ myche wele
But brynge þou him no womman   3235
Of þe kynde of canaan
Sir he seide what shal I do
Þis ilke mayde if þat sho
Wiþ no catel come wiþ me
Þen of þin oþ I holde þe fre   3240
For ysaac wiþ no forward
Wol I he wende þidirward
Gladly he seide hit shal be done
Þis mon [m]ade him redy soone
Fast he hyed to his goyng   3245
Wiþ tresour greet & preciouse þing
Suche as maydenes han mistere
Al þat ten camels myʒte bere

3216   wedded] wed B.
3217   And] A L; He B.
3220   frendes] kyn B. weldand] wonnand L; duellande B.
3221   seriaunt] servaunt LB. sone] þo B.
3227   And]In L.
3228   To] for to B.
3230   Vnto] vnt T; Into B.
3232   second to] for B.
3241   no] non B.
3242   Wol] Wolde B. wende] weddyd B.
3244   made] nade H.
3246   tresour greet] grete tresoure B. preciouse] ryche B.
3247   mistere] of mistere TLB.

Ringe & broche þat were proude
Gold & stoon for mayden shroude   3250
Þat whoso him say myȝt vnderstonde
He comen was fro a riche londe
To mesopothanye soone coom he
And soone he fonde þat cite
Whenne he coom nyȝhonde þe toun   3255 fol. 19r col. 2
By a wel he liȝte doun
A preyere made he in þat plas
And þus bisouȝte god of gras
Lord he seide þat al welde may
Þat my lord honoureþ euery day   3260
For whos loue he wolde not warn
To sacrifise his owne barn
To whom to seke a wyf I fare
Lord þou sende me oon sumwhare
And so my seruyse set to seme   3265
Þat to þi worshepe may be queme
And siche a wyf to ysaac
Þat may be good him to tak
Him to ioye & menske to þe
Lord þou graunt þat hit so be   3270
And graunte me bi þis welle here
Tristy to be of my preyere
For bi þis welle wol I byde
What of myn ernede wol bityde
Here wol I be til þat I se   3275
Maydenes come fro þis cite
Her watir at þis welle to drawe

3249   Ringe...þat] Ryngys brochys þere B.
3250   stoon] stonys B. shroude] schulde B.
3251   whoso] who TLB.
3252   comen was] was come B.
3254   þat] þat riche B.
3255   nyȝhonde] nerhande B.
3256   liȝte] sett hym B.
3257   A] And L. in...plas] of hys grace B.
3258   of gras]MS B *has* of h *crossed out*; in þat place B.
3259   welde] well B.
3263   *second* to] I B. I] to B.
3266   to] may be to B. may be] *om* B.
3268   him...tak] withouten lak B.
3269   & menske] & plesur L; honoure B.
3273   byde] abide L.
3274   What...wol] What soeuyr of me B.
3275   til] to B.
3276   þis] þat B.
3277   watir] *om* B. welle] welle watyr B.

Þere shal I my woman knawe
She þat [shal] bete my þirst
I shal hir holde as for best   3280
He nadde rested but a þrowe
Of maydenes he say come a rowe
Þe formast was vnlauȝter mylde
Hir semed no þing to be wylde
Was she not of semblaunt liȝt   3285
Rebecca hir name hiȝt
Batuel hir fadir snel
Hir semed alle hir werkes wel
Sittyngly hir watir she tooke
Þis mon faste dud on hir loke   3290
He was witty and deuyse
He seide to hir on þis wyse
Mayden he seide ȝyue me drynke
Myche I haue on þe to þinke
I am a man faryng þe weye   3295 fol. 19v col. 1
Myn harnay[s] dide I here doun leye
Of my passage I was in doute
For no man knowe I here aboute
Me were loþ if I myȝte were
Men dude me harm on my gere   3300
Frend she seide þyn askyng
Nis not but litil þing
Þou shalt hit haue wiþ good wille
And þi camailes to drynke her fille
For here vs wanteþ no vessel   3305
Bolle ne boket ny no fonel

3278   woman] mayden B.
3279   shal] om H. bete] bote L; here bete B.
3280   as for] for þe B.
3281   nadde] ne had L; had B.
3282   Of] When B. a] on a B.
3283   formast] fayrest B. vnlauȝter] of laghter B.
3286   hiȝt] was ryght B.
3287   Batuel] Batuel het TLB.
3288   first Hir] Her B. second hir] he B.
3289   hir] þere B.
3290   faste dud] did fast L.
3291   deuyse] wyse B.
3296   harnays] harnay H.
3298   knowe] knew T.
3300   my] any B.
3301   she] she she L. þyn] thyng L.
3302   Nis not] Ne ys B. litil] a litell B.
3304   fille] The edge of MS B is torn here, & this word does not appear.
3306   ne] om B. no] om B.

She drouȝe hem alle ynouȝe of drinke
Lefte she not for no swynke
Þis oþer man myȝte not blyn
To biholde þis fair maydyn 3310
How alle hir dedes dude hir seme
Þi[s] mon þouȝte hem to queme
Mayde he seide by þis hond
Hastou any fadir lyuond
ȝe she seide & modir wiþ al 3315
To house gladly þat wol þe cal
Fodder and hay þou shal be boun
No feirere Inne in al þe toun
He hir ȝaf a ȝifte anoone
A golde ring þat briȝte shoone 3320
Þankynge god to erþe he fel
Þe mayde ran hoom of hym to tel
She had a broþer het laban
He ran forþ aȝeyn þe man
Bi tokene soone were þei knawe 3325
To ryche gestenyng was he drawe
Þenne wist þei bi þis messangere
Abraham was sib hym ful nere
Ete ne drynke nouþer he wolde
Til he hadde his eronde tolde 3330
And þe sikernes was made
Likenes to rauen he not hade
Wel be siche a messangere
His message forþ to bere
Þat of himself reccheþ nouȝt 3335 fol. 19v col. 2

3307   of] to B.
3308   Lefte] Lett B.
3309   oþer] ilk B.
3312   þis] þi H. hem] hym L.
3313   þis] þi TLB.
3317   Fodder] Corne B. þou...be] schaltow have B.
3318   Inne] *om* B. þe] þis TLB.
3320   þat...shoone]*with* a stone B.
3321   þankynge] He þankyd B. erþe] þe erþe B.
3323   het] þat hight B.
3325   tokene] tokyns L. were þei] was he B.
3328   sib] hid L. sib...ful] to hem sybbe B.
3329   wolde] nolde B.
3330   Til] Or B.
3331   sikernes]sckyrnes L.
3332   rauen] a ravyn L. not] ne B.
3333   be] fare L; worþe B.
3334   His] That so his L. forþ to] will L. to] so to B.
3335   reccheþ] restyþ L; recchyd B.

Til his nedes be ful wrouʒt
Þe mariage dide he þenne make
Bitwene rebecca and ysaake
To vchone ʒaf he ʒiftis sere
Aftir þat þei worþi were 3340
And clad þe may in ryche wede
As was lawe in þat lede
To vchon he ʒaf sum þing
Batuel hym made good gestenyng
A morwe in goddis benesoun 3345
Rebecca was lad of toun
Hir modir als wiþ hir ladd
Til þei coom nyʒe þere hir radd
Þere wonynge sir Abraham was
Isaac was not fer fro plas 3350
As Isaac went hym to roo
And þouʒte of þingis he hadde to do
He ʒeode walkynge bi þe strete
And coom aʒeynes hem to mete
Rebecca seide what man is he 3355
Þat towarde vs comynge I se
He drouʒe hir neer & stille spak
Þat is my lord sir ysaac
Hit is þe caiser shal be þyn
Of him shal þou haue soone seesyn 3360
To his bihoue I þe souʒt
In sely tyme & wiþ me brouʒt
Þis seriaunt dide hir doun to liʒte
In better aray for to diʒte

3336   Til] To B. his] he L. wrouʒt] Iwrought B.
3337   þenne] þere B.
3339   vchone...he] eche he ʒafe B. sere] in fere B.
3341   þe] þat B.
3343-4 om in B.
3344   hym made] made him TL.
3345   A morwe in] On morne with B.
3346   of] from L; oute of B.
3347   als] as T.
3348   nyʒe] nere B.
3349   wonynge...Abraham] Syr Abrahamys woning B.
3351   hym...roo] to hym þo B.
3352   of þingis] one þing B.
3354   coom] came B. hem] hym L.
3356   vs comynge] ys come B.
3359   shal] þat schall B.
3360   shal þou] schaltow B. haue soone] soone haue TB.
3363   seriaunt] servaunt LB. to] om B.
3364   for to] to be B.

She hir in bett*er* wede arayed   3365
A mantel of reede aboue she layed
And þei she shameful was I wis
She lest no countenau*n*ce wiþ þis
Rebecca and ysaac are samen
Mette wiþ myche ioye & gamen   3370
Wiþ myche myrþe for to mene
Was brouȝte to house þ*a*t may shene
Þenne þei made þe mariage
Þat fel to riche heritage
Þe michel loue of rebecca   3375 fol. 20r col. 1
Falled þe sorwe of dam sara
Suche are nowe alyue ful þike
Forȝete þe dede for þe quyke
But þei hit dide for sum resou*n*
And þourȝe significacioun   3380

Thre wyues had Ismael
Twelue kyngis com of hi*m* to tel
Þei helde as myȝtyest þat day
Þe londes þat in þe eest lay
Wondir hit were þe kyn to tel   3385
Þat multiplied of Ismael
Abraham aftir dame sara
Took a wyf het cephura
Of hir he geet a sone madan
And anoþ*er* hett madian   3390
Not for lust of leccherye
But his seed to multiplye
As god him hadde tofore hiȝt
He took a wyf for hit was riȝt
Bitwene his childre he delt his auȝt   3395

3365   hir] *om* B. wede] wede her B.
3367   þei] þouȝe T; ȝef B. shameful was] schamfast wer B.
3368   no] non B.
3369   are] in B.
3370   wiþ myche] togedyr w*ith* B.
3371   myrþe] ioye B.
3372   shene] so schene B.
3376   Falled] fellyd B.
3377   alyue] on lyfe B.
3380   significacioun] singnificacion B.
3384   þe] As B.
3388   cephura] Sepura L.
3390   And] *om* B.
3391   Not for] Bote for no B.
3393   him] hem L. him...hiȝt] before had hym behight B.
3394   for hit] & þat B.

His lond to ysaac he bitauȝt
For he firste born was in mariage
Bi riȝte he hadde his heritage
An hundride ȝeer seuenty & fyue
Whenne abraham had lad his lyue   3400
He diȝed in trouþe & holyhede
His sones douȝty were of dede
Þei wepte his deeþ & so dide moo
Bi sara þei leide hym þo
In god was euer his feiþ fest   3405
Oure lord brynge vs to his rest
Siche a reste to to come
Þat we may wiþ himseluen wone   3408

Now is good to vndirtake
Þe story to telle of sir ysaake
Oure lord þat is of goodnes boun   3411
To ysaac ȝaf his benisoun
Wyse he was & god he dradde
And gladly dide þat he him badde
Wiþouten childe his wyf was longe   3415 fol. 20r col. 2
Þat þouȝte him ful stronge
He preyed him þat may al mende
Þat he wolde him childre sende
For of his wyf he dredde soore
She shulde be bareyn euermore   3420
Þe gode childre geten of grace
Vnneþe coom þei forþ in place
But whenne þei coom wel is knowe

3397   firste...was]was borne fyrst B. born] bone L.
3398   his] þe B.
3399   seuenty] seventyn B.
3400   lad] lefft B.
3402   douȝty were] þat were doughty B.
3403   wepte] wepe L.
3406   to his] alle to B.
3407   Siche] To swich B. first to] om L; for B.
3408   wone] wone. Amen B.
3409-10   om CGHTLB.
3410a   vndirtake] vndirstonde & take B.
3410b   sir] om B.
3414   he] god B.
3416   þat þouȝte] And þat forþought B. ful] swyþe B.
3417   preyed] previd L.
3418   wolde] schuld B. childre] a chylde B.
3421   childre] chyld B. geten of] gete no L.
3423   is] it is B.

Þat þei of goddis grace are sowe
Childe but oon had dame sara   3425
Rebecca hadde rachel & anna
Nor ȝitt holy Elizabeth
To haue hir childe coom not eth
Þat was Ion þe baptist
Þat to men shewed crist   3430
Also semeþ riȝt to deme
Beþ of rebecca barnteme
She hadde hem not sooþ to say
Ar þei were souȝt mony a day
God het hem childre not forþy   3435
Þat of her seed shulde multiply
And saide I shal ȝitt be
As wiþ þi fadir so wiþ þe
Ysaac ȝaf to god his tende
And preyed he shulde childer sende   3440
So long he preyed his preyere
Wel was herd wiþ god so dere
She þat longe had childe forgone
Now she bereþ two for oone
Of twynlyngis hir þouȝte no gamen   3445
Þat fauȝt ofte in hir wombe samen
So fast in hir dude þei fiȝte
Þat she had reste day ne nyȝte
To preye to god ay was she prest
To counsel hir wat were best   3450
What were beste hir to rede

3426   rachel] rechella B. anna] nanna B.
3427   Nor ȝitt] Noþe B.
3428   childe] chyldre B. eth] eyght B.
3429   þe] *om* B.
3431   riȝt] it for B.
3432   Beþ] Boþe B.
3434   a] *om* B.
3436   her] hys B.
3437   I shal] *om* L.
3438   wiþ] well *with* L. so] as L.
3439   to] *om* B.
3440   shulde] shuld hym L; wolde hym B. childer] child L.
3441   his] þat his TL; at hys B.
3442   herd] he herde B.
3443   childe] chyldyrn B.
3444   bereþ] bredeþ T.
3445   hir] sche B.
3446   ofte] awght L. samen] in same B.
3447   dude þei] wombe þey did B.
3448   þat] *om* B. had] ne had L; hathe no B. ne] nor T.

Hir lyf was licly to be dede
Wondir strong was her were
Þei wolde not þat stryf forbere
Til þei had of hemself myȝt   3455 fol. 20v col. 1
To se wherfore þei shulde fiȝt
Fro þe bigynnyng of þe werd
Of siche a werre was neuer herd
Ne siche a stryf of childre twynne
Þat lay þe modir wombe wiþynne   3460
Btiwene vnborn a batail blynde   3463
Sichon was wondir to fynde
He þat on þe riȝt syde lay   3465
His broþer ofte wrast him away
And he þat lay on þe left
His broþer ofte his stide him reft
Þe lady was ful myche a drad
As womman þat was harde stad   3470
But oure lord god þat is
Had done hir into sikernis
Þourȝe his verrey prophecie
Þat shulde be þo childer nye
Of her were and of her lyf   3475
And what ensaumple bar þat strif
Þerfore buxomly she hit bare
And knew coueryng to come of kare
Hir bredynd was ful sore
And hir childyng myche more   3480
Þo wex þe fiȝte more, þen toforn
Whiche shulde be firste born   3482

3452   Hir lyf] Sche B. was] were L.
3453   strong] stronk B. her] he L; þat B.
3454   wolde] nold L. þat stryf] her B.
3455   of] om B.
3458   werre] worlde B.
3459   twynne] tweyn B.
3461-2   om HTLB.
3463   vnborn] two vnborne B.
3464   Sichon] Swich B. to] for to B.
3466   wrast him] him wrast TL. ofte... him] hym ofte wreght B.
3468   ofte] om B. him] oft hym B.
3470   stad]bestad B.
3472   into] to B.
3474   be þo] þo be B.
3475   were] werke B.
3478   And knew] A new L. to...of] of her B.
3481   more] moche B. toforn] beforne B.
3482   Whiche] Which chylde B. be firste] fyrst be B.
3483-4   om HTLB.

Of þese two breþeren þat we mote   3485
Þe lasse þe more took bi þe fote
In trauelynge & drouȝe aȝeyn
Miche was þe modir peyn
Þe first born was rouȝe of hare
Þe oþere childe sleȝt & bare   3490
He þat was rouȝe was reed wiþ alle
Esau men dide him calle
Iacob hett þe ȝonger broþer
Þe modir him loued more þen þat oþer
Þerfore nowhere was he sent   3495
But to þe hous took he tent
To tente þe mete & hous to kepe
Þerto was he good & meke
Þe fadir loued esau for fode   fol. 20v col. 2
For he was an archer gode   3500
Whenne he wolde euer was he boun
To gete his fadir venisoun
And as he was as formast born
He dalt al wiþ tilþe & corn
Wiþ oþere þingis delt he sere   3505
Wiþ beestis wode foule & ryuere
His fadir olde and vnfere
Ofte he fedde wiþ good dynere
Good was þe world in þat ceesoun
Miche availede benesoun   3510
Of fadris þat wel helde her fay
On childre whenne þei wolde hit lay
Of blessyng may men ensaumple take
Bi þese childer of ysaake
How þe ȝonger of þe two   3515
Þe blessynge stale his broþer fro

3485   breþeren] chyldryn B.
3489   born] was borne & B.
3490   oþere] toþyr B. sleȝt] sleygh B.
3494   þat oþer] þe toþer TLB.
3496   took he tent] he toke entent B.
3497   &] þe B.
3498   meke] mete L; ȝepe B.
3503   *second* as] *om* B.
3506   &] of TB; in L.
3509   ceesoun] tyme B.
3510   benesoun] þis benyson B.
3512   childre whenne] þayre chyldre B.
3514   Bi...childer] Of þe blyssyng B. þese] this L.
3516   þe] Hys B.

But firste is to be tolde
How esau his broþer hit solde
// Esau went forþ to hunte
A day as he was ofte wonte   3520
Fer & neer he had souȝte
Þat day gamen fonde he nouȝte
For haue man neuer so myche nede
Vche day is not tyme of spede
But ofte þat day þat men faile   3525
Moost aboute hit þei trauaile
Whenne he was wery forgoon
Hoom he took his weye anoon
Hauke is esy I here say
To reclayme þat haþ lost his pray   3530
His broþer he fond þat toke tent
To diȝte a noble mete present
Of þis mete broþer he seide
ȝyue me sum þat here is greyþede
Mete & drynke þou hast at wille   3535
And longe is siþ I eet my fille
Iacob seide nay god hit wit
For þe haue I not diȝt hit
Þis mete my modir me bitauȝt   fol. 21r. col. 1
For þou and I are selden sauȝt   3540
Aboute oure forburþe are we wrooþ
ȝif þou wolt swere me an ooþ
Þat þou shalt neuer fro þis nyȝt
Of þi forburþe cleyme no riȝt
Forburþe he seide what serueþ me   3545
Broþer at þi wille shal hit be

3517   is] it is B.
3519   forþ] oute B.
3520   A] On a B. ofte] om B.
3521   he] om T. he had] had he B.
3522   fonde] ne founde B.
3523   man] a man B.
3524   of] to B.
3526   hit] om B.
3529   Hauke] Hang B.
3531   þat] & B. tent] entent B.
3532   To] To a B.
3538   haue I] I haue yt L.
3540   are] be B.
3541   Aboute] For B. are we] or we were B.
3544   þi] this L. cleyme no] calang B.
3545   me] it me B.
3546   Broþer] Broþere he seyde B. shal hit] it schall B.

Wiþ þat forwarde he made a vow
Almest for hongur I deȝe now
And for his fille of þat potage
As wrecche he solde his heritage   3550
He eet & dronke & went his way
And lost his blessyng fro þat day
N[o] bote him was him forþouȝt
God wolde hit were his þat hit bouȝte

Þis yssac þat worþi man   3555
Sekenes & elde on him ran
Of body failed him þe myȝt
And of yȝen also þe siȝt
Þe body þat so in elde is nome
His day is goon his nyȝt is come   3560
Haue a man ben neuer so bolde
Whenne þat he bicomeþ olde
Vnwelde put at him a pulle
His body waxeþ dryȝe & dulle
His heed bigynneþ þenne to shake   3565
His hondes oþerwhile to quake
Hit crepeþ crulyng in his bake
Þenne his boones bigynne to crake
Þe frely faire to falle of hym
And þe siȝte to wax al dym   3570
Þe frount frounseþ þat was shene
Þe nese droppeþ ofte bitwene
Teeþ to rote breeþ to stynke
Only to lyue trauaile him þinke

3548   I] *om* B.
3549   his] þe B.
3550   As... solde] He solde awey B.
3552   And] He B. fro] for L.
3553   No] Ne H. bote] boto T; butt B. *first* him] yt LB. was] nas TL; were B.
3554   hit] that L.
3555   þat] þis B.
3556   elde] age B.
3558   yȝen] hys eyen B.
3563   Vnwelde] Vnweldy L.
3566   oþerwhile] & hys lymes B.
3567   crulyng] crokyng B.
3569   *om* B.
3570   al] *om* B.
3571   frount frounseþ] forhede to fronte B.
        extra line in B: hys fayrnes to fall hym fro.
3572   droppeþ... bitwene] to drop þe mowthe also B.
3573   Teeþ] þe teþe B. rote] schake þe B.
3574   lyue] leue B.

Eȝeþ hit is þenne to sporne   3575
He falleþ wiþ his owne torne
He preyseþ þingis þat ben gone
Þat þenne bene he preyseþ noone
Soone þenne he wole be wrooþ   fol. 21r col. 2
To be at oon sumdel looþ   3580
To teche men of his witt
He holdeþ noon so wise as hit   3582
No þing þenne may hym pay   3585
Boldely þenne may we say
He þat in þis state is stad
Nis no gle may make him glad
Elde is now a wondir þinge
Alle desiren hit þat are ȝinge   3590
Whenne þei hit haue þei are vnfayn
Þenne wolde þei ȝonge be aȝayn
Þei wolde be as þei were ore
And þat þei may neuermore

So haþ elde þis ysaac led   3595
Þat he sike liþ in his bed
Him wantede siȝte as I seide er
And calde his sone esau þer
Esau leue sone he seide
Go loke þi takel be purueide   3600
And fonde for to stalke so nere
Þat þou may sle sum dere
If þou myȝte any venisoun gete
Gladly wolde I þerof ete
Sone þou hast hidur tille   3605
Gladly done þi fadir wille
Þou art archere wiþ þe best
Boþe in felde and in forest

3575   Eȝeþ] Erþe B.
3577   He preyseþ] Hys preuy B. ben] þan be B.
3578   he preyseþ] þay praysed B. noone] sone L.
3583-4 om HTLB.
3588   Nis] þere is B.
3590   are] be B.
3592   ȝonge be] be ȝong B.
3594   þei may] will be B.
3595   elde þis] age B.
3596   he sike] seke he B.
3597   wantede] wantyþ LB.
3604   Gladly... þerof] þerof wold I blyþely B.
3605   hast] haste þe B.
3606   Gladly done] For to do B.

If þou may brynge me any beest
Diȝte hit me feir and honeste   3610
Þeraftir now me longeþ so
Þere I lyue in bed of woo
Sone he seide I wol not lye
Hit beþ not longe ar I dyȝe
To brynge me venisoun be boun   3615
And þou shalt haue my benisoun
He seide sir gladly & soone
Wiþ goddes helpe hit shal be done
His modir tent to ysaac
And herde þo wordis þat he spaak   3620
And wist of longe lyf was he nouȝt   fol. 21v col. 1
She went bi syde and hir biþouȝt
Iacob hir sone she calde hir to
And þus to him seide sho
My leue sone I wol þe warn   3625
For þou art my derrest barn
Þi fadir bad þi broþer snelle
To fett him mete & not dwelle
If he any what myȝte gete
He shulde him diȝte þerof to ete   3630
For were he ones þerwiþ fed
Ar he dyȝed in seke bed
His benisoun he wolde him ȝyue
For longe he woot he may not lyue
Leue sone looþ me wore   3635
Þat he þi benisoun fro þe bere
Vnhappy wrecche he haþ ben ay
Þi ȝele shal he not bere away
Þou shal do now my counsel
I woot hit wol availe wel   3640

3609   me] *om* L.
3611   now] *om* B.
3612   bed of] my bed full L.
3613   wol] shalle L.
3614   beþ] shalle L; will B. longe] be long LB. ar] or þat B.
3615   be] þou be B.
3620   þo] þe B.
3622   bi... and] & besely B.
3629   what] *om* B.
3630   him] it B. þerof] for B.
3632   seke] hys B.
3633   benisoun] blissyng B.
3634   he may] may he TL.
3638   ȝele] hele B.
3639   my] be my B.
3640   hit... wel] well it will Avayle B.

Hyȝe þe sone þat þou not blyn
Ar þi broþer be comen In
Of fatte kydes fet me two
I shal þe teche how þou shalt do
I shal hem diȝte to his byhoue   3645
Siche as he was wont to loue
Hit shal him sauour al at wille
Ete he shal þerof his fille
Whenne hit is diȝt þou hit him reche
Do wel as I þe teche   3650
Þat he may þe lasse mystrau
Say þou art his sone esau
Fro þe forest newely comen
Venisoun þou hast Inomen
Deyntily diȝte to his pay   3655
Þou bidde hym ryse & assay
Þat þou may gete bi þis resoun
Of þi fadir his benisoun
Modir he seide wise is þi lore
But o þing I drede soore   3660
Þou woost my hondis are al bare   fol. 21v col. 2
And esaues rouȝe wiþ hare
If my fadir þat is blynde
May me so wiþ gile fynde
Of þat benisoun sore I drede   3665
Lest he me curse in his dede
Dowey sone rebecca sayde
Þat malisoun on me be layde
Þat I þe bad brynge me soone
Gladly he seide hit shal be done   3670
Iacob went into þe folde

3641   þat] & B.
3643   kydes] kyddis fete L. fet] fech B.
3644   how] what L.
3647   Hit] He L; I B. him] it B. at wille] to well B.
3648   he shal] & drynk B.
3650   Do] Do now B.
3652   his sone] om B.
3653   newely] þou art B.
3654   Venisoun] And venison B. Inomen] him nomen TL.
3656   þou] þan B.
3657   þis] om B.
3661   are] is L.
3662   rouȝe] now T. wiþ] & full of B.
3664   me] we L. so wiþ] with swich a B.
3665   benisoun] blissyng B.
3671   into] vnto L; to B.

And brouȝte þe kides I of tolde
His modir smertly hem diȝte
As she tofore had hym hiȝte
And clad him wiþ þo cloþes mete   3675
Of his broþer þat smelled swete
Wiþ a rouȝe skyn hid his hals
And hiled þerwiþ his hondis als
For his fadir shulde trowe trewe
He were his sone esawe   3680
His modir him þis mete bitauȝt
He hit to his fadir rauȝt
Fadir he seide sitt vp & ete
I haue þe brouȝte þi ȝernyng mete
What art þou his fadir seide   3685
Sir . esau þi mete haue greide
What maner mete . sir venisoun
Ete and ȝyue my benisoun boun
How was hit þou sped so soone
Sir god of myȝte herde my bone   3690
And sende hit smartly to my honde
Men owe to þonke him his sonde
Come nere sone & lete me fele
If þou be he I loue so wele
Whenne he felde his smellyng clooþe   3695
And his necke & his hondis boþe
Þis voys he seide . þat I here
Is of iacob wiþouten were
But hondis & hals as I trowe trew
Is my dere sone esaw   3700
Þe sauour of þi vestiment   fol. 22r col. 1
Saŭereþ as þe pyement

3672   And] A L. I] þat I LB.
3675   wiþ] of LB. þo] þe B. mete] swete L; meke B.
3676   smelled swete] wer hym mete L.
3677   a] *om* B. hid] aboute B.
3680   He] þat it B.
3681   bitauȝt] taught B.
3682   He] And he B.
3684   þi] þe L.
3686   haue] hath LB
3688   my] me my L; me þy B. boun] *om* B.
3690   of myȝte] Almyghty B.
3692   Men] Me B. his] of hys B.
3696   And] *om* B. necke] nick L.
3697   here] here her B.
3699   hals] als L; nek B. trowe trew] trew trowe B.
3701   þi] the L.

I shal forþ wende þou dwellest here
My blessyng haue þou sone dere
Þi broþer be þyn vndirloute   3705
And alle þat wonen here aboute
Alle þo sone þat blessen þe
Blessed shal hemseluen be
And alle þat bidde þe malisoun
Shal bere hit on her owne croun   3710
He eet & dranke at his wille
And þenne his [son] cald him tille
His broode blessyng he him ȝaue
Þat his broþer wende to haue
He made him lord of al his kyn   3715
Siche þen was his modir gyn
His modir counsel was þerto
But god wolde hit shulde be so
// Iacob went whenne þis was done
And esau coom aftir soone   3720
Fadir he seide sitt vp in bed
I haue þe brouȝte to be of fed
Of venisoun þat I þe brynge
Ete and ȝyue me þi blessynge
His fadir asked what he was   3725
Sir esau þi sone in plas
Sone he seide for my prow
Þou were here at me riȝt now
I he seide nay god woote
Miȝte I not be so liȝte of fote   3730
Wiþ þis ȝaf yssac a grone
Sone he seide riȝt now was one
Þat firste me fedde & þenne me kist
And me bigyled ar I wist
My benesoun now haþ þi broþer   3735

3705   vndirloute] andyrloute B.
3709   þat] þo þat B. þe] þis B.
3711   wille] owne wylle L.
3712   son] om H.
3713   broode blessyng] broþer blessid L. ȝaue] than L.
3714   his] þe oþer L.
3716   þen] om B.
3719   went] wend L.
3720   coom aftir] þo come B.
3722   of] with B.
3728   here... me] wiþ me here B.
3730   Miȝte I] I myght B.
3733   þenne] om B.
3735   now] om B.

Fadir he seide is þer noon oþer
No sone als haue I mede
Allas he seide I am in nede
Away he haþ my blessyng born
So dude he als þe ʒondur morn   3740
He haþ me done mychel shome   fol. 22r col. 2
Skilful is iacob his nome
Þat is to say in riʒt langage
Putter out of heritage
For I first born shulde ha be   3745
Wiþ strengþe aʒeyn drouʒe he me
And done me als þis vnresoun
To reue me þus my benisoun
Me is so wo almest I wede
Fadir þis was no broþerhede   3750
Counsel me fadir nowe to lyue
What counsel sone shal I þe ʒyue
And is þer fadir no blessyng left
No þi broþer hit haþ þe reft
And is þer fadir noon oþer woon   3755
Soþely he seide is noon but oon
In þe dew & gras also
Shal be þi blessyng where þou go
Wiþ erþe trauaile so þou do
And preye god sende his dew þerto   3760
Lord he seide what is me best
Myn hert beþ neuermore in rest
Til þat þis iacob be deed
If I may gete him to any sted
Þus esau wiþ his manace   3765
Out of þat lond dide Iacob chace

3737   als] he sayde so B.
3740   þe ʒondur] þis endyr B.
3745   ha] *om* B.
3747   And] Hath L. vnresoun] treson B.
3749   Me is] I am B. almest] þat nere B.
3750   broþerhede] broþer dede B.
3752   shal] schuld B.
3753   And] *om* B.
3754   hit haþ] hath yt L.
3757   þe] *om* B. gras] þe gres B.
3760   his] þe B. þerto] also B.
3761   me] my L.
3762   beþ neuermore] schall neuer be B.
3763   þis] ilke B.
3764   to] in B.
3766   þat] þe B.

Whenne her modir say hit so
He souȝte his broþer for to slo
She sent him soone into aran
To hir broþer þat het laban   3770
Þere to soiourne for þat sake
Til his broþer wratthe wolde slake
By nyȝte þe flom iurdan he wood
And þourȝe a wildernesse he ȝood
He loked where him were best   3775
By þe weye to make his rest
A stoon he took þat lay hym by
And þeronne leyde his heed on hy
In sleep he say a ladder strauȝt
Fro his heed to þe skye hit rauȝt   3780
On þat ladder say he boun   fol. 22v col. 1
Aungels clymbynge vp & doun
Open him þouȝte þe ȝate of heuen
Of god he herde siche a steuen
God and lord he seide I am   3785
Of Isaac and of Abraham
Iacob he seide þou shalt haue twynne
Wyues of þyn owne kynne
Two douȝteres of laban þyn eeme
Þat þou shalt haue wiþ barnteeme   3790
Wiþ þe wol I be in þi nede
And make þyn osprynge wyde to sprede
For þine eldres to þe I take
And esau for þe forsake
Glad he was of þat siȝt   3795
Him þouȝte he slepte softe þat nyȝt
On þe morne whenne hit was day
Iacob roos fro þenne he lay
He seide oure lord out of were
I wist not his wonynge here   3800
Here is nowe þenne seide he

3769   aran] aram T.
3771   soiourne] socour B.
3772   Til] To B.
3773   wood] wolde B.
3774   a] þe B.
3780   hit] om B.
3787   twynne] tweyne B.
3792   wyde] om B. to] & L. sprede] spede B.
3793   eldres to] ordres for B.
3794   for] fro L. þe forsake] þi sake T.
3798   þenne] þennes T; þere B.
3799   out of] with owen B.

Goddes hous & heuen entre
Þe stoon þat his hede lay on þat nyȝt
In tokene he hit set vpriȝt
And oyle he put vpon þat stoon   3805
And made to god a voys anoon
He seide if god be my frende
And lede me in my waye to wende
And sende mete drynke & clooþ
And brynge me aȝeyn wiþouten loþ   3810
Into my kiþthe þere I coom fro
If I fynde þat he lede me soo
He shal be my god and kynge
Þis stoon shal stonde in tokenynge
And þis place fro nowe shalle   3815
Be cleped goddis owne halle
Of al þe good he doþ me welde
Trewely tiþe I shal hym ȝelde
// Iacob wente him forþ his way
Where þre flockes of beestis lay   3820
Byside a welle vpon a felde   fol. 22v col. 2
And Iacob say and bihelde
A mykel stoon vpon hit lay
Þat beestis dronk at euery day
Þe herdes fonde he bi hem þere   3825
And asked hem wheþen þei were
Sir þei seide we are of aran
And knowe ȝe ouȝte he seide laban
Sir ȝee . & is he hool and fere
ȝee hool þei seide out of were   3830
ȝondir I se his douȝtir Rachelle
Dryuynge his beestis to þe welle
For alle þe flockis comen hidur
Vche day to drynke togidur

3802   &] of B.
3803   þat nyȝt] ryght B.
3805   þat] þe B.
3809   mete] me mete B.
3812   þat] *om* B.
3814   stonde in] be þe B.
3821   vpon] in B.
3824   þat] þe B. dronk] *om* L. at] þerof B.
3825   fonde he] he founde B.
3826   hem] hym L; þe herdys B. wheþen] whennes TB.
3827   are] be B. aran] Aram B.
3828   And] *om* B.
3830   hool] *om* B.
3834   Vche... drynke] To drynke iche day B.

Þenne coom rachel þat mayden briȝt   3835
Iacob lift vp þe stoon ful wiȝt
He spak so wiþ þat damysel
And knowleched him þere wiþ rachel
He seide what art þou lemman
Sir my fadir hett laban   3840
Aboute þe necke he hir hynt
And cust hir þryes ar he stynt
I am Iacob þi cosyn nere
For þi loue am I comen here
Whenne she bigan to vndirstonde   3845
Þat iacob shulde be hir husbonde
To laban tolde she þat tiþande
And she hym ladde bi þe hande
Þei freyned of her frendes fare
And he hem tolde of þat vnswere   3850
Laban þenne he dide to calle
For fayn of him his frendes alle
Soone he dide him to say
What was þe chesoun of his way
Sir he seide I wol þe telle   3855
For to spouse þi douȝtir rachelle
Þenne shal þou serue me seuen ȝere
Ar þat þou haue my douȝter dere
Gladly he seide so shal hit be
Stille wiþ laban so dwelt he   3860
Þe elder suster he forsoke   fol. 23r col. 1
For she gliȝed seiþ þe boke
For to serue for rachel fre
He was maystir herde of fe
Hit was myche wondir þere   3865

3836   wiȝt] riȝt L.
3838   him... wiþ] so to B.
3839   lemman] woman B.
3841   hynt] hin T.
3847-8   reversed in B.
3847   To] And to B. she] om B.
3848   And] om B. hym ladde] led hym home B.
3849   freyned] fayned B.
3851   he... to] dyd hym B.
3852   For] And B.
3856   þi] your L.
3857   shal þou] schaltow B.
3860   dwelt] lefft B.
3862   seiþ] so sayth B.
3864   herde] here B.
3865   myche] om B. þere] for to here B.

How myche multiplied þei were
Whenne þo seuen ȝeer were gone
Iacob asked his lemmone
Laban seide ful bliþely
But þere he dide a tricchery   3870
Whenne he hadde rachel wedde
Lya he stale to his bedde
Bisyde lya al nyȝte he lay
His vnwityng til hit was day
But whenne he wist on þe morn   3875
Wo was him þat he was born
Fro hir he roos & siked soore
And asked who brouȝte hir þore
Laban she saide . allas þe while
Who wende he wolde me þus bigyle   3880
He asked laban to resoun
Whi he dide him siche tresoun
Oure lawe he seide þat we Inne lyue
Wol firste oure elder douȝter be ȝyue
But mourne þou no maner ȝet   3885
Þou shalt haue rachel as I þe het
But þat may be noon oþere wyse
But for oþer seuen ȝer seruyse
Þe while holde lya in bedde
Penne shal þou rachel wedde   3890
Þis newe forwarde was made þan
Bitwene iacob and laban
His ȝeres past & seuen dayes
Rachel he weddid þe story sayes
//Lya bred childe sone had oon   3895

3867   þo] þe B. were] was B.
3868   Iacob] Iakyd L.
3870   he] þay B.
3873   Bisyde] Be B.
3874   til] to B.
3877   &] *om* L.
3878   who] hire who B.
3882   siche] þat B.
3883   lyue] leve L.
3885   maner] more B.
3887   noon] on none B.
3888   ȝer] yeris L.
3889   þe] þere B. in] to þy B.
3890   shal þou] schaltow B.
3892   Bitwene] Betwyx B.
3893   His] þe B.
3895   sone] & sone LB.

Ruben & siþen symeon
Þenne leuy þenne Isacar
Zabulon Iudas sixe breþer war
A douȝtir she hadde hiȝt dyna
But þenne of oþer wymmen twa   3900
Hadde foure sones geten of hym   fol. 23r col. 2
Dan . Gad . Asser . Neptalym
Rachel bar Iacob sones twyn
First Ioseph & þenne beniamyn
Þat was þe cause of hir ende   3905
Of hem she dyȝed in gesin hende
What of his wyues two in spouse
And als of hondwymmen in house
Twelue sones of þo hadde he
And a douȝter dyna to be   3910
Iacob wex riche his childer þroof
Þourȝe þe grace þat god him ȝoof
Talent bigan to take him þo
To his owne londe to go
Wyf and childe wiþ oon assent   3915
Vchon in hond wiþ oþere went
Laban of leue seide hem nay
And þei on nyȝt stale away   3918
A god had laban in his boure   3921
Whiche he was wont to honoure
In her flittyng rachel hit fond
Forþ she bare hit in her hond
Laban hit missed oueral hit souȝt   3925
But his god fonde he nouȝt
Iacob went forþ his way
On þe feld wiþouten he lay
On þe to side of flum iurdon

3897   leuy] leve I L. *second* þenne] *om* L; and B.
3902   Dan] Van B. Asser] Assere & B.
3903   twyn] twey L; tweyn B.
3904   First] Fyrst was B. &] *om* B.
3906   hem] hym B. dyȝed] dide L.
3907   of] *om* L.
3908   als] alle L; *om* B. in] of B.
3909   he *is added in a later hand* L.
3911   wex] with B.
3914   To] Vnto B.
3919-20   *om* in HTLB.
3924   Forþ] How L; And B. bare hit] yt bare B.
3925   *second* hit] he B.
3926   fonde] ne fonde B.
3927   way] was T.

And sent his auȝte ouer vchon   3930
Iacob lay bi himself þat nyȝt
In hond he kauȝte an aungel briȝt
So in honde wrastled þay
Al þat nyȝt til hit was day
Þe aungel seide let me go   3935
He seide þat wolde he neuer do
Lete him passe for no þing
Til he hadde ȝyuen him his blessyng
Long þei wrasteled togider þore
Þat iacob was hurt ful soore   3940
Þe maistir synewe of his þee
Þat euer aftir haltide hee
And for þis resoun here new   fol. 23v col. 1
Of synewe eteþ neuer no Iew
Þenne asked god wiþouten blame   3945
And bad hym say soone his name
Iacob I het . Iacob seide he
So shal þi name no lenger be
Þou shalt be calde israel
Þat is mon seyng god of hel   3950
For þou aȝeyn god strong is
More worþ aȝeyn mon be fro þis
Iacob sent þenne to fonde
Esau wiþ sauȝtelynge sonde
For he was ferde in alle þinge   3955
For to come to his metyng
Whenne he of his comynge herde
Ful wroþely to him he ferde
Foure hundride men soone he fonde
To kepe iacob fro his owne londe   3960
And so he shal þat woot I wele
For he is al bisett wiþ sele
Iacob sent him of his auȝt

3930   auȝte] meyne B.
3932   he] hym B.
3934   til] to B.
3939   Long] So long B.
3943   new] now LB.
3947   I het] he sayde B.
3950   mon seyng] to sey B.
3952   be fro] before B.
3953   þenne] þo B.
3958   wroþely] worþely L.
3960   owne] *om* L.
3962   bisett] besyde B.

ȝiftis large hym to sauȝt
Þe messangere brouȝte vnswere 3965
He coom aȝeyn him wiþ greet powere
Iacob led myche folk of his kyn
For doute he dalt hem in twyn
For greet doute he hadde þan
He dalt in two beest and man 3970
Whil esau smoot oon of þoo
þat oþer part shal skape him fro
Iacob dredde Esau sare
For he was fel wiþouten spare
Þat if he myȝte him ouergo 3975
Wiþouten pite he wolde him slo
Þus he made his preyere
Lorde he seide my god so dere
Þat madest Adam mon of lyf
And siþþen of him Eue his wyf 3980
Hadde þei holden þat þou hem bad
Þei hadde in endeles ioye ben stad
And also noe trewe and good fol. 23v col. 2
Þou sauedest fro þat ferly flood
Þou woost lord þat hit is soo 3985
My broþere nowe is my foe
For I þourȝe my modir roun
Stale fro him his benesoun
Here ouer þis flum last whenne I ferde
I bare in hond but a ȝerde 3990
And now my lord blessed þou be
Two flockis of folk come wiþ me
Lord now sende me sum rede
Aȝeyn esau lest I be dede
For man þat þou wolt helpe in nede 3995

3964   ȝiftis large] Large ȝefftys B.
3966   him] om B.
3968   in] on B.
3969   greet doute] doute of hym B.
3970   beest] boþe best B.
3971   of] om B.
3972   þat] þe B. þat oþer] þe toþer TL. shal] schuld B. skape] skyp L.
3980   of him] madest B.
3983   And] om B. trewe and] þe B.
3984   þat] þe B.
3988   Stole] Toke B.
3989   last] om B.
3993   Lord] Now lorde B. now] om LB.
3994   Aȝeyn] Ayenst LB.
3995   man] men B. helpe] kepe B. nede] dede L.

Þar hym neuermore drede
Of þis auȝte þou hast me lent
Þerof I haue bifore me sent
For ar he alle þo haue slayn
He shal be mased of his mayn   4000
Þat while if þou wol þei shul pase
And come not in his hond percase
Esau coom breem wiþ greet route
Now is iacob in mychel doute
He swore if he myȝte hym mete   4005
Formast he shulde his lyf lete
But whoso god helpe wolle
May sauely go at þe folle
Whenne esau say him & his auȝt
Soone he souȝte hym wiþ sauȝte   4010
And for his come was ful bliþe
Þat gan he wiþ kissyng kyþe
Of siche strengþe is þe holy goost
To oonen hem þere wraþþe is moost
He welcomed iacob ful feire   4015
And knewe him for his fadir heire
Wiþouten wraþþe or any wrake
Of loue & pees togider þei spake
Whenne þei had seid þat þei wolde say
Esau went hoom his way   4020
Vnto syer þer he coom fro
And iacob to his fadir to go
For ȝitt þo he was lyuonde   fol. 24r col. 1
Rebecca his modir dede he fonde
Þis ysaac þat I of rede   4025
In bookis is calde þe lastyng sede
He ladde his lyf wiþouten blame

3996   þar] Dare L; Than B. neuermore] not nevirmore L; no more B.
3997   auȝte] gode B. lent] sent B.
3999   alle... haue] haue all þo B.
4000   mased] marryd L.
4001   þat] þe B.
4004   Now is] *om* L. in mychel] was in grete L.
4007   But] For B.
4008   þe] *om* B.
4011   for] of L. come] comyng B.
4012   þat] Than L; And B. he] hym B. wiþ kissyng] hym L.
4014   oonen] oven L; corde B.
4017   or] and L.
4018   þei] *om* B.
4022   to] gan B.
4023   þo] *om* B. lyuonde] leuande B.

And buried is bisyde abrahame
Nyne skore ȝeer ouergoone he hadde
Whenne he of þis world was ladde   4030
Whenne þis douȝty man was ded
Þese breþeren two toke hem to red
To dele her londes hem bitwene
Þenne myȝte þei lyue out of tene
To esau fel Ebron   4035
And to Iacob þenne Edon   4036

Þe story of iacob bigynneþ here
And also of his sones dere
Iacob was wondir riche of fe   4037
Of alle goodis he had plente
He was ful riche as we rede
Trewe and loued of vche lede   4040
Wel he loued his sones vchone
But so wel as Ioseph noon
He was fair wiþouten sake
Of briþeren hadde he noon his make
His breþeren alle were herdes I saye   4045
But he dwelt at home alwaye
Þis was trew Ioseph þat dredde
His loue word wyde spredde
Þat wise chaste þat gentile
Þat aftir sufferide greet perile   4050
Of þo periles þat he was ynne
Sumwhat to telle I shal bigynne
How he coom out of his woo
Into his wele here also
Ioseph say a nyȝte in sweuene   4055

4028   is] *om* B.
4029-31   *In MS B the lines are in the following order*: 4030, 4031, 4029.
4031   Whenne þis] And hys B. man] name B.
4032   hem] them L.
4033   hem] them L.
4034   lyue] leue B.
4036   þenne] *om* B.
4040   of vche] euery B.
4043   sake] lak B.
4044   noon] not B.
4045   alle were] were all B.
4046   he] Ioseph B.
4048   word wyde] wolde wyde be B.
4049   *second* þat] and B.
4052   shal] will B.
4055   say] se in B. in] a B.

Þat is worþi for to neuene
Him þouȝte his fadir her corn shere
Þere his elleuen breþeren were
Hymself was on þe felde bisyde
To geder corn in heruest tyde   4060
His breþer sheeues he say loutynge   fol. 24r col. 2
To his alone þat was stondynge
Anoþer he mette þeraftir soone
Him þouȝte boþe sunne & moone
And of [þe] grettest þat were on heuen   4065
Honoured him sterres elleuen
Alle louted hym on her manere
Riȝt as he her lorde were
He hem tolde & þei seide how
May þis bityde what wenes þow   4070
For to be lord ouer vs alle
Þat blisse shal þe neuer bifalle
Fro þis tyme forþ neuer þe les
Wiþ Ioseph were þei neuer at pes
Þei hadde enuye to hym strong   4075
Þei souȝte to greue him ay wiþ wrong
Wolde þei neuer vpon him se
Fro þat day but wiþ enemyte
At hoome was moost Ioseph þat childe
His breþeren in wildernesse wilde   4080
Wiþ her fee þe lowes bitwene
As þei were þen wont to bene
Bi þis story may men se
Men lyued moost þo bi fe
Þese breþeren þat I spak of ere   4085

4056   worþi] worþe B.
4057   her] *om* B.
4063   mette þeraftir] þought þat afftyr B.
4064   boþe] þat boþe B.
4065   þe] *om* H. on] of L; in B.
4067   louted] honourid L.
4073   forþ] forwarward B.
4074   at] in LB.
4076   souȝte] þought B. ay] euer L; *om* B.
4077   vpon] syþ on B.
4078   enemyte] envyte L.
4079   was moost] moost was TB.
4080   His] And hys B. wilde] wyde B.
4081   her] he B. lowes] londys B.
4082   þen] *om* L.
4083   may men] men may L.
4084   fe] þe fe B.

Among þe feldes dwellynge were
Þat noon couþe of hem typing telle
Til on a day hit bifelle
Her fadir of hem wite walde
Ioseph his sone to him he calde   4090
Sone he seide þou must algate
Go wite of þi breþer astate
Longe is siþ I of hem herde
Or of her fee how þei ferde
Fadir he seide I wol ful fayn   4095
Þi biddyng not to stonde aȝayn
He went forþ & wiste not where
Soþely þat his briþeren were
But ar he to his breþeren coom
Whil he went he mette a mon   4100
What sekest þou here sone seide he   fol. 24v col. 1
My breþer sir my fadir fe
Þen vnswered þat mon to him
Þou shalt hem fynde in dothaym
He went forþ and forþer past   4105
Til he hem fonde at þe last
He went forþ & ferþer souȝt
Til he hem fond lafte he nouȝt
Whenne þei seȝe Ioseph come her broþer
Vchone of hem seide to oþer   4110
Lo where þe dremere is comen
Bi myȝty god he shal be nomen
Lete vs do hym to þe dede
Loke what his dreem wol stonde in stede
Fayn þei were þere hym to fynde   4115
For to haue her wille blynde
If þei bifore him ouȝte forbare
Now wol þei hym not spare

4086   feldes] fendes L. were] þere B.
4088   hit] þat it B.
4089   Her] þe B.
4092   þi] ȝour B. astate] state B.
4096   to] *om* B.
4101   sekest þou here] sekestow my B.
4105-6   *om in* CFG
4106   hem fonde] fonde hem B.
4107-8   *om in* B.
4109   seȝe] sye L; sawe B. come] *om* B. her] their L.
4111   comen] ecomyn L.
4114   wol stonde]stant hym B.
4116   her] their L.
4117   bifore him] hym afore B.

// Oon eldest of þe elleuen was
Þat ruben hette in þat plas   4120
Whenne he herde þei wolde him slo
Þerfore was him wondir woo
Stynte hit wolde he if he myȝt
Þe foly þat his briþeren tiȝt
Alle he say hem in o wille   4125
Her broþer giltles to spille
Breþer he seide dooþ not so
I rede ȝe not ȝoure broþer slo
Þat is ȝoure owne flesshe & blode
[T]o murþer him hit is not gode   4130
If ȝe do forsoþe my wille
Shul ȝe neuer haue þertille
If ȝe hit do I ȝow teche
Sikur may ȝe be of wreche
And ȝoure shame shal be couþ   4135
Alle men to haue ȝou in mouþ
Þat baret rede I not ȝe brewe
Þat ȝe foreuer aftir rewe
He haþ no þing done why
ȝe haue not to hym but envy   4140
Wite his fadir he be sloone   fol. 24v col. 2
His lyf dayes telle I goone   4142
For mon lyuyng þei seide ne wyf   4145
Shal he skape wiþ his lyf
Whenne ruben seye þer was noon oþere

4119 eldest... elleuen] of þe ten þat þere B.
4120 *first* þat] *om* B.
4122 þerfore] þerto B.
4123 Stynte] Synt L. *first* he] *om* L.
4124 his] þe B.
4126 to] for to B.
4128 ȝe] you L. ȝe not] noght ȝe B.
4129 ȝoure] oure B.
4130 To] So H.
4133 ȝe] you L.
4134 may] mow B.
4137 baret... ȝe] bale I rede you not L. baret rede] bare in nede B.
4138 foreuer aftir] after euyr L; euyr afftyr B.
4139 no þing] not to ȝow B.
4140 not] *om* LB. to] vnto B.
4142 telle... goone] bene ydone L; be nere gon B.
4143-4   *om in* FGHTLB.
4145 lyuyng] lying B. ne] no B.
4146 skape] not scape L.
4147 þer] it B.

But algate þei wolde sle her broþere
For goddes loue do wey he seide
þat noon honde be on him leide   4150
Þat no blood of hym be shede
But if he algate shul be dede
Do hit þenne wiþ siche a wyle
Þat ȝe not ȝoure hondes fyle
In þis waast I woot a pitt   4155
Drye and watirles is hit
Þerouer stondeþ a mychel tre
Caste him þerynne & lete him be
Til þat he of lyue be brouȝt
Þen may we saye we soȝe him nouȝt   4160
His curtel wol we ryue & rende
And blody to his fadir hit sende
And telle him þat we hit fonde
In þe wildernesse lyonde
Say we þat he rent es   4165
Wiþ wilde beestis in wildernes
Þenne wole no man saye vs by
Þat we han slayn hym felonly
Do seide Ruben as [I] ȝow say
He þouȝte to stele him quyke away   4170
Anoon þei grauntide þat bihete
Þei hent Ioseph bi honde & fete
Made him naked & kest him doun
And lafte hym þere in prisoun
Siþþe sett hem doun and ete   4175
Þei say þo comyng bi þe strete

4148   algate] þat B.
4150   noon] no L. be... him] on hym be L.
4151   þat] And that L. be]we T.
4153   wyle] wille L.
4154   fyle] soyle L.
4155   þis waast] the west L.
4161   ryue &] al to B.
4162   blody] om B. hit sende] schall it be sent B. his] our L.
4163   telle] tell we B.
4164   lyonde] on þe grounde B.
4165   Say we] þan may we saye B.
4166   in] in þe B.
4169   I] om H.
4170   stele] take B.
4173   Made] þey made B.
4174   þere] in that pytte L.
4175   Siþþe] And þo þay B.
4176   þo] þan B.

Marchau␣dis of on vnkouþ londe
Of egipte as we in bookis fonde
Wiþ camailes þat grete burþens bare
Of spicis and of oþere ware   4180
Among þese breþere oon þer was
Whoos name was calde Iudas
What boote he seide were hit to vs   fol. 25r col. 1
To fordo oure broþer þus
Take we him out of þat den   4185
And sille we him to þese chapmen
Þat þei may lede hym to fer londe
To be her þral euer lyuonde
If hit so be he dye þare
Hit is to vs but litil care   4190
And if he be þere lyuynge
His fadir of him haþ no tiþinge
Þere was Ioseph to seruage solde
For twenti besau␣tis taken of golde
Now is Ioseph lad out of londe   4195
God holde ouer hym his holy honde
Ruben of hem moost was wys
He wiste not of þis marchau␣dys
On þe morn he coom & souȝte
Þe pyt but Ioseph fonde he nouȝte   4200
He mourned more þen I con telle
Almest in swou␣ doun he felle
To his briþeren went he soone
And þei him tolde as þei had done
What bote is hit to make mone   4205

4177   on] *om* L. vnkouþ] vnkond T.
4178   we... bookis] in bokis we L. bookis] boke B.
4179   Wiþ] Of B. burþens] packys B.
4180   spicis] spycery B. *second* of] *om* LB. ware] chafare L.
4182   calde] *om* B.
4185   þat] þis B.
4186   we] *om* B.
4187   to] in L. fer] her B.
4188   To] And B. her] their L. lyuonde] lenande B.
4190   litil] mochell B.
4192   His] Our L. him haþ] shalle haue L.
4193   þere] þan B. seruage] sarvis L.
4194   twenti] þretty B. taken] chosyn L.
4195   Now] Anon L.
4198   He] *om* L.
4200   þe pyt] *om* L. fonde] there found L.
4202   Almest... swoun] In swownyng allemost L.
4204   as] how L.
4205   hit] *om* L.

For þing þat cou*e*ringe [of is] none
His fadir þei sent witterly
Ioseph curtil al blody
// Whenne his fadir þe curtil knew
Soone bigan he to chau*n*ge hew   4210
A beest he seide my sone haþ rent
Allas þat euer I hym out sent
Into þat wylde weye to wende
Þat al my loue on hym gan lende
Alas wittles was I þat day   4215
Beestis of hym han made her pray
Þis was his clooþ hit is wel sene
A þis beest was ful kene
Þat haþ me refte my derlyng dere
My ioye my gladnes & my chere   4220
Ioseph þou wast my ioye allon
Now art þou deed & I haue noon
Ioseph þat was fre and fair   fol. 25r col. 2
Of al myn auȝt shulde ha ben myn heir
For þi goodnesse & þi fair hew   4225
My kare shal be euere new
I wolde sinke to helle depe
Wiþ my sone þere to wepe
But al his mournyng for to rede
Ouþer to speke hit myȝte not spede   4230
His oþere sones coom vchone sere
For to amende her fadir chere
But for nouȝte þei coomen alle
To counfort wolde he noon falle
No þing may his mournyng mende   4235

4206   of is] is of H. of] *om* B.
4207   His] Hir L.
4209   knew] sawe B.
4210   bigan he] he began B. to] *om* T.
4214   on... gan] was on B.
4215   Alas] As L.
4216   her] their L
4217   is] was LB.
4218   A] *om* LB. beest]cruelle best L. ful] boþe strong & B.
4221   wast] were B.
4222   art þou] ertow B.
4223   was] was so L; were B.
4224   myn] *om* TLB.
4229   his] þe B.
4230   Ouþer] Or softyr L; Or B.
4231   coom] *om* B.
4232   For] Com B. her] hys B.
4234   noon] not B.

Neuer to his lyues ende
Leue we nowe of iacobus care
To telle of Ioseph & of his fare
// Þese chapme[n] þat Ioseph bouȝt
Into egipte han him brouȝt   4240
Þere he was eftsones sold
To a douȝty man and bold
To putifar stiward wiþ þe kyng
Was he sold þat childe ȝyng
He helde Ioseph in menskful lore   4245
Þouȝe her layes on not wore
For þei were of sarasene lede
And Ioseph helde his owne in dede
Sir putifar wel vndirstood
Þat Ioseph was of gentil blood   4250
In alle þe dedis þat he wrouȝt
God was euer in his þouȝt
Þe keping of al his auȝt
Haþ putifar Ioseph bitauȝt
Ioseph þenne was loued & dred   4255
Wiþ wisdoom he his werkes led
For he was curteys and hende
Of alle folk fonde he frende
Putifar went into cuntre
Ioseph dwelt wiþ his meyne   4260
And haþ his goodis vndir honde
Vndir himself al weldonde
Ioseph was wondir fair in face   fol. 25v col. 1
And filde al wiþ goddis grace
His lady hir yȝe on hym cast   4265

4238   To] And LB. of... his] we now of Iosephis LB.
4239   chapmen] chapme H; marchauntys B.
4240   han] þey haue B.
4243   wiþ] to B.
4244   childe ȝyng]yong thyng L.
4245-8   *om* L.
4245   menskful] gode B.
4246   þouȝe her] ȝef þe B. on] it B.
4247   sarasene] sarsynes TB.
4248   in] *om* B.
4249   wel] *om* B.
4250   Ioseph was] he was comyn L.
4253   þe] In B.
4255   þenne was] was þenne T; was þo B.
4259   cuntre] þat contre L; þe contre B.
4261   And haþ] with alle L.
4263   in] of LB.
4264   filde al]fully fillyd B.

Forward of fool is eþ to fast
Foly hit was & she so fond
Hir loue to sett but hit wolde stond
She kid hit euer & on hym souȝt
And Ioseph lett he wiste hit nouȝt   4270
He wiste & helde hit stille as wyse
And euer she preysed his seruyse
So longe she haþ in hert hit hidde
At þe last hit most be kidde
For whosoeuer be glad or bliþe   4275
At þe ende wol pryue loue out wryþe
Ofte she mened to him hir mone
But euer she fonde him in one
Whenne she þat say hir hert was soor
And longynge had she moor & moor   4280
In hir foly she was so fest
Þat nyȝt nor day had she rest
What is more hert brest
Þan want of þing men loue best
Into siche prisoun to be put   4285
Þat reueþ man myȝte & wit
In prisoun I calle hym bistad
Of whom þe hert is neuer glad
Whenne hert haþ þe wille I wis
Þe body may haue no more blis   4290
Ne no more woo þen likyng woone
Wiþouten wille Is likyng noone   4292
Þe strengþe of loue noon may stere   4295

4266   fool] foly L. is eþ] her ye B. eþ] euer L. fast] last T.
4267   &] om B. she so] so she TL; so sche yt B.
4270   And] om B. he] as he L.
4271   hit] hym B.
4273   hit] in L.
4274   most] mote B.
4275   whosoeuer] whoso will B.
4277   she... him] to hym she nemyd L. mened] mevyd B.
4278   But euer] And L. in] euyr in L.
4280   longynge... she] euyr mornyd B.
4282   nor] ne B. rest] no rest B.
4284   of] a B. men] þat men TL.
4286   þat] Hyt L. reueþ man] renewith manys B.
4287   calle] holde B.
4289   hert] þe hert B.
4290   no] the L.
4291   Ne] No B. þen] þat B.
4293-4   om HTLB.
4295   noon] men L. noon may] may no man B.

Þouȝe his herte al steel were
Hert of steel & body of bras
Strenger þen eu*er* sampson was
Þat loue ne may meke wiþ myȝte
Su*m*tyme alone wiþ oon yȝe siȝt   4300
Ful harde hit is wiþ him to dele
Mannes flesshe he makeþ ful frele
Whe*n*ne his loke alone may bry*n*ge
Into his þraldome þe kynge
And maugrei his do him loute   4305 fol. 25v col. 2
For euer he ledeþ him wiþ doute
Þ*er*fore if þou be siche a gome
Þat þou algate wolt loue ou*er*come
Whe*n*ne þou seest him loue to þe
Stalworþely fro hym þou fle   4310
Fle & turne þou not þyn yȝe
Or ellis but þou be ful slyȝe
Þourȝe þyn yȝe þou shalt be shent
As þing wiþ wilde fyre forbrent
Firste to brenne þi herte wiþynne   4315
And siþen to st[r]angle þe in synne
Fle and folwe not I rede
For elles may þou come to dede   4318
Bett*er* is in tyme to be forborn   4321
Þen folwe þe pray þat is forlorn   4322
Who so doþ shal rewe soore   4325
And venge his harme wiþ foly more
So dide þis wyf þat I of rede
She folwede Ioseph where he ȝede

4296   þouȝe] ȝef B. al] of B.
4299   ne] me B. wiþ] hys B.
4302   ful] *om* B.
4303   alone] a love L; of loue B.
4305   his] in hys B.
4306   wiþ doute] aboute B.
4307   gome] grome LB.
4309   loue] lene B.
4310   Stalworþely] Strongly B.
4312   þou] ȝef þou B. ful]ryght B.
4314   þing wiþ] þin in B.
4316   strangle] stangle H.
4317   folwe] folowe it B.
4318   For] Or LB. may þou] maistou T; þou maste B.
4319-20   *om* HTLB.
4321   is] it is B. in time] bityme TB; the tyme L. to] *om* B.
4322   forlorn] lorn TLB.
4323-4   *om* HTLB.
4328   where] whereu*er* L.

And for she folwynge fond a sporn
She waited hym euel torn 4330
Hirself hadde þe grame & gilt
Almest also she had him spilt
How she bigan hym to fonde
For to telle I wol not wonde
She souȝte on him mony a day 4335
And euer he vnswered hir wiþ nay
Ioseph þat was hir purueoure
On a day wiþ mychel honoure
In chaumber gret hir hendelye
And seide madame to mete ȝe hye 4340
ȝus she seide [but] er þou go
Speke wiþ me a word or two
Longe he seide may I not dwelle
Þenne bigon she þus to telle
Ioseph lemmon for þi sake 4345
To þe now my mone I make
Bitwene þiself alone & me
Now wole I shewe my pryuete
Þat loue me haþ brouȝte to grounde fol. 26r col. 1
Þat I may neuermore be sounde 4350
But if my bote ryse on þe
Þat þou wolt my lemmon be
Worldes welþe to welde in wone
Inowȝe þou shalt haue allone
To my lord shal þou be dere 4355
Oþer noon shal be þi pere
She toke him aboute þe necke wiþ þis

4329-30 *om* L.
4329 folwynge] folowyd B.
4330 euel] *with* an euill B.
4331 gilt] þe gylt B.
4334 I wol]will I B.
4335 a] *om* B.
4339 hendelye] kyndly L.
4340 ȝe] you LB.
4341 but] *om* H. but er] or þat B.
4342 Speke] I will speke B. me] þe B.
4344 þenne... she] And than she gan L. þus] for B. telle] spell B.
4346 now] *om* B. make] will make B.
4348 Now] *om* L.
4351 ryse] aryse B.
4353 Worldes] Worldeles B. welde] welle L.
4355 To] *om* B. shal þou] schaltow B.
4357 wiþ þis] to kys B.

And proferede hir mouþ to kis
And drowe him towarde hir bed
But Ioseph þat mychel god dred   4360
Do wey he seide þi foly wille
Wolt þou þi self & me als spille
Putifar me haþ bitauȝte
Lond and lithe & al his auȝte
And for he tristeþ my lewete   4365
To kepe his godis he toke hem me
Al is me take & not forgone
But þou art his wyf allone
Of þe haue I no maner myȝt
If I hadde hit were no riȝt   4370
He þat ȝaf me suche pouste
To bitraye god forbede me
Wiþ no resoun we ne owe
To oure lord suche tresoun showe
Leuer me is be pore & trewe   4375
Þen falsely wynne catel newe
Þerfore lady wiþ myȝt & mayn
Drawe þi foly wille aȝayn
For whoso bigynne wol suche þing
Hym owe to þenke on þe endyng   4380
She seide allas Ioseph þis day
Hast þou vnswered me wiþ nay
If I lyue þou shalt me proue
An euel frend to þi bihoue
I shal þe make wiþ my housbonde   4385
Þe moost hated in al þis londe

4358   proferede] anon she profyrrid L; proferyd hym B. hir mouþ] hym for L. to
       kis] with þis B.
4359   hir] þe B.
4361   wille] dede B.
4362   Wolt þou] þou wilt B.
4363   me haþ] my lord hath me L.
4364   lithe] lede B.
4365   tristeþ] troweth in B.
4366   godis] gode B. hem] yt B.
4367   is me] me ys B.
4369   haue I] I haue L.
4370   no riȝt] nought B.
4372   bitraye] bretay L; betray hym B. forbede] he forbade L; forbede it B.
4373   we ne] ne with B.
4374   suche] schuld B.
4378   foly] foule L.
4379   bigynne wol] begynneþ B. suche] eny L.
4382   Hast þou] Hastow B.
4386   þe] om B. hated] Ihatyd B. þis] þe L.

She drouȝe his mantel bi þe pane
Whenne Ioseph say no better wane
He drouȝe she helde þe tassel brak   fol. 26r col. 2
Þe mantel lafte & he ȝaf bak   4390
Þenne fel she into felony
And soone souȝte a tricchery
She made a cry alle to here
Þat þat tyme in þe pales were
Lady þei seide what is ȝow   4395
She seide herde ȝe not how
Þat traytour iewe wolde me shende
Þat my lord halt his frende
He wolde haue forsed me in hye
Nadde I þe suuner made a crye   4400
Whenne I cryed soone he fledde
And lafte wiþ me a tokene wedde
His mantel is bilefte wiþ me
Here þe soþe may vche man se
Here may men se þe vilany   4405
Þat he souȝte on his lady
Sir she seide to putifar lo
Was neuer lady serued so
Þis shame he haþ me done in dede
Þis gedelyng of vncouþe sede   4410
Þis Ioseph souȝte on me in bour
To do me þis dishonour
Such hit was þe vilany
Þat he gon seche on my body
Þerfore as þou art man for þe   4415
Loke þou on him wroken be
Putifar commaundide soone

4389   tassel] mantell B.
4390   lafte] kaste B.
4392   souȝte] þought B.
4393   alle to] that alle might L.
4394   þat þat tyme] Of tho that L.
4395   Lady... seide] þey sayde lady B. is] eilis L.
4397   þat] þis B. wolde... shende] will shend me L.
4398   halt... frende] hath take to me L. halt] holdeþ B.
4400   Nadde] Ne had LB; þe] om B.
4402   wedde] in wedde TL; in bed B.
4403   is] he B. wiþ] om B.
4404   soþe] trewþe L. may... man] eche man may LB.
4405   may men] men may L; man may B.
4409   shame] schame syr B. me done] do me L; don B.
4410   þis] þe T. vncouþe sede] þe vncouþe lede B.
4413   was] is L.
4416   þou] þat þou B. on... wroken] awrokyn on hym L.

Ioseph for to take & done
In kingis prisoun for to lye
Wiþouten raunsoun for to bye   4420
Allas Ioseph þe war & wyse
Euel is quytte þi trewe seruyse
For þi goodnes & þi trewe dede
Ful euel is ȝolden þe þi mede
Suche is tresoun of wommon   4425
Stronger in world is founden noon
God amende hem þat suche ben
And ȝyue men grace hem to flen
Now is Ioseph in prisoun stronge   fol. 26v col. 1
And lowe liþ wiþ myche wronge   4430
And aftir lyked him ful wele
For al was turned him to sele
Soone was Ioseph holden dere
Wiþ þe mayster iaylere
Þourȝe þe myȝte of goddes grace   4435
Ouer alle þe prisouns pat þer wase
Alle þat in prisoun were in bonde
Ioseph had hem vndir honde
He ferde wiþ so mychel þrifte
Þat al was done as he wolde shifte   4440
Þus con god helpe mon in nede
Þo þat wol hym loue and drede
Whil Ioseph þus ferde þere
Tweye men of þe kyngis were
To prisoun sende for her mysdede   4445
What hit was I con not rede
Þe spensere and þe botilere boþe

4418   for] *om* B. take] bytake L. done] in preson done B.
4419   kingis] þe kynngis LB. for] *om* B.
4420   Wiþouten] Boute B. bye] dye B.
4421   þe] so B.
4422   quytte] þe quit T; he quyt L. þi] þe L.
4423   goodnes] trewnes B. trewe] gode B.
4424   ȝolden] quit B.
4426   Stronger... founden] In all þis worlde ys stronger B.
4428   men] hem B. hem] swich B. flen] slen B.
4431   aftir] after yt L.
4432   was] þat B. him] in L. sele] ȝele L.
4438   hem] *om* L.
4441   in] at L.
4443   Ioseph þus] Iosophus B.
4444   were] þer wer L.
4445   her] their L; hys B.
4447   spensere] bakar L. botilere] panter B.

Þe kyng wiþ hem was ful wroþe
But þe mayster iaylere
Toke hem Ioseph vnto fere 4450
Whenne Ioseph say hem swiþe
Hem to counfort he was bliþe
But as þei lay in þat prisoun
A nyȝte þei mette a visioun
Of a sweuene þei hadde sene 4455
Eiþer gan to oþere mene
Ioseph say her droupynge chere
And asked why þei mournyng were
Þe botillere for boþe vnswerde
Sir he seide we are aferde 4460
For two sweuenes we say in siȝt
In oure slepe þis ilke nyȝte
What were þo for þi lewete
Þyn owne sweuene firste telle me
Me þouȝte I say a wyn tre 4465
And a bouȝe wiþ braunches þre
On þis tre on vche bowȝe
Heng grapes þicke ynowȝe
Of þo grapis þat þer hong   fol. 26v col. 2
In a coupe me þouȝte I wrong 4470
Þe kyng was at his mete faste
And in his hond þe coupe I þrayste
Ioseph seide wiþ myȝte of heuene
I shal arede wel þi sweuene
Or hit be þis þridde day 4475

4448   was] were B.
4450   Ioseph... fere] vnto Ioseph þere B. vnto] hym to L.
4451   Whenne] When þat B.
4454   A] At L.
4455   þei] þat þey B.
4456   mene] nevene L.
4457   her] their L. droupynge] dropenyng T.
4458   asked] askyd hem B. mournyng] drowpyng L.
4460   Sir... seide] And seid sir L. are] ben B.
4461   sweuenes] dremys B.
4464   firste] om B. me] þou me LB.
4465   Me] My L. wyn]vyne L.
4467   bowȝe] a bowgh LB.
4469   þo] þe B. þat] þer T.
4470   me]my L.
4472   And] om B.
4473   wiþ] þorough B.
4474   arede] rede B.
4475   þis] þe B.

Of prisoun shal þou be take away
And ben aquyt bifore iustise
And put aȝeyn in þi seruyse
Whenne þou in wele art wiþ þe kyng
For goddis loue on me haue menyng   4480
Þat I may by helpe of þe
Of þis prisoun delyuered be
Firste solde was I fro my þede
And now prisoned sackeles of dede
Þe spensere seide me þouȝte I bere   4485
A leep as I was wonte do ere
Wiþ breed I bar hit on my hede
Me þouȝte rauenes hit me reuede
A myche rauen my basket hent
Aboute my hede hit al to rent   4490
Ioseph sei[d] hit beþ not longe
Or þat þou on galwes honge
Hit shal wiþynne þre dayes be
Shal no raunsoun go for þe
Riȝte as Ioseph seide biforn   4495
He was honged þe þridde morn
Þe botillere scaped þe same day
And Ioseph stille in prisoun lay
Wiþ myche kare and also wo
Longe he was forȝeten so   4500
Wildenes of welþe of þis botillere
Forȝat Ioseph his dreme redere
For man þat waleweþ al in ȝeles
And for þat ioye noon angur feles

4476   shal þou] schaltow B.
4478   in] to B.
4480   on... haue] haue on me B.
4481   by] be þe B.
4482   Of þis] Oute of B.
4483   solde... I] was I solde B. þede] stede L; ched B.
4485   spensere] bakar L; þantyr B.
4486   do] to do B.
4488   reuede] berewyd B.
4489   my... hent] in me behent B.
4490   hit]my baskett B.
4491   seid] seiþ H. beþ not] shalle not be L.
4492   Or... þou] But þou shalt L.
4493   Hit] And yt L. þre] þis þre B.
4499   also] sum dele L; mochell B.
4501   Wildenes] Welding B. þis] þe B.
4503   waleweþ] walkyþ L; weldyth B. ȝeles] welys B.
4504   noon] no B.

Þouȝe he haue frend þat is in wo   4505
Oft he is forȝeten soo
ȝore was seid & ȝitt so beþ
Herte forȝeteþ þat yȝe not seeþ
But I dar saye god woot euer   fol. 27r col. 1
Whoso trewely dooþ forȝeteþ he neuer   4510
Ioseph lay in þat longyng
Til þat pharao þe kyng
Say in sleep a sweuene on nyȝt
He comaundide to him brynge riȝt
Clerk knyȝt erle & baroun   4515
To telle to hym his visioun
To wite if any man were
Coude telle what ende hit bere
But þer was noon of hem alle
Coude say what shulde bifalle   4520
Þenne bigan þe botillere speke
Of Ioseph in prisoun steke
To þe kynge he seide þan
Sir he seide I knowe a man
Þat if he were brouȝte in place   4525
I vndirstonde he haþ þat grace
Of þi dreem wiþouten abyde
He shal þe telle þat wol bityde
Sir whenne ȝe were wiþ me wrooþe
& wiþ þe maystir spensere boþe   4530
In prisoun were we done in bonde
Þerynne a iewes childe we fonde
Eyþer of vs a dreem we sawe
And he bad vs to hym hem shawe

4505   þouȝe] ȝef B. in] om B.
4507   ȝore] Euyr B.
4508   not] ne LB.
4510   Whoso] Who B. forȝeteþ he] he forȝete B. he] om L.
4513   Say... on] A sweuyn se in slepe a B.
4514   comaundide] comaunde B. him] om B. riȝt] lyght B.
4515   Clerk... erle] Clerkys knyghtys B.
4517   any man]þere any B.
4518   telle] wite to B.
4519   hem] om B.
4520   say] wite B. shulde] it schuld B.
4521   þenne] Tho L.
4522   in] that in L. prisoun] þe preson B.
4527   abyde] byde B.
4528   þat wol] what schall B.
4530   maystir spensere] panter B. spensere] botelar L.
4533   we] om B.
4534   hem]yt L.

And we bigan al to telle   4535
He tolde vs al þat aftir felle
Go to þe prisoun seide þe kynge
And do hym swiþe to me brynge
Þat cloþing on him newe be done
And þat he come bifore me soone   4540
Þe botillere to þe prisoun went
Soone þerof ioseph he hent
And dide on him newe cloþing
And brouȝte him siþen bifore þe kyng
On Ioseph hit was wel sene   4545
Þat he had longe in prisoun bene
Lene he was & won in face
As he þat longe was fro solace
Þe baronage wondir þouȝt   fol. 27r col. 2
Þat he to kyngis counsel was brouȝt   4550
Þe kyng called ioseph nerre
And seide I haue souȝt nere & ferre
To fynde a mon my dreme to rede
But hiderto myȝt I not spede
Coudes þou telle me what hit wore   4555
My grace I graunte þe euermoore
Sir he seide shewe hit þon
And I shal rede hit as I con
I am redy þi wille to do
If god wole ȝyue me grace þerto   4560
// Me þouȝte þat þis ȝondur nyȝt
I coom in a medewe briȝt
Flouris & greses þerynne I fond
And ky fourtene þerynne goond

4535   bigan al] gan hym L.
4536   He] And he L. al] *om* L.
4539   on... newe] newe on him TL; now on hym B.
4542   þerof] oute B.
4545   On] Of LB. sene] wene B.
4546   had] *om* L. bene] had bene L.
4547   in] of B.
4548   he... was] long þat he had ben B. þat] had L. was] be L.
4550   kyngis] þe kynggis LB.
4552   nere &] *om* L.
4555   Coudes] Canst L. Coudes þou] Coudestou T; Canestow B.
4556   euermoore] for euermore B.
4559   þi wille] the while L.
4560   me] *om* L.
4561   ȝondur] other B.
4562   in] into B.
4563   greses] gres B.
4564   ky] bestys B.

Of þe seuen me þouȝte ferly   4565
Þei were faire and fatte ky
Þe oþere seuene I ȝeode to se
And als myche wondir þouȝte me
Her hyde was clongen to þe boon
S[o] lene say I neuer noon   4570
Hongry & lene boþe were þei
Þe[i] droof þe oþere seuene away
In þat medewe so longe þei ware
Þei hadde eten to þe erþe bare
Þenne me þouȝte I folwede a sty   4575
Into a felde and sawe me by
Fourtene eres stonde of whete
Summe of hem were wondir grete
Ful of corn were þei set þo
But þe toþer were not so   4580
Þei were clongen dryȝe & tome
Of þis Ioseph saye me þi dome
ȝyue me her of good counsaile
And I shal þe neuer faile
Good offis shal þou haue in plas   4585
And be forȝyuen al þi trespas
Þenne seide Ioseph leue sir kyng
God haþ þe shewed fair warnyng
Þerfore owe þou bi riȝt   fol. 27v col. 1
To honoure him wiþ al þi myȝt   4590
Siþ he bifore haþ warned þe
Of þi woo saued to be
For þourȝe þis ensaumple here
Wite þer shal be seuen ȝere
Of plente in þi kyngriche   4595
Þat is þese seuen fatt beestis liche

4569   hyde... clongen] skin were closyd B.
4570   So]S H.
4572   þei] þe H.
4575   folwede] went on L.
4576   felde] þat feld L. and] I B. me by] þereby B.
4577   stonde] I sawe B.
4578   Summe] Sevyn B.
4580   toþer] oþer sevyn B.
4581   clongen dryȝe] drye clongyn B.
4583   her of] now a B.
4586   al] of B.
4587   Ioseph] om L.
4589   owe þou] þou owe B.
4594   Wite] Whete L. The h is inserted with a caret. be] come B.
4595   þi kyngriche] þat kyngdom ryche B.
4596   þese] þe LB.

Þes oþere seuen woful neet
Bitokeneþ seuene ʒeer hongur greet
Þat oþere ʒeeres shul be folwonde
Þat neuer were siche bifore in londe   4600
Suche defaute shal ben of breed
Þe folk shal be for hongur deed
Sir kyng þis is þi auysioun
Loke þiself bi al resoun
For boþe þi dremes ben as oon   4605
Þerfore I rede þou anoon
Gete þe a good purueour
Þat in þis nede may þe socour
In vche lond men for to sett
To geder vche fifte mett   4610
Of þat tyme þat is plente
Certis he seide so shal hit be
Ioseph þou art mychel of prys
And þerto boþe war and wys
Noon I se is founde þe liche   4615
Here in al my kyngriche
Stiwarde þou shalt be & hyʒe iustise
For wel I triste in þi seruyse
Nay sir he seide take not to spit
For firste wol I make me quyt   4620
Of gilt of putifares wyf
Do wey he seide þerof no stryf
Sakles sire haue I dere bouʒt
I woot þou tellest hit me for nouʒt
Þis sakles shame sene hit is   4625
God is wiþ þi werkis I wis

4597   þes] þis B.
4598   seuene] oþer sevyn B. hongur] of hunger B.
4599   þat] þe B.
4600   þat... were] þer was neuer B. bifore... londe] beforhande B.
4602   þe] þat B. shal] þat schall B.
4603   auysioun] vision B.
4606   þou] þe L; þat þow B.
4607   Gete þe] þat þow gete B.
4608   in... þe] may þe att þy nede B.
4609   men] om B.
4610   geder] gete L. fifte] fyfty L.
4611   Of... þat] In þe toune þere B.
4618   in] to B.
4619   spit] quite B.
4620   I am a presoner and endyte B.
4621   gilt] þe gylt B.
4623   sire... I] I have þat B. bouʒt] abouʒt TL.
4624   hit me] me yt L.

Whenne þe baronage of egip
Say him haue siche worship
Wondir þei hadde how þat he   fol. 27v col. 2
To þe kyng was made priue   4630
For he was a man vnseene
And hadde in greet myslikyng bene
We wende he had be deed þing
Nay god forbede seide þe kyng
He was prisound wiþ false rede   4635
So haþ he lyued in mychel drede
Þat is wel [s]ene in his visage
Men han him done greet outrage
Of my dremes now haþ he
Tolde me what of hem wol be   4640
For I woot nowere his make
I wol þat he here vndirtake
Al þe worshipe of my londe
Þat I wol ʒe vndirstonde
And al be wrouʒte bi his counsaile   4645
For al my londe hit shal availe
Þe seuene craftis wel he kan
He is a wondir wyse man
Al his baronage him biforn
To Ioseph han an ooþ sworn   4650
To him as her keper to tent
And to done his comaundement
Of his owne hond toke þe kyng
And dude on iosephs his ryng
Cloþing on him he lette falle   4655
Suche as himself was clad wiþ alle
To ride and go wiþoute lettyng
And knele bifore him as kyng

4636   So] Wo B. in] with L.
4637   sene] wene H. in] on B.
4638   him done] done hym B.
4639   now] me tolde B.
4640   Tolde... wol] And sayde what þe menyng may B.
4641   nowere his] þat he haþe no B.
4642   I... þat] þerfore I will B. here] om B.
4644   ʒe] he B.
4646   shal] may B.
4647   wel] full well B.
4650   an] her B.
4651   as... keper] & to hys kepe B.
4654   iosephs] Iosephis hond LB. his] þe B.
4656   him... clad] he was cloþyd B.
4658   knele] knelyd B.

Þenne seide Þe kyng Ioseph lo
Þou woost þat I am pharao   4660
Shal noon so bolde be in my londe
Wiþouten þe stire foot or honde   4662
His name þei chaungide for þat honoure   4665
And called him þe worldis saueoure
Þe kyng him made a wyf to take
Hiȝt assener a douȝti make
Ioseph þouȝte on his mistere
Made geder him seruaunt & squyere   4670
To gete him wriȝtes in a stounde   fol. 28r col. 1
Where euer þei myȝte be founde
Bernes he made in þat ȝere
A þousande sett in stides sere
And aftir he commaundide himselue   4675
Depe seleres for to delue
And bi grace wiþ his witty dede
Filled hem of wyenes whyte & rede
Whenne þe folk þus sawe h[i]m dele
Wiþ wyn & corn flesshe & mele   4680
And filde þo bernes here & þore   4681
Þe londis of egipt lesse & more   4684
Þus ferde he þo seuene ȝeeris   4685
Þat mo þen a þousande seleres
Filde he wiþ wynes newe & fresshe
And larderes wiþ salt flesshe
Graungis gerneris filde he wiþ seed
Moo þan I con wiþ tunge reed   4690

4662   or] no B.
4663-4   *om in* MSS CGHTLB.
4666   worldis] weryd B.
4671   a stounde] þat londe B.
4672   Where euer] Wheresoeuyr B.
4675   commaundide] comaund LB.
4677   wiþ] be B.
4678   of] with LB. wyenes] wyne B.
4679   folk] folde B. him] hem H.
4680   *first* &] *om* B.
4681   þo] the LB.
4682-3   *om in* MSS CGHTLB.
4684   þe... of] þoroughoute B.
4686   þat] *om* B.
4687   he] hid L; *om* B. wynes] wyne B.
4688   larderes] larderhous B.
4689   Graungis] Granges & B. filde] found L. he] *om* B.
4690   con... tunge] wiþ tonge con TLB.

In euery stide laft a wardeyn
Þenne went he to þe kyng aȝeyn
For to reste him wiþ þe kyng
Aftir his greet trauailyng
Whenne þo seuen ȝeer were oute   4695
Plowemen oueral þe londe aboute
As þei were wont her seed dide sawe
But al welþe bigon wiþdrawe
Þe erþe clang for hete & drye
And so þe wo bigon vp hye   4700
For þat drouȝt þat was so strong
Corn ne gras on erþe noon sprong
Þe beestis dyȝed vp al bydene
For þat hongur was so kene
Þat bi þe firste ȝeer was goon   4705
Vnneþe was þere beest laft oon
Þe wrecched pore fonde no fode
Þei were so fele beggynge þei ȝode
Togider þei flocked in þat lond
By hundrides & bi þousond   4710
Þei souȝte hem rootis as done swyn
Sorwe hit was to se þat pyn
Þe childre & þe men of elde   fol. 28r col. 2
For hongur lay dede in þe felde
Bifore þe kyng þei coom wiþ cry   4715
And seide lord þou haue mercy
Of þi folke for hongur is deed
Was neuer moore nede of breed
Þouȝe men ouer al sowe feldis
Of corn nouȝt hit vp ȝeldis   4720

4691   laft] he lefft B.
4692   went] left L.
4695   þo] þe fyrst B.
4697   dide] to B.
4698   welþe] þe welþ B.
4704   þat] þe B.
4705   þat] And B.
4706   beest] bestis L. oon] none B.
4708   fele] sely L.
4709   þat] þe B.
4710   hundrides] hundred B.
4711   as] so B. done] doþe L; don þe B.
4712   þat] þe B.
4716   þou] om B.
4717   Of] For B. folke] folde B.
4718   Was] Was þer B.
4719   þouȝe] Thy L; ȝef B.
4720   hit] om B.

Þe qualme haþ beestis ouergoon
But if sum bote be þe on
Þe folke shul dyӡe alle bidene
Wiþ qualme þis hongur is so kene
// Þe kyng say þis & wepte soore   4725
How mennes bodyes bolned wore
Wite we wel in þat tyde
Hadde he in his herte no pryde
Lordyngis he seide wel wite ӡe
Ioseph my stiwarde fedeþ me   4730
For derworþely is he þertille
He is al lord þat is skille
But gooþ & falleþ him to fote
And pray hym to do ӡow boote
Þat he ӡyue ӡow of his corn   4735
Or ӡe for hongur be forlorn
To Ioseph went þei cryinge þon
Rewe on vs þou blisful mon
And lene vs sumwhat of þi seed
Was neuer eer so myche need   4740
Sumwhat lene vs bi þi skep
I shal ӡow lene seide Ioseph
// Ioseph was ful of pite
Lete þresshe soone in þat cuntre
Whenne þe seed was al boun   4745
He solde vchone his porcioun
So þat þei myӡte skilfully
Þei & her meyne lyue þerby
In bokis fynde we of a wyle
Þat Ioseph dide þat was sotile   4750
Þe chaf of corn he cast oþerwhyle
Into a watir men calle nyle
For þat watir þat ran þare   fol. 28v col. 1

4722   if... on] it be fewe þer leuyth none B.
4723   þe] Thy L.
4725   say þis] sayde B.
4726   mennes] manys B. bolned] bollen B.
4727   we] ӡow B.
4729   wite] wote LB.
4731   For] Full B.
4732   al] a TB. þat] and þat B.
4735   þat he] Pray hym B.
4738   blisful] blyssyd B.
4741-2 *om in* L.
4743   was] that was L.
4744   þat] þe B.
4752   men calle] þat ys callyd B.

To iacobus hous hit hadde þe fare
Þis hongur þat I here of telle   4755
In londis al aboute hit felle
Men mist hit nowhere in no lond
Seuen ʒeer hit was lastonde
Þenne Iacob & his sones wore
Wiþ hongur in poynt to forfare   4760
Sorweful þei were no selcouþ
Nouʒte hadde þei putte in her mouþ
Siluer þei hadde & golde rede
But þei myʒte fynde to bye no brede
For hongur soore þis childre dide grete   4765
Iacob wiste not how hit to bete
Ofte he helde vp his hende
To god him for to helpe sende
And þat he myʒte menskely dyʒe
Ar he þat [h]ongur longe shulde dryʒe   4770
But oure lord god of myʒt
Hereþ monnes preyer in riʒt
For þouʒe he preue his frend wiþ pyne
Þerfore wol he not him tyne
Whenne Iacob was moost in fray   4775
God him counfortide þat al do may
Soone aftir in a litel whyle
Iacob ʒeode bi þe watir of nyle
He say vpon þe watir gleem
Chaf coom fletyng wiþ þe streem   4780
Of þat siʒte wex he ful bliþe
And to his sones tolde hit swyþe

4755   þis] His L; þe B.
4756   londis al] all londys B.
4757   mist] wist B. nowhere] neuer B.
4760   Wiþ] For B. forfare] fare L; mysfare B.
4761   no] & L; non B.
4762   hadde þei] þat hadde B. putte] to put TLB.
4764   fynde to] no where B.
4765   þis] þese TL. childre] breþer B. dide] om LB.
4767   hende] sond L.
4768   To] þat B. him... to] for L; wolde hym B. sende] to fond L.
4769   menskely] lightly L; sone B.
4770   hungur] longur H.
4771   of myʒt] almyght B.
4773   þouʒe] ʒef B.
4774   he] hym L.
4776   counfortide] comforte B. do] om B.
4781   þat] þe B. wex] was LB. ful] om B.
4782   tolde] he tolde B.

Childer he seide ȝe liste & lete
I saw chaf on þe watir flete
Wheþen hit comeþ I con not rede   4785
But doun hit fleteþ ful good spede
If hit be come fro fer lond
Loke whiche of ȝow wol take on honde
For vs alle to trauaille
Herof is good we take counsail   4790
Aȝeyn þe fleem to fynde þe chaue
Corne þer shul we fynde to haue
// Ruben seide to his resoun   fol. 28v col. 2
Lo I am al redy boun
Oure alþer nedis to take in place   4795
ȝyue me tresour & let me pace
His broþer seide go we alle
In goddes name & so we shalle
Tresour ynouȝe wiþ ȝow ȝe take
And I ȝow pray for goddes sake   4800
Whenne ȝe founden han þat þing
Þat ȝe make not long dwellyng
But goþ wisely in vncouþe lond
God holde ouer ȝow his holy hond
Þese breþer went fro canaan   4805
For þer was iacob wonynge þan
Her ȝongist broþer þei left at hame
Beniamyn was his name
Þei hyed hem vpon her weye
Soone to egipte comen þeye   4810
Whenne þe[i] saye of corn plente
Gladder men myȝte noone be

4783   seide] *om* L.
4784   saw] shaw L.
4785   Wheþen] When L; Fro whens B. I con] con I TLB.
4786   fleteþ] comeþ B.
4788   on] in L.
4789   For vs] Of ȝow B.
4790   we] to B.
4792   þer] we L. we] ther L.
4794   al] *om* B.
4795   nedis] nede B.
4797   broþer] brethryn LB.
4798   &] *om* B.
4800   ȝow pray] pray ȝow B.
4803   wisely] willyngly L.
4806   wonynge] duellyng B.
4809   hyed] sped B. her] þe B.
4811   þei] þe H. of] þe B.

Breed to selle þei fonde & bouȝt
And to Ioseph soone þei souȝt
Men hem tauȝte whiche was he   4815
Doun þei kneled on her kne
Couþe þei of hym no knowleche take
And vncouþely to hem he spake
Childer he seide wheþen are ȝee
Sir þei seide of a cuntre   4820
Þerynne is mony a nedy man   4822
Þe lond men calleþ canaan   4821
Þenne seide Ioseph ful vncouþelye
What are ȝe comen þis lond to spye
Nay þei seide lord vs forbede   4825
But we are comen for greet nede
For bittur hongur þat is bifalle
Oon mannes childer are we alle
Þere is hongur in oure kyngryche
Was þer neuer noon hit lyche   4830
Þe folk dyȝeþ vp al bydene
Suche hongur was neuer er sene
Þerfore haue we hider souȝt   fol. 29r col. 1
A party of money wiþ vs brouȝt
Redy pens haue we to telle   4835
If we may fynde corn to selle
Þerfore we prey þe lord hede
Þat þou vs helpe in þis nede
Of þi michel plente here
To selle vs be hit neuer so dere   4840
Haue ȝe lorde no mystrowyng
Þat we shulde come for oþere þing
// I shal ȝow selle but telleþ me
What maner man ȝoure fadir is he

4813   to... &] þay fonde & sum þey B. bouȝt] broght L.
4816   her] their L.
4817   of... knowleche] no knowlege of hym B.
4819   wheþen] whens LB.
4821-2 *are reversed in* MSS GHTLB.
4821   calleþ] callid L.
4823   þenne... Ioseph] Ioseph sayde B.
4825   lord] god B.
4827   þat] *om* B.
4829   þere] For þere B.
4831   vp] *om* B.
4832   er] arst B.
4837   þe] þi TLB.
4842   shulde] shulle L; *om* B.
4843   selle] yt selle L.
4844   man] of man L. is he] be B.

Sir iacob is oure fadir nome   4845
An olde man we lefte at home
Elleuen breþer are we lyuonde
Oon at home & ten in þis londe
What he seide is he þe leest
Sir beniamyn het þe ȝongest   4850
Whenne he bihelde hem on rowe
Wel vchone he couþe hem knowe
His fadir care þouȝte he on þore
And þerfore he syked ful sore
For siluer he took & ȝaf hem corn   4855
And to her In dude hit be born
He lete wayte at a pryue tyde
And dide his siluer coupe to hyde
In a sekke bysyde her corn
And bad hem byde to mete þat morn   4860
Whenne þei had eten & were boun
For to wende hoom out of toun
Ioseph bigan to sermoun go
And þus shewed hem his resoun þo
//Gode men he seide ȝe shul fare   4865
But of oure kyng I warne ȝow ȝare
I am not kyng ouer þis londe
Vche man shal vndirstonde
Oure kyng hett pharao
And al his wille con make be do   4870
Ouer al I drad and also ryche
Nas neuer eer mon him lyche
Of him I telle ȝow witturly   fol. 29r col. 2
Of þeof wole he haue no mercy

4845   Sir] *om* L.
4848   &] *om* B.
4852   couþe] coude T; did L.
4853   þouȝte he] he þought B. þore] are B.
4854   ful] *om* B.
4855   For] Ther L.
4857   lete] did B.
4858   his] a B.
4859   bysyde] among L. her] þe B.
4860   to] at L. þat] at B.
4862   For] *om* B. toun] þe toun B.
4863   to] *om* B.
4866   But of] Vnto L. oure] ȝour B. ȝare] þar B.
4867   ouer] of B.
4870   al] by L. con... be] I must L; I con make B.
4871   I] he is L; is B.
4872   Nas] Was TB. eer mon] man non B.
4874   þeof] theris L. wole... haue] hath he L.

Whoso is taken wiþ stole þinge   4875
He wole hym do soone to hynge
I say not þis but þat ȝe
Seme trewe men to be
God graunte ȝow wel to founde
And brynge ȝow hool hoome & sounde   4880
ȝoure fadir to se hool & fere
God ȝou graunte lorde dere
God ȝow forȝelde seide þay
To alle ȝoure gode & haueþ good day
// Whenne þei alle were forþ goon   4885
Ioseph seruauntis called anoon
Childre he seide we serue þe kyng
We misse sumwhat of his þing
If he wite he wol be wrooþ
God hit forbede þat were vs looþ   4890
ȝondir be þeues we trowe wende
And he a þeof hem hider sende
Folweþ hem & ransake her ware
Or þei forþer fro vs fare
If in her seckis be ouȝt founde   4895
Loke þei alle be take & bounde   4896
// Þe sergeauntis þenne breme as boore   4899
Ran & ouertook hem þore   4900
Þeues þei seide ȝe shul abyde
Wende ȝe þe kyngis tresour to hyde
He þat ȝow haþ done socour
Stolen ȝe haue of his tresour
In euel tyme dide ȝe þis d[e]de   4905
For siche þerof wol be ȝoure mede

4876   do] done B.
4877   þis] þus L. þat] not L.
4880   hool hoome] hoom hoole TB.
4884   To... ȝoure] And save ȝow B. &] om L.
4885   alle were] wer all B. were forþ] forþ were TL.
4886   seruauntis] his seruauantis LB.
4889   wite] wist B. wol] wolde B.
4891   we] I L. trowe] trow ye L; trew B.
4892   he] ye fynde L. hem]hym L.
4895   be ouȝt] oght be B.
4897-8   om in CGHTLB.
4899   þe] om B. þenne... boore] anon went therfore L.
4900   Ran... hem] They gon ouyrtake them L. þore] ȝore B.
4901   þei] he B.
4902   Wende] Wene LB.
4903   ȝow haþ] hath you L.
4905   dede] dide H.
4906   siche þerof] which þerfore B.

// Certis þei seide leue lordyngis
Haue we not stolen þe kyngis þingis
We are trewe men and lele
Were we neuer wont to stele   4910
We haue wiþ vs trussed nouȝt
But þing þat we trewely bouȝt
And so is oure trewe geten þing
For goddes loue do vs no lettyng
Vpon her sackes leide þei hond   4915 fol. 29v col. 1
Þe coupe þei souȝte & soone fond
Traitours þei seide now is sene
Wheþer ȝe be foule or clene
Anoon were þei bounden harde
And brouȝte bifore þe stiwarde   4920
And prisounde to þe þridde morn
Þat moo folke myȝte þei come biforn
Þat while Ioseph sent þen
To kepe her harneys of his men
// Þe þridde morn comaundide he   4925
A gederynge of þe londe to be
Forþ were brouȝte þo breþer ten
Were þer neuer soryere men
Þei fel doun at Ioseph fette
And mercy souȝte wiþ reuful grete   4930
Þe folke asked what þei shulde be
Þeofes quod Ioseph of a cuntre
Þat is hennes fer as þei me tolde
So is sene on her dedes bolde
Whil I solde hem of my sede   4935

4907   lordyngis] lordyng B.
4908   not] none B. þe... þingis] þing B.
4909   lele] sele L.
4912   trewely] haue truly B.
4913   trewe]tewe T.
4915   leide þei] þey leyde her B.
4916   fond] þey fonde B.
4917   is] yt ys B.
4918   ȝe] þat ȝe B.
4920   bifore] tofore B. stiwarde] high styward B.
4922   moo] no B. þei] hem B.
4923   þat] The L; þer B. while] whyles B.
4924   her] their L. of] by L.
4926   to] schuld B.
4927   þo] þe TB; their L.
4928   þer] they LB. soryere] so sory B.
4930   souȝte] cryed B.
4933   hennes fer] fer hens B.
4934   is] it is B. on] be B.

My coupe þei stale away to lede
Sergeauntis I sent soone on honde
And in her gere my coupe þei fonde
I serued hem & warned nouȝt
Of al þat þei me bisouȝt   4940
Mete & drynke I ȝaf hem boþe
And bad hem kepe hem ay fro loþe
Siþen I preyed god al weldonde
Lede hem sauely to her londe
Here vpon þei stale my þing   4945
If ȝe ȝyue dome men shul hem hyng
// Þonne spak ruben þe eldest broþer
Stille menyng to þat oþer
Now is comen oure aller sake
Into woo synne and wrake   4950
I seide ȝow so þis oþer ȝere
ȝe wolde not my resoun here
As of Ioseph oure broþer lele
Wiþ wrong ȝe solde him for catele
ȝe solde hym out of myn assent   4955 fol. 29v col. 2
Þat fynde we nowe here present
Done ȝe haue þis synne in ȝow
ȝoure repentaunce late comeþ now
Furþer may we not stere
Her wille mut we suffere here   4960
Helpe lord þat al haþ wrouȝt
In oþer helpe me triste I nouȝt
He mened him þus wiþ mournyng chere
And wende Ioseph myȝt hit not here
Allas þei seide þat euer we ware   4965

4937   Sergeauntis] Seruantys B. sent] sende T.
4938   my] þe L. my... þei] sone þey it B. þei] was L.
4939   I] om B.
4940   me] had me B.
4942   ay] euer B.
4946   If] ȝefe B. ȝyue] þe B. shul] sayde B.
4948   Stille menyng] Full styll mornyng B. þat] þese T; all þe B.
4952   ȝe] And ȝe B. wolde] nold L.
4955   out of] withoute B.
4956   we] ȝe B. here] in B.
4957   in ȝow] now B.
4959   Furþer] For hens B.
4960   Her... we] Nedys mvst vs B.
4961   Helpe] Help now B.
4962   me] ne LB.
4963   mened] mornyd B.
4964   myȝt hit] it myght B.

Born if we shul þus forfare
// Ioseph roos vp fro his stede
To galewe þei wende he wolde hem lede
Ioseph herde her mournyng soore
And left hem as nouȝt ne wore   4970
His wille was but to make hem gast
And aftir rewe on hem at þe last
Whenne he say her mournyng moone
To þe court he spak anoone
Listeneþ alle þat hider beþ come   4975
Ar ȝe ȝyue here any dome
A word he seide sooþ may falle
Al þouȝe þei be þeues alle
Whenne þei were breþer alle at home
Þei menged me þe ȝongist nome   4980
I wol do to hem þat grace
Þat þei þe ȝongist brynge in place
Þat þei lafte at her faderes In
Whiche is called beniamyn
Þe whyle wole I haue oon of ten   4985
Þat þei ȝyue to name ruben
To dwelle in hostage here wiþ me
Til þat þe ȝongest comen be
Þis terme is fourty dayes sett
Þat þei þis commaundement not lett   4990
But þei me þenne my couenaunt bringe
Elles her hostage shal I hynge
And if þei couenaunt holde I wis
I shal forȝyue hem al þis mys   4994
And þus wol I hem preue now   4995

4966   shul þus] þus schull B.
4967   his] þis B.
4971   but to] not bot B.
4972   þe] *om* LB.
4973   say] *om* B.
4976   here] *om* B.
4978   þouȝe] ȝef þat B.
4980   menged... nome] neuenyd a ȝonger son B.
4981   to] *om* B. wol] wolde TL.
4982   þe] þat B.
4984   Whiche] þe which B.
4985   þe] þer B. ten] þe ten LB.
4986   þat... name] Which that is callyd L; þe which þat þey call B.
4989   þis] The L. is] shalle LB. sett] by sette LB.
4991   þei me] ȝef þay B. couenaunt] comaundment L; comenant B.
4992   shal] wylle L.
4993   couenaunt] conaunt B.
4995-5318   *missing from* H (2 *leaves*). *Printed here from* T.

Sir þei seide god ȝelde ȝow
For if þat we haue lif þerto
ȝoure commaundement shul we do
Her leue þei toke & were bliþe
And hyȝed in her weye swiþe   5000
Oure lord lad hem in her fare
Þei coom to her fadir ȝare
Þei him cussed swiþe soone
And dude her sackes to be vndone
Say me quad Iacob how is þis   5005
Þat of my childre oon I mis
He is in egipte allas why
For þere vs toke þe heȝe baily
To skape wiþ gile were we fayn
What hope ȝe shal he be slayn   5010
Nay þei seide god hit shilde
Him shal delyuer ȝoure ȝongest childe
How shal beniamin com þare
Sir elles þei wol Ruben forfare
ȝoure eldest son to hede or honge   5015
Haue ȝe terme he seide how longe
Fourty dayes we drede hit sare
ȝe most haste ȝou on ȝoure fare
Hadde þei soiourned but a stounde
Iacob seide tyme is to founde   5020
Fetteþ me home ruben blyue
O[r] elles holde ȝe not my lyue
Ledeþ wiþ ȝou beniamyn
God graunte ȝow grace þider to wyn
// Lord myȝtful kyng he seide   5025
Þat paradis to mon purueide

4997   For] And B.
4998   we] be L.
5000   hyȝed] sped B. in] hem L; hem in B.
5001   lad] had L.
5002   þei coom] þan com þay B.
5008   þere] theve L; þere ys & B.
5009   gile] lyffe B.
5010   hope] trow B.
5014   þei wol] wylle they L.
5015   to] om B. or] ar B.
5016   terme] day B. how] so L.
5018   ȝe] ȝow B.
5021   Fetteþ] Fech B.
5022   Or] O T.
5023   Ledeþ] Lede ȝe B.
5026   mon] men B.

And adam tauȝte þere to abyde
With eue þat wrouȝte was of his syde
Fro flood þou sauedest noe here
And Abraham temptidest to þe dere   5030
Of his o son offryng to make
And he hit grauntid for þi sake
Þat was my fadir Isaac
Til þe aungel for him spak
And sauedest me my broþer fro   5035
Esau þat wolde me lord slo
Saue my childre hool to me   fol. 32r col. 2
And haue of Iosephes soule pite
// Þese childre toke wiþ hem to spende
And redied hem forþ to wende   5040
So longe þei went in her wey
Into egipte soone coom þey
Þei souȝte & soone þe stiwarde fond
At a gerner him stondond
Þere he lyuerey made of corn   5045
Þei grette him alle on kne biforn
Whenne [Ioseph] gan his breþeren se
Muchel ioye in herte hadde he
Ruben þat for him was nomen
Had muchel ioye whenne he was comen   5050
Muchel ioye was Ioseph wiþinne   5052
He bihelde þenne beniamynne   5051
For whenne þe ton þe toþer seȝe

5027   tauȝte] broght B.
5028   þat] *om* B. was] þer B.
5029   flood] þe flode B. sauedest] sauest B.
5030   temptidest] temptist LB.
5031   o] owne B.
5032   þi]hys B.
5034   for]to B.
5035   sauedest me]sauyd my lyfe B.
5036   lord]a B.
5037   Saue] So saue B.
5039   childre] folke B. wiþ] *om* B. to]for to B.
5040   redied]sped B. forþ]in her wey B.
5042   soone coom]come ar B.
5043   fond] fode B.
5044   a]þe B. him]*om* B.
5045   he]*om* L ; þey B. lyuerey]delyueraunce B.
5046   þei grette]And fell B.
5047   Ioseph]*om* T.
5051-2   *reversed in* MSS GHTLB.
5051   þenne] *om* B.
5052   Muchel]Was L.
5053   For]And B.

No lenger myȝte þei nouþer dreȝe
But bent hem in armes þore   5055
And cussed sixty siþe & more
Ioseph wepte ful tenderly
And siþ on benche set him him by
How fareþ he seide oure fadir fre
Mi fadir sir fareþ wel seide he   5060
Knowyng of ȝoures haue I noon
Mafay broþer and al is oon
Knowes þou not me he seide nay
I sawe ȝou neuer bifore þis day
We are not sibbe sir seide he   5065
ȝus he seide I telle to þe
Furst wolde þei ha slayn me þes ten
Siþ me þei solden to vncouþe men
Al was for I tolde a dreme
Þat now is comen to good teme   5070
I hatt Ioseph ȝoure broþer am I
Þei fel in swoun & cryed mercy
Þo þei wende wiþouten wene
To haue ben honged al bidene
But Ioseph coumfortid her chere   5075
And wepyng seide breþeren dere
ȝoure gult I haue forȝyuen ȝow   fol. 32v col. 1
Forȝyue me myn I preye ȝow now
Forȝyue me þat I dud ȝou take
Into bondes wiþouten sake   5080
Þe coupe into ȝoure secke put I
And pursewed ȝou dispitously

5054   nouþer]lengger L.
5055   hem]hym L. þore]ȝore B.
5056   siþe]tymys B.
5057   wepte]went B.
5058   him him by]hym truly L; hem B.
5059   oure]my L.
5060   sir]om L. seide]ser seid L.
5061   ȝoures]ȝow B.
5062   Mafay]My fayre B.
5063   Knowes þou]Knowestow B.
5064   ȝou]þe B. bifore] or B.
5066   to]om B.
5067   ha... me]me haue slawe B. þes]þis LB.
5068   me þei] þey me B. vncouþe]straunge B.
5074   To... ben] For to be B.
5077   ȝow]you yow L.
5081   þe] Oure B.
5082   dispitously]spytusly B.

And shamed ȝou *in* me*n*nes siȝt
I am aknowe I dud vnriȝt
Mi wraþþe is clene fro me goon 5085
To me I p*r*eye ȝou ȝe haue noon
B[ut] hyȝe ȝou swiþe hoom to go
I wol algate hit be so
Makeþ ȝoure gere redy to drift
ȝoure sackes shal I fille of ȝift 5090
To fette my fadir shul ȝe fou*n*de
Seiþ hi*m* I am hool & sou*n*de
For ȝitt haue we to com & bide
Fyue ȝeer of þis hongry tide
Þ*a*t make shal mony mon & wyf 5095
Ar þei be done lese her lyf
Beþ not ferde but makeþ good chere
For ȝoure hele god sende me here
Not ȝoure reede but goddes sonde
Was I sende into þis londe 5100
For pharao kyng haþ made me
Lord of al þis londe so fre
// Sir gladly at ȝoure biddyng
Shal hit be to vs a co*m*mau*n*dyng
Als soone as we may be purueide 5105
We wol do as ȝe haue seide
Oure misdede we repente ay
Forȝyue vs lord we ȝou pray
Siþ god wolde suche caas shulde falle
He seide I haue forȝyuen ȝou alle 5110
To ȝoure fadir now hiȝe ȝe
And telle hi*m* þ*a*t ȝe sou*n*de be

5083   me*n*nes]manys B.
5084   aknowe]beknow B.
5087   But]Bi T.
5088   hit]þat it B.
5089   gere]ȝere B.
5091   fette]fech B. shul ȝe]ȝe schull B.
5092   I]þ*a*t I B.
5095   make shal]schall make B.
5096   lese]to les B.
5097   ferde]aferde B.
5101   kyng]þe kyng B.
5102   so fre]and fe L; to be B.
5104   hit... a]we do ȝour B.
5108   we]I B.
5109   wolde]will B. shulde falle]befalle B.
5110   have forȝyuen]will forȝefe B.
5111   ȝoure]oure B. now]ye L; sone B.
5112   And]*om* L. be]me se L.

He makeþ deol for ȝoure sake
Þis tiþing shal his sorwe slake
We shul þei seide make no dwelling   5115
Til þat we him to ȝou bring
Takeþ ruben hoome wiþ ȝow   fol. 32v col. 2
And leuep me beniamyn now
He clad him wiþ pal of affrik here
And siþen ȝaf hem ȝiftis riche & dere   5120
He cussed hem alle in token of sauȝt
And siþen to god hem bitauȝt
Þenne ȝede he hoom to his In
Wiþ his ȝonge broþer beniamin
He dud on him pal cloþing   5125
And on his hond sett riche ring
Þese breþer ȝode forþ her way
To her fadir soone coom þay
Siluer & golde þei wiþ hem ledde
And cloþing als for backe & bedde   5130
Forȝeten haue þei al þat care
Þat Ioseph had done hem þare
Hoome þei coom not prisoners liche
But as þei were knyȝtis riche
Clad þei were wiþ riche wede   5135
Her camails charged alle wiþ sede
Her fadir lay vnhol in bedde
He miȝte not sture of þat stedde
To him coom a messangere

5113   deol]sorow B.
5114   his... slake] hym ioyfull make B.
5117   ȝow]ȝou so dere B.
5118   om in B. me]with me L.
5119   him] hem B. of... here]dere L. of] & B.
5120   And] om B. siþen]om L. hem] hym L. riche... dere] that riche wer L.
5121   sauȝt]pees L.
5122   hem]he hem B. bitauȝt]byches L.
5123   ȝede]went B.
5124   ȝonge] om B.
5125   pal]fayr B.
5126   riche]a B.
5127   þese breþer] This brothir L.
5129   þei... hem] with hem þay B.
5130   cloþing... for]also cloþis to B.
5132   done hem] hem done B.
5133   not]not as B.
5135   wiþ]in B.
5136   alle wiþ] with rich B.
5137   vnhol]syk B.
5138   of]fro L. þat]þe B.

And tolde him soþely in his ere   5140
Sir he seide here good tiþinge
Þi sones are knyȝtis here comynge
Þou lyest he seide bi god so dere
Ar þei no knyȝtis ny knyȝtis fere
Sir bi þe feiþ I owe to ȝow   5145
Þei are knyȝtis as I trow
For þei are clad in riche pal
And riche ȝiftis ȝyuen ouer al
Siluer & golde þei haue plente
Seistou soþ he seide sir ȝe   5150
If þou trowe not my tale
Rise vp & se þiseluen shale
I may not rise he seide for lame
Wiþ þat word þei coom alle hame
In at þe dor vpon a route   5155
Heilsynge her fadir for to loute
Sir þei seide tiþingis here   fol. 33r col. 1
Fro þi tweyne sones dere
Oon fro beniamyn oure broþer
And fro Ioseph is þe toþer   5160
Whenne iacob in bed þat lay
Herde Ioseph named þat day
Anoon his herte bigon to liȝt
And in his bed sat he vpriȝt
His heed was al bare for elde   5165
Vpon his sones he þenne bihelde
And say hem clad in riche pal
Seiþ me he seide now ȝe shal
What makeþ ȝou to mene now
Of my son Ioseph bitwixe ȝow   5170
Þritty ȝeer hit is agone

5140   soþely]softly L.
5144   Ar]Be B. ny... fere] no squyer B.
5150   Seistou]Seist þou L. sir]*om* LB.
5154   alle hame] attane L.
5155   vpon]on B.
5157   tiþingis]tyþing B.
5159   fro]ys B.
5161   in... þat]þat in B.
5162   named]neuyn in B.
5164   sat he]he sat B.
5166   þenne]*om* L.
5167   hem]þen L.
5168   now... shal] how is þis full B.
5169   mene]neme L; meve B.
5170   my... bitwixe] Ioseph betwene B.

Siþ he of beestis wilde was slone
ȝe gabbe & also done greet synne
Of him to me for to mynne
Fadir þei seide mistrowe nouȝt   5175
Þat we any gabbynge haue brouȝt
For ioseph hool & sounde lafte we
Lorde he seide I wolde him se
Certis þei seide þat may god ȝyue
I wolde he seide no lenger lyue   5180
ȝe shul haue lif longer þen þider
Haue ȝe brouȝte him wiþ ȝou hider
Nay sir but ȝe mot to him fare
He haþ sent aftir þe his chare
We shul ȝou make þerynne a bed   5185
Into egipte ȝe shul be led
Þo wex iacob swiþe fayn
His body bigon to quyke aȝayn
ȝyue me my cloþes þenne seide he
Hastily þat we redy be   5190
Childer he seide go we stronge
Into egipte þinke me longe
Israel wiþ þis vp leep
Þat myȝte bifore stire no step
Wiþouten helpe of any son   5195
Þat quake with vche a lymme was won   5196
Iacob hiȝed as he ȝong were   5199 fol. 33r col. 2
Þenne seide ruben fadir dere   5200
I rede studfastliere þou go
What art þou þat biddest so
Ruben ȝoure son & what þing
Is of Ioseph wiþouten lesing

5172   of]with B. beestis wilde]wyld bestis LB.
5174   mynne]nymme L.
5179   god ȝyue] not ȝet B.
5183   but... mot] ȝow most B.
5184   aftir þe] for ȝow B. þe]you L.
5187   swiþe]wondyr B.
5192   þinke me] me think B. me]we L.
5194   myȝte] om L. stire no]aneþe myȝt L; styrt ne B.
5195   helpe]the help L.
5196   with]byfor L. a]om LB. was] & was B.
5197-8   om HTLB.
5199   Iacob]Israel B.
5200   seide ruben] Ruben sayde B.
5201   rede] rede the L. studfastliere þou] ȝow stedefastly or ȝe B.
5202   art þou]ertow B. biddest]sayest B.
5203   &... þing]to telle typyng L.
5204   Is]om L. lesing]lettyng B.

Of egipte sire þat riche londe   5205
He is maistir al weldonde
How so is þere noon oþer kyng
ȝus sir but he tenteþ no þing
Þe warde he haþ of þat kyngriche
Pore & riche to deme I liche   5210
He deleþ þe corn of þat cuntre
Þis is þe soþe leue ȝe me

Israel mad oon offringe swiþe
As þei were wont in þat siþe
God coom to him in a visioun   5215
And seide to Iacob his resoun
Iacob he seide listen to me
Wiþ þi fadir I was & I am wiþ þe   5218
Wende to egipte among þat lede   5220
For I myself shal þe þere fede   5221
And þere forsoþe shal þou d[ie]   5223
Ioseph þi sone shal louke þin eȝe
Þenne was Iacob redy ȝare   5225
Wiþ his meyne redy to fare
His sones alle & her flittyng
Wyf & childe & oþere þing
In weynes were þei put to lede
Þat Ioseph sent hem ful of sede   5230
His meyne þat him folewed þider
Whenne þei were gedered alle togider
Six & sixti somme on lyues

5206   al]and all B.
5208   no]to no B.
5210   I]in B.
5213   swiþe]bliþe B.
5214   siþe]kiþe B.
5215   a]*om* B. visioun] vecyon L.
5216   to]*om* B.
5218   &]*om* B. I am]so L.
5219   *om* TLB.
5220   among]into B.
5221   For]And B.
5222   *om* TLB.
5223   die]dreȝe T.
5224   þin eȝe]þy nye B.
5225   þenne was]When B. redy ȝare] was redy þare B.
5226   redy]for LB.
5227   & her]were L.
5228   *first* &] *om* L.
5231   him] hem L.
5233   Six... sixti]Sexty & sex B.

Þei were wiþouten sones wyues
And Ioseph hadde sones twyn   5235
Manassen and effraym
Þo in egipte his wif him bare
Whiche þe kyng had geten him þare
Whenne iacob coom egipte nere
He sende Iudam his messangere   5240
To telle Iacobes coome to londe   fol. 33v col. 1
And bere Ioseph þerof tiþonde
Whenne Ioseph þerof herde
Wiþ his court aȝeyn him he ferde
Whenne þei had cussed a mile & more   5245
His blessyng ȝaf he him riȝt þore
Whenne Ioseph wiþ his fadir met
Tenderly wiþ eȝe he gret
Þei grett for gladnes as I trowe
Iacob seide to Ioseph nowe   5250
Of dede wol I me neuer mene
Now I þi face son haue sene
But certeynely þe soþe to say
Whoso had be bistad þat day
And had þat swete metyng sene   5255
Þei he þre dayes had fastyng bene
Of mete ne drynke bi myn entent
He shulde haue had no talent
Son he seide longe is gone
I wende wilde beestis hade þe slone   5260
Wherfore I fel in greet sekenes
Blessed be god þou lyuynge es
Son whi helde þou þe fro me
What clooþ was hit brouȝte me to se

5234   þei]þere B. wyues]& wyfes B.
5235   Ioseph]Iacob B. twyn] tweyn B.
5238   Whiche] þe which B. him]hem LB.
5241   Iacobes]þat Iacob is B.
5242   And]To B.
5243   Whenne]When þat B.
5244   aȝeyn]aȝens B. he] om B.
5245   Whenne] As L. had cussed]mette L. &]or L.
5246   His]Iacob hys B. he... riȝt]hem B.
5247   wiþ]om L.
5251   me]om L.
5252   I]I haue B. son haue]om B.
5254   bistad]ther LB.
5255   þat]þe B.
5256   þei he]ȝef he had B. had] om B.
5257   ne] and LB.
5264   Whan that blody cloþe was broȝt me L. hit... se] þat þey broght me B.

Þat blody was & I noot how   5265
Not of me fadir þat se ȝe now
Into sichen whenne I þe sent
To seche þi breþeren þat þider went
So dud I fadir mystrowe hit nouȝt
Her mete to hem I redy brouȝt   5270
But soone as I þere was comen
Wiþ euel counsel was I nomen
Whi leue son I shal ȝou say
Þenke ȝe not how mony a day
Of a dreem is gone ful ȝore   5275
Leue son were þou take þerfore
ȝe fadir vnneþes scaped I
Til marchaundis coom me for to by
To þis londe þei me con bringe
And siþen solde me to þe kynge   5280
In prisoun aftir is not to leyn   fol. 33v col. 2
Was I done to suffer peyn
And was þourȝe putifares wif
Þat wolde haue brouȝte me of lif
To prisoun so whenne I was gone   5285
Me borwed noon but god allone
He þat to his in nede is best
In him I haue my hope fest
He haþ delyuered me of my woo
And þut me to welþe no mon so   5290
Þe lordshipe of al þis lond
To reule & kepe is in myn hond
Þerfore fadir lete ȝe nouȝt
Al ȝoure wille hit shal be wrouȝt
Boþe for my breþer & ȝow   5295

5265   *om* B.
5266   þat]bote B. ȝe] þou L. now]how B.
Extra line in B, Bot þis is þe soþe trow, *after* 1.5266.
5270   I redy]redy I B.
5271   soone]as sone L. þere] thedir LB.
5277   vnneþes]vnneþe B.
5279   me con]me gon L; gan me B.
5281   is...to]soþe I B.
5283   And]þat B.
5284   of]from L.
5285   so]þo B.
5286   borwed]sorowye B.
5287   his]vs L.
5288   In]To L.
5290   me]om B.
5295   ȝow]for ȝow B.

For I ouer alle haue pouste now
To my lord ȝe com wiþ me
I shal ȝou do aqueynted to be
I shal ȝou aske sum rescet
Wel I woot I shal ȝou get   5300
Gladly son go we soone
To þanke him þat haþ for þe done
Knele I shal al bifore þe kyng
And þanke him of his grete helping
As his owne in al þat I may   5305
And þou shal bene his seruaunt ay
I shal to þe kyng þe biteche
And siþen þe my blessynge reche
Þenne I wol me leye to deȝe
To lyue may I no lenger dreȝe   5310

Iacob went þen wiþ his route
His sones twelue him aboute
His berde was side with myche hare
On his heede his hatt he bare
As mon of elde longe forlyuen   5315
Many baret tofore had dryuen
Whenne þei were comen tofore þe king
Þei loutide him alle wiþ hailsyng
Of his come þe kyng was fayn   fol. 30r col. 1
And of his sete roos him aȝayn   5320
Kust & sette him on benche him by
And honoured him ful derworþely
Þe kyng lete write lettres ȝare

5296   I... haue]all is in my B.
5298   to]om B.
5302   haþ]om L. done]hath done L.
5303   al]om LB.
5304   his]þy B.
5307   I]And I L. to]the to LB. second þe]om LB.
5308   þe]to þe B.
5309   I... to]will I to deþe sone B.
5310   may I]I may LB.
5312   aboute]al aboute B.
5314   second his]an B.
5315   longe forlyuen] þat long had liuen B.
5316   Many]And many B. Many... tofore]Byfore many a day L.
5317   tofore]afore B.
5318   him]hem L; to hym B. alle]om B.
5320   roos him] him roos TL.
5321   Kust]He hym kist B. on benche]doun B.
5322   derworþely]worþely B.
5323   lete]did B.

To geder alle wiþ hasty fare
Þe beste in þat londe vnliche   5325
And dide to make a feeste riche
Whenne Iacob say alle plentes were
And alle aboute to make him chere
He preyed þo þat þere were lent
To here a litel of his entent   5330
Þe kyng to alle bad pees þan
Þus iacob his tale bigan
Pees haue phareo þe kyng
God ȝyue hym his brode blessyng
Gode men I am as ȝe may se   5335
An olde man pouȝe ȝe knowe not me
Nor I ȝow to vndirstonde
For I am here in vncoupe londe
Out of ebron born am I
Þere liþ oure elderes & so shal I   5340
Þere liþ adam þe formast man
And Eue of whom we alle bigan
Þe folke þat of hem firste was bred
For þei noþing god ne dred
On hem he took vengeaunce sore   5345
But eiȝte on lyue he lefte no more
Oon was noe riȝtwis of wham
Bicoom oure feiþful Abraham
Þat dredde god & loued hym so
Þat for his loue his sone wolde slo   5350
Þat was ysaac his childe dere
Whoos sone I am þat ȝe se here
I am sixe score & ten ȝeer olde

5324   To geder] To gider T.
5326   dide]bad L. to]om B.
5327   plentes] blyþe L.
5328   aboute]bygan L.
5330   entent]talent L.
5332   þus]This L.
5334   brode]dere L.
5336   þouȝe]ȝef B.
5339   ebron]Ebrew L. am]was B.
5340   liþ]lyf B. &... I]witterly B.
5343   of... firste] fyrst of hem B.
5344   god]of god B. ne]om L; wer B.
5345   On]Of L.
5346   on]of B.
5347   riȝtwis]right B.
5349   hym so]also B.
5351   his]þat B.
5352   ȝe se]stondeth B.

My fadir het ysaac as I tolde
Whenne he was to his endinge boun 5355
I hadde of him my broþer benesoun
My broþer esau me bysouȝt
To disherite me if he mouȝte
He flemed me out of my londe fol. 30r col. 2
Þourȝe god I haue hit ȝitt in honde 5360
Þese twelue are my sones vchone
Pritty ȝeer hit is ful gone
Þat I hadde lost my sone so dere
Ioseph þat I haue founden here
Of his fyndynge þonke I god so 5365
He saue him fro þe fend his fo
He ȝaf hem alle his blessyng
And to Iacob seide þe kyng
A wyse man is þi sone Ioseph
In al egipte is noon so ȝep 5370
His witt haþ saued me & myne
Fro mychel nede & myche pyne
Firste was he here as our þral
Now vndir me mayster of al
I ȝyue him wonynge stide to lende 5375
For euermore wiþouten ende
To him & his breþer elleuene
To chese where þei wol hit neuene
Iacob whenne he leue had lauȝt
Wiþ his sones & her auȝt 5380
Went to a stide hem to plese
Of pasture greet & hett ranese
In þat stide her lyf þei ledde

5354 tolde]ȝou tolde B.
5357 bysouȝt]sought B.
5358 mouȝte]had moght B.
5360 god]om T. ȝitt]om L. honde]my hond L.
5362 ful]om B.
5364 Ioseph]om B. I]I now B.
5365 þonke I]I þank B. so]also B.
5366 saue]sauyd B. fend his]fendys B.
5368 And]þan B.
5370 ȝep]lef L.
5372 nede]woo B.
5375 lende]bende B.
5376 For]om B.
5377 his]to hys B.
5379 he]his L.
5380 her]with his L; hys B.
5382 &]that LB. ranese]gessen B.

Ioseph hem ӡaf wherof to be fedde
Faut of breed þat ilke tyde   5385
Was ouer al þe world so wyde
But in no londe so myche wan
As in egipte & canaan   5388
So longe hadde þei bouӡte her sede   5391
Þat her siluer wexe al gnede
Whenne þei hadde no þing ӡare
Þat þei myӡte to her lyflode spare
Þe folk of egipte coom bydene   5395
Byfore Ioseph hem to mene
Lord þei seide to þe we saye
Al oure auӡte hit is awaye
Now haue we noon wherwiþ we may
Lengþe oure lyf fro day to day   5400
No þing is lefte vs but erþe bare   fol. 30v col. 1
And alle oure bodyes ful of kare
Londes & liþes wiþ body we bede
Þat þou vs take in þi bondhede
In þraldome take oure londis ӡe shal   5405
For seed þenne may we sowe wiþal
Þei solde her londis al for nede
Ioseph bouӡte hem al for sede
In al egipte lefte he no lond
Vnbouӡte into þe kyngis hond   5410
Outake þe lond of þat lede
Þat was bitauӡte *pre*stis to fede
To kepe[n] hemself for her holde
Þe kyng hem fonde as hit is tolde

5384   hem ӡaf]ӡafe hem B. wherof]wherw*ith* B.
5386   so]*om* B.
5389-90   *om* CGHTLB.
5392   wexe]was B.
5393   ӡare]þare B.
5395   þe... of]Vnto B.
5396   mene]nevene L.
5397   þe we]ӡow I B.
5398   auӡte hit]stuf B.
5399   noon]noght B.
5401   vs]*om* B.
5404   bondhede]nede B.
5405   ӡe shal] w*ith* all B.
5410   Vnbouӡte]Bote bought it B.
5411   Outake]W*ith*oute B.
5412   *pre*stis] þe prestys B.
5413   kepen]kepem H. for]fro B.
5414   fonde]fed B.

// Þus couþe Ioseph as I seide ȝow   5415
Awayte his lord þe kyngis prow
His lord he profitide erly & late
And halpe þe nedeful in her state
Whil hem lastede þat seesoun dere
Iacob þere lyued seuentene ȝere   5420
In a cuntre þat hett Iessen
Of him were bred mony men
Whenne hit drouȝe to his laste day
To Ioseph þus gon he say
If I fonde euer grace in þe   5425
Lay þi hond vndir my þe
And hete me trewely bi couenaunte
Þat I not grauen be in þis lande
But hete mi trewely þou þi selue
Shal me wiþ myne elderes delue   5430
Fadir I bihete þe riȝt
Hit shal be done wiþ al my myȝt
Þerto þere an ooþ he sware
Now lyþ Iacob in bed of care
He draweþ fast to his endyng   5435
And Ioseph dide tofore him bryng
Boþe Effraim & manasse
To blesse his childre preyed he
Iacob in bed him leyde vpriȝt
For elde al dym wex his siȝt   5440
He leide aboute hem eyþer arm   fol. 30v col. 2
And kiste hem ofte'vpon his barm
My swete sone Ioseph he seide

5415   couþe]coude T. seide]tell B.
5416   Awayte]Wayte B.
5417   profitide]sauyd B.
5418   her]þe B. state]estate L.
5419   hem]them L.
5420   Iacob... lyued]Ther lyvid Iacob L.
5422   were]was TLB.
5423   his]þe L.
5425   euer grace]grace euer B.
5426   my]in L; þy B.
5427   bi]om L. couenaunte]couand B.
5428   not... be] be not grauyn B.
5430   Shal]þou schall B. elderes]erdres B.
5433   þere]þeron B.
5439   him]om B. leyde]led L; lay B. vpriȝt]full right LB.
5440   For]And B. al]& B. wex]was B.
5441   eyper]oþer L.
5442   ofte]of B.

Of þe am I not vnpurueyde
Þi fruyt I se bifore myn eȝe   5445
Now recche I neuer whenne I deȝe
He leide his hond vpon her croun
And ȝaf hem dyuerse benesoun
Soone he seide to Ioseph now
Most I passe god take I ȝow   5450
God þat was oure elderes wiþ
Gnaunte ȝow goyng into ȝoure kiþ
Þei ȝe be flemed here a whyle
He wol ȝow brynge fro þis exile
His sones he bifore hym calde   5455
And many resouns to hem talde
Boþe þat þei shulde ouerbyde
And in her laste dayes bityde
Whenne he endide of his sawe
His sones he blessed on a rawe   5460
To vche he ȝaf dyuerse benysoun
And aftir leide his heed adoun
He went out of þis wrecched werde
And to his formest fadris ferde
And brouȝte is into grace of griþ   5465
Lord vs grante to dwelle him wiþ
Nyȝe seuen score ȝeer of elde
Was þis Iacob at his dounhelde
But þre ȝeer þerof was wan
His sones him beer to canaan   5470
And leyde him þere his elderes by
Þere he desired for to ly
By ysaac & by Abraham

5444   am I]I am B.
5445   eȝe]nye B.
5449   Soone]Son TL.
5450   take I]thanck L.
5453   þei]ȝef B.
5455   he]om L. hym]hem L.
5456   talde]he tolde B.
5457   ouerbyde]euer bide B.
5460   a]om L.
5464   fadris]fadir TLB.
5465   And]om B. is into]he ys to B. of] & B.
5466   Lord... grante] God ȝefe vs grace B.
5467   Nyȝe]om B. ȝeer] & nyne ȝere B.
5468   at... dounhelde]þat now is doun & tolde B. dounhelde] helde L.
5469   þerof... wan]þerby cam L.
5473   *second* by]om B.

In ebron bisyde olde Adam
Þis Iacob þat I of melle   5475
Het boþe iacob & Israelle
Þe folk of israel of him sprong
Þat pharao kyng helde in wrong
In egipte helde he hem ful harde
As I shal telle soone aftirwarde   5480
Siþen he dyȝed Ioseph þe wyse   fol. 31r col. 1
And endede in oure lordis seruyse
Firste was he buryed in þat cuntre
Siþen borne to his lond was he
Þe osprynge þat of Ioseph bredde   5485
Was mychel in þat londe spredde
What of him & of his breþer sede
Were þritty þousande as we rede
Half sixe skore was Ioseph þat day
Whenne he of world went away   5490
Whil þat Ioseph regnede þere
His breþere in egipte þei were
Aftir þei lyued hadde mony a day
Dede & doluen þere were þay

Of moyses now wole we telle
If ȝe wole a stounde dwelle
Þe whyle roos þere a newe kyng   5495
Þat of Ioseph had no knowyng
He made þenne a parlement
And seide gode men takeþ tent

5474   In... bisyde]By Abraham & by B. ebron]Ebrew L. olde]om L.
5478   kyng helde]had B.
5481   he]so L.
5482   oure lordis]godis B.
5483-4   *reversed in* MS T.
5483   Firste]For firste T.
5484   Siþen]And syth B.
5485   þe]To L.
5486   þat]þe B. spredde]praysed B.
5487   *second* of]om B.
5489   Half... skore]þre score ȝere B.
5490   world]wolde T; þis worle B.
5492   breþere]brothir L. þei]om LB.
5493   lyued hadde]had levyd L. hadde]om B.
5494   doluen]grauyn B.
5494a   we]I B.
5496   had]haue L.
5497   þenne]there L.
5498   tent]entent B.

How þe folk of Israel
Is bred among vs so fel   5500
But we kepe vs fro her kynne
Oure lond wol þei fro vs wynne
Sir kyng þat is sooþ þei seyde
Þei haue ȝoure lond al ouerleyde
Iosephs kyn ouergooþ al   5505
Þat to ȝoure elderes first was þral
Wiþ oure penyes bouȝte was he
Now wol his kyn disherite þe
Sir takeþ counsel herfore
Was neuer nede of counsel more   5510
Lete vs loke pryuelye
For vs bihoueþ to be slye
Holde we hem so in doute
Þat þei be euer oure vndirloute
If þei aȝeyn vs take þe fiȝt   5515
And ouercome vs bi her myȝt
I dar saye wiþouten fyne
Þat we shul so oure londis tyne
Holde we hem þerfore in awe   fol. 31r col. 2
In trauaile boþe to bere & drawe   5520
In werkes þat we han to make
We shul fynde werke for her sake
Vpon her neckis shul þei bere
Bolles wiþ stoones & mortere
On hem þe kyng set mony stiwarde   5525
To holde hem in werkis harde
Wiþ hardenes he helde hem Inne
Soone hadde þei made townes twynne

5499   þe]þis B.
5502   Oure]þis B. lond]lord L. wol þei]þey will B.
5504   al]om L.
5505   Iosephs]Ioseph his L.
5506   ȝoure]our LB. was]wer B.
5507   oure]ȝoure TLB.
5510   of]to B.
5513   we]we euer B.
5514   þei]bey L. euer]ovir L.
5515   aȝeyn]aȝens B. þe]om B.
5516   her]om B.
5520   boþe]for LB.
5521   werkes]werk B. to]for to B.
5523   om in B.
5524   Bolles]Belles L; Bolle B. wiþ stoones]of stone B.
5525   On]Of L.
5527   Wiþ]þis B. he]þey B.
5528   twynne]tweyn B.

Rameses and Fyton hiȝte þei
Þat goddis folk bar to hem cley   5530
But euer as þei dide hem wo
Þe folke multiplied moo & moo
Þe londis folk þat þei wiþ were
Greet enemyte to hem þei bere
Ofte wiþ her wordis smert   5535
Greet tene þei sette to her hert
Þe kyng wex wondir felle
Aȝeyn þe folk þat I of telle
Þei hem wiþhelde as her foos
And wolde no fruyt of hem roos   5540
Whenne wymme[n] were in childing stad
Bremely commaundide he & bad
Midewyues to be of þat same lond
And alle þe knaue childre þei fond
Wiþouten griþ þei shulde hem slo   5545
And mayde childre let hem go
Þe midwyues for god were drad
And did not as þe kyng hem bad
But þei saued þo childre lyues
Þe kyng let calle þo mydwyues   5550
Of whiche þat þer were twa
Phua þe ton hiȝt þat oþer sephora
To þese two spak þe kyng
Why do ȝe not my biddyng
Wiþ þo childer of ebrew lay   5555
Sir for þis resoun gon þei say

5529   Rameses] Rames B.
5533   londis folk]folk of þat londe B.
5534   þei]om B.
5535-6 om L.
5535   Ofte]Offtyn tymes B. her]om B.
5536   tene]þen B.
5537   þe]þis B.
5538   Aȝeyn]Ayens B.
5540   roos]arose L.
5541   wymmen]wymme H. in]with B.
5542   Bremely]Brevely L.
5543   Midewyues]þe medwifes B. to be]om B. þat]þe B.
5544   And]om B. knaue]chave L. þei]þat þey B.
5545   shulde]shulle L.
5546   mayde]mayden T. hem]forþ B.
5549   þo]þe B.
5550   let... þo]callyd þe B.
5551   þat]medwifes B.
5552   þe ton]þat oon T. hiȝt]om B. þat oþer]þe toþer TLB.
5555   Wiþ] Of B. þo]the L; þes B. lay]þe lay B.

Þo wymmen ȝe shul vndirstonde
Are not like wymmen of þis londe
Vchone con stire fer and nere   fol. 31v col. 1
Whenne þei come to þat mistere   5560
For ar we come to hem wiþ myȝt
Þei are liȝter bi her owne sleiȝt
And for þo wymmen dide so wele
God hem sent hap and cele
// Þenne comaundide kyng pharao   5565
Þat alle þat folke wolde fordo
Ouer al his kyndam euerywhere
Whenne wymmen any childe bere
Þat of þe kynde of ebrew ware
Men shulde hit in þe flom for fare   5570
Lord he was wicked & wode
Aȝeyn þat folke so mylde of mood
For nouȝte he wende to sle þat sede
Þat god himself wolde of brede
May no man for no chaunce   5575
Fordo þat lordes puruyaunce
Of Israeles seed he þouȝte
Be born þat þis world wrouȝte
And of his ferþe sone þat was
Geten of lay þat hett Iudas   5580
Þen wolde he drawe his monhede
Of hym coom kyngis of þat lede

5557   þo]The L.
5558   Are]Be L.
5559   Vchone]Eche B. stire]þe crafft B.
5561   ar]ȝef B. to]wiþ L.
5562   liȝter]light L. sleiȝt]flight L; sight B.
5563   þo]the L.
5564   sent] sende T. cele]lele L.
5565   comaundide]comaundyng B.
5567   al]om B. euerywhere]euer dele L; euerwhere B.
5568   Whenne]What L. wymmen]wommon TL.
5569-70   om B.
5570   Men]They L. flom]flore L.
5571   wode]wood thare L.
5572   þat]þe B.
5573   For evir he thoght to distroy þat food / And of that blissid sede L.
5574   þat]om L. wolde of]thoght to L.
5575   May]þer may B.
5576   lordes]is goddis B.
5578   þis]all þis B. wrouȝte]haþe wroȝt B.
5579   And... his]Of Iacobis B.
5580   of lay]alay L.
5582   of... lede]as we rede B.

And of his broþer leuy bredde
Þe prestis þat her lawes ledde
Prest and domesman seye I   5585
Boþe coom of þis leuy
Whiche moyses was formaste
As I shal telle ȝow in haaste
How he coom firste in place
And saued was bi goddes *gra*ce   5590
Fro pharao þe kyng feloun
Þat bad þo children to droun
Siþen aftir shal be rad
How moyses goddes folk lad
How he þe comaundementis toke   5595
As hit is writen in holy boke
Whenne I se tyme þerto
Þe kyngis kyn I shal vndo
Of whom sprong oure saueour   fol. 31v col. 2
And brouȝte vs alle to socour   5600
Þe firste broþer þat het leuy
A mon was of his genealogy
Fro hym but þe oþere degre
Þat of his wyf had childre þre
Moyses & aaron þese twa   5605
And a douȝter het Maria
In þat tyme born was moyses
Whenne þat folk was in þat pres
Whenne he was born wiþouten *pr*ide
His modir dide him for to hyde   5610

5583-4   *om* B.
5585   Prest]Prestys B. domesman]domysmen B. seye]also sey L.
5586   þis]*om* B. leuy]lely L.
5587   Whiche]With L.
5588   ȝow]þe L.
5590   bi]thorogh L.
5592   bad]had B. þo]the LB. droun]drom B.
5593   be rad]I rede B.
5594   folk]chyldre B.
5595   How]And how B.
5597   tyme]þe tyme B.
5598   vndo]fordo L.
5601   þe firste]þat ilk B.
5602   A mon]Adam L. his]þe B.
5603   but]brought B.
5604   of]be B.
5605   Moyses]Moyser B. þese twa]also B.
5606   a]hir L.
5608   in þat]so in B.

When she two moneþis hade him hidde
And hit paste into þe þridde
Þat she lenger hidde him nouȝt
A cofur of ȝerdes dide she be wrouȝt
Dide piche hit so wiþoute & Inne   5615
Þat þourȝe myȝte no watir wynne
In þis chiste þe childe she dide
And sperde hit wiþ þe lidde
Not fer fro þe kyngis home
She leide hit on þe watir fome   5620
Among þe risshes in an yle
Soone þeraftir in a whyle
Þe kingis douȝtir þere pleyinge ȝode
And say þat vessel in þat flode
She lete men fette hit to þe lond   5625
A squelyng childe þerynne she fond
Þat was wondir fayre to se
Of þat childe she hadde pite
Forsoþe she seide trowe þar noon
Of ebrew childre þat þis is oon   5630
Þe childis sistir stood þerby
Wolt þou I go she seide lady
To fecche a womman of þat lede
ȝe go she seide I shal hit fede
She went & fonde þat she souȝt   5635
Þe childis modir soone she brouȝt
Þe lady toke hit hir to fede
And for hir seruyse het hir mede
Þe womman vndirtoke hit þo   fol. 32r col. 1
And fedde hit til hit couþe speke & go   5640

5611   she]sche hym B. him]om B. hidde]kept L.
5612   hit paste]om L. þridde]third lept L.
5613   þat]When B. lenger]no lenger myȝt B.
5614   wrouȝt]broght L.
5617   chiste]coffre B.
5618   sperde]kevyrd L; closyd B.
5621   þe risshes]þo richesses T.
5623   þere]on B.
5624   þat]þe B.
5625   lete]made B. fette]fech B.
5626   squelyng]smylyng L; squekyng B.
5629   trowe þar] I trow yt is L. þar noon]þeron B.
5630   childre... oon] child born L. þat]om B.
5631   þe]þis T. stood]stote L.
5632   þou... go] ȝe þat I B.
5635   went]wend L.
5637   hit hir]hir hit T.

Whenne hit was þryuen of good elde
To þe lady she dide hit ȝelde
For hir childe penne she him chees
And ȝaf hit to name moyses
Moyses was herfore his name   5645
For he was of þe watir tane
Alle þat him sawe in lede
Wondir hadde of his fairhede
Bi þis coom moyses to elde
Þat he myȝte hymseluen welde   5650
Þenne went he out vpon a day
To se þe breþer of his lay
To knowe his broþer how þei ware
Filed in þat lond wiþ care
He say a gipcian ful sore   5655
Smyt a iewe bifore him þore
Þat braunche of kyn calde Iewes was
Þat coom of Iacob sones Iudas
Moyses say þer were no mo
But himseluen and þei two   5660
To þat egipcian he drouȝe
Siche a dynt þat he him slouȝe
When he had slayn him wiþ his honde
He dalf him soone vndir sonde
Anoþer day he went also   5665
And fiȝtynge fonde he iewes two
He seide to him þat hadde þe wyte
How dorst þou þus þi broþer smyte

5641   of]to B.
5642   dide]gan B.
5643   þenne]om B. him]yt B.
5645   herfore]þerfore B.
5646   of... tane]founde in watris fame B.
5647   him sawe]saw hym B.
5648   Wondir hadde]Had wondir L.
5651   vpon]on L.
5652   breþer]chyldryn B.
5653   how]who LB.
5654   þat]þe B.
5655   gipcian]egipcian TLB. ful sore]þore B.
5656   bifore... þore]hym before B.
5657   of... Iewes]kyn of Iewis callid L. Iewes]om B.
5658   sones]son TB.
5659   were]was B.
5661   þat]þe B.
5664   He]þey B. vndir]in þe B.
5666   he]om B.
5668   dorst þou]diddist þou L; dorstow B.

Þenne vnswered him þat oon
Siþ whenne was þou oure domesmon   5670
Wolt þou me sle herfore
As þou didest þe egipcian not ӡore
Moyses for þis vmbreyde
Was dredynge in his herte & seyde
Þourӡe whom is þis how may hit be   5675
Who brouӡte vp þis worde on me
Þe kyng hit herde & bad also
Men shulde moyses seke to slo
Moyses say no bettur won   fol. 32r col. 2
But fledde into madyon   5680
He sette hym þere a welle bisyde
Tiþingis to here þere to abyde
Þe prest of þis stide þat I neuene
He hadde at home douӡteres seuene
Þei coom to watir wiþ her fe   5685
Wherof her fadir hadde plente
As þei to watir drof her beest
Coom herdis & awey hem kest
Moyses say þei dide hem wrong
Soone he medeled hem among   5690
Þo herdis fro þe welle droof he
And dide to drynke þe maydens fe
Þo wymmen went hoom aӡeyn
And at hem gan her fadir freyn
How had ӡe so smartly done   5695

5669   þenne]He L. þat oon]þe ton TB.
5670   was]were B. was þou]wastou T.
5671   Wolt þou]Wystow B.
5672   ӡore]ore L.
5673   for]of B. vmbreyde]vnbraid L; vpbrayde B.
5675   hit]þis B.
5676   on]of B.
5678   Men]þat men B. moyses seke]seke moyses L. to] & B.
5679   say]had B. won]wene B.
5680   But]*The* t *is obliterated by a blot in* L. fledde ...madyon] fle vnto þe Mayden B.
5681   welle]whyle B.
5682   Tiþingis]Tyþing B. þere]for B. abyde]bide B.
5683   þis]þe B. þat]om L.
5685   fe]ke L.
5687   drof]drow L; com *with* B.
5690   Soone he]And sone þay B.
5691   þo]þe TLB.
5692   fe]ke L.
5693   þo]The LB.
5694   hem]home TL.
5695   smartly] smerly B.

Þat ȝe are comen home so soone
Sir þei seide bi a ȝong man
Þat semed to be egipcian
Sir þe soþe to ȝow to say
He putte þe herdes alle away   5700
And wiþ vs he oure watir drouȝe
And ȝaf oure beestis drynke ynouȝe
Where is þat man doþ him calle
Sir þei seide gladly we shalle
Moyses þei fette faire & swete   5705
And wiþ þe prest raguel he ete
Whenne þei were queyntid so to tel
Þis moyses & sir raguel
He weddede of his douteris oon
Sephoram a hende wommon   5710
Two childre dide she to him bere
Gersan and elyezere
// Þis whyle was in Israele
Þe folk lad in mychel vnwele
Her soor was sorwe onne to se   5715
And for to here was greet pite
Hem þei helde harde as þral
On god þei gan to crye & cal
Aȝeyn þo folke so wiþ hem ferde   fol. 32v col. 1
So longe þei calde þat god hem herde   5720
He herde her menynge & vnquert
And shope þerfore in litil sterte
On þat biheste he þouȝte þan

5697   þei]he L.
5698   to]om L. be]be an TLB.
5699   to ȝow]the L. second to]I B.
5700   þe]þo T.
5701   he]om B. oure]vs L.
5704   þei]she L. gladly]þat do L.
5706   ete]hete LB.
5707   queyntid]aqueynted T. *The a was inserted later in a different hand.*
5708   sir]þis B.
5710   hende] fayre B.
5711   dide]om B.
5712   Gersan]Sirsan L.
5713   Israele]fra ele L.
5715   onne to]vnto L.
5718   On]To B. gan]can T. to]om B.
5719   þo folke]þefolde B
5720   calde]cryed B.
5721   &]& her on B.
5722   in] a B. sterte]smert B.
5723   þat]þe B.

Þat he made to olde Abraham
For þat forwarde he wiþ him fest   5725
His yȝe of reuþe on hem he kest
Boþe he halpe hem of her wo
And delyuered hem of her fo
// Moyses þat tyme took kepe
To his eldefadris sheepe   5730
Þat was þe *pre*st of madian
Whos douȝtir he had him tan
His folke he fedde vpon a tyde
By a wylde wodes syde
And as he welke þe*re* wiþ wille   5735
Bisyde eȝeb a litil hille
He sawe a selcouþe siȝt to se
Him þouȝte bre*n*nynge a tre
As hit wiþ lowe al were bileyde
& to hymseluen soone he seide   5740
To þat tre I wol go nerre
Þat brennyng semeþ as on ferre
Whenne he þis buske coom to sene
Wiþ blome & leof he fonde hit grene
Þis was a forshewyng shene   5745
Of modir boþe & mayden clene
Þat siþen longe out of prees
Bar a chylde & she wemles
As þe tre semed to brynne
And þe*n*ne was þe*re* no fyre þe*r*ynne   5750
As moyses on fer þouȝte
Þe tre bre*n*nyng & brent nouȝt

5724   olde]eld L.
5725   For]Fro L. him fest]fyrst B.
5728   of]*om* B. fo]enemyes B.
5731   þe]a B. madian]maryan L; Madan B.
5732   him]*om* L.
5733   folke]flok B. vpon]on B.
5735   welke]went B.
5736   eȝeb]Ebell L; eȝev B.
5739   hit]he B. al were]were all B.
5740   &]*om* B.
5742   brennyng semeþ]semyth brennyng B. on]eny L; *om* B.
5744   blome]flour B. & leof]a lyf L; & gres B.
5745   forshewyng]feir shynyng L; ensample B.
5746   modir boþe &] þe modyr B.
5747   þat] And TL.
5748   wemles] wenyngles L.
5750   And]*om* B. no]non B. þerynne]wi*th*in B.
5751   fer]fyre L; þe tre B.

Þenne calde on him oure lord of myȝt
Out of þe mychel lemyng liȝt
Twyes moyses he calde by name   5755
What woltou lorde here I ame
I am þyne eldres god seide he
For I hem ledde þat loued me
My folk of israel is woo   fol. 32v col. 2
Þei haue ben ledde wronge also   5760
But I wol now her mournynge mende
To pharao I wol þe sende
Pharao of egipte þe kynge
Out of his londe hem for to brynge
Lord he seide what am I þerto   5765
Suche a greet nede to do
Go forþ he seide wiþouten drede
For I myself shal þe lede
Þat þei not ȝeynsaye my sonde
Wiþ my tokenes þou shalt hem fonde   5770
Whenne þou hast brouȝte hem fro þat lande
Do hem to make to me offrande
Vpon þe top of þis hille
He seide lord say me þi wille
What shal I saye is þi name   5775
God vnswered wiþouten blame
If þei my name wol at þe freyn
Vnswere hem þus aȝeyn
To ȝow me sendeþ he þat es
Þis is my name more ne les   5780
Os he þat is my name þou calle
My menyng shal neuer falle
Do moyses as I þe kenne

5753   on]om B. oure]þe B.
5754   mychel lemyng]leme B.
5756   here]om B.
5757   eldres]eldist L.
5758   ledde]lede B. loued]louyth B.
5760   wronge]wiþ wrong B.
5761   I... now]now I wille L. mournynge]monyng L.
5768   For]om B.
5769   not]ne L; schull not B. ȝeynsaye]forsay B.
5770   Wiþ]om B. tokenes]tokyn B.
5771   fro]to T.
5772   first to]om B.
5773   Vpon]Vp B.
5778   hem]thow L.
5780   ne]nor B.
5781   Os... is] I am þat I am B. þou]þat þou B.

Go geder togider þe eldest menne
Of alle my folk of Israel   5785
And seye þat I haue herde hem wel
Þei are in wandrynge & in wo
Wel I woot þat hit is So
Say I shal hem soone pay
Perto shal not be longe delay   5790
I shal hem brynge of þat þralhede
Into lufsom londe hem lede
A lond rennynge hony & mylke
In al þis world is noon swilke
Siþen shal þou wende also   5795
To pharao þe kyng þou go
Bidde hym lete my folke away
Þat he haþ holden to þis day
Doynge to hem so greet trowage   fol. 33r col. 1
Þat þei may make to me no knowlache   5800
Into wildernesse londe
I wol hem brynge out of his honde
Wel I woot he is ful þro
Looþ him is to lete hem go
He shal me drawe forþ on lengþe   5805
Til I delyuere hem wiþ strengþe
Moyses seide take not in greue
Lord pharao wol me not leue
What hast þou seide god in þi hande
Lorde he sayde I bere a wande   5810
Caste hit on þe gras I bidde

5784   Go]Do B.
5785   my]þe B.
5789   pay]pray L.
5790   þerto]Say þat B.
5791   of þat]oute of B.
5792   Into]Vnto L; And into B. lufsom]losir L.
5794   world]lond L.
5797   away]haue wey L.
5798   to]vnto B. þis]his L.
5799   hem]hym L. greet]good L.
5800   to]om TLB.
5801   Into]Into a B.
5803   Wel]om L.
5804   him]he L.
5806   Til]To B.
5807   take]lorde take B.
5808   Lord]om B.
5809   hast þou]hastou TB.
5811   on]fro þe on B.

Gladly lord & so he didde
Whenne hit was on þe gras cast
An eddur hit was & he was gast
So ferde þat he to fle bigon   5815
To moyses seide oure lorde þon
In þi honde þou not forsake
By þe tail þou hit vptake
Whenne moyses hit hade in hande
Hit wex as hit was er a wande   5820
To moyses spake god almyȝte
Þi honde putt in þi bosum riȝte
He put his hone in al in hele
And out he toke hit as mysele
He put hit efte in his speyere   5825
And out he toke hit hool & fere
Go forþ he seide & if þe kyng
Wol not leue þi firste tokenyng
Who so þe firste wol not trowe
To leue þe oþere is his prowe   5830
If þei leue nouþer of þese two
To þe watir of þe flum þou go
And poure of hit vpon þe londe
And certeynly þou vndirstonde
Al þat þou drawest out of þat flode   5835
Hit shal be turned into blode
Take wiþ þe aaron also
To pharao kyng seye ȝe two
Þat he lete my folke aperte   fol. 33r col. 2
Passe to worshepe me in desert   5840
Her sacrifise to make to me

5812   he] I L; om B.
5813   cast]Icaste B.
5814   eddur]neddyr B. hit]he T. was gast]agaste B.
5815   ferde]aferd L. to]om B.
5817   þou]it B.
5818   vptake]take B.
5819   hit hade]had it B. hande]hys honde B.
5823   first in]om L.
5824   as]alle L; as a B.
5825   in... speyere]þer it was er B.
5828   þi]þe B.
5829   trowe]know L.
5830   þe... his]that othir it is L. oþere]todyr B.
5831   þese]this L.
5835   out]om L. second þat]þe B.
5836   into]to rede B.
5837   aaron]A, then a blank space left in L.
5838   kyng seye]þe kyng B. two]go B.

Out of his londe iurneyes þre
Now makeþ moyses him boun
As god hym tauʒte his lessoun
His broþer aaron he mette   5845
For god himself her metynge sette
To warne þe eldest of israele
And pharao þei went wele
Þei seide god hymseluen bad
His folk þat vndir him was stad   5850
To lete hem of his londe hem dresse
To worshepe him in wildernesse
Kyng phareo ʒaf his vnswere
What is he þat god & where
Þat I shulde for his sonde   5855
Let þat folk out of my londe
Nouþer I knowe him þat ʒe sey
Ne I wol lete þe folke awey
ʒus þei seide þus wol he
Þat alle his folke come Iurneyes þre   5860
In wildernesse offerynge to make
Þat swerde on ʒow take no wrake
He seide wondir of ʒou me þinke
Wolde ʒe my men take fro swynke
Þei ryse & brede ay more & more   5865
And more if þei ydel wore
Blame haue þat hem spare
To holde hem euer harde & bare
Fro þat tyme he bad þat þay
Shulde do two iourneyes on a day   5870
Vpon hem sett he men to aske
Euery day to ʒelde her taske

5848   pharao]to pharao TB. wele]om L.
5850   His]þe B.
5851   of his]oute of B. hem]to L; om B.
5852   To]And to B.
5853   his]þat B.
5854   he]om B. &]or TL.
5856   þat]my B.
5857   him]hem L.
5858   Ne]Nothir L; Nor B. lete þe]not lete my B.
5859   ʒus]Thus LB. þus]om B.
5862   on]of L. ʒow... wrake]þou none vengaunce take B.
5865   ay]euer B.
5866   more]more wolde TLB.
5867   haue]haue he B.
5869   Fro]For L. þay]day L.
5870   on a]oon L.
5871   he]om B.

To stonde lete ȝe hem not byde
As ȝe haue done mony a tyde
Whoso doþ not ȝoure biddynge 5875
Wiþ sharpe scourgis þat ȝe hem swynge
Now wolde þei make a wiþsawe
Fro her werkes hem to wiþdrawe
For to wende to wildernesse fol. 33v col. 1
To her lord I noot what he esse 5880
As I euer brouke my hond
I shal hem do dwelle in my lond
Þenne spak god al weldonde
To moyses his trewe seruonde
Whenne pharao askeþ ȝow 5885
By what tokene he shal ȝow trow
Bidde þi broþer aaron þon
Caste þe ȝerde bifore pharaon
Into a nedder hit shal be lent
Anoþer tyme forþ þei went 5890
Bifore þe kyng into his halle
Þere he sat wiþ his knyȝtis alle
But not he of her erned herde
Þenne took aaron his ȝerde
And on þe flore he kest hit doun 5895
Hit bicoom a worm feloun
Þen calde þe kyng his enchauntours
Þe craftiest of his iogelouris
Doun þei caste a ȝerde vchone
Dragouns þei bicoom anoon 5900
But aarons ȝerde wexe so kene
Þe oþere hit woryed al by dene

5873   byde]abide B.
5875   Whoso]Whos L.
5876   þat]om TLB. ȝe]he L.
5877   wiþsawe]wyȝt saw L; wis lawe B.
5878   wiþdrawe]drawe B.
5879   first to]om L.
5885   askeþ ȝow]askyd how B.
5886   he] I B. trow]know L.
5888   ȝerde]Erthe L.
5889   hit]his T.
5891   into]in B.
5892   wiþ]and B.
5893   he]om B. herde]he herd B.
5894   took]take L. his]the L; forthe hys B.
5898   craftiest]crafftys B.
5899   a... vchone]ȝerdys euerychon B.
5901   wexe]yt wax L.
5902   þe]þo T. hit]he B.

Þe kyngis herte wex harde as bras
Þe folke he seide ʒit shal not pas
God seide þo to moysen   5905
Þe herte of pharao I ken
Now I woot hit is more
Harder for me þen hit was ore
For þat he wol not me here
Hardenesses shal I sende him sere   5910
Boþe on him & his kyngryche
He shal make mony men myslyche
For he wol þus debate on me
I shal him drenche in þe see
Þe firste vengeaunce he on him sende   5915
Men shul mone to þe worldes ende
Þenne hit was þe firste sonde
Alle þe wattris of his londe
Soone wex into blood reed   fol. 33v col. 2
Þat alle þo fisshes þerinne were deed   5920
For þe root þat þeron felle
Boþe þen stanke ryuere & welle
Þer was in house no vessel fre
Þat watir helde of stoon ny tre
So foule al þis watir stonke   5925
Wo was hem þat hit dronke
// Þe toþer venieaunce þat him felle
Were frogges þat no tunge coude telle
Þat out of banke & wattris bredde
And ouer al egipte londe spredde   5930
Al þe erþe þei couered so

5904   ʒit... not]schuld not ʒit B.
5906   I ken]is kene L.
5908   for]fro B.
5910   Hardenesses]Hardnes L. him]hem B.
5912   men]a man L.
5916   mone to]into B.
5918   Alle]þat all B.
5919   wex]waxyn L. reed]om L.
5920   þo]þe TLB. fisshes þerinne]fysch þen B. þerinne deed]to ded yode L.
5921   root]rewþe L. þeron]þerof B.
5922   Boþe... stanke]Stynkyd boþe B.
5925   al þis]þerof þe B.
5926   hit]of it B.
5927   þe]That L. toþer]othir L; seconde B. þat]on B.
5928   Were]þe B. frogges]froshis L.
5929   banke]bankys B. wattris]water B.
5930   spredde]þey spred B.
5931   Al]Also B. þei]om B.

Men myȝte not fre sette a to
Boþe in house & wiþoute
And ouer al þe londe aboute
Þen bad þe kyng soone anoon   5935
Calle moyses & aaron
Preye ȝoure lord þat he
Do þese froggis away fro me
Þei seide set vs tyme whenne
To preye for þe & þi menne   5940
Tomorwe he seide sir we shal
Faste on god þo gon þei cal
To delyuer þe folk of þat wreche
And god was ful soone her leche
Þe frogges dyȝed al bydene   5945
Þe hepes wondir was to sene
Þat men gedered on þe grounde
Whenne pharao hadde reste a stounde
He wex al greet in greue
Þe folk wolde he ȝyue no leue   5950
For to passe out of his londe
Þe þridde vengeaunce coom on honde
Al þe poudir of his lande
Wexe flyȝes foule sore bitande
Boþe þei boot mon & beest   5955
To flesshe flyȝes were þei likest
Al for nouȝte hit was no bote
Þe folke lete he passe no fote
Þenne sent god on hem a fleȝe   fol. 34r col. 1
A sharper say neuer noon wiþ eȝe   5960
On pharao and his to drauȝt
Þat ouer al his lond hit rauȝt
Saue in þat londe þat het Iessen

5932   fre sette]sett fre L.
5935   soone]om B.
5938   froggis]frosshis L.
5941   Tomorwe]Tomorn B. he... sir]on god they seid L; syr he sayde B.
5942   on]to B.
5943   þe]om B.
5944   ful]om B.
5945   þe frogges]For froshis L.
5947   þat]om L; And B. gedered]togedyr B.
5951-2 reversed in B.
5951   his]þe B.
5953   poudir]power B. his]þe B.
5954   foule]full LB.
5960   A sharper]As waspys B. noon]mon TL.
5962   his]this L; þe B. hit]om B.
5963   Saue]Seue B.

Þere woned goddis owne men
Coom noon of þo flyȝe[s] þare   5965
Wel he couþe his owne spare
Þouȝe þei woned in þat cuntre
Feire he made his owne fre
For pharao shulde vndirstonde
Miȝty he was oueral his londe   5970
Pharao ful false of pees
Calde aaron and moyses
Gooþ he seide here in my londe
And to ȝoure lord make offronde
Wherto shulde ȝe for þer go   5975
Do wey þei seide hit is not so
God wol no worshep take of hem
Þat dwelle among curside men
Suche is þe folk of egipt
Þat make to beestis her worship   5980
Thre iourneyes more ne lesse   5983
Most þei wende into wildernesse
To make oure lord worshepe to   5985
As he haþ bede to be do
Wendeþ he seide siþ ȝe wol go
But furþer go ȝe not þen so
For me ȝe preye ȝus þei seide
Tomorwe shal þo fleȝes be leyde   5990
Bigyle vs no more in kare
Þe folke þo he lete forþ fare
Moyses preyed þat oþer day

5965   þo]the LB. flyȝes]flyȝe H.
5966   couþe]coude T.
5967   þouȝe]ȝef B.
5970   his]þe B.
5973   seide]seith L.
5974   And to]Vnto B.
5975   Wherto shulde]Whete schull B. go]gro B.
5976   þei]he L.
5977   no]not L.
5979   is]as is L.
5981-2   *om in* CGHTLB.
5983   Thre]Hir L. more]no more B.
5984   þei]hem B. into]in B.
5986   bede to be]bodyn vs to B.
5987   wol]schull B.
5988   furþer golwendith B. ȝe]they L. þen]& L; ferþer þan B.
5989   ȝus]þus LB.
5990   þo]the LB. Tomorwe]Tomorne B.
5992   þo]*om* B.
5993   þat oþer]þe toþer T; anoþer B.

Þe flyȝes were alle quyt away
Þat al þe lond wex so clene   5995
Þat neuer a fleȝe þerInne was sene
ȝit þe kyng hem helde ful þro
For wolde he not lete hem go
// Þen sende god a qualme of alle
In þat kyngdome on beestis to falle   6000
Horse and asse mule & camel   fol. 34r col. 2
Doun þei dyȝed al her catel
Goddis folke þat hadde any beest
Dyȝed noon of hem moost ne leest
Pharao sende þat to se   6005
Hool & fere he fonde hor fe
But euer was pharao in oon
Þe folk awey let he not goon
// Þe sixte vengeaunce coom on honde
False pharao for to fonde   6010
Byle and blister bollynge soore
On alle his folke lasse & moore
Hem was wo on her bodyes alle
Her kyng þei waryed greet & smalle
ȝit for nouȝte þat men myȝte sey   6015
Wolde he lete þe folk awey
// Þe seuenþe vengeaunce to tel
Hit was a weder wondir fel
A þondir wiþ a hayl so kene
Suche anoþer was neuer sene   6020
Hayl & fuyre menged samen
Þat hit ouertoke þouȝte no gamen
Boþe hit slouȝe fro hit bigan

5994   þe] All þe B. alle quyt]om B.
5995   þat]And B. so]all L.
5996   neuer a]no B.
5997   hem helde]held hym LB. ful]om B.
5999   of]on L.
6000   In... on]Among þe B. to]vnto B.
6001   camel]catell B.
6002   al]om T. al... catel] & camell B. her]their L.
6006   fe]ke L.
6007   pharao]he B.
6010   for]om TLB.
6011   Byle]Byles B. blister]blesterys B. bollynge] boundyn L; bolled B.
6016   Wolde]Wylle L.
6020   anoþer was]one was þere neuer B.
6021   menged]menqillid L. samen]in same B.
6022   þouȝte]hem þought B.
6023   slouȝe]snowe B.

Wiþouten house beest & man
Þe trees hit brast þe erþe brynt   6025
At iessen lond þere hit stynt
Of israel for þat tempest
Was nouþer harmed mon ne beest
Þen seide þe kyng I haue þe wrong
Al þis wreche is on me longe   6030
Preye þi lord sir moyses
Þat he wol do þis þunder cees
He is riȝtwis þat ȝe on leue
His folke shal go wiþouten greue
I and myne mys han done   6035
He preyed þe wedur ceesed soone
Whenne pharao had þat he souȝte
Longer forwarde helde he nouȝte
// Þenne sent god hem a litil beest
Of tooþ is not vnfoulest   6040
Locuste hit hette in book I fond   fol. 34v col. 1
I trowe noon siche be in þis lond
Þat beest gnow vp al bidene
Þat þonder lafte rype & grene
Of hem were so mony bred   6045
Ouer al þe lond þei were spred
Þat men myȝte nowhere se
Gras on erþe ne leef on tre
But ȝit was pharao forsworn
& false as he was biforn   6050
Þenne dide god wiþdrawe his liȝt
And merkenes made more þen nyȝt

6024   beest]boþe best B.
6025   trees]treest T. hit]om B.
6028   ne]nor T.
6030   is on me]on me ys B. longe]lond L.
6032   þunder]wedyr B.
6034   His folke]ȝe B.
6035   mys... done]haue mysdone B.
6036   He]þay B. þe] & þe B.
6038   forwarde]comenaunt B.
6039   sent]sende T.
6040   Of alle other the fowlest L. too þis]tethe of yen B.
6041   Locuste]Lobest B. I fond]we fynd B.
6043   gnow]knew L.
6044   þonder lafte]þe thundir brast L.
6045   Of]That of L.
6046   þei were]were þay B.
6047   nowhere]ne þyer L.
6050   as]om L.
6052   merkenes]derkenes B.

So merke noon myȝte oþere se
And þat lasted dayes þre
No man out of stide myȝte stere   6055
Gessen cuntre was al clere
ȝit god fondide pharaon
And sende þe tenþe wrecche him on
Moore þen alle þes oþere smert
To sette him sorwe at his hert   6060
Aaron god seide and moysen
Dooþ he seide as I ȝow ken
Saye to my folke on þis wyse
Þat þei make me a sacrifise
Firste þei me an auter make   6065
And siþen vchone to hous In take
A clene lomb þat is honest
Þe blood ȝe kepe þe filþe out kest
And whenne hit is to offerynge bed
Þe meyne þerwiþ shul be fed   6070
Loke þei be shod vchone
Þat lomb shal ete & barfote noone
Whoso for pouert is bihynde
Þe toþere alle shul him fynde
Þat lombes blood in alle þinge   6075
ȝe make þerwiþ a tokenynge
On euery post on vche dernere
Þe syne of tayu make ȝe þere
Wiþ þerf breed & letus wylde
Whiche þat groweþ in þe felde   6080
Hit shal not soden be but bredd   fol. 34v col. 2

6053   merke]dyrke þat B.
6055   out]myght oute B. stide myȝte]þe sted B.
6058   tenþe]trenþe H. him on]vppon L.
6059   þes]this LB.
6062   seide]seith L.
6063   wyse]avyse B.
6064   a]om B.
6066   hous]his hous T. In]om T.
6070   meyne]men þat B.
6071   þei]that they LB.
6072   lomb]þe lombe B.
6074   þe toþere]That othir for L; þe oþere B. him]hem L.
6075   þat]þe B. alle]þat B.
6076   ȝe]The L.
6077   euery]eche a B. dernere]dore here B.
6078   tayu]Taev L; þe tayle B. ȝe]you L.
6079   þerf]bakyn L. letus]lecon B.
6081   soden]soþyn B.

Þe lom þat ȝe shul be wiþ fed
Þei shul hit ete feet & heued
Ouer nyȝte no þing þerof be leued
And ȝif ouȝte leue or hit be tynt   6085
Do hit in þe fyre be brynt
Beeþ alle gurd wiþ staf in honde
Ne hones not whil ȝe are etonde
And I myself seide god almyȝt
Shal passe þourȝe egipt þat nyȝt   6090
Alle þe forbirþes shal I slo
Boþe of mon & beest also
On her godis I wole wrake
On hem I shal my venieaunce take
In mynde shal ȝe holde þis day   6095
Boþe ȝe & ȝoure osprynge ay
Solempnely in ȝoure lawe
Wiþ alle worshipes þerto to drawe

Þenne calde moyses þe olde
Men of israel and tolde   6100
Al þat god had hym seyde
And how þis lomb shulde be purueyde
On her poste & her derner
Þe blood þei shulde anoynte þer
Straytly he forbeed þat þay   6105
Shulde out of house come ar day
To delyuer hem haþ god mynt
And ȝyue egipcians a dynt
Þe folk was fayn & loutid doun

6082   be wiþ]wiþ be TLB.
6084   no... þerof] þere schall of noght B.
6085   And] *om* B.
6087   Beeþ alle] Loke ȝe be B.
6088   hones] hovis L; tary B.
6091   Alle] And B. forbirþes] forebodis L.
6092   Boþe]*om* B. mon] men B. beest] of beste B.
6093   godis]goodis L. wole]schall B.
6094   On]Of L.
6096   Boþe]*om* B.
6098   worshipes]worschip B. to]*om* TLB.
6101-2   *reversed in* B.
6101   Al]And all B.
6102   And]*om* B. shulde]shal L.
6103   poste]postys B. &]of L. derner]dores here B.
6104   shulde]shalle L.
6106   house come]her hous B.
6108   ȝyue]yef L; ȝefe þe B. egipcians]Egipcian L.

Þei went to make her lambes bou*n*   6110
Of þis bodeword were þei glad
And duden riȝt as moyses bad
Soone aftir þat ilke nyȝt
God as he bifore had hiȝt
Sent anoon his au*n*gel dou*n*   6115
Thourȝe al egipte in vche tou*n*
And souȝte her housis al bidene
Of þo þat were egipciene
Of þat meyne lafte he noon
At þe laste þat he slouȝe vchon   6120
At þe kyng he firste bigan   fol. 35r col. 1
Þe forburþe slouȝe beest & man   6122
Wroþerhele roos vp þe kyng   6125
And þo þat were wiþ hym dwellyng
Ouer al egipte þe cry was
Mony þ*er* were seide allas
Þer was no hous in þat lond
But þerynne was deed mon ligond   6130
By nyȝte þe kyng sent pon
Aftir moyses and aaron
Gooþ he seide out of my kith
ȝe and al ȝoure folk ȝow wiþ
Make sacrifise ȝoure god tille   6135
Where and how þat ȝe wille
Take ȝoure beestis wiþ ȝow boun
Gooþ & ȝyue me ȝoure benysoun
Þe folk bigan on hem to crye
Gooþ & doop forþ in hye   6140
Dwelle ȝe lenger any whyle

6110   þei]And B.
6115   anoon... au*n*gel]one of hys aungelys B.
6116   al]*om* B. vche]eche a B.
6117   housis]hous B.
6118   þo]*om* L; hem B.
6119   þat]þe B.
6120   þe]*om* B. þat]*om* LB. slouȝe]sowȝe T.
6121   kyng]kine B. firste]*om* B.
6122   þe forburþe]And so forth L; þe forborogh he B.
6123-4   *om* GHTLB.
6128   seide]þ*a*t seyde B.
6129   no]none B.
6130   þerynne was]þere were B. mon]men B.
6131   By nyȝte]Anon L.
6135   ȝoure]yon L. god]goddis B.
6140   dooþ]do ȝow B.
6141   ȝe]we B.

We drede deþ wol vs gyle
Fro þis folk þat was in sorwe
Þe folk of israel to borwe
Asked siluer vessel sere   6145
And cloþes of prys ful dere
God þat grace to hem ȝaue
Her askyng he dide hem haue
For to reue þat folk so snel
And helpe his folk of israel   6150
Þei were whenne þei to go bigon
Six hundride þousand fotemen þon
Wiþouten childer wymmen & broode
Þat noon þe noumbre vndirstood
Laft þei not þat horen was   6155
Sheep ne kow oxe ne as
Her wonyng þere wiþouten wene
Foure hundride ȝeer & two had bene
Whenne þis tyme coom to ende
Of egipte goddes hoost out wende   6160
Þis oweþ euer to be in mynde
To israel and al her kynde
To moyses oure lord þo tolde   fol. 35r col. 2
What wyse þei shulde paske holde
And neuermore þat day to ete   6165
Sour breed ny noon oþere mete
Ny no day wiþinne þo seuen dayes
Seuen þe firste þe story sayes

6142   We]I B. gyle]bigyle TB.
6143   Fro]For L. was]were B.
6144   to]for to B.
6147-8 *reversed in* B.
6147   þat]gat B. to]*om* L.
6150   his]this L.
6151   þei]þere B. to go]*om* B. to... bigon]bygan to gon L.
6152   Six] iij¹ L.
6153   wymmen... broode]of women brode L.
6155   horen]heren T; hirs L; þerin B.
6156   *first* ne]nor B. oxe]oxe hors B.
6157   Her]For L.
6160   hoost]*om* B.
6161   oweþ]oþer B.
6162   her]for L.
6163   oure]þo oure B. þo]*om* B.
6164   paske]he paske B.
6165   neuermore]euyrmor L.
6166   ny] & L. noon]*om* B.
6167   þo]the LB.
6168   Seuen]Sen L; Sene B. *second* þe]*om* B.

Þe forburþe of her children alle
Fro þat tyme to god let falle   6170
And to him offere at þe leste
Þe forburþe of vche a beste
Mannes childe wiþ pris be bouȝt
And sheep . hors . & asse [h]e brouȝt
In mynde þis was to vndirstonde   6175
Þat he delyuered hem of þat londe
Bi strengþe of egipte he hem drouȝe
Of mon & beest forbirþe he slouȝe
Whenne pharao had hem forþ sende
God bad hem to wildernesse wende   6180
Or philistiens wolde wiþ hem mete
And let hem for to wende her strete
Þat folk took þe wylde way
Bysyde þe rede see hit lay
Þus goddes folk armed were   6185
Iosephs bones wiþ hem þei bere
Whenne Ioseph in lyf was stad
ȝerne he preyed þe folk and bad
Þat whenne god sende hem visitynge
Men shulde his boones penne brynge   6190
By a myche wodes syde
Þei made hem logges to abyde
God himself hem led her way
Hem to kepe nyȝte and day
Wiþ clouden piler on þat dayliȝt   6195
Wiþ fyre piler vpon þe nyȝt
In no tyme hem wantide nouþer

6169   forburþe] forborogh B.
6172   forburþe]forborough B. a]om B.
6173   Mannes]Many L. be]he LB.
6174   hors] & hors B. & asse]as B. he]be H.
6176   of þat]oute of þe B.
6178   forbirþe]forborow B. he]she L.
6182   for]om B.
6183   þat]The L.
6184   Bysyde]Before B.
6186   bones]his bonys L.
6187   lyf]hys lyffe B.
6189   god]men L.
6190   þenne]þennes TB.
6191   om L.
6192   hem]her B. to abyde]for to byde B.
6193   hem... her]led hem þe B.
6195   þat]þe LB.
6196   vpon]on B. þe]þat T.
6197   In no]Into L. hem]þey B.

Nyȝt or day þei hadde ouþer
God hem bad drawe ynnermore
Aȝeyn on slont þere þei were ore   6200
Into pharaons syde
On hym wolde he shewe his pryde
He shulde wene hem loke þere   fol. 35v col. 1
Þat þei furþer myȝte nowhere
Him shulde þenne rewe his cast   6205
Whenne þe folk were fro him past
He shulde þenne himseluen peyn
Algate to brynge þat folke aȝeyn
Of þe woo he wolde hem mynt
For euer þenne he shulde be stynt   6210
Þe folk dude so & were glade
And Innermore her loggyng made
Soone in londe was tiþing spred
Þe folk was turned aȝeyn þat fled
His folke gedered pharaon   6215
Lordyngis he seide what haue we don
Shul we þus lete þis folk away
Þat shulde vs serue euer and ay
His folke armed dide he calle
And lete couple his cartes alle   6220
Six hundride cartis wiþ her geris
On al þe hoost he set lederes
Whenne he had redy made his hoost
He went wiþ myche pride & boost
Whenne goddis folke his coom herde   6225
Þei bigonne to wexe aferde

6198   or]no B. þei]þat þey B.
6200   on slont]oon slowte L; þe slogh B.
6201   Into]Into þe B.
6204   furþer]furþermor L; slouþere B.
6205   Him]He B.
6208   Algate]For B. folke]flok L.
6209   þe]þat B.
6210   he]om B. be]hem L.
6212   Innermore]euermore B. loggyng]longyng L.
6213   londe]þe londe B. was tiþing]typing was B.
6214   þe]Hys B. þat fled *is crossed out in* B.
6217   þus lete]lete þus B. þis]the L.
6218   euer and ay]euery day B.
6219   armed]of armys B.
6221   Six]With sex B.
6223   redy made]made redy B.
6224   wiþ myche]forþe with B.
6225   his]of his L.

Whenne þei him seȝe aftir hye
Þe folk of israel bigan to crye
On god and to moyses seide
In egipte was noon euel vs leide   6230
Þerfore hast þou vs led hit may falle
To wildernes to sle vs alle
Why woldes þou vs lede fro þat lond
Seide we not þere dwellond
To leue vs for vs leuer were   6235
Þe egipcians to serue þere
Al disese for to dryȝe
Þen here in wildernesse to dyȝe
// Moyses vnswered and seide
Noon of ȝow beþ myspayde   6240
Stondeþ & biholdeþ seide he
Goddes myracle shul ȝe se
Goddes miracle and his myȝt   fol. 35v col. 2
Himself today for ȝow shal fiȝt
Gooþ hardily forþ ȝoure wey   6245
And god to moyses gon say
Moyses þou take þi wande
Þat þou were wont to bere in hande
Do þe to þe wattris syde
Þe see þou smyte wiþouten abyde   6250
Þou shalt se hit cleue in two
And ȝyue ȝow redy weye to go
Þat shal kyng pharao se
Wiþ his host and his meyne
He shal wene ȝou ouertake   6255
But þenne shal he haue my wrake
ȝe shul come alle hool to londe
Suche is þe vertu of þi wonde

6227   him seȝe]se hym B.
6228   bigan]gan B.
6229   to]vnto B.
6231   hast... led] hastow led vs B.
6233   woldes... lede]woldestow lede vs TLB.
6235   leuyr vs were woo to drye B. *second* vs]we L.
6236-7 *om* B.
6238   here]*om* B.
6240   myspayde]euyll apayd B.
6242   shul ȝe]ȝe schall B.
6248   to]*om* B. hande]þy hande B.
6249   Do þe] And go B.
6252   ȝow]the L.
6255   ȝou]ȝow to B.
6258   þi wonde]my honde B.

//Moyses dude as god him bad
  For pharao was he not drad   6260
  In þe see his ȝerde he smate
  Hit cleef & ȝaue him redy gate
  Þe see on eyþer syde vp stood
  As walles whil þei forþ ȝood
  Til þei were passed al þat drede   6265
  Whenne þe kyng þis say in dede
  He folwed wiþ hoost on hors & fote
  For nouȝt caytif was him no bote
  He say þe see wiþdrawen in twynne
  Þe brood watir he dide him Inne   6270
  Moyses wiþ his folk al hale
  Wiþouten wantyng of his tale
  He helde his hoost vpon þe londe
  And smoot þe watir wiþ his honde
  Þen was þere no lenger byde   6275
  Togider þe see went boþe syde
  Boþe bihynde hem & bifore
  And drenched mony hundride skore
  Kyng knyȝt squyere ne swayn
  Coom neuer noon of hem aȝayn   6280
  Þus wreked him þe lord of myȝt
  On hem þat wiþ him wolden fiȝt
  His folke haþ he saued sounde   fol. 36r col. 1
  His enemyes brouȝte to grounde
  Þo Israelis seide hem amonge   6285
  Cantemus domino a newe songe
  To god þat had hem saued so
  Of al her sorwe and her woo

6260   drad]adrad B.
6261   In... ȝerde] With his yerd the se L. In]On B. his]þe B.
6262   Hit cleef]Hymself L.
6265   þat]þe B. drede]brede L.
6266   þis say]se þis B.
6272   his tale]a male B.
6273   helde]had B.
6274   honde]wande B.
6276   þe... went]went þe see on B. went]went on L.
6277   hem]om B.
6278   hundride]an hundird L; a M¹ B.
6279   ne] & B.
6280   neuer... hem]þere neuer one B.
6282   On]With B. wiþ... wolden]wille with hym L; wold with hym B.
6284   His]And his L. brouȝte]hathe he broȝt B.
6285-6   om B.
6287   had hem]hem hathe B.
6288   Of]Fro B. sorwe and]care & all B.

And so mot he delyuere vs
Oure dere lord swete ihesus   6290
Þese were þe folk of israele
Oure lord chees to hym for lele
For whom he mony miracle wrouȝt
Til himself hem turned to nouȝt
Ofte fro hym þei dide out reche   6295
Wherfore ofte þei fonde his wreche
As ȝe may here redily
Forþermore in þis story
Wiþ her grucchyng on moyses
Ofte dide þei greet males   6300

Of þe tree of lyf shal I tel
And of þe folk of Israel
Whenne moyses þat folk had lad   6301
Ouer þat see as god him bad
He and his broþer aaron
Out of pharaos seruage þon
In sirie vpon þat oþer syde   6305
Þei made her loggyng to abyde
Whil þei dwelled þere to rest
Of watir hadde þei mychel þrest
Wyde þei souȝte hit here & þere
Watir myȝte þei fynde nowhere   6310
Þe folke þat þere aboute him lay
Vchon gon to oþere say
Wheþer we shul in wildernes
Dyȝe for þirste þourȝe moyses
What shul we drynke seide þay   6315
Moyses þat nyȝte in sleep lay

6289   And]om B.
6293   miracle]a myracle L; myracles B.
6294   Til]To B. hem]he B. to]om B.
6295   fro]on B. out reche]vnrech B.
6296   Wherfore... þei]þerfore þey offte B.
6300   dide þei]þay did B.
6301   moyses þat]þat moyses þe B.
6302   Ouer þat]þurgh þe B. as] & B.
6304   seruage þon]seruys is gon B.
6305   vpon]on B.
6306   loggyng]longgyng L. to abyde]for to byde B.
6307   Whil]When B. to]in B.
6308   þrest]brest B.
6309   here... þere]farre & nere L.
6313   Wheþer]Wher TLB.
6316   þat... sleep]in slepe þat night B.

Þat nyȝt he ȝeode & took rest
Slepyng he lay in þat forest
On morwe he loked him by
He say þat him þouȝte ferly   6320
At his heed he say stonde   fol. 36r col. 2
Waxen of cipres a wonde
On his lift hond loked he
Anoþer he say of cyder tre
Þo he loked on his riȝt hand   6325
Of palme tre þe þridde he fand
Bi þo leues þat þei bere
Þei kidde of what tre þei were
But moyses for goddis awe
Durst hem not vp drawe   6330
Þat oþer day he went eke
Wiþ þat folk watir to seke
Þere he slepte at morwe tyde
He fonde þo ȝerdis hym bysyde
Þe þridde tyme so he hem fonde   6335
Þat dide him wel to vndirstonde
Þat sum tiþing shulde þer be
Closed in þo ȝerdis þre
Selcoupe þing he seide wiþ In
Is closed in þes ȝerdis þryn   6340
Þei bitokenen persones þre
And o godhede in vnite
Þenne he drouȝe hem vp first
Wiþouten any skaþe or birst
Whil þei in wildernes were   6345
Þo ȝerdis wiþ hem þei bere

6317-8   *om* B.
6319   morwe]þe morne B.
6322   Waxen]Wexyng LB.
6325   þo]*om* B.
6326   Of]A B.
6327   þo]þe B.
6328   kidde of]schewyd B.
6331   þat oþer]þe toþer TL.
6332   þat]þe B.
6333   slepte]sleepe B. morwe]þe morn B.
6334   þo]the B.
6337   shulde]shulle L.
6338   þo... þre]þe þryd tre B.
6339   Selcoupe]Sercouþe B.
6340   þryn]treyen L; þrye B.
6342   godhede]god B. vnite]trenite B.
6345   in]in þe B.
6346   þo]þe B. þei]euer þay B.

Siþ þei fonde þat firþe wiþyne
Watir bittur as any bryne
As bryne hit was & no swetter
To drynke was hit neuer þe better 6350
Whenne þo ȝerdis were In done
Þe watir wex swete ful soone
Þat watteres þat so foule stank
Of swetter þo neuer man drank
Þat myracle þei say apert 6355
Þat dwellyng were in desert
Fro þat tyme held moyses
Þo ȝerdis boþe in pris & pres
Where he walked here or þere
Þo ȝerdis algate wiþ him were 6360
Whenne he clomb mount synay   fol. 36v col. 1
Þo he hidde hem pryuely
Whil he fasted lenten tyde
In erþe he dud hem to hyde
Nouþer for dryȝe ne weete algate 6365
Þei chaungide neuer her state
But euer þei helde lyf & floure
Sauerynge wiþ a swete sauoure

Of þis moyses lordyngis
I haue ȝow tolde summe þingis 6370
Of hym may I not al telle
For hit were to longe to dwelle
But of his trauaile telle I shal
He suffered froward folk wiþal
He hem ladde sooþ hit is 6375
Fourty wyntur in wildernis

6347   þat]om B.
6350   was hit]it was B.
6351   þo]þe B. In]þer in B.
6352   ful]om B.
6353   watteres]watir LB. þat]þat þere B.
6355   say]sayde B.
6356   dwellyng]duellid L; wellyng B. desert]þe ȝerd B.
6358   þo]þe B. boþe... pres]all of grete pryce B. pres]pees L.
6360   þo]þe B.
6361   clomb mount]went vp þe mount of B.
6363   fasted]fastyn L; fastyd þe B.
6365   ne]nor B.
6366   her]hys B.
6368   wiþ a]euyr with B.
6371   may I]I may B.
6374   wiþal] & þrall B.
6375   ladde] fed B.

God fond hem fode in her nede
Wiþouten sowyng any sede
God hymself hem sende foode
Fonde þei neuer noon so gode 6380
Hit snew to hem as hit were floure
Of hony hit hadde lickest sauoure
Þe mete þat þei were fed wiþ so
Manna þei cleped hit þo
Hit coom at morwe & at euenyng 6385
Volatile hem sende þat kyng
Þat kyng owe men loue & loute
Wiþ alle worshipes to menske & doute
Þere þei hadde myche watir wone
Moyses of þe harde stone 6390
He smoot wiþ his forseid wonde
And out brast of þat watir a stronde
Þenne hadde þei watir in þat lond
Plente boþe to foot & hond
But for alle þo dedes gode 6395
Þat god hem sent to her fode
Þe mouþes þat of wille were wlank
ȝalde him euer litel þank
Þey her tungis speke resoun
Her hertis euer were tresoun 6400
In þis tyme þat I of spek 6403 fol. 36v col. 2
Was a lordynge het amalek
Þat on hem fauȝte & þei on him 6405
In a stide hett rapidym
Moyses calde sir Iosue
And made him mayster of þat semble

6378   any]of eny LB.
6379   hem] *om* B. foode] flode B.
6381   snew]snowyd B.
6381   were]was L.
6385   morwe]morn TL; þe morne B. euenyng]þe evenyng B.
6386   Volatile]Vetaile L.
6387   owe men]men owe to B.
6388   menske]drede L.
6390   of]oute of B.
6391   forseid wonde]ȝerd gode B.
6392   Oute of þe stone brast a flode B.
6397   of... wlank]euyr were wranke B. wlank]lank L.
6398   ȝalde]holdeth B. litel]at litell B.
6399   þey]ȝef B.
6400   tresoun]in treson B.
6401-2   *om in* CGHTLB.
6404   Was]þer was B. lordynge]lorde B.
6407   sir]*om* B.

He seide chese þe men and diȝt
Wiþ sir amalec to fiȝt   6410
And I shal on þat hil stonde
And goddes ȝerde holde in honde
To þis fiȝte þei wente anoon
Moyses þo and aaron
Þei wente vpon þat hille   6415
In hope allone of goddis wille
Whil moyses helde vp his hende
Wel was hit in þat bataile kende
Euer þat whyle witerly
Had goddes folk þe victory   6420
And if he slaked hem any siþe
Amalec won also swiþe
So longe he helde hem vp wiþ þis
Þat slake hem most he maugre his
Of werynesse was no wondir   6425
Þei gedered stoones & leyde him vndir
Euer helde he vp and aaron
His hondes til þe fiȝte was don
Vndir eiþer hond was oon
Þat helde hym stille as any stoon   6430
Bi þe sunne was at doun helde
Wiþ Israel was lafte þe felde
// Ietro þe prest of madian
Þat was moyses kynnesman
Whenne he herde how þei had don   6435
Bitwene Israel and pharaon
To speke wiþ moyses he cam
Brouȝte him his wyf sephoram
Wiþ two sones she by hym beer

6409   þe]thy L.
6410   to]for to B.
6412   holde]om B. honde]my honde B.
6415   vpon þat]vnto þe B.
6417   Whil]When B. hende]held L; hede B.
6418   þat]om B.
6420   þe victory]þo maystery B.
6421   hem]om B.
6422   Amalec]Amale L.
6424   slake]slaked B. maugre his]maw greis L; magr is B.
6425   werynesse]werying B.
6427   helde he]he held B.
6431   at]om L.
6436   Bitwene] Bytwe L.
6438   Brouȝte him]And with B.
6439   om B.

Gersan and Elyaser   6440
Þis ilke folke was vntoun to fonde
Þat moyses hadde vndir honde
Þei dide him wondir greet *tra*uaile   fol. 37r col. 1
Til Ietro ȝaf him counsaile
Vndir bailis to set hem þen   6445
In riȝt for to kepen hem
Of mony wrongis þat þer were
Of whiche men greet charge bere
But þat . þat fel to goostlynes
Shul be tauȝte bi trewe moyses   6450

Listeneþ now to my sawe
Telle I shal of moyses lawe
Þenne bigan þe folk to say   6451
To moyses go gete vs lay
Moyses seid þat is riȝt
We shul hit aske of god almyȝt
To faste bihoueþ ȝow and me   6455
How longe shal þe terme be
Þe terme shal laste fourty dayes
Whil I go to gete ȝow layes
Here on þe mou*n*t of synay
Sir þei seide ful bleþely   6460
Moyses wente vpon þat felle
Fourty dayes þere gon dwelle
Whiche he fasted as we rede
To gete lawe his folk to lede
Oure lord coom to hym anoon   6465
And toke him tables two of stoon
Wiþ his co*m*mandementis ten
And bad him teche hem to his men

6440   *After* 6440, *an extra line in* B: Which Ietroys chyldyr wer.
6441   ilke]ille TL. vntoun]wantou*n* TB.
6443   wondir]vndyr B.
6445   bailis]bay leuys B. hem]om B.
6448   men]wysemen B.
6449   *first* þat]*om* L; þo B. goostlynes]gostely liues B.
6450   bi]to LB.
6450b shal]wol T.
6452   go]to LB.
6453   þat is]to his B.
6460a&b *om* CGHTLB.
6461   þat felle]þe hyll B.
6462   þere gon]he gon þere B.
6463   Whiche]þe which B.
6464   To] Go L.
6468   him]hem L.

For we owe hem holde for det
In þis book I haue hem set 6470
//Trowe þou in no god but oon
//Ny ooþ þat þou swere noon
//Holde wel þi holy day
//Fadir & modir worshepe ȝe ay
//Reue no mon his lyf þon 6475
//Do no lecchery bi no wommon
//Loke ȝe no þing ne stele
//Bereþ witnes noon but lele
// Þi neiȝebores wif wiþ wronge þou naue
// Nor beest of his mayden ny knaue 6480
Þese are þe commaundementis ten fol. 37r col. 2
Þat god took to moysen
Firste þe iewes to teche
And siþen þe cristen to preche
If we hem kepe out and Inne 6485
Þei wol vs saue fro dedly synne

Whiles moyses was awey
Þat false folke wiþouten fey
Þei seide Moyses was slayn
And neuer wolde come aȝayn 6490
And summe seide þat he
Was lyuynge & in lyf shulde be
Þei toke her counsel as þei wolde
To make hem a god of golde
Þo foolis seide hem among 6495
So stalworþe shulde he be & strong
Þat he shal holde vs hool & fere

6469 we]ȝe B. hem holde]to holde hem B.
6470 book]koke T.
6474 ȝe]om B.
6475 Reue]Reue ȝe TLB. lyf]wyfe B.
6477 ȝe]þat ȝe B. ne]om TB; ȝe L.
6478 noon]not L.
6479 þou naue]þou nam L; ne haue B.
6480 knaue]man L.
6482 took]ȝafe B.
6483 þe]to þe B.
6484 cristen]cristen men B.
6487 Whiles]Whyles þat B.
6488 þat]þe B.
6490 wolde]more schuld B.
6492 lyuynge]lying B.
6495 þo]The LB.
6496 shulde he]he schuld B.
6497 shal]schuld B.

And kepe vs euer in oure mistere
Whenne manna wol vs wantynge be
He shal vs sende good plente   6500
Þus bigan her gyle wiþ gamen
Her tresour of gold þe[i] gedered samen
A golden calf þerof þei blewe
And as god honourid hit newe
Oure god þei seide þis is he   6505
Þat brouȝte vs þourȝe þe rede see
Fro pharao and his powere
Þerfore honoure we him here
Þis moyses was dere & kynde
To god men may hit here fynde   6510
He toke hym tables of þe lawe
As ȝe herde in my sawe
Whenne he had hem hym take
Þe folke he seide haþ don wrake
Siþ þou coom fro hem laste   6515
Þou shalt hem fynde vnstidefaste
Lordingis to þis false lede
Manna fel ȝe herde me rede
Fro heuen fel so greet plente
As a ryme frost onne to se   6520
Whil moyses hym helde a way   fol. 37v col. 1
For to do hem haue þe lay
Summe of hem þis fast forsoke
And þis riche manna toke
And vndir erþe in hoolis hidde   6525
Aȝeyn forbode þus þei didde
Þus þei were þat tyme vnwyse
Þei dide aȝeynes goddes enprise

Whenne moyses coom fro þat felle
Soone herde he tiþing telle   6530
Þat þis folk ful euel had done

6500   shal]will B.
6501   her]þey B.
6502   Her]Hys B. of]& B. þei]þe H.
6503   golden]colden T.
6504   god]a god T; a god þey B.
6505   þei]he B.
6514   þe]þy B. wrake]wrong B.
6520   a]om B. onne to]vnto B.
6525   hidde]þey hyd B.
6526   Aȝeyn]Aȝens B.
6529   felle]hyll B.
6530   tiþing]tydyngis B.

Þerof fonde he tokene soone
Whenne he was comen into desert
Þe calf fond he þere set apert
He herde þe greet noyse þare   6535
Aboute þis calf wiþ mychel fare
So greued he wex in his mode
He myȝte say euel ny gode
He ne wist wheþer better wore
To turne or wende him forþermore   6540
Þe tables þat he in hond bere
In peces he hem brak riȝt þere
Þerwiþ forþermore he ȝede
For to se her cursed dede
He say hem knele þis calf aboute   6545
As god hymself to loue and loute
What deuel is þis he seide in greue
Is þis ȝoure god þat ȝe in leue

Whenne þei were war of moyses
Þei fley awey al in a res   6550
ȝonge and olde lasse & more
Þe calf alone laft þei þore
Moyses þenne called hem togider
Lordyngis he seide I am comen hider
Aboute ȝoure eronde haue I bene   6555
Why fle ȝe fro me þus bidene
Comeþ aȝeyn wiþouten doute
Haue ȝe þese dayes alle fasted oute
þat I ȝow bad ar I went
Haue ȝe holde my commaundement   6560
Who haþ made þis calf byfore   6561 fol. 37v col. 2
Hit shal heraftir ȝow rewe ful sore   6568

6531   þis]his TLB.
6532   tokene]tyþing B.
6534   set]om B.
6535   þe]a B.
6537   wex]was L.
6538   euel]ney þer euil B.
6539   He... wist]Ne wist he neuer B.
6540   him]om B.
6542   hem brak]brak hem B.
6544   her]þat B.
6547   is... seide]he sayde is þus B.
6548   ȝoure]þe B.
6558   fasted]faste B.
6559   ȝow]om B.
6562-7   om HTLB.
6568   heraftir ȝow]ȝow afftyr B.

Who made þis calf I most him ken
Who helde þe fast among þese men   6570
Who haþ holden my comaundement
And who not siþen I went
Who forȝat me & who nouȝt
And who þis gold togider brouȝt
Whiche are þo togider hit blew   6575
Whiche are þo for her god hit knew   6576
Alle þei made hemseluen quyte   6578
Vchone seide I haue no wyte   6577
Par fay seide moyses for nouȝt
Pe soþe algate shal be souȝt   6580
I wol myself knowe þe fals
And vche man shal knowe him als
Ful euelhel brake ȝe þat day
Pat I fasted so shul ȝe say
Allas shul ȝe say þat siþe   6585
For whenne I weped ȝe made ȝow bliþe
ȝe made þis god in to trowe
Whil I went to preye for ȝowe
Mychel foly dide I þan
Pat euer to helpe ȝow I bigan   6590
Whenne I ȝow ladde þourȝe þe stronde
Out of alle ȝoure enemyes honde
Siþen I asked ȝoure fode
And god sende ȝow manna gode
Pat ȝe in erþe ha hud vndir   6595
Mony men on ȝow shal wondir
Oure lord shal me on ȝow wrake

6569   I... him]hym must I L.
6570   þe]þis B.
6574   togider]hedyr B.
6576   for her]þat for B.
6577-8 *reversed in* HTLB.
6578   seluen]seuen T.
6580   shal]it schall B.
6583   Ful]For L. euelhel]euyll B. þat]þe TL.
6585   Allas]Alle B. þat]the L.
6586   weped]wepe L. ȝow]ye L.
6588   Whil]When B. to]in to B.
6590   to]om B.
6591   þourȝe]oute of B.
6592   honde]bonde B.
6594   sende ȝow]ȝow grauntyd B.
6595   in]þe B. ha hud]a had L.
6596   men... shal]a man schull on ȝow B.
6597   me]om B. wrake]do wrak B.

And saue þo þat haue no sake
Alle are ȝe trewe by ȝoure sawes
Is noon of ȝow þis calf knawes   6600
ȝe saye þat ȝe made hit nouȝt
Ne neuer coom hit in ȝoure þouȝt
Nor ȝe honourid hit neu*er* ȝe say
Al of þis ȝe make hit nay
But say me þe*n*ne wherfore & why   6605
ȝe made so myche dene & cry
Þat I ȝow say make alle bidene   fol. 38r col. 1
Þourȝe þe watir hit shal be sene
Sheweþ me soone hit shal be kid
Wher ȝe haue þis manna hid   6610
Þo puttis whe*n*ne þei hem vndid
Þei fonde but wormes crulyng Imyd
Whe*n*ne þei sey þis sooþ to say
Þat gilty were þouȝte no play
Þis golden calf he made to brest   6615
To precis & into watir kest
And of þis watir he made vchon
To drynke wheþ*er* þei wolde or noon
Alle þo men þat gilty were
Gulden berdes soone þei bere   6620
Þo þat were wiþouten pliȝt
And helde his co*m*mau*n*dement riȝt
And trowed to no maumetrye
As was þe kynreden of sir leuy
Þe watir proued hem for clene   6625
Was no gold on her berdis sene
Moyses to her ȝatis ȝode
Þus he seide whe*n*ne he þ*er*e stode

6598   sake]lak B.
6602   hit]*om* B.
6604   of]*om* B.
6605   me þe*n*ne]ȝe me B.
6607   make]*om* B.
6611   þo]The LB. puttis]pytte B.
6612   crulyng]cruly L; krepy*n*g B.
6613   sooþ]þe soth B.
6615   made]did B.
6616   To]In ij° L; In B. into]in þe B. kest]yt kest LB.
6618   To]*om* B. or noon]ar now L.
6620   Gulden]W*i*t*h* goldyn L. bere]wer L.
6622   helde]hold L. his]her B. co*m*mau*n*dement]comandement*is* B.
6624   kynreden]kynred L. sir]*om* B.
6626   berdis]berd B.
6627   her]þe B.

Alle þat are in goddis partye
Hider ʒe come & stonde me bye   6630
So dude þat were in goddis half
And honoured not þe gilden calf
Gooþ he seide þat hit be sene
Sleeþ vp þo caitifs al bydene
Vchone went wiþ swerd in honde   6635
And slowʒe þere twenty þousonde
Þenne gon moyses to hem say
Wite ʒe what ʒe haue done today
ʒe haue to god holden vp ʒoure hondes
And slayn þat goddis wille wiþstondes   6640
// ʒit spak oure lord to moysen
Do he seide as I þe ken
Hewe þe siche tablis he seide
As I bifore þe purueyde
Whiche þou brake & I shal soone   6645
Wryte hem newe hit is to done
Vpon þe morwe whenne hit was day   fol. 38r col. 2
Moyses went to fett þe lay
He toke comaundementis ten
For to lede wiþ his men   6650
Writen wiþ goddis owne honde
He sent hem þere a fair presonde
Whenne moyses hadde brouʒt þe lawe
And his folk In face him sawe
Hem þouʒte him horned on heed fer   6655
And douted to come him ner
Þenne þe lawe he hem vndide
As oure lord to hym gon bide

Off oon arke to hem he spake
In goddis worshipe for to make   6660

6631   þat]they that LB.
6632   And]þat B. gilden]goldyn LB.
6634   Sleeþ]And sleyth B. þo]þe B. al bydene]clene B.
6647   morwe]morne TLB.
6648   fett]sett B.
6649   toke]toke þe B.
6651   owne]om B.
6652   þere]om B.
6653   hadde]om B.
6654   In]hys B. him]om B.
6655   him horned]he hornis B. fer]fro fer B.
6657   þenne]When he B. he]to B.
6660   In... worshipe]And tabernacles B.

A tabernacle als for to diȝt
Þerof he shewed hem þe riȝt
Þe þre ȝerdis vp he toke
And þeryn dide so seiþ þe boke
To bere wiþ hym to euery stede   6665
Whider he wolde þat folk lede

Listeneþ now a litil þrawe
For I wol telle of moyses lawe
Now shul ȝe of þo domes here   6667
Þat god ȝaf to moyses sere
Alle to telle hit were gret swinke
But summe are gode to here me þinke   6670
Whoso smyteþ man in wille to slo
He shal himself be slayn also
Whoso sleeþ any man wiþ wille
And bifore haþ waited þertille
If he to myn autere flyȝe   6675
Men shal him þennes drawe to dyȝe

Who þat fadir or modir smyte
Or elles hem waryeþ in despite
Dyȝe þei shal for þat sake
Wiþouten raunsoum noon to take   6680

If two chyde & þat oon
Þat oþer smyte wiþ fuste or stoon
So þat he lye short whyle or long
Siþen whenne he may go strong
Þe smytere shal quyte his lechyng   6685 fol. 38v col. 1
And þe skaþe of his liggyng

6661   A... als]In goddis hous B.
6662   þerof]þerfore B.
6663   vp he]he vp B.
6664   dide]did hem B.
6666   Whider]Wheþer L; Whedyr þat B. þat folk]hem B.
6667   þo]þe B.
6669   swinke]stynk B.
6671   Whoso]so L. in]I L.
6673   Whoso]so L.
6676   þennes]þan L.
6677-80   *are displaced in B, appearing after* 1.6686.
6677   þat]so B.
6678   hem]om B.
6680   take]make B.
6681   chyde & þat]childyr þat þe B. þat oon]the tone LB.
6682   þat oþer]þe toþer TLB.
6683   lye... whyle]lay litell B.
6686   þe... his]hys harme for B.

Whoso smyteþ his seruaunt wiþ a wand
And he be deed vndir his hande
He shal be gilty of his synne
But if he lyue a day or twynne   6690
Þe lord shal vndurly no peyne
For as his catel is his sweyne

If mon smyte wyf wiþ barn
Wherfore þe childe is forfarn
If so be þat þe modir lyue   6695
To hir husbonde þenne shal he ȝyue
Medis þat men saye is riȝt
By lokyng of trewe mennes siȝt
And if she deȝe þerfore þe wyf
Þenne shal he lose lyf for lyf   6700
Eȝe for eȝe tooþ for toþ
Hond for hond loke þis be sooþ
Foot for foot too for too
Wounde for wounde woo for woo

Whoso smyteþ out his þralles yȝe   6705
And makeþ hym vnsiȝtilyȝe
Or tooþ out of his mouþ smyte
He shal him make fre & quyte

Þe ox þat sleeþ mon wiþ horn
And so was not wont biforn   6710
To deþe men shal þat beest stone
But of þe flesshe ete no mon none
Þe beestis lord shal go quyte
Of alle chalengis & wyte

6687   Whoso]so L.
6689   synne] fyne B.
6690   if]om B. twynne]tweyne B.
6692   is... sweyne]he is slayne B.
6693   mon]a man B.
6694   forfarn]mysfarne B.
6695   þat]om B. lyue]leue B.
6696   hir]þe B. þenne]he B. he]om B.
6697   Medis]Godes B.
6701   eȝe]ȝeȝe H.
6705   Whoso]so L. out]om B.
6708   him]hymself L.
6709   mon]a man B.
6711   stone]stond L.
6712   But]And B. ete... mon]men ete B.
6713   beestis lord]lorde of þe beste B.
6714   chalengis]þe chalaunge B.

If his lord knowe h*im* kene of horn   6715
Þre dayes þer biforn
If he sle wo*m*mon or mon
Þe beest to slauȝte shal go þon
And þe lord þat hit iȝt
Shal vnswere þerfore at his myȝt   6720
If he sle any mo*n*nes sweyn
Thritty shillyng of mone[y] aȝeyn
Shal men ȝyue þe lorde to mende
Þe beest shal wiþ stoonyng ende

[I]f any man makeþ a pit   6725 fol. 38v col. 2
And siþþen wol nat stoppe hit
If ox or asse or oþ*er*e beest
Falle þerynne leest or meest
Þe man þat þis put auȝte
Be he wrooþ or ellis sauȝte   6730
Of his beest shal ȝelde þe prys
But þe dede beest shal be hys
If þat myn oxe firste sle þyn
Þus biddeþ god almyȝtyn
Þat þe quyke beest be solde   6735
Þe prys bitwixe hem dalt & tolde
And þe dede careyn also
Shal be delt bitwene hem two
And if he wist hit at þe leest
Þre dayes bifore of þis beest   6740
And no kepyng dude on þat wylde
Ox for ox þe*n*ne shal he ȝilde

6717   he]it B.
6718   slauȝte]slawght*ir* LB.
6719   iȝt]hight L.
6721   sweyn]swyne LB.
6722   shillyng] £ B. money]mone H.
6723   þe lorde schall ȝeue to amend B.
6725   If] *The I in* MS H *is very faint,* merely the scribe's guide to the rubricator,
        which the latter missed.
6727   *first* or]*om* L.
6728   leest... meest]meest or leest TLB.
6729-30   *om* CFG.
6731   his beest]þe dede B. þe]a B.
6732   beest]*om* B.
6736   þe]And þe B. dalt &] *om* B.
6737   careyn]body B.
6740   bifore]afore B. þis]þe B.
6741   no]non B. þat]þe B.
6742   þe*n*ne]*om* B. he]be B.

Whoso steleþ sheep ox or cow
To sle or selle or oþer prow
Oxen fiue for oon he pay   6745
For oon sheep foure hit stonde for lay

Þeof housbrekynge or digynge grou*n*d
If mon hi*m* smyte wiþ deþes wou*n*d
And þe dede be done bi ny3t
Þe smyter þe*n*ne shal haue no pli3t   6750
But if þe su*n*ne be vp þon
Hit shal be tolde for slau3te of mon

If þeof haue no fyn ne 3ift
Þat he a3eyn may 3elde his þift
He shal be solde but if þat he   6755
Haue any au3te may founden be
If he haue any 3onge or olde
He shal a3eyn 3elde double folde

If fyre be kyndeled by vnhap
Þour3e felde or corn mowe or stak   6760
He þat hit kyndeleþ in þat felde
He ow3e þe harmes for to 3elde

If I 3yue þe forto kepe
Ox or cowe . asse or shepe
Hors or any oþ*er*e au3te   6765 fol. 39r col. 1
And hit wiþ þeofis be lau3te
Or deed or done into euel my3t
Or done away fro monnes si3t
Wiþ þin ooþ make þe clene
And þou go quyt of þ*a*t I mene   6770

6743   Whoso]Who TL.
6744   prow]þrow L.
6745   he]schall he B.
6747   þeof]Of B. or digynge] & breking B.
6748   mon hi*m*]it man B.
6750   no]þe B.
6751   vp þon]vpon L.
6752   slau3te]slaghtyr B.
6753   þeof]þe þefe B. haue... ne]may fynde no B.
6754   may]maþ T.
6755   shal]shalbe L.
6756   may founden]þ*a*t fonde may B.
6757   *om in* B.
6758   He]It B. a3eyn]be solde & B.
6759-62   *om in* B.
6761   kyndeleþ]kyndeled TL.
6764   *first* or]*om* L.
6766   lau3te]caught B.

But if þis auȝte be stolen in chaunce
Þou shalt him make restoraunce
And if I lent þe siche a beest
Þat deed or spilt be at þe leest
And I myself not present   6775
Þou shalt hit quyte bi iugement
And elles not namely in dede
I lete to hyre for any mede

Þo þat to wicked dedes drawe
God wol þat þei be done of dawe   6780

Whoso doþ wiþ beest þe foul synne
He shal be done to deþe þerynne

Who þat honoureþ goddes newe
Of his sleyng shal no mon rewe
To comelyngis loke ȝe do no gyle   6785
For siche were ȝoureself sum whyle

Widewe nor childe fadirles
Do no wronge ny noon vnpees
If ȝe do crye to me þei shal
And I forsoþe wol here her cal   6790
Þenne shal my wreche kyndel so
Þat soone þeraftir I wol ȝow slo
Widewes I shal make ȝoure wyues
ȝoure childer haue no fadris in lyues

If þat þou lenest any þing   6795
Þou lene hit not wiþ okeryng
If þat þou whenne þou art wrooþ

6771   auȝte]oxe B. in]wiþ B.
6774   þe leest]þyn hest B.
6775   not]be not B.
6777   And]Or B.
6778   I]And T.
6779   to]þe B.
6780   þei]þo B. of]on B. dawe]law L.
6781   Whoso]Whos L. beest]þe beste B. þe]þat L.
6783   Who þat]Whoso TB; Whoso þat L.
6785   comelyngis]ȝong aires B.
6786   ȝoureself]ȝe ȝourselff B. sum]a B.
6788   ny]vp L.
6790   her]their L.
6792   þeraftir]afftyr B.
6793   ȝoure]you LB.
6794   no fadris]godfadyr B. fadris]fadir TL. in]on L.
6795   þat]om B.
6796   okeryng]vsuryng B.

Of sympel mon take wed or clooþ
ȝelde aȝeyn þat clooþ I say
Ar þe sunne go doun þat day   6800
In hap he haþ on bak nor bed
Clooþ to hile hym but þat wed
Elles if þat he to me cryȝe
I shal him here þourȝe my mercyȝe

Missaye no prest þat precheþ in londe   6805 fol. 39r col. 2
ȝyue gladly þi tende & þyn offronde
Þe formast sheues of ȝoure corn
Þe firste childe to ȝow is born
Not þat alone I bid ȝow
But als þe firste of sheep & cow   6810
Þe childe þat ȝe to offring brynge
ȝe bye aȝeyn for oþere þinge
Þe forburþes þat I of telle
Shal seuen dayes wiþ modir dwelle
Þe eiȝteþe day to offred be   6815
As I haue comaundide þe

Þe flesshe þat beest bifore haþ taast
Ete ȝe not þerof þe last

Lerne not of hym þat is lyere
Ny false witenes noon ȝe bare   6820
Folewe hem no more þen þi foos
Þat vnto wickede dedis goos

Holde wiþ none þouȝe þei be fele
Aȝeyn þe doom þou woost is lele
To riche & pore þou seest in pliȝt   6825

6798   sympel mon]semble men B.
6801   on]to B. bak]bat T. nor]no L.
6802   hym]hym wiþ B.
6806   ȝyue]yf L. tende]tiþe TLB.
6807   sheues]scheff B.
6809   þat]om B.
6810   als]om B.
6811   þat ȝe]ȝe fyrst B.
6812   bye]bye it B. þinge]offryng B.
6813   þe]þese TL; þis B. forburþes]forbodis L; forbode B.
6814   modir]þe modyr B.
6815   eiȝteþe] viij L. to offred]offred to B.
6817   flesshe... beest]beste flesh that best L.
6819   lyere]a lyer B.
6821   hem... þi]not hem þay or ȝour B.
6823   þouȝe]ȝef B.
6824   Aȝeyn]Aȝens B. doom... is]dedys þat be B.
6825   &]ne B.

In dome spare þou not þe riȝt

Þin enemyes beest þou fyndes o stray
Þou brynge hit hoom þat wol þi lay

If þou fynde of þyn euel willonde
Vndur birþen his beste biggonde   6830
Helpe hym or þou forþer wende
And so þou maist make þi frende

Sle no man wiþouten sake
Blendyng ȝiftis noone þou make

To pilg[r]ym & to vncouþ   6835
Bere þe feire of dede & mouþ
ȝe knowe þe state of comelynge
Of pharaos tyme þe kynge
ȝoure lond ȝe sowe seuen ȝere
And repe þerof cornes sere   6840
Þe eiȝteþe lete hit lye stille
Pore mennes hongur to fille

Six dayes shul ȝe worche I say
And ȝe shul reste þe seuenþe day
Hors & asse wommon and knaue   6845 fol. 39v col. 1
Þat day shul þei restyng haue

Trowe on no goddes fals
[S]wereþ not I bidde ȝow als
Holdeþ þis wel I bidde ȝow now
Myn aungel shal go bifore ȝow   6850
Þat shal ȝow wisse & sumdel lede

6826   not]neuer B.
6827-8 om B.
6827   þin enemyes] In enemyest L.
6828   wol]weld L.
6830   birþen]brethyn L. his]hest B. biggonde]liggonde T; lyand B.
6834   Blendyng]Blynde B. make]take TL.
6835   pilgrym]pilgym H.
6836   feire] Syr B. &]of B.
6837   state]estate L. comelynge]comyng L.
6838   tyme]come L.
6840   cornes]corn L.
6841   eiȝteþe] eyght ȝere B.
6842   Pore mennes]Purvyaunce B.
6843   shul ȝe]ȝe schull B.
6845   asse]also B.
6846   shul]schuld B.
6847   Trowe]Throw L. no]none B.
6848   Swereþ]wereþ H. *The rubricator has evidently forgotten to draw the* S.
6849   now]om B.
6851   wisse]wysshe L.

Into a lond of blisfulhede
ȝoure foos þat ȝow wolde wiþstonde
Shul haue no myȝte in foot nor honde
I myself wol for ȝow fiȝt   6855
Shal noon ouer ȝow haue no myȝt
I shal holde ȝow my sawe
Whil ȝe folwe my riȝt lawe
Suche was þe lessoun and þe lore
And ȝitt a þousonde siþis more   6860
Þat god shewed to moysen
To do his folk hym knowe & ken
But lordyngis for þat I
By witenessynge of prophecy
And þourȝe preef of þe selue dede   6865
To cristis burþe I wol vs lede
Ar he had take flesshe & blode
Þe firste was Abraham of her brode
To whom was het þat of his sede
Shul alle þe blessed folke brede   6870
And so dide prynce & als prophete
As god dide to hym bihete
And lordyngis for þat I
May not telle al her prophecy
Þat of þat blissed burþe was seyde   6875
Þat longe tofore was purueyde
Of somme of hem þat seyde moost
Of his birþe bi þe holy goost
I shal ȝow shewe wiþouten les
As anentis þis moyses   6880

6852   a]þe B. blisfulhede]lofesomhede B.
6853   ȝow wolde]wolde ȝou T; ye wille L.
6854   nor]ne B.
6856   no]om B.
6857   ȝow]for ȝow B.
6858   folwe]fullfyll B.
6859   lessoun]lofesom B.
6860   siþis]syþe B.
6862   hym]om B.
6864   witenessynge]witnes B.
6866   burþe]burgh B.
6867   &]or B.
6869   het]yt L; behight B. þat]om B.
6870   Shul]Schuld B.
6871   als]om B.
6872   to]om B.
6874   her]holy L.
6876   tofore]bifore TB.
6880   anentis]aventus L.

Þis moyses þat I rede of here
Was tauȝte þe folke to lede & lere
Þat dalt weren in kynredens twelue
Moyses hem bad hymselue
Þat vche kynreden to bere a wond   6885 fol. 39v col. 2
His biddyng durst þei not wiþstond
And vche wande þat þei þere bare
He spered hem in her seyntware
And wroot þe name & seled also
Þat noon shulde oþere gyle þo   6890
Whenne he hem loked on þe morn
He fonde oon wiþ leef & flour born
And for hit was an almaunde wonde
Þat same fruyt þeronne þei fonde
Almaundis grewen þo þeron   6895
Þe ȝerde þat fel to aaron
To al þe folk in þat londe
Moyses soone shewed þe wonde
But he tolde hem not þat tyde
What þe tokene wolde abyde   6900
For he her frowardenesse knewe
And þei were of trouþe vntrewe
Þis ȝerde was done vp to holde
As god of myȝt himself wolde
In tokene for to take & telle   6905
Aȝeyn þe folk þat was rebelle
To vndirstonde þat god mouȝt
Al þing do þat hym good þouȝt
Þis ȝerde bitokened oure lady trewe
Þe fruyt hir sone swete ihesue   6910

6882   Was]þat B.
6883   kynredens]kynredes TL; kyndys B.
6885   kynreden]kynred LB. to]schuld B.
6887   þere]om B.
6888   spered]schett B. her]þe B.
6891   loked]lokis B.
6892   leef]levys B. flour]flourys B.
6893   almaunde]almon L.
6894   þat]þe B. þei]yt L.
6895   Almaundis]þe almondis B. grewen]growe B.
6897   in]of B.
6898   þe]þat B.
6902   trouþe]her trouþe B.
6904   of myȝt]allemyȝty L.
6905   &]om B.
6906   was]were B.
6909   ȝerde]yern L. bitokened]betokenyth B.

Of þis matere mut I now cees
To telle ȝou more of þis moyses
Whenne he as god him chees bifore
He lad þe folke in wildernesse þore
Fourty wyntur and no las   6915
Dede in þat desert he was
Al his elde was sixe score ȝeer
For he was to god so der
Himself byryed him & hid
In a pryue place vnkid   6920
For wiste þe iewis where he lay
Honoure him as god wolde þay
Þes iewes went wiþouten resoun
Into þe londe of promissioun
Þourȝe moyses ne coom þei nouȝt   6925 fol. 40r col. 1
But Iosue hem þider brouȝt
God aftir good moysen
Made hym leder of his men
Wiþ his felawe þat calef hiȝte
Þo two brouȝte hem to riȝte   6930
Þis Iosue coom of þat kyn þo
Þat men calle effraym also   6932
In egipte born but fed he was   6935
And leder als wiþ maystir moyses
Þis ilke moyses riȝtwis of rede
Forȝat not ar he were dede
To sette þese holy ȝerdes þre
In a stide he fonde pryue   6940
Þere þei grew lasse ne more
But euer as þei were bifore

6911   now]*om* B.
6912   To]And B.
6914   þore]ȝore B.
6915   and no]more ne B.
6917   elde]age B.
6919   Himself]He hymselffe B. him]*om* B. & hid]in hide L.
6923   þes]þe B.
6924   Into]Vnto L; To B.
6925   ne]þere B. þei]þe B.
6926   Iosue]Ihesu L.
6931   Iosue]Iesew L.
6932   calle]callyd B.
6933-4   *om* HTLB.
6935   but]& B.
6936   als]he was B. maystir]*om* B.
6937   riȝtwis]þat right was B.
6940   stide]place B.
6941   grew]grow B.

Riȝt to kyng dauid dayes
Þat lad þe folk in goddis layes
He bi warnynge of goddis sonde
Brouȝte þe ȝerdis to his londe   6945

Whenne aaron was deed þe prest
His sone eliazar was neest
And his fadir astate he beere
Til Iosue we speke of here   6950
Þis iosue was wondir liȝt
And maistry had in mony a fiȝt
Trewely he fauȝte for goddis lay
Þerfore god doubled him his day
And made þe sunne stille to stonde   6955
Til Iosue had þe hyȝer honde
And whil he past þe flum iurdon
Þe watir stood stille as stoon
Til he þe folk had ouer brouȝt
Into þe same lond þei souȝt   6960
Ioseph boones þei wiþ hem lede
And þer grof hem in þat stede
In a lond þat het sichym
Was ȝyuen in lot to Ioseph kyn
For as þei wan hit wiþ her honde   6965
Þei dalt bitwixe hem þat londe
Vche kynreden of þo twelue   fol. 40r col. 2
Had a lodesmon hemselue
Þat shulde her owne kynreden lede
Whenne þat þei to bataile ȝeode   6970
For þei fonde strong folk hem aȝeyn
Wiþ were þat dide hem myche peyn
And wiþstood hem þe londe to wynne

6946   þe]þo T.
6949   astate]state B.
6950   speke]spak B. here]are B.
6953   fauȝte]thoght L.
6954   doubled]dobbyd B.
6960   Into]To B. same]om B. þei]þat he B.
6961   þei]om B.
6962   grof]graued T; did grafe L.
6964   Was... lot]þat ȝeffyn was B.
6965   For as]þere B.
6966   þei]And B. bitwixe]betwene B. þat]þe B.
6967   kynreden]kynrede TB. þo] the LB.
6968   lodesmon]Sodec man B.
6969   her]he T. kynreden]kynrede TLB.
6972   Wiþ]þat with B. þat]om B.
6973   þe]þat B.

But þat was for her owne synne
For whil þei helde her lawe in londe   6975
Was no folk myȝte hem wiþstonde
Þat alle oþere dude myȝte not avayl
Whil þei helde goddes counsayl
Hem þurte drede no man in place
But her fiȝte lasted litil space   6980
Whenne þei moost had of her wille
Moost þei dide hemself vnskille
Of god almyȝty þei laft þe lawe
To sarasenes feiþ gan hem drawe
And made wiþ hem her mariagis   6985
Who herde euer suche men in ragis
Suche a kyng coude no man knawe
Hem helde from vche mannes awe
And euer þei vnskil on him souȝt
Til þei hemself in þraldom brouȝt   6990
In þraldome were þei worþ to be
Þat wolde not suffere to be fre
// Calef coom aftir Iosue
Of israel demer was he
In his tyme were þo fablis writen   6995
Þat ȝitt are as bookis witen
Saturneus & sir Iubitere
Þat we nowe in fables here
And þe first sibile of pers
Men fynden of in olde vers   7000
// Calef had a sone othomel
He demed þe folk of israel

6974   But]And B.
6976   no folk]none þat B.
6977   dude]*om* L.
6978   helde]did B.
6979   þurte]nede L.
6980   her]his B.
6981   had]herd L. of]*om* B.
6982   Moost]þe most B.
6983   þei... lawe]þoght þey non awe B.
6984   hem] þay B.
6986   herde]sawe B. men]*om* B.
6988   Hem]He hem L.
6990   in]þe B.
6991   worþ]worþy B.
6994   demer]þe rote B.
6995   þo]þe B.
6996   as]ab B.
6997   sir]*om* B.
6998   in]of in TLB.

By fourty ȝeer in his tyme was
Þe cite made of thebas
Ayoth was þenne demestere   7005
Of israel foure score ȝeere
In his tyme was a bataile grym   fol. 4Ov·col. 1
Bitwene Israel & beniamyn
For loue of a deknes wyf
Mony a man lost her lyf   7010
Fourty þousande of israele
Of beniamyn nyȝe also fele
// Sanygath coom aftir hime
Troye was bigonne in his tyme
Ten ȝeer had he þe folk to ȝeme   7015
Siþ his two sones hem dide deme
// Barach & wiþ him delbora þo
Þei demed fourty ȝeer & moo
Þenne was oon sibile of libye
And apollo wiþ his melodye   7020
Aftir coom Gedeon
Þat worshepe in his tyme won
Slouȝe fourty kyngis of heþen sede   7024
Wiþ þre hundride of hys lede   7023
Þen was oreb & salmana   7025
Zeb and zebee þes oþere twa
In tyme of þis Iudeon was
Boþe orpheus & ercules
// Tola ladde þe folk þo
Lastyng fourty ȝeer & mo   7030
Þenne roos þe þridde sibila
Þat men cleped delphica
Of troye & grece þe batailes bolde

7004   thebas]thobas B.
7005   þenne demestere]þe domysman B.
7006   ȝeere]ȝere þan B.
7010   her]his B.
7013   Sanygath]Sanytath B.
7015   Ten ȝeer]Syth B.
7016   hem dide]þey did hym L; did hym B.
7017   wiþ him]sith B.
7023-4   *reversed in* MSS GHTLB.
7024   kyngis]knyghtys B. sede]syde B.
7026   Zeb]Zele B. and]om B.
7027   tyme]þe tyme B. þis]om B. was]Iwis B.
7028   Boþe orpheus]Was oleffernus B.
7030   &]or L.
7033   þe]tho L. batailes]batayle B.

Þis sibile myche tofore of tolde
Sir Iare was also long 7035
Her maister & ledere strong
In grece þenne regned preamus
As þe olde story telleþ vs
In þis ilke iare tyme
Were lettres founden of latyne 7040
// Iepte firste þei helde bastarde
Siþen he helde six ȝeer her warde
Zamazinis þat tyme bigon
Þe wymmen lond wiþouten mon
// Ezebon aftir seiþ þe boke 7045
Toke israel to lede & loke
He ladde hem seuen ȝeer & more fol. 4Ov col. 2
Alisaundre in þat tyme þore
Þat parys auȝte rauysshed Elayn
Wherfore many men were slayn 7050
Þe ferþe sibile in þat siþe
In babiloyne bigan to kyþe
Achialon coom aftir hard
Her leder was & her stiward
He had þat folk ten ȝeer to get 7055
In his tyme was troye biset
// Labdon had hem vndir honde
And ouer hem was eiȝte ȝeer lastonde
In his tyme was troye nomen
And wiþ þe grekes ouercomen 7060
Þere mony modirsone was colde
As hit is in þe story tolde
Þat werre lasted so long a pece
Þer was slayn of hem of grece
Eiȝte hundride siþe sixty & ten 7065

7034   tofore of]before B.
7036   Her]For L. ledere]leryd B.
7037   þenne]þo B.
7041   firste... helde]þey held fyrst B.
7042   her warde]forward L.
7044   þe... lond]þay wonde landys B.
7047   hem]*om* B.
7049   auȝte]aght þat B.
7050   were]was TL.
7053   coom]*om* L.
7055   ȝeer]*om* B.
7057   had]*om* B. vndir honde]vndirhold L.
7060   þe]*om* L.
7061   colde]solde B.
7062   þe]*om* B.
7065   siþe... &]tymes B.

Of þousandis diuerse tyme of her men
Six hundride foure score six þousand
Men of troye fauȝte for her land
Herof ben no men in were
For why þe sege lasted ten ȝere   7070
Wiþouten brekyng of þat werre
Þat greued boþe nyȝe & ferre
Þat werre semed to be noon oþer
But as þat oon half aȝeyn þat oþer
And al þis world haþ risen bene   7075
So was þer mony cayser kene
But myȝte þei neuer wynne þe toun
Til þei hit wan wiþ tresoun
And al þe chesoun of þis stryf
Was for rauysshyng of a wyf   7080
Al for fairhede of Elayn
Was þere so mony þousande slayn
// And siþen aftir þis labdon
Her domesman was sir sampson
Þat was so strong & so wiȝt   7085
Childeles was his modir mony nyȝt
In hir elde bi goddis grace   fol. 41r col. 1
An aungel het hir childe in place
Þat bi his heer shulde so myȝty be
As twenty men to fele & se   7090
Vndir philistiens þei were
Þat iewes were holden þo þere
Sampson souȝte chesoun of stryf
Of philistiens he wolde haue wyf
Vpon a day he went & sawe   7095
A fair womman of hir lawe
He tolde his frendis soone anoon

7066   tyme]tymes B. her] þeir L; om B.
7067   Six]Sexty B. six]om B.
7069   men]mon TB.
7071   brekyng]þe brekyng B. þat]þe B.
7072   nyȝe]nere B.
7074   þat oon]þe ton TLB. aȝen]aȝens B. þat oþer] þe toþere TLB.
7075   And]Bote as B. þis]þe B. haþ]had TLB.
7076   So]þere B. þer]made B. cayser]a cayzar LB.
7077   þe]þat B.
7078   hit wan]wan yt B.
7081   for]forþe B.
7082   þousande]thowsandis L.
7084   Her... was]Was her domysman B.
7086   Childeles]Gohiller L; Childes B. mony nyȝt]riȝt L.
7088   hir]he B.

Þat he hade chosen siche a wommon
He toke hem wiþ him for to proue
Hir to gete to his bihoue   7100
If hir frendis wolde him late
As he wente walkyng bi þe gate
A leouns whelpe ran ouerþwart
Raumpyng to sampson he start
// Sampson slouȝe þat leon kene   7105
Þe spirit of god in hym was sene
Whenne he hadde his eronde done
Homwarde he went also soone
But a litil fro þat gon
He wente to take his lemmon   7110
As he went þat way aȝeyn
He fond in þe leon mouþ sleyn
A swarm of bees þerynne were bred
And wiþ þe hony he hem fed
His wyues fadir & modir fre   7115
Of þis hony to ete ȝaf he
But not he made hem vndirstonde
How he þat hony fonde
At þe feest þere he was stad
A redeles vndo hym he bad   7120
He hett men to ȝyue hem mede
ȝif þei couþe hit riȝtly rede
And þei to ȝyue þe same aȝeyn
If þei hit redde not certeyn
Of þe etyng þe mete out sprong   7125
And þe swete out of þe strong
Þis was al whenne þei souȝte   fol. 41r col. 2
Þre dayes þei studied aboute nouȝte
Þo þei bisouȝte his wyf þat sho

7101   him]hyt L.
7103   leouns]lyon B.
7104   Raumpyng]Rapyng B. he start]smert B.
7105   þat]þe B.
7106   in... was]was in hym B.
7109   gon]place B.
7110   to take]þere B. lemmon]leman was B.
7111   way]day B.
7112   in]om L. sleyn]flayne L.
7114   And]þat B.
7116   þis]hys B.
7118   he þat]þat he B.
7120   redeles]redell B. vndo]vnto TL. hym he]he hem B.
7122   þei]he B. couþe]coude T. riȝtly]trewly

Shulde make hir lord to telle hit hir to   7130
Þat bruyd was of biddyng bolde
Sampson al þe soþe hir tolde
And she to þo þat were hir kid
Soone aftir hit vndid
And þat was a greet folye   7135
Hir lordis counsel to discrye   7136
Sampson for wraþþe hir forsooke   7145
And she anoþer husbonde toke
Whenne sampson þerof herde saye
Now he seide fro þis daye
Owe I to haue no maner wyte
Þouȝe I philistiens do despite   7150
Þre hundride foxes togider he knyt
I ne woot how he on hem hit
To her tailes fire he bond
And folwynge vche fox a brond
Into philistiens cuntre   7155
Þourȝe þe felde he made hem fle
Whenne þei were ripe he let hem renne
And so her curnes dide he brenne
Her olyues wiþ her wyne trees
Þes foxes brent wiþ her rees   7160
Þes philistiens wenten oute
And souȝten sampson alle aboute
Þe iewes were vndir her walde
Sampson bounden soone þei ȝalde
Þo philistiens wiþouten les   7165
Ran on sampson in a res
But sampson was ful smart
Out of her handes soone he start

7130   to]om TLB.
7132   al]as B.
7133   to]afftyr to B.
7137-44   om in CGHTLB.
7150   þouȝe... philistiens]Philistiens to B.
7151   he]om B.
7152   ne woot]note B.
7155   Into]Into þe B.
7156   made]did B.
7157   let]made L.
7158   curnes]turvis L.
7159   wiþ]& B. wyne]vyne B.
7162   sampson]þe phelistiens B.
7163   her]his B.
7164   bounden]bounde hem B.
7165   þo]þes B.

He ȝaf a breyd so fers & fast
Þat alle his bondes soone he brast   7170
By chaunce he fonde an asse boon
Oþer wepen had he noon
Of þat heþen folke he felde
A þousande by tale telde
Siþen he went into a toun   7175 fol. 41v col. 1
To a wyf þat was comoun
Bisydis hir al nyȝt he lay
Þe philistiens herden say
Þei bisett þi toun aboute
Þat if sampson coom oute   7180
By nyȝt or in þe mornynge
To doolful deeþ þei wolde hym brynge
But sampson þat was so wiȝt
Vp he roos amydde þe nyȝt
And bar þe ȝatis of þe toun   7185
And leyde hem on an hyȝe doun
Aftir he chees a wyf þo
Dalidam him brouȝte in wo
Þe philistiens so ful of stryf
Bihet to dalidam his wyf   7190
ȝiftis grete al for to frayn
Where were sampsons mayn
Longe she freyned hym þat bolde
And siche a gabbyng he hir tolde
Wiþ seuene senewes who so me bond   7195
I lost my strengþe foot & honde
His foos þo she bad take kepe

7169   He] And B. breyd]bronde L.
7170   soone he]all to B.
7174   by]and mo by L. telde] I tellyd B.
7176   wyf]woman B.
7177   Bisydis]Besyde B.
7179   þi]þe TLB.
7181   in þe]be B.
7182   doolful]þe B. brynge]bryȝt L.
7183   But]ȝett B.
7184   amydde... nyȝt]att mydnyght B.
7186   an hyȝe]þe hight B.
7188   him brouȝte] which broȝt hym L.
7189   þe]þo TL. so]om B.
7192   were]was TLB.
7193   Longe]om B. þat]in þat L; long þat B.
7194   And]þat B.
7196   my]þe B. foot]by fote B.
7197   þo]om B.

And þe while he was on slepe
Soone she his fomen calde
To do wiþ hym what þei walde   7200
Sampson waked of his nap
His bond dide he al to crak
Alle his bondis he brak in two
As þei had ben but a stro
But ȝit his wyf laft not þus   7205
Þourȝe eggyng of his enemyus
Til she þe soþe made him say
Wherynne al his strengþe lay
She seide leef telle me where
Hit is he seide in my here   7210
If hit were of I were not þon
No strenger þen anoþer mon

Now haþ sampson taken his lyf
In wille to welde to his wyf
Was neuer sampson eer in drede   7215 fol. 41v col. 2
She had in hond his lyf & dede
In hir wille hadde he boþe done
Þat shulde ben aftir sene soone
His firste wyf him lered wit
If he coude haue holden hit   7220
Þis oþer wyf þat he had now
Auȝte he not wel to trow
Soore shulde man drede þe brond
Þat bifore haþ brent his hond
And hard hit is to stond aȝeyn   7225
Þe wif þat leueþ not to freyn

7198   on slepe]aslepe B.
7202   bond... al]bondis al gan B. crak]knap L; clap B.
7203   he... in]brast on B.
7204   þei]it B. but]om B.
7206   enemyus]envious B.
7209   where]wheþer B.
7211   I were]were þow B.
7212   No]om B. mon]þan B.
7213   lyf]lyth L.
7215   Was... eer]Sampson was neuer arst B.
7216   &]in B.
7217   he]þey B.
7218   þat afftyr schall be sore sene B.
7219   lered]leuyd B.
7221   had]hath LB.
7222   he]hym B.
7223   man]men B.
7226   leueþ]lyueþ B.

Þat ouþer for loue or drede of awe
Doþ man his priuetees to shawe
By dronkenes als may bityde
Doþ man his priuetees to vnhyde 7230
In fondyng ofte men fynde hit so
Pryuyest to man is moost his foo
Þer is noon so myche may greue
As traitour derne & pryue þeue
And so dide dalida þen 7235
Worþe hir worste of alle wymmen
Hir lordis counsel tolde sho
Hir lordis moost foos to
Hir tyme she tooke a leyser þere
And whil he slept kut his here 7240
Wiþ hir sheeris wo worþe her hende
And to his foos hym bikende
Þenne myȝte þei do as þei had mynt
Þourȝe his here his myȝt was tynt
Þei dude hym wondir myche loþe 7245
Beten hym & prisound hym boþe
Whenne he was done in prisoun
A mon of þat same nacyoun
Gat dalida his wyf to wedde
Sampson was to þe brydale ledde 7250
For he was slyȝe of harp glew
By þat his heer was waxen new
By a piler was his sete
To myrþe men at her mete
Whenne þei were gladdest at þe feest 7255 fol. 42r col. 1

7227 loue... of]drede or love L. of]or B.
7228 man]men L; a man B. priuetees] counsayle B. to]om B.
7229 By]In B.
7230 man]hym B. vnhyde]be hyde L.
7232 Pryuyest to]His preuyest B. to man]with men L. moost]ofte T.
7233 so... may]þat may so mochell B.
7234 traitour]wyffe and traytur B. &]in L. pryue]om B. þeue]tene L.
7235 And... dide]Also B.
7236 alle wymmen]any woman B.
7238 Hir]Vnto her B. foos to]foo B.
7240 kut]kyt of B.
7241 wo]om T.
7242 To his lete wyttond L.
7243 þei]he B.
7245 wondir myche]moche wondir L; mochell B.
7246 second hym]om B.
7247 done]bound L.
7251 of]and L. glew]& glow B.
7253 his sete]he sett B.

Sampson coude wel geest
Somdel waxen was his heer
Þe post þat al þe hous vp beer
Wiþ boþe his hondis he hit shook
So fast þat al þe hous quook   7260
Þe hous he falde ȝaf no man griþ
His foos he slowȝe himself þerwiþ

Aftir sampson aldur nest
Was domesmon Ely þe prest
And þouȝe himself was clene of synne   7265
For gult þat his sones were Inne
Whiche he wist & chastised nouȝt
Her synne on himself he brouȝt
Whil he laft at home for elde
Þei went to fiȝte on þe felde   7270
Slayn were þei þere in sake
And goddes hooly arke I take   7272
Elye his horn panne brake bi chaunce   7277
God sent hit him for vengeaunce
Þei made drede siche vncele
Þat chastise not her childre wele   7280
Ofte on fadir falleþ wrake
Þat sent is for þe childer sake
Fourty ȝeer demed he israel
And aftir coom samuel
He was a selcouþe douȝty þing   7285
Þe firste þat noynted mon to kyng

Prophete was sir samuele
Dere to god for he was lele
Þe Iewis wiþ her mychel pride
Sent aftir hym on a tyde   7290

7261   he falde]þat felle B.
7265   þouȝe]ȝef B.
7266   For]þe B.
7267   Whiche]þe which B. chastised]chastyd B.
7268   synne]synnes B.
7270   on]in B.
7271   þere in]in þat B.
7273-6   om in CGHTLB.
7277   horn panne] lorn þat B.
7279   made]may TB.
7280   chastise]chastieth B. childre]child L.
7281   fadir]þe fadyr B.
7283   ȝeer]wyntyr B.
7284   aftir]afftyr hym B.
7286   þe] He was þe B. noynted]notid L. mon to]om B.

Lordyngis he seide seiþ me wher tille
Haue ȝe me fet what is ȝoure wille
Gete vs a kyng . What are ȝe wode
Haue ȝe not a kyng ful gode
Þat fro ȝoure foos þourȝe see ȝow ledde   7295
And wiþ riche manna ȝow fedde
And mony werkis for ȝow haþ wrouȝt
Sir þei seide þou seist for nouȝt
Gete vs a kyng þat may vs lede   fol. 42r col. 2
As we se oþere haue in dede   7300
Parfay seide samuele
ȝe are to frowarde wiþ to dele
Nouþer are ȝe war ne wyse
For ȝoure richesse to hyȝe ȝe ryse
Now are ȝe boþe in rest & pees   7305
ȝe longe ful sore to haue males
Forsoþe I saye & shal avow
Ful sore hit shal repente ȝow
Not ȝow allone but ȝoure ospryng
Shal rewe ful soore ȝoure ȝernyng   7310
Hit is wel worþi þat who
May þole no wele þole wo
// Sore wepte samuel wiþ þis
To him coom oure lord of blis
Þryes he calde on samuel   7315
Lord he seide I here þe snel
My folk seide god ful frowardly
Þei seche & worche greet envy
Þei aske anoþer kyng þen me
Euelhele þe tyme shul þei se   7320

7291 he seide]*om* L.
7292 fet]sent B.
7295 see]þe se B. ȝow]ye L.
7296 riche]*om* B. ȝow]hape ȝow B.
7297 werkis]a þing haþe B. haþ]*om* B.
7302 are]rek B. dele]duell B.
7303 are... ne]ȝe ar not B.
7304 For]To B. ȝe]you L.
7306 ȝe]ȝow B. ful]to B.
7307 &]I L.
7309 ȝow]ȝe B.
7310 ȝernyng] seruyng B.
7311-2 *om* B.
7312 *first and second* þole]suffir L.
7316 snel]wel B.
7317 seide]he sayde B.
7320 Euelhele]Ylle hayle L; In euyll B. þe]*om* B.

Þat þei desire þei shul hit haue
To her owne heed a staue
Among þis folk shal þou fynde oon
Þat saul is calde a stalworþe mon
Wiþ shulderes boþe þicke & brade   7325
He shal her kyng be made
Siþ þei haue þus forsaken me
He shal be souȝte her kyng to be
// Soone þei dide saul be souȝt
Founden & forþ was he brouȝt   7330
He was hyȝer þan any man
By þe shuldres founden þan
Þis saul haue þei made her kyng
Wiþ anoyntyng & corounyng
Wroþerhele to her bihoue   7335
Soone on hem gon hit proue
Þenne was þere no lenger abyde
Men werred on hem on vche syde
So þat wiþinne a twelmonþe stage   fol. 42v col. 1
Þei were put out of her heritage   7340
Þenne bigon þei to calle & cryȝe
Þat god on hem shulde haue mercye
And samuel þat wist her woo
Calde on god for hem also
God him bad fille his horn   7345
Wiþ oyle & wende forþ biforn
Vnto a man þat hett iesse
In bedleem shal he founden be
Þou shalt him fynde in bedleem
Seuen sones he haþ to barnteem   7350
Oon of hem make þou kyng
For saul dredeþ me no þing
Þerfore wiþ caytif and care
Out of þis world shal he fare

7323   shal þou]þou schalt B.
7324   is calde]hight B. stalworþe]strong B.
7329   be]to be B.
7330   Founden]þey founde hym B. was he]hym B.
7333   þis]Thus L.
7334   anoyntyng]oynement B.
7336   on... hit]it gan vpon hem B.
7337   abyde]byde B.
7342   on]of B.
7347   hett]om L.
7351   hem]he T.
7353   caytif]kaytyfhede B.
7354   shal he]he schall B.

For or þat he be slayn in were   7355
Þe fend he shal in body bere
He shal hym trauail day & nyȝt
And lodly his body diȝt
// Maffay lord seide samuel
I here not of þat Iesse tel   7360
Nor his sones ny him I knowe
Þe childes name ȝe me showe
ȝis he seide I shal þe kenne
Him to knowe by oþere menne
In visage is he briȝte & clere   7365
In reed of hew wiþ lawȝynge chere
His fadir in alle haþ sones seuen
Þe ȝongest is he þat I neuene
Boþe wys hende & of good fame
Dauid he hette bi his name   7370
And for þat he is war & wys
I haue hym chose to þis seruyse
His seed forsoþe al bydene
Ouer alle men shal I mayntene
His foos shul not aȝein hym vaile   7375
Him ne his shal I not faile
To be kyng not wol him dere
My benesoun shal he bere
// Samuel went sechyng þe lond   fol. 42v col. 2
Til he þe hous of Iesse fond   7380
Iesse hym resceyued feire
And samuel him called his heire

7358   his]schall his B.
7360   Iesse tel]Iestell L.
7361   ny]by L; nor B.
7362   þe...name]His childre namys B.
7364   by]fro B.
7365   is he]he ys B.
7366   In reed]Feyre L. wiþ]& L.
7367   in]and L; of B. haþ]his B.
7368   þe]*om* B. is he]he ys B.
7369   hende]and hende B.
7370   hette bi]sayde is B.
7373&4   *are merged in* B.
7373   bydene]wey schall I maynten B.
7375   aȝein]aȝens B.
7376   ne]nor B. shal I]I schall B.
7377   not...him]schall he not B.
7378   My benesoun]Beneson myne L.
7380   þe...Iesse]Iesse hous B.
7382   him]*om* B.

Comen he seide I am iesse
To se oon of þi sones [f]re
Sir he seide wiþ good entent   7385
ȝoure word is to me commaundement
His sixe sones þat were at home
Alle he called hem forþ by nome
But þe ȝongest was away
Samuel seide sir iesse say   7390
Where is þyn alþer ȝongest sone
He is he seide þere he is wone
Wiþ oure sheep vpon þe lowe
Do fet me him I wol him knowe
Þei hym fett wiþ cheer ful swete   7395
He heilsed hendely þat prophete
He knewe him whenne he had biholde
Bi tokenyngis bifore of tolde
Anoynt he was wiþouten abade
And kyng of þo iewes made   7400
But þouȝe he were anoyntide kyng
Þe kyngdome to haue in gouernyng
He entermeted him of no þing in dede
But to his sheep aȝeyn he ȝede
Goddes goost in him was sent   7405
Fro þenn fro saul hit was went
Dauid coude of dyuerse note
He coude myche of harpe bi rote
Whenne he wiþ his gle wolde game
His sheep assemblede soone same   7410
Of his menstralcy to here

7383   Comen] I am come B. I am]om B. iesse]of Iesse L.
7384   fre] H had orig. fre, emended to þre.
7390   say]nay B.
7392   is]was B.
7394   fet me] fech B.
7395   ful]om B.
7396   He]And he B. hendely]om B.
7397   biholde]hym behold B.
7398   tokenyngis]tokenys LB. bifore of tolde]tofore Itolde]B.
7399   Anoynt]Anoyntyd B. abade] a lade L.
7400   þo]the LB.
7401   anoyntide]noyntid TB.
7403   entermeted]entirmete L.
7405   in]to B.
7406   þenn... saul]saule to hym B.
7408   He... of]Of croud michis B. bi]& B.
7410   assemblede]semblyd B. soone]soþe L. same]in same LB.
7411   menstralcy]menstalcy T.

Mony were wont to drawe him nere
// Saul was ȝitt in stide of kyng
But he myȝte do no gouernyng
Þe fend was in his body fest   7415
Wherfore he myȝte haue no rest
Þenne seide þei alle what is to do
Of oure kyng þat haþ no ro
He is euer out of witt & wood   fol. 43r col. 1
How shul we amende his mood   7420
He is ful of wickedhede
Wo is hym þat he shal lede
Þenne seide a good man of þat þrom
And seide do we litel dauid com
Wiþ his harp bifore þe kyng   7425
He shal him do to lauȝe & synge
Whil he to him takeþ kepe
Þe kyng he shal make to slepe
Forþ dud þei dauid brynge
Harpyng a song bifore þe kynge   7430
He made him wiþ his melodye
Falle on slepe þat was werye
Oþerwhile wiþ harp sumtyme wiþ song
Þus he serued þe kyng ful long
Þat euer whenne he was trauailed moost   7435
Þourȝe þat foule sory goost
If he bigon to harpe & synge
Of his vnro he had restynge

7412   were wont]went L. him]om L.
7415   in]of L.
7416   Wherfore]Where þurgh B.
7419   &]om B.
7420   shul]schuld B.
7421   wickedhede]wrechydhede B.
7422   he]hym B.
7423   of... þrom]anon L.
7424   And seide]om LB. com]to come B.
7426   shal]will B. do]make B.
7428   þe kyng]om B. make to]hym make to fall on slepe B.
7429   dud]do L. dud þei]þey did B.
7430   Harpyng... song]He harpyd & song B.
7431   him]om B.
7432   Falle]Hym falle B.
7433   Oþerwhile]Somtyme B.
7434   ful]om B.
7436   þat]þe B.
7437   he... to]þat he gan B.
7438   vnro]travayle B.

Þat while coom philistiens in þore
Her feloun foos þat paynemes wore   7440
Her hoost in al þat cuntre spred
Þei wasted godes & awey led
Þei brouȝte wiþ hem goly an eteyn
Þat in foul hoordome was geteyn
Greet he was & also hy   7445
He semed sathanas vnsly
Bitwene his eȝen þre fote he hade
Loþely was his visage made
Of body greet & greynes long
Sternely semed he to be strong   7450
Sixe ellen fully he was in hiȝt
Al redy armed for to fiȝte
Of his mete was mesure noon
Seuen sheep he wolde ete his oon
// He seide where is saul kyng   7455
And I myȝte ones wiþ him myng
Shulde he neuer bere no croune
I wolde him sle by seynt mahoune
Why comeþ he not or sent his sonde   fol. 43r col. 2
Wiþ him I wolde my fors fonde   7460
Ouþer sende he to me hidur
A mon þat we may fiȝte togidur
Wheþer oþer ouercomeþ in felde
Þe toþers folke al to him helde
A mon of his aȝeyn oon of ouris   7465
If oure may wynne his in stouris
Þat þei be ouris & her heires

7439   while]tyme B. þore]þere B.
7440   Her... þat]þat his fone were and B.
7441   Her]þe B. þat]þe B. spred]sped L.
7442   led]lent L.
7443   goly]om B. an]& L.
7449   & greynes]of armys B.
7450   Sternely... he]He semyd well B.
7451   in]on B:
7452   Al]And B.
7454   his oon]alone B.
7455   kyng]þe king B.
7456   And]I wolde B.
7459   sent]sendiþ B.
7461   Ouþer]Or ellys B. he to]vnto B.
7462   A mon]Anon B.
7463   oþer]of vs B.
7464   toþers]toþer B. al]schall B. helde]yeld LB.
7465   aȝeyn]aȝens B.
7466   oure... in]ovres wyn may in any B.

If þei wynne ouris we be þeires
Here I byde myself redy
For to fiȝte for oure party   7470
Vche day [h]e come in place
And batail bede wiþ siche manace
Euer whenne þe folk him sawe
Hem stode þen of him ful greet awe

Allas seide saul þe kyng þan   7475
Where shal we fynde a man
Þat dar þe bataile for my sake
Aȝeyn þis þeof vndirtake
Whoso wolde fiȝte him aȝeyn
And him ouercome in bataile pleyn   7480
He shulde be ryche al his lyue
And haue my douȝter to his wyue

Dauid þis herde & forþ gan stonde
Sir he seide holde me couenonde
I trowe trewely in goddis myȝt   7485
Þat I shal vndirtake þat fiȝt
Aȝeyn goly þat is so grym
Wiþ goddis *grace* sle shal I hym
Aȝeyn þe ȝonder wrecched þing
Forsoþe haue I no drede sir kyng   7490
He tristeþ al in his owne hand
And I in ihesu al weldand
// To dauid seide saul þe kyng
I drede þerto þou art ful ȝyng
Hit is a stalworþe batail wriȝt   7495

7468   ouris]vs B. we]they L. be]ar B.
7471   he]we H.
7472   And]*om* L. bede]to byd L ; bade B.
7474   Hem]They L ; Off hym þey B. þen]*om* LB. of him]*om* B. ful]in L.
7475   þe kyng]*om* B.
7476   a]swich a B.
7478   þis]þe B.
7479   wolde]wille L.
7480   him ouercome]ouercome hym B.
7481   al]and all B. lyue]kyn B.
7484   couenond]comenond L.
7485   in]by L.
7486   *second* þat]þe T.
7487   Aȝeyn]Aȝens B. goly]Golias B.
7488   *grace...* I]help I schall sle B.
7489   Aȝeyn þe]Aȝens þat B. ȝonder]wond*ir* L. wrecched] cursyd B.
7491   owne]*om* B.
7492   ihesu]god TB.
7495   stalworþe]strong B.

And þou lernedest neuer to fiȝt
If he þe sle as god forbede
Alle most we holde of heþen lede
What bote to lese þi lyf leue page   fol. 43v col. 1
And aftir we do hem omage   7500
Do wey he seide sir hit is no nede
Þere god wol helpe þar no man drede
Vpon a day my sheep I gette
A bere a lyoun boþe I mette
I hadde no helpe but from aboue   7505
Of god þat lent me his loue
Þei souȝte me to rende & ryue
I leide hond on hem ful blyue
I shook hem by þe berdes so
Þat her chaules I wrast in two   7510
Wiþouten ouþer swerde or knyf
Boþe I refte hem hor lyf
He þat me þere þe maystrye ȝaue
May do me here hit to haue
Hit is not good leue sir kyng   7515
Þat mon in god haue mystrowyng
Go þenne he seide in goddis griþ
And god himseluen be þe wiþ
Gooþ he seide & feccheþ in hy
Myn armure to childe dauy   7520
Helme haburioun on him þei dyde
And girde him wiþ a swerd amyde
Whenne dauid was armed so
Forþ a fote myȝte he not go

7498   heþen] þe heþyn B.
7499   to]is to B. leue]om B.
7500   do]to L.
7502   þar]ther L; þere B. no man]is no B.
7503   gette]kept B.
7504   *first* A]And a B. *second* a]& a B. boþe]om B.
7505   no]none B.
7507   &]on L.
7508   hond]om B. ful]my handis B.
7510   chaules]chawis L; cheke bonys B. wrast in]brak on B.
7511   ouþer]any B.
7512   hor]of her B.
7513   þere]first L.
7514   hit to]þe maystry B.
7515   is]nys L. leue]to leue B.
7516   mon]non L.
7518   himseluen] of hevyn B.
7521   haburioun]havberk B.
7522   amyde]Imyd T; myd L.

Nouþer forþ ny ȝit on bake   7525
But stille stood as a stake
His armure fro him gon he swyng
And toke him but a staf slynge
Whiche he was wont to haue in honde
Aboute his flocke of sheep walkonde   7530
He took fyue stoonys rounde
And put in his scripp þat stounde
Do wey he seide þis oþere gere
For I kan noone armes bere
Wiþ my slynge I shal him felle   7535
Go we þider wiþouten dwelle
// Whenne dauid went forþ in route
He saw þe folk þat were in doute
To make hem in hope bolde   fol. 43v col. 2
Þis resoun he hem tolde   7540
Why shulde men ben adred
Þat are in riȝtwis batail sted
And who þat fiȝteþ in þe wronge
Hit helpeth not him ful longe
Nouþer may yren nor stele   7545
Were monnes wrongfulnesse wele
God is euer on riȝtwis syde
Werryng aȝeyn wrongwis pryde
Þerfore god wol for vs fiȝte   7550
Wel ȝe woot we haue þe riȝte   7549
He vs helpe of his grace
Wiþ þat he went into place

7525   ny]nor B. on bake]abak LB.
7526   stille stood]stode still B.
7527   swyng]swynk L.
7528   him]he L.
7529   Whiche]Whihe T.
7534   noone]no B.
7538   þat]om B.
7540   hem]to hem B.
7541   Why]While L.
7542   þat are]This is L; þat be B. riȝtwis]right B.
7543   And...þat]For whoso B.
7544   not]om B. ful]wel TL; not B.
7545   nor]ne L.
7546   monnes]was B.
7547   on]on the LB.
7548   wrongwis]wrong & LB.
7549-50   *reversed in* GHTLB.
7549   ȝe]he T. þe]om B.
7551   He]And he B.
7552   place]þe place B.

Whenne golias on him biheld
Litil he set bi him in feld
But helde hym al in despit   7555
And þus bigan him to flite
Sey wenesþou an hound I be
And wiþ þi stoon to stone me
Come forþ fast wiþouten abade
Þi flesshe shal foulis fode be made   7560
// Dauid seide if god wol nay
In god I haue fest al my fay
Armed comest þou me aȝeyn
And I aȝeyn þe al pleyn
I come aȝeyn þe in his name   7565
Þat þou hast don despite & shame
Hym hast þou & his in despit
Wiþ his grace I shal hit þe quyt
Þi body shal I ȝyue to ȝift
To ete þe foulis of þe lift   7570
Þat alle may wite þat god of myȝt
Saueþ not mon in wanhope piȝt
But fully to trowe in him stidfaste
And stabel in his lawe to laste
// Þenne seide goly þou art but dede   7575
Dauid seide god be my rede
Goly seide wolt þou fiȝte wiþ me
I rede bityme þou heþen fle
Fle þat weneþ haue þe werre   fol. 44r col. 1
For ar I fle I shal come nerre   7580

7555   But]And B.
7556   bigan]gan to B.
7557   Sey]He sayde B.
7558   þi stoon]þo stonys B.
7559   Come]He sayde com B. fast]om B. abade]bade B.
7561   nay]may B.
7562   god...haue]hym haue I B. al]om B.
7563   comest þou]comestou TB.
7564   And...þe]I come to þe aȝen B.
7566   despite]spite B.
7567   om B. & his]om L. hast þou]hastou T.
7568   hit]om L. hit þe]þe it B.
7569   ȝift]smyte B.
7570   first þe]to L. of þe lift]as they left L.
7571   of myȝt]almyght B.
7574   stabel]stably B.
7577   seide]he seid L. wolt þou]woltou TB.
7578   heþen]hennes TB. fle]om L.
7579   þat]he þat B. haue]to haue B.
7580   fle]wend L.

Anoon a stoon he leide in slynge
So myȝtyly he lete hit swynge
Þat in his frount þe stoon he fest
Þat boþe his yȝen out þei brest
Anoon he fel was no ferly   7585
And out his swerd drouȝe dauy
And heded him wiþ his owne brond
And brouȝte þe kyng to *pre*sond
Þo sarazines þere bisyde
Fledde alle & durst not abyde   7590
Þere were mony felde to grou*n*de
And mony fled wiþ deþes wou*n*de
// Dauid went hoom wiþ greet honoure
Alle þanked god her creatoure
Miche he was sooþ to say   7595
Loued and drad fro þat day
Pore and ryche ȝonge & olde
Loued him alle mony folde
To ierusalem þe heed bar þey
Þere dau*n*sed wy*m*men bi þe wey   7600
In her dau*n*se þis was þe song
Þat þei for ioye seide among
Saul haþ smyten a þousond
Ten þousond smyte*n* in dauid hond
For þis word was saul wrooþ   7605
And ofte boþe breme and looþ
Haue I a þousonde felde how so

7582   swynge]oute swyng B.
7584   þei]he L.
7585   no]none B.
7587   And]He B. heded]he did L.
7588   þe]it þe B.
7589   þere]þ*a*t were B.
7590   abyde]byde B.
7592   fled]fley TL.
7594   þanked]þankys B. creatoure]criat hono*ur* B.
7595   he was]was he B. sooþ]sone L.
7596   Loued]Leuyd L. fro]afftyr B.
7597   *first* and]*om* B.
7598   alle]þo B.
7599   To]þo to B.
7601   þe]her B.
7602   seide]made B.
7603   Saul]Kyng Saule B. smyten]slayne B.
7604   smyte*n*...dauid]slowe dauy wi*th* B.
7605   was saul]Saule was B.
7606   breme]grym L.
7607   how so]also L.

And dauid ten þousonde & mo
Bi þis is hym nouȝt wone
But þat he is not kyng allone   7610
For loos þat dauid won þat siþe
Wolde neuer saul loke on him bliþe   7612
He hated him as his foo   7615
Fro þenne he wayted him to slo
Ofte be þei quyt þis wyse
Þat done to liþer lord seruyse
Þat oþer day aftirwarde
Þe fend trauailed saul harde   7620
As he was wont bigon to rage   fol. 44r col. 2
And as dauid cam him to swage
Þe kyng smoot to him wiþ a spere
In tene he wolde him þourȝe bere
And þourȝe he had his body born   7625
Ne hadde he blenched him biforn
Away þoo drouȝe him soone dauy
But saul dredde hım not forþy
Of a þousande men bi tale
He made him ledere & marchale   7630
He þouȝte þus in his mood
Þat I him sle hit is not good
But I shal lete hym allone
Philistiens shul ben his bone
He asked dauid if he wolde   7635
His douȝter wedde to haue & holde
In þat couenaunt for to brynge
An hundride hedes to þe kynge
Of þat folk of heþen dede
Dauid went forþ good spede   7640

7612   neuer saul]Saule neuer B.
7613-4   om HTLB.
7617   Ofte]Ought L.
7618   liþer]þer L.
7619   þat oþer]þe toþir TLB.
7620   harde]had L.
7621   bigon]om B.
7622   as]om B.
7624   tene]tyme L.
7625   he...body]his body had he B.
7626   him]hem L.
7627   soone]om L.
7634   his]in his L.
7636   to]and B. &]in B.
7639   dede]lede TB
7640   good spede]in good speke L.

Wiþ þat folk soone he mett
And wiȝtly wan of hem þe bet
Aȝeyn þat hundride þat saul souȝt
Dauid to him þe double brouȝt
Þe kyng him ȝaf his douȝter anoon   7645
Þat het michol a fair wommon
Þe kingis sone het ionathas
To dauid trewe frend he was
Þe kyng bad whoso myȝt go
Dauid his sone in lawe to slo   7650
As his foo him to seche
Ionathas was not payed of þat speche
He preyed boþe day & nyȝt
To make þe kyng & david liȝt
Bifore þe kyng þei dauid brouȝt   7655
But aftir soone was al for nouȝt
Soone aftir batail roos
And dauid went aȝeyn his foos
Þis bataile was harde ynouȝe
And dauid of his foos fast slouȝe   7660
Mony a mon fel vndir sheeld   fol. 44v col. 1
But wiþ dauid lafte þe feld
And efte þe fend ful of greef
Trauailed þe kyng to myscheef
And dauid harped wiþ his harp   7665
Þe kyng hent a spere sharp
To smyte him þourȝe into þe wowȝe
Dauid blenched in litil þrowe
Into his hous þen dauid fled
But ar þe kyng wolde go to bed   7670
He sett his men þe hous aboute
To wayte at morwe when he coom oute
To sle him if he myȝte be mette

7642   And]A L. wiȝtly wan]smertly had B. bet]best L.
7643   Aȝeyn]Ayenst L. souȝt]besought B.
7645   him...douȝter]his doughtyr hym ȝafe B.
7648   frend]fend L.
7650   lawe]londe B.
7658   aȝeyn]aȝens B.
7660   And]om B. of]fast of B. fast]he B.
7661   fel]went B.
7662   lafte]lastyd B.
7666   hent]caught B.
7668   Dauid]Bote Dauid B. in]a B.
7669   his]an B. þen]om B.
7672   at]a B. morwe]morn TLB.

But his wyf by nyȝt him out lette
Out at a pryue posterne   7675
He fledde to samuel ful ȝerne
Þat in ramatha was dwellyng
Soone hit was tolde to þe kyng
Þenne his messangers he sende
To rauysshe dauid wel he wende   7680
But þerto myȝte þei neuer wyn
For company þat he was yn
And goddis grace þat him was wiþ
Saued him euer in good griþ
Among his kyn in pryuyte   7685
As outlawe þo woned he   7686
// Saul souȝte ofte here & þere   7689
Dauid as his foo he were   7690
He wiste if he to lyf myȝt stonde
He shulde be kyng of his londe
And þo childer of saules sede
Shulde be out dryuen for nede
Þerfore he hett hem ȝiftis ryf   7695
Þat myȝte brynge dauid of lyf
In felde & toun friþþe & felle
Saul souȝte dauid to quelle
Often fel so þe chaunce
Was þere but goddis desturbaunce   7700
Dauid þat was mylde of mood
Dide euer aȝeynes euel þe good
Ofte he myȝte saul haue take   fol. 44v col. 2
And slayn hym in his owne sake
For fro þe kyngis owne bed   7705
Þus he brouȝte a pryue wed
On a tyme whenne saul him souȝt
Wiþ al þe myȝte þat he mouȝt
He sett his tentis in a dale

7674   lette]gett B.
7678   to]om L.
7680   rauysshe]take B. wende]went LB.
7684   euer]om B.
7687-8   om HTLB.
7689   ofte]ought L; om B. þere]here B.
7694   for]of londe for B. nede]mede L.
7695   ȝiftis]richis L.
7696   þat]Thai L. of]on L.
7700   Was þere]þat þere was B. desturbaunce]troblance B.
7702   euerevr L. þe]om LB.
7703   Ofte]Ought L.
7705   For]om B.

Þerof to dauid coom þe tale 7710
Whenne hit was nyȝt cald dauy
Of his men ful pryuely
Wiþ him allone stille þei went
To þe kyngis owne tent
Hymself & his folk þei fonde 7715
In her beddes fast sleponde
Þe squyere hiȝt Abisay
Þat to þe tent coom wiþ dauy
Sir he seide bi leue of ȝow
I shal hym sle liȝtly now 7720
Þourȝe his body I shal him smyte
Þat euer of hym shul we be quyte
Dauid seide god hit forbede
Þe to þenke to do þat dede
Or euer him do despite or shame 7725
Þat noyntide is in goddis name
Of al þat ilke kyngis gere
He took but a coupe & spere
No more brouȝte he wiþ him oute
Whenne alle slepte him aboute 7730
He ȝeode til noon myȝte him dere
Þus he cryed to þat here
How haue ȝe kepte ȝoure kyng seide he
His coupe his spere where may hit be
Þat boþe were set at his heued 7735
Where be þei now bileued
Whenne saul herde þat cry
Is þat he seyde my sone dauy
Dauid seyde I was þore
Why sekest þou me & wherfore 7740

7710 to]*om* B.
7712 pryuely]*pr*euy B.
7715 þei]he B.
7716 her beddes]hys bed B.
7720 now]enow L.
7721 þourȝe]þorough oute B.
7722 þat]And B. shul we]we schall B.
7725 him...despite]do hym spyte B.
7726 noyntide...goddis]mayntenyth his gode B.
7728 spere]the spere L; a spere B.
7731 til]to B.
7734 hit]þay B.
7735 þat]þey B. heued]bed hede B.
7736 be]ar L.
7738 seyde]may B.
7740 sekest þou]sekestou TB.

Now þat þou be aknowen
Why sekest þou me & I am þyn owen
Saul seyde wiþouten wene   fol. 45r col. 1
Þe mys is myn wel is sene
Here I leue þe kyngis gleyue   ,7745
Sendeþ a man hit to receyue
He þat al riȝteþ wiþouten roos
Wol vche mon ȝelde aftir he doos
// Soone aftir not ful long
Coom batail vpon saul strong   7750
Þe saresines hym vmbeset
In harde shour togider þei met
So sharpe was þat shour & snel
Alle fled þe folk of israel
Þere þei fel þat myȝt not fle   7755
On þe mounte of gelboe
Þe douȝty childer þere were sleyn þan
Þe kyngis sones & Ionathan
Of þis batail þat was so snel
Þe wors on kyng saul fel   7760
Mony a goode archer þore
Woundide þe kyng himseluen soore
Þe kyng seide to his squyere
Drawe þi swerd & sle me here
Ar I in þis place be ouergone   7765
And wiþ sarazines hondis slone
Þe squyere dude not as he bad
For he was ful soore drad
Saul himself drouȝe his sworde
And ran euen vpon þe orde   7770
Whenne his squyere say him dede

7742   sekest þou]sekestou TB. &]om B. I]om TL.
7744   wel]wece L.
7745   leue]beleue B. gleyue]glebe L.
7748   vche mon]echon L.
7750   vpon]on B.
7751   hym]all hym B. vmbeset]were byset L; besett B.
7753   þat]þe B.
7757   þere were]was B.
7758   sones]son B. &]of L; om B.
7759   þis]þat B.
7760   on]om B. fel]befelle B.
7762   þe...soore]hymselffe þe king þore B.
7764   Drawe]Drawe oute B.
7766   sarazines]þe sarsyns B.
7768   drad]adrad B.
7770   euen vpon]hymselffe on B. orde]word L.

He dude himself þat same rede
Vpon his owne sword he ron
And dyȝed wiþ his lorde þon
A mournynge day most þat be 7775
Of saul & his sones þre
And his folke þat were so kene
Now are slayn alle bydene
// Þe sarazines on þat oþer day
Fond where saulis body lay 7780
Þe heed þei smoot of of þat kyng
And sende þe body for to hyng
His men coom bi nyȝturtale fol. 45r col. 2
Wiþ hem away his body stale
Pryuely þei dude hit hyde 7785
And dalf hit in a wode syde
Fourty wyntur was he kyng
Now haue ȝe herde his endyng
Þenne was dauid comen aȝayn
Fro amalec þat he had slayn 7790
Þat was a strong philistiene
Dauid had ȝyuen him batel kene
By goddes grace þe felde he wan
Of saul hoost he mett a man
Bifore dauid to fote he felle 7995
Whennes comes þou anoon þou telle
Fro þe folke of israele
I com to telle tiþingis lele
Þei are discoumfite in þat plas
Saul is slayn and Ionathas 7800
Ar þei boþe slayn wherby
Woost þou þat sayde dauy
Bi chaunce he seide I coom rennonde

7772   þat]þe B.
7776   his]of his B. sones]fois L.
7777   And]Alle B. so kene]token B.
7778   Now...slayn]Were þo slaw B.
7779   þat oþer]þe toþer B.
7781   þe]om L. of]om L.
7782   þe]hys B.
7784   his]þe B.
7790   had]om L.
7791   philistiene]philissiende L.
7793   By]With B.
7796   comes þou]comestou TB.
7798   tiþingis]tyþing B.
7800   is]om B.
7802   Woost þou]Wostou TB. þat]ought B.

On mou*n*te Gelboe & fonde
Saul lenynge on his spere   7805
Wou*n*dide wiþ þe sarsynes here
He me bisouȝte whe*n*ne I hi*m* sawe
Þat I shulde brynge hi*m* of dawe
Þourȝe his body my sword I reef
His hert in two I woot I cleef   7810
I wiste no lenger lyue he myȝt
Lo here his coroune briȝt
He wende wel for his tyþing
To haue payed dauid þe kyng
Þerwiþ payed he not dauy   7815
Þat shulde he soone dere aby
// Dauid for þis ilke disport
Was he neu*er* of wors cou*m*fort
He wrong his hondis & his me*n* alle
Þat goddes folk shulde so mysfalle   7820
Þei wept þ*a*t day til hit was goon
Þan spak dauid to þat mon
Why dreddest þou not god he seide   fol. 45v col. 1
Whenne þou hondis on saul leide
For to do despite or shome   7825
Þat noyntide was in goddes nome
Out of my siȝt ȝe lede hym soone
To deolful deeþ þat he be done
Þat fouler deþ may no mon dryue
So alle may knowe mon & wyue   7830
Þat whoso leiþ honḍ in felony

7805   lenynge]lying B.
7806   þe]þo TL. here]þere B.
7808   of]on B.
7809   þourȝe]þoroughoute B.
7810   His]And his B. I woot]*om* B. I]yt L.
7811   myȝt]ne myght B.
7814   payed]plesid L.
7815   payed]plesid L. payed he]he payed B.
7816   þat shulde]þerfore schull B. dere]*om* B.
7817   þis]þat B. ilke]ille TL.
7820   þat]For B. mysfalle]befall B.
7821   til]þ*a*t L. goon]don L.
7823   dreddest þou]dredystow B.
7824   þou]þy B.
7825   despite]hym spyte B.
7826   noyntide...in]was noyntyd on B.
7828   done]sone L.
7830   So alle]þ*a*t in B. mon]boþe man B.
7831   whoso]who B.

On kyng or seiþ him tricchery
Or ellis him waiteþ wiþ despite
And may not her of him quyte
By doom of fuyr wiþouten griþ   7835
He diȝe if he bitake þerwiþ
// Þe þridde elde now is past
Þerof þis saul was þe last
Þat elde bygan at abrahame
And endeþ here in goddes name   7840
Nyne hundride ȝeer fourty & two
Hit lasted hit is writen so
Foure þousande six skore & foure told
Was þis world þat tyme olde
Bytwene abraham & kyng dauy   7845
Herkene now þe genealogy
Abraham in lawe so lele
Þat fadir was of folk so fele
Ysaac his sone in spousaile was
Of him iacob of hym Iudas   7850
Of him phares of him Esrom
Vchone of þese of oþere coom
Of whiche aaron wiþouten gabbe
Of him coom amynadabbe
Of amynadab coom nason   7855
Of nason coom salmon
Of hym coom boz of him obeth
Of hym iesse þis elde is eth
Firste fro abraham to taste
And so to iesse þe laste   7860

7832   or...him]in any B.
7833   him]þat B. wiþ]in B.
7834   And]þat B. her...him]hym hereof B.
7835   By doom]Bodon B. griþ]grefe L.
7836   He diȝe]þe deþe B. þerwiþ]wiþ B.
7838   þis]om B.
7839   at]of L.
7841   ȝeer]om B.
7842   lasted]laste B.
7843   six]four B.
7844   þis]þe B.
7846   Herkene]Here B.
7847   so]to B.
7848   so]om B.
7850   iacob]com Iacob B.
7854   him]hem L.
7857   coom boz]cay boye L. obeth]com obeth B.
7858   is eth]seþe B.
7859   Firste]þe fyrst B. taste]cast B.

Here bigynneþ witterly
Þe ferþe elde at kyng dauy
Saul is slayn þat sorweful kyng   fol. 45v col. 2
In his stude dauid douȝty þing
Þei set a septure in his hond
Þat men calle þe kyngis wond
Alle honourid him wiþ hailsyng   7865
Heil be þou lord dauid oure kyng
Saf & sounde euer mot þou be
Whil þe folk is vndir þe
Dauid was a ful wyse mon
Riȝtwisly he regned þon   7870
Fro þat he was kyng in londe
Was noon durst his word wiþstonde
Fair a courte wiþ him he ledde
His folk boþe him loued & dredde
He nadde regned but a stounde   7875
Whenne he an hous bigon to founde
A myche tour longe & brade
In ierusalem he let be made
But þe [w]iliest of wynne
Ryuely ofte þei falle in synne   7880
Dauid þat many had in wone
Raft hym his wyf þat had but one
He hadde a douȝty knyȝt of fame
His wyf barsabe by name
Alas she was fair & briȝt   7885
Þe kyng cast ones on hir siȝt
He asked what was þat lady
ȝoure knyȝtis wyf þei seide vry

7860b   at]of LB.
7861   is]was B. sorweful]sory B.
7862   douȝty þing]kyng L. douȝty]is þat doghty B.
7866   lord]om B.
7867   mot]om B.
7869   ful wyse]rightwis B.
7870   Riȝtwisly]Riȝtfuly T; And rightwisly B. regned] resceyuyd L.
7872   durst...wiþstonde] þat durst in wer hym stonde B.
7873   a]om B.
7874   boþe him]hym boþe B.
7875   nadde]ne had L; had B.
7879   wiliest]viliest H.
7880   Ryuely ofte]Lyghtyly oft L; Ryvelyest B.
7881   þat...wone]his wifes had mane one B. in]& L.
7884   by]was her B.
7885   she]þat sche B. fair &]so B.
7886   ones]om B. siȝt]a syght B.
7888   þei seide]Syr B.

Þat vry þo was not þare
In kyngis hoost was he forþ fare   7890
Whil þis knyȝt was away
Þe kyng bi þat lady lay
Þe lady was wiþ childe in hye
Þe kyng sende þo to fette vrye
Whenne vry coom wiþouten wite   7895
Þe kyng lete soone lettris wryte
And toke hem vry for to bere þo
To his marchal of his hoost so
Wiþ biddyng he hym bisouȝt
Þat vrye þat þo lettres brouȝt   7900
Into bataile so shulde be led   fol. 46r col. 1
Þat he shulde soone be deed
Vrye þo lettres took & bare
But he wiste not what þei ware
Þe kyngis commaundement was done   7905
Slayn he was in bataile soone   7906
Whenne vry was þus brouȝte of lyue   7909
Dauid took barsabe to wyue   7910
And hulde hir in his hous fro þan
Til oure lord seide to natan
Go to dauid kyng an say
He haþ mysdone aȝeyn my lay
Þenne coom þat prophete to þe kyng   7915
And seide him þis in tokenyng
Tweye men were late in londe

7889   þo...not]was not þo B.
7890   In]*With* þe B. was...forþ]he was B.
7892   þat]þe B.
7893   wiþ]þo wiþ B.
7894   fette]seke B.
7896   lete soone]sone lett B.
7897   for]*om* B.
7898   his]þe B. so]þo T.
7899   *om* B.
7900   *After* l. 7900, *an extra line appears in* B: Schuld be slayne & lettyd noght B.
7901   so]*om* B.
7903   þo]þe B.
7906   he was]was he B.
7907-8   *om* HTLB.
7909   was þus]þus was L. of]on B.
7911   hous]hond L. fro]to B. hulde]held TLB.
7912   Til]þat B.
7914   aȝeyn]aȝens B. my]the L.
7915   þat]þe B.
7916   þis]þus L. in tokenyng]typing B.

A pore & a ryche wononde
[Pe] riche hadde mychel fe
Of alle godis greet plente   7920
Of welþe he hadde myche wone
Þe pore hadde no sheep but one
Þat he had wiþ his siluer bouȝt
And fro a lamb hit vp brouȝt
Þe riche man wiþ euel hert   7925
To a gest coom ouerþwert
For to spare his owne auȝt
Þe pore monnes sheep he lauȝt
To his mete dide hit be slone
Of his þat nadde but þat one   7930
Þe man þat haþ done siche dede
Sir kyng what shulde be his mede
Of þis tale þe kyng was wrooþ
By god on lyue he sweer his ooþ
Þat man he seide is ful of quede   7935
And shal by riȝte suffere dede
Sone he seide take good gome
ȝyuen þou hast þyn owne doome
God made þe kyng of israel
To lede þe folk in lawes wel   7940
Þou shuldest han holde þe lawe in stede
And hast broken þe lawe þat he forbede
Slayn þou hast þi knyȝt vry   fol. 46r col. 2
And taken his wyf & layn hir by
Of god himself stood þou noon awe   7945
Þerfore I coom þe to shawe
Þat þi hous he sendeþ þe word
Shal neuer twynned be fro sword

7918   pore]riche B. ryche]pore B.
7919   þe]om H.
7921   welþe]sheep TLB.
7924   fro]fre B. vp]out L.
7928   monnes]mennys L. lauȝt]caght B.
7930   nadde]ne had L; had B. þat]om B.
7931   siche]þis B.
7932   shulde]schall B.
7933   Of...kyng]þe king with þis tale B.
7934   on lyue]alyve L. sweer]swore L.
7936   And shal]Schuld B.
7940   folk in]folkes in his B.
7943   þi]þat B.
7944   &...by]in avowtry B.
7945   þou]þe B.
7946   þe...shawe]to do þe knawe B.

Reyse euel he shal on þe ful kene
And þus he seiþ þe bidene   7950
Þi wyues þat þou hast alle
Be ȝyuen to oþere men shalle
Þi synne þat þou in priuyte did
Byfore folk hit shal be kid
Synned I haue seide dauid þan   7955
Þat is sooþ seide nathan
Þerfore shal þou not dyȝe I wate
For god haþ het þe transolate
Þou shalt wite I shal not lye
Þe sone of barsabe shal dye   7960
Dauid gat ȝit a son þonne
Þat wyse was & het salomonne
Whenne dauid knewe his cost of care
Rewed him neuer þing so sare
In tokene þat he rewed his sake   7965
An orisoun soone gon he make
Þat het miserere mei deus
Hem owe to say hit þat synnes rewes
Of alle þe salmes of þe sautere
Þis salme for penaunce haþ no pere   7970

Dauid regned kyng þore   7973
Wyntres twelue or ellis more
Not wiþouten stryf & fiȝt   7975
ȝitt helde he wel his owne riȝt
Oure lord hym shewed a siȝt to say
A nyȝt as he in bed lay
He þouȝte on þe philistiens
Þat had hym done mony tenes   7980
Þat souȝte his folke to brynge to grounde
Gladly wolde he hem confounde
To make hem sore for him to gryse

7950   And]*om* B.
7953   þi]þe B.
7956   nathan]þan nathan B.
7957   shal þou]I schall B.
7958   haþ het]had yt L. het þe]sent me B.
7961   ȝit]on her B. þonne]*om* B.
7962   wyse]*om* L.
7963   cost of]syn & B.
7966   An]In an L. soone]*om* B.
7968   synnes]syn B.
7969   salmes]phalmus L. of]in B.
7971-2   *om* FGHTLB.
7977   hym shewed]schewyd hym B.

He him biþouȝte on what wyse
He him bitauȝte to god to kepe   7985 fol. 46v col. 1
Blessed him & fel on slepe
Þenne coom an aungel clere
Was goddes owne messangere
And louesomly to dauid spake
Of sleep dauid now I þe wake   7990
Comen am I þe to counsaile
Folewe hit & hit shal þe availe
Sir god þe chees kyng of kiþ
His hert haþ euer ben þe wiþ
He biddeþ þe wende anoone   7995
Þat þou passe flum iurdone
Into þat ilke stide þou pase
Where moyses hym doluen wase
Þe stide woot no mon but himselue
Oure lord þat þere hym gon delue   8000
A relyk shal þou fynde þere dere
In al þe world is not þe pere
Bitwene erþe and þe lift
May no man ȝyue a riccher ȝifte
Þou shalt fynde þre ȝerdes þere   8005
Þat moyses ofte wiþ hem bere
Of cyder palme & of cypres
Þere were þei sett by moyses
Out of a stide þat hett helym
Þider brouȝte he hem wiþ him   8010

7984   him]hem L.
7985   him]hem L. *first to]om* TLB.
7986   Blessed]And blissyd B. &]that L.
7987   clere]dere B.
7988   Was]þat was B. owne]om B.
7989   louesomly]louely B.
7991   Comen...I]I am come B.
7992   shal]may B.
7994   hert]will B.
7995   wende]þat þow wende B.
7996   flum]þe flom B.
7998   Where]þere B. hym doluen]bedoluyn B.
7999   but]bun T.
8001   shal þou]schaltow B.
8002   not]none B.
8003   Bitwene]Betwix þe B.
8004   ȝyue] fynde B.
8005   þre]þe B.
8006   hem]him TLB.
8007   *second* of]om B.
8010   hem]home L.

Is no mon forsoþe con say
Of how greet vertu & grace are þay
No mannes tunge may telle ny mele
What þei shul bere of soulis hele
Of hem shalt þou haue greet vauntage   8015
To þe and to þi baronage
Whoso resteþ him vndir þat shadowe
May no þing him cumber nowe
Haue good day now wende I
Geder þyn hoost togider in hy   8020
// Whenne dauid had þis counsel herde
To geder his hoost soone he ferde
He past þe flum his hoost him wiþ
And wenten hem þourȝe felde & friþ
Til he was comen into þat place   8025 fol. 46v col. 2
Þat him was beden go to bi grace
He fonde þe ȝerdes þo he coom þere
Eth was to know whiche þei were
He knew hem at þe firste siȝt
Þe þre were alle of oon hiȝt   8030
Of o likenes þouȝe þei were sere
Passed was a þousande ȝere
Siþ þei were set in þat place
And euer grene in goddis grace
Togider þei were in grounde knytt   8035
On o stok þe soþe is hit
Þe stok was on þat þo stode vndir
But þe croppes were alle sondir

8011   Is]þere is B.
8012   how]whome L.
8013   mannes]manere B.
8014   of soulis]for manys B.
8015   shalt þou]schaltow B.
8017   him]om B. þat]þe B.
8018   May]May hym B. him]hem L; om B.
8020   in]om T.
8024   þourȝe]þurghoute B.
8025   into]to B.
8026   þat him]þere he B. go]om B.
8027   þo]whan LB.
8028   Eth]Eche L. Ech...know]He knew anon B.
8030   þre]ȝerdys B.
8031   þouȝe]ȝef B.
8032   a þousande]many a B.
8034   grene]grew L.
8037   þo]þey B. vndir]on þere B.
8038   sondir]on sonder B.

By fruyt & leef myȝt men se
Of what kynde was vche tre   8040
Whenne þe kyng coom nyȝe þo trees
He kist hem crepyng on his knees
He drouȝe hem vp softe ynouȝe
Wiþouten brekyng any bouȝe
Whenne þe kyng had hem vp twiȝt   8045
His hoost honoured hem wiþ riȝt
Þe kyng held hem vp to se
A leem shone of þo ȝerdis þre
Þat al his hoost myȝt se euene
How hit rauȝt vp to heuene   8050
Þenne bicoom þat folke ful blyþe
For fond þei neuer fro þat siþe
Mon nor beest þat þei met
Þat myȝte hem of her weye let

A riche man woned bi her wey   8055
Was seke & to him turned þey
He hadde ben seke mony a day
Wiþouten helpe of hele he lay
His folk wiþouten stille abade
To se þat seke a turne he made   8060
I[n] sekenes sore he fond him stad
Of þe kyng he was ful glad
Whenne he bigon þo ȝerdis to se
On hem he wept for greet pite
Þenne was he hool & sounde in hye   8065 fol. 47r col. 1
Þe swote smel rauȝte to þe skye
Wiþ þe kyng he ȝeode away

8039   By...&]þere þe B. &]of L. men]ech man B.
8040   vche]þe B.
8041   nyȝe]nere B. þo]the LB.
8043   softe]sought L.
8044   any]of eny LB.
8048   A leem]þe light B. of þo]on þe B.
8051   þat]þe B.
8053   nor]ne L.
8055   woned]was B. her]þe B.
8056   Was]þat was B. &]om B.
8059   abade]he bade B.
8060   se þat]þe B.
8061   In]I H.
8063   þo]þe B.
8064   On]Of B. wept]wepe B.
8065   sounde]saue B
8066   rauȝte]laft B.
8067   away]on way B.

And tauȝte hem god & good day
Faire was þat processioun
Þere was many a bolde baroun 8070
As þei wente þe hyȝe strete
Sarazines foure þe kyng can mete
Blak & blo as leed þei were
Miche richesse wiþ hem þei bere
Men say neuer bifore þat houre 8075
So frowarde shapen creatoure
Of her blac hewe was selcouþe
In her brestis þei bare her mouþe
Longe & syde her browes weren
And rauȝt al aboute her eren 8080
In her forhede was her siȝt 8083
Loke myȝt þei not vpriȝt
Her armes hery wiþ blak hyde 8085
Her elbowes were set in her syde
Crompled knees & bouche on bak
Þe kyng wondride on hem & spak
Whenne hem bihelde þe kyngis oost
Þei lowȝen alle leste and moost 8090
On her knees þei hem sett
And hendely þe kyng þei gret
To þe kyng seide þay
Saaf be þou sir now & ay
What þou berest lat vs se 8095
To fonde if goddis wille hit be
Shewe vs þe sauyng tre sir kyng
For wel woot we wiþouten lesyng
Peyne on þat tre suffere he shal
Þe kyng of blis for his folk al 8100
Shewe vs þe tre out of were

8071　þe hyȝe]be þe B.
8072　can]gon TLB.
8074　richesse]riches TL.
8076　So]Iso H. frowarde]loþely B. creatoure]a creatur L.
8077　was]þey were B.
8081-2　*om* HTLB.
8084　not vpriȝt]but forþer right B.
8086　in]on B.
8087　bouche]bunche L.
8088　on...&]& to hem B.
8094　Saaf]Sauyd B. þou]ȝow B. sir]*om* LB. now]now ser L.
8095　þou]ȝe B.
8096　goddis wille]his goddis B.
8098　woot we]we wote B. we]ye L.

Þerfore are we comen here
Byholden vs ynouӡe hastou
Oure froward shap þou seest now
Ful loþely are we but also looþe   8105
Is euel mannes soule & body boþe
Þes ӡerdes þre wiþynne her roote   fol. 47r col. 2
Aӡeyne alle eueles are bote
Þei shul vs ӡelde bifore þi siӡt
Feirenes bi grace of god almyӡt   8110
Of hem shal ryse oure raunsoun
And of alle oure synnes pardoun
To hem þat mercy for her synne
Cryeþ to ihesu of dauid kynne
Þe myӡte of hem sir lete vs proue   8115
Wiþ þat þe kyng took of his gloue
Þo braunchis of so mychel blis
He helde hem to hem for to kis
Þei kneled & kist hem also tite
Als soone her hyde bicoom white   8120
And of þe fre blood had þei þe hew
Al her shap was turned new
Of mankynde hadde þei þe met
In riӡt kynde were þei set
Bifore þe kyng þenne fel þei doun   8125
And maden vchone her orisoun
Þei wepte & þanked god of myӡt   8128
Al þat folk þat say þat siӡt   8127
Þe richesse þat þei wiþ hem ladde
Þei offered þat þat þei hadde   8130

8102   are]be B.
8103   ynouӡe]myght L; þorough B.
8104   þou seest]se ӡe B.
8105   also]all to B.
8106   soule]sone T.
8107   her]one B.
8108   Aӡeyne]Aӡens B. eueles]euil B.
8109   þi]the L.
8113   To...þat]Tho þat call L.
8114   Cryeþ]Or cry L; Comeþ B. ihesu]þat lorde B. kynne]kyng L.
8115   hem]god B.
8117   so]om B.
8118   hem for]þo men B.
8120   hyde]hede B.
8123   þe]om B.
8127-8   in reverse order in HTLB.
8127   þat]the L.
8128   of]alle L. of myӡt]almyght B.
8130   first þat] om L; þere B.

Hemself aȝeyn þei toke þe sty
And wenten hoom to ethyopy

Þe kyng went forþ þourȝ a feld
Toward a felle bi a doun helde
An heremite þer fond þei at hoome   8135
In þat mounteyne was halt & lome
Mychel had he vnhele
Thritty ȝeer had ben mesele
Ouer al his body was he sore
Þerfore he lyued his one þore   8140
Of grete londes had he lord bene
But alle he lafte hem in þat tene
And for hardenes of his vnhele
He ȝaf him al wiþ god to dele
And for to ende in his seruyse   8145
Þe nyȝte toforn of paradyse
Him þouȝte he was euen þerby   fol. 47v col. 1
And þat þe good kyng dauy
Wesshe wiþ a wande his body clene
Þat no sekenes was on hym sene   8150
Suche was þe sweuene þat him þouȝt
But of þo branchis wiste he nouȝt
Þat þei hem had souȝte & founde
And brouȝt to cuntre þat stounde
He wook & þouȝte on þat siȝt   8155
And seide lord god of myȝt
Why ne were I as hool & fere
As me þouȝt riȝt nowe here
Vnneþe had he mened his mood
A leem from þo ȝerdis stood   8160
Riȝt into þe ermytage

8131   þei]om B. þe]to L.
8133   forþ]doun B.
8134   felle]hill B.
8135   þer]þay B. þei]þere B.
8138   ȝeer]wynter B.
8139   Ouer]On B. was he]he was B.
8140   lyued]louyd L. lyued...þore]is lafft þere allone B.
8142   he]is B. tene]teme L.
8143   vnhele]vnselle B.
8150   sekenes...hym] filþe þeron was B.
8152   þo]the L.
8156   of myȝt]allmyght B.
8157   I as]om B. & fere]as fyre L.
8159   mened]nemyd L.
8160   þo]þe B.

Þe kyng coom & his barnage
Whenne þei mett wiþ þat hermyte
Þei heilsed hym wiþ greet delite   8164
Whenne þat he þe kyng had knowen   8167
He seide welcome to ȝoure owen
Bi þese sir kyng I mysele
Shal be saaf of al vnhele   8170
Me þouȝte tonyȝte on þis wyse
Þat we were boþe in paradise
And þat þou wiþ þo wandes wesshe
Al þe vnhele of my flesshe
As any fisshe þou mades me fere   8175
Wiþ þese ȝerdes þou berest here
He kissed þo ȝerdes knelynge þere
Was he neuer holer ere
Þe kyng þat kynde was in coost
Ladde him forþ wiþ his hoost   8180
And al his lyf did wiþ him lende
To þe kyng was he ful hende
Knyȝte he was myche of prys
Þe kyng hym quyt wel his seruys
Forþ went þe kyng soone þan   8185
Til he coom to flom iurdan
He took þe ȝerdis in his honde
Þe streem stille bigan to stonde
Hit stode þe folk on eyþer syde   fol. 47v col. 2
Þe kyngis passage for to abyde   8190
Whenne þei were passed ouer þe stronde
And comen into þe toþer londe
Wite ȝe wel þei were ful glad
To þe folke þe kyng þen bad

8162   &]in L.
8164   heilsed]hayled B.
8165-6 om HTLB.
8167   þe]om T.
8169   þese]þe T; this LB.
8170   Shal]I schall B. be]om L. vnhele]vnsell B.
8172   we]om L.
8174   of]fro B.
8175   As...fisshe]Of all filþ B.
8177   þo]þe B.
8179   kynde]kyd L. kynde was] was kinde B.
8182   was he]he was B.
8187   þe]þo T.
8188   streem]stremys L.
8190   abyde]byde B.
8191   ouer]on L.
8192   And comen]þei coom T.

Vchon to sett her pauyloun   8195
As for þat nyȝt wiþouten þe toun
And on þe morwe whenne þei shul so
Into ierusalem þenne go
Þo ȝerdis wolde he sette in warde
Wiþinne his owne orcharde   8200
Þat while wolde he make hym boun
To ordeyne faire processioun
Þe nyȝte þei rested in þat slade
And of þo ȝerdis greet ioye made
Þe kyng aboute hem was ȝerne   8205
He put hem into a cisterne
And dude bisyde hem laumpes liȝt
And made men wake hem al nyȝt
Þenne went þe kyng for to slepe
But god þat al haþ to kepe   8210
And al ouerlokeþ in his siȝt
His wille to lette haþ noon myȝt
Is no þing þat may forbarre
His wille bifore hit is so warre
He þat so myȝty is and wyse   8215
He dide þo ȝerdis for to ryse
In þat cisterne þe rotis honeste
Togider grewen & were feste
Myȝt no man hem atwynne wynne
Wiþouten brekynge for no gynne   8220
// Whenne dauid say noon oþere bote
But alle þo ȝerdis hadden o rote
Þat fastened were in erþe so faste

8197   morwe]morne TLB. whenne]om L. shul]schuld B.
8198   þenne]for to B.
8199   þo]þe B.
8203   rested...þat]rist doun þe B.
8204   þo]þe B.
8206   a]om B.
8208   nyȝt]þat night B.
8210   al haþ]hathe all B.
8211   ouerlokeþ]oþer lokeþ B.
8212   His]And L.
8213   no]non B. may]my B.
8214   hit]he B.
8216   þo]þe B.
8218   grewen]growyn B.
8219   atwynne wynne]take on twyn B.
8220   no]non B.
8222   þo]þe B.
8223   erþe]þe erþe B.

In his hert he was agast
And seide al nacyoun and lede   8225
Oweþ oure good lord to drede
Miȝtful is he & þat is skil
Of vche dede to done his wil
Þe kyng seide no man hem ster   fol. 48r col. 1
Fro henne siþ god sett hem þer   8230
Þe kyng made to kepe þat syde
To make þe orcharde more wyde
A wal dide he aboute hit reise
And plauntide trees þat were to preyse
Of cidre palme and of lorere   8235
Þat ȝerde shulde be hymseluen dere
Oþer riche trees he souȝt
In mony stedes and þider brouȝt
Alle fruytes he plauntide in þat place
For his walkyng and his solace   8240
Whenne hit was cloos aboute þat tre
A cercle of siluer nayled he
For to knowe bi þat strengþe
What he wexe in greet & lengþe
Suche cercles made he sere   8245
Thritty wyntir vche a ȝere
He dide oon on as I ȝow say
Euer whenne he took anoþer way
Pritty wyntir wex þat tre
Þat hit was selcouþe for to se   8250
Of cercles þat he tooke away
Offrynge he made to mone on ay
Hit was so charged vche a bowe

8225   nacyoun]nacions B.
8226   good lord]god for B.
8227   Miȝtful]Mochell B. þat]yt L.
8230   henne]hennes T; heuyn LB. god]þat god B. þer]her LB.
8232   To]And L.
8235   *second* of]om B.
8236   shulde]schull B.
8238   stedes]a stede B.
8241   cloos]closyd B.
8242   nayled]naylyd þere B.
8243   þat]þe B.
8244   he wexe]it grew B. greet]brede B.
8246   vche a]euery B.
8247   oon on]an oon L; one þere B.
8248   way]away TB.
8250   þat]om L. selcouþe]wondyr B.
8251   Of]þe B.
8252   mone] many L.

Wiþ leef flour & fruyt ynowe
Alle seide þat hit say lasse & mare   8255
Was neuer tre siche blossum bare
Anoþer tre of siche kynde
Myȝte no man in worlde fynde
Of worshepe was þis tre to wondir
Þe kyng ofte kneled þervndir   8260
In bedes þat he had to say
Knelyng he þervndir lay
Whenne he had made his orisoun
Vndir þat tre he sette him doun
And þouȝte vpon mony a þinge   8265
As he þat was a greet lordynge
A temple he þouȝte þenne to make
To goddis worshepe & for his sake
Bisily he him biþouȝte   fol. 48r col. 2
How þis tempel shulde be wrouȝt   8270
To kepe in his relikes þan
And saue hem in his kyndam
Þe holy arke þat þei bare
Aboute wiþ al her holy ware
Oon was þe tables tweyn   8275
Þat þe ten commaundementis were In
Þat god wroot his owne honde
And þerinne was aarons wonde
Þat bar fruyt þo hit was drye
And als of manna sum partye   8280
Þe gilden oyle of þe propiciatory
To cherubins as seiþ þe story
Þese þingis þat I telle here
Þe kyng hem helde tresour dere

8254   leef flour]leuys flourys B.
8257   kynde]a kynde B.
8258   worlde]þe worlde B.
8259   Of]In L. þis]the L; þat B. to]om L.
8262   he þervndir] þerevndyr he B.
8264   þat]þe B.
8267   þenne]for B.
8270   þis]þe B.
8272   And]To B.
8275   þe]þo T; of þo B. tweyn]twyn TL.
8277   his]with his B.
8279   þo]to L; when B. drye]dight LB.
8280   als of]also B.
8281   gilden]Eyldyn L.
8282   cherubins]cherubin B.
8284   hem helde]held as B.

Herfore þouȝte dauid kyng   8285
To make hem a riche wonyng
Vndir þis tre þat I of sey
A stapul was of marbul grey
And as he þouȝte what was to done
An auɳgel coom from heueɳ soone   8290
On a bouȝe he made his sete
Of þat tre þat was so swete
For wiþ þat flour þat was so newe
Þer stood a selcouþe louely hewe
Þis aungel þat so briȝt shone   8295
Spak to þe kyng þere allone
And seide god þe loke sir kyng
Wel I woot al þi ȝernyng
Þi wille is worshepe for to wirche
To god himself [a] crafty chirche   8300
But þou shalt wite on what wyse
Þat þis werke owe to ryse
God wol not þiself hit make
Of þi hondis he wol not take
Siche a werke hit were vnriȝt   8305
For werriour art þou ful wiȝt
And many hast slayn wiþ þi hond
But þou shalt ellis vndirstonde
Al may hit not bi þe be done   fol. 48v col. 1
Ende hit shal þi sone salamone   8310
Þou shalt ordeyne hit in þouȝt
By salamon hit shal be wrouȝt
He shal be a man of peese
And mychel haue worldes ese
He shal be kyng aftir þi day   8315
Þis is sooþ þat I þe say

8285   kyng]þe king B.
8288   stapul]stabyll L.
8289   what]om L.
8290   soone]trone TL.
8291   bouȝe]bowght L.
8293   was]stodeB.
8295   þat]þat þere B.
8296   allone]anone B.
8300   a]& H.
8301   But]om B.
8303   make]made L.
8305   hit...vnriȝt]of þe full right B.
8306   art þou]ertow B.
8307   hast]hastow B.
8311   þouȝt]thy thoght L.
8316   þat]as B.

In reste & pees regne shal he
Þe temple by hym made shal be
He shal haue wite riches & cele
To reule al his kyndom wele   8320
Hit shal be preciouse & ful proude
Þe werke he shal so semely shroude
Relikes shul þereynne be loken
Þat euermore shul of be spoken
Bytwene þis & þe worldes ende   8325
Haue good day now I wende
Dauid vndirstode þis skil
To leue his dede had he no wil
Fully he þouȝte to do so
As þe aungel seide him to   8330
Þe kyng to his chaumber went
And soone aftir þe queen he sent
For of his lawes þis was oon
Of al his baronage was þer noon
Mon nor womman ȝonge nor olde   8335
Þat in his chaumber was so bolde
O foot to sette but þei were calde
When þe kyng speke wiþ him walde
Ny not þe queen wiþouten leue   8340
Ny noon oþer wiþouten greue   8339
Þerfore entrede bersabe
Þe queen his spouse & his priue
Þe kyng þat he in hert had hid
To þe queen he vndid
But neuerþeles tolde he nouȝt   8345
Þe bodeword þat þe aungel brouȝt
But elles wisely & ful shert
He tolde as hym lay on hert

8318   þe]That L.
8319   wite]*with* L. riches]richesse T.
8321   ful]*om* B.
8324   þat]And L. euermore]euer B. of]þerof B.
8326   I]will I B.
8327   vnderstode]vndirstonde H.
8334   al]*om* B.
8335   *first* nor]ny T; ne B.
8336   þat]*om* B.
8337   O]One B. þei]he B.
8338   speke...him]*with* hym speke B.
8339-40   *reversed in* MSS HTLB.
8344   vndid]it vndid B.
8348   as hym]þat B. on]in his B.

Dame I dud þe hidur calle   fol. 48v col. 2
As for my weddide wyf of alle   8350
In elde am I waxen now
Of my kyndam what redes þow
To whom shal I hit ȝyue to lede
Me to turne to menske & mede
Þat lady to hir lorde dide loute   8355
Wiþ buxom reuerence and doute
She kneled aftir she had stonde
Þe kyng took hir vp bi þe honde
As he þat of hir counsel wolde wite
And boþe dud hem doun to sitte   8360
He bad hir say & lett nouȝt
What were best as he[r] þouȝt
Of his kyndam þat was to say
Who shulde hit haue aftir his day
// Sir she seide now I se   8365
Þat ȝe wole counsel haue of me
Gladly wolde I if I couþe   8368
Þe beste shewe ȝow wiþ mouþe   8367
Þe kyndam sir þat is þyn
Þou hit wan wiþ myche pyn   8370
Also þou haddest greet malese
For to stabel hit in pese
Sir she seide ȝe haue in lyues
Mony children wiþ ȝoure wyues
Þat desiren now in stryf   8375
To haue þe kyndam in ȝoure lyf
Þou frely kyng ful of blis
Þe beste red me þinke is þis

8349   þe]ȝow B.
8351   am I]I am B.
8352   redes þow]redestow B.
8353   hit ȝyue]ȝyue hit TB. to]to do B.
8354   Me...to]God to worschip & me B.
8355   þat]þe B. dide]gan B.
8359   þat]om B.
8360   dud]þay sett B.
8362   were]was L. her]he H; sche B.
8365   I se]is he L.
8366   wole counsel]counsayle wold B.
8367-8   reversed in HTLB.
8371   haddest]holdyst L.
8374   wiþ]be B.
8376   To]Now to L. þe]om L. in]be B.
8377   frely]fre L.
8378   is þis]yt is L.

ȝe ȝyue hit to whom ȝe wol
My grau*n*te shul ȝe haue fol   8380
I þat am þyn owne wo*m*mon
Aȝeynsawe wol I make noon
For salamon my sone is ȝing
But myȝte ȝe mone vpon sir kyng
Wel ȝe woot ȝe me hiȝt   8385
Ar ȝe to spouse me trouþ pliȝt
A sone if ȝe myȝt gete wiþ me
ȝoure heire forsoþe shulde he be
And siþ so is I haue me kept   fol. 49r col. 1
Þat neu*er* oþ*er* siþen wiþ me slept   8390
But oon bifore oþ*er*e had I nouȝt
For ȝoure loue was I widewe wrouȝt
On what wise þar me not tel
Wel ȝe woot how hit bifel
Blessed be god of myȝt   8395
Forȝyuen is ȝow þ*er*of þe pliȝt
I say not now so god me rede
For noon vmbreyd ny for mede
Ny for no desyre þat I haue
Ny couenau*n*t of ȝow to craue   8400
For nouþ*er* kepe I gabbe ny glose
To say þe soþe is my purpose
Þouȝe salomon my sone be ȝong
He is wyse and of redy tong
Þat neu*er* dide ne [d]isserued vileny   8405
And geten is wiþ þi body
He þat bett*er* con mende ny peyre
Best worþi is to be þyn heyre
Not forþy whom god wol chese

8380   fol]þertyll B.
8385   Wel]Will L. me hiȝt]due behight B.
8386   ȝe]þat B.
8387   wiþ]on B.
8388   he]yt B.
8390   siþen...me]wiþ me siþen T.
8391   oþere]ne B. had]huaue L.
8393   þar]dar L; nede B.
8394   Wel]Wille L.
8395   myȝt]his might B.
8398   vmbreyd]vnbraide L; vpbrayde B. mede]no mede B.
8399   for no]none B.
8400   Ny]Any TLB. couenau*n*t]couau*n*t B.
8403   þouȝe]ȝef B.
8405   disserued]sisserued H; desyryd B.
8406   is]he is TLB.
8407   bett*er*...mende]can bettyr mede B.

Aftir þi day kyng he bese 8410
Wiþ siche a knott þe queen him knytt
Þe kyng herkened wel hir witt
And curteysly as was to done
He grauntide hir al hir bone
// Dame he seide to þe I say 8415
Þat salomon aftir my day
Shal be kyng of þat I wan
If god wol þat hit be þan
He is not ȝitt but wondir ȝing
Sett hym faste to good teching 8420
Til he be lerned himself to lede
Boþe of clergye & knyȝthede
Lerne of clergye wel he shal
Of wisdome þat is groundwal
Þe childe is þewed & mylde of mode 8425
Loke þat he haue maister gode
But hit be on himseluen longe
He shal be boþe riche & stronge
Dame hele þis vpon þi lyf fol. 49r col. 2
For looþ me were to rere stryf 8430
Til we se þe tyme and day
He shal be kyng whoso saiþ nay
Þerto haue þou no mystrowe
Þerfore make I here þat avowe
Þis childe was soone set to boke 8435
Clergy wel he vndirtoke
Al his hert he ȝaf to lore
Myȝte noon loue clergy more
By grace of only god of heuen
Soone he couþe þe artes seuen 8440
Whenne he couþe of londis lawe

8411   queen]kyng LB. him]sche B.
8415   he]I L.
8419   is]nys L. not...but]bote ȝete B.
8421   be]haue L.
8422   of]in B. &]& in B.
8424   Of]þat of B. þat]om B. groundwal]ground of alle L.
8425   mylde of]of mylde B.
8426   maister]a maistir T; maystrys B.
8427   longe]along B.
8430   For]om B.
8432   whoso]who LB.
8433   þou no]I here non B.
8434   þerfore]þerto B. þat]om LB.
8436   vndirtoke]vndirstode L.
8439   only]holy B.

Þei made him kyng in litil þrawe
Was noon aȝeyn hit olde ne ȝinge
Þat salomon þenne was ma[d]e kynge
His fadir biddyng dide he holde   8445
And al þat euer his modir wolde
He helde þat tre dere and derne
Þat dauid kyng honoured ȝerne
Ofte vndir þat tre he sat
And lered mony selcouþe what   8450
For vndir þe shadowe of þat tre
Þe kynde of þingis lerned he
Boþe of trees & greses fele
Whiche were her vertues lele
For what euel vchone myȝ[t] geyn   8455
Wherso þei grewe in wode or pleyn
And wheþer þe medicyne & boote
Founden were in croppe & roote
Of lore þat he lerned vndir þat tre
He made goode bookis þre   8460
Douȝtily he hem vndid
Wiþ saumplis of trees & herbes amyd
Þe firste book wiþouten lees
Men calle ecclesiastises
Þat moost spekeþ & wol not wonde   8465
How fals þis world is to fonde
Of prouerbis is þe secounde booke
Þat techeþ aboute hem to loke
Aȝeynes þe worldes wrecched hede   fol. 49v col. 1
How þei shul hem reule and lede   8470
Þe þridde boke aftir two
Cantica men calleþ hit so
A noteful boke of holy writt

8442   litil]a B.
8443   aȝeyn]aȝens B.
8444   þenne]*om* B. made]make H.
8446   euer]*om* B.
8450   lered]lernyd L. mony]many a B.
8452   lerned]leryd B.
8455   myȝt]myȝ H.
8456   Wherso]Wheþer B.
8458   &]or TB.
8459   Of]Or L. *first* þat]*om* B. lerned]lered TB.
8462   saumplis]ensample B.
8464   calle]calliþ it B.
8465   wol...wonde]wel notande B.
8470   shul]schuld B. lede]rede L.
8471   two]þe two B.

Þe book of loue men clepeþ hit
Of þat loue hit spekeþ moost   8475
Bitwene monnes soule & þe holy goost
So crafty was no clerke to say
Fro þat tyme to þis day
Þat him myȝte wiþ clergy mate
Ne couþe þe bookis þat he wrate   8480
Whil he sat vndir þe bowȝe
Of al wisdam he hadde ynowȝe
// Studfaste stood þat marbul stoon
Ful fer þe golden lettres shoon
Þei seide sumtyme men shul se   8485
God himself regne in þat cuntre
Þat plaunted was bitwene þo flouris
Þere þe sternes helde her coures
Wel I woot neuer is hit wan
Of floure ne fruyt þat hit haþ tan   8490
And in his tyme siche fruyt shal ȝyue
Þat alle his frendis þerof shul lyue
Of þat fruyt shulde no mon byte
But he shulde loue hit also tyte
Þis writ wiþ fele was red & sene   8495
But fewe wiste what hit wolde mene
Bytwene þat he whom bare marye
Heng þeron his folke to bye
Bi barnetem of olde adame
Þourȝe a bite brouȝt alle in blame   8500
An appul bite boþe man & wyf

8474   clepeþ]calliþ B.
8476   Bitwene]Betwix B.
8479   him]he hym B.
8480   Ne couþe]Nor B.
8481   þe]þat B.
8484   þe golden]þo gold B.
8485   shul]shuld LB.
8486   regne]regnid L. cuntre]tre B.
8487   plaunted]paynted B. þo]þe B.
8488   sternes]stremys L; sernes B. coures]colourys B.
8492   shul]shulde T.
8493   shulde]shalle LB.
8494   shulde]schall B.
8495   þis]om B.
8496   what]that L.
8497-8 om L.
8497   he]tyme B.
8498   Heng]Hong B.
8499   Bi]The L; Be þe B. barnetem]barnten L.
8501   bite]boote B.

Þe tre was deþ þis shal be lyf
And writen is in parchemyn
Þat hit coom out of þat pepyn
Þe wrecched adam fel fro   8505
And brouȝte himself in mychel wo
For so bigan þe cros I wis
Of ihesu cryst kyng of blis

Now is good to go to oure style   fol. 49v col. 2
Þat we haue left of a whyle   8510
And turne to oure story aȝeyn
To make hit hool & certeyn
Dauid þat I red of here
Was kyng & regned fourty ȝere
His regnyng was of siche renoun   8515
His foos wiþ him hadde no foysoun
Childer by wyues had he sere
Of whiche I make no menyng here
For he þat myche haþ to telle
Þe shorter mot nede be his spelle   8520
Þis was þat kyng dauy
Þat myche spake of prophecy
Of cristis burþe long biforn
Þat shulde of a mayde be born
Whiche mayde of dauid sede   8525
Was aftir geten as we rede
As oure lord biforne him hiȝte
Of hym to sprynge alle þinge to riȝt
Þis dauid made þe sautere
Þat is rad boþe fer & nere   8530
Homer þe poete þat was so ryf
Lyued in þis kyng dauid lyf
And of affryk þe strong barnage
Dide make þe cite of cartage
Þat to rome was euer queed   8535

8502   þe]þat TLB. þis]om L; þis tre B.
8503   parchemyn]þerchemyns B.
8504   þat pepyn]þre peppyns B.
8506   And]om B.
8512   To]And B.
8515   regnyng]reigne B.
8516   foysoun]seson B.
8517   by...he]he had be his wifes B.
8518   I make]he makeþ B.
8520   mot]mor L.
8521   kyng] worþy king B.
8525   of]afftyr of B.
8535   euer]neuer L.

Siþ whenne þe kyng was deed
He bad his men þat he shulde ly
In bedleem his fadyr by

Aftir dauid deeþ salomone
Was kyng sittyng in his trone 8540
He was a boldly bachilere
In al þis world had he no pere
Of witt & wisdam as we rede
Was neuer a wyser lawe to lede
In bed he lay on a nyȝt 8545
Biforn him stood an aungel briȝt
And to him spak wiþ blisful chere
He seide I am a messangere
My lord haþ sende þe word by me fol. 5Or col. 1
To ȝyue þe choys of þingis þre 8550
Of strengþe riches and of witt
Chees whiche þou wolt & haue hit
If þou him serue wiþ hool hert
Of þre þou shalt haue oon in quert
// Salomon þis vndirstood 8555
Of þis message þouȝte him good
Witles he seide what is catele
Or what is strengþe wiþ to dele
Þat mon no witt haþ wiþ to lede
I ches me witt for greet nede 8560
I þonke him þat chois wolde me ȝyue
I shal hym serue whil I lyue
Wiþ al my myȝte & my wille
He ȝyue me grace hit to fulfille
To salomon seide þe aungel þo 8565

8538a   om CGHTLB.
8539   salomone]was Salamon B.
8540   Was]om B. kyng]the kyng L. his]om L.
8541   boldly]bodely L; bolde B.
8542   had...no]was non his B:
8543   &]of L.
8544   a...lawe]so wise a londe B.
8548   He...am]I am he sayde B.
8549   þe]me T. me]þe T.
8551   riches]richesse T. and]or B.
8553   If]yeve L.
8554   þre]þre þingis B.
8559   no]þat B. wiþ]for B.
8561   chois]me choys B. me]om B.
8562   serue]thanck L.
8563   myȝte]witt B. &]& al TLB.
8564   hit to]to yt L.

In chois hastou wisely go
And for þou wel hast chosen oon
Þou shalt haue hem euerychon
Þou shal be ful war in dede
Alle folk shal þe drede   8570
And drednes shal þou haue of [n]on
Of riches shal þou haue greet won
// Þus regned salmon wiþ þis
In myche ioye & mychel blis
He loued þe folk of his kyngdome   8575
And þei hym alle chylde & mon
Alle þat aȝeyn him dud males
Wiþ wisdome he hem toke to pes
Al þat his fadir myȝt nouȝt
Salamon to ende hit brouȝt   8580
Ierusalem loued he moost of alle
Þere was he sett in kyngis halle

In his kyngdome þe forme dawes
Among his folk he set his lawes
And did hem streitly to ȝeme   8585
Miȝte no man more riȝtly deme
Among his riȝtwis domes ryf
Here how he felde a stryf
Mister wymmen were þer twynne   fol. 50r col. 2
Þat lad her lyf in sake & synne   8590
Housyng had þei noon to note
Boþe þei dwelt in a cote
Boþe on a nyȝte liȝter were þai
And boþe at onys in gesyn lay
Boþe were knaues þat þei bare   8595

8566   hastou]hast þou L. wisely go]well I go B.
8570   Alle]As B. drede]rede B.
8571   drednes]drede B. shal þou]schaltow B. non]mon H.
8572   shal þou]shaltou T; þou schalt B.
8574   In]Wiþ B.
8576   alle]leuyd boþe B.
8578   hem toke]toke hem B.
8580   hit]om B.
8582   halle]stalle B.
8582a   om CGHTLB.
8583   þe forme]in þe first B.
8586   more riȝtly]no righter B. riȝtly]lightly L.
8588   he felde]þere fyll B.
8589   Mister]Comon B. twynne]tweyn B.
8590   lad]had L. sake]wrongh B.
8592   Boþe...dwelt]þey duellyd boþe B.
8593   on a]in oon L. liȝter]lyghtyd L.

Her moderes ful nedy ware
Þei had no credeles ne wiþ to by
But dide her childre bi hem to ly
Her beddyng was to hem so nede
Hit myȝt not be depardide in dede 8600
Of þese wymmen soone þe ton
In bed slepyng hir sone had slon
As wymmen done ryuely
Þat ȝonge childre leyn hem by
Whenne she fond hir childe was dede 8605
Coude she fynde no better rede
Fro hir fere she stale hir barn
And laide hiren þere þat was forfarn 8608
So in bed stille she lay 8613
As she had slepte til þe day
Þat oþer wommon whenne she woke 8615
And bigan hir childe to loke
She fond hit ded liggyng hir by
Alas she seide þat born was I
My childe Is slayn & I noot how
Colde haþ slayn hit as I trow 8620
Þe childe in barme to fire she bare
Wel she wende to quyke hit þare
Al for nouȝt hit was forleyn
Hit myȝte not quyke to lyue aȝeyn
She hir biþouȝte in short while 8625
Þat of hir childe she had gyle
Whenne she soþely had knowen
Þat þe childe was not hir owen
To hir felowe she lep in hy
And þerwiþ ȝaf a mychel cry 8630

8597   ne]no B.
8598   to]om B.
8600   depardide]parted TB.
8601   þese]this LB. soone]anon L.
8602   bed]her bed B. had]haþe B.
8608   hiren]hir L. hiren þere]her hers B.
8609-12   om CGHTLB.
8613   in...stille]it beffell þat B.
8614   til]to B.
8615   þat oþer]þe toþer TLB.
8619   slayn]dede B.
8620   Colde]God L.
8626   gyle]a gyle B.
8628   þe]þat B.
8630   ȝaf]sche ȝaffe B. mychel]om B.

She seide wicked be þe wo
Why hastou me bygyled so
Of my childe þat myself bere   fol. 5Ov col. 1
ȝyue hit me anoon now here
ȝyue me my childe þou fro me stal   8635
Þe toþer seyde þou lyest al
I hit bar and hit is myne
Þe dede childe soþely is þyne
Þat þou slouȝe whil þou slept
Ful wel haue I myn kept   8640
She seide þou lyest wik wommon   8643
Þou shalt þerof be ouergon
My quyk childe þou hast stolen to þe   8645
But þi dede childe leyd by me
Þou shalt hit ȝelde to me al
Whenne iuggement þerof be shal
Wiþ þis þei coom bifore þe kyng
Alle folwede hem olde & ȝin[g]   8650
Mychel pepul of mony toun
Of þat doom to here resoun
Soone wiþ salomon þei met
Vndir þe tre þere he was sett
Þere he moost his witt souȝt   8655
Of alle þingis þat he wrouȝte
Whenne þei were biforn him þere
First spak she þe quyk childe bere
She seide saf be þou salomone
Kyng sittyng in þi trone   8660
Lord þi pore wommon þou here

8631   þe]þy B.
8632   hastou]hast þou L. me bygyled]begyled me B.
8634   hit me]me hit T.
8635   þou]þat þou L.
8636   al]hall B.
8637   and]om B.
8638   soþely]it B.
8639   þat þou]þou it B.
8640   haue I]I haue B.
8641-2   *om* CGHTLB.
8643   wik]wickyd B.
8645   childe]*om* L.
8646   But]And TLB. by]to B.
8648   Whenne]Tyll B. be shal]befall B.
8650   Alle folwede]As folowyth LB. olde]boþe olde B. ȝing]ȝin H.
8651   toun]a toun LB.
8655   witt]wyf L.
8658   quyk]furst T.
8659   saf be]saue me L ; hayle be B.

And riʒtwis deme in þis mistere
Pese *wim*men þat ʒe se here stonde
We are boþe in o hous dwellonde
Boþe at onys wiþ childe we were   8665
And boþe at ones oure childre we bere
In wonyng were we stad not wyde
And layde oure childre by oure syde
But weilawey hit so bifel
My fere in bed hir childe dud quel   8670
Siþ she layde hit *pri*uely
Whil I slepte in bed me by
And stal my lyuyng childe away
Til I knewe wel by liʒt of day
Of þis tresoun she had me done   8675 fol. 50v col. 2
I hir resouned also soone
But myʒte I neu*er* hidur tille
No childe gete for good nor ylle
// Pou lyʒest seide þat oþer þon
Ful bitturly as euel wom*mon*   8680
Pouʒte I neu*er* þi childe to stele
But wom*mon* am I trew & lele
Pis childe in myn arme is myn
And þat þat is dede hit is þyn
Of my wombe þis childe was born   8685
And þou wiþ shame þin hast lorn
Pe ded is þyn & myn þe quyke
Suche wordis spak þat wom*mon* wike
Pat oþer seide allas sir kyng
And þerwiþ gon hir hondis wryng   8690
I se my childe is me wiþdrawen
And shal not come to myn awn

8662   deme]dome B.
8663   þese *wim*men]*þis* woman B.
8666   oure]*om* B. we]*om* TL.
8667   In]Of B.
8672   Whil]Whils B. slepte]slepe B.
8674   wel]it B.
8675   had]hath B.
8678   No]My B.
8679   þat oþer]þe toþer TLB.
8683   arme]armys B.
8684   *second* þat]which L; *om* B. hit]þat B.
8687   & myn]myn is B.
8688   þat...wik]þe women þek B.
8689   þat oþer]þe toþer TLB.
8690   hir]our L.
8692   And]I TLB.

Þou do me bote aȝeyn þis bolde
For al þe soþe I haue þe tolde

Þe kyng þat was so sleȝe a cle[r]k   8695
War & wyse in al his werk
Of þis pleynt meruailed sore
A caas þat hadde not come bifore
Lordyngis he seide þis wommon here
Seiþ þat þe quyke childe she bere   8700
Þer aȝeyn seiþ þat oþer
She is þe modir & noon oþer
Part in þe dede haue þei noon
Þei clayme þerof blood nor boon
But of þe quyke boþe wolde be   8705
Modir as ȝe here and se
But modir may hit haue but oon
To proue hit shul we soone goon
And eyþer wolde haue hit al
But þarto may þei not fal   8710
Me þinkeþ by al maner art
Bytwene hem we mot hit part
And siþen þat þei wol so
Wiþ swerd hit shal be delt in two
Eyþer shul to o syde stonde   8715 fol. 51r col. 1
Anoon fet me my swerd in honde
// Þe womman þat þe modir was
Fel to grounde & cryed allas
And seide lord god hit shylde
Þat þou sir kyng sle my chylde   8720
ȝyue hir al my childe allone

8693   bote]botee L. aȝeyn]aȝens B.
8694   tolde]take B.
8695   þe]The The L. clerk]clek H.
8696   War]Wyse B. wyse]ware B.
8697   pleynt meruailed]playntis wondryd B.
8698   A]As TLB. come]be B. bifore]tofore TL.
8700   Seiþ]Sayde B. þat]om B.
8701   þat oþer]þe toþer TLB.
8702   noon]not þe B.
8704   nor]ne L.
8710   þei]it B.
8711   Me]Be B.
8712   we...hit]it mvst be B.
8715   o]þe ton B.
8716   fet] fech B.
8717   womman]modyr B. modir]chyldis B.
8718   cryed]sayde B.
8720   sir kyng]in dome B.
8721   hir]I it her B.

Þat is better þen hit be slone
Of him I ȝyue to hir my riȝt
Or he shulde so be diȝt
// Þe toþer seide not shal [h]e   8725
Hool be ȝyuen to me ne þe
But baldely dalt mot he be
As þe kyng haþ seide in se
Euer þat oþer seide in sawe
Lord lete not my childe be slawe   8730
For no þing þer may bifalle
Lordyngis he seide þis here ȝe alle
To whiche of þese shal I hit deme
Say me what wol best biseme
Þei seide sir bi þis day   8735
We noot bitwene hem what to say
He seide herde ȝe not þat oon
Wolde haue him quyke anoþer sloon
Þat oon wolde dele þe childe in two
Þat oþer wolde not lete hym slo   8740
Wherfore I ȝou rede
Þe childe be not done to dede
But bitake hym to þat wyf
Þat so fayn wolde haue his lyf
For she þat halt his lyf so dere   8745
His modir is wiþouten were
Þis doom þei seide is of prise
Alle þonked salomon þe wyse
Hir childe she toke & hoom she gos
Of þis doom fer sprong þe loos   8750
Alle þat spake of salomon

8722   be]to be B.
8723   Of him]to þe todyr B. to hir]om B.
8724   Or he]Raþer þan it B. he]yt L.
8725   he]be H.
8726   Be ȝevyn hoole to þe nor me B. me]þe T. þe]me T.
8727   dalt]dresst B.
8729   þat oþer]þe toþer TLB.
8731   no]þis B. þer]þat TLB.
8733   þese]þis B.
8734   me]me best B. best]om B.
8736   what]is best B.
8737   ȝe]you L. þat oon]þe tone B.
8738   him]yt L. anoþer]þe toþer B.
8739   þat oon] þe ton TLB.
8740   þat oþer]þe toþer TLB. hym]it B.
8741   I ȝou]it is my B.
8744   þat]þat wolde B. wolde]om B. his]þe B.
8745   halt]holdith B.

Seide so wyse was neuer noon
Ny craftiere in werke of honde
Was neuer founden noon in londe
Ne neuer noon þat had I wis   8755 fol. 51r col. 2
So myche wele of worldly blis

Whenne salomon was wel at ese
And al his kyndome in pese
In worchynge he bigan to wake
In det he was þe temple to make   8760
Þat his fadir him of bisouȝt
But of a þing wondir him þouȝt
Whil he was tymberyng to þat þing
Þat while þe tre bigon to clyng
Þe tre þat I bifore of tolde   8765
Þo bigon to waxen olde
Vche man seide þat hit seȝe
Þat hit for elde bigon to deȝe
And semed wel bi þat purpos
Men shulde no more hit holde in cloos   8770
Þe short tale þerof to telle
Men þe raþer shulde hit felle
Whenne nede were to be souȝt
And to þe temple werk be wrouȝt
Þe kyng cast by scanteloun   8775
And dide make al þe tymbur boun
Whenne al was purueide in place
And bounden togider beem & lace
Þei fond gret merryng in her merk
Þe wriȝtes þat shulde reise þe werk   8780
Þe best beem þat þerynne shulde be
Þerof wanted hem a tre

8753   in]of B.
8754   founden...in]non founde in no B.
8759   to wake]awake B.
8761   of]om B.
8762   him]he B.
8763   to]of B.
8764   þat]þe B.
8768   elde]age B. deȝe]driȝe TLB.
8769   And]þat B.
8771   þerof]þan B.
8772   þe]schul B. shulde]let B.
8774   be wrouȝt] Ibroght B.
8775   þe kyng]King Salamon B.
8776   þe]his B.
8778   bounden]boun L. beem]bone L. lace]brace B.
8782   wanted]lackyd B. hem]þerof L.

Þe beem þat moost þe werk shulde bynde
Þei souȝte anoþer for to fynde
Mony a wod haue þei þourȝe gon 8785
But siche tre fonde þei noon
When þei had souȝt wiþouten spede
Sir kyng þei seide we doute oure dede
Shal þerisshe & al left werk vchone 8789
And spak to kyng salomone 8792
Þei seide sir durst we for awe
Oure þouȝte wolde we to ȝow shawe
We haue souȝt fer & neer 8795
To fynde a tre to þis mister
For to fest wiþ compas slyȝe fol. 51v col. 1
Oure werk togider lowe & hyȝe
If we durst seye ȝow sir kyng
Þat ȝe took not in greuyng 8800
Þe tre þat is in orcharde þin
Wolde brynge oure werk wel to fyn
Þe kyng of þis tre vndirstood
Almost menged him his mood
Neuerþeles he graunt þat tre 8805
Whenne hit myȝt noon oþer be
Soone was þat hewen doun
And squyre on leyd & scanteloun
Þe tre was also mete & queme
As any man couþe þerto deme 8810
But whenne hit was vp bi strengþe
Hit wanted large ań ellen lengþe
Anoon doun þei hit let
And fond hit mete ynouȝe bi met
Efte þei lifted vp þat tre 8815

8786   tre]a tre TLB. fonde þei]couþ þey fynd B.
8787   When]With L.
8789   al]om B.
8790-1   om HTLB.
8793   sir]om B.
8794   shawe]knaw B.
8796   second to]of L; at B.
8797   wiþ]oure T.
8800   ȝe]you L. not in]it noght to B.
8801   þe]This L; þat B.
8804   him]was B.
8805   Neuerþeles]Neþeles B.
8807   Soone]Sith B. was þat]that was L; it was B.
8810   couþe þerto]myght B.
8812   wanted]lackyd B. lengþe]of length B.
8814   fond]om B. mete...bi]toke anoþer B.
8815   lifted]lefft B.

Hit was to short greet quantite
Þus þei proued hit þre dayes
As hit in þe story sayes
But for no profu[r] þat þei dude
Hit wolde not þere stonde in stude   8820
Whenne þei say no bote ellis
Þei wente to seche friþþe & fellis
Fynde anoþer tre wolde þay
Þei hit fonde þe firste day
Þe same day þei hit founden   8825
Þe beem was in his burþen bounden
Þis tre þei took of cypres
And dude hit in worshepe & in pees
In þat holy temple griþ
And þe þritty cerclis þerwiþ   8830
Þat kyng dauid so good
Dude aboute hit whil hit stood
To wite how hit grew by ȝere
And offered hem as tresour dere
To haue of þat tre lastynge mynde   8835
Of dyuerse tokenes as we fynde
At þe temple for þis resoun   fol. 51v col. 2
Þei were wiþ tresour in comoun
Ne were þei neuer þenne spende
Til þei were Iudas bikende   8840
To hym were þei bitauȝte & tolde
Whenne he for hem his lorde solde
Þus seiþ sum opynyoun
But so seiþ not þe passioun
Þe tre þenne ful richelye   8845

8816   greet]a grete L.
8819   no]to L. profur]proful H.
8820   þere...in]stonde þere in no B.
8821   no]non LB.
8822   seche]fecche L.
8824   firste] fourþe B.
8825   þei]þat þey B.
8826   beem]tre B. his burþen]cariage B.
8828   dude]putt B.
8837   At]Oute of B.
8838   comoun]to moun B.
8839   þenne]þerin B.
8840   were Iudas]to Iudas were B.
8841   bitauȝte]taght B.
8842   Whenne he]Whem þey B. his]oure B.
8843   seiþ]sayn B.
8844   so]þus B.
8845   þe]þis B.

Was in þe temple don to lye
Þerof was neuer made ouȝte
Til þe cros þerof was wrouȝt
Þis chirche was made of marbul stoon
Suche anoþer in world was noon   8850
As was tempel salomone
Þerynne were alle her relykes done
Mony selcouþes to se
He wrouȝte þere in stoon & tre
Was neuer noon þat couþe wirche   8855
Ne ordeyne siche anoþer chirche
But god had ȝyuen siche wisdome
As he ȝaf to salomon
As seye þe men þat þere han been
Wiþynne & oute boþe han seen   8860
Pritty ellen whenne hit was made
Hit hade on lengþe & ten brade
And on heiȝte hit hadde fiftene
Bi crafte ouer al wrouȝt bydene
Þerfore þe beem I tolde of ore   8865
Of elnes was fiftene & more
Whenne þe temple halwed wes
Þe tre lay euer stille in pees
Mony hit wolde haue done away
Miȝte þei not stille hit lay   8870
And aftir salomones dawe
Coom a prest of her lawe
Þerto fyue hundride men he ledde

8846   Was]Was done B. don]for B.
8847   neuer made]made neuer B.
8850   world]þe world B.
8851   tempel]þe temple of B.
8852   alle her]þe B.
8853   selcouþes]mervayles B.
8855   Was neuer]þere was B. couþe]coude T.
8857   But]For B. siche]non swich B.
8858   ȝaf]did B.
8860   oute boþe]withoute þat B. seen]it sene B.
8862   on]of B. brade]on brade T; of brade LB.
8863   on]of B.
8864   wrouȝt]made B.
8865   of ore]beffore B.
8866   was]hit was T; length B.
8868   euer]ovyr L. in pees]by gras L.
8870   stille]so still B.
8871   dawe]days B.
8872   lawe]lawys B.

Þei myȝt not stire hit of þat stedde
Wiþ ax he wolde haue kut hit þon   8875
Al to soone he bygon
Out of þat tre brast a blase   fol. 52r col. 1
And brent hem alle in þat plase
Coom noon of hem hoom quik
Cirillus het þat prest wik   8880
Þis was a tokenyng of þat tre
Þat halwed was as ȝe may se

Salomon þo was ful wele
And vmbset wiþ hap & cele
His wyues were wondir to neuene   8885
Queenes had he hundrides seuene
Þre hundride lemmons he sayes
Aftir þe lawe in þo dayes
Wiþinne þe tyme þat I of rede
Þer coom a lady of þat lede   8890
For to honour hit in þat stude
As mony of þat cuntre dude
She þouȝte to make hir orisoun
But vnwisely she sette hir doun
Vpon þis ilke tre wiþ chaunce   8895
Þat men hadden In affiaunce
Soone was þere seen a wondir
Hir cloþes bigunne to brenne hir vndir
As þe tre in fire had bene
Þat ilke wommon þat I of mene   8900
Þe tre aferd she stirte fra
Hir name was maximilla
Þenne bigon she for to crye
Wiþ a voys of prophecye
She seide on þat tre shulde hynge   8905

8874   þat]þe B.
8877   þat]þe B. blase]blast B.
8880   wik]quik T.
8881   a tokenyng]þe tokyn B. þat]þe B.
8883   þo was]was þo B.
8884   And...wiþ]All aboute hym B. vmbset]vnbyset L.
8887   he]it B.
8888   þo]om T.
8894   But vnwisely]Vnhappely B.
8895   þis]þat B.
8896   affiaunce] fyans B.
8900   of]om B.
8901   þe tre]Sore B. fra]þerffra B.
8905   shulde]schall B.

Þe lorde of hele þe blisful kynge
Ihesu crist of mayden born
To saue þe world þat was forlorn
Þat shulde þe iewes here & se
Þat shulde þe cros make of þat tre   8910
For þe loue of þis sooþ sawe
Þe felle iewes wiþouten awe
For þenne nemed she cristis name
On god seide þei þou hast seide shame
She is wod wiþ fend Itake   8915
Anoon þei heueded hir wiþ wrake
Send was þere an aungel clere   fol. 52r col. 2
And vp to heuen her soule bere
Þere in al þe folkes siȝt
And seide þat cristiane she hiȝt   8920
Þerfore were þo iewis wrooþ
Þat nome to here hem was looþ
Þis womman was þe first men knew
Martired for loue of crist ihesew
Þese iewes þouȝte not ȝitt ynouȝe   8925
Þis tre out of þe temple þei drouȝe
A pyt þer was ful litil hem fra
Was cald piscina probatica
Þe iewes þat were wont to wrong
ÞerInne þe kyngis tre þei slong   8930
Whersoeuer þis tre lay
God shewed þeron his myȝtis ay
Vche day a certeyn hour
Þer liȝt doun fro heuen tour
Aungels þat were selcouþe shene   8935
To stire þe watir al bydene

8906   hele]all B. þe]that L; a B.
8909   shulde]schall B.
8910   þat shulde]om B. make]be made B.
8911   þe]om B.
8912   awe]lawe B.
8914   On]Off B. seide þei]þey sayde B. hast seide] schalt haue B.
8915   fend] fendis B.
8920   And]þey B.
8921   þo]þe B.
8924   loue]þe loue B.
8926   þis]þe B. þei]om B.
8927   ful]om TL; a B.
8929   were]was L.
8930   slong]clong B.
8932   myȝtis]myȝt B.
8935   Aungels]And B. selcouþe]fulleryght & B. shene]shent L

Whenne þat hit was stired so
Men þat lay seek in wo
Whoso to þat watir coom anoon
Of soor hadde he lenger noon   8940
Were his sekenes neuer so strong
Or hadde he lyued neuer so long
Þes iewes þo crabbed & kene
Whenne þei hadden þis Isene
Þei drouȝe hit þenne & made a brigge   8945
Ouer a litil ryuere to ligge
Þe watir of siloe & þei seide
Whenne hit was ouer þe watir leyde
If her Inne any vertu be
Of olyue wiþynne þis tre   8950
Bi synful mennes feet seide þei
Wiþ goynge shal be done awey
On þis maner þis tre þere lay
Til aftirwarde mony a day
Til sibile coom fer fro kiþ   8955
To salomon to speke him wiþ
For to here of his Wisdom   fol. 52v col. 1
Whenne she to þe cite coom
She coom in at þulke ȝate
Þere þe tre lay in hir gate   8960
Doun she bowed to þe grounde
Þe tre she honoured þere a stounde
She laft hir sherte neuer þe latir
And barfot wolde she ouer þe watir
To þat tre she gan hir folde   8965
And prophecye þerof she tolde
And of domes day namely
How mony men shulde be sory
Whenne þat sibile wiþ þe kyng

8939   Whoso]Whos L. þat]þe B. coom anoon]first com B.
8943   þo]om B.
8944   Isene]sene B.
8945   þenne]þennes TB.
8946   ryuere]watyr B.
8947   & þei]it is B.
8951   Bi]Wiþ B.
8955   Til]To B. fer fro]from fer B.
8959   þulke]þe B.
8960   hir]þe B.
8961   bowed]lloutyd B.
8963   sherte]smok B.
8964   barfot]barfort H.
8968   men]a man B.

Disputed had of mony þing   8970
Þe kyng ȝaf hir ȝiftis faire
And hamwarde she dide repaire
Þis ilke tre þat I of say
Þere hit lay mony a day
But hit was in þe temple boun   8975
At tyme of cristis passioun

Let we hit ligge þere hit lise
Speke we of salomon þe wyse
His dedis couþe no mon amende
Suche grace god hym sende   8980
But harde hit was þe dede of synne
Þat ordeyned was to adames kynne
Þat sorweful werk hemself hit souȝte
Þat al her sede in sorwe brouȝt
Man to falle in fulþe of flesshe   8985
Þourȝe fourme of kynde þat is nesshe
Ouer þast hym haþ þat caytif kynde
And made kyng salomon al blynde
Blynde of witt & wisdoom als
And also in his feiþ ful fals   8990
Þourȝe wymmen þat he loued fele
He fel fro lyf & soulis hele
Aȝeynes goddis forbode dide he
And loued ladyes of vncouþe cuntre
Þat made him god to renay   8995
And to forsake his owne lay
Lord god so mychel of myȝt   fol. 52v col. 2
Where bicoom al his insiȝt
Þat dude himself so to spille
Folwynge wicked wommonnes wille   9000

8970   Disputed had]Had dispited B. þing]a þing B.
8973   ilke]ille B.
8976   tyme]þe tyme B.
8978   Speke]And speke B.
8979   dedis]dede TB.
8980   hym]had hym B.
8982   to]for B.
8983   hit]*om* B. souȝte]thoght L.
8984   þat al]And B.
8988   And]þat B. kyng]*om* B.
8990   ful]*om* B.
8994   And loued]To loue B. vncouþe]oþer B.
8996   to]*om* B.
8997   so mychel]full B.
9000   wicked]*om* B. wommonnes]womens LB.

[A]llas erly þi gyle bigon
At adam þat was formast mon
Sampson þat strengest was in lyf
Was bigyled þourʒe a wyf
Kyng dauid for a wyues siʒt   9005
To deþe dude a sacles knyʒt
Salomon þat I rede of here
Þat neuer hadde of wisdome pere
Siþ wymmen han bigyled him so
Who may of hem be siker who   9010
Certis I trowe neuer oon
In þis world of wicke wommon
Þe man she haþ in hir bandoun
She bryngeþ to confusioun
Þerfore I say blessed is he   9015
Þat doþ hym not in hir pouste
For if he loue hir more þen nede
To foly wille she wol him lede
Be he neuer biforn so sly
Þenne shal he falle into foly   9020
Mistrowe no man herfore þat I
Wol speke of wymmen vileny
If I so dude I were vnhende
I þenke no good wommon to shende
Certis þat þar no man wene   9025
For in þis world is noon so clene
Creature wiþ god & mon
To loue as good wommon þon
Þis euel to hem I hit telle

9001   Allas]*A space is left in* MS H *for a rubricated* A, *and a faint a appears as a guide.* erly]to sone B. þi] þis TLB.
9002   At]That L.
9003   þat]the L. strengest was]was strengest B.
9005   Kyng]*om* B.
9006   dude]*om* L; did do B. sacles]doughty B.
9008   hadde]*om* B. pere]had no pere B.
9009   Siþ]When B. han]had L.
9011   oon]non B.
9012   wicke]wicked TB.
9014   to]hym to B.
9018   wille]forsoþe B. wol]*om* L.
9019   neuer biforn]ner toforn L; neuer toffore B.
9021   herfore]þerfore T.
9023   If]And ʒeff B. so]*om* B.
9025   þat þar]þer nedeþ B.
9028   wommon]women LB. þon]can L.
9029   to...hit]I to hem B.

Þat are founden false & felle   9030
Þe goode are neuer þe wors to preyse   9035
What so men of þe wicked seyse
Whiche are to lacke & whiche to loue
Her owne werkis wol hem proue
But god þat dyȝed vpon þe rode
Amende þe wickede & saue þe gode   9040

Whenne salomon his wille had wrouȝt   fol. 53r col. 1
Wo him was þat euer he hit þouȝt
God to wraþthe his soule to fyle
Þenne repentide hym a whyle
Wiþ boþe his yȝen sore he gret   9045
And dude prophetis to be fet
Patriarkis hem coom wiþ alle
Biforne her feet he doun con falle
And saide haueþ of me mercy
Is noon so synful wrecche as I   9050
I se wel I haue mysgoon
I haue honoured himself saton
I haue laft my lordis lawe
And to þe fendis fully drawe
// Hastou þei seide þi lawe reneyed   9055
ȝe ȝe wayleway he seyed
Whi þei seide dost[ou] so
A womman wrouȝt me þis wo
My mysgilt I am aknowen
I were worþi to be drawen   9060
I haue done a wickede dede
Þourȝe a wommon of heþen lede
ȝe rede me now for goddis sake
ȝoure counsel I wol vndirtake

9031-4   om HTLB.
9036   so...of]euer B.
9037   &]om B. second to]ar to B.
9039   vpon]on B.
9040   wickede]ill B.
9042   him was]was hym B. he]om B.
9044   repentide]repent he B.
9046   prophetis]prophecy B. fet]lett B.
9048   doun]om B. con]gan LB.
9049   of]on LB.
9050   synful] foule a B.
9054   fully]foly B.
9055   Hastou þei]Hast þou he L. reneyed]renewid L.
9057   dostou]a blot obscures the ou in H; dudes þou T; dedist þou B.
9059   mysgilt]gilt B. aknowen]beknawe B.
9062   lede]rede B.

Alle þei seide what rede con ȝe   9065
Þe reede is holly in þe
Þou þiself þat art so wys
Firste saye vs þyn avys
We shul be to þi biddyng boun
He seide takeþ of my croun   9070
Þat I no lenger owȝe to were
My kyngis robe of me ȝe tere
For my synne fer wol I fle
To vncouþe lond fro þis cuntre

[D]o wey þei seide kyng salomon   9075
Þis þing owȝe not we to don
Nouþer we wole ne haue myȝt
Fordo þe lawe of kyngis riȝt
Þe lawe þat god haþ leyd on kyng
We owȝe to breke for no þing   9080
What seide he what saye ȝe now   fol. 53r col. 2
Shal I haue no rede of ȝow
What rede may we saye to þe
I wol þat ȝe vncroune me
Mi lord I haue laft alas   9085
Helpeþ me in þis caitif caas   /
Leiþ on me harde penaunce
Sore is hit my repentaunce
Siþ I haue serued to haue shame
ȝyue me shrifte in goddis name   9090
// Þat shrifte was sorweful to sene
Al þe cite say bidene
Olde & ȝonge gon on him wondir
Þe shrifte þat solomon ȝeode vndir

9065   ȝe]we T.
9066   þe]Thy L; þis B. is]hit is TL. holly]all hoole B.
9071   þat I]I owe B. owȝe]it B.
9072   of...tere]ȝe of schere B.
9073   For]Fro L.
9074   To vncouþe]Oute of þis B. fro þis]to fer B.
9075   Do]*The d was intended as a guide to the rubricator in* H.
9076   not we]we not TB.
9077   myȝt]no myght B.
9080   for]it for B.
9081   seide...ȝe]he sayde ne schall I B.
9082   rede]drede L.
9083   may]schall B.
9086   caitif]careffull B.
9088   is hit]it is B.
9089   Siþ]Sith þat B. to haue]om B.
9093   gon...him]on hym did B.

His synne bifore þe greet cite 9095
Wiþ woful wepyng shewed he
His riche croune of stoon & gold
He dide firste take of his molde
Of his robe he gan to ryue
And his body al to dryue 9100
He scourgid him bare in þat þronge
Out of his backe þe blood sponge
Suche soor shame & marterynge
Was neuer seyn on siche a kynge
Al he toke in goddis name 9105
And þoled mekely þat shame
Him þouȝte al þat to be lite
For to þole for siche a wyte
Wherof tofore he loued þe lust
He let ryue hit al to dust 9110
Þerfore hit semed wel bi þis
Þat he gat mercy of his mys
What for þe reuþe of his mysdede
And for his shrifte he vndirȝede
Aftir þe tyme þis was done 9115
A While regnede salomone
Blisfuly ouer al þat lond
His werkis ȝitt ben lastond
His craftis shul be lastyng ay
Til hit come to domes day 9120
Miche of hym haue I to telle fol. 53v col. 1
Miȝte I for oþere þingis dwelle
On oþere þingis most I mynne

9096   woful]sorouffull B.
9097   of...&]þat was of B.
9098   firste]hit furste T. of]fro B.
9102   sponge]sprong L.
9104   seyn]sith B.
9105   Al]As B.
9106   þoled mekely]suffyrd mekyll L.
9107   þat]om B. be]om B. lite]to lite T.
9108   þole for]suffir L.
9109   lust]loste B.
9110   ryue]rent B.
9111   þerfore]Wherfore B.
9113   þe]om B.
9114   his]om B.
9115   þis]þat þis B.
9118   ȝitt ben]ben ȝitt B.
9121   haue I]I haue B.
9122   for]of hym fro B. þingis]þing B.
9123   þingis]þing B.

To reken forþ oure lady kynne
For þerfore moost I vndirtoke   9125
For to make þis englisshe boke
To telle how þat lord of myȝt
To hele men ofte had hiȝt
Þat of her seed a mon shulde springe
Monkynde out of wo to brynge   9130
Longe was þis het biforn
Ar ihesu crist to vs was born
// Of salamon now we ende
Þat regned fourty wynter hende
He had hade boþe of wele & wo   9135
His elde was fourty ȝeer & two
In bedleem grauen was he boun
Þat was his owne fadir toun
Wiþ menske & worshepe aftir wham
Regnede his sone þat hett roboam   9140
Þis roboam þat I of mene
Regnede wynteres seuentene
// His sone coom aftir abya þo
Þre ȝeer he regnede & no mo
// Asa his sone hool & fere   9145
Regnede oon & fourty ȝere
// Josephat his sone in lyue
Regnede twenty ȝeer & fyue
Þat was elyas þe prophete
God of hym so mychel lete   9150
He styntede reyn bi his preyere
Six moneþes & þre ȝere
And whenne he preyed eft aȝeyn
God hem sende plente of reyn

9126   englisshe]ilk B.
9127   lord]our lorde B.
9128   had]haue I B.
9129   þat]þat her B.
9130   Monkynde]þat mankynde B. to]schuld B.
9131   het]yt L.
9134   wynter]ȝerys B.
9135-6 *om* B.
9135   hade]*om* L.
9139   menske &]muche L. aftir]atir T.
9140   þat hett]*om* B.
9141   þis]*om* B. þat...of]of whom I B.
9142   wynteres]ȝerys B.
9143   abya]abra B.
9147   in]on LB.
9153-4 *om* B.

He was þe firste storyes sayes   9155
Þat dede men reysed in þo dayes
Of Ioseph coom Ioram
Þat eiȝte wynter regnede wiþ wham
Was a prophete elizeus
And as þe story telleþ vs   9160
Ely was þat tyme þare
Translated in golden chare   fol. 53v col. 2
// Of þis Ioram coom osyas
Of regne fifty wynter þat was
In þat tyme þat I of mele   9165
In þat lond were prophetis fele
Isaias . Ioel . Osee . Abdyas .
Amos . Ionas . & mecheaas
Þe eiȝteþe sibile bigan to ryse
Þat was of prophecye ful wyse   9170
Of ozias coom Iothan
Sixtene ȝeer he regned þan
Romulus was þe firste man
Þat regned in rome & hit bigan
// Achaz his sone aftir him coome   9175
Þat tyme was made þe toun of rome
Sixtene ȝeer regnede achaz
Of him coom ezechias
He regnede nyne & twenty ȝeere
Wel was he loued wiþ ihesu dere   9180
Þenne regned manasses
Þat was his sone wiþouten lees
Þat tyme was seiþ þe story
A sibile þat het of samy

9155   storyes]as stories L; as story B.
9157   Ioseph]Iosophath B.
9159   a]þe B.
9162   golden]a goldyn L; a briging B.
9163   osyas]Asias B.
9164   Of...wynter]Offring fifften ȝere B.
9166   In...were]Were ther many LB.
9167-8   reversed in B.
9168   & mecheaas]melchias B.
9169   began]gan B.
9175   Achaz]Achaar L.
9177   Sixtene] Ix L. achaz]Achaar L.
9178   ezechias]Echias L.
9180   was...loued]he was belouyd B. ihesu]god T; our lord B.
9183   seiþ]so saiþe B.
9184   of]MS L has of crossed out.

Of þis manasses coom amon þo   9185
As his fadir tofore dide go
Foles were þei boþe vnslye
Þei honoured euer maumetrye
Amon sone het Iosyas
Douȝty kyng in his tyme was   9190
Fordide þe toun of nynyue
Þat was aboute Iourneyes þre
Þat stonden had in tyme þore
Fourty hundride ȝeer & more
Þat tyme was prophete Ieremye   9195
Spekyng in his prophecye
Iosias gat Ieconyam
Þe transmigracioun was þan
Þat þe book of mynde mas
Þere was a kyng sedechias   9200
In þis tyme was þe Iewes lond   fol. 54r col. 1
Wonnen al into sarazines hond
Ierusalem was stryed & take
Þat kyngdome fel into wrake
And as we in þe story descende   9205
In þat tyme was þe temple brende
Thourȝe a kyng of babilone
In þraldome he had hem done
Nabugodonosor he hiȝte
Stronge he was of myche myȝte   9210
Twelue moneþe biseged he hit þon
And for defaute of mete hit won
Þe kyng fley out bi nyȝt
Wiþ his boldest men & wiȝt
He was take as he fley   9215
His sone slayn in þat wey

9186   go]do B.
9187   vnslye]onely B.
9188   euer]boþe B.
9189   Amon]A mannys L.
9190   Douȝty]A Dowghty LB.
9199   of mynde]mynde of B.
9200   sedechias]hight Sedechias B.
9202   into]to B.
9204   into]all into B.
9210   Stronge...was]He was strong & B.
9211   moneþe]moneþis B. biseged he]he biseged TB.
9212   hit]þus he it B.
9213   fley]went B.
9214   boldest men]eldest son B.
9216   His]And his B. þat]þe B.

And himseluen dide þei bynde
And kest him into prisoun blynde
Þe iewes were put out of state
And her kyngdome al transolate   9220
Þat foure hundride ȝeer had stonde
And fifty at þat day ne[re]honde
Þe ferþe elde of þe world is tolde
Þat was foure hundride wynter olde
And fyue & sixty ȝeer & þre   9225
But siþ þis world bigan to be
Is foure þousande six hundride fol
Who so redily rekene hit wol

9218   kest]led B. into]to B.
9222   nerehonde]neuerhonde H.
9223   elde]age B. þe]þis B.
9224   wynter]ȝere B.
9226   þis]þe B.
9228   hit]om B.

Explanatory Notes

LIST OF ABBREVIATIONS USED

The abbreviations of biblical books are the standard ones listed in *Biblia Sacra,* Denuo ediderunt complures Scripturae Sacrae Professores Facultatis theologicae Parisiensis et Seminarii Sancti Sulpitii (Rome, 1956), xli.

Linguistic abbreviations are also standard:

ME — Middle English
OE — Old English
OF — Old French
OI — Old Icelandic
ON — Old Norse

In the following list, the abbreviation used is followed, if necessary, by the full title of the work, and the first word or words of the entry in the Bibliography, where full information can be found.

Ad. & Ep. — Adrian and Epotys in SMITH, Lucy Toulmin, *A Commonplace Book.*
Adnot. in Pent. — Adnotationes Elucidatoriae in Pentateuchon. HUGH OF ST. VICTOR.
Anc. Corn. Dr. — Ancient Cornish Drama. NORRIS, Edwin, ed.
Anc. Test. — Traduction anonyme de l'ancien testament.
Ancrene Riwle — DAY, Mabel, ed.
Apocalypse of Moses — in CHARLES, R. H., ed. *Apocrypha and Pseudepigrapha.*
Auch. — Canticum de Creatione aus MS Auchinleck in HORSTMANN, C., ed. *Sammlung Altenglischer Legenden.*
Ayenbite — Ayenbite of Inwit. MORRIS, Richard, ed.
Book of the Knight of LaTour-Landry — WRIGHT, Thomas, ed.
Cant. Creat. — Canticum de Creatione aus MS Trin. Coll. Oxf. 57 in HORSTMANN, C., ed. *Sammlung Altenglischer Legenden.*
Chester — Chester Plays. LUMIANSKY, R. M., ed.
Cleanness — GOLLANCZ, Israel, ed.
CM-Cursor Mundi. MORRIS, Richard, ed.

Conf. — *Confessiones.* AUGUSTINE.

Creat. of World — *Creation of the World,* STOKES, WHITLEY, ed. and trans.

DCD — *De Civitate Dei.* AUGUSTINE.

Dest. of Troy — *"Gest Hystoriale"* of the Destruction of Troy. PANTON, ed.

DGAL — *De Genesi ad Litteram.* AUGUSTINE.

DGALIL — *De Genesi ad Litteram Imperfectus Liber.* AUGUSTINE.

DGCM — *De Genesi Contra Manichaeos.* AUGUSTINE.

Dict. théol. cath. — VACANT, A. et al., eds. *Dictionnaire de théologie catholique.*

DIM — *De Imagine Mundi.* HONORIUS AUGUSTODUNENSIS.

Elucid. — *Elucidarium.* HONORIUS AUGUSTODUNENSIS.

I *Enoch,* II *Enoch* — in CHARLES, R. H., ed. *Apocrypha and Pseudepigrapha.*

Etym. — *Etymologiarum.* ISIDORE.

Fall of Princes — *Lydgate's Fall of Princes.*

Fest. — *Mirk's Festial.* MIRK, John.

G & E — *Middle English Genesis and Exodus.* ARNGART, Olof, ed.

Harley fragment — MEYER, P. "Notice et Extraits...", *Romania* (1907).

HIGDEN — *Polychronicon Ranulphi Hidgen.* HIGDEN, Ranulph.

Hist. Jos. — *L'Histoire de Joseph.* STEUER, Wilhelm.

Hist. Schol. — *Historia Scholastica.* PETRUS COMESTOR.

I & I — *Iacob and Ioseph.* NAPIER, Arthur S., ed.

Index — BROWN and ROBBINS.

JOSEPHUS — *Jewish Antiquities.* JOSEPHUS.

Jubilees — *Book of Jubilees.* CHARLES, R. H., ed.

KEMBLE — *Dialogue of Salomon and Saturnus.* KEMBLE, John M., ed.

Kildare — *Die Kildare-Gedichte.* HEUSER, W., ed.

Leg. Aur. — *Legenda Aurea.* JACOBUS A VORAGINE.

Legende — LAZAR, Moshé.

Life of Christ — FOSTER, Frances A., ed.

Lud. Cov. — *Ludus Coventriae.* BLOCK, K. S., ed.

"Lydgatiana" — MACCRACKEN, H. N.

Life — Vernon — "The Life of Adam and Eve" in BLAKE, N. F., ed. *ME Religious Prose.*

MANDEVILLE L — *Mandeville's Travels.* LETTS, Malcolm, ed.

MANDEVILLE S — *Bodley Version of Mandeville's Travels.* SEYMOUR, M. C., ed.

MED — *Middle English Dictionary.* KURATH, Hans and Sherman M. KUHN, eds.

Met. Para. — *A Middle English Metrical Paraphrase of the Old Testament.* KALÉN, Herbert, ed. Vol. I. OHLANDER, Urban, ed. Vols. II-IV.

Midrash — *Midrash Rabbah.* FREEDMAN, H. and Maurice SIMON, eds.

Myroure — *Myroure of oure Ladye.* BLUNT, John Henry, ed.

Newcastle Noah — *Newcastle Play of Noah's Ship,* in DAVIS, Norman, ed.

North. Homs. — the Northern Homily Cycle. *Northern Homilies.*

OED — *New English Dictionary.* MURRAY, James A. H., ed.

OEGen. — *Genesis* in KRAPP, George Philip, ed. *The Junius Manuscript.*

Ormulum — HOLT, Robert, ed.

Piers Plowman — SKEAT, Walter W., ed.

Pilg. Life of Man — *Pilgrimage of the Life of Man.* DEGUILEVILLE, Guillaume de.

Pricke of Conscience — MORRIS, Richard, ed.
Queen Mary's Psalter — WARNER, George, ed.
"Questiones" — "Questiones be-twene the Maister of Oxenford and his Clerke". HORSTMANN, C., ed.
RASHI — *Pentateuch with... Rashi's Commentary*. ROSENBAUM, M. and A. M. SILBERMANN, eds.
Rev. Meth. — "Middle English Metrical Version of the *Revelations* of Methodius". D'EVELYN, Charlotte.
SEL — *South English Legendary*. D'EVELYN, Charlotte and Anna J. MILL, eds.
SELTemp. — *South English Legendary, Temporale.*
Sent. — *Sententiæ*. PETRUS LOMBARDUS.
Speculum Vitæ — in ULLMANN, J. "Studien zu Richard Rolle de Hampole".
Story of the Holy Rood — *Legends of the Holy Rood*. MORRIS, Richard, ed.
Sum. Theol. — *Summa Theologica*. THOMAS AQUINAS.
Targ. of Jon., Targ. of Onk. — *Targums of Onkelos and Jonathan Ben Uzziel on the Pentateuch*. ETHERIDGE, J. W., ed.
Towneley — *Towneley Plays*. ENGLAND, George and Alfred W. POLLARD, eds.
Trad. anon. — *Traduction anonyme de la Bible entière.*
Trin. Camb. — "Zwei Gedichte aus der Handschrift..." BRUNNER, Karl.
WM. OF SHOREHAM — *Poems of William of Shoreham*. WILLIAM OF SHOREHAM.
WYNTOUN — *Original Chronicle of Andrew of Wyntoun*. ANDREW OF WYNTOUN.
York — *York Plays*. SMITH, Lucy Toulmin, ed.

EXPLANATORY NOTES

1ff The *Trad. anon.* opens in a similar way. The poet mentions several popular romances, and then urges his hearers to abandon them and listen to something more edifying. BONNARD, p. 85 prints the relevant passage from the Old French poem. Cf. also the opening of William of NASSYNGTON's *Speculum Vitæ*, 11.35-48; Karl BRUNNER's edition of *Richard Cœur de Lion*, 11.7-20.
3 Only one extant Middle English Alexander Romance could conceivably have been known to the *CM* poet. The rest were all composed later. See SEVERS, *Manual*, I, pp. 104-13, 268-73.
4 Julius Caesar was not a popular romance character.
5 On ME Troy poems see Severs, pp. 114-8, 274-7. The story was told in French from the twelfth century.
7 The story of Brutus, who came from Troy to found Britain was known from at least the ninth century.
13 DICKENS and WILSON, *Early ME Texts*, p. 223 point out that C's "wawan" is the French form of the name.

15   The best known story of Charlemagne and Roland is, of course, the *Chanson de Roland*. See also SEVERS, pp. 80-100, 256-66.

17-8   Only one ME poem is wholly devoted to Tristan. See SEVERS, pp. 75-9, 253-6. MSS CF refer to a specific incident in the Tristan legend, now known only in two MSS of the French *La Folie Tristan*. See BOSSUAT, *Manuel*, items 1657-68, 6312. The reference in MSS GTLB is much more general.

19   Ioneck, MSS CF, is now known only in Marie de France's lai *Yonec*. The name seems to have been unfamiliar to the scribes also, for it is corrupted to "kyng Ion" in MSS GTLB.
     The story of Isombras is told only once in ME, in an early fourteenth century poem. See SEVERS, pp. 122, 279.

20   The story of Amadas and Ydoine is now extant only in French. See BOSSUAT, items 1232-40. However, the pair were obviously well-known to ME writers. See *Emaré*, 11.122-3; *Sir Degrevant*, 11. 1493-4.

37-8   This exact proverb is not recorded in Whiting *Proverbs*, but cf. his items F.685 and F.689.

83   MS C's "loue" is an error for "life", as in FGTLB.

111-130   This is the *CM* poet's own statement of purpose and his description of the structure of his work.

122   The idea of "running over" the history of the world has analogues in other languages. Cf. the explanation of the title of Hugo von Trimberg's historical work *Der Renner*, which is roughly contemporary with the *CM*:
     Renner ist ditz buch genant,
     wanne ez sol renne durch di lant.

131-222   Two French paraphrases have versified tables of contents. The one in *Trad. anon.* is only about 20 lines long, but that of Geoffroi de Paris takes up eight folios.

188   MSS GHTL have the man sick for 28 years. Only CFB have the correct reading of 38 years. Cf. *Ioan.* 5:5.

217-20   Neither the sorrows of Mary nor the institution of the Feast of her Conception is found in the southern translation, which ends at 1.23,898.

219-20   MS E breaks off after 1.24,968, and is the only extant MS of the *CM* which ends where this table of contents says it should.

231-50   The poet declares his intention of writing in English for the common people. Cf. GROSSETESTE, *ME Translations*, 261/35-8, 362/73-4; MORRIS, ed., *Pricke of Consc.*, 336-9.
     The southern translator omitted some of the references to French (11.237-42). The original author of the poem was writing at a time when the English language was only beginning to oust Anglo-Norman as a literary language. As his sources were almost all in French or Latin, he must have been conscious of himself as a pioneer writer of biblical paraphrases in English. The southern translator, however, would be unaware of the language of the sources. Also by the time he was working on the *CM*, the use of Anglo-Norman must have been well on the wane. See LEGGE, *Anglo-Norman Lit.*, pp. 5-6. Cf. ÉVRAT's discussions of the French language as a vehicle for translation, *Gen.*, fol. 2v col. 1, fol. 25v col. 2.

233-5   These lines are much discussed in connection with the *CM*'s provenance. Certain linguistic evidence suggests the poem was written in

Scotland. See KALUZA, "Zu den Quellen", p. 453; STRANDBERG, *Rime-Vowels*, xiv-xv; KAISER, *Zur Geographie*, p. 6; BENNETT and SMITHERS, *Early ME Verse and Prose*, p. 367. These lines, however, seem to rule against that possibility. Kaiser, pp. 5-14, tries to prove that the term "England" applied to all the territory south of the Clyde-Forth line in the fourteenth century. Recent research into Scottish mediaeval history, however, strongly suggests that a fourteenth century poet speaking of "England" is referring to exactly the same territory as a twentieth century reader would understand by the term. See esp. BARROW, "Anglo-Scottish Border", pp. 21-42.

258 Morris' emendation of C's "fro" to "frote" is unnecessary. See *MED* "fro" n. [Cp.OI *fro*], meaning "profit, comfort, relief".

267-8 The southern translator missed another chance to explain the title of his poem here. Cf. 11.121-2 above.

270ff As promised in the prologue, 11.125-30, the poet grounds his work in the Trinity.

279-88 These lines are suggested by *Elucid.* I 6, a work which the *CM* poet here begins to use extensively. The Father created the world ("ordayned" 1.285), the Son maintains it ("gouerneþ" 1.286), and the Holy Ghost gives it life ("multeplied" 1.286).

289-308 From *Elucid.* I 3. Similar comparisons are in AUGUSTINE, "Sermo de Quarta Feria" vi, *PL* XL 692 and "De Symbolo: ad Catechumenos Sermo Alius" ix, *PL* XL 658; ANSELM, *De Processione Sancti Spiritus* xiii-xiv, *PL* CLVIII 306-7; OTLO of ST. EMMERAN, *Liber de Admonitione Clericorum et Laicorum* ii *PL* CXLVI 247; AELFRIC ed. Thorpe, I 282.

Honorius in the *Elucidarium* lists the properties of the sun as "ignea substantia, splendor et calor". The *CM*'s "bodi rond" is a poor translation of the first. Aelfric also had trouble with the phrase, and called it "seo lichamlice edwist þaet is þere sunnan trendel". The *CM* poet's version sounds more like Otlo's: "corpus in modum rotae constans, et splendorem atque calorem ipsius."

In the *CM*, the noun "heat" of MSS CF has been miscopied as the adjective "hot" in GHTLB. In these latter MSS, therefore, the three attributes of the sun seem erroneously to be roundness, heat and light, but cf. 1.303, where the body of the sun more correctly symbolizes the Father.

299 MS C's "erth" is an error.

309-13 God is sometimes referred to as a fountain in scripture. See *Ier.*2:13, *Ier.* 17:13, *Ps.*35:10. Honorius *Elucid.* I 4, calls Him "fons et origo", a very common Latin phrase. The "welle þat neuer is dry", however, seems an echo of *Is.*58:11: "sicut fons aquarum cujus non deficient aquæ".

311 The corruption of "for" or "forþi" to "ouer" in MSS GHTLB obscures Honorius' original meaning: God is the fountain "a quo omnia procedunt". *Elucid.* I 4.

314-22 *Elucid.* I 6.

316 MS C, although unmetrical, is closest to the original reading, translating "ne in nihilum dissolvantur".

319-22 The southern translation omits the widely known Augustinian description of the Trinity as "minning" *(memoria)*, "vnderstanding" *(intelligentia),* and "will" *(voluntas).* See AUGUSTINE, *De Trinitate* X xii, *PL* XLII 984. Cf. below 11.562-8.

323-30   *Elucid.* I 15. L1.327-30 lack a context in *CM.* In the *Elucid.* they answer the pupil's question about whether God lived alone before the creation of the world. By the end of the fourteenth century, the idea that God was not older in time than his creation was condemned as heresy by Nicholas EYMERIC in the *Elucidarius Elucidarii.* See *Elucid.* p. 491.

331-4   The *CM* poet picks up the "artifex" image of the previous lines and carries it further. This passage does not come from *Elucid.* Cf. AUGUSTINE's *DGCM* 1 vi, *PL* XXXIV 178.

332   MSS CF have the better reading. The point is not God's supreme dignity, as it appears to be in MSS GHTLB, but his difference from other workmen. The line was probably rewritten to eliminate "sere" (ON *sér*).

335-6   These lines pose both a linguistic and theological problem. The linguistic problem concerns the meaning of "euene". Kaluza in *CM* p. 1704 glossed this word as "image, resemblance, likeness", but this is quite wrong. The *OED* prints this line from the *CM* under "euene" sb.1: "material; subject matter", but this raises the theological issue. If "euene" means material, then the *CM* poet is saying that God created the world from Himself, *ex deo,* rather than from nothing. The idea of creation *ex deo* does appear in the Middle Ages, most notably in the work of Scotus Erigena and Nicholas of Cusa. However, the Church strongly supported creation *ex nihilo.* Less than 100 years before the *CM* poet wrote, it condemned the works of Erigena and of two of his twelfth century followers, Almeric of Bena and David of Dinant. People were burned in France in the 1220's for subscribing to this pantheistic heresy. On this subject see esp. WULFSON, "Meaning of Ex Nihilo" and COHN *Pursuit of the Millennium.* This is not the sort of doctrine to appeal to a conservative ME poet writing for "lewed folk".

I suggest that the *CM* poet may be using the word "euene" either to mean "ability, resources, means", as in *MED* "evene" (b), or, as in *MED* "evene" (c), to mean "occasion, cause". Honorius writes at this point: "Quae fuit causa ut crearetur mundus? Bonitas Dei, ut essent quibus gratiam suam impertiret."

337-54   *Elucid.* I 17, 19-20.

341   In spite of Morris' note, *CM* p. xxxii, MSS CF are closer to the poet's original, translating "In ictu oculi, id est quam cito possis oculum aperire".

342   Not in *Elucid.*

343ff   This is the fullest explanation of creation in Middle English. The story in *Genesis* posed two main problems for mediaeval theologians: (1) did creation occur all at once, as suggested by *Eccli.* 18:1 and *Gen.* 2:4, or over a period of time, as told in *Gen.* 1; and (2) what exactly was produced by God's first creative act? The *CM* poet follows received opinion by saying that God, in a single act, created the matter from which the world would be shaped, and then spent six days separating it into elements and ornamenting his work.

344   MSS CG's "first" translates *Elucid.*'s "semel".

345   Cf. n. to 11.335-6 above.

346   *Eccli.* 18:1.

347 Perhaps suggested by *Sap.* 11:21: "sed omnia in mensura, et numero, et pondere disposuisti".

348-58 The poet's first explanation of the nature of the "prima materia" comes from *Elucid.* I 20. The matter is a jumbled mixture of the four elements (11.349-50), which is later given shape in the six day period described in *Genesis* (11.351-2). Cf. PETRUS LOMBARDUS, who said that matter existed "in forma confusionis ante formam dispositionis". See *Sent.* II xii, *PL* CXCII 676.

351 MSS CF read "sythen"; G has "fin", an error for "sin". This latter reading the southern translator miscopied as "ful".

353 The six day period of the Hexaemeron following the *opus creationis* is further divided. The first three days consist of the *opus distinctionis*, during which the elements are separated from each other and arranged in a hierarchy. Cf. GEOFFROI DE PARIS, fol. 1v col. 2:

> Li secons chapistres dira
> Coument Diex le monde estora,
> Les iiij ellemens a compas,
> L'un plus haut et l'autre plus baz.

354 Honorius writes that in the last three days of the Hexaemeron, God shaped those things "quae sunt infra elementa", that is those things which are made up of the elements. "Infra" was miscopied as "intra" in some Latin MSS, such as BL Harley 5234 fol. 90r col. 1. This error in Latin produces the *CM*'s nonsensical line. The error was widely circulated, however, for it turns up in many of the European translations of the *Elucidarium*. See SCHMITT, *Die Mittelenglische Version*, p. 5; the Old French Translation I in MS BL Add. 28260 fol. 37v; REYNAUD, "Elucidarium", p. 221 (Provençal); JONES and RHYS, *The Elucidarium*, p. 5 (Welsh); HELGASON, *The Arna Magnæan Manuscript 674A*, fol. 4v (Old Icelandic).

355-8 Not in Honorius. HAENISCH, *CM*, p. 4* suggested that the poet took these lines from *Hist. Schol. Gen.* i, *PL* CXCVIII 1055-6, where Comestor names the elements in refuting the atomic theories of Epicurus. In any event, their names would be familiar to the poet from other sources.

359-72 This is a second explanation of the nature of the first created matter, a division which is blurred in the southern translation by the substitution of "And" for "Or" (CF) or "Ayder" (G). The poet attributes this theory to Augustine (1.360) although it is taken from HUGH OF ST. VICTOR's *Adnot. in Pent. Gen.* v, *PL* CLXXV 34. Hugh was sometimes called the second Augustine, however, and some of his works may have been attributed to Augustine. See Roger BARON, "Hugues de Saint-Victor", p. 224. L1.362-8 sum up the Augustinian position. See *DGCM* I iii, *PL* XXXIV 176; *DGALIL* iii-iv, *PL* XXXIV 222-7; *Conf.* XII ii, v-viii, *PL* XXXII 826-9; *DGAL* II xi, *PL* XXXIV 272-3; *DCD* XI vi.

362 An exact translation of "angelicam naturam", Augustine's interpretation of the "coelum" of *Gen.* 1:1.

363 *Adnot. in Pent. PL* CLXXV 34. "þe world" is the physical universe, the "terram" of *Gen.* 1:1. Time cannot exist without motion and change. Motion and change cannot occur in God, but only in a created thing. Therefore time begins simultaneously with the first motion and change, i.e. with the first creature. See *DGCM* I ii, *PL* XXXIV 174-5; *DGALIL* iii, *PL* XXXIV 222-4; *Conf.* XI x-xiii, *PL* XXXII 814-5; *DCD* XI vi;

Hist. Schol. Gen. i, *PL* CXCVIII 1056; *Sum. Theol.* Q.LXVI art. 4. Thus for Augustine the world is created simultaneously with the beginning of time rather than before time began, as in BEDE, *In Pent., PL* XCI 191, whose opinion appeared in the *Glossa Ordinaria, PL* CXIII 69, or in time, as in Thierry of Chartres. See HARING "The Creation and Creator", p. 186 no. 5.

366-7 This is not the same jumbled mixture of elements described in 11.349-50. It seems at first to be Augustine's *prima materia*, which he conceived to be absolutely without all form (in the scientific sense of the word), as his Old Latin translation of the Bible declared: "Terra autem erat invisibilis et incomposita" (*Gen.* 1:2).

Cf. a Picard fragment quoted by BERGER, *La Bible française*, p. 266: "Au commencement du monde crea Dieu le ciel et le tierre mais devant chou li eliment n'estoient mie devisé li un de l'autre..."

368 MS F mistakes "serenes" for "sternes", but this is meaningless as exegesis.

369-72 Even Augustine admitted that matter could not exist absolutely without form, but his solution was to state that the priority of matter over form was not a temporal but a causal one. See *DGAL* I xv, *PL* XXXIV 257-8. The explanation given here by the poet, however, is Hugh of St. Victor's modification of Augustine's idea: "[materia] creata est autem informis, non ex toto carens forma; sed ad comparationem sequentis pulchritudinis et ordinis, informi potest dici." See *Adnot. in Pent., PL.* CLXXV 34.

Note that "shaples" here is used in the technical sense to translate "carens forma". The *OED* gives the earliest instance of this usage in *Piers Plowman* A. Cf. 1. 350 above, where "shaples" is used loosely to mean simply "having no definite or regular shape". Similarly, "of forme vnshapen" (CF "mischapen") in 1. 367 translates Hugh of St. Victor's "informis", although the *MED* gives the earliest instance of this technical meaning of "forme" (14b) as Gower's *Confessio Amantis* 7.214.

371 "how" in MSS GHTLB is a miscopying of "I tru" (CF).

373-408 A mixture of the accounts of *Genesis*, Honorius and Hugh of St. Victor: 11.373-81, *Adnot. in Pent.* vi, *PL* CLXXV 35; 11.382-94, *Gen.* 1:10-8; 11.395-402, *Elucid.* I 20; 11.403-4, *Adnot. in Pent., loc. cit.*; 11.405-6, *Elucid.* I 68; 11.407-8, *Gen.* 2:2-3.

375 MS F's "lift" is the original reading. C's "light" is an error.

The poet passes to the works of the second day without mentioning the creation of the light. This may reflect the author's Augustinian interpretation of the "lux" of *Gen.* 1:3-5 as the creation or perfection of the "angelicam naturam" or "aungel kynde". See *DGALIL* I iii, *PL* XXXIV 222-4; *Conf.* XIII iii, *PL* XXXII 846; *DGAL* I iii, *PL* XXXIV 248-9; *DCD* XI ix, xxxiii, *PL* XLI 323-5, 346-7. Cf. *Elucid.* I 20 and 27, and also *G & E* 61-4 and *Met. Para.* 51-4.

This line erroneously implies that the stars were created with the firmament, although in fact they did not appear until the fourth day. The poet may have wished to imply that the particular "sky" created on the first day was that which would later house the stars. He may have been thinking of *DIM* I lxxxvii, *PL* CLXXII 141 which says of the firmament

"stellis undiqueversum ornatum". Cf. also BEDE, *Hex.* I, *PL* XCI 18:
"Hic nostri coeli, in quo fixa sunt sidera, creatio describitur".

376   MS C's reading "sonded" is a corruption of an original "wit water
      sonde als cristale", translating *Adnot. in Pent.* vi, *PL* CLXXV 35:
      "de aquis solidatis quasi crystallinus lapis". Cf. *DIM* I lxxxvii, *PL*
      CLXXII 141. See *OED* "sound" a. 4.a.: "solid, massive, compact".
      The readings "clere" or "shynynge" in the other MSS come about
      because of the widely known properties of crystal. Cf. WHITING,
      Proverbs, C587-C594.

377-8 MORRIS, *CM,* p. xxxii suggested emending "sondid" (C) to "sond-
      erd", which makes much better sense. Without this change, the poet
      gives no idea of the function of the firmament in separating the waters
      above from those below. Cf. *Gen.* 1:7. MS F's reading is a scribal re-
      working of corrupt lines.

      Morris also suggested emending his reading of C, "þ[e]se", to
      "yse", but "yse" seems to me to be the reading of the MS itself. Two
      sources known to the *CM* poet thought of the firmament as made of ice.
      See *DIM* I lxxxvii, *PL* CLXXII 141; *Hist. Schol. Gen.* iv, *PL* CXCVIII
      1058; cf. *G & E* 97.

384   Most of the scribes had trouble with this line. MSS CG read "gress and
      frut", translating "herbam... et... fructum" (*Gen.* 1:11). F makes no
      sense with "and bad hit [the earth?] grow and frute forþ bringe". The
      southern translator mistook "and" for the northern ending of the present
      participle. He wrote "grisyng", (HT), as in *MED* "grassen" v. (a) "to
      become covered or decked with grass, produce grass". This modifies
      "hit" (the earth): "And bade the grass-producing earth bring forth
      fruit". The scribe of L was dissatisfied with "grisyng", however, and
      wrote "cresyng", as in *MED* "cresen" v. (1) "To become larger, in-
      crease". The scribe of B came close to reproducing the original form
      of the line by writing "grape &".

401   "goynge beestis" is an anticipation of *Gen.* 1:28.

402-6 The poet follows the example of *Genesis* in giving only a brief ac-
      count of Adam's creation here and reserving the full details for the be-
      ginning of the story of his fall. The biblical structure results from the
      fusion of two narratives. For details see ACKROYD and EVANS, *Cam-
      bridge History of the Bible,* I, pp. 71ff.

403-4 Perhaps from HUGH OF ST. VICTOR, *loc. cit.*: "Et merito post omnia
      factus est homo, qui omnibus praeferendus erat".

405-6 *Elucid.* I 68 quotes the popular Jewish tradition that Adam was
      created in Hebron. Cf. *Legende* 44/2, 45/18; KEMBLE 283; GROSSETESTE,
      ME Translations 264/126, 356/73; *Creat. of World* 340; *Ad. and Ep.*
      517; WYNTOUN I 67. The *CM* poet must also have known the equally
      popular tradition that Adam was created "in agro... Damasceno". See
      Hist. Schol. Gen. xiii, *PL* CXCVIII 1067; *G & E* 207; *Life of Christ*
      6185-8; HIGDEN 219; WYNTOUN I 65; *Fall of Princes* 500; CHAUCER'S
      "Monk's Tale" 2007-8; MANDEVILLE, ed. Letts, p. 48.

411-24 *Elucid.* I 23, perhaps suggested to Honorius by ANSELM's *De
      Similitudinibus* xliii, *PL* CLIX 623-4.

420   The number of angels created was usually left vague. The pseudo-
      Dionysius himself declared that the number was known only to God and

that earthly intelligence was incapable of comprehending it. See *De Caelesti Ierarchia* ˙vi and xiv, *PL* CXXII 1049, 1064. Cf. *Dan.* 7:10.

425-8 *Elucid.* I 26.

429-32 *Elucid.* I 23.

430 The nine orders of angels derive from the tradition of the *Celestial Hierarchies* of the pseudo-Dionysius, in which the nine orders are ranged in groups of three. The Gregorian tradition does not subdivide the nine orders. See GREGORY's *XL Hom. in Evang. II Hom.* xxxiv, *PL* LXXVI 1249-50.

432 Cf. GREGORY, *loc. cit.* and note to 11.514-6 below.

437ff The story of the fall of Lucifer is based on *Is.* 14:12-5, *Ez.* 28:2-19, *Luc* 10:18, *Apoc.* 12:3-9.

441-2 DUSTOOR, "Legs. of Lucifer", p. 232, suggests that these lines are translated from Bonaventura: "Dictus est autem Lucifer quia prae ceteris luxit." However, the connection of the name Lucifer with light is popular in vernacular writings. See WM. OF SHOREHAM 389; "Lydgatiana" I 13; KILDARE 18; Trin. Camb. 10; *North. Homs.*; CHAUCER's "Monk's Tale" 2004.

445-6 The meaning of these lines has been altered in transmission. The original version said that Lucifer ceased to know God who had created him:

> Allas! caitif he kneu him noght,
> þat hee drightin þat had him wroght; (CF)

MSS GHTLB, however, by omitting the second "þat", alter the sense to mean that Lucifer forgot that God had created him at all. In these MSS, Lucifer takes a Manichean position on the origins of the powers of darkness. See AUGUSTINE, *DGAL* XI xiii, *PL* XXXIV 436. The idea that Lucifer denied that God had made him is found in RUPERT OF ST. HERIBERT, *De Victoria Verbi Dei* I, xii-xiii, *PL* CLXIX 1227-8, where it is based on *Ez.* 28:2 and 29:3-4. Cf. *Paradise Lost*, V 833ff, 853ff, and McCOLLEYː "Milton's Battle", 230-5.

450 *Is.* 14:14.

451 Lucifer's pride can manifest itself in several ways. Augustine stressed his self-love, which is expressed as vanity in a number of vernacular works. See *Cleanness* 209; *Met. Para.* 61-4; *Ancrene Riwle*, 22/34-6; *York* I 49-56, 65-72; *Creat. of World* 114-33; *Ayenbite* p. 16; *Pilg. Life of Man* 12564-87; *Dest. of Troy* 4409. Augustine also said that pride gives rise to envy in *DGAL* XI xiv, *PL* XXXIV 436, cf. *Sent.* II, Dist. v, *PL* CXCII 661. Envy, either of God (*G & E* 273-6) or of the newly created man (as in the Latin *Vita Adae et Evae* and all its vernacular derivatives, see MOZLEY, p. 132), is often stressed as the chief sin of Lucifer. By contrast, the author of the *CM* is most indignant over Lucifer's disloyalty to God who had given him all he had. This interpretation, tinged by feudal concepts, is also found in *Piers Plowman* B I 110, 112, cf. B XII 41-6, and in *Cleanness* 210, and is much stressed in the *OE Gen.* (267, 277, 283, 291, 743).

457-9 *Is.* 14:13.

465-6 Cf. 11. 488-90.

469 The tradition that Michael cast out the devil is based on *Apoc.* 12:7, but is found also in I *Enoch* 10:11-16. Few vernacular works, except those specifically in honour of St. Michael, tell of his part in defeating the

rebels. See *SEL* 407/189ff; Mirk's *Fest.* 259; possibly also Trin. Camb. 35-6.

485-6 Perhaps suggested by *Elucid.* I 43. Cf ANSELM, *Cur Deus Homo* II xxii, *PL* CLVIII 430, and Woodburn O. ROSS, ed., *ME Sermons,* p. 314.

488-90 *Elucid.* I 36. The length of Lucifer's stay in heaven is problematical. *Ez.* 28:13 could indicate that the devil enjoyed a short period of happiness before his fall, but *Ioan.* 8:44 could mean that he did not. Many commentators agreed with Honorius that there was no interval between Lucifer's creation and his fall. See AUGUSTINE *DGAL* XI xvi, *PL* XXXIV 437; ISIDORE, *Sententiae* I x, *PL* LXXXIII 555; *Sum. Theol.* Q LXIII art. 6; so too, by implication, *Met. Para.* 53ff, cf. 1.66.

495 *Elucid.* I 40. The southern translator miscopies "air" (CFG) as "erþe". B corrects this.

In line 478 the poet simply followed *Is.* in assigning the fallen angels to hell. Here, however, he follows a long patristic tradition which put some of the demons on earth and some in the air. The devil's access to earth is mentioned in *Is.* 14:12, *Ez.* 28:17; *Iob.* 1:7, 2:2; *Apoc.* 12:9. Cf. AUGUSTINE, *Ennarrationes in Psalmos* CXLVIII 9, *PL* XXXVII 1943; *Sent.* II, iv, Dist. vi, *PL* CXCII 663 quotes *Ioan.* 14:30: "princeps aeris (alias mundi)"; *Hist. Schol. Gen.* viii, *PL* CXCVIII 1061. In Middle English see *G & E* 288; Trin. Camb. 14; *SEL* 408/192, 194, 409/219-21; *Life* — Vernon 106/78-9; *Piers Plowman* B I 123; "Quaestiones" 286; MIRK's *Fest.* 259; *Ad. & Ep.* 387-92; *Myroure,* p. 303.

497-502 *Elucid.* I 43, 50. The subsequent fate of both good and bad angels was discussed fairly often. See AUGUSTINE, *DCD* XI xiii and XXII i; *Enchir.* xxix, *PL* XL 246; GREGORY, *Moralium* XXVII xxxix, *PL* LXXVI 438; XXXIV vii, *PL* LXXVI 724; *Hom. in Ezech.* I vii, *PL* LXXVI 849; PETRUS LOMBARDUS, *Sent.* II Dist. vii, *PL* CXCII 664-5; HUGH OF ST. VICTOR, *Summa Sent.* Tract II 84, *PL* CLXXVI 84; and THOMAS AQUINAS, *Sum Theol.* Q. LXIV art. 2. While many vernacular writers mention the devil's eternal damnation, suggested by II *Pet.* 2:4, and *Iudae* 6, few are concerned with the confirmation of the good angels. Cf. however, *Life* — VERNON 106/71-5; WM OF SHOREHAM 412-4.

503-4 The poet is characteristically vague about the number of angels who fell. A frequent estimate is one tenth of the number who were created, for Gregory had suggested that man was created as a tenth order to fill up the gap left by the falling angels. See *XL Hom. in Evang.* II xxxiv, *PL* LXXVI 1249. Cf. *Cleanness* 216; *Kildare* 30; *North. Homs.;* *York* I 256-7; VII 19; *Cant. Creat.* 340-2; *Piers Plowman* C II 106; *Life of Christ* 4007-8; *Ad. & Ep.* 103-6; *Towneley* I 142; *SEL* 408-9.

505-6 Some paraphrases convey the distance through the time it takes the angels to fall, either seven days and seven nights (*Auch.* 44; *Kildare* 25), three days and nights (*OE Gen.* 306-8), forty days (*Cleanness* 224), or nine days (*Piers Plowman* B I 119).

507-10 The ultimate source of this estimate of the distance from heaven to earth is a passage in Moses Maimonides' *Guide of the Perplexed,* III 14. Largely through the *Legenda Aurea,* this *topos* reached many vernacular works. See JACOBUS A VORAGINE, *Legenda Aurea,* p. 321; *Life of Christ,* 8925-38; *Pricke of Consc.* 7671-86; an anonymous poem of 20-odd lines found in two MSS, BROWN and ROBBINS, *Index* 2794;

"On the Leaps which Christ Took", ed. Person, *Camb. ME Lyrics,* p. 29; as a page filler in a sermon book, MS BL Harley 2250, fol. 83 v; and in a garbled version in Mirk's *Fest.* 152/24-8. A slight variant on the tradition is found in the French and English versions of the *Image du monde.* See O. H. Prior, ed., *L'Image du monde,* pp. 194-5; the verse version of the same work as in MS BL Harley 4333, fol. 65v; Prior, ed., *Caxton's Mirrour* p. 171; cf. *SEL,* "Michael III", 418/489-96.

The *CM* poet attributes this calculation to Bede. I have not found such a passage in Bede's works. However, in one MS, BL Add. 36983 fol. 255r col. 1, the third legend of Michael from the *SEL,* which contains this passage, is said to have been translated from Latin to English by Bede. This suggests a mediaeval tendency to credit Bede with writings of this kind because his works on the natural sciences were so well known.

514-6   Cf. 1.432. The poet has used two traditions here. The earlier line implies that nine orders of angels were created and some of each order fell. Man was always intended to be the tenth order. Honorius maintains this in the passage translated there: "novem quidem ordinibus angelorum et decimo hominum." Cf. Gregory, *XL Hom. in Evang.* II xxxiv, *PL* LXXVI 1249. In line 516, however, the *CM* poet suggests that all the angels who fell belonged to a tenth order, and that man was created to replace this order. Ten orders of angels appear in II *Enoch* 20:3.

517-8   This seems flatly to contradict *Gen.* 2:7, where Adam is said to be made of earth alone. However, commentators who wished to see man as a microcosm of the physical universe could say that the "limo terrae" was made up of several of the basic elements. See e.g. Thomas Aquinas, *Sum. Theol.* Q. XCI art. 1. Cf. also *SEL.,* Laud MS, 318/668-9.

517-52   *Elucid.* I 59. This passage deals with Adam's physical nature. My analysis of it is based largely on Lefèvre's, *Elucid.* p. 115. First the writer says that Adam is composed of the four elements (11.519-20). Secondly he says that various parts of his body resemble the four elements: his head is like the sky or fiery element (521-30), his chest is like the air (531-4), his stomach resembles the sea (535-6), and his feet are like the earth (537-8). Then man's five senses are said to come from the five elements of Aristotelian tradition, which distinguished air from ether as two separate elements. See Aristotle, *On the Heavens,* Bk. I. Thus Adam's sight comes from fire (539), his hearing from the upper air or ether (540), his sense of smell from the lower air (*Elucid.* I 59), his sense of taste from water (*loc. cit.*), and his sense of touch from earth (542). Cf. Augustine, *DGAL* III iv, *PL* XXXIV 281. In addition, the hardness of his bones comes from stones (543-4), his nails are like the trees of the earth, his hair like grass (545-6), and in his senses he is one with animals (547-8).

The *locus classicus* for this kind of statement about man's physical composition is II *Enoch* 30:8. The tradition was extremely popular in the Middle Ages, both in Latin and in the European vernaculars. See esp. Förster, "Adams Erschaffung", 477-529. J. M. Evans, "Microcosmic Adam" also deals with this *topos.*

Honorius repeats this description of man in his *Sacramentarium* I, *PL* CLXXII 773. For an illustration of Honorius' conception of man as a microcosm in a twelfth century German MS, see M. W. EVANS, *Medieval Drawings*, pl. 81.

Certain corruptions have crept into the *CM* text.

519 Adam's blood is made from water, as in MSS CF, but GHTLB contain the scribal error "body" for "blod". His flesh is made from earth.

520 Adam's heat comes from fire, as in CF. MSS GHTL all contain the corruption of "heet" to "heer", but B corrects it again to "hete". Adam's breath comes from air.

521-2 MS F alone preserves the original translation of *Elucid.* I 59: "Caput ejus est rotundum in caelestis sphaerae modum." The lines are not spurious, as Morris suggests, *CM*, p. 38.

527 The seven master stars translate Honorius' "septem caeli", that is the seven planets which are supposed to control men's actions.

531-4 Honorius in fact compares the chest to the air, for breathing and coughing simulate wind and thunder. The *CM* poet has padded 1.533 by the meaningless addition of lightning with the thunder.

534 The reading "breed" in FGHTLB is a scribal corruption of C's "spred", Lat. "versantur".

539 Adam's sight comes from the fiery element. Scribal error corrupted CFG's "þe ouer fir", Honorius' "ex caelesti igne", into HTLB's "Thonder fyre".

540 His hearing comes from the upper air. Similar scribal error gives "Thonder eyer" in HLB for Lat. "ex superiore aere". MS T has further corrupted "eyer" into "oþer".

541 His breath comes from the under air, or wind. MSS HTLB have corrupted "þis vnder wynd", Lat. "ex inferiore aere", to "þis wondur wynde".

542 His senses of touch ("fele") and taste ("fond") come from the earth. None of the MSS correctly translates Honorius' "ex aqua gustum, ex terra habet tactum".

546 Many other versions have veins instead of nails here. Honorius, however, has "unguibus". Note that this is plural, as is B's "nayles".

547-8 This translates Honorius' "sensum cum animalibus".

556 The image of God in man mentioned in *Genesis* is usually considered to be the soul. See, e.g., *Elucid.* I 61; *Sent.*, II Dist. xvii, *PL* CXCII 685-6; *Hist. Schol. Gen.* ix, *PL* CXCVIII 1063.

557 Honorius used this image to describe the making of the angels in God's image in *Elucid.* I 54.

558 MS C errs in writing "licam" for "likeness". The resemblance between God and man is, of course, not physical but spiritual.

561-80 *Elucid.* I 61. The soul is here a microcosm of the Trinity as the body is a microcosm of the physical universe. Cf. 11.319-22, n.

564 MORRIS, *CM*, p. xxxiii was puzzled by C's "min" and preferred the readings of GT. However, the rhymeword "thrin" in 1.563 is probably original. "Thrin" (ON þrinnr) in C is usually translated to "three" in the other MSS.

585-7 Adam is usually said to have been created a fully formed adult, so that he would be capable of working the land in the Garden. The reference to Augustine is probably to *DGAL* VI xiii, *PL* XXXIV 348, but cf. *De Peccatorum Meritis* xxxvii, *PL* XLIV 149. The *CM* poet could also have found this in *Hist. Schol. Gen.* xii, *PL* CXCVIII 1066.

The tradition was so well known in the Middle Ages that the Monk of Sawley added it to his translation of GROSSETESTE's *Chateau d'Amour*. See GROSSETESTE, *ME Translations*, 321/29. Cf. GINZBERG, *Legends* V, p. 21 n. 21.

588   *Gen.* 2:8, 15. Cf. 11.405-6 and note above.

589-94   *Elucid.* I 64. The interpretation of Adam's name depends on the initial letters of the Greek words for the four directions — *anatole, duses, arctos* and *mesembris*. The tradition is a very old one. See *Sybilline Oracles* iii 24-6; II *Enoch* xxx 13-4. It became popular with the Fathers. See JEROME, *Expositio Quatuor Evang.*, *PL* XXX 533; AUGUSTINE, *In Joannis Evang.*, IX ii, *PL* XXXV 1465; *Enarratio in Psalmum* xcv 15, *PL* XXXVII 1236; BEDE, *In Pent.*, *PL* XCI 216; HUGH OF ST. VICTOR, *De Arca Noe Mystica* iv, *PL* CLXXVI 686. It is also frequent in Irish exegesis. See MCNALLY, *The Bible*, p. 26. It is attached to many MSS of the *Vita Adae et Evae* and their translations. See MOZLEY, 147-8/57. See also KEMBLE 178-80; *Quaestiones* 285; *Ormulum* 11.16384-16419; MACÉ, 369-85.

589   MSS CG's "not þe" is preferable to the "now ʒe" or "mow ʒe" of the southern scribes.

598-602   *Elucid.* I 64.

617   This begins the account of earth history. Throughout the Old Testament narrative, the poet stresses the world's decline from this state of perfection.

617-38   A conflation of *Gen.* 1:26 and *Gen.* 2:19-25.

625-6   The ME poet has Adam sleep during Eve's creation simply to keep him from knowing how God created her. Some MSS of the *Elucidarium* add the long-standing tradition that Adam's sleep was an ecstatic one, during which he received visions of the future. See *Elucid.* I 71a, and p. 232. Cf. *Hist. Schol. Gen.* xvi, *PL* CXCVIII 1070, and in ME, *G & E* 224-6; *Chester* II 137-40. Jerome, however, objected to this interpretation on linguistic grounds, in *Quaest. in Gen.*, *PL* XXIII 990.

The southern translator seems to have rewritten 1.625 because of the excess of verbs in the sentence.

633-4   *Gen.* 2:23 depends on a Hebrew pun. The woman is first named *Issa* (woman) because she came from *Is* (man). The Old Latin translation "mulier" completely ignored the pun, as Augustine complained in *DGCM* II xiii, *PL* XXXIV 206. Theodotian had tried to translate the word as "assumptio: quia ex viro sumpta est". See JEROME, *Quaest. in Gen.*, *PL* XXIII 990. Jerome, however, fixed the Latin translation as "virago" from "ex viro sumpta est" in *PL* XXIII 990.

The *CM* simply repeats the Vulgate translation, although the pun makes no sense in English. Other ME writers tried to do something with the pun. Some English versions of the *Vita Adae* give it literally: "this shalle þe cleped mannes deede [*vir ago*], for she is taken of man". See "Nachträge zu den Legenden" 355/6-7; DAY, ed., *Wheatley MS*, 78/31-2. Only *G&E* ingeniously tries to render an English pun:

> Mayden, for sche was mad of man,
> Hire first name ðor bi-gan (235-6).

637　The first "hem" is plural, but the second must be read as singular, referring to Adam, who is to multiply with "her" (1.638). Originally all three pronouns were plural, as in MSS CFG.

659　An intensification of the prohibition in *Gen.* 2:17 that they must not eat the fruit. Cf. *Piers Plowman* B XVIII 192; C XXI 200. Other accounts go even further, warning Adam and Eve not to go near the tree. See *Rev. Meth.* 31; *SELTemp.* fol. 1r col. 1.

660　The "double deeþ" is a favourite phrase of the *CM* poet, picked up from *Trad. anon.* See fol. 215v col. 2, e.g. Exegetical tradition said that after the Fall, man can suffer the death of both the body and the soul. See, e.g., *DCD* XIII i-xii; REMIGIUS OF AUXERRE, *Comment. in Gen., PL* CXXXI 62. Cf. *Pricke of Consc.* 1683-99.

663-8　Cf. Honorius' brief discussion of free will in *Elucid.* I 73. The *Trad. anon.* also discusses it, fol. 214r. The *CM* poet is not translating either one exactly, however.

672-82　*Trad. anon.* fol. 214r col. 2.

683-98　The idea that no animals would have been allowed to be harmful in Paradise is frequently met. See, e.g., ISIDORE, *De Ord. Creat.* x, *PL* LXXXIII 938; AELFRIC, *Homs. of Aelfric,* 678/39-40; Alexander NECKHAM, *De Nat. Rerum* II clvi, p. 249; COLI, *Il Paradiso terrestre,* 136, GRAF, *Miti,* 52-4. However, this catalogue of animals in the *CM* is almost unique among descriptions of Paradise in the vernacular biblical paraphrases. The poet translated it, slightly abridged, from *Trad. anon.,* fol. 214r col. 2.-214v col. 1.

　　The idea of this catalogue of animals in the French poem comes from *Is.* 11:6-8. This speaks of harmony between wolf and lamb, panther and kid, calf, lion and sheep, calf, bear and dog, asp and basilisk. Latin commentators usually glossed this to refer to the future triumph of Christ and his Church. See, e.g., HAYMO OF HALBERSTAT, *Comment. in Isaiam* II, *PL* CXVI 781; HERVÉ OF BOURGDIEU, *Comment. in Isaiam* II, *PL* CLXXXI 142-4. However, the future concord of animals was sometimes seen as a return of a past Golden Age. Jerome dismissed this opinion as one of the "fabula poetarum", in a passage which was widely circulated in the *Glossa Ordinaria.* See JEROME, *Comment. in Is.* IV xi, *PL* XXIV 150-1; *Glossa, PL* CXIII 1251.

691　The griphon does not come from *Isaiah.* Cf. *Hist. Schol. Gen.* xxiii, *PL* CXCVIII 1074 where, in a similar passage, it is paired with its traditional enemy, the horse.

693-4　A southern reviser has altered the Scandinavian word "stang" (ultimately from the Old Norse verb *stanga*) to "tonge". This is an error of biology, of course, but an understandable one, for the word sting was sometimes erroneously applied to the tongue of a poisonous serpent in the Middle Ages. See *OED* Sting sb¹ 2.

698-700　*Gen* 3:1.

701-10　Translated from GROSSETESTE's *Chateau d'amour,* 11.48-59. *Is.* 30:26 prophesies that the brightness of the sun and moon will increase in this manner in the future. The earth's loss of brightness after the Fall, however, is a Jewish tradition, well known to Latin commentators and English writers alike. See *Jew. Encyc.* "Adam"; JEROME, *Com-*

ment. in Is. IX xxx, *PL* XXIV 362; ISIDORE, *De Ord. Creat.* v and x, *PL* LXXXIII 923-4, 938; HAYMO OF HALBERSTAT, *Comment. in Is.* II, *PL* CXVI 869; AELFRIC, *Homs. of Aelfric,* ed. Pope, 679/56-65; *Pricke of Consc.* 6356-63; Lydgate, *Fall of Princes* 596-604; ROSS, *ME Sermons* 317/35-318/2; MACÉ 285-8. Cf. *CM* 9381-4.

702   MSS GHTLB preserve better readings than MSS CF. Grosseteste wrote "ke ne est ores".

708   MSS CFG preserve the original reading, translating "En terre, en mer, a val, a munt" (56).

712   "Selly" is a miscopying of G's "felly", but can be read as modifying "hym" (Adam).

713-20   *Trad. anon.* fol. 214v col. 2. Cf. n. to 1.451 above.

725   The word "warlau" (CF) is frequently used to refer to the devil in ME. See *OED* Warlock. MSS GHTLB make the reference even more explicit by calling him Satan.

731   "on hyȝe" (GHTLB) probably originated in a misreading of "on drei", at a distance. Cf. 1.757 and n. The scribe, however, could have visualized the devil looking up at Adam on the heights of Paradise from his own position below in hell.

735   *Genesis* nowhere connects the serpent with the devil, but other biblical books do. Cf., e.g., *Sap.* 2:24. Most commentators see the serpent as the devil himself in disguise, but the *CM* poet speaks of him here as a messenger sent by the devil. In the *OE Gen.,* 11.442ff., a subordinate demon is sent, disguised as a serpent, to do the tempting. Cf. also the *Apocalypse of Moses* 16:1-5 in which the devil tempts the serpent to rebellion first by persuading him that he should not have to eat Adam's tares. The history of the same motif as it appears in the tenth century Irish work *Saltair na Rann* is traced in MURDOCH, "Early Irish Adam and Eve". For a brief discussion of this motif in art see TRAPP, "Iconography of the Fall", pp. 240-2.

The *CM* poet oddly omits to mention the serpent with the human face which appears in many vernacular works from the twelfth century on. The latest discussion of this motif is in KELLY, "Metamorphoses", which refers to older scholarship.

738-40   Cf. *Gen.* 3:1.

741-3   The usual reason given for the devil's tempting Eve first is that she is the weaker of the two. See *DCD* XIV xi; BEDE, *In Pent., PL* XCI 212; *Sent.* II Dist. xxi, *PL* CXCII 694; *Hist. Schol. Gen.* xxi, *PL* CXCVIII 1072; WM. OF SHOREHAM 647-51; HERMAN, fol. 1v.

745   Why did Satan teach the serpent, his messenger, how to tempt Adam (above, 1.735 and note) if he himself is to be in the serpent's skin? The line may be intended metaphorically to suggest that Satan's intentions have completely taken over the serpent's, or it may indicate a second source for the scene. Cf. *DGAL* XI xxviii, *PL* XXXIV 444; *Hist. Schol. Gen.* xxi, *PL* CXCVIII 1072; *Elucid.* I 85. A twelfth century Irish work makes the scene more clearly understandable. There the devil persuades the serpent to help him and then says: "Take my counsel... and make we covenant and friendship and go thou not to wait on Adam and give me a place to me in thy body, that we may go, both of us [*lit.* in our duality], unto Eve and enjoin upon

her to eat the fruit of the forbidden tree;..." From MacCarthy, ed., *Codex Palatino Vaticanus*, 51f.

749-54   Cf. *Elucid.* I 73.

757   Cf. the *Vita Adae et Evae*, in which the temptation takes place when Eve is alone, after Adam has very reluctantly left her. See Mozley 138/33 and the English translations.

758-90   The dialogue between Eve and the serpent is a fairly close rendering of *Gen.* 3:1-6.

764   CFG's "midward" translates *Gen.* 3:3 "quod est in medio paradisi".

767   Cf. n. to 1.659 above.

768   Cf. 1.660 and note. MSS CFG do not repeat the reference to the "doubel deeþ".

775-84   Eve's first sin is wishing to be like God. Cf. *Gen.* 3:5. The *CM* poet ignores the difficulties created by the plural noun "dii" in the Vulgate, as do most vernacular writers. Others translate "dii" as the Trinity (Kildare 64) or as angels (possibly *G&E* 332), or say that Adam and Eve wanted to be "As two godes, with god" (*Piers Plowman* C xxi 320).

776   This phrasing is not from *Gen.*, but recalls Lucifer's own desires. See 1.450 above.

787-8   Eve's second sin is sensuous curiosity about the fruit, *Gen.* 3:6. Cf. *DGCM* II xv, *PL* XXXIV 207; Bede, *In Pent.*, *PL* XCI 214; *Sent.* II Dist. xxi, *PL* CXCII 696; *Hist. Schol. Gen.* xxii, xxiii, *PL* CXCVIII 1072, 1074; Hugh of St. Victor, *De Sacramentis Christ. Fid.* I vii 10, *PL* CLXXVI 290-1; *Sum. Theol.* Q. CLXIII art. 1. Cf. also the moral lesson taught in *Ancrene Riwle* 22/36-23/10.

791-27   The poet is here using a source which I have not been able to identify.

792   The correct reading is hard to reconstruct here. Perhaps the original line stated that the devil's promise was immediately shown to be false.

794   C's line is probably original. Its "wayth" (ON *vaoi*) is often changed in the other MSS. G's "king" is a miscopying of "kin". The southern translator glossed the "king" of his exemplar as "oure lord god". The line is acceptable as it stands in these latter MSS, but is clearly not the original.

795   The fruit is universally called an apple in the vernacular, as in Latin Christianity generally. Von Rad, *Genesis*, p. 88 suggests this identification may have arisen through the association of "malus"/bad, and "malum"/apple. Quinn, *The Quest of Seth*, p. 128 traces it to a Targum translation of *Cant.* 2:3 and 7:9 as "paradise apple". Petrus Comestor, however, suggests that the fruit was a fig. See *Hist. Schol. Gen.* xxiii, *PL* CXCVIII 1073. Cf. Isidore, *De Ord. Creat.*, *PL* LXXXIII 941: "ficum, maledictum delicti Adae, quae totam terram inficeret". Cf. Rashi, 13.

795-6   The apple of Eden is here metaphorically identified with the sour grapes of *Ier.* 31:29: "Patres comederunt uvam acerbam,/et dentes filiorum obstupuerunt." Cf. *Ez.* 18:2. Cassidy, "The Edged Teeth" 227-36 suggests that the identification is first made in the fifth century in Sedulius' *Carmen Paschale*, from which the *CM* passage is "a

lineal descendent". See *PL* XIX 595, 11.20-5. AUGUSTINE, *Enchir.*
xlvi, *PL* XL 254 also quotes the passage from *Ez.* in speaking of the
consequences of the Fall. Cf. Old English *Phoenix,* 11.402-9; *Pirke,*
xiii, p. 95; GINZBERG, *Legends* V, p. 68 n. 68.

823   For Petrus Comestor, as for most commentators in the Augustinian
tradition, the immediate effects of the Fall are mainly sexual. See
Hist. Schol. Gen. xxii, *PL* CXCVIII 1072-3; cf. AUGUSTINE, *DCD*
XIV xv-xxvi. The *CM* poet, however, takes from the *Trad. anon.*
this description of the disharmony in Paradise after the Fall. It neatly
balances the previous description of the harmony in the animal world
(11. 671 ff. above).

828-38   *Trad. anon.* fol. 215r col. 2-215v col. 1.

828   *MED* suggests that MS C's "blurded" is an error for "blered".
However, G's "lourid" is probably the original reading. *Trad. anon.*
has "Toutes [les bêtes] li firent laide chiere". The southern translator,
or his exemplar, miscopied "lourid" as "lord", and a much weaker
couplet resulted.

877-84   These lines, like much of this conversation, sound more like *Trad.
anon.* fol. 215v col. 1 than like *Gen.* 3.

897-8   These lines are obviously reversed in MSS GHTLB.

901-12   *Trad. anon.* fol. 215v col. 2.

901-2   The reference to the serpent's warm nature ultimately comes from
a misreading of *Gen.* 3:1 *calidior* 'hotter' instead of *callidior* 'more
clever'. Cf. ELLIS, *Golden Legend,* I, 172: "Then the serpent which
was hotter than any beast of the earth..." Cf. WHITE, *Book of Beasts,*
pp. 186-7.

905   Cf. 1.660 above and note.

909-10   The subjection of woman to man might have called to the French
poet's mind the passage from I *Cor.* 11:3-10 which urges women to cover
their heads as a sign of their subjection and shame. Cf. however *Pirke*
xiv, p. 100, where part of Eve's penalty is that "her head is covered
like a mourner".

911-6   The poet makes clear Eve's function as the antitype of Mary, the
usual mediaeval interpretation of *Gen.* 3:15. See the references in
Dict. théol. cath., "Eve", V 1651-2.

937-42   The southern translator garbled CG's close translation of *Gen.*
3:22. He has God addressing Adam (11.937-8) and wrongly asserting
that He gave Adam knowledge of both good and evil.

944   The southern translation errs in the pronoun "þei". Only Adam was
made in the world, while Eve was formed in Paradise. This is of some
interest to commentators such as PETER ABELARD, *PL* CLXXVIII
243, and is made the subject of a riddle in the prose *Life* — Vernon
107/90-3.

945-51   God lectures Adam in somewhat similar terms in *Trad. anon.*
fol. 216r col. 1. The French poem does not mention the oil of mercy
(1.955) because this part of the legend does not appear there.

952   Cf. 1.660 above and note.

967-70   *Trad. anon.* fol. 215v col. 2. The rest of the conversation is not
in the French poem.

975-88 MSS GHTLB all omit these lines. A scribe's eye mistook "Adam" on 1.989 for "Adam" on 1.975.

975-9 Possibly suggested by Hugh of St. Victor, *Adnot. in Pent.* vii, *PL* CLXXV 44.

981-8 The poet implies that the Fall occurred immediately after Eve was created, for Adam was formed at 9 am ("vndern tide"), and Eve at midday, and Adam lived only three hours in Paradise before the Fall (1.982). Cf. *DGAL* IX iv, *PL* XXXIV 395-6; Trin. Camb. 41; *North. Homs.*

985-8 *Elucid.* I 91.

994 The southern scribes are clearly dubious about this line. MS H's "fully flecched"/completely turned away, is at least innocuous. T's "fouly flecched" seems to question God's justice in turning Adam out of Paradise, but cf. a similar construction in *Anc. test.* fol. 3r col. 1: "Vilement en fu iete de parais". Morris, *CM,* p. xxxiv reads "flecched" as a variant of "flekked", and thus reads fouly spotted, but this is unconvincing.

995 The wall of fire surrounding Paradise is found in ISIDORE, *Etym.* XIV iii 3; RABANUS MAURUS, *De Universo* XII iii, *PL* CXI 334; *DIM* I viii, *PL* CLXXII 123; etc.

999ff. This description of Paradise includes many of the conventional topoi, and represents a vision of still-existing but unattainable delight. Cf. the present tense used in 1.1006 and n. to 11.1030-1. The *loci classici* for Christian descriptions of Paradise are Lactantius, *De Ave Phoenice*, trans A.S. Cook, in *OE Elene,* p. 124, PSEUDO-TERTULLIAN, *De Judicio Domini* viii, *PL* II 1151-2; and AVITUS, *De Mosaicae Historiae Gestis, PL* LIX 323-30. See discussions by COLI, *Il Paradiso terrestre*; GRAF, *Miti*; Patch, *The Other World;* GIAMATTI, *The Earthly Paradise;* Witke, *Numen Litterarum;* and DUNCAN, *Milton's Earthly Paradise.* Graf, Appendice I, prints relevant extracts from twenty sources.

Because the *topos* is so wide-spread, I shall comment only on unusual features in the *CM.*

1006 In *Gen.* 2:8, the Septuagint and Old Latin read "ad orientam" instead of "a principio". Most mediaeval writers thus place Paradise in the east. HAENISCH, *CM,* p. 4* suggests that this detail in the *CM* comes from Petrus Comestor, but the poet could have picked it up almost anywhere.

1007 Man worked in the Garden without fatigue. See, e.g., *DGAL* VIII x, *PL* XXXIV 381; ERNALDUS OF BONNEVALLE, *Hexaemeron, PL* CLXXXIX 1536; *Hist. Schol. Gen.* xv, *PL* CXCVIII 1068.

1009 The idea of a perpetual day without night is found in the pseudo-Tertullian poem, *PL* II 1151 and 1152, but, as Lactantius speaks of a dawn, 1.35, his vision of Paradise presumably includes nights. Cf. CHAUCER's *Parliament of Fowles* 209-10, and above, 1.646.

1010 Cf. below, 11.1288-90.

1012 The perpetual leafiness of Paradise is stressed in *Trad. anon.* fol. 212v col. 1. Augustine said that the fruits in the garden would not decay, and referred to *Ioan.* 6:27 to support the idea. However, he interpreted the passage allegorically. See *DGCM* ix, *PL* XXXIV 202. Cf. PSEUDO-TERTULLIAN, *loc. cit.*

1014 GIAMATTI, p. 70, lists the stress on the beautiful odours of Paradise as characteristic of Christian as opposed to classical, descriptions of Paradise. This may arise from the mention of *bdellium*, an aromatic gum, in *Gen.* 2:12. Cf. *Trad. anon.* fol. 212v col. 1.

1015-26 This description of the four trees comes from *Elucid.* I 69. Cf. somewhat similar passages in AUGUSTINE, *DCD* XIV xxvi; ROBERTUS PULLUS, *Sententiae* II xix, *PL* CLXXXVI 746.

1027 The "orcharde of delices" exactly translated "hortus deliciarum", which in turn translates the Hebrew words rendered by *Paradisus (hortus)* and *Eden (deliciae)*. See JEROME, *Quaest. in Gen.*, *PL* XXIII 988; ISIDORE, *Etym.* XIV iii 2; etc.

1028 Cf. n. to 1.1014 above. The pseudo-Tertullian poem mentions cinammon and amomum, Avitus cinammon and balsam. Cf. ERNALDUS, *op. cit.*, 1535. In the *Apocalypse of Moses*, Adam and Eve take spices with them when they are expelled from Paradise. In the *Vita Adae et Evae*, Eve and Seth return from Paradise bringing Adam three herbs. See MOZLEY, 142/10-11.

1030-1 The sweet bird songs of Paradise are stressed by Ernaldus, for instance, *Hex.*, *PL* XXXIX 1537, and in the *Legende*, p. 46/27. The original reading of the *CM* however seems to have referred to the songs of saints in the earthly Paradise rather than to those of birds. Cf. MSS CF. Strictly speaking, the existence of saints is impossible in Adam's time, because they had not yet been born. Their appearance in this passage emphasizes that this is a description of the earthly paradise as it exists now. Cf. above, n. to 1.999ff.

1032-8 The well and four streams are also characteristic of the Christian paradise. See GIAMATTI, p. 70.

1037-8 The names of the rivers are corrupt only in MSS of the southern translation. MS C now has the biblical forms of the names, "gyon" and "fison", although these are written in a later hand. MSS FG and probably originally C make the common identification of Phison with Ganges and Gehon with Nile. See JOSEPHUS, p. 19; JEROME, *Quaest. in Gen.*, *PL* XXIII 989; *DGCM* II x, *PL* XXXIV 203; BEDE, *Hex.*, *PL* XCI 45; *In Pent.*, *PL* XCI 207; *Hist. Schol. Gen.* xiv, *PL* CXCVIII 1068.

The first part of the southern translator's "Iulespigre" was a scribal misreading of the minims in "nilus". The second half of the word, "pigre", began in the exemplar of the southern MSS as an attempt to copy an original "phison", but after one letter the scribe's eye slipped upward to the ending of "tigre". Hence the meaningless "Iulespigre".

1039-40 According to Giamatti, p. 70, the precious stones of Paradise are a special characteristic of Christian tradition not found in classical literature. They originate in *Gen.* 2:11-2. The Septuagint translates the Hebrew word in *Gen.* 2:12 as "carbuncle" instead of "bdellium", as in the Vulgate, thus reinforcing the tradition.

1041 Paradise is always thought to be remote and inaccessible. Some writers say that it is inaccessible because it is so far away, separated from us by vast spaces of land, sea or desert, sometimes filled with wild beasts. The most popular Christian tradition said that Paradise was inaccessibly high, perhaps because it shared something of earth and heaven, as Patch suggests, *The Other World*, p. 135. This belief is reinforced by II *Cor*. 12:2-4, whose "tertium Coelum" the Greek Fathers identified with the lunar sphere. See Giamatti, *loc. cit.*

1042-4 The idea that Paradise, because of its height, escaped the great flood, is often found also, even in pagan authors. The *CM* poet probably takes his version from PETRUS COMESTOR, *Hist. Schol. Gen.* xiii, *PL* CXCVIII 1067.

1050 MSS CFG state that Adam and Eve were the first people to have to work hard. The reading of the southern translation, "þe firste þei were to sawe bigan", results from scribal corruption of "sua"/so to "sau"/ sow. Cain is usually supposed to be the first cultivator. See JOSEPHUS 27; *Hist. Schol. Gen.* xxvi, *PL* CXCVIII 1076.

1052 Cain is not yet cursed, of course, but many vernacular works cannot resist the alliteration. See *Cant. Creat.* 447; *Rev. Meth.* 58; *Met. Para.* 234; cf. *Hist. Schol. Gen.* xxvi, *PL* CXCVIII 1076, the probable source here. *Piers Plowman* says that Cain was conceived while his parents were still unrepentant and was therefore cursed (C XI 212-5).

1056 "fode" here means offspring, an allusion that Emerson, "Legs. of Cain", p. 832, missed in discussing the devilish origin of Cain. The idea is a Jewish one, given authority for Christians by *Ioan* 3:12. See *Jew. Encyc.* "Cain". Cf. AUGUSTINE, *In Epistolam Joannis ad Parthos*, Tract. V iii, *PL* XXXV 2012-3; BEDE, *In Primam Epistolam Sancti Joannis*, *PL* XCIII 102.

1063-6 *Gen.* 4:4-5 says simply "et respexit Dominus ad Abel, et ad munera ejus. Ad Cain vero, et ad munera illius, non respexit;" without specifying why Abel's offering was more acceptable. The most popular explanation was that Abel gave his in a better spirit. Cf. *Hebr.* 11:4 and references in "Abel", *Dict. théol. cath.* I 29. See also WEATHELY, ed., *Speculum Sacerdotale*, pp. 66, 95-6. The mystery plays, especially the Towneley "Matacio abel", make great fun out of Cain's unwilling sacrifice.

1070 The original reading must have been C's "sacrilages". The word is plural because it refers both to the coming murder of Abel (*OED* under "sacrilege... any kind of outrage on consecrated persons or things") and more immediately back to the grudging offering of the tithe. In the Middle Ages, sacrilege was a branch of avarice. See Chaucer's "Parson's Tale": "Espiritueel thefte is sacrilege, that is to seyn, hurtynge of hooly thynges, or of thynges sacred to Christ,... they that withdrawen falsly the rightes that longen to hooly chirche" (X[I]800-1). Cf. MORRIS, ed., *Ayenbite of Inwyt*, p. 41.

Probably by missing or omitting a superscribed abbreviation sign for "ri", a scribe has corrupted "sacrilege" to "sacles" (FG), which can only refer very awkwardly to Abel.

1073 C's "chafte ban" (ON; cp. OI *kjapt-r*)/jaw-bone, is the original reading. The tradition that the weapon used to murder Abel was the jaw-bone of an ass is firmly entrenched in vernacular literature and in art in the Middle Ages. The tradition has been discussed by EMERSON, "Legs. of Cain"; BONNELL, "Cain's Jaw Bone", 140-6; SCHAPIRO,

"Cain's Jaw Bone"; HENDERSON, "Cain's Jaw-Bone"; COOMARASWA-
MY, *Art Bulletin;* BARB, "Cain's Murder-Weapon". In England the
ass's jaw-bone appears in KEMBLE, 180; Trin. Camb. 86; *Life* — Ver-
non 112/255; *Met. Para.* 236; *Lud. Cov.* III 149; *Towneley* II 324;
Creat. of World 1117. Cf. *Anc. Corn. Dr.* 539-40 where Cain strikes
Abel on the jaw-bone, obviously a corruption of the same tradition.
The jaw-bone appears also in *Anc. test.* fol. 3r col. 1, quoted in BON-
NARD, p. 97. The earliest picture of Cain holding a jaw-bone is in the
illustrations to Aelfric's translation of the Hexateuch, MS BL Cotton
Claudius B iv, fol. 8v, dated in the second quarter of the eleventh
century.

1075-82   Cf. MALAN, *Book of Adam* I 79; *Apoc. of Moses,* xl 4.

1083-4   Cf. *Hist. Schol. Gen.* xxvii, *PL* CXCVIII 1077. This is the earliest
citation for this proverb in WHITING, *Proverbs,* M806.

1087-1110   *Trad. anon.* fol. 216v.

1087-90   Adam instinctively knows that Cain has done an evil deed. Cf. the
Vita Adae, Mozley 134-5/23, in which Eve dreams, before the deed,
of Cain with Abel's blood in his mouth.

1093-6   In *Gen.* 4:9 these words are part of the dialogue between God and
Cain. Petrus Comestor was apparently bothered by God's asking Cain
where Abel was. He explains that God really knew the answer all
along, but intended his words as a cry against fratricide. The vernacular
poets have evaded Comestor's difficulty by transferring the question
to Cain's earthly father. See *Hist. Schol. Gen.* xxvii, *PL* CXCVIII
1077.

1098   *Genesis* does not mention the offering being burned, but the tradition
was of long standing. The Hebrew word which appears in the Vulgate
as "respexit" was translated as "kindled" by Theodotian, and this
was widely reported in the Middle Ages. See Jerome, *Quaest. in Gen.,*
PL XXIII 992; cf. BEDE, *In Pent., PL* XCI 215; HUGH OF ST. VICTOR,
Adnot. in Pent. iv, *PL* CLXXV 44; *Hist. Schol. Gen.* xxvi, *PL* CXCVIII
1077; "Abel", *Jew. Encyc.* Various legends grew up in the vernacular.
Sometimes God kindled Abel's sacrifice and not Cain's, as in MALAN,
Book of Adam I lxxviii, p. 98; Trin. Camb. 77-84; *Life of Christ* 2337-
40; *Chester* II; *Lud. Cov.* II 131-6; *Townely* II 275ff; ÉVRAT, *Genèse,*
fol. 13r col. 2. Sometimes the smoke of Abel's sacrifice ascends to
heaven, while Cain's drifts downward and chokes him, as in *Life*-Vernon
112/243-6; *Townely* II 275; GEOFFROI DE PARIS, fol. 12r col. 2. This may
have evolved from a Midrashic interpretation of *Gen.* 4:5, which translated the Hebrew "wayyihar" (Vulgate "iratus") as burnt up or black-
ened. See *Midrash*, p. 184; GINZBERG, *Legends* V, p. 137 n. 13. In the *Trad.
anon.*, which the *CM* poet has been following, Abel's sacrifice gives off a
sweet smell, while the odour of Cain's is foul.

1099   Cf. *Gen.* 4:8. Instead of the Vulgate's "Egrediamur foras", the Old
Latin read "Eamus in campum". Hence the murder of Abel frequently
takes place in a field. See EMERSON, "Legs. of Cain", pp. 857 ff.

1116   "his owne ymage" of course refers back to *Gen.* 1:26-7.

1119-20, 1123-42 *Trad. anon.* fol. 216v col. 2-217r col. 1.

1123-6   Cf. n. to 11.1093-6 above.

1134-42   This is the curse on Cain, *Gen.* 4:11, strongly mixed with the curse on Adam, *Gen.* 3:17-8.

1143-60   These lines do not appear in the source the *CM* poet has been using.

1149-54   Cf. *Gen.* 4:12.

1153   MS H's unique reading "knowen" for "holden" was accidentally taken over from the previous line.

1161-72   *Trad. anon.* fol. 217r col. 1.

1172   Cf. *Gen.* 4:14.

1175-82   *Trad. anon., loc. cit.*

1177-8   There are various traditions about the mark of Cain. Some Jewish sources said it was a horn. See *Midrash* xxii 12, p. 191, which also mentions other traditions. This horn appears in the Cornish *Creat. of World* 1373. The Septuagint translation, however, instead of making Cain a wanderer, said that he would be groaning and trembling on the earth. This trembling became the mark of Cain in several different works. See MALAN, *Book of Adam* I LXXIX, pp. 102-3; BUDGE, *Cave of Treasures* 78, HUGH OF ST. VICTOR, *Adnot. in Pent., PL* CLXXV 44; *Hist. Schol. Gen.* XXVII, *PL* CXCVIII 1078; *Life* — Vernon 113/269-70; Macé 593-6. Cf. EMERSON, "Legs. of Cain", p. 869; GINZBERG, *Legends* V, p. 143 n. 37.

   The *CM* poet implies that the mark of Cain is a piece of writing. This is a Jewish tradition, apparently suggested by *Ez.* 9:4, 6, and found in *Pirke* xxi, p. 156; RASHI 19. The only other vernacular work known to me which describes this as the mark of Cain is the *Trad. anon.* fol. 217r col. 1:

> Niert pas ansic *com* tu las dist
> En fronc te metrai un escrist
> Qui te u*er*ra quil ne te toiche
> [Mais conoisse ta felonie]
> Mon signe de ta penita*n*ce
> Qui te fera lou amia*n*ce

(One line, missing in MS BN fr. 763, is here supplied from MS Arsenal 3516 fol. 6r col. 1.)

1187-9   The same riddle appears in dialogue literature, especially from German sources. See KEMBLE, p. 290, 295-8. Cf. *Parzifal* IX 464. The answer here is Abel. He was born before his parents because they were never born at all, but created. His grandmother was the earth, and he had her maidenhead because his was the first blood to be shed on her. The riddle may have been suggested to the *CM* poet by the following passage from the *Hist. Schol. Gen.* xviii, Add. 1, *PL* CXCVIII 1071: "Terra proprie adhuc virgo erat, quia nondum corrupta homine opere, nec sanguine infecta."

1191-1202   *Elucid.* I 93. HAENISCH, *CM*, p. 4* thought that this came from Petrus Comestor.

1191   The Vulgate says only that Adam was 130 years old when he begat Seth (*Gen.* 5:3). This story of his continence for 100 years after Abel's death is widespread. See *Hist. Schol. Gen.* xxix, *PL* CXCVIII 1080; Trin. Camb. 101-2; *SELeg.* 168/27-8; *Cant. Creat.* 496-8; *Life*—Vernon 113/278-81; *Myroure*, p. 191; *Rev.* Meth. (English translation only), p. 158/73-80, cf. p. 183; *Anc. Corn. Dr.* 619-39. For a variant of this story see MALAN, *Book of Adam*, lxxiii; R. H. CHARLES, *Apocrypha*, p. 137; and *G&E* 389-408, 421-2. Cf. also GINZBERG, *Legends* V, pp. 148-9 n. 50.

1206   Cf. I *Cor.* 15:45 where Christ is referred to as the new Adam. Cf. also I *Cor.* 15:20-2; *Rom.* 5:12-21.

1210   An echo of Christ's commandment in *Matth.* 22:39: "Diliges proximum tuum, sicut teipsum." The poet changes "proximum" to "breþer", thus suggesting that Seth is both an anti-type of Cain, who did not love his brother, and a type of Christ, the enunciator of the new law. This is one of the *CM* poet's rare hints of a figural interpretation. Cf. n. to 1.1206 above.

1211-3   *Elucid.* I 93. C's reading is closest to the Latin. Cf. the etymology of Seth given by ISIDORE, *Etym* VII vi 9: "Seth... positio, quia posuit eum Deus pro Abel."

1216-8   From *Hist. Schol. Gen.* xxix, Add. 1, *PL* CXCVIII 1080. *Gen.* 5:4 merely says of Adam: "genuitque filios et filias". In other vernacular works, the number of sons varies from 30 to 33, depending on whether Cain, Abel and Seth are counted. The number of daughters varies between 30 and 32, according to whether or not the author knew of Cain's and Abel's twin sisters.

1223-36   The author winds up the stories of Cain and Abel and the offspring of Adam by looking ahead to the death of Cain's kindred in Noah's flood.

1237ff.   The *CM* poet here begins to tell the story of Seth's quest for the Oil of Mercy and the history of the wood of the Cross, both immensely popular in the Middle Ages. The pioneering work of classification was carried out by Wilhelm MEYER in "Die Geschichte des Kreuzholzes vor Christus", and "Vita Adae et Evae". An excellent study has been produced by Esther Casier QUINN, *The Quest of Seth*. I will not attempt to reproduce her discussion of the variations in the tradition and their transmission throughout the Middle Ages. For work which has been done since her book appeared, see SEVERS, ed., *Manual* II 441-6 and 635-9.

　　Briefly, the history of the Holy Cross began in two parts. One told of the life of Adam and Eve after their expulsion from Paradise, and of Seth's journey back to Eden on behalf of his dying father. This is told in the Greek *Apocalypse of Moses* and, in the form known in the West, in the Latin *Vita Adae et Evae*. I refer throughout to the text of the *Vita* published by J. H. MOZLEY, "The 'Vita Adae'". Mozley used English manuscripts for his edition, and classified several details in their texts which are specifically English.

　　A separate legend began with Moses finding rods in the desert, and told of their history through various owners until they were used to form Christ's cross. The introduction to Arthur S. NAPIER, *Rood Tree*, contains a good early description of the texts. See also Quinn.

　　These two separate stories were combined to produce what Meyer called the *Legende* version, telling the history of the cross wood from Seth's quest for its seeds in Paradise. I quote from the *Legende* text printed by Moshé LAZAR, "La Légende de l'Arbre de Paradis".

The *CM* poet has used the Latin *Legende* as his source for the Adam section of the rood story, and *Trad. anon.* for the rest.

1237ff. *Legende* 45/11ff.

1239 *Legende* 45/11 has "bipennam", a double-edged axe. This was translated "hak" in MSS CF, with the spade added for the rhyme. The spade alone survives in GHTLB and is substituted for the "hak" in 1.1241. Henning LARSEN, "Origo Crucis", 30 adduces the appearance of an *oxi*/pick-axe in the Old Norse *Hauksbók* version of the legend as a striking parallel with the *CM*. The source is much more likely to have been the Latin, however.

1240 MSS CF's "sad" is original, translating "cepit ... tristari". HL's "mate" (OFr. *mate*) is equally good, but GTB's "made" is inferior.

1241 The reviser who dropped "hak" as the rhyme word has left Adam in a very awkward position, with his breast somehow resting on his spade.

1245 BENNETT and SMITHERS, p. 1245, point out that "yate ward" was originally two words, "ward" being a verb. Thus C's line, without Morris' suggested interpolation of "es", translates "ad Cherubin... qui custodit... atrium" (*Legende* 45/13).

1246-50 Not in *Legende*.

1251-64 *Legende* 45/17-9.

1256 C's "gren" was accidentally re-copied from the previous line. The original rhyme word was probably "sene", as in GHTLB.

1265-77 *Legende* 45/14-5.

1271-2 Not in *Legende*.

1283-1394 *Legende* 45/20-46/23.

1288-90 This may be the great light of Paradise itself, or it may be the burning wall surrounding it.

1291 Henning LARSEN, "*Cursor Mundi* 1291" seeks to derive this from an Old Norse version of the story, but MSS CF translate the Latin "signavit se signo theta".

1295-1302 This is in direct discourse in the Latin.

1299-1300 Not in *Legende*.

1303 The poet uses the word "cherubin" as a proper name. Cf. *Life* — Vernon 108/138.

1305-88 *Legende* 46/25-47/48.

1311 The *CM* poet is not being vague again, but is simply translating his source, *Legende* 46/26.

1315 Latin "lucidissimum".

1334 "þat made him doute". The Latin has "stupefactus rediit", 46/34.

1343 The child is obviously Christ. The "swaþelynge bonde", Latin "pannis involutum", 46/35, echoes *Luc.* 2:7, 12.

1344 As the angel later explains, Christ is weeping for the sins of Seth's parents. The ME poet, though he translates the restrained "deflet" as "wepeþ" at 1.1357, here uses the realistic "squelonde".

1348-9 "in quo cognovit animam fratris sui Abel", 46/36.

1372 Not in Latin.

1375 Latin "infra os ejus pones", 47/42. Cf. below 1.1417, *Legende* 47/51.

1377 The three trees in the *Legende* are cedar, cypress and pine, 47/43. MSS CFG preserve the original reading here, but the southern translator has changed all the references to the three trees to cedar, cypress and palm. The palm was often cited in other places as one of the woods of which the cross was made. See QUINN's discussion, *Quest of Seth,* p. 70 and n. 3, p. 151, n. 3.

When he changed the third tree in his source, the southern translator of the *CM* may have had in mind the verses of *Eccli.* 24:17-8:

> 17 Quasi cedrus exaltata sum in Libano, et quasi cypressus in monte Sion;
> 18 quasi palma exaltata sum in Cades,

These images were very often applied to the Virgin. See RABY, *Christian-Latin Poetry,* p. 366. Thus the southern translator has deliberately altered his original to refer, however obliquely, to the Blessed Virgin, to whom the *CM* is dedicated.

1380 MSS CF's reading is the original, translating "universis arboribus alcius crescere consuevit" (47/45).

1389-98 This conversation is not in the *Legende.*

1399-1405 *Legende* 47/49-50.

1406-12 Not in *Legende.*

1409 According to *Gen.* 5:5, Adam lived 930 years. However the *Legende* says he was 932 (45/11). Aware of the two different figures, the *CM* poet here begs the question. Cf. *SEL* 168/31.

The southern translator's new rhyme word "ȝare", meaning "alert, nimble, active, brisk, quick" (*OED* Yare *a* 2) exactly contradicts the intent of the passage as a whole, and especially the following line.

1413-9 *Legende* 47/51-2.

1421, 1424-30 *Legende,* 47/53.

1435-48 Cf. *Life* — Vernon 117/385-8, where Adam is said to have spent 4604 years in Hell. Cf. also GEOFFROI DE PARIS, fol. 13v col. 2.

1438 The southern translator's change from "ras" to "diȝed" weakens the line.

1449 The sisters (and' wives) of Cain and Seth have various names in ancient tradition. See *Jubilees* 4:9,11; MALAN, *Book of Adam,* I lxxiv, lxxv. Calmana and Delbora are the names most often used in mediaeval texts. See *Rev.* Meth. 192; *Hist. Schol. Gen.* xxv, *PL* CXCVIII 1076. Cf. below, 1.1501.

1451ff. The *CM* tries to reproduce the genealogy of Seth as given in *Gen.* 5, but gets the ages of four out of the eight men wrong.

1453-4 *Gen.* 4:26.

1455 i.e. 912 years. Cf. *Gen.* 5:6-7.

1459-60 MSS CFG preserve the name as "Cainan" (*Gen.* 5:12-4). The southern translator has corrupted it to "Caym". Cainan lived 910 years.

1461-2 T miscopies the name "maladial", but HLB have the correct form. He lived 895 years (*Gen.* 5:17). Perhaps a Roman numeral xcv was miscopied as xxv.

1463 Jared lived 962 years (*Gen.* 5:20). MSS CF come closer to the correct figure.

1464 MS C preserves the original "kne". See *MED* kne n. 3, a somewhat uncommon usage, which GHTLB change to "kyn".

1465-6 These lines are based directly on a short text of the *Revelations* of Methodius: "Quadragesimo autem anno tempore Jareth, transiuit

primum miliarium seculi." See *Rev.* Meth. p. 193. Cf. below, n. to
11.2001-6.

1468   Henoch lived 365 years (*Gen.* 5:23). The poet may have misread
Gen. 5:22.

1469-70   From *Hist. Schol. Gen.* xxx, *PL* CXCVIII 1081. Cf. *Jubilees*
4:17; I *Enoch* 12:4, 14:1; *DIM, PL* CLXXII 165. In ME, Higden
223 and Wyntoun 269-74 also translate this information from Comestor.

1471   The standard interpretation of *Gen.* 5:24, which says, "Ambulavitque
cum Deo, et non apparuit, quia tulit eum Deus." The tradition begins
very early. See *Jubilees* 4:23; I *Enoch* 70:1-3; II *Enoch* 67:2; JEROME,
Comment. in Amos III xi 2ff, *PL* XXV 1087; BEDE, *Hex., PL* XCI 73;
Hist. Schol. Gen. xxx, *PL* CXCVIII 1080; HIGDEN 223; WYNTOUN
275ff; KEMBLE 200, 213; *Creat. of World* 2094-2145. A possible explanation of the ideas connected with Enoch comes from Babylonian tradition. Enoch was the seventh in line from Adam, and the seventh
ante-diluvian king of Babylon was also said to have received divine
illumination. Interestingly, the Babylonian king was in the service of
the sun god, and Enoch's life lasted 365 years, the duration of one
solar year. See DRIVER, *Genesis,* 78.

1471-4   Probably from *Hist. Schol. Gen.* xxx, *PL* CXCVIII 1080.

1475-80   Enoch and Elijah are the two men of the Old Testament who did
not die but were taken to Paradise bodily to await the second coming.
The story of their fatal struggle with Anti-Christ is very old and is
based on their identification with the two witnesses of *Apoc.* 11:3-7.
See BOUSSET, *The Antichrist Legend,* pp. 203-17. The *CM* poet may
have taken his account of this from Adso's widely known *Libellus de
Antichristo.* See KALUZA, "Zu den Quellen", p. 451.

1481-2   The *CM* poet now begins to use *DIM* as a source: "Hujus tempore
mortuus est Adam," *PL* CLXXII 165. KALUZA, "Zu den Quellen",
p. 451 first pointed out the poet's indebtedness to this work, but he
reported that the *CM* poet used *DIM* only in 11.6993-7082 and 9133-
9222.

1493-5   Petrus Comestor discusses various estimates of the length of the
first age, *Hist. Schol. Gen.* xxx, *PL* CXCVIII 1081. However, Comestor
does not give this figure. Adding the ages of each man at the birth of
his eldest son, plus the 612 years of Noah's life before the beginning of
the second age, gives a total of 1668, not 1662, as in MSS CF. Cf. WYN-
TOUN, who gives the number of years as 1667, 11.283-4.

1496ff.   The *Trad. anon.* spends considerable time on the family of Cain,
having his sons discover the seven liberal arts among other things.
The *CM* poet chose not to translate this. Cf. *Gen.* 4:16-24.

1501-2   See note to 1.1449 above.

1505   MSS CFG preserve the better reading "mad" for "took". Cf. *Gen.*
4:17.

1506   The ages are not given for the descendants of Cain in *Gen.* 4:17ff.
In any event, they all perish in Noah's flood.

1508   From *Rev.* Meth. 193: "hec prima facta est ante deluuium". The
phrase does not occur in Petrus Comestor. In the *Revelations,* however,
and in works derived from it, the city is called Effrem. Cf. Trin. Camb.
88. The *CM* poet has corrected this to the biblical Enos, 1.1504.

1509   According to the Vulgate, *Gen.* 4:18, the line runs from Enoch to Irad. However, the Septuagint and Old Latin translations gave the name Irad as Gaidad. This is the name used here in *DIM,* and therefore the one used by the *CM* poet, as preserved in MSS CG. The scribe of F was apparently puzzled by this "Gaidat", and rewrote the line. The southern translator made a similar adaptation.

The forms "mamael" (C) and "Mainael" (F) are scribal corruptions of the Vulgate "Maviael" (*Gen.* 4:18). MSS GHTLB's "malaliel" is a further corruption of this, probably influenced by the "malaliel" in Seth's line. Cf. above 1.1461.

1513-4   This refers to the usual mediaeval interpretation of *Gen.* 4:23-4 as a song of lament sung by Lamech when, old and blind, he accidentally kills Cain. This story was often told at length in the Middle Ages, especially by authors who knew PETRUS COMESTOR, *Hist. Schol. Gen.* xxviii, PL CXCVIII 1079-80. Cf. GINZBERG, *Legends,* V 146-7, n. 44; MALAN, *Book of Adam,* II xiii, p. 122; BUDGE, *Cave of Treasures* 78-9; RASHI 21; *Rev.* Meth. 193; *Glossa,* PL CXIII 101; HUGH OF ST. VICTOR, *Adnot. in Pent.,* PL CLXXV 44-5; see also JAMES, *Lost Apocrypha,* 10-11. In ME the story is found in *G&E* 471-86; HIGDEN 229-31; WYNTOUN 191-202; *Fall of Princes* 735; MANDEVILLE L 81; *Lud. Cov.* IV 142ff.; *Creat. of World* 1465-1712. In French, both ÉVRAT, fol. 15r col. 2 and MACÉ 709-44 tell the story.

The abbreviated version is unusual, and probably comes from *Rev.* Meth. 193 which says simply: "filii lamech ceci, qui fuit primus cecus. qui interfecit Caim." D'Evelyn does not note this parallel with *CM,* and HAENISCH, *CM,* p. 5* gives Comestor as the source of the passage.

1516-24   Cf. *Gen.* 4:20-22.

1517   MS C's "loger" is original, from OF *logier.* The line refers to *Gen.* 4:20: "pater habitantium in tentoriis".

1525-8   From COMESTOR, *Hist. Schol. Gen.* xxviii, PL CXCVIII 1078-9.

1529-30   This story is told of Seth's descendants in JOSEPHUS 33; *Creat. of World* 2146-2210; and in the *Vita* — MOZLEY 145/52 and its ME translations. Cf. GINZBERG, *Legends,* V pp. 149-50 n. 53. Comestor, however, had already switched it to the sons of Lamech who recorded the secrets of their crafts. See *Hist. Schol. Gen.* xxviii, PL CXCVIII 1079; *G&E* 461-4; *Rev.* Meth. 163-90; HIGDEN 233; WYNTOUN 223-40; MACÉ 679-92.

1541-52   From *Hist. Schol. Gen.* xxxvi and Add. 2, PL CXCVIII 1087. Comestor got the idea from JOSEPHUS 57. Cf. HIGDEN 231. D'Evelyn suggested that the ME translation of the *Revelations* of Methodius took this passage from the *CM.* See *Rev.* Meth., 11.191-214. Both the *CM* and the *Revelations* say the Great Year takes 100 years to pass, whereas Comestor and Higden both say 600 years.

1548   "mychal spire" translates "magnus annus".

1553ff   The story of Noah's flood begins in *Genesis* with the account of the intercourse between the sons of God and the daughters of men which bred a race of giants. This was originally interpreted as describing the fall of man. See N. P. WILLIAMS, *Ideas of the Fall.*

The sons of God have been variously interpreted. Jewish tradition thought of them as sons of noble families. See DRIVER, *Genesis* 82-3;

SKINNER, *Genesis* 142 n.; *Targ. of Onk.* 46; *Targ. of Jon.* 176; *Midrash* 26:5, p. 213; RASHI, p. 25. The Septuagint translation calls them angels, as do Josephus 35 and *Jubilees* 5:1, and some early Fathers. See references in EMERSON, "Legs. of Cain", 919-21. However, *Matth.* 22:30 specifically denies sexual activity to the angels. Later Christian authorities assumed a prohibition on marriage between the descendants of Seth, from whom Christ was to come, with the descendants of the wicked Cain. See EMERSON, "Legs. of Cain", 921.

The *CM* poet barely glances at the problems of this passage, tacitly accepting the latter interpretation and concentrating on the wickedness of the descendants of Cain.

1553-6   From *Rev. Meth.* p. 193, as d'Evelyn points out. Comestor gives the date without reference to Jareth. See *Rev. Meth.* pp. 148-9; cf. *Hist. Schol. Gen.* xxx, *PL* CXCVIII 1081.

1557-8   The *CM* poet sees the early history of the world as a continuing decline from the blessedness of Adam's state. Cf. AQUINAS, who asserts that the effects of the Fall made themselves felt over a period of time. See *Sum. Theol.* II

1569-84   The southern translator has expanded and changed these lines somewhat. Morris' numbering gives a false picture of correspondances.

CFG	HTLB
—	1569-72
1569-76	1573-80
1577-8 (CG only)	—
1579-82	1581-4
1583-4	—

Originally the *CM* poet mentioned only lust, adultery with their brothers' wives and rape (ll.1567, 1573-4, 1577-8 CFG). The southern translator took up the suggestion of the sin against nature and inserted four lines to show that lesbianism and homosexuality were the abhorrent sins (ll.1569-72 HTLB). He has much in common with other ME writers who use this story to fulminate against whatever sin they most disapprove of. Thus the *SELTemp.*, fol. 1v col. 1, calls the sin incest, and *I&I* 13-20 blames gluttony. Cf. the note to 1.2907 below. The author of the *Book of the Knight of LaTour-Landry* 62 attributes the flood entirely to women's dress.

1570-1   The poet's description of the two laws is preserved in MSS CG: "þar lau/þat es o settnes and o kind", i.e. the positive law and the natural law. The *Dict. théol. cath.* XI 875 distinguishes the two:

> [La loi] est naturelle, si l'obligation qu'elle impose dépend de la nature des choses, positive, si cette obligation dépend de la volonté positive et libre du législateur.

The *CM* poet could have picked up the concept of the two laws from his reading of GROSSETESTE's *Chateau d'amour*, ll.111-128.

Isidore's first example of natural law is "viri et feminae coniunctio", in *Etym.* V iv 1. This explains the stress on sexual irregularities as being "aʒeyne kynde".

1574 (CFG)/1578 (HTLB)   This comes from *Rev.* Meth. and is also found in *Hist. Schol. Gen.* xxxi, *PL* CXCVIII 1081. Cf. *G&E* 529-30.

1602   *Gen.* 6:6.

1621   "feluns", MSS CFG, is original, a better antithesis with "þe gode" than "foolis" of HTLB which is probably scribal corruption.

1625-6   The genealogical diagram in MS C is not reproduced in the other MSS, although these lines promise one. Only MSS FL omit the lines altogether.

1627-30   Cf. *Gen.* 5:32. HAENISCH, *CM*, p. 5*, attributes this to PETRUS COMESTOR, *Hist. Schol. Gen.* xxxi, *PL* CXCVIII 1081.

1633-60   Based on God's speeches in *Gen.* 6:7, 13, 17-8.

1636   Cf. 1.482 above.

1644   Cf. *Gen.* 8:21; *Lev.* 1:9; *Phil.* 4:18; and *Eph.* 5:2. In the latter, the sweet smell of Christ's sacrifice is contrasted with fornication and uncleanness.

1652-5   Perhaps from *Trad. anon.* fol. 219r col. 1, but the similarity is not striking.

1664ff   Two interesting studies have appeared concerning the ark of Noah: ALLEN, *Leg. of Noah,* and Grover ZINN, "Hugh of St. Victor and the Ark of Noah".

Mediaeval ideas of the ark usually conformed to one of three basic shapes:

(1)   Based on the Septuagint reading of *Gen.* 6:16, Origen's ark was pyramidal in shape. See *In Gen. Hom.* II, *PG* XII 161-7; *Contra Celsum,* IV, *PG* XI 1095-8; BEDE, *Hex., PL* XCI 89-91; *In Pent., PL* XCI 221; ALLEN, *Leg. of Noah,* p. 71. Cf. also *Hist. Schol. Gen.* xxxii Add. 1, *PL* CXCVIII 1083: "Quasi agricolae locutus est Dominus, ut faceret scilicet navem, instar arconii, id est ad conum tendentis, vel forte ab arcendo, quia undique clausa."

(2)   Augustine's ark was cubic, having vertical sides with the same floor space on each level. He left the sea-worthiness of such a box-like craft in the hands of Divine Providence. See *DCD* XV xxvii.

(3)   Hugh of St. Victor interpreted *Genesis* differently. In his ark, the walls are only 15 cubits high, while the roof rises a further 15 cubits, at a slope of one cubit. The two upper stories of the ark are under the slope of this roof. See *De Arca Noe Morali,* I iii, *PL* CLXXVI 627. ALLEN, *Leg. of Noah,* p. 140 describes the ark in the *CM* as "up-to-date... a poetical version of Hugh of St. Victor's ark". This is not the *CM* poet's conception, however, as is shown by the measurement "Fro grou*n*de to þe tabulment" (1.1678). The tablement is a feature of wall construction, not of roofs. The *CM* poet, then, is saying that the full height of the ark, 30 cubits or 15 ells, is the same as the height of its walls. His ark, therefore, is more like Augustine's than like Hugh's.

1664   The Vulgate reads: "Fac tibi arcam de lignis levigatis" (*Gen.* 6:14). The Septuagint, however, has the ark built of square timber, as here. Comestor gives the Old Latin reading "quadratis" as an alternative to the Vulgate's. See *Hist. Schol. Gen.* xxxii, *PL* CXCVIII 1082; cf. *Glossa, PL* CIII 105. Cf. *York* VIII 73-4, which combines the two readings.

The *Trad. anon.* says "Larche feras de legiers fuz q*u*arrez", which is interesting as MSS GL use the ME derivative of this Old French word: "quarid" or "quarry".

1666   *Trad. anon.* fol. 219v col. 1: "et il meismes fuit maistres charpentiers".

1669-74   The *CM* poet does not seem concerned to describe the hull of the ark. SALZMAN, *Building in England* is useful in understanding the structure that Noah is working on here. The *CM* poet describes it as a timber frame structure filled in with wattle and daub. This is a typical mediaeval building, less grand than a stone structure, but not as humble as the wattle and daub huts of the peasants. See SALZMAN, pp. 192, 194.

The poet speaks of Noah as the master wright (1.1666), who directs his helpers and is himself responsible for fastening in place the main beams of the building (1.1728). See SALZMAN, pp. 201-205. The poet speaks of cutting the timber (1.1724) and fastening it (1.1669). This is the process of laying the groundsills in the desired shape, and then attaching to them the uprights, or studs. See SALZMAN, p. 189. The uprights are then bound together with "balks or horizontal timbers, as opposed to the... studs, or uprights" (SALZMAN, p. 542, n. 2), and "bands" or "laces", that is tie beams, running across the structure from side to side (11.1671, 1728). See SALZMAN, pp. 204, 211, and the illustration between pp. 196 and 197. Then the wattling process is begun, that is the spaces between the uprights are filled with vertical stakes, interwoven with small branches or "wands" (11.1670, 1672). See SALZMAN, pp. 188-9. Then the wall is daubed with earth, clay, mortar or plaster to fill in the interstices. See SALZMAN, p. 188. The *CM* poet has the ark daubed with pitch, as the Vulgate specifies (1.1673, *Gen.* 6: 14), and with plaster (1.1674). See SALZMAN, p. 189.

I have found no comparable description of the ark in written sources, but similar woven arks are to be seen in three illuminated MSS of the period. See

(1) COCKERELL, ed., *Book of Old Testament Illustrations,* p. 79 pl. 14; also in a partial reprint, *Old Testament Miniatures,* p. 32 no. 13. The hull of this ark, painted about 1250 in Paris, is wickerwork.

(2) WARNER, ed., *Queen Mary's Psalter,* pl. 10 and p. 57. The upper part of the hull is woven in this early fourteenth century work.

(3) HASSALL, ed., *Holkham Bible Picture Book,* fol. 7v, where the superstructure has a timber frame woven with reeds. The pictures were probably done in London, later in the fourteenth century.

The texts in these MSS sometimes try to explain the pictures, usually by saying that Noah was rushed and at the last minute had to finish his ship by weaving rather than continue nailing planks onto the frame. HASSALL, pp. 73-4, offers this explanation of the legends. "The conflicting explanations seem to be rationalizations of a natural misinterpretation of a traditional way of representing the fabric of the ark. This is exemplified in the fifth or sixth century in the *Cotton Genesis* and perhaps in the bronze door of Monreale Cathedral (c.1180-90). The original intention was not to represent wickerwork at all but to show "a form of panelling which became common in Cairene work... In its origin it seems to have depended on forms of the Greek fret which are frequently found as pattern on Coptic textiles. This form of panelling was doubtless used because it required only small pieces of timber...'" The suggestion Hassall quotes was made by LETHABY, "The Painted Book of *Genesis*", p. 98.

See my article "'A Schippe Behoues þe to Dight'".

In spite of the unusually detailed description of the ark in the text of the *CM,* the sketch of the "archa noe" found at the bottom of fol. 12v of MS C is of a conventional ship with mast and rudder.

1675-6 *Gen.* 6:15 says that the ark was 300 × 50 × 30 cubits in size. The *CM* says 150 × 24 × 15 ells. In his reckoning, then, 2 cubits = 1 ell. Exegetical writers usually agreed that a cubit contained 1½ feet, as it did in Roman linear measure. See, e.g., PETRUS COMESTOR, *Hist. Schol. Gen.* xxxii, *PL* CXCVIII 1083; HUGH OF ST. VICTOR, *Adnot. in Pent., PL* CLXXV 46. An English ell, on the other hand, was 45 inches.

The *CM* poet is here either using a Scottish ell (37.2 inches) as a rough equivalent for 2 cubits, or he is using a standard Anglo-Saxon unit of measurement. For building purposes the Germanic tribes, both in England and on the Continent, had reckoned 1 cubit = 2 feet and 4 feet, or 2 cubits = 1 "cloth-elne". This unit of linear measure was eliminated some time between 1266 and 1303 by the document *Compositio ulnarum et perticarum.* On the subject see ZUPKO, *British Weights and Measures,* pp. 10, 20-1, 143.

1678 From *Hist. Schol. Gen.* xxxii Add. 2, *PL* CXCVIII 1083 "id est, a fundo usque ad tabulatum".

1679-86 *Gen.* 6:16. The Vulgate said "mansiunculas in arca facies," (*Gen.* 6:14) and "deorsum, coenacula, et tristega facies in ea" (*Gen.* 6:16). This would have been a structure of impressive scale in mediaeval times, where two story houses were the rule even in London. See Salzman, *Building in England,* p. 197.

1683 Cf. n. to 11.1759-60.

1687-90 Cf. *Gen.* 6:19-20.

1691-1700 The *CM* poet describes the arrangement of the decks. Haenisch gives the source of this passage as *Hist. Schol. Gen.* xxxii, *PL* CXCVIII 1083. Cf. also HUGH OF ST. VICTOR, *De Arca Noe Morali* I iii, *PL* CLXXVI 627.

1692 MSS CF preserve the correct meaning, that the birds are to be beside Noah, not beneath him as in MSS GHTLB.

1699-1700 Many descriptions of the ark mention these sanitary arrangements, which are not those of a ship, but of a house constructed over a cess-pit which would be cleaned periodically. See SALZMAN, pp. 283-5. The commentators obviously conceived the only apertures in the ark to be the door and window specifically mentioned in *Gen.* 6:16, and even these are kept closed at all times during the flood.

1701-6 *Gen.* 6:3. Early commentators interpreted the 120 years as the span of a man's life from then on. See JOSEPHUS 35; *Jubilees* 5:8; cf. *Pricke of Conscience* 11.738-41. The Fathers say, however, that 120 years was the length of time given to men before the Flood in which they might repent. See *Quaest. in Gen., PL* XXIII 997; *DCD* XV xxiv; BEDE, *In Pent., PL* XCI 221; PSEUDO-BEDE, *Quaest. super Gen., PL* XCIII 292; *Adnot. in Pent., PL* CLXXV 46; *Hist. Schol. Gen.* xxxi, *PL* CXCVIII 1082. So too the *Targ. of Jon.* This is the point of view of the *CM* poet.

This explanation still leaves a difficulty however. By comparing *Gen.* 5:32 with *Gen.* 7:6, one sees that the Flood came only 100 years after God's promise to Noah. See Augustine's attempt to explain the discrepancy in *DCD* XV xxiv.

1709-18 Cf. *Gen.* 6:18-21.

1723-30   *Trad. anon.* fol. 219v col. 1.

1725   Most literal commentaries also assume that Noah had helpers when he built the ark. See ALLEN, *Leg. of Noah,* p. 141; AUGUSTINE, *Quaest. in Hept.* I v, *PL* XXXIV 549; *Piers Plowman* C XII 238-43; *Chester* III 49ff. However, the *Anc. Corn. Dr.* says that Noah built the ark alone (11.1009-16).

1728   Cf. n. to 11.1669-74 above.

1729-34   Noah's entire sermon is given in *Trad. anon.* fol. 219v col. 1-220r col. 1. The *CM* poet summarizes it.

The idea that Noah preached to the onlookers while he worked on the ark is an ancient tradition, found in JOSEPHUS 35; MALAN, *Book of Adam* III ii, pp. 144-5; BUDGE, *Cave of Treasures* 100. Cf. II *Petr.* 2:5; I *Petr.* 3:20. In the twelfth century it appeared again in the commentary of Rashi on *Genesis,* p. 28. Cf. GINZBERG, *Legends,* pp. 174-5 n. 19 for other references. In vernacular paraphrases the motif is rare, occurring only in *CM, Trad. anon.,* the Cornish *Creat. of World* 11.2294ff, 2346, and *OEGen.* 1317-9.

1759-60   The window must be capable of being opened from inside so that Noah can later release the birds (*Gen.* 8:6ff). This seems to be a fairly unusual feature of mediaeval windows, which were more often simply holes in the wall over which shutters would be fastened. See SALZMAN, *Building in England,* pp. 198, 256.

The other MSS have mistaken C's verb "loke"/lock for "look", to produce a line which makes little sense in its context.

1761   The *CM* poet here omits two traditional additions to the Noah story, of which he might easily have been aware. He does not name the women in the ark, as so many commentators did. See UTLEY, "One Hundred and Three Names". Neither does he make Noah's wife a source of difficulty for her husband or a figure of comedy, as so many ME sources did. The tradition that Noah's wife tried to thwart the project is an ancient one. See M. R. JAMES, *Lost Apocrypha,* pp. 13-5; MILL, "Noah's Wife". In ME it appears in *Chester* III; *Towneley* III; *York* IX; the *Newcastle Play of Noah's Ship* 95ff; WARNER, *Queen Mary's Ps.* p. 57 and plates 10-12; GOLLANCZ, *Caedmon MS* pp. 66, xlv; and cf. GARVIN, "Note on Noah's Wife". Note, however, that the *Lud. Cov.* and the *Anc. Corn. Dr.,* like the *CM,* ignore the comic character of Noah's wife.

The suggestion made by W. YOUNG "Noah and his Wife" pp. 20-1, that the scoffing of the bystanders while Noah is building the ark in the *CM* may have suggested Noah's wife's scorn to the dramatists is wrong.

1761-98   The *Trad. anon.* fol. 220r col. 2 has a few lines about the storm, but nothing like this elaborate description. Several of the lines come from the *Bible* of Herman de Valenciennes, the *CM* poet's first use of this source. Compare HERMAN's *Bible* in University of Chicago MS H.27.B.6.12 fol. 4v and *CM* 11.1763-4, 1770-4.

Such lengthy descriptions of the storm which caused the flood are most unusual in ME versions of the Noah story. Cf. only *Cleanness* 373ff. The *CM*'s storm has two functions. As MARDON, *Narrative Unity,* p. 69 points out, its savagery prefigures the storms which herald the arrival of doomsday, thus establishing Noah's flood as a type of the final destruction of the world. The scene also calls to mind very clearly the *CM*'s descriptions of Paradise both before and after Adam's fall. See above 11.639-710, 825-36, 999-1044. Rather than perpetual light and a much brighter sun and moon, all is darkness and night. The sight of men and animals swimming together in terror with all enmity forgotten is an ironic recollection of Paradise, when all had lived together in perpetual harmony. L. 1793 may recall the rebellion of Lucifer, which the *CM* poet had particularly considered to be a struggle over lordship (1.482).

1766, 1768   These descriptions of flood conditions interpret the biblical "fontes abyssi" (*Gen.* 7:11; 8:2). In Hebrew cosmology, these referred to the great deep under the earth.

1786   MSS CF's "wolf and ram" is probably original. Cf. above 1.685.

1835-6   The story of the Flood in *Genesis* is compiled from two sources. The J narrative (*Gen.* 7:4, 12; 8:10, 12) conflicts with the calculations of the P narrative (*Gen.* 7:11, 17, 24; 8:3-5) about the length of the Flood. The Septuagint and Old Latin readings add further complications. The length of the Flood was a problem to Latin scholars. See ALLEN, *Leg. of Noah*, p. 70, cf. Roger BACON, *Opus Majus*, p. 220.

The *CM* poet has the rain last for forty days (11.1835-6), and the waters prevail for 140 days (1.1851) instead of 150 days as in *Gen.* 7:24; 8:3. The Flood lasts 12 months in all (11.1917-22). This would agree with the Septuagint text, and also with Petrus Comestor, who argued that the Hebrew calendar differed from his own, and that the Vulgate text meant to state that a whole year had elapsed. See *Hist. Schol. Gen.* xxxv, *PL* CXCVIII 1085-6.

1837-8   *Gen.* 7:20 says fifteen cubits. The *CM* poet has again used his rough equivalent of two cubits equals one ell. Cf. n. to 1.1675-6 above.

1851   Cf. n. to 1.1835-6 above.

1856   C's "knyue" is surely an error.

1860ff.   Cf. *Gen.* 8:1ff.

1869-70   *Gen.* 8:4: "super montes Armeniae".

1871-88   BUEHLER, "*CM*", p. 487, pointed out that this passage was translated from 11.312-25 of HERMAN's *Bible*. Noah does not consult his sons elsewhere in ME.

1885-8   Cf. *Gen.* 8:7. This legend is told to explain the continued absence of the raven in almost every version of the flood story. See, e.g., "Flood", *Jew. Encyc.*; AUGUSTINE, *Quaest. in Hept.* I xiii, *PL* XXXIV 551; PRUDENTIUS, *Dittochaeum*, *PL* LX 93; ISIDORE, *Myst. Expos. Sac.* vii, *PL* LXXXIII 233; *Hist. Schol. Gen.* xxxiv, *PL* CXCVIII 1085; *OEGen.* 1446-8; *SELTemp.* fol. LV col. 2; *Cleanness*, 459ff; WYNTOUN 408-10; *Pilg. Life of Man* 2405-72; *Lud. Cov.* IV 246; *Towneley* III 499-504; *Creat. of World* 2464-5; *Anc. Corn. Dr.* 1103-81.

1889-92   Cf. below 11.3332-4.

1911-2   This may reflect the Augustinian speculation that the carnivorous animals had lived on figs and chestnuts during the voyage. See *DCD* XV xxvii; REMIGIUS OF AUXERRE, *Comment. in Gen.*, *PL* CXXXI 76; *Hist. Schol. Gen.* xxxiii, *PL* CXCVIII 1084.

1917-20   See note to 11.1835-6.

1921   "perus maior", as HAENISCH, *CM*, p. 6* pointed out is a corruption of C's "piers mayner", a translation of Petrus Manducator, i.e. Petrus Comestor.

1923ff. Cf. *Gen.* 8:15ff. MSS CF's "spak" is original, for Latin "Locutus est".

1952 MS C's "therst" is surely an error for "theft" as the glossary suggests, *CM,* p. 1773.

1953-60 From *Trad. anon.* fol. 220v col. 2-221r col. 1. The poet begins with the dietary prohibition of *Gen.* 9:4. This evidently calls to his mind the passages from *Lev.* 11:3 and *Deut.* 14:6 which permit the eating of cloven-hoofed beasts only if they chew the cud. The *CM* poet describes the dietary laws more fully than does the French poet.

1961 *Deut.* 14:19.

1962 *Deut.* 14:12-8.

1963-4 Perhaps based on *Deut.* 14:9. The southern translator corrupted "fixs" to "flesshe".

1966 The southern translator also corrupted "blod" to "body".

1967-78 The poet returns to *Gen.* 9:5-6, 9-16.

1985-6 *Trad. anon.* fol. 220v col. 2. Once again the poet takes an opportunity to emphasize the need for tithing.

1993-4 *Hist. Schol. Gen.* xxviii, *PL* CXCVIII 1079.

1995-2000 *Hist. Schol. Gen.* xxxii, *PL* CXCVIII 1082.

2001-6 *Rev.* Meth. p. 194. As d'Evelyn points out, *Rev.* Meth. p. 147-8, the *CM* poet borrows this directly from the short text of Methodius, the "Metody" of 1.2004, and not from Comestor. Comestor does not mention the 612th year of Noah's age.

2013ff. Noah's drunkenness and the curse on Canaan (*Gen.* 9:20-7). Two main problems arise out of the narrative in *Genesis*: why was it so disastrous for Ham to see his father naked, and why, if Ham was guilty of an offense, did the punishment fall on Canaan? For the *CM* poet's answers to these questions, see notes to 11. 2028 and 2051-2 below.

2015 MS C's "sloght" is not a mistake for "soght", as the Glossary, p. 1763 states. Rather it must come from OE *sleccan,* a weak verb meaning to smooth.

2018 The word "vnwarres" reflects the discussions among exegetical writers who sought to excuse the drunkenness of the righteous Noah. See ALLEN, *Leg. of Noah,* p. 73; ALANUS DE INSULIS, *Contra Haereticos* I xxxvii, *PL* CCX 341, 343. Cf. *Piers Plowman,* which condemns him for it (C XI 175-7).

2021-40 BUEHLER, *"CM",* p. 488, has shown that these lines are translated from HERMAN's *Bible,* 11.370-81.

2025 Herman refers to "L'ainsnés des fius" (1.372), but the *CM* poet calls Ham "His mydelest son", as is implied by the order of names in *Gen.* 10:1.

2028 Several traditions exist to explain the harshness of Ham's punishment. Latin commentators tend to follow Josephus in saying that Ham's crime lay in mocking his father's nakedness, as here. See JOSEPHUS 69; BEDE, *Hex., PL* XCI III; *Hist. Schol. Gen.* xxxvi, *PL* CXCVIII 1087. Cf. MALAN, *Book of Adam* III xiii, p. 160; BUDGE, *Cave of Treasures,* 118.

2047-8 *Hist. Schol. Gen.* xxxvi, *PL* CXCVIII 1087. The statement is also found in HUGH OF ST. VICTOR, *Adnot. in Pent., PL* CLXXV 48.

2051-2 In *Gen.* 9:25, the curse falls on Canaan, the son of Ham. The *CM* poet follows Herman who also has Noah curse Ham himself. For conjecture about the biblical curse, see ALLEN, *Leg. of Noah,* 77; "Ham", *Jew. Encyc.*; VON RAD, *Genesis,* 131-2.

2051 MS C's "þam" is an error for "cham", for only one brother was cursed.

2069-80 From HERMAN's *Bible,* 11.398-406. See BUEHLER, *"CM",* 489.

2070-2 Ham is the natural successor to Cain after the Flood. See EMERSON, "Legs. of Cain", p. 489.

2082 *Gen.* 9:28: "Vixit autem Noe post diluvium trecentis quinquaginta annis." The reading "fourty ʒeer" in all MSS is plainly an error. Morris seems to have added the figures in 11.2082-3 to get his running head-line "Noah lived 990 years", *CM,* p. 127.

2087-90 Long tradition assigns these parts of the world to the sons of Noah. See JOSEPHUS 59-73; BEDE, *Hex., PL* XCI 123; *In Pent., PL* XCI 228; HUGH OF ST. VICTOR, *Adnot. in Pent., PL* CLXXV 49; *Hist. Schol. Gen.* xxxvii, *PL* CXCVIII 1087; cf. *Rev.* Meth. 354-65; MANDEVILLE L 155.

2091ff. This passage does not come from any of the *CM* poet's usual sources. A comparison with Isidore's *Etymologies,* the basis of most mediaeval geography, shows that the *CM* poet's information is con-densed from Isidore. The information may have reached the ME poet through an intermediate source, however.

2096-8 ISIDORE, *Etym.* XIV ii 2-3. Cf. HUGH OF ST. VICTOR, *Adnot. in Pent., PL* CLXXV 49.

2102 *Etym.* XIV iii 20 and 23 mention Judea and Galilee. The heathens are probably the marvellous inhabitants of Asia mentioned in so many travel-lers' tales.

2103 *Etym.* XIV iii 5, 6, 7 enumerates the spices and precious stones of India.

2104 *Etym.* XIV iii 2.

2105 *Etym.* XIV iii 5 on India; 12 on Persia; 15 on Arabia.

2106 *Etym.* XIV iii 14 on Babilonia, 20 on Judea. "Sulie" is a corruption of "surie"/Syria, as Kaluza suggests in his glossary, *CM,* p. 1818. Note MS B's "Surry". Cf. *Etym.* XIV iii 16.

2108 *Etym.* XIV iii 14 on Babylon.

2109-10 *Etym.* XIV v 1, "De Libya" begins "Libya... hoc est Africus."

2113 *Etym.* XIV v 8 on Carthage.

2115-6 These lines are corrupt and may have been transposed. "Mortaygne" is Mauretania. "Ienile" is a corruption of Gaetulia ("Ietule" being misread by a scribe as "Ienile"). "Indie" cannot refer to India, which was discussed in its proper place under Asia, at 1.2105 above. Rather, it is a corruption of Numidia ("Numidie" having lost some initial minims). The same misreadings occur in TRETHEWEY, ed., *La Petite Philosophe,* p. 40, 1.1231 and n., pp. 117-8: "Puis est Genilie e Indie".

Morris punctuated MS C to suggest that "þis land" of 1.2117 refer-red to Africa or possibly to "Indie". If the lines are reversed, how-ever, "Ienile mortaygne & indie" carry on the enumeration of other countries and cities of Africa begun in 11.2111-4. The passage would then continue:

þe myche londe of ethiopye
þat lond is moost into þe souþ
þere þat blo men are ful couþ

Lines 2115-8, then, clearly translate Isidore's discussion:

> Proxima autem Hispaniae Mauretania est, deinde Numidia, inde regio Carthaginensis, post quae Gaetuliam accipimus, post eam Aethiopiam, inde loca exusta solis ardoribus... Aethiopia dicta a colore populorum, quos solis vicinitas torret (*Etym*. XIV v 17, 14).

Furthermore, of the *MED*'s citations under "blo-man", six connect them with Ethiopia, and only this one line in the *CM* with India.

2119 The poet says almost nothing about Europe, the best known part of the world in the Middle Ages.

The original reading was CFG's "lest". The southern translation's "best" contradicts 1.2090.

2132 One would expect the figure 72 here. The Vulgate text enumerates 15 descendants of Noah in Japheth's line, 30 in Ham's and 27 in Shem's (*Gen*. 10). Similarly the number of workmen engaged in building the Tower of Babel and the number of languages there created was usually 72. See BEDE, *Hex., PL* XCI 123; HUGH OF ST. VICTOR, *Adnot. in Pent., PL* CLXXV 49; ISIDORE, *Etym*. IX ii 2; *Hist. Schol. Gen*. xxxvii, *PL* CXCVIII 1087; McNALLY, *Bible,* 38. The figure is important, for it reappears in the New Testament as the number of missionaries sent out to preach, excluding Christ's disciples, in *Luc* 10:1.

In ME, *G & E* 669-70 mentions the 72 workmen, as does the *Quaestiones* 285, although later on in the dialogue the number of languages is said to be 62. See *Quaestiones* 287.

The *CM* poet probably gets his figure from *Trad. anon.* fol. 222r col. 1 which says that 62 languages were spoken after the Tower of Babel was abandoned. Although the correct figure, 72, appears everywhere else in the *Trad. anon.*, the *CM* poet stays with the incorrect one. At various times he says that Noah's descendants numbered 60 (1.2132), and that 60 workmen built the Tower of Babel (1.2214), but 62 speeches resulted (1.2270), although no descendants of Shem took part in the work (11.2279-80). Also the Tower was 62 fathoms broad (1.2241).

2133-6 The passage is an elaboration of *Gen*. 9:26-7. Its immediate source is Honorius Augustodunensis' *DIM*. After the Flood, men are divided "in liberos, milites, servos. Liberi de Sem, milites de Japhet, servi de Cham." See *PL* CLXXII 166.

The three classes usually mentioned in this context are priests, slaves and knights. The *CM* passage is the earliest instance in English of the subdivision of the class of commoners into thralls and freemen. See THRUPP, *Merchant Class,* 289-91. However, as early as the tenth century (probably), the *Rígsþula* had given mythological sanction to this commonplace of Scandinavian social organization. See Gwyn JONES, *History of the Vikings,* pp. 145ff.

2140 Shem lived to be 600 years old (*Gen*. 11: 10-1).

2141-2 *Hist. Schol. Gen*. xlvi, *PL* CXCVIII 1094: "Huic Melchisedech, aiunt Hebraei fuisse Sem filium Noe."

2151-2 The quotation given in the note to 11.2141-2 above continues "et vixisse usque ad Isaac." The poet's seventy years (MS C wrongly has seven) is a puzzle. Calculations from the Vulgate involving the age of each man at the time of the birth of his first-born son would indicate that Isaac was 110 years old when Shem was 600. *DIM* says Shem died in Jacob's time. See *PL* CLXXII 168.

2154-6   The poet realizes that the genealogy given in *Gen.* 11:10-27 is only of the succession of eldest sons from Shem to Abraham. Cf. Augustine's discussion, *DCD* XVI x.

The genealogy which follows is found also in *DIM, PL* CLXXII 166.

2157-8   *Gen.* 11:12-3. MS C's reading "tuenti" is wrong.

2159-60   This Cainan does not appear in the Vulgate here. The *CM* poet takes him from *DIM, PL* CLXXII 166, where he is said to have lived 438 years. He comes ultimately from the Septuagint, *Gen.* 11:12-3, where he has a life span of 460 years. Petrus Comestor points out that the name appears in the genealogy of *Luc.* 3:36 in the Vulgate as well. See *Hist. Schol. Gen.* xli, *PL* CXCVIII 1090. Cf. *DCD* XVI x; HIGDEN 241.

2163-4   *Gen.* 11:16-7. Heber lived 464 years, not 444.

2165-6   "anen" is a mistake for "nine" in MS C.

2172   *Gen.* 11:24-5. Nahor did not live to be 88, but 148. The correct reading would be "seuen score and eiȝte".

2177-8   *Gen.* 11:1.

2181-94   *Gen.* 10:2-7. The order of names is often rearranged for the sake of rhymes.

2186   "Togoriens" is a scribal corruption of "Togorma", as in MSS CF. Cf. the Vulgate "Thogorma".

2187   MS C's "antechim" is an error.

2189-90   *Gen.* 10:5. GHTLB's "foly" is probably a scribal corruption of C's "folk".

2193   MSS CF have "euila" for the Vulgate's "Hevila". G's "enila" should also be transcribed "euila". The southern translator's "ielula" results from a misreading of minims.

2195   The poet skips the sons of Regma (*Gen.* 10:7) and the rest of the genealogical information in *Gen.* 10. to pursue the story of the last son of Chus, Nimrod.

Genesis does not say exactly who built the Tower of Babel, but a very early tradition assigned it to Nimrod because of *Gen.* 10:10. See "Babel, Tower of", "Nimrod", *Jew. Encyc.*; DRIVER, *Genesis*, 122-3; MENNER, ed., *Solomon and Saturn*, pp. 122-3.

2199-2209   I know no source for this passage. The wickedness of Nimrod was well known, however. See *Hist. Schol. Gen.* xxxvii, *PL* CXCVIII 1088.

2208   The southern translator's line is probably a rationalization of a corruption of "maistri" (CF) to "merci" (G).

2210-1   *Trad. anon.* fol. 222r col. 1.

2212-3   *Gen.* 11:2. C's "felauscap", meaning a crew of workmen, is preferable to readings in the other MSS.

2214   Cf. note to 1.2132. The *Trad. anon.* says he brought 72 people.

2218   Nimrod and his followers were idolaters, traditionally worshippers of the sun. See the homily "De Falsis Diis" in *Homs. of Aelfric* II, ed. POPE, 68/82-4 and the sources there cited. Cf. HUGH OF ST. VICTOR, *Adnot. in Pent., PL* CLXXV 49; *Hist. Schol. Gen.* xxxvii, *PL* CXCVIII 1088. A Jewish tradition held that the people built the tower of Babel to the heavens to war on God. See GINZBERG, *Legends* V, pp. 201-2 n. 88; ISIDORE, *Etym.* VII vi 22; WYNTOUN 1439-40; GOWER, Prol. to *Confessio Amantis* 1020-1. In these lines, the poet presumably made the logical connection and had Nimrod make war on the sun and moon. Cf. another Jewish tradition, which said Nimrod wanted to ruin heaven, in GINZBERG, *loc. cit.* Cf. also below, 11.2232-6.

2224-8 Nimrod's speech reflects the other traditional reason for building the tower, that in it the people would be safe from another flood. See *Hist. Schol. Gen.* xxxviii, *PL* CXCVIII 1089. Cf. *Trad. anon.* fol. 221v col. 2; EVRAT, fol. 25r col. 1; MACÈ 1178-84; *G & E* 659-62; *Rev.* Meth. 326-9; HIGDEN 249. Lydgate has Nimrod build two towers in the *Fall of Princes,* one to escape another flood (1079-85) and the second to take heaven away from God (1191ff).

2231 The square and scantillon were both carpenters' tools, the scantillon used for measuring thickness. The two frequently appear as an alliterative formula. See the citations in *OED.*

2232-6 See note to 11.2217-8 above.

2233-4 From *Trad. anon.* fol. 221v col. 1.

2238 From *Trad. anon.* fol. 221v col. 2.

2241-2 The *Trad. anon.* fol. 221v col. 1 gives some dimensions of the building, but none which correspond with these measurements. Cf. n. to 1.2132 above. Jewish tradition held that the Tower of Babel was 70 stairs high because of the 70 families which built it. See GINZBERG, *Legends,* V, pp. 202-3 n. 88.

2242 The groundwall was a low wall of stone or brick upon which the timber groundsills of a building were often set to preserve them from rotting. See SALZMAN, p. 201.

2245-6 *Gen.* 11:3. Bricks were called "tiles" until the fifteenth century, when the word brick came into use. See SALZMAN, pp. 140-2.

2248-52, 2256-61 From *Trad. anon.* fol. 221v col. 2.

2265-6 MSS CFG preserve the original reading "schending", meaning confusion. This is the usual interpretation of the word Babel, as in *Gen.* 11:9.

2269-70 *Trad. anon.* fol. 222r col. 1:

Deuant nauoit ou monde que i langaige
Sesante & ii enfut par cel outraige

Cf. n. to 1.2132 above.

2279-81 *Trad. anon.* fol. 222r col. 1.

2289-2302 *Hist. Schol. Gen.* xl, *PL* CXCVIII 1090. Comestor attributes the beginnings of idol-worship to Ninus, which the *CM* poet alters to Nimrod. From the fourth century on, however, Ninus, the founder of Ninevah, had sometimes been identified with Nimrod the founder of Babel, of which Ninevah itself was a colony. See *Gen.* 10:11. On this subject see COOKE, "Euhemerism", 396-410, and MENNER "Two Notes on Mediaeval Euhemerism", 246-8. The ultimate source of the concept is *Sap.* 14: 15-21.

2303-4 These lines are added to the *Hist. Schol.*'s description of the beginning of idolatry. The idea that devils enter into statues or idols to mislead the people is widespread. Jewish sources describe this happening to a statue made by Enosh, one of the descendants of Seth. See GINZBERG, *Legends,* V, pp. 150-1, n. 54. French paraphrases tell of it happening to the image of the golden calf. See HERMAN, 1. 2117; GEOFFROI DE PARIS, fol. 25v cols. 1-2; MALKARAUME, fol. 54r col. 1. However, PANTON and DONALDSON, ed., *Destruction of Troy,* 11.4332-57 agrees with *CM* in having the incident happen to Nimrod's statues. Cf. AELFRIC, ed. POPE, 687-8/197-201.

2307-8   *Gen.* 22:20-2 names eight children of Nahor, including Hus, Buz and Bathuel.

2309   *Hist. Schol. Gen.* lviii, *PL* CXCVIII 1105.

2310   *Gen.* 22:23 says Bathuel begat Rebecca. The reference to her brother Laban is an anticipation of *Gen.* 24:29.

2311-2   MSS CF mention two daughters of Aran, while GHTLB say he had three, presumably counting Lot as a daughter. However, some genuine confusion did exist over this family. A mysterious Jescha appears in *Gen.* 11:29 but is never mentioned again. For the sake of neatness, Jewish tradition identified Jescha with Sarah. See JOSEPHUS 75; *Targ. of Jon.* 192; RASHI 47; SKINNER, *Genesis*, 238. Later commentators accepted the identification, as did ME paraphrasers. The scribe responsible for the reading "three" in MSS GHTLB, then, might have been counting Sarah, Melcha and Jescha as three different daughters of Aran. Cf. however, 11.2333-4.

2315-8   *Trad. anon.* fol. 222r cols. 1-2. L.2316 appears in French as "Et fuit racine de crestiene foi". The MS which the *CM* poet used must have had "loi" instead. Abraham, whose obedience is everywhere stressed, makes more sense as a root of Christian faith, rather than of law.

2315-26   Abraham's place in the genealogy of the Virgin is now made clear.

2333-4   Cf. note to 11.2311-2.

2335-6   This was later specifically prohibited by *Lev.* 18:9 and 20:17.

2343-50   Cf. *Gen.* 13:16, 15:5-6, and below, 11.2568-72. The "graueles in þe see" metaphor in 1.2347 and 1.2571 comes from *Gen.* 22:17.

2355   *Genesis* contains some discrepancies in the ages of the patriarchs here. Thare is 70 when he begets Abraham (*Gen.* 11:26), and Abraham leaves Haran at 75 (*Gen.* 12:4). At this time, Thare would only have been 145 years old, yet his death in Haran at 205 has already been described (*Gen.* 11:32). Jerome and Augustine both tried to solve the apparent discrepancy. See *Quaest. in Gen., PL* XXIII 1006; *Quaest. in Hept.* I xxv, *PL* XXXIV 553-4.

The *CM* poet does not notice the difficulty. He assumes that Abraham left Haran immediately after his father's death (11.2357ff) and the figure sixty-five (1.2355) is a straightforward error for seventy-five. Cf. *G & E* 731-2, 739-40.

2357ff   The *CM* poet seems to take his account more or less from *Genesis*, but various lines come from *Trad. anon.* fol. 222v, esp. 11.2364-7, 2395-7, 2410, 2430, 2438.

2364-7   *Trad. anon.* fol. 222v col. 1.

2364   MSS CG have the original reading, the northern imperative form "ta" of the verb "take", with the k suppressed. The southern translator, or his exemplar, misread this as "to".

2367   This is the only mention of Ur of the Chaldees, the original home of Abraham (*Gen.* 11:31), here incorrectly identified with Haran. The biblical account contains a confusion resulting from the joining of the J and the P narratives. The compiler of *Genesis* tried to reconcile two traditions by having Abraham leave Ur, move to Haran, and then move on from there. However, when Abraham sends his servant to procure a wife for Isaac, he speaks as if Haran, not Ur, were his native city. See *Gen.* 24:4, 7, 10; 27:43; 28:10; 29:4.

2395-7, 2410 *Trad. anon.* fol. 222v col. 2 and 223r col. 1.

2419 The *CM* poet does not mention Pharaoh's offers to Abraham, nor the plagues which God sent (*Gen.* 12: 16-7).

2430 The silver and gold which Pharaoh gave to the departing Abraham comes from *Trad. anon.* fol. 223r col. 2.

2438, 2441-2, 2445 *Trad. anon.* fol. 223r col. 2.

2447-56 Two reasons are given in *Genesis* for the separation of Abraham and Lot. The P document says that there was not enough pasture for both flocks (*Gen.* 13:6) while J says that the herdsmen were quarrelling (*Gen.* 13:7). The *CM* poet reconciles the two versions.

2470 *Trad. anon.* fol. 223v col. 1.

2480 Both the poet of the *Trad. anon.* and the *CM* poet omit God's promise in *Gen.* 13: 14-7.

2481 *Gen.* 13:18 speaks of "convallem Mambre", but the *CM* calls it a hill, as does *Met. Para.* 556, and *Anc. test.* fol. 5r col. 2.

2489-90 *Trad. anon.* fol. 223v col. 2.

2491-2528 Much of this account of the war among the kings is taken from *Trad. anon.* fol. 223v col. 2-224r col. 2. See esp. 11.2491-8.

Modern commentators agree that *Gen.* 14 came from a different source from the rest of the book, and is probably a later interpolation. See DRIVER, *Genesis,* p. 155, VON RAD, *Genesis,* p. 169. The gusto with which the battles are treated in the *OEGen.* (11.1960ff) is unmatched in ME.

2520 "themas" is a scribal error for "demas", *Trad. anon.* "damas", probably by confusion of capital Đ with capital D. However, Petrus Comestor mentions a place called "Themam" in connection with Ishmael, and the *CM* poet may have confused the one with the other. See *Hist. Schol. Gen.* lvi, *PL* CXCVIII 1104.

2535-44 Cf. *Gen.* 14: 18-24, though the speeches are much abbreviated in the ME version.

2537-8, 2540 Probably from *Trad. anon.* fol. 224r col. 2. Cf. *Hist. Schol. Gen.* xlvi, *PL* CXCVIII 1094-5.

2551-76 *Genesis* reports two separate visions, one waking and one sleeping (*Gen.* 15:1, 12). The *CM* poet takes the setting of his one dream from the latter verse. The *Trad. anon.* also has only one vision, but it is a waking one.

2571 *Trad. anon.* fol. 224v cols. 1-2. Cf. fol. 225r col. 1.

2577-8 The poet omits the details of the sacrifice in *Gen.* 15:7-11, 17.

2579-2634 Cf. *Gen.* 15:13-16, 16:1-12.

2595ff. Some commentators were uneasy with the idea of the virtuous Sarah suggesting her husband commit adultery. Josephus 93 had her do it at God's command, while Augustine excused it because the deed was motivated by a desire for progeny rather than by lust. See *DCD* XVI xxv.

2613-4 *Gen.* 16:6 reads "Affligente igitur eam Sarai." Augustine, for one, was bothered by the virtuous Sarah, frequent symbol of the Church, having persecuted her slave. See *Epist.* CLXXXV ii, *PL* XXXIII 797. So too the *Met. Para.* 517-26, but not the *CM* poet.

2637-48 Cf. *Gen.* 16: 15-6; 17:1-16.

2643   Abraham was, in fact, 99 years old, not 109. See *Gen.* 17:1. Cf. below, 1.2699.

2650-1 The change of name is from "Abram" to "Abraham" in *Gen.* 17:5, although few ME scribes make the distinction.

2653-4 Petrus Comestor makes the etymology rather clearer than does the Vulgate. See *Hist. Schol. Gen.* 1, *PL* CXCVIII 1097.

2689   The *CM* poet does not describe Abraham's laughter at God's promise of a child in his old age, nor record His promises for Ishmael (*Gen.* 17: 17-22).

2693-2700 Cf. *Gen.* 17:23-7.

2697   MS F has the correct reading thirteen years. Cf. *Gen.* 17:25. The other MSS all read 30.

2699   Cf. note to 1.2643 above.

2701-2 Cf. Josephus 95; *Hist. Schol. Gen.* 1, *PL* CXCVIII 1097; *G & E* 1004; Higden 293; cf. above 1.2666.

2703-4 Cf. *Gen.* 18:1.

2705-12 Buehler, "*CM*", pp. 289-90 first suggested that these lines are based on Herman's *Bible*, 11. 423-6.

2709-10 The angel who speaks to Abraham in the Vulgate is referred to as "Dominus" (*Gen.* 18:3, etc.) which led most commentators to see the three angels as a manifestation of the Trinity. See, e.g., Isidore, *Allegoriae, PL* LXXXIII 104; Bede, *Hex., PL* XCI 167; Von Rad, *Genesis*, p. 201. Cf. also *G & E* 1010-2; *SELTemp.* fol. 2r col. 1; *Met. Para.* 573-6 and *Piers Plowman* C XIX 242-8. These latter two works both use the formula quoted in *Piers Plowman*: "Tres vidit et unum adoravit."

2713   Cf. *Gen.* 18:4. By having Abraham himself wash their feet, a further parallel with Christ is brought out. Cf. also *Trad. anon.* 225v col. 1 and *Anc. test.* fol. 5r col. 2 which also have Abraham washing their feet.

2714-5 Cf. *Gen.* 18:5-8. This passage bothered early commentators, for according to biblical authority angels did not eat human food. See *Iud.* 13:16; *Tob.* 12:19; Skinner, *Genesis*, p. 300; Von Rad, *Genesis*, pp. 201-2. Several Jewish commentators say that the angels only gave the appearance of eating. See Josephus 97; *Targ. of Jon.* 211, 214; *Midrash* xlviii 14, p. 415; Rashi, 72; Ginzberg, *Legends*, V p. 236 nn. 143-4. Principally through Comestor, this idea spread widely. See *Hist. Schol. Gen.* li, *PL* CXCVIII 1098-9; *G & E* 1015-8; *Cleanness* 641-2; Geoffroi de Paris fol. 14r col. 2; Évrat fol. 42r col. 1.

The poet of the *CM* was not troubled by this problem, apparently, but an annotator in MS F was aware of it, for he wrote in the margin "hou god et botter [sic] & botter". See Morris, *CM*, p. 164, MS F.

2716-48 Cf. *Gen.* 18:9-21.

2741-2 *Trad. anon.* fol. 225v col. 2.

2742, 2744 Cf. 1.1644 above, and note.

2749-64 The haggling between God and Abraham recounted in *Gen.* 18: 23-33 is here much abbreviated. This is standard practice among paraphrasers. See Josephus 99; *Hist. Schol. Gen.* lii, *PL* CXCVIII 1099-1100; *G & E* 1041-6; *SELTemp.* fol. 2r col. 1; *Met. Para.* 577-84. Among English works, only *Cleanness* gives a full account of the conversation, 11.713-66.

2761-2 *Trad. anon.* fol. 225v col. 2.

2765-2846 Cf. *Gen.* 19:1-25.

2810 The Bible does not mention the cities sinking. Cf. however, HERMAN 469; *G & E* 1114.

2848 See WHITING, *Proverbs,* B529, where many other occurrences of this proverb are cited.

2849-55 From HERMAN's *Bible,* 467-74. See BUEHLER, *"CM"*, pp. 490-1. Lot's wife also turns back on hearing the cry from the city in MAL-KARAUME fol. 5v col. 2; GEOFFROI DE PARIS, fol. 14v col. 2; *Anc. test.* fol. 5v col. 1; *OEGen.* 2562-5.

2854 Cf. JOSEPHUS 101; *Hist. Schol. Gen.* liii, *PL* CXCVIII 1101; *OEGen.* 2567-71; *Met. Para.* 612; MALKARAUME, fol. 5v col. 2; GEOFFROI DE PARIS, fol. 14v col. 2; *Anc. test.* fol. 5v col. 1.

2856-60 A similar legend is found in *Pirke* xxv p. 186, but this is the only other occurrence of this legend that I have found. Beasts are briefly mentioned in *SELTemp.* fol. 2r col. 1.

2861-80 *Hist. Schol. Gen.* liii, *PL* CXCVIII 1101; cf. xliv, and Add. 1, 1092 and 1093.

2877-80 The story of the dead sea apples is a very popular one. See *G & E* 1127-30; MANDEVILLE S 63/1-5; *Cleanness* 1041-8; TACITUS *Hist.* V vii; JOSEPHUS, *History of the Jewish War* III 143-5; ISIDORE, *Etym.* XIV iii 25; FULCHER OF CHARTRES, *Historia Hierosolymitana* II iv, *PL* CLX 867.

2879 The poet originally compared these fruits not merely to round balls but to puff-balls (C "fise bal", F "pis balle").

2881ff This is one of the *CM* poet's rare direct, moralistic interpretations of the story which he has been telling. Many mediaeval writers delighted in describing the sexual sins of Sodom. See esp. *SELTemp.* fol. 2r col. 1 and *Cleanness* 689-712.

2907 Another popular interpretation of the sin of Sodom, based on *Ez.* 16:49: "Ecce haec fuit iniquitas Sodomae, sororis tuae: superbia, saturitas panis et abundantia, et otium ipsius, et filiarum ejus;" See JOSEPHUS 95; *Hist. Schol. Gen.* lii, *PL* CXCVIII 1099 (where the *CM* poet must have seen it); PETRUS CANTOR, *Verbum Abbrev.* cxxxviii, *PL* CCV 333-4. In ME, see *Piers Plowman* C XVI 232-3, cf. B XIV 74-80; *Ayenbite of Inwit* 206.

2912-6 Cf. *Gen.* 19:30.

2914 The original reading was CFG's "fell", Latin "in monte". Cf. 1.2832 below.

2917-26 Cf. *Gen.* 19:27-8.

2929-51 Cf. *Gen.* 19: 30-38.

2953-8 *Trad. anon.* fol. 226r col. 2-226v col. 1.

2961-3006 Cf. *Gen.* 20:1-15. This is essentially the same story as that told in *Gen.* 12 (see above, 11.2357ff). Many commentators ignore the new telling of the same story, except to wonder how Sarah could still have been so dangerously attractive at the age of 90. See AUGUSTINE, *Quaest. in Hept.* I xlviii, *PL* XXXIV 560; *Hist. Schol. Gen.* lv, *PL* CXCVIII 1102. Like the *CM*, *Trad. anon.* and *G & E* also tell the story for the second time, however.

2961 "cadades" (C "cades") is evidently the "Cades" of *Gen.* 20:1, although the Vulgate says Abraham lived "inter Cades et Sur".

2974   CF's "talking" was miscopied as "tokening" in GHTLB.

3006   The poet omits the curse which had fallen on Abimelech because of his treatment of Sarah (*Gen.* 20:17-8).

3007-82   Cf. *Gen.* 21:1-21.

3013-4   This is a loose translation of Comestor's etymology, *Hist. Schol. Gen.* lvi, *PL* CXCVIII 1103. Cf. JEROME, *Liber de Nominibus Hebraicis, PL* XXIII 824; ISIDORE, *Etym.* VII vii 4.

3024-6   The reason for Sarah's demand that Ishmael be banished is unclear in the Vulgate, which says simply that Sarah saw "filium Agar aegyptiae ludentem cum Isaac filio suo" (*Gen.* 21:9). The *CM* poet does not look farther than this, although many explanations were provided in the Middle Ages. See SKINNER, *Genesis,* 322; DRIVER, *Genesis,* 210-1; VON RAD, *Genesis,* 227; "Isaac", "Ishmael", *Jew. Encyc.; Jubilees,* 17:4; JOSEPHUS 107; *Targ. of Jon.* 221; *Hist. Schol. Gen.* lvi, *PL* CXCVIII 1103; *G & E* 1213-4.

3050   MSS CF have the more accurate reading "trused" for the Latin "imposuit scapulae ejus", *Gen.* 21:14. This is weakened in MSS GHTLB to "tok".

3055   As Hagar and Ishmael are dying of thirst, the poet's statement that they stay by a well is incongruous. It is, of course, an anticipation of the revelation of 1.3066 (*Gen.* 21:19).

3061-7   *Trad. anon.* fol. 227v col. 1.

3065   The reading "blinde" (in MS F and originally in MS C also) may have been suggested by the sequel in *Gen.* 21:19: "Aperuitque oculos ejus Deus;". However the line is now corrupt in all MSS.

3083-94   This is not found in the Vulgate, which continues with the story of the covenant of Beersheba, omitted altogether by the *CM* poet. BUEHLER, *"CM"* pp. 491-2, has demonstrated, however, that the ME poet has selected a few details from a long passage in HERMAN's *Bible,* 11.419-22, 507-11, describing Abraham's longevity and character.

3095-3116   This passage is even more obviously borrowed from HERMAN, 11.513-35. See BUEHLER, *"CM",* pp. 492-3. It continues to detail the degeneration of the world from its original state, a view which is thematic in the *CM.* The further mention of tithing in connection with sacrifice is also a continuing motif.

3115   MS C's "wil" is an error for "wit", as comparison with the source shows.

3117ff   The story of Abraham's willingness to sacrifice Isaac was a very popular one with mediaeval audiences. The *CM* poet does not follow the Vulgate in his retelling of it, nor does he stress the importance of the incident as a figure of the sacrifice of Christ, an allegorical interpretation much favoured in exegesis.

3119-24   HERMAN, 11.557-63. See BUEHLER, *"CM",* 494. The lines serve to underline the deep and longstanding emotions involved in the incident.

3131   Cf. HERMAN, 1.571.

3133-46   The poet begins to stress Abraham's absolute obedience to God's order. This is one of the rare places where the *CM* poet steps in to interpret his story.

3147-80   Cf. *Gen.* 22:2-8, 10-13.

3152   Isaac is consistently referred to as a child here, which greatly increases the pathos of the situation. A strong mediaeval tradition, ultimately Jewish, made Isaac a man at the time of the sacrifice. See "Isaac", *Jew. Encyc.*; VON RAD, *Genesis*, 238; JOSEPHUS 113; *Pirke* XXXI 225; *Hist. Schol. Gen.* lviii, *PL* CXCVIII 1104; *G & E* 1284; *SELTemp.* fol. 2r col. 2; *York* X 821. His maturity is also implied in *Met Para.* 714-6, 729. The other Abraham and Isaac plays in ME agree with the *CM* in calling Isaac a child, however. So too does GEOFFROI DE PARIS fol. 14r col. 1. See WELLS, "The Age of Isaac", 579-82.

3168-72 Abraham is concerned lest the boy see the sword as he draws it. Cf. *Chester* IV 337-40; *Lud. Cov.* 179-82 and the Malvern windows described in M. D. ANDERSON, *Drama and Imagery*, 109.

3189-98 Although based on *Gen.* 22:15-8, the angel's speech has been altered to stress Abraham's obedience further.

3203-6 Abraham's swearing Isaac to secrecy is not in *Gen.*, but was borrowed from HERMAN's *Bible*, 11.613-7. See BUEHLER, "*CM*", 494.

3209-14 The ME poet has already given the genealogy of Nahor, in *Gen.* 22:20-4, cf. *CM*, 11.2307-10. He omits virtually all of *Gen.* 23 dealing with the purchase of land for Sarah's burial. This is true of the other ME and most of the French paraphrases.

3215-3400 Most of the following story comes from *Trad. anon.* fol. 228r col. 1-228v.

3225 *Genesis* and the *Trad. anon.* both describe the Hebrew custom of swearing with the hand under the thigh. The *CM* poet substitutes a more mediaeval tradition.

3230 Mesopotamia is not mentioned here in *Gen.* or in *Trad. anon.*

3246-50 The treasure comes from *Trad. anon.*, but the camels are from *Gen.* 24:10.

3260 MS C's "now" is an error for "my".

3283 Kaluza glosses "vnlaghter" as "without fault", (OE *leahter*). Cf. MORRIS' note *CM*, p. xxxvii. The French, however, reads "qui ne uint pas riant", so the English was more probably intended to mean "without laughter".

3286-7 From *Gen.* 24:15, not *Trad. anon.*

3295-3300 Not in the Vulgate or *Trad. anon.*

3313-5 There is some confusion over Rebecca's father. Although he never appears, he is usually called Bethuel (*Gen.* 22:23, 24:15, 24). The negotiations for the marriage are carried on by her brother. Josephus and, following him, Comestor speculated that Rebecca's father was dead. See JOSEPHUS 123, *Hist. Schol. Gen.* lx, *PL* CXCVIII 1107. The *CM* poet ignores the latter opinion to state plainly that Rebecca's father is alive.

3327-31 A condensation of *Gen.* 24:33-49, in which the messenger retells the whole story.

3332 Cf. above 11.1889-92.

3337 A condensed version of the negotiations in *Gen.* 24: 53-9 and *Trad. anon.* fol. 228v col. 2.

3347 "foster moder" is closer to the Vulgate's "nutricem" than is the "moder" of MSS GHTLB. The line does not appear in *Trad. anon.*

3349-62 Details come from *Gen.* 24: 63-5, rather than from *Trad. anon.*

3363-6 *Trad. anon.* fol. 229r col. 1. *Gen.* 24:65 calls the garment simply a "pallium". COMESTOR, *Hist. Schol. Gen.* lxi, *PL* CXCVIII 1107, says that this was an Arabic woman's costume and that it was white. The red mantle comes definitely from the French.

3369-80   The poet expands on the couple's joy in each other which is suggested briefly in *Trad. anon.* The poet also continues to stress the contrast between the purposefulness of those times and that of his own, a concept which is not in the French work.

3375-80   *Gen.* 24:67 and the poet's own reflections.

3381-2   *Gen.* 21:21 and 25:12-6 mentions the twelve princes which came of Ishmael, but give him only one wife. Cf. *Hist. Schol. Gen.* lvi, *PL* CXCVIII 1103-4, which mentions the two events together.

3384   Cf. *Hist. Schol. Gen.* lxv, *PL* CXCVIII 1109, which says that Ishmael's sons ruled India.

3387-94   *Trad. anon.* fol. 229r col. 1:

    Sa darrienne femme ot en nom securra
    Ne fut pas lealte *que* avec li se aiosta

MS Arsenal 3516 has the same reading. The MS which the *CM* poet consulted may have had "licherie", not "lealte". Cf. AUGUSTINE, *DCD* XVI xxv who excuses Abraham's affair with Hagar on the same grounds.

3415-42   This passage links the children of Isaac, born late after much prayer, with other similar children in history.

3426   This line, perfectly clear in C, is meaningless in the southern translation.

3443-88   BUEHLER, "*CM*", p. 495 says these lines are a condensed version of HERMAN's 11.640-754. The other ME paraphrases brush hastily over the entire event, as does the *Trad. anon.*

3491-2   This is the etymology of the name Esau. See JEROME, *Liber de Nom. Hebr.*, *PL* XXIII 823; ISIDORE, *Etym.* VII vi 33; cf. *Hist. Schol. Gen.* lxvi, *PL* CXCVIII 1110.

3494-8   The Vulgate merely says "Jacob...habitabat in tabernaculis...et Rebecca diligebat Jacob" (*Gen.* 25:27-8). The *CM* poet makes this into a cause and effect ralationship: because Rebecca loves Jacob, she keeps him at home. The *Met. Para,* on the other hand, says that Rebecca loved him because he stayed at home (1.800).

3499-3500, 3506-16   From HERMAN's *Bible,* 11.794-805. See BUEHLER, "*CM*", 495-6.

3506   The line is garbled in the southern translation. MSS FG have the best reading.

3509-16   The comment about the former efficacy of blessings continues the theme of the present degeneracy of the world. Here the poet stresses the seriousness of Esau's crime in selling the blessing which should have been his.

3529-30   See WHITING, *Proverbs,* H200.

3553-4   The *CM* poet has followed the Vulgate in simply attributing Esau's folly to his great hunger. Here, however, he adds a note to say that this was all part of God's design. Cf. *Hist. Schol. Gen.* lxvi, *PL* CXCVIII 1110; "Creditur enim in utero jam tunc sanctificatus fuisse Jacob." Cf. note to 11.3717-8 below.

    The *CM* poet, like most other ME paraphrasers, omits the matter of *Gen.* 26, which includes another version of the story of the patriarch telling strangers his wife is his sister, and an account of Isaac's adventures in Gerar and Beersheba. Only the ME *G & E* mentions this at all, and the dullness of its brief account of Isaac's moves (11.1513-26) amply justifies their exclusion from the other works.

3555-94   COFFMAN, "Old Age", discusses this passage. He traces the *topos* of old age from Horace through Maximianus and down to the Middle Ages. Coffman believes that the immediate source of the *CM*'s lines was the *Pricke of Conscience*, 11.766-803, which, however, was written after *CM*.

3595-3700   Based on *Gen.* 27:1-22, with some expansions in the dialogue.

3701-2   The odour of "piement" comes from HERMAN, 11.904-5. See BUEHLER, "*CM*", 496.

3705-10   *Gen.* 27:29.

3717-8   Cf. *Met. Para.* 1.864 and *G & E* 1558-60 which also stress that this is part of God's plan. *The Book of the Knight of LaTour-Landry* goes so far as to praise Rebecca's vision in engineering the misplaced blessing (p. 106).

3719-72   Cf. *Gen.* 27: 30-44.

3731   *Trad. anon.* fol. 230r col. 1: "Ysaac se meruoille fait exclamantion." In *Gen.* 27:33-4 it is Esau who cries out.

3773-86, 3791-2 *Gen.* 28: 11-3.

3783   *Hist. Schol. Gen.* lxxiii, *PL* CXCVIII 1114.

3787-90   The *Met. Para.* 918 also has God specify that Jacob will marry twice.

3794   The scribe of MS T has miscopied the end of the line.

3797-3818   Cf. *Gen.* 28:16-8, 20-22.

3806   C's "voo" (Latin "votum") is original, but GHTLB's "voys" is an interesting substitute.

3819-34   Cf. *Gen.* 29:1-6. The ME paraphrasers are in general not much interested in this incident. The *SELTemp.* fol. 2r col. 2; and *Met. Para.* 79-82 reduce the whole romantic story of the meeting of Jacob and Rachael to a businesslike announcement of the final arrangement.

3835-62, 3867-94   Based loosely on *Gen.* 29:9-23, 25-8.

3862   Leah's eye trouble varies slightly. The Vulgate says "lippis erat oculis" (*Gen.* 29:17), — her eyes were inflamed or watering. The Authorized Version calls her "tender-eyed". The ME poet is less gallant. He calls her "gliȝed", having a squint or cast in one or both eyes. GEOFFROI DE PARIS, fol. 17v col. 2 and Jean MALKARAUME, fol. 11r col. 1 simply say she was ugly.

3863-6   The *Trad. anon.* fol. 230v col. 2 displaces the story of Jacob's work with Laban's cattle, *Gen.* 30:37ff, and tells it here.

3873-4   The *CM* poet does not report the tradition that Jacob was too drunk to know the difference. Cf., however, JOSEPHUS 145; *Hist. Schol. Gen.* lxxiv, *PL* CXCVIII 1115; *G&E* 1675; *SELTemp.* fol. 2v col. 1.

3896-3904   *Trad. anon.* fol. 231r col. 1. Cf. *Gen.* 35:23-6. The *Met. Para's* format is very similar, 11.985-96.

3913-7   The *CM* poet omits the story of Jacob's trick to increase his herd, and the difficulties he encountered on leaving Laban (*Gen.* 30:25-31:18).

3921-6   Cf. *Gen.* 31:19-35. Only MS C preserves the original mention of Laban's pursuit of the fleeing family.

3931-52.   Cf. *Gen.* 32:24-32, slightly rearranged.

3952   The author's etymology of the name Israel is from *Hist. Schol. Gen.* lxxxi, *PL* CXCVIII 1121: "vir videns Deum." Cf. *Etym.* VII vii 6.

3953ff   The poet has grouped the whole story of the meeting with Esau to-gether, rather than interpolate the wrestling episode in the middle, as is done in *Genesis*. L1.3953-60 condense *Gen.* 32:3-8.

3963-4   *Gen.* 32:13.

3968-72   *Gen.* 32:7-8.

3973-4010   BUEHLER, *"CM"*, 497-9, points out the similarities between this passage and HERMAN's *Bible*, 11.1118-54, especially in Jacob's prayer which begins with a recapitulation of history. Cf. *Gen.* 32:9-12.

4022-4   *Hist. Schol. Gen.* lxxxv, *PL* CXCVIII 1123.

4029-30   *Gen.* 35:28. *Trad. anon.* fol. 232r col. 2 says 170 years.

The poet has entirely omitted the story of the rape of Dinah (*Gen.* 34). This story appealed to the moralists of the Middle Ages. See M. DAY, ed., *Ancrene Riwle*, pp. 23-4, *Book of the Knight of LaTour-Landry*, pp. 73-4. However, it does interrupt the story of Jacob's life somewhat. *G&E* 1847-62 is the only ME paraphrase to include even an abbreviated version of it.

4035-6   In fact, Esau received Edom and is the father of the Edomites. See *Gen.* 36:1,8,9,19,43; *Hist. Schol. Gen.* lxxxv, *PL* CXCVIII 1123.

4041-3   Early Jewish traditions credit Joseph with exceptional beauty in his youth. See the excellent article by Frederic E. FAVERTY, "Legends of Joseph", 79-81. Petrus Comestor quotes Josephus on this point, and Joseph's early beauty gets into many vernacular paraphrases. See JOSEPHUS 173; *Hist. Schol. Gen.* lxxxvii, *PL* CXCVIII 1125; *G&E* 1910; *I&I* 189-92, GEOFFROI DE PARIS fol. 19v cols. 1-2; MALKARAUME, fol. 18r cols. 1-2; ÉVRAT, fol. 129v col. 1; MACÉ 2281-8.

4045-6   *Trad. anon.* fol. 233v col. 1. This detail comes from the story of Jacob's youth; cf. above 11.3494-8 and note.

4049   MSS FGHTLB's "wise" is probably original. Comestor called Joseph "sapientior caeteris" in *Hist. Schol. Gen.* lxxxvii, *PL* CXCVIII 1125, also reflecting Jewish tradition. See also FAVERTY, "Legs. of Joseph", p. 82, and *G&E* 1910.

4055-78   Based on *Gen.* 37:5-11.

4075, 4079-80   *Trad. anon.* fol. 233v col. 1.

4083-4   A further indication that the poet looks on this scene as occurring in a past time essentially different from the present.

4085-4118   Cf. *Gen.* 37:12-20.

4105-8   The first two lines appear only in the southern translation. They are obviously not original, but are a ballad-like restatement of a single idea.

4119-68   The speech of Reuben against Joseph's murder is considerably expanded from *Gen.* 37:21-2.

4145   L1.4143-4, which appear only in MS C, indicate the change of speaker. The scribes of FG did not notice the discrepancy, but the southern translator shows the new speaker by inserting "þei seide" in this line.

4161-9   The actual course of action followed by the brothers is here made part of Reuben's speech of advice. Cf. *Gen.* 37:20, 31-3.

4170-94   Cf. *Gen.* 37:22-8.

4174   The southern translator omitted "als" which appears in MSS CFG, thereby changing the statement from a simile foreshadowing Joseph's later imprisonment under Pharaoh (''They left him as if he were in prison'') to a literal statement of fact ("They left him there in a prison", i.e. in a place from which he could not escape).

4194 Because Joseph was seen as a type of Christ, commentators often changed the price paid for him from 20 to 30 coins, to correspond with the money paid to Judas in the New Testament. See BEDE, *In Pent.*, *PL* XCI 263; Roger BACON, *Opus Majus*, p. 244; *G&E* 1956; *SELTemp.* fol. 2v col. 2; ÉVRAT, printed in BONNARD, p. 118. Editions both of Petrus Comestor and of the Vulgate differed in their readings. See BONNARD, p. 118. Compare *Hist. Schol. Gen.* lxxxvii, *PL* CXCVIII 1126 with Joseph HALL, *Selections from Early ME* II 643.

The *CM* poet must have been aware of the alternative readings for the *Trad. anon.* fol. 234r col. 2 gives both: "Quar lour ue*n*dons ioseph xx ou xxx besans". He deliberately chose the Vulgate's number.

4197-4211 Cf. *Gen.* 37:29-33.

4212-36 Jacob's grief is described in much greater detail here than in *Gen.* 37:34-5. L1.4215-6, 4227-8 are probably from *Trad. anon.* fol. 234v col. 1, which also has a very long speech by Jacob here. Cf. also *Anc. test.* fol. 7v col. 2.

4237-8 The *CM* poet, like many mediaeval paraphrasers, omits entirely the story of Judah and Tamar in *Gen.* 38. In ME, only the *Met. Para.* pp. 31ff includes it.

4243 Interpreters encountered a very real difficulty in the story of Joseph's captivity, for his new owner is called Potiphar "eunuchus Pharaonis" (*Gen.* 37:36, 39:1), yet he has a wife who later tries to seduce Joseph. Furthermore, this Potiphar is often identified with Potipherah, priest of On, whose daughter Joseph marries (*Gen.* 41:50). What is to be done with a eunuch who possesses a wife and child?

Several ME paraphrases, like the *CM*, respond by translating "eunuchus" simply as an officer or steward. See *G&E* 1991; *SELTemp.* fol. 2v col. 2; *Met. Para.* 1239. Modern commentators agree that this explanation is etymologically probable. See "Potiphar", *Jew. Encyc.*; VON RAD, *Genesis*, 350.

Other, more colourful, explanations were well known in the Middle Ages. Jewish tradition said that Potiphar himself was first attracted to Joseph's beauty, but God moved to protect His favourite by castrating the Egyptian. See *Midrash* lxxxvi 3, p. 802; GINZBERG, *Legends*, V pp. 337-8 n. 101; JEROME, *Quaest. in Gen.*, *PL* XXIII 1046; *Hist. Schol. Gen.* lxxxviii, *PL* CXCVIII 1126-7; *G&E* 1995-2008; HIGDEN, p. 305; FAVERTY, "Legs. of Joseph", p. 85. In contrast the *CM* poet inserts a long passage in praise of Potiphar's broadmindedness, in spite of his Saracen faith. See below, 11.4245-54.

The substitution of Pharaoh's queen for Potiphar's wife which occurs in so many versions of the story, might also have arisen to avoid the awkwardness of a eunuch with a wife. Cf. n. to 1.4259ff.

4245 MSS CF's "are" is corrupted to "lare" in G. The southern translator, trying to correct the line, produced the virtually meaningless "in menskful lore".

4248 Perhaps suggested by *Trad. anon.* fol. 234v col. 2: "Por ce quil doutoit deu et q*ue* sa loy gardoit".

4249-58   This is reminiscent of HERMAN's *Bible*, 11.1190-1204. Cf. especially *CM* 3908 and HERMAN 1.1201, *CM* 3909-10 and HERMAN 1199, *CM* 3914 and HERMAN 1197, *CM* 3916 and HERMAN 1200.

4255   This seems to be a misinterpretation of *Trad. anon.* fol. 234v col. 2: "Li estrange lamerent et li sien le despirent".

4259ff   The story of Potiphar's wife, a favourite in the Middle Ages, is given a greatly expanded treatment in the *CM*. On this whole subject see FAVERTY, "Story of Joseph and Potiphar's Wife".

Several of the French sources used by the *CM* poet say that the Queen of Egypt rather than Potiphar's wife tried to seduce Joseph. This version of the story was very wide spread and of long standing. It occurs in Tertullian and was especially popular in France, where it appears in HERMAN's *Bible*, 11.1205ff; *Trad. anon.* fol. 234v-235v; GEOFFROI DE PARIS fol. 19v col. 2; MALKARAUME fol. 23v col. 2, (cf. BONNARD, pp. 86-7, 43, 59); WARNER, ed., *Queen Mary's Psalter* p. 62 and pl. 29; and KER, *MS BM Harley 2253*, fol. 93r. In English the story of Pharaoh's queen is found in *I&I* 195ff; WYNTOUN pp. 333-4; and in the Book of the *Knight of LaTour-Landry*, p. 76.

FAVERTY, "Legs. of Joseph", p. 88 says simply that "The role of the wicked queen was familiar in popular stories, and temptation by a queen would serve to increase the moral virtue of Joseph." Equally, of course, this version avoids the difficulty of the eunuch's wife. See above, note to 1.4243.

4259   *Gen.* 39:11 does not specify where the others of the household had gone when Potiphar's wife tempted Joseph. Hebrew legend said that the men had gone to a public festival. See FAVERTY, "Legs. of Joseph" p. 92; JOSEPHUS 187 and n.; *Hist. Schol. Gen.* xc, *PL* CXCVIII 1128; HERMAN 11.1215-9. Like the *CM*, however, *I&I* 1931-4 has the servants leave for the country to hunt.

4273-4326   A surprising digression on the force and dangers of love. The moralist gets the better of the historian here, and any similarity with the power of love as extolled in the romances is negated by the concept of sin brought in at 1.4316. Cf. 11.4425-8.

The French paraphrases often seem to pause for reflexion at this point in the story. *Anc. test.* fol. 8r col. 1 has a few lines on the torments of love, but without the *CM*'s moralizing. Cf. *Hist. Jos.* 301/623ff, 364/831ff. Two other paraphrases contain a monologue by the rejected queen at this point. See *Trad. anon.* fol. 235r and MALKARAUME fol. 23v col. 2, the latter printed in BONNARD, "Monologue de la reine d'Égypte".

4276   This is the only citation of this proverb in this particular form in WHITING, *Proverbs*, L494.

4302   Only MS C preserves the original "mangonele"/a seige engine. The *Trad. anon.* refers to this weapon in another context on fol. 234r col. 1.

4316   MSS CF's "slokend"/quenched is the better reading, carrying on the metaphor of love's fire burning the heart. GHTLB's "strangle" is limp by comparison.

4345-80   The courtly love situation is here reversed, with the lady speaking of love and begging for favours, while the young man stands off.

4357-8   Cf. *Trad. anon.* fol. 234v col. 1 and HERMAN, 1.1210.

4381-6   Potiphar's wife adds threats to her promises of riches to tempt Joseph. Cf. *G&E* 2021-4.

4387-4419   Cf. *Gen.* 39: 12-20.

4389   Cf. *Anc. test.* fol. 8r col. 2: "e le le tint ferm & rumpent li tassel".

4395   The misreading of CF's "aleis" as "is" makes the question virtually meaningless in the southern translation.

4407   Potiphar has apparently returned from the country. In the Vulgate the wife has to wait until her husband returns to show him Joseph's cloak, but in HERMAN's *Bible,* 11.1234-6, the husband himself hears his wife's screams and runs to hear her first complaints.

4408-9   The southern translator has rephrased the lines and eliminated the run-on line of MSS CFG.

4425-8   Other paraphrases declaim against women at this point. See esp. *Anc. test.* fol. 8r col. 2-fol. 8v col. 1; *Hist. Jos.* 301/607ff, 363/807ff.

4433-98   Cf. *Gen.* 39:21-40:23.

4446   *Trad. anon.* fol. 235v col. 2.

4454   The *Trad. anon.* also uses the word "uision" here. Furthermore the French poet has a digression on dreams, fol. 236r col. 2, in which he shows that a "uision" is the only kind of dream to be trusted.

4473   Some mediaeval commentators were disturbed by any hint of magical powers. In the phrase "wiþ myȝte of heuene", the *CM* poet firmly establishes Joseph's powers of interpretation as divinely given. Cf. 1.4560 below and *Gen.* 41:16. Cf. also FAVERTY's discussion of *Gen.* 44:15, "Legs. of Joseph", 98-100, 102-3.

4491   The southern translator carelessly used the present tense "seiþ" here, though the scribe of MS L corrected it.

4498-4500   HERMAN, 11.1297-8.

4503-10   This is one of the poet's rare general moralizations.

4508   WHITING, *Proverbs,* E216 cites several other occurrences of this proverb.

4510   The southern translator corrupted "loues" to "doþ". Cf. WHITING, *Proverbs,* L565. The saying also appears in French: "Qui bien ayme tard oublye."

4511-8   Cf. *Gen.* 41:1, 8-23.

4514-5   In the Vulgate Pharaoh summons "conjectores" and "sapientes". See *Gen.* 41:8. The *CM* is closer to Herman's *Bible* here, 11.1312-3:
Manda tous ses barons et tous ses conseilliers;
Dont i viennent baron prinches et chevaliers;

4545-50   A passage of visual description and emotional sympathy which is extremely rare thus far in the *CM*. The poet takes it from HERMAN, 11.1336-9.

4561-4600   The dream is told as in HERMAN's *Bible,* 11.1346-67.

4572   Like the *CM*, Herman does not mention the lean cattle eating the fat ones. Cf. *Gen.* 41:20.

4579   The southern translation has here preserved a better reading than MSS CFG. "Ful of corn were þei set þo", translates HERMAN, 1.1355: "Les VII cargiés de blé".

4581   Like the *CM* poet, Herman omits the concept in *Gen.* 41:24 that the thin ears ate the fat ones.

4605-11   Cf. *Gen.* 41:26, 33-4.

4612-46 The remainder of the dialogue in which the king aquits Joseph of the crime against Potiphar's wife is not in *Genesis*. Cf. however the interchange in HERMAN's *Bible*, 11.1369-98 in which Joseph brings up the matter of Pharaoh's wife and is told "Joseph, oublié l'ai". The remarks of the barons also come from Herman.

4647 HERMAN, 1.1401.

4650-2 HERMAN, 11.1404-6.

4653-68 Cf. *Gen.* 41: 42-5.

4668 Several legends about Joseph's wife Aseneth were current in the Middle Ages. See BURCHARD, *Untersuchungen zu Joseph und Aseneth*, and DWYER, "Asenath of Egypt in ME". The ME paraphrasers ignore her, however.

4669ff From this point on, Borland recognizes that the *CM* poet translates constantly from Herman's *Bible* for about 800 lines, beginning with Herman, 1.1408. See BORLAND, *CM*, p. 3.

4674, 4686 The thousand barns and thousand cellars come from HERMAN, 11.1412, 1416, 1423.

4678 The food is more concretely specified in *CM* and HERMAN than in *Genesis*.

4679-83 This is an incomplete sentence in MSS CGHTLB. The *CM* poet, or an early scribe, erred in writing a preterite tense "filde" instead of another infinitive "fill" in 1.4681. MS F corrects the lapse by supplying a subject, but the original had:

> La gent de la contree, quant le voient venir
> Et prendre leur aumaille et leur blé departir
> Et faire ches greniers tous de leur blé emplir,
>   (HERMAN's *Bible*, 11.1417-9)

MS F alone preserves the original completion of the sentence, 11.4682-3, translating Herman's 11.1420-1:

> Les barons de la terre faire tous son plaisir,
> Tout le vont enclinant, et tout le vont servir.

4690 A typical expression of the *CM* poet, perhaps suggested by *Gen.* 41:49: "copia mensuram excederet".

4695-4747 The harrowing description of famine conditions is added to the Vulgate's bare narrative by Herman, 11.1429-63.

4705 C's "thrid" is an error. Herman writes of "le premier an", 1.1433.

4725 HERMAN, 1.1445, has the king see, rather than hear, his subjects' distress, as do MSS GHTL.

4732 MSS CFGHL read "He is al lord", the result of an accidental scribal doubling of the "1". Herman has "sires est et sera" in 1.1449. The scribes of MSS TB have apparently corrected the clumsy reading of their exemplar to "he is a lord".

4749-4803 The Vulgate says simply "audiens autem Jacob quod alimenta venderentur in Ægypto" (*Gen.* 42:1), without specifying how Jacob came to know this. Several Old French paraphrases, with more sense of drama than of geography, tell how Jacob saw chaff floating down the Nile from Egypt to Canaan and sent his sons to its source. The *CM* poet presumably took his version from HERMAN's *Bible*, 11.1464-93; cf. GEOFFROI DE PARIS, fol. 21v col. 1, reported in BONNARD, p. 43; the HARLEY fragment, 210/22-3; WARNER, *Queen Mary's Psalter*, pl. 33 and p. 63; *Hist. Jos.* 377/1340-75. Napier conjectures that the legend was probably recorded also on a lost leaf of the ME poem *Iacob and Ioseph*. See his introduction to *I&I*, pp. xii-xiii. The *CM* is the only other work in ME to record the story, but it also appears as the only legendary subject in the carvings of the chapter house of Salisbury Cathedral. See COCKERELL, *Book of Old Testament Illus.*, p. 20 n. 1.

4749-50 The *CM* poet makes Joseph's action in casting the chaff on the water a deliberate lure for his father and brothers. HERMAN's *Bible* merely states that this is what Joseph did, but *Queen Mary's Psalter* and *Hist. Jos.* both agree with the *CM* version. Cf. GEOFFROI DE PARIS, fol. 21v col. 1 who has Joseph order the chaff to be thrown into the river, but without specifying why.

4754 MS C's "ioseph" is clearly an error.

4771-6 The *CM* poet adds these lines to the narrative showing God dominating the course of history.

4797-8 Not in Herman. Jacob begins to speak at 1.4799.

4805-19 These lines are translated from *Gen.* 42: 3-4 rather than from Herman, who persists in his geographical error by having the brothers sail on the river to Egypt in 11.1494-9. Cf. above, note to 11. 4749-4803. Cf. GEOFFROI DE PARIS, fol. 19r col. 2 and the Harley fragment, 201/36ff.

4811-22 From HERMAN, 11.1500-7.

4821 Herman has the brothers say they come from Jerusalem, 1.1507. The *CM* poet corrects this to Canaan, as in *Gen.* 42:7.

4825-42 Not in Herman.

4843-50 HERMAN, 11.1514-9.

4851ff In the Vulgate, the brothers make three journeys to Egypt. On the first, Joseph takes Simeon as a hostage until they return with Benjamin. He also puts the money they paid for the grain back into the grain sacks. See *Gen.* 42. Jacob is reluctant to send Benjamin with his brothers, but as the famine persists, he finally agrees. This time, Joseph again puts the payment money back into the grain sacks, and also puts his own silver cup into Benjamin's sack. The cup is discovered, Joseph threatens the apparent culprit, and Judah offers to suffer in his place. See *Gen.* 43-44. The third journey is made simply to bring Jacob to see his son Joseph.

HERMAN's *Bible* alters the Vulgate's account considerably. As soon as they discover corn is for sale in Egypt, four of the brothers return to their ship immediately. Only six brothers, therefore, attend the first audience with Joseph. Joseph sends these six to the ship to fetch the other four. He then puts the gold and silver they have paid him into the grain sacks and has his servants discover this. The cup is never mentioned, and Benjamin is still at home with his father. Ruben, not Simeon, is left as a hostage while the others go to fetch Benjamin at 1.1610. Joseph reveals himself to Benjamin and the brothers go to fetch Jacob to Egypt.

The *CM* uses Herman's version in the main, but corrects some of it from the Vulgate. The incident of the four brothers who return to the ship is omitted. Also, the ME poet has Joseph put his cup, rather than simply the brothers' gold and silver, into the sack. This leads to some confusion; see note to 1.4888 below. The rest of the story is the same as Herman's.

Of the other ME paraphrases, *G&E, SELTemp.*, and the *Met. Para.* follow the Vulgate in their order of incidents. However, like HERMAN's *Bible* and the *CM, I&I* also has the episode of the cup take place on the first journey, while Benjamin is still at home. See 11.400ff.

4851-5126   From HERMAN, 11.1529-1720.

4856   HERMAN, 1.1533, has "Porté l'en ont as nés". The *CM* poet changes the ship to an inn, as in *Gen.* 42:27 *et passim*.

4858-62   This is not in Herman, who says that Joseph put gold and silver in the sacks (1.1534), as in *Gen.* 42:25.

4871-2   MSS CF preserve the sense of Herman, 11.1539-40 better than the other MSS do.

4886   MSS CFG's "sargantz" is original, translating Herman's "serjans", 1.1550.

4888   The *CM* poet has already stated that the object in the sack was Joseph's own cup, 1.4858, and he reiterates this in 11.4916, 4936, 4938 and 5081. Herman, however, had the king's money stolen instead, and the *CM* seems to hedge in calling the object "þe kyngis þingis" or "þe kyngis tresour" here and in 11.4902 and 4908 below. Cf. *I&I* 1.401.

4899   "breme as boore" is an alliterative formula found frequently in ME. See *MED* "breme" a. II b.

4921, 4925   The third morning is not specified in Herman. The *CM* poet could have taken this detail from *Hist. Schol. Gen.* xciii, *PL* CXCVIII 1131.

4924   HERMAN, 11.1569-70, has Joseph send men to guard their ship and their corn.

4967-72   This is not in Herman. The *CM* poet reassures his audience of Joseph's motives and the ultimate outcome of the event.

4975   CF's reading is correct.

4995-5000   The ME poet here condenses the conversation and omits some details of the journey found in HERMAN 11.1617-32.

5052   MSS CFG translate Herman, 1.1671: "tous li sans li mua". The southern translator has altered and weakened the line.

5056   MSS GTLB say they kissed sixty times or more, while C says more than forty times. HERMAN, 1.1674, specifies 100 times. The numbers are indefinite, used simply to indicate a large quantity.

5098-5102   This is not in Herman. BORLAND, *CM*, p. 28, suggests that the passage is close to the variant reading of HERMAN's *Bible* printed in Vol. II, Appendix, p. 132. This could equally well come from *Gen.* 45:8, once again showing God's will worked out in history.

5119   Herman says Joseph gave all his brothers African garments. Thus the pronoun "þam" in MS C is plural. However, MSS FGHTLB have the singular, perhaps influenced by *Gen.* 45:22 and HERMAN 11.1718-9, in which Benjamin gets more clothes than the others.

5127-5377   From Herman, as printed in BARTSCH, *Chrestomathie*, 11.3-189.

5136   Herman, of course, had their ships loaded, not their camels.

5143   Not "pantener", as Morris printed in MSS CF, but "pautener", Herman's "paltoniers", "A vagabond, rascal" *(OED)*.

5171   The Vulgate does not mention the length of time which has elapsed. Cf. HERMAN, 1.177 and below 1.5362.

5184   In Herman, Joseph sends a boat.

5197-9 The southern translator, having accidentally omitted 11.5197-8 changed "cries" to "hiȝed" to make sense of the passage. MSS CFG preserve something like the original reading. Cf. HERMAN, 11.57-8.

5213-30 At this point Herman has the family board their boat once again to sail for Egypt, and more conversation takes place. See 11.67ff. The ME poet omits this, and reverts to another source, not the *Trad. anon.,* for the story of Jacob's sacrifice and departure. Cf. *Gen.* 46:1-6.

5231-8 The poet omits the long list of names from *Genesis,* mentioning only Joseph's offspring. See *Gen.* 46:26, 20.

5239-42 Cf. *Gen.* 46:28.

5243-8 From HERMAN, 11.91-4. The court goes with Joseph in Herman, but not in the Vulgate.

5250-2 Cf. *Gen.* 46:30. Herman omits this and instead has Jacob fail to recognize his son, 11.95-7. Herman seems to stress Jacob's senility. Cf. 11.68-71 where the brothers laugh merrily at their father's failure to realize that he is already at sea. The *CM* poet omits such episodes, while keeping many of Herman's other emotional embellishments.

5253-5378 From HERMAN, 11.99-189.

5280-4 Herman has Joseph say he was sold to the king and tempted by his wife. The *CM* poet remembers to mention Potiphar's wife instead of the queen, but forgets that he had followed *Gen.* 39:1 in having Joseph sold to Potiphar instead of to the king. Cf. above 11.4241-4.

5281 Herman has "pestrin" at 1.121, which MSS CF translate as "mister". MSS GHTLB substitute "prisoun".

5313 Apparently from HERMAN 1.196, although the narrative itself has only reached HERMAN 1.138.

5333 MSS GHTLB preserve the original "Pees", which C miscopied as "þis". See HERMAN, 1.151.

5353 Not in Herman. Cf. *Gen.* 47:9.

5373-4 HERMAN, 1.187: "je l'acatai a serf, mais or le franchison". Cf. MS C.

5375-6 MSS CF's reading is preferable.

5378-5414 Cf. *Gen.* 47:11-3, 15, 19-20, 22. Herman omits these events and passes straight on to the deaths of Jacob and Joseph.

5420-39 *Gen.* 47:27-48:2.

5426 MS C's "kne" is an error for "þe". Cf. the Vulgate's "sub femore meo".

5440-8 Cf. *Gen.* 48:10-4. The *CM* poet has left out the dying Jacob's retelling of his own history.

5448 The poet avoids the squabbling over the final blessing in *Gen.* 48:14, 17-9. Cf. below 1.5461.

5449-54 Cf. *Gen.* 48:21.

5455-68 This summarizes all of *Gen.* 49.

5467-9 *Gen.* 47:28 gives Jacob 147 years, not 137 as the *CM* poet elaborately calculates.

5470 The *CM* poet ignores the magnificent funeral described in *Gen.* 50. Cf. also the description of Egyptian burial customs in *Hist. Schol. Gen.* cxiv, *PL* CXCVIII 1140, which appealed to the poet of *G&E* 2447-67.

5481-8 From HERMAN, 11.215-8.

5489-90 110 years, i.e. 5 1/2 score. See *Gen.* 50:26.

5495-5502 Cf. *Ex.* 1:8-10. The *CM* poet drops Herman as a principal source, apparently because the French poet greatly condenses the biblical narrative, touching only on the highlights of Moses' career. A few odd lines from Herman do appear, however. Many of these parallels were not noticed either by Borland or by Buehler. The *CM* poet is not using the *Trad. anon.* here either.

5503-8 HERMAN, 11.1959-62.

5519-70 Cf. *Ex.* 1:11-22. For the first few lines, the *CM* poet seems to invent more dialogue in the style of Herman, fitting in the Vulgate detail which the French poet omits.

5571-5600 The ME poet pauses to recapitulate his themes.

5609-46 Cf. *Ex.* 2:1-10.

5621 The original reading was probably "rushes".

5647-8 Probably from HERMAN 1.1987, although Moses' beauty was well known. See JOSEPHUS 265; *Hist. Schol. Ex.* v, *PL* CXCVIII 1144; *G&E* 2659; *Met. Para.* 1529-36; *SELTemp.* fol. 3v col. 1; MALKARAUME fol. 42v col. 1; MACÉ 3429-31.

5649-5710 Cf. *Ex.* 2:11-21.

5658 The sense demands that "son" should be singular here, as in MSS CFTB. The southern translator must have copied a plural form from his exemplar, as GHL all have "sones". The scribes of TB presumably corrected their copy.

5711-28 Cf. *Ex.* 2:22-5.

5729-44 Cf. *Ex.* 3:1-3.

5733 Not "folke", as in MSS HTL, but "flock", as in CFG. Cf. *Ex.* 3:1: "cumque minasset gregem...".

5736 "eʒeb" is, of course, Latin Horeb.

5745-50 One of the *CM* poet's rare typological interpretations. This interpretation of the burning bush as a type of the Blessed Virgin is found in hymns and in the Victorine sequence described in RABY, *Christian-Latin Poetry*, p. 370; BERNARD OF CLAIRVAUX, *Sermones de Tempore*, *PL* CLXXXIII 63; WM. OF SHOREHAM, 127/19, "Hours of the Blessed Virgin" in LITTLEHALES, *Prymer*, p. 24; MACÉ 3541-52 and n.

The closest analogue to the *CM*, however, is in HONORIUS AUGUSTODUNENSIS' *Speculum Ecclesiae*, *PL* CLXXII 904: "quam ignis Spiritus sancti prole illuminavit, nec tamen flamma concupiscentiae violavit." Cf. note to 11.6909-10.

5753-5806 Cf. *Ex.* 3:4, 6-7, 10-14, 16-20. The poet does not describe the Jewish custom, referred to in *Ex.* 3:5, of Moses removing his shoes in a holy place.

5807-36 Cf. *Ex.* 4:1-4, 6-9. The ME poet omits Moses' humility and God's further instructions, as told in *Ex.* 4:10-14.

5837 Cf. *Ex.* 4:14.

5838-42 Cf. *Ex.* 3:18.

5843-7 Cf. *Ex.* 4:29.

The *CM* poet omits all mention of Moses' speech defect, the reason why Aaron always accompanies him. See *Ex.* 4:10-6, 30. Jewish legend traced this defect to an incident in Moses' infancy, and the story was often retold, in one version or another. See GINZBERG, *Legends* V, p. 402 n. 65; *Hist. Schol. Ex.* v, *PL* CXCVIII 1144; *G&E* 2633-58; *Met. Para.* 1549-84; *SELTemp.* 3v col. 1; MACÉ 3473-3508.

Cf. MALKARAUME fol. 42v col. 2; JOSEPHUS 267. G. L. HAMILTON's "La Source" is an excellent discussion of this legend in European literature.

5848-80   Cf. *Ex.* 5:1-6, 8.

5859   MS F and the southern translation get the pronoun right, showing that the Israelites, and not Pharaoh, are speaking here.

5862   MS C alone translates correctly the "nobis" of *Ex.* 5:3 as "hus". The other MSS give the pronoun in the second person.

5883-5908   Cf. *Ex.* 7:8-14.

5918-26   Based on *Ex.* 7:19-20. Herman's account of the life of Moses is so greatly abbreviated that he scarcely describes the plagues. On the other hand, the *Trad. anon.* deals with Moses' story in great detail. The *CM*'s version falls between the two extremes. It must be considered an abridgement of the Vulgate, unless another source, perhaps in French, is discovered.

5927-36   Cf. *Ex.* 8:3.

5935-51   Cf. *Ex.* 8:8-10, 12-5.

5953-5   Cf. *Ex.* 8:17.

5959-70   Cf. *Ex.* 8:21-2.

5971-98   Cf. *Ex.* 8:25-32.

5999-6008   Cf. *Ex.* 9:2-4, 7.

6001   Of all the *CM* MSS, C's line is closes to the list in *Ex.* 9:3.

6009-16   Cf. *Ex.* 9:9, 12.

6017-38   Cf. *Ex.* 9:23-8, 33, 35.

6025   CF's "gresse" is original, translating *Ex.* 9:25's "herbam agri".

6039-50   Cf. *Ex.* 10:14-5, 20.

6051-6   Cf. *Ex.* 10:22-3.

6061-98   Cf. *Ex.* 12:3, 5, 7-12, 14.

6099-6121   Cf. *Ex.* 12:21-3, 29.

6125-64   Cf. *Ex.* 12:30-3, 35-8, 40-3. The translation of the Vulgate is quite close. The ME poet omits repetitious verses, but does not condense material as he had done in his story of the plagues.

6158   The correct figure is 430 years. See *Ex.* 12:40. MSS CG have 400 years, F 100. MS G has mistaken "to" in the expression "to þen"/ until that time, for the numeral "tua". From a similar MS, the southern translator took his reading 402 years.

6165-78   The instructions in *Ex.* 12:43-9 concern who is allowed to partake of the feast. The *CM* poet skips to *Ex.* 13:3, 12-5.

6179-98   Cf. *Ex.* 13:17-22.

6199-6252   Cf. *Ex.* 14:2-8, 10-4, 16.

6230   MSS CF have "graues", correctly translating "sepulcra". G reads "ill", and the southern translation "euel".

6253-8   Cf. *Ex.* 14:17-8. The ME poet has omitted any mention of the statement, frequently repeated in *Exodus,* that it is God who hardens the hearts of Pharaoh and the Egyptians. See *Ex.* 14:17; cf., e.g., 7:13, 9:12, 10:1, 10:20, 10:27.

6259-80   Cf. *Ex.* 14:21-3, 27-8.

6285-8   The "newe songe" is found in *Ex.* 15:1-19, and would be known to the *CM* poet as the most frequently used canticle in the liturgy. See CABROL and LECLERCQ, eds., *Dict. d'archéologie chrétienne,* II 1978.

6289-90   The poet interjects a prayer of his own.

6301ff   The *CM* poet here interpolates the section of the story of the wood of the holy cross which is chronologically appropriate. He had translated an earlier part of this story from the Latin prose *Legende*. See note to 1.1237ff above. From now on, however, the *CM* poet uses the version of the story found in the latter part of the *Trad. anon*. He evidently kept his copy of the Latin *Legende* at hand, however, as well as his Vulgate, for he uses both to insert several details lacking in his principal source.

NAPIER, *Rood Tree*, p. xxiii *et passim* first identified the source of these lines. He prints several extracts from the French poem on pp. 63-7 of his book and a further extract appears in Bonnard, pp. 88-9. References to line numbers in the *Trad. anon*. are to these printed extracts. Citations from the MS continue to be identified by folio numbers.

QUINN, *The Quest of Seth*, is again invaluable for tracing the development of this legend and the different versions of it. See also MEYER, "Die Geschichte des Kreuzholzes".

6301-10   *Trad. anon*. (in Napier), 11.29-37.

6305   The Old French poem says they came to "Elyn" (1.34), the *Legende* "Ebron" (47/54). The *CM* poet apparently uses his geographical knowledge to place these in Syria.

6308   The southern translation's "þrest" is a closer translation of "Sitivit" (*Ex*. 17:3) than is CFG's "brest"/need.

6311-5   Cf. *Ex*. 17:3. This is not found in the Old French poem.

6319-68   *Trad. anon*. (Napier), 39-87.

6320   MS C's "selly" is probably an error for "ferly".

6326   The Old French poem has "pin" here (1.43), as do MSS CFG. Cf. note to 1.1377 above.

6347   NAPIER, *Rood Tree*, p. xxvi suggested that this line originally read "Siþen þai fand ín Raphindin", translating the Old French "A ra-phin*d*in les a portees;" cf. *Ex*. 17:1.

6347-56   The cross story combines several biblical episodes here. The sweetening of the waters occurred at Mara in *Ex*. 15:23-5, but the Old French poem places the incident at Raphidim. At the biblical Raphidim, in *Ex*. 17:1-7, Moses struck the rock to being forth water.

The wood which will become the true cross is here substituted for the biblical tree in *Ex*. 15:25, or the rod of Moses in *Ex*. 17:5.

6348-9   The Old French says "Qua*r* plus ere amere q*ue* suie:" (1.71).

6369ff   The *CM* poet drops the *Trad. anon*'s cross story here and begins to abbreviate the biblical adventures of Moses.

6373-8   HERMAN, 11.2088-91.

6379-86   The story of the manna is found in *Ex*. 16. Herman dismisses it in one line (1.2092). The *CM* poet gathers together various details from the account in *Exodus*.

6381   Cf. *Ex*. 16:14.

6382   Cf. *Ex*. 16:31.

6383-4   Cf. *Ex*. 16:15, 31.

6385   Cf. *Ex*. 16:8, 12. In fact, God sent flesh to be eaten in the evening and manna in the morning.

6386 Cf. *Ex.* 16:13. MS F's unique reading "angel mete þai dide hit calle" could be from the original version of *CM*. The idea of manna as the food of angels is based on *Ps.* 77:25 and *Sap.* 16:20. See GINZBERG, *Legends,* VI p. 17.

6389-95 Cf. *Ex.* 17:1-7. Herman dismisses the story in two lines (11.2093-4).

6403-32 Cf. *Ex.* 17:8-12.

6414 MS C alone preserves the correct reading. The other MSS omit Hur. Cf. *Ex.* 17:10.

6427 Again MS C preserves the mention of Hur, which the other MSS have dropped. Cf. *Ex.* 17:12.

6433-40 Cf. *Ex.* 18:1-4.

6433 MS F corrupts "Ietro" to "Petro".

6441-50 A condensed version of *Ex.* 18:13-26.

6441 MSS CFG probably preserve the correct reading "þis ilk folk was vntelland," (C). The line is a gloss on *Ex.* 18:13, 18, 22, verses which imply that the administration of law was becoming too time-consuming for one man to manage. The southern translator's "þis ilke folke was vantoun to fonde" makes good sense, however. It implies that the work increased because the people were more evil, rather than more numerous.

6451-67 The prologue to the giving of the commandments is from HERMAN, 11.2095-2106. In *Ex.* 19, God initiates all the action, but here the people themselves are the first to ask for the law, as they do in GEOFFROI DE PARIS, fol. 25r col. 2.

6461-4 Herman takes the idea of Moses' fasting forty days from *Ex.* 34:28, which deals with the renewal of the tablets after Moses had broken them.

6471-80 The *CM* poet gives a ten line resumé of the ten commandments. Cf. *Ex.* 20:3-17. Herman does not even list the commandments here.

6487-6504 The *CM* poet turns once again to HERMAN, 11.2109-16 for the narrative of the golden calf.

6505-7 Expanded from *Ex.* 32:4.

6513-6 Cf. *Ex.* 32:7.

6514 MSS CF's rhyme word, "suik"/deceit has been mis-copied in G as "suilk", probably because of confusion with the same word in the previous line. This error makes the line meaningless in G. The southern translator seemingly recognized the lapse of sense and rewrote the line.

6517-6614 From HERMAN, 11.2127-2194.

6520 The frost comes from *Ex.* 16:14.

6525 The southern translation has preserved a better reading "hoolis", translating Herman's "fosses", 1.2133. MSS CFG have "hepes" (G "helpis"). Cf. below, 1.6611, where CF refer to "holes".

6527-8 MS C has preserved the better reading, translating HERMAN, 11.2134-5:

Mont crient el veel la gent maleüree
Se donques fu salvage, encor n'est pas senee.

6562-7 These lines are omitted from the southern translation but are evidently authentic, translating HERMAN, 11.2161b-2165.

6615-8 Cf. *Ex.* 32:20.

6619-26 *Ex.* 32:20 simply says that Moses ground the golden calf to powder and made his people drink it. A wide spread mediaeval legend added that the powder stained the faces of the idolators but left the faces of the innocent clean. The two French sources which the *CM* poet has been using report that the mouths of the guilty were gilded. See *Trad. anon.* fol. 256r col. 1. HERMAN, 1.2196. PETRUS COMESTOR, *Hist. Schol. Ex.* lxxiii, *PL* CXCVIII 1190, like the *CM* poet, says their beards were affected, and HAENISCH, *CM*, p. 8*, pointed to this as the source. The golden beards are found in many places. See *SELTemp.* fol. 4r col. 1; *Met. Para.* 1975-80; MACÉ, 5247-52; GEOFFROI DE PARIS fol. 26r col. 1; cf. *Pirke* XLV 356-7.

6627-40 Cf. *Ex.* 32:26-9. This is not in Herman.

6636 Cf. *Ex.* 32:28 which says 23,000, not 20,000.

6641-8 Cf. *Ex.* 34:1, 4.

6651 Cf. *Ex.* 34:27-8 which says that Moses himself wrote the second set of commandments, at God's direction. The original tablets were written by God's own hand. See *Ex.* 31:18, 32:16.

6653-6 Morris' proposed reading of "horud" for "hornd" in his note on this line is wrong. See *CM*, p. xlii. *Ex.* 34:29 reads "et ignorabat quod cornuta esset facies sua ex consortio sermonis Domini." The horns of Moses are a result of Jerome's translation of the Hebrew word "qeren", which can mean either "horns" or "rays of light".

Some commentators did not believe literally in the horns of Moses. Rashi, the influential Jewish commentator of the twelfth century, said that the horns indicated merely the shape of the rays of light which came from Moses' head. See RASHI, II 196. This explanation was taken up by various scholars, including PETRUS COMESTOR, *Hist. Schol. Ex.* lxxvii, *PL* CXCVIII 1192. The idea is reflected in *CM* 1.6655: "Hem þouȝte him horned on heed fer". The *Trad. anon.* similarly says: "Et fu au puiple descenduz/Si lor sambla estre cournuz". However, nothing in the context suggests that the *CM* poet is translating here. Cf. MACÉ 5469-71; *SELTemp.* 4r col. 1.

On the whole subject, see the excellent study by MELLINKOFF, *The Horned Moses.*

6657-66 *Trad. anon.* fol. 267v col. 2-268r col. 1.

6667ff This is a selection of the laws given by God to Moses in *Ex.* 21ff. Herman ignores them, as do most other paraphrase writers.

6671-2 *Ex.* 21:12.

6673-6 *Ex.* 21:14.

6677-80 Based on *Ex.* 21:15.

6681-6720 *Ex.* 21:18-30.

6698 *Ex.* 21:22 reads "arbitri judicaverint." The English poet instead refers to trial by jury.

6703-4 After "pedem pro pede", *Ex.* 21:25 goes on to list "adustionem pro adustione, vulnus pro vulnere, livorem pro livore." CF's "bla for bla" is thus more correct than MSS GHTLB's "too for too".

6706 CF's "vnmighti for to seie" is original, translating *Ex.* 21:26 "luscos". G's corruption of "vnmighti" to "vnsihti" would make the servant invisible. The southern translator changes G's reading to "vnsiȝtilyȝe", which could possibly mean blind, but probably means simply ugly. See *OED.*

6721-58 *Ex.* 21:32-*Ex.* 22:4.

6727-30 The southern translator altered 1.6728, perhaps to do away with the unaccustomed caesura in MSS CFG:
> And ox or hors, or oþer aght
> Fall in, þe man þat þis pitt aght

Because he completed 1.6728 with a meaningless filler, "Falle þerynne leest or meest", the translator had to compose two new lines to convey the meaning of the passage.

6759-62 *Ex.* 22:6.

6763-72 *Ex.* 22:10-2.

6773-8 *Ex.* 22:14-5.

6779-82 The paragraphing marks in MSS FHTLB indicate that two separate laws are involved here, translating *Ex.* 22:18-9. A later hand in MS C, however, has interpreted the first two lines to refer to the fate of the beast involved in the sin mentioned in the next couplet:
> [to dele wit best what man him draws
> Godd wil þe best] be don o daus.
> C 6779-80

6783-6831 *Ex.* 22:20-23:5.

6797-8 *Ex.* 22:26 is talking about taking a neighbour's clothes as a pledge ("pignus"), but the *CM* poet apparently understands this as taking them in anger.

6805-6 The *CM* poet has translated into contemporary terms of priests and tithes the instructions of *Ex.* 22:28-9.

6811-2 Not in *Ex.*

6833-48 *Ex.* 23:7-13.

6834 The "Blendyng ʒiftis" translates "Nec accipies munera, quae etiam excaecant prudentes", *Ex.* 23:8.

6839-41 *Ex.* 23:10-11 orders the people to cultivate the land for six years and leave it fallow the seventh. All the MSS wrongly read seven for six in 1.6839. CF correctly read "seuend" in 1.6841, while all the others have "eiʒteþe".

6850-8 *Ex.* 23:20, 22.

6859-80 The *CM* poet here speaks more of the shaping of his history. He omits the rest of *Exodus,* all of *Leviticus* and part of *Numbers,* to arrive at the story of Aaron's rod.

6884-98 Cf. *Num.* 17:6-9.

6903-8 Cf. *Num.* 17:10.

6909-10 The interpretation of Aaron's rod as a type of the Virgin is found in several places in the Middle Ages. See the Victorine sequence described in RABY, *Christian-Latin Poetry,* pp. 361, 370; BERNARD OF CLAIRVAUX, *Sermones de Tempore, PL* CLXXXIII 63; WM. OF SHOREHAM, 128/27. The closest analogue to the *CM*'s interpretation is in HONORIUS AUGUSTODUNENSIS, *Speculum Ecclesiae, PL* CLXXII 904: "Arida virga quae nucem protulit est virgo Maria quae Christum Dominum et hominem mundo progenuit." Cf. n. to 11.5745-50 above.

6915 The figure of forty years is common knowledge, of course, but may be suggested to the poet here by *Trad. anon.* fol. 268r col. 1; "xl ans les auoit porteis/Moyses...".

6918-20 Probably from *Trad. anon.* fol. 268r col. 1. Cf. *Deut.* 34:5-6.

6921-2   Taken from *Hist. Schol. Num.* xx, *PL* CXCVIII 1260: "Quod ideo factum autumant Hebraei ne ipsi Moysen pro Deo colerent". Cf. *SELTemp.* 4r col. 2.

6923-30   The *CM* poet translates Herman's summary of events, 11.2206-10.

6937-46   *Trad. anon.* fol. 268r col. 1.

6947-50   Cf. *Num.* 20:23-8.

6951ff   The *CM* poet greatly abbreviates Joshua's part in history, but HERMAN's *Bible* mentions none of his acts at all.

6953-4   *DIM* remarks of Joshua "sol stetit spatio duorum dierum." See *PL* CLXXII 168. Cf. *Met. Para.* 2967-8.

6955-6   Cf. *Ios.* 10:12-4.

6957-60   Cf. *Ios.* 3:7-4:24.

6961-4   Cf. *Ios.* 24:32.

6983-4   Cf. *Iud.* 2:11 *et passim.*

6984   The *CM* poet uses "sarasenes feiþ" as a synonym for all idolatry, a common mediaeval practice.

6985   Cf. *Iud.* 3:6.

6993-7082   These lines are a rapid summary of the Judges of Israel, with a passing reference to events in other kingdoms occurring at the same time. For the Middle Ages, the ultimate source of such comparative time schemes was the work of Eusebius of Caesarea. Eusebius and other canonists of the third and fourth centuries were trying to establish that the Christian religion, which seemed so new, was actually older than the state religions it sought to supplant. Jerome's translation of the work is printed as *Translatio Chronicorum Eusebii Pamphili, PL* XXVII 11-507. Parts of the work were copied into many later chronicles and histories, among them the *Hist. Schol.*

   HAENISCH, *CM*, pp. 8*-9* believed that some of the details in the *CM*'s lines came from the *Hist. Schol.* The immediate source of these lines, however, unless otherwise noted, is HONORIUS' *De Imagine Mundi, PL* CLXXII 169ff. This source was first noted by KALUZA in "Zu den Quellen", p. 452.

7001   Othoniel in *Iud* 3:9 is the younger brother of Caleb, not his son. Morris prints the word as "Othomel" in all MSS, but the minims should be read as "ni" instead of "m".

7007-12   This is based on *DIM*: "Hujus tempore fuit bellum inter populum Israel et Benjamin, propter uxorem Levitae apud Gabaam constupratam, et a Israel quidem occisa sunt quadraginta millia, de Benjamin triginta quinque et centum viri," *PL* CLXXII 169.

   In the Vulgate, "Ayoth" was indeed a Benjamite, but the enemy he fought was the Moabites. See *Iud.* 3:15-30. The battle between Benjamites and Israelites occurs in *Iud.* 19-21 because of the death of the wife or concubine of a Levite, the "deknes wyf" of 1.7009. *DIM* and hence the *CM* telescope the two separate incidents into one, and exaggerate the numbers killed. See *Iud.* 20:35, 46.

7013-4   These lines may be reversed. *DIM* puts the construction of Troy in the reign of Aioth.

7015   From *DIM*. The Vulgate gives no length of reign for Samgar, nor does he appear in Eusebius' chronology. Comestor mentions him, but does not give the length of this reign. See *Hist. Schol. Iud.* vi, *PL* CXCVIII 1275.

7016 The two sons are apparently Deborah and Barack. The poet does not know that Deborah is a woman. Neither is, in fact, the child of Samgar. Barrack is frequently called "filium Abinoem". See *Iud.* 4:6, 5:1, 5:12.

7020 *DIM* does not mention Apollo here. Haenisch has no note on these lines, but he might have cited the passage from Comestor which mentions both Delphos (although not the sybil) and Apollo: "Obiit Liber pater, cujus sepulcrum est apud Delphos juxta Apollinem aureum." See *Hist. Schol. Iud.* vii, *PL* CXCVIII 1277.

7023-6 These lines do not correspond to anything in *DIM*. MSS CF preserve the lines in their original form. First they mention the three hundred men of Gideon's army, as in *Iud.* 7:7 *et passim*. Then they name the four kings: Oreb and Zeb from *Iud.* 7:25, Zebee and Salmana from *Iud.* 8:5. MSS GHTLB have corrupted the four kings to forty and reversed the order of the first two lines. This leaves the four names dangling. "þat" of CF 1.7025 becomes "þan" in GHTLB and the four rulers of the Midianites are transformed into Judges of Israel.

7027-8 From *DIM*, *PL* CLXXII 169, although Haenisch cited Petrus Comestor.

7029 The *CM* poet skips over the story of Abimilech to get to Thola. He thus ignores Abimelech's three year reign, which is mentioned in *DIM* as well as in *Iud.* 9.

7030 *DIM* and *Iud.* 10:2 both say he reigned twenty-three years. MSS CFG are correct, but the southern translator corrupted 20 to 40. This is the length of reign of many of the other Judges.

7033-4 *DIM* says simply "Priamus in Troja", without connecting the city with the sibyl.

7037-8 Both *DIM* and *Hist. Schol. Iud.* x, *PL* CXCVIII 1283 mention Priam under the reign of Thola.

7039-40 Not in *DIM*. Haenisch, *CM*, p. 8*, pointed out that Petrus Comestor has this notice under the reign of Jair: "Carmentis nympha litteras Latinas invenit." See *Hist. Schol. Iud.* xi, *PL* CXCVIII 1283.

7041 Cf. *Iud.* 11:1. *DIM* does not mention his supposed bastardy.

7043-4 *DIM* mentions the amazons here, but the explanation of the word is given only by the *CM* poet.

7045 HAENISCH, *CM*, p. 8*, suggested that the form of the name, Esebon, is taken from *Hist. Schol. Iud.* xiii *PL* CXCVIII 1285. *Iud.* 12:8 has Abesan, *DIM* Abessan.

7047 *Iud.* 12:9 says Abesan led Israel for seven years exactly. MSS CGHTLB all say seven years and more. MS F has seemingly corrected this to "in rowte". The meaningless rhyme which the scribe provides in 1.7048 makes clear that this was probably not the original reading.

7048-50 This is not in *DIM*. HAENISCH, *CM*, p. 9* pointed to *Hist. Schol. Iud.* xiv, *PL* CXCVIII 1285: "Eo tempore Paris Helenam rapuit, bellum decennale surrexit." Comestor refers these events to the reign of Achialon, however.

The *CM* poet himself was aware that Alexander was another name of Paris the Trojan. Hence C's lines "Alexandre, in þat siquar,/þat paris hight, raiuist helayn,—" (7048-9). Later scribes, less familiar with the Troy story, apparently knew only one Alexander, Alexander the Great. By changing only one word, "hight" to "auȝte", one such copyist altered the lines to read "Alexander [the Great], who owned [the city of] Paris,...ravished Helen." This is the meaning in GHTLB. The scribe of MS F rewrote the lines entirely, producing a very ,weak version.

7056   See note to 11.7048-50.

7059   HAENISCH, *CM*, p. 9*, pointed to *Hist. Schol. Iud.* xv, *PL* CXCVIII 1285. The source, however, is once again *DIM*.

7060-3   This is not in either *DIM* or *Hist. Schol.*

7064-8   HAENISCH, *CM*, p. 9*, supposed that the *CM* poet used another source here, or that he invented the figures which are not found in *Hist. Schol.* In fact, he is using *DIM* again, but his lines are now garbled. *DIM* says the number killed was 877,000 Greeks and 686,000 Trojans. The number of Trojans is correct in all *CM* MSS, but the number of Greeks is expressed very unclearly. The original line may have read "Eight hundred sixty seven and ten".

7069-82   Nothing in *DIM* corresponds to this summary of the Trojan war, although Kaluza said the borrowing from *DIM* continued until 1.7082. See KALUZA, "Zu den Quellen...", p. 451.

7083-7101   The story of Samson's birth and courtship is greatly abbreviated from the Vulgate. Cf. *Iud.* 13:2-14:4. The *CM* poet may be using another source here. Cf. the *Met. Para.* 3601ff, which treats the story of Samson at greater length than does the *CM*.

7102-34   Cf. *Iud.* 14:5-9, 12-5, 17.

7137-44   These lines appear only in MS F, although they translate *Iud.* 14:18, and are added to complete the story. They must have been missed out in an early exemplar, when a scribe's eye skipped from "priuate" in 1.7136 to the same word in 1.7144, thus causing most later copies to omit entirely the solution of the riddle.

7145-6   Based on *Iud.* 14:19-20.

7147-60   Cf. *Iud.* 15:3-5.

7161-74   Abbreviated from *Iud.* 15:11-5.

7175-7204   Abbreviated from *Iud.* 16:1-9.

7198   MSS GHTLB have a corrupt version of this line, from which all mention of the binding of Sampson has disappeared. In these MSS, Samson breaks bonds which the reader never knew were on him.

7205-12   Cf. *Iud.* 16:16-7.

7213-36   The *CM* poet draws the obvious moral from the story.

7237-46   Based on *Iud.* 16:18-9, 21.

7246   MSS CF have the better reading "blinded", whereas GHTLB read "beten". Cf. *Iud.* 16:21.

7247-51   In *Iud.* 16:23, the feast is in honour of the Philistine god Dagon. The *CM* poet, or his source changes this into a bridal feast for Delilah and her new husband, and endows Samson with special talent as a harper.

7252-62   Cf. *Iud.* 16:22, 25, 29-30.

7265-77   Cf. I *Reg.* 4:3-18.

7273   "ware þai" must originally have been "was it", for the ark of the covenant was captured, not the sons of Eli.

7274-6   These lines, found only in MS F, correspond to I *Reg.* 4:18. Cf. 1.7277 in the other MSS.

7278-82   This is a bit of moralizing from the poet.

7283   Cf. I *Reg.* 4:18.

7287-7454   From HERMAN's *Bible*, 11.2213-2317. See BORLAND, *CM*, p. 47.

7287-96   HERMAN, 11.2213-20.

7297-7300   This reiteration is not in Herman. It comes from I *Reg.* 8:19-20.

7301-10   HERMAN, 11.2221-6.

7311-2   This proverbial saying is added by the poet.

7313-42   HERMAN, 11.2229-43. The biblical narrative is greatly abridged here.

7343-58   Herman reports God's instructions in direct discourse in 11.2244-52, as do MSS CF of the *CM*. In GHTLB, however, the discourse is indirect. The *CM* poet is also using the Vulgate here, for Herman does not mention that Jesse lived in Bethlehem. See *CM* 11.7348-9 and cf. I *Reg.* 16:1.

7359-7432   From HERMAN, 11.2253-2306. The expansion and contraction of the Vulgate narrative of I *Reg.* 16:10-18, 23 definitely indicates Herman as the source.

7405-6   Not in Herman.

7407-12   Beryl ROWLAND, *Blind Beasts*, p. 7, believes that this picture of David playing to his sheep is influenced by the Orphic myth.

7439-54   HERMAN, 11.2309-17.

7451   I *Reg.* 17:4 says "altitudinis sex cubitorum et palmi". This number does not appear in Herman. The *CM* poet is here treating ells and cubits as if they were equal. Cf. n. to 11.1675-6 above.

7455   Borland found no more traces of Herman's influence until 1.8979. However, I feel that the *CM* poet has continued to combine HERMAN's *Bible* and the Vulgate.

7455-7474   Goliath does not make a speech in Herman. The *CM*'s version is based on I *Reg.* 17:8-11.

7475-82   Cf. HERMAN, 11.2319-21.

7481-2   HERMAN, 1.2321, says merely "Qui vaintre le porra, mon regne li donrai." The reference to the king's daughter is evidently an anticipation of I *Reg.* 18:27. Cf. below, 11.7645-6.

7483-9   From HERMAN, 11.2322-4.

7487   On MS C's "gerard" see DICKENS, "Gerard as a Goblin Name".

7491-2   David's brother Eliab, in I *Reg.* 17:28, accuses David of pride: "Ego novi superbiam tuam, et nequitiam cordis tui;". Both Herman and the *CM* poet are defending David against this charge.

Herman has already expanded from the Vulgate David's references to his trust in God. The *CM* translates all Herman's points and gives them greater emphasis. These lines in the English version summarize mediaeval ideas about pride. A Christian hero, to avoid the sin of pride, need not humble himself by not doing the great deeds of which he is capable. Rather he must be sure to attribute his prowess to God alone, and not to himself. The proud man may *do* exactly the same things as the Christian hero, but he will attribute all his triumphs to his own abilities. See, e.g., THOMAS AQUINAS, *Sum. Theol.* I Q. lxiii art. 3.

7493-7518 Saul's fears for David are not expressed in Herman, but are based on I *Reg.* 17: 33-7.

7519-36 The arming of David is from HERMAN, 11.2327-35.

7531 Herman says three stones, 1.2332. The *CM* poet has corrected the number to five from I *Reg.* 17:40.

7537-50 HERMAN, 11.2336-42.

7541-2 MSS CF have "man...es". MS G, however, reads "men...es", a grammatical error which obviously found its way into the southern translation. Scribes corrected it in various ways: "mon...is" T; "men... are" H; "men...be" B.

7544 The *CM* poet, or perhaps his later copyists, seem to have had trouble with the French idiom in HERMAN, 1.2339: "ne li valt pas .1. gant". The English poet renders "valt" as "helpes" and then searches for a subject. MS C's "Irinnes" was probably suggested by the following line, while F's "hardines" and G's "dredness" are similar attempts to find a subject for the sentence. The southern translator gave up the struggle and allowed the vague "hit" to stand by itself with no obvious antecedent.

7553-71 Cf. I *Reg.* 17:42-6.

7575-90 From HERMAN, 11.2349-56.

7593-8 From HERMAN, 11.2363-4.

7599-7612 Cf. I *Reg.* 18:6-9.

7613-5 From HERMAN, 11.2370-1. Herman skips the events between David's fight with Goliath and his accession to the throne. The *CM* poet accordingly turns to the Vulgate for his material.

7617-8 A philosophical reflection of the poet's on the usual rewards of faithful service.

7619-26 Cf. I *Reg.* 18: 10-11.

7628 All the *CM* MSS state that Saul was *not* afraid of David, but this may be an error for an original "now". Cf. I *Reg.* 18:12: "Et timuit Saul David".

7629-36 Cf. I *Reg.* 18:13, 17.

7637-46 Cf. I *Reg.* 18:25, 27.

7647-52 Cf. I *Reg.* 19:1-2.

7653-4 MSS CF preserve the original reading "paind". MSS GHTLB have corrupted this to "preyed". In I *Reg.* 19:3-5, Jonathan does not pray to God, but intercedes with his own father, Saul, for a reconciliation.

7655-75 Cf. I *Reg.* 19:7-12.

7676-84 Cf. I *Reg.* 19:18-20.

7685-98 From HERMAN, 11.2368-75.

7705-6 A reference to I *Reg.* 24.

7707-46 Cf. I *Reg.* 26:3-13, 15-8, 21-2.

7749-86 Cf. I *Reg.* 31:1-6, 8-13.

7785-6 The Middle English poet omits the burning of the body in I *Reg.* 31:12.

7789-7828 Cf. II *Reg.* 1:1-12, 14-5.

7791-3 This parenthetical reference is to the action described in I *Reg.* 30. David there fights the nation of the Amalekites, not an individual named Amalek, as the *CM* poet states. Cf. I *Reg.* 15 in which Saul defeats the Amalekites and kills their king Agag. Amalek himself was defeated by Moses and Joshua. See *Ex.* 17:8-16 and above, 11.6401-32.

7827-36 From HERMAN, 11.2390-6. Herman expatiates on the sin of regicide here, although in II *Reg.* 1:14 the crime seems more like sacrilege: "Quare non timuisti mittere manum tuam, ut occideres christum Domini?"

7835 In II *Reg.* 1:15 the penalty is swift in coming. This Herman renders correctly as "mort soubite", in 1.2396. This is translated in *CM*, MSS CG as "ferings ded". MS F changed the death to an "euel" one however and the southern translator apparently misinterpreted "ferings" as "fiery".

7837-60 The *CM* poet, as usual, marks the end of an age and the beginning of a new one. HAENISCH, *CM*, p. 9* refers this passage to *Hist. Schol.*, but the *CM* is closer to *DIM* here. Both *CM* and *DIM* calculate the total age of the world at this time, although the totals they arrive at are different. Cf. *DIM, PL* CLXXII 170.

The summary of the genealogy between Abraham and David is in none of the sources the poet has been using, but is consistent with his avowed purpose of providing a continuous genealogy for the Virgin Mary.

7861-77 HERMAN, 11.2397, 2401, 2403-9.

7869 The *CM* poet evidently translated Herman's "fiers" as "aghful", making David an awe-inspiring man. See *MED* "aueful" adj (b). The other MSS corrupt this, however, G to "waful", and the southern translation to "wise".

7879ff Herman does not go into details about the beginning of the liason of David and Bathsheba. The *CM* poet reverts apparently to the Vulgate for his story.

7883-7906 Cf. II *Reg.* 11:2-5, 14-7. The translation of the Vulgate is not close, however. The poet may be using another source here.

7909-60 Cf. II *Reg.* 11:27-12:7, 9-14.

7936 In II *Reg.* 12:6, David proposes only that the rich man restore the lamb four-fold.

7961-2 Cf. II *Reg.* 12:24.

7963-7 This story of the composition of the *Miserere* may have been suggested to the *CM* poet by the Latin *Legende*. In that work, David composes the Psalm after his great sin, while sitting under the tree which has grown from Moses' wands. See *Legende*, 50/86.

The *CM* poet has inserted the passage here, after the biblical version of the story of Bathsheba. He has to omit all mention of the sacred tree, however, because he has not yet told of David's part in its history. When he does tell of it, he uses the version from *Trad. anon.* which does not mention Bathsheba's adultery, nor the composition of the Psalm.

7973ff The *CM* poet translates the next 1000 odd lines from the cross story in *Trad. anon.* Cf. above, n. to 1.6301ff. The first 56 lines, corresponding to *CM* 7973-8033, are reproduced by NAPIER, *Rood Tree*, pp. 64-5.

7974 The Old French says ten years (1.128).

8007   Once again, MSS CFG agree with the *Trad. anon.* 1.159, in having the rods of cedar, pine and cypress. Once again, the southern translator has consistently altered the pine to palm. Cf. above, note to 1.1377.

8009   The *Trad. anon.* does not here name the place where Moses found the rods: "Dun leu lai ou il les troua" (1.161). However, "Elyn" has already been named in 1.34.

8053-8193   NAPIER, *Rood Tree*, pp. 65-7 prints 11.202-332 of the cross story section of *Trad. anon.*, which correspond to these lines.

8058   MSS CFG correctly preserve "hope" for "esperance" (1.207).

8066   The sweet smell is not mentioned in *Trad. anon.*, but came to the *CM* from the Latin *Legende*. Instead of the light which shines from the rods when David finds them, as above 11.8047-50, the *Legende*, 49/74, speaks of a beautiful odour.

8078   *Trad. anon.* 1.225 has "Au pis lour tienent li manton".

8080, 8106   The Old French lines corresponding to these are missing from the MS. See NAPIER, *Rood Tree*, p. 66, n. to 11.226, 250.

8081-2   These lines were accidentally omitted from the southern translation. They correspond to *Trad. anon.* 1.227.

8119   According to 1.8091, the Saracens are already kneeling. There had been no mention of kneeling in the Old French poem, 11.235-7, and there the poet says merely that they kissed the wands "deuotement" (1.263).

8121   The *CM* poet translates the French "de gentil sanc" (1.265) by "of þe fre blood".

8125-6   Once again the Saracens kneel. Here, at least, the Old French says "et se mettent a orison" (1.270).

8127-8   These lines are reversed in the southern translation. However, the subject is still the onlookers, not the Saracens.

8132   The Old French says simply that they returned "ou desert" (1.275). However, the Old French poet had already established that they came from Ethiopia (1.220).

8134   See NAPIER, *Rood Tree*, p. xxvi n. 2. The Old French MS has "Tant quil uint a une fontaine" (1.277). This is a scribal error for "montaine", the original reading, which the *CM* poet has translated "felle" and, at 1.8136, "mounteyne".

8138   *Trad. anon.* says forty years, 1.279.

8150   The idiom of MSS CF, "þat he was hale sume ani trote", does not appear here in *Trad. anon.* Cf. below 1.8175. The southern translation is closer to the French: "Et apres se trouoit tout sain" (1.291).

8152-3   MS C has the original reading. Cf. *Trad. anon.* 11.294-5. The scribe of G seemingly misunderstood "barun" as "branchis", and the southern translator rewrote the couplet accordingly.

8164   MSS F and the southern translation preserve the original reading here, translating Old French "Molt lont doucement salue" (1.306).

8165-6   These lines are omitted from the southern translation. They correspond to 1.307 of the Old French poem.

8169   MSS CFT preserve the correct reading "Thoru þe" or "Bi þe", translating the Old French "Par uos ert gariz li lieprous" (1.310). HLB, however, alter the pronoun, probably on purpose, to refer to the rods rather than to the king.

8175   This translates the Old French idiom "sainz *com*me .i. poissons" (1.319). Cf. above, 1.8150 CF.

8206-33   As NAPIER, *Rood Tree*, p. xxvii pointed out, the *CM* poet has here combined details from the Latin *Legende* with the *Trad. anon.*

8206   The *Legende* says "Posuit ergo illas in cisterna" (49/79). The *Trad. anon.* has them planted "a t*e*rre dure" (fol. 269r col. 2).

8207-8   *Legende* 49/80: "Apposuit quidem lumina et custodes."

8210-7   *Legende,* 49/81.

8218-24   *Trad. anon.* fol. 269r col. 2.

8224   For the sake of the rhyme, the English poet has exaggerated David's state of mind. The Old French has simply "Porpe*n*sa soi q*u*il feroit" (fol. 269r col. 2).

8225-33   *Legende,* 49/83-4.

8234-8460   *Trad. anon.* fol. 269r col. 2-270v col. 2.

8235   The southern translator has changed the original pine to a palm even in this line, where the woods in question are not those of the three branches which became the cross.

8240   MS C's "schirting" does not mean comfort, as Kaluza's glossary states, but amusement, from OE *(ge)scyrtan.* See *OED* "shurt" v. The *Trad. anon.* says "ce ert ses depors. ce ert ses desouiz", fol. 269r col. 2.

8271   *CM*'s "relike" translates Old French "*v*ertuz", fol. 269v col. 1.

8274   *Trad. anon.* has "sacrement", fol. 269v col. 1. Perhaps the *CM* poet is consciously avoiding the anachronism.

8288   For "stapul", *Trad. anon.* has "p*e*rron".

8420-6   The French original lays more stress on the knightly virtues than the clerical English translator allows:
> Or gardez quil soit bien noriz
> Apres de proesces et dars
> Quil ne soit vilains ne couars
> Et saiche les p*a*rs de clergie
> Prouesce de cheualerie
> Li aufes est de bons mors
> Gardez quil ait m*o*lt b*on*s doctors (fol. 270v col. 1).

8449-62   The connection of these lines with the following passage describing the writing of Solomon's books is tenuous. L. 8452 is promising: "þe kynde of þingis lerned he", or in Old French "Veoit des choses la nature" (fol. 270v col. 1). Insights into the "nature of things" might well result in books such as *Ecclesiasticus, Proverbs* and the *Canticum Canticorum.* However, when he comes to describe Solomon's new knowledge, the Old French poet produces only some allusions to folk wisdom about the medicinal properties of plants.

8463-82   The *CM* poet does not accept the Old French descriptions of the three books, nor even their order of composition. Rather, he composes these lines according to what he knows of the meaning of each of Solomon's books.

8482   After his résumé of the three books, the Old French poet recapitulates the kind of knowledge that Solomon obtained:
> Toutes les h*e*rbes cognoiscoit
> Et q*ue*l u*e*rtuz chasc*un*ne auoit (fol. 270v col. 2).

The ME poet omits the lines. Cf. n. to 11.8449-62.

8483-8508 *Trad. anon.* fol. 270v col. 2.

8488   MS G alone preserves the correct reading "stremis", translating the Old French "Des aigues qui ont lou droit cors". MSS CHT have "sternes", an easy scribal error to make, and one rendered more likely by the common occurrence of phrases such as "the stars in their courses". However, MS L also has "stremys", which suggests that the southern translation may also have preserved the original reading.

8497   The awkward word order is dictated by the need to use "marie" as a rhyme word. The inflected ending of the pronoun "whom" makes the meaning unmistakable, however. The Old French simply has "li filz marie".

"Bytwene þat" is a very awkward translation of the original "Bitwix and" (CFG).

8509-12   The *CM* poet inserts these lines as he leaves the *Trad. anon.* and reverts to Herman as a source.

8513-7   HERMAN, 11.2425-7.

8514   Herman says only that David reigned "longuement" (1.2425). The forty years comes from *DIM, PL* CLXXII 172.

8521-6   HERMAN, 11.2429-31.

8531-4   *DIM, PL* CLXXII 172.

8536-8   Cf. III *Reg.* 2:10.

8539-71   From HERMAN, 11.2432, 2435, 2438-57.

8575-81   HERMAN, 2460-3.

8583-8614   HERMAN, 11.2474-87. Borland pointed out these parallels in *CM*, pp. 52ff.

8583   MS C's "fourte" is an error for "forme" GHTL, Herman "primes".

8589-90   The *Trad. anon.* agrees with the Vulgate in calling the women "putains", fol. 271v col. 1; cf. III *Reg.* 3:16 "mulieres meretrices". Herman has softened this to "femes...menestrés", which the *CM* poet translates "Mister wymmen". However, his next line shows that the poet still thinks of them as sinful.

8603-4   The *CM* poet adds this generalization and warning, which is not in his sources.

8609-12   These lines, appearing only in MS F, have no counterpart in Herman.

8615-52   From HERMAN, 11.2490-2508.

8641-2   These lines, appearing only in MS F, are not found in Herman.

8653-6   The *CM* poet got this idea from *Trad. anon.* fol. 271v col. 1. Herman does not deal with the cross story at all.

8657-73   HERMAN, 2509-19.

8658   Herman, 1.2510, says the woman who carried the dead child spoke first. The *CM* poet means the same woman, but describes her as the mother of the living child.

8679-92   From HERMAN, 2520-27.

8695   The *Trad. anon.* here raises a point of mediaeval law: the problem cannot be settled either by "sairemens", that is by swearing, nor by combat. None of the barons is sufficiently convinced of the rights and wrongs of the case to take up the defence of either woman. See fol. 271v col. 2.

8699-8716 This recapitulation of the case does not appear either in Herman or in the Old French cross story. Cf. however III *Reg.* 3:23-4.

8717-20 HERMAN, 2533-5.

8721-2 Cf. III *Reg.* 3:26.

8723 *Trad. anon.* fol. 271v col. 2. The Old French poem uses legal terms here: "Je li clain quite ma partie". Cf. *CM* 1.8723.

8729-31 From HERMAN, 2537. The remainder of the mother's speech in Herman is very moving, but it has been omitted by the *CM* poet.

8732-44 HERMAN, 2541-6.

8747 Herman has the barons say merely "Sire, jugié l'avés" (1.2547). The *Trad. anon.* has:

Certainnement sceuent li baron
Quil a iugie droit et raison (fol. 272r col. 1).

8748-56 HERMAN, 2550-6.

8757-8842 The *CM* poet returns to the *Trad. anon.* as a source. See fol. 272r col. 1-272v col. 1.

8768 MSS CF preserve the correct reading "dei", for Old French "moroit".

8775-8808 The technical building terms are not found in the Old French poem. Cf. above, 11.1669-74, 2231 and notes.

8843-4 The *CM* poet is already aware of the sources he will use for the passion section of his poem, and knows that this story of Judas getting the silver from the temple is found only in *Trad. anon.* which he does not plan to follow.

8845-8 *Trad. anon.* fol. 272v col. 1.

8849-66 The description of the temple does not appear either in the *Trad. anon.* or in the Latin *Legende* or in Herman. The description is based on III *Reg.* 6-7. Several of the Old French paraphrases have quite elaborate descriptions of the Temple, however.

8854 Cf. III *Reg.* 6:7, 9.

8861-3 Cf. III *Reg.* 6:2. As he did in the description of Noah's ark, the English poet has here changed the unit of measurement from the biblical cubits to ells. Cf. n. to 11.1675-6.

8867-80 *Trad. anon.* fol. 272v col. 1, 11.916-31. L1.918-31 are printed by NAPIER, *Rood Tree*, p. 67.

8873 *Trad. anon.* 1.924 says 700 men.

8880 The extant Old French MS names the priest Arillus, not Cirillus, in 1.930.

8883-9 These lines are not in the *Trad. anon.* Cf. III *Reg.* 11:3.

8894-8921 *Trad. anon.* fol. 272v col. 1-2, 11.934-56. L1.932-53 are printed in BONNARD, pp. 88-9.

8902 *Trad. anon.* 933 calls the lady "Sebile". She is also called "sibilla" in the earliest form of the cross-wood story in MS Bodl. 343. See QUINN, *Quest of Seth*, pp. 59 *et passim*.

The name Maximilla is used only in the *Legende* version of the story. See *Legende* 51/106 and Quinn's discussion, *Quest of Seth*, pp. 128-9. The *CM* poet must call this woman Maximilla, however, because he plans to use the *Legende*'s story of another Sebilla. See below 11.8953-76.

8922 This line summarizes several lines in the French which elaborate the significance of the name for Christians and the Jews' abhorrence of it. See fol. 272v col. 2, 11.957-63.

8923-4   Napier, p. xxviii pointed out that these lines come from the *Legende* 51/109.

8925-42   After the story of "Sebile", the *CM*'s Maximilla, the *Trad. anon.* goes on to tell how the wood stayed in the Temple and was honoured there until Christ's time.

However, the episode, told in *CM*, of the wood's being thrown into the "piscina probatica" is found in the earliest Latin cross story known to Meyer, the *Historia*. It recurs in many versions including the Latin *Legende* 51/110-3, which the *CM* poet translated here.

The healing pool stirred by an angel is obviously based on *Ioan.* 5:2-4. See QUINN, *Quest of Seth*, pp. 65-6.

8927   MSS CF's "stank" (OF *estanc*) is a better translation of "piscina" than GHTLB's "pitt". Cf. 1.8936.

8943-76   The story of the wood's being used as a bridge is also found in the *Legende* 51/114-20. The ME version is considerably expanded from the Latin here, and may in fact have been translated from another source.

8947   The name comes from II *Esdr.* 3:15 and *Ioan.* 9:7, 11, where it is a pool rather than a stream. Cf. QUINN, *Quest of Seth*, pp. 107, 129.

8977-8   Again the *CM* poet uses this formula when he changes from one source to another.

8979-9000   This is probably an expansion of HERMAN, 2564-7. Cf. especially *CM* 8997-8 and HERMAN, 2567: "Dix, que devint ses sens".

9001-10   The diatribe against women is not found in any of the sources the poet has just been using. The conjunction of Adam, Sampson, David and Solomon as men deceived by women is common in mediaeval proverbs. See H. WALTHER, *Proverbia, Sententiaeque* I, 519ff, 5026a. The four appear in this context in a *Planctus* of Peter Abelard. For a discussion of the *topos* see Dronke, *Poetic Individuality*, 124-5. For other parallels in mediaeval literature cf. FRIEND, "Sampson, David and Salomon" and R. W. KING, "A Note on *GGK* 2414ff".

9014   MS C alone has the word "crachon" (OF *cracheron*) a worthless person. GHTLB prefer Chauntecleer's remark: "Mulier est hominis confusio". Cf. Carleton BROWN, "Mulier...".

9041-85   From HERMAN, 2573-94.

9060   Solomon does not go quite this far in his repentance in Herman.

9086-90   The *CM* poet omits Herman's further discussion between Solomon and his advisors, 11.2595-2601. He resumes with HERMAN, 2602.

9091-9104   HERMAN, 2603-16.

9097-8   Herman does not mention the crown here.

9099-9100   Herman has "Li rois oste ses dras et sa char a livree/A .IIII. de ses hommes toute l'ont desciree;" 11.2609-10. Thus MS C's 1.9099 is corrupt and that of GHTLB is to be preferred, while C's unique reading in 1.9100 is correct.

9105-14   The *CM* poet elaborates more than Herman on the sin and penitance.

9115-20   HERMAN, 2618, 2621.

9121-32   The *CM* poet returns to his genealogical theme.

9133-9203   These lines are taken from *DIM, PL* CLXXII 172-3 unless otherwise stated. Kaluza first pointed this out in "Zu den Quellen", p. 451.

9133-9 *DIM, PL* CLXXII 172 says simply that Solomon reigned for forty years. Cf. III *Reg.* 11:42-3.

9150-2 *DIM* gives the length of time simply as three years and does not give God's motive for the drought.

9162 *DIM* does not mention how Elijah was translated. Cf. IV *Reg.* 2:11.

9163 The *CM* poet here omits several reigns, and skips to Ozias.

9164 *DIM, PL* CLXXII 172 gives Ozias' reign as 52 years. Cf. IV *Reg.* 14:21, 15:1-2. Ozias is really the son of Amaziah, whom the *CM* poet does not mention, rather than of Joram.

9169 MSS CF correctly refer to the sixth sibyl. Cf. *DIM, PL* CLXXII 172.

9173-6 These lines have been transposed in all the MSS. Ahaz is the son of Jotham, and 11.9175-6 obviously must follow 1.9172. The couplet about Romulus and Rome, 11.9173-4, follows 1.9176.

This order is confirmed by *DIM, PL* CLXXII 173, which mentions Romulus and the founding of Rome in the reigns of Ahaz and Ezechias.

9179 Ezechias reigns 28 years in *DIM*, 29 in IV *Reg.* 18:2. MSS CFG share the erroneous reading 39, which the southern translator has apparently corrected from the Vulgate.

9180 Not in *DIM*. Cf. IV *Reg.* 18:3.

9183-4 These lines do not appear here in *DIM*, but come from *Hist. Schol.* IV *Reg.* xxxiii, *PL* CXCVIII 1415, as Haenisch pointed out, *CM*, p. 9*. *DIM, PL* CLXXII 173 mentions this Sibyl along with the prophet Jeremiah under the reign of Josias. The *CM* poet has consciously chosen Petrus Comestor's version.

9186-8 There is nothing about this idol-worship in *DIM*. Cf. however IV *Reg.* 21:2-9; *Hist. Schol.* IV *Reg.* xxxiii, *PL* CXCVIII 1415.

9194 MS C alone preserves the correct numbers. *DIM, PL* CLXXII 173 says that Ninevah had stood 1470 years.

9197 HAENISCH, *CM*, p. 9*, points to *Hist. Schol.* IV *Reg.* xxxviii, *PL* CXCVIII 1418 as the source for the name Ieconias, but this name is found here in *DIM* also.

9200-18 Cf. IV *Reg.* 25:1-10.

9204-20 Not in *DIM*.

9221-2 *DIM, PL* CLXXII 173 says Jerusalem had stood for 549 years before the transmigration.

9223-8 *DIM, PL* CLXXII 173 says the fourth age of the world occupied 475 years and the total age of the world at that time was 4610 years.

APPENDIX A

Errors in Morris' Texts

7   baron]T barou*n*
23   sa[nge]s]F sa⟨nge⟩s. Similarly 25 ⟨re⟩de, 29 lath⟨e⟩, 34 ⟨ver⟩tue,
        41 b⟨e⟩takenes, 46 h⟨*im*⟩.
33   the]C þe.
39   þat]C þ*a*t.
58   smert]G snert.
67   wito*u*ten]C witoten.
70   [nede me dos socur*e*] G ⟨nede me dos socur*e*⟩.
84   þat]C þ*a*t.
85   [mater] C ⟨mater⟩.
91   þat]C þ*a*t.
93   *delete* ? C.
101   Lady]G *does not have a decorated capital here.*
110   him]G hi*m*.
120   Bre[fl]i]C Bre ⟨fl⟩ i.
134   siþen]C sithen.
139-40   [ʒo]u, Es[au]e]T *the letters are somewhat rubbed, but legible.*
178   bigonne]T bigo*n*ne.
185   womman]C wom*m*aM. þat]G þ*a*t.
186   þat]C þ*a*t.
187   How]G Hou.
188   þat]C þ*a*t. aht]C aght.
192   the]C þe.
219   last]C laste. alle]C all.
222   þat]C þ*a*t.
225   think]G thinck.
227   worlde]T world.
230   world]C werld.
232   is]C it.
236   understand]C vnderstand.
241   the]C þe.
252   þat]C þ*a*t.
257   to]G so.
270a   sou*n*day]C sonu*n*day.
275   þ*a*t]T þat.
313   his]F h ⟨is⟩.
364   þins]F þing.
372   þat]C þ*a*t.
378   þ[e]se]C yse. sou[n]did]C sondid.

384 *gr*ifyns]T *gr*isyng.
386 h[am]]F h ⟨am⟩.
387 iiij]F iiii *(twice)*.
409 ensau*m*ple]T ensauple.
428 with]C wit.
454 anttour]G auctour
518 element[e]s]C element*es*
519 water]G watir
520 and]*om* C.
549 things]C thing*es*
570 Wouen]T Wonen
587 heþ]T lieþ
604 lussum]T lufsum
611 vnbroken]T vnbrokon
635 tway]G tuay
654 tre]F tree
712 þat]C *þa*t
734 has]F had
740 þat]C *þa*t
746 Wonþer]G Wonþ*er*
766 /ho]F *originally* sho, *with s erased. So also* 772.
770 othere]C oth-r
844 ransumed]G ransuned
888 þat]C *þa*t
897 wom*m*ones]T wo*m*mo*n*nes
920 werld]G world
921 and]C an
1001 þareof]G þarof
1012 is]G es
1022 werines *is the reading in* F, *not* wermes, *as Morris' note states.*
1031 sautes]C santes
1093 Sun]C Su*n*
1136 hi[t]]T hi ⟨t⟩
1182 Ye]G þe
1185 birijing]G birijng
1253 yu]G þu
1255 greene]G grene
1287 [he]]C he *written in margin*
1291 seuid]C senid
1305 ȝe]G þe
1312 frott]G frort
1335 eet]T eer
1352 þat]G *þa*t
1359 Que*n*]G Qu*e*n
1401 namare]C namar
1417 pepinis]G pepins
1434 þritte]C thritte
1435 When]T Whe*n*n
1440 at]G þat
1446 harwede]T harwide
1462 yer]C þer

1486   seuenti]G seuinti
1495   a[r þe t] oþer]C a ⟨r þe t⟩ oþer
1516   son]G sun
1520   soñ]F sou*n*. sonne]G soune. soñ]T sou*n*
1553   Whēn]T Whe*n*n
1554   hundid]G hundrid
1559   amang]G emang
Genealogical table following 1.1626: Mattussael] C Matussael
1628   geten]G getin
1656   graunted]C grauntid
1661   vengeance]G vengance
1770   din*n*ed]G di*m*med
1785   swan]T swam
1806   miste]T nuste
1834   noh*u*t]G noht
1859   þer]T þ*u*s
1878   þe]*om* F
1908   dam*n*yng]T da*m*myng
1917   with]C wit
1919   rode]T ȝode
1929   Ti]C Til
1943   þouȝ]T þouȝt
1946   sul]G sal
2019   he]G lx
2039   broiþer]C broiþ*er*
2126   one]T owe
2129   speede]T sprede
2141   seder]T sedec
2165   witterli]G witt*er*li
2169   hundrid]G hundred
2176   lete]G lele. good]T goood
2193   and]G a*n*d
2194   regma]G regina
2199   [þ] is F þis
2210   þat]C þ*a*t
2218   a*n*d]G a*n*
2223   syn]F kyn
2265   þ[*at*]]C þ ⟨*a*t⟩
2268   diu*er*is]G diu*er*s
Genealogy after 1.2314: *The blank space on the right has* om*er in a
later hand.*
2317   is]G es
2324   mayd*en*e]G mayd*er*e
2330   of]C o
2348   be]C bee
2359   su[ilka]] C su ⟨ilka⟩
2360   l[oke]]C l ⟨oke⟩. þ[e b]une]C þ ⟨e b⟩une
2414   þat]G þ*a*t
2420   her]G hir
2421   þat]G þ*a*t
2426   wij]C wijf

2483 heȝt]F het
2491 þat]G þat
2499 bat]T bac
2500 to]C til. pit]T putt
2506 graunted]G granted
2508 getun]G getim
2520 þat]G þat
2522 he]T þe
2530 miht]G mitht
2578 on on]C on
2580 uoice]G voice
2602 mine] mñe
2631 cruell]C cruel
2636 her]T hir
2657 sal]C sol
2691 [þis]]F' ⟨þiis⟩
2692 bl[is]]F bl⟨is⟩
2695 scare]C sitre
2709 onered]G onerd
2729 chide]T childe
2739 [þou]]F' ⟨þou⟩
2772 wald]C watd
2779 and]G an
2796 pressed]T preesed
2847 vn-suukyn]F vnsunkyn
2903 þat]G þat
2915 did]C hid
2970 ȝorne]F ȝerne
3008 langer]G langer
3009 þat]G þat
3016 make]F mak
3051 þat]G þat
3118 lete]G lele
3135 Morris' note l: schild]C child
3166 immolatur]C imnolatur
3171 [þat]]F ⟨þat⟩
3172 [or]]F ⟨or⟩
3198 out]G vut
3219 her]C hir
3220 were]C ware
3268 þat]C þat
3318 toune]G toune
3386 multeplied]G multiplied
3414 bidinge]F bidding
3439 godde]G godd
3474 uye]T nye
3514 þose]T þese
3593 þie]T þei
3638 ȝele]T zele
3653 For]T Fro
3693 leue] crossed out in G.

3747 [mali]sou*n*]F ⟨mali⟩sou*n*
3764 sa]F so
3781 be]T he
3896 simeon]F symeon
3935 lete]C lett
3941 s[ine]]F s⟨ine⟩
3965 messag[er]s]C messag*er*s
3981 hi*m*]T he*m*
3993 [now þi rede]]F ⟨now þi rede⟩
4003 cumis]G cu*m*is
4024 his moder]*copied twice in* C.
4027 liue]C luue
4055 auyʒt]T anyʒt
4086 felles]F folles
4127 saide]G [saide]
4218 þat]G þ*a*t
4248 in]G iu
4254 pantifar]F pautifar
4297 [of]]F ⟨of⟩
4298 samp[son was]]F samp⟨son was⟩. Similarly, all the [ ] in F, 11.4299,
   4329-31 should be ⟨ ⟩.
4348 priuete]G p*r*iuete
4355 lauerd]G lau*er*d
4365 lente]T leute
4424 ye]G þe
4434 maister]T maistir
4464 dreme]G drem
4466 bouʒe]T bowʒe
4482 l[i]u*er*id]G liu*er*d
4484 p*r*isou*n*]T p*r*isou*n*d
4493 me]T ine
4494 rau*m*son]T rau*n*son
4505 þat]G þ*a*t
4506 is]G es
4508 hert]G herte. þat]G þ*a*t
4510 nouer]T neuer
4513 saghe]F sagh
4568 þai*m*]G þ*a*m
4569 ban]F bane
4585 pla]T plas
4596 fat]G fac
4627 Qu[e]*n*]C Qu*e*n
4629 þat]G þ*a*t
4668 asseuer]T assener
4729 Lauerding*es*]C Lau*er*ding*es*
4731 Forder worþely]T For derworþely
4751 he]G be
4752 hait]C hatt
4785 Wheþon]T Whepen
4821 hait]C hatt
4829 kingriche]T kyngriche

4843 hit]T but
4861 Qu[e]n]C Q*ue*n
4990 cuu*n*and]C cu*n*nand
4991   "   "
5000 þar]C þair
5022 elles]G ellis
5024 *gra*untt]G grau*n*tt
5058 sitt]C sett
5067 slayn]G slay*n*
5095 wiif]G wijf
5114 his]G sal his
5118 beniamin]G beniamyn
5220 þat]G þ*a*t
5225 yare]F þare
5280 sold]G sald
5287 is]C es
5305 [his aghen in]]C ⟨his aghen in⟩
5342 bigann]G bigam
5370 to ȝepe]F so ȝepe
5382 þat]G þ*a*t
5420 þaire]C þare
5529 Fitou]G Fiton
5547 godd]G god
5553 wi*mm*en]G wi*m*en
5557, 5558 wi*m*men]G wi*m*nen
5623 kingis]T kyngis
5633 fetche]T fecche
5638 se[r]uis]C s*er*uis
5657 branch]G brau*n*ch
5662 þat] G þ*a*t
5756 lauerd]G lau*er*d
5765 Lauerd]G Lau*er*d
5770 takins]G taknis
5781 Of]T Os
5821 mightin]G mihtin
5851 hand]G ha*n*d
5874 his]F þis
5889 neddir]G nedd*ir*
5957 al]G all
6018 suel]F snel
6042 non]G nan
6098 now]G nou
6101 MS C *does not repeat* had, *as Morris' note states, but* MS G *does,*
      hadd]G hadd had.
6154 numb*er*]G nunb*er*
6156 or [ox]]G ox
6167 wi*th* me]T wi*th*ine
6173 he]T be
6235 vs]G us
6251 *The first* shal *is cancelled in* T.
6287 quite]C quitte

6303   aron]G aran
6332   water]G wat*er*
6352   wa*t*er]G wat*er*
6397   þat]G þ*a*t
6400   were]F ware
6491   oþer]C eþer
6530   ȝe]G þe
6610   ȝe]G þe
6611   putis]G pittis
6646   it]*om.* G.
6685   lechyng]C leching
6696   þen]T þe*n*n
6697   Nedis]G Medis
6734   mightin]G mihtin
6744   oþer]G oþer
6747   grubband *correct in* G. *Not* grulband *as in Morris' note.*
6758   dubbil *correct in* G. *Not* dulbil *as Morris' note states.*
6783   þat]G þ*a*t
6796   leue]T lene
6813   forbirths]G forbirthis
6814   dwel[le]]F dwel⟨le⟩
6819   ȝou]F þou
6864   prophesi]G pr*o*phesi
6866   cristes]T cristis
6896   aaro*n*]C aaron
6913   Quen]C Que*n*
6916   wes *does not appear in* C, *as Morris states. The scribe first wrote* be es, *altered this to* he es, *then crossed it out and re-wrote* he es.
6955   still]T stille
6965   þat]G þaii
6996   ay]F ar
6997   Saturnens]T Saturneus
7094   wal[d] ha]C *originally had* wal ha, *altered by a later hand to* wald haf.
7157   late]C lete
7162   soghte]G soght
7219-22   *The alterations in a later hand are as follows:*
    7219   þi]C erased. þe]C hi*m*
    7220   þou]C he
    7221   þou]C he
    7222   þou]C hoo
7228   priuetes]C pr*i*uetes
7251   fleȝe]T sleȝe
7269   left]C lelft
7278   wengaunce]G wengance
7281   oft]G ofte
7312   no]C na
7316   ȝe]G þe
7339   þat]G þ*a*t
7342   godd]G god
7363   ȝe]F þe
7377   king]T kyng

7399 [Enoynted]]C *written in a later hand.*
7401 þoure]T þouȝe
7443 þat]C þat
7462 þat]G þat
7463 queþer]G queþer
7488 grace]G grace
7495 is]G es
7507 ren[d]]C *originally* rent, *changed in a later hand to* rend.
7519 fotte]F fottes
7535 mi]G my
7546 men]G man
7614 at]C þat
7625 hody]F body
7649 [wha]]C who *is inserted in a later hand.*
7659 [þi]s]C <þi>s. So also 1.7660 <And>, 7661 ⟨þer⟩.
7731 him]C him
7745 gleyne]T gleyue
7746 resceyne]T resceyue
7755 sle]G fle
7778 þei]C þai
7785 priuelie]C priuelic
7792 gunen]G guuen
7826 þat]C þat
7833 waites]C wattes
7840 nam]C name
7843 [and]]F &
7851 Efrom]T Esrom
7857 boȝ]T boz
7858 is]C es.
7859 cast]T tast
7883 du[ȝti]]F du⟨ȝti⟩
7900 letter]F letter
7902 hem]F him
7908 þar]G þai
7926 t wert]F thwert
7932 what]G quat
7946 cum]G cum
7989 lonesomly]T louesomly
7997 þat]G þat
8031 ware]F were. a]T o.
8032 thousande]F thonsande
8034 greue]T grene
8075 þat]C þat
8087 Crumpled]C Crumpeld
8110 All]C Al
8131 þe]T þei
8150 þat]C þat
8174 And]G All
8175 þal]F þat
8195 pauyl*i*on]F pauyloun
8202 processioune]G proscessioune

8203   þe]T þei
8214   ls]T is
8221   // *in left margin of* T.
8255   þat]G þat
8275   þe]G þa
8283   alle]F atte. pat]G pat
8297   kyng]F king.
8323 sa]F sal
8335   womman]G womman. ȝonge]G ȝong.
8363   þat]G þat
8365   siþen]G siþen
8407   þen]F þen
8438   clilde]F childe
8457   medicine]C medecine. queþer]G queþer.
8459   þat]G þat
8465   þat]C þat. maist]F mast
8485   þat]G þat
8506   in]G in
8542   werld]G world
8559   þat]C þat
8577   þat]G þat
8597   þa]G þai. na]G ne.
8613   stiffe]T stille
8638   þede]T dede
8733   queþer] F queþer
8777   puruaid]G puruaid
8804   mengid]G menged
8816   quantite]G quantite
8831   þat]G þat
8848   þat]G þat
8872   þat]G þat
8883   *There is a paragraph mark before this line in* C.
8895   chance]C chaunce
8950   olyne]T olyue
9024   womman]G womman
9040   and]G and
9163   orias]F ozias
9204   [þan]]F ⟨þan⟩
9228   tell]G telle

BIBLIOGRAPHY

PRIMARY SOURCES

AELFRIC. *Homilies of Aelfric*. Ed. John C. Pope. London: Oxford University Press, 1967-8. EETS OS 259, 260.
———. *Sermones Catholics, or Homilies of Aelfric*. Ed. Benjamin Thorpe. London: Aelfric Society, 1844.
ANDREW OF WYNTOUN. *The Original Chronicle of Andrew of Wyntoun*. Ed. F. J. Amours. Edinburgh and London: William Blackwood, 1903-1914.
AQUINAS, THOMAS. *Summa Theologica*. 60 vols. Cambridge: Blackfriars, 1964-6.
ARISTOTLE. *On the Heavens*. Trans. W. K. C. Guthrie. London: Heinemann, 1953.
ARNGART, Olof, ed. *The Middle English Genesis and Exodus*. Lund: C. W.K. Gleerup, 1968. *Lund Studies in English*, 36.
AUGUSTINE. *Confessiones. PL* XXXII.
———. *De Civitate Dei contra Paganos*. Ed. J. E. C. Welldon. London: SPCK, 1924.
———. *De Genesi ad Litteram. PL* XXXIV.
———. *De Genesi ad Litteram Imperfectus Liber. PL* XXXIV.
———. *De Genesi contra Manichaeos. PL* XXXIV.
———. *Quaestiones in Heptateuchum. PL* XXXIV.
BACON, Roger. *The Opus Majus of Roger Bacon*. 2 vols. Philadelphia: University of Pennsylvania Press, 1928.
BEDE. *Hexaemeron. PL* XCI.
———. *In Pentateuchum Commentarii. PL* XCI.
BENNETT, J.A.W. and G.V. SMITHERS. *Early Middle English Verse and Prose*. 2nd ed. Oxford: Clarendon Press, 1968.
BLAKE, N.F. *Middle English Religious Prose*. London: Edward Arnold, 1972.
BLOCK, K.S., ed. *Ludus Coventriae*. London: Oxford University Press, 1922. EETS ES 120.
BLUNT, John Henry, ed. *The Myroure of oure Ladye*. London: N. Trübner, 1873. EETS ES 19.
BOAS, Marcus, ed. *Disticha Catonis*. Amsterdam: North-Holland, 1952.
BONNARD, Jean. "Monologue de la reine d'Égypte dans le poème biblique de Malkaraume", in *Mélanges de philologie romane et d'histoire littéraire offerts à M. Maurice Wilmotte*. Paris: Honoré Champion, 1910. Pp. 49-56.
BONNARDOT, F. "Fragments d'une traduction de la Bible en vers français", *Romania*, XVI (1887), 177-213.
BRANDL, A. and O. ZIPPEL. *Mittelenglische Sprach-und Literaturproben*. Berlin: Weidmannsche Buchhandlung, 1917.
British Library, MS Harley 3375, fols. 140-9.
BROWN, Carleton, ed. *Religious Lyrics of the XIVth Century*. 2nd ed. rev'd by G.V. Smithers. Oxford: Clarendon Press, 1952.
BRUNNER, Karl, ed. "Zwei Gedichte aus der Handschrift Trinity College, Cambridge 323 (B.14.39)", *Englische Studien*, LXX (1935), 221-243.
BUDGE, E.A. Wallis, ed. *The Book of the Cave of Treasures*. London: Religious Tract Society, 1927.
BURCHARD, Christoph. *Untersuchungen zu Joseph und Aseneth*. Tübingen: J.C.B. Mohr, 1965. Wissenschaftliche Untersuchungen zum Neuen Testament, 8.

CHARLES, R.H., ed. *The Apocrypha and Pseudepigrapha of the Old Testament in English.* 2 vols. Oxford: Clarendon Press, 1913.
———, ed. *The Book of Jubilees.* London: Adam and Charles Black, 1902.
CHAUCER, Geoffrey. *The Works of Geoffrey Chaucer.* Ed. F.N. Robinson. 2nd ed. Boston: Houghton Mifflin, 1957.
DALY, Saralyn Ruth. *The Historye of the Patriarks.* Diss. Ohio State, 1950.
DAVIS, Norman, ed. *Non-Cycle Plays and Fragments.* London: Oxford University Press, 1970. EETS SS 1.
DAY, Mabel, ed. *The English Text of the Ancrene Riwle.* London: Oxford University Press, 1952. EETS OS 225.
———, ed. *The Wheatley Manuscript.* London: Oxford University Press, 1921. EETS OS 155.
DEGUILLEVILLE, Guillaume de. *The Pilgrimage of the Life of Man.* Trans. John Lydgate. Ed. F.J. Furnivall. London: Kegan Paul, 1899-1904. EETS ES 77, 83, 92.
DEIMLING, Hermann, ed. *The Chester Plays.* London: Kegan Paul, 1893. EETS ES 62.
D'EVELYN, Charlotte. "The Middle-English Metrical Version of the Revelations of Methodius; with a Study of the Influence of Methodius in Middle-English Writings", *PMLA,* XXXIII (1918), 135-203.
——— and Anna J. MILL, eds. *The South English Legendary.* 3 vols. London: Oxford University Press, 1956-9. EETS OS 235, 236, 244.
DICKENS, Bruce and R. M. WILSON, eds. *Early Middle English Texts.* London: Bowes & Bowes, 1951.
DÜWELL, Henning, ed. *Eine altfranzösische Übersetzung des Elucidarium.* Munich: Wilhelm Fink, 1974. *Beiträge zur romanischen Philologie des Mittelalters,* VII.
ELLIS, F. S., ed. *The Golden Legend.* I. 1900; rpt. New York: AMS Press, 1973.
EMERSON, Oliver Farrar, ed. *A Middle English Reader.* New and rev'd ed. London: Macmillan, 1924.
ENGLAND, George and Alfred W. POLLARD, eds. *The Towneley Plays.* London: Kegan Paul, 1897. EETS ES 71.
ETHERIDGE, J.W., ed. *The Targums of Onkelos and Jonathan Ben Uzziel on the Pentateuch.* Vol. 1. London: Longman, 1862.
EVRAT. *Genèse.* MS BN fr. 12,456.
FOSTER, Frances A., ed. *A Stanzaic Life of Christ.* London: Oxford University Press, 1926. EETS OS 166.
FREEDMAN, H. and Maurice SIMON, eds. *Midrash Rabbah.* London: Soncino Press, 1939.
FURNIVALL, F.J., ed. *Adam Davy's Five Dreams About Edward II.* London: N. Trubner, 1878. EETS OS 69.
GEOFFROI DE PARIS. *La Bible des sept états du monde.* MS BN fr. 1526.
Glossa Ordinaria. PL CXIII.
GOLLANCZ, Israel, ed. *Cleanness.* London: Oxford University Press, 1921.
GOWER, John. *Confessio Amantis,* in *The Complete Works of John Gower.* Oxford: Clarendon Press, 1901.
GROSSETESTE, Robert. *Le Château d'amour de Robert Grosseteste Évêque de Lincoln.* Ed. J. Murray. Paris: Champion, 1918.
HAHN, A. "Zu Pricke of Conscience v. 7651-7686", *Archiv,* CVI (1901), 349-50.
HARING, N. "The Creation and Creator of the World According to Thierry of Chartres and Clarenbaldus of Arras", *Archives d'histoire doctrinale et littéraire du moyen âge* (1955), 137-216.
HELGASON, Jón. *The Arna Magnaean Manuscript 674A, 4to. Elucidarium.* Copenhagen: Ejnar Munksgaard, 1957. *Manuscripta Islandica,* 4.
HERMAN DE VALENCIENNES. *La Bible von Herman de Valenciennes.* II Ed. Otto Moldenhauer. Greifswald: Hans Adler, 1914.

——. "Herman de Valenciennes, *Bible de Sapience*", in Karl BARTSCH, ed. *Chrestomathie de l'ancien français*. 10th ed. Leipzig: F.C.W. Vogel, 1910. Pp. 71-6.

——. *La Bible*. MS University of Chicago H.27.B.6.12.

HEUSER, W., ed. *Die Kildare-Gedichte*. Bonn: P. Hanstein, 1904.

HIGDEN, Ranulph. *Polychronicon Ranulphi Higden*. Trans, John Trevisa. Ed. Churchill Babington. London: Longmans, 1869.

HILL, Betty. "The Fifteenth Century Prose *Legend of the Cross before Christ*", *Medium Ævum*, XXXIV (1965), 203-22.

Historical Manuscripts Commission. 6th report. Appendix. London: Eyre and Spottiswoode, 1877. Pp. 319-20.

HOLT, Robert, ed. *The Ormulum*. 2 vols. Oxford: Clarendon Press, 1878.

HONORIUS AUGUSTODUNENSIS. *De Imagine Mundi*. PL CLXXII.

——. *Elucidarium* in Yves Lefèvre, *L'Elucidarium et les lucidaires*. Paris: de Boccard, 1954. *Bibliothèque des Écoles françaises d'Athènes et de Rome*, fasc. 180.

HORSTMANN, C., ed. *Altenglische Legenden. Neue Folge*. Heilbronn: Gebr. Henniger, 1881.

——, ed. *The Early South-English Legendary*. London: N. Trubner, 1887. EETS OS 87.

——, ed. *The Minor Poems of the Vernon Manuscript*. London: Kegan Paul, 1892. EETS OS 98.

——, ed. "Nachträge zu den Legenden", *Archiv*, LXXVI (1887), 459-70.

——, ed. "Questiones by-twene the Maister of Oxenford and his Clerke", *Englische Studien*, VIII (1884-5), 284-7.

——, ed. *Sammlung Altenglischer Legenden*. Heilbronn: Gebr. Henninger, 1878.

HUGH OF ST. VICTOR. *Adnotationes Elucidatoriae in Pentateuchon*. PL CLXXV.

——. *De Arca Noe Morali*. PL CLXXVI.

——. *De Arca Noe Mystica*. PL CLXXVI.

ISIDORE. *Etymologiarum*. Ed. W. M. Lindsay. 1911; rpt. Oxford: Clarendon Press, 1966.

JACOBUS A VORAGINE. *Legenda Aurea*. Ed. Th. Graesse. Lipsiae: Impensis Librariae Arnoldianae, 1850.

JEROME. *Liber Hebraicarum Quaestionum in Genesim*. PL XXIII.

JONES, J. Morris and John Rhys, ed. *The Elucidarium and other Tracts in Welsh*. Oxford: Clarendon Press, 1894.

JOSEPHUS. *History of the Jewish War Against the Romans*. Trans. H. StJ. Thackeray. London: William Heinemann, 1930.

——. *Jewish Antiquities*. Trans. H. StJ. Thackeray. London: William Heinemann, 1930.

KALÉN, Herbert, ed. *A Middle English Metrical Paraphrase of the Old Testament*. I. *Göteborgs Högskolas Årsskrift*, XXVIII (1922).

KANE, George, ed. *Piers Plowman: The A Version*. London: Athlone Press, 1960.

KEMBLE, John M. *The Dialogue of Salomon and Saturnus*. London: Ælfric Society, 1848.

KER, N. R. *Facsimile of British Museum MS Harley 2253*. London: Oxford University Press, 1965. EETS OS 255.

KRAPP, George Philip, ed. *The Junius Manuscript*. New York: Columbia University Press, 1931.

LAZAR, Moshé. "'La Légende de 'l'Arbre de Paradis' ou 'bois de la croix'", *Zeitschrift für romanische Philologie*, LXXVI (1960), 34-63.

LITTLEHALES, Henry, ed. *The Prymer or Lay Folks Prayer Book*. London: Kegan Paul, 1895. EETS OS 105.

LUMIANSKY, R. M. and David MILLS, eds. *The Chester Mystery Cycle*. London: Oxford University Press, 1974. EETS SS 3.

LYDGATE, John. *Lydgate's Fall of Princes.* Ed. Henry Bergen. 4 vols. London: Oxford University Press, 1924-7.

McCARTHY, B. *The Codex Palatino Vaticanus No. 830,* Royal Irish Academy, Todd Lecture Series, Vol. III. Dublin: Royal Irish Academy, 1892.

MacCRACKEN, H. N. "Lydgatiana", *Archiv,* CXXXI (1913), 40-63.

———, ed. "The Storie of Asneth", *JEGP,* IX (1910), 224-64.

MACÉ DE LA CHARITÉ. *La Bible de Macé de la Charité.* Vol. I ed. J. R. Smeets. Vol. IV ed. H. C. M. Krabben. Leiden: Universitaire Pers Leiden, 1967, 1964.

MALAN, S. C., ed. *The Book of Adam and Eve.* London: Williams and Norgate, 1882.

MALKARAUME, Jehan. *Bible.* MS BN fr. 903.

MANDEVILLE, John. *Mandeville's Travels.* Ed. Malcolm Letts. 2 vols. London: Hakluyt Society, 1953.

———. *The Bodley Version of Mandeville's Travels.* Ed. M. C. Seymour. London: Oxford University Press, 1963. EETS OS 253.

MENNER, Robert J., ed. *The Poetical Dialogues of Solomon and Saturn.* New York: Modern Language Association of America, 1941. Modern Language Association of America Monograph Series 13.

MEYER, Paul. "Notice de MS Egerton 2710 du Musée Britannique. i. Poème anglo-normand sur l'Ancien Testament", *Bulletin de la Société des Anciens Textes français,* XV (1889), 72-97.

———. "Notice et extraits d'un fragment de poème biblique composé en Angleterre", *Romania,* XXXVI (1907), 184-202.

———. "Notice sur deux anciens manuscrits français ayant appartenu au Marquis de la Clayette", *Notices et extraits des manuscrits de la Bibliothèque Nationale et autres bibliothèques* XXXIII, Part 1 (1890), 71-5.

———. "Notices sur quelques manuscrits français de la Bibliothèque Phillipps a Cheltenham", *Notices et extraits des manuscrits de la Bibliothèque Nationale et autres bibliothèques,* XXXIV, Part 1 (1891), 198-211.

———. "Notice sur la *Bible des sept états du monde* de Geufroi de Paris", *Notices et extraits des manuscrits de la Bibliothèque Nationale et autres bibliothèques,* XXXIX, Part 1 (1909), 260, 273-4.

———, ed. *Recueil d'anciens textes.* Paris: F. Vieweg, 1877.

MEYER, WILHELM. "Die Geschichte des Kreuzholzes vor Christus", *Abhandlungen der Philosophisch-Philologischen Classe der Königlich Bayerischen Akademie der Wissenschaften,* XVI (1881), 101-166.

———. "Vita Adae et Evae", *Abhandlungen der Philosophisch-Philologischen Classe der Königlich Bayerischen Akademie der Wissenschaften,* XIV (1898), 185-250.

MIRK, John. *Mirk's Festial.* Ed. Theodor Erbe. London: Kegan Paul, 1905. EETS ES 46.

MORRIS, Richard, ed. *Ayenbite of Inwit.* London: N. Trubner, 1866. EETS OS 23.

———. ed. *Cursor Mundi.* 1874-93; rpt. London: Oxford University Press, 1961-6. EETS OS 57, 59, 62, 66, 68, 99, 101.

———. *Legends of the Holy Rood.* London: N. Trubner, 1871. EETS OS 46.

———. ed. *The Pricke of Conscience.* Berlin: A. Asher, 1863.

———. and Walter W. Skeat, eds. *Specimens of Early English.* 2nd ed. Oxford: Clarendon Press, 1889.

MOZLEY, J. H., ed. "The Vita Adae", *Journal of Theological Studies,* XXX (1929), 121-49.

"Nachträge zu den Legenden", *Archiv,* LXXIV (1885), 327-65.

NAPIER, Arthur S., ed. *History of the Holy Rood-Tree.* London: Kegan Paul, 1894. EETS OS 103.

———, ed. *Iacob and Ioseph.* Oxford: Clarendon Press, 1916.

NORRIS, Edwin, ed. and trans. *The Ancient Cornish Drama.* 2 vols. Oxford: Oxford University Press, 1859.

Northern Homilies. MSS BL Harley 4196 fol. 107r-107v, and BL Addit. 22, 283, fol. 5r.

OHLANDER, Urban, ed. *A Middle English Metrical Paraphrase of the Old Testament.* II *Gothenburg Studies in English,* V (1955), 1-112.

————, ed. *A Middle English Metrical Paraphrase of the Old Testament.* III, *Gothenburg Studies in English,* XI (1960), 1-131.

————, ed. *A Middle English Metrical Paraphrase of the Old Testament.* IV *Gothenburg Studies in English,* XVI (1963).

PANTON, G. A. and D. DONALDSON, ed. *The Gest Hystoriale of the Destruction of Troy.* 1869; rpt London: Oxford University Press, 1968. EETS OS 39.

PERSON, Henry A., ed. *Cambridge Middle English Lyrics.* Seattle: University of Washington Press, 1962.

PETRUS COMESTOR. *Historia Scholastica. PL* CXCVIII.

PETRUS LOMBARDUS. *Sententiarum. PL* CXCII.

PICKERING, F. P., ed. *The Anglo-Norman Text of the Holkham Bible Picture Book.* Oxford: Blackwell, 1971. *Anglo-Norman Texts* XXIII.

PRIOR, O. H., ed. *Caxton's Mirrour of the World.* London: Kegan Paul, 1913. EETS ES 110.

————, ed. *L'Image du monde de Maître Gossouin.* Lausanne and Paris: Payot, 1913.

REMIGIUS OF AUXERRE. *Commentarius in Genesim. PL* CXXXI.

REYNAUD, Georges, ed. *"Elucidarium", Revue des langues romanes,* XXXIII (1889), 217-50.

ROSENBAUM, M. and A. M. SILBERMANN, eds. *Pentateuch with Targum Onkelos, Haphtaroth and Rashi's Commentary.* 5 vols. New York: Hebrew Publishing Co., n.d.

ROSS, Woodburn O., ed. *Middle English Sermons.* London: Oxford University Press, 1940. EETS OS 209.

SAJAVAARA, Kari, ed. *The Middle English Translations of Robert Grosseteste's Château d'amour.* Helsinki: Société Néophilologique, 1967. *Mémoires de la Société Néophilologique de Helsinki,* XXXII.

SAMPSON, G., ed. *Cambridge Book of Prose and Verse.* Cambridge: Cambridge University Press, 1924.

SARGENT, Michael G. "The McGill University Fragment of the 'Southern Assumption'", *Mediaeval Studies,* XXXVI (1974), 186-98.

SCHMITT, Friedrich, ed. *Die Mittelenglische Version des Elucidarium des Honorius Augustodunensis.* Burghausen: W. Trinkl, 1909.

SKEAT, Walter W., ed. *The Vision of William Concerning Piers the Plowman.* 2 vols. London: Oxford University Press, 1886.

SMALL, John, ed. *English Metrical Homilies from Manuscripts of the Fourteenth Century.* 1862; rpt New York: AMS Press, 1973.

SMALLEY, Beryl. "A Commentary on the Hexaemeron by Henry of Ghent", *Recherches de théologie ancienne et médiévale,* XX (1953), 60-101.

SMITH, Lucy Toulmin, ed. *A Commonplace Book of the Fifteenth Century.* London: Trubner, 1886.

————, ed. *York Plays.* 1885; rpt New York: Russell and Russell, 1963.

South English Legendary, Temporale. MS Bodl. Eng. Poet. A. 1.

STEUER, Wilhelm. "Die altfranzösische 'Histoire de Joseph'", *Romanische Forschungen,* XIV (1903), 227-410.

STOKES, Whitley, ed. and trans. *The Creation of the World.* London: Williams and Norgate, 1864.

SUCHIER, Hermann. *Denkmäler provenzalischer Literatur und Sprache.* I. Halle: Max Niemeyer, 1883.

Traduction anonyme de la Bible entière. MS BN fr. 763, fols. 211-77.

Traduction anonyme de l'Ancien Testament. MS BL Egerton 2710, fols. 1-97.

TRETHEWEY, William Hilliard, ed. *La Petite philosophe.* Oxford: Basil Blackwell, 1939. *Anglo-Norman Texts* I.

ULLMANN, J. "Studien zu Richard Rolle de Hampole", *Englische Studien,* VII (1884), 415-72.
WEATHELEY, Edward H., ed. *Speculum Sacerdotale.* London: Oxford University Press, 1936. EETS OS 200.
WILLIAM OF SHOREHAM. *The Poems of William of Shoreham.* Ed. M. Konrath. London: Kegan Paul, 1902. EETS ES 86.
WRIGHT, Thomas, ed. *The Book of the Knight of LaTour-Landry.* London: N. Trübner, 1868. EETS OS 21.
ZUPITZA, Julius. *Alt-und mittelenglisches Übungsbuch.* 12th ed. Wien und Leipzig, 1922.

SECONDARY SOURCES

ADAMSON, J. H. "Milton and the Creation", *JEGP,* LXI (1962), 756-78.
ALLEN, Don Cameron. *The Legend of Noah.* Urbana: University of Illinois Press, 1949. *Illinois Studies in Language and Literature,* XXXIII, nos. 3-4.
ANDERSON, M. D. *Drama and Imagery in English Medieval Churches.* Cambridge: Cambridge University Press, 1963.
AREND, Zygfryd Marjan. "Linking in *Cursor Mundi*", *Transactions of the Philological Society* (1925-30), 200-59.
BARB, A. A. "Cain's Murder-Weapon and Samson's Jawbone of an Ass", *Journal of the Warburg and Courtauld Institutes,* XXXV (1972), 386-9.
BARON, Roger. "Hugues de Saint-Victor: contribution à un nouvel examen de son œuvre", *Traditio,* XV (1959), 223-97.
BARROW, G. W. S. "The Anglo-Scottish Border", *Northern History,* I (1966), 21-42.
BARTH, Curt. *Der Wortschatz des Cursor Mundi.* Diss. Königsberg, 1903.
BEICHNER, Paul E. "La Bible versifiée de Jehan Malkaraume et l'*Aurora*", trans. Paul Mertens, *Moyen âge,* LXI (1955), 63-78.
———. "The *Cursor Mundi* and Petrus Riga", *Speculum,* XXIV (1949), 239-250.
———. "The Old French Verse *Bible* of Macé de la Charité, a Translation of the *Aurora*", *Speculum,* XXII (1947), 226-39.
BERGER, Samuel. *La Bible française au moyen âge.* Paris: Imprimerie Nationale, 1884.
BLISS, A. J. "The Auchinleck Life of Adam and Eve", *Review of English Studies,* new ser., VII (1956), 406-9.
BONNARD, Jean. *Les Traductions de la Bible en vers français au moyen âge.* Paris: Imprimerie Nationale, 1884.
BONNELL, John Kester. "Cain's Jaw Bone", *PMLA,* XXXIX (1924), 140-6.
BORLAND, Lois. *The Cursor Mundi and Herman's Bible.* Diss. Chicago, 1929.
———. "Herman's *Bible* and the *Cursor Mundi*", *Studies in Philology,* XXX (1933), 427-44.
BOSSUAT, Robert. *Manuel bibliographique de la littérature française du moyen âge.* Melun: Librairie D'Argences, 1951. 2 Supplements.
BRADLEY, H. "The Caedmonian *Genesis*", in *Essays and Studies by Members of the English Association,* VI, 7-29. Oxford: Clarendon Press, 1920.
BRASWELL, Laurel Nichols. *The South English Legendary Collection: A Study in Middle English Religious Literature of the Thirteenth and Fourteenth Centuries.* Diss. Toronto, 1964.
BRIQUET, C. M. *Les Filigranes.* 4 vols. Genève: A. Jullien, 1907.
BROWN, Carleton. "The *Cursor Mundi* and the Southern Passion", *Modern Language Notes,* XXVI (1911), 15-8.
———. "Mulier est Hominis Confusio", *Modern Language Notes,* XXXV (1920), 479-82.
——— and Rossell Hope ROBBINS. *The Index of Middle English Verse.* New York: Columbia University Press, 1943. *Supplement.* Lexington: University of Kentucky Press, 1965.

BUEHLER, Philip. "The *Cursor Mundi* and Herman's *Bible* — Some Additional Parallels", *Studies in Philology*, LXI (1964), 485-99.

CABROL, Fernand and Henri LECLERCQ, eds. *Dictionnaire d'archéologie chrétienne et de liturgie*. Paris: Letouzey et Ané, 1924-50.

Cambridge History of the Bible. Vol. I ed. P. R. Ackroyd and C. V. Evans. Vol. II ed. G. W. H. Lampe. Cambridge: Cambridge University Press, 1969-70.

CASSIDY, Frederick G. "The Edged Teeth" in *Studies in Old English Literature in Honor of Arthur G. Brodeur*. Ed. Stanley B. Greenfield. Oregon: University of Oregon Books, 1963. Pp. 227-36.

COCKERELL, Sydney C., ed. *A Book of Old Testament Illustrations of the Middle of the Thirteenth Century*. Cambridge: Cambridge University Press, 1927.

COFFMAN, George R. "Old Age from Horace to Chaucer. Some Literary Affinities and Adventures of an Idea", *Speculum*, IX (1934), 249-77.

COHN, Norman. *The Pursuit of the Millenium*. Rev. ed. New York: Oxford University Press, 1970.

COLI, Edoardo. *Il Paradiso terrestre dantesco*. Firenze: G. Carnesecchi, 1897.

COOMARASWAMY, Ananda K. *Art Bulletin*, XXIV (1942), 383-4.

COOKE, Daniel. "Euhemerism: A Mediaeval Interpretation of Classical Paganism", *Speculum*, II (1927), 396-410.

DAREAU, Margaret Grace and Angus MCINTOSH. "A Dialect Word in Some West Midland Manuscripts of the *Prick of Conscience*", *Edinburgh Studies in English and Scots*. Ed. A. J. Aitken, Angus McIntosh and Herman Pálsson. London: Longmans, 1971. Pp. 20-6.

DEANESLY, Margaret. *The Lollard Bible*. Cambridge: Cambridge University Press, 1920.

DICKENS, Bruce. "Gerard as a Goblin Name", *Times Literary Supplement* (Feb. 1, 1941), 55.

DRIVER, S. R. *The Book of Genesis*. London: Methuen, 1904.

DRONKE, Peter. *Poetic Individuality in the Middle Ages*. Oxford: Clarendon Press, 1970.

DUNSTAN, A. C. "The Middle English *Canticum de Creatione* and the Latin *Vita Adae et Evae*", *Anglia*, LV (1931), 431-42.

DUSTOOR, P. E. "Legends of Lucifer in Early English and in Milton", *Anglia*, LIV (1930), 213-68.

DWYER, R. A. "Asenath of Egypt in Middle English", *Medium Ævum*, XXXIX (1970), 118-22.

EMERSON, Oliver F. "Legends of Cain, Especially in Old and Middle English", *PMLA*, XXI (1906), 831-929.

———. "A Note on the M. E. Cleanness", *Modern Language Review*, X (1915), 373-5.

EVANS, J. M. "Microcosmic Adam", *Medium Ævum*, XXXV (1966), 38-42.

EVANS, M. W. *Medieval Drawings*. London: Paul Hamlyn, 1969.

FAUSBØLL, Else. *A Study of the Phonology and Accidence of the Fairfax Manuscript of the Cursor Mundi*. Diss. Manchester, 1954.

FAVERTY, Frederic E. "Legends of Joseph in Old and Middle English", *PMLA*, XLIII (1928), 79-104.

———. "The Story of Joseph and Potiphar's Wife in Mediaeval Literature", *Harvard Studies and Notes in Philology and Literature*, XIII (1931), 81-127.

FÖRSTER, Max. "Adams Erschaffung und Namengebung", *Archiv*, XI (1908), 477-529.

FOWLER, David C. *The Bible in Early English Literature*. Seattle and London: University of Washington Press, 1976.

FRIEND, Albert C. "Sampson, David and Salomon in the Parson's Tale", *Modern Philology*, XLVI (1948), 117-21.

FURNIVALL, F. J. "How Cato was a Paynym and a Christian Too", *Notes and Queries*, 4th ser., II (1868), 176.

GARVIN, Katherine. "A Note on Noah's Wife", *Modern Language Notes*, XLIX (1934), 88-90.

GEROULD, Gordon Hall. *Saints' Legends*. Boston and New York: Houghton Mifflin, 1916.

GIAMATTI, A. Bartlett. *The Earthly Paradise and the Renaissance Epic*. Princeton: Princeton University Press, 1966.

GLUNZ, H. H. *History of the Vulgate in England from Alcuin to Roger Bacon*. Cambridge: Cambridge University Press, 1933.

GOLLANCZ, Israel. *The Caedmon Manuscript*. London: Oxford University Press, 1927.

GRAF, Arturo. *Miti, leggende e superstizioni del Medio Evo*. Torino: Giovanni Chiantore, 1925.

HAENISCH, Dr. "Inquiry into the Sources of the *Cursor Mundi*", in Richard MORRIS, ed., *Cursor Mundi*. VI London: Kegan Paul, 1892. EETS OS 99. Pp. 1-56.

HAMILTON, G. L. "La Source d'un épisode de Baudouin de Sebourc", *Zeitschrift für romanische Philologie*, XXXVI (1912), 129-59.

HASSALL, W. O., ed. *The Holkham Bible Picture Book*. London: Dropmore Press, 1954.

HENDERSON, George. "Cain's Jaw-Bone", *Journal of the Warburg and Courtauld Institutes*, XXIV (1961), 108-114.

HOLTHAUSEN, F. "Zu dem mittelenglischen Gedicht *Cleanness*", *Archiv*, CVI (1901), 349.

HORRALL, Sarah M. "The *Cursor Mundi* Creation Story and Hugh of St. Victor", *Notes and Queries*, n. s. XXIII (1976), 99-100.

_____. "An Old French Source for the *Genesis* Section of *Cursor Mundi*", *Mediaeval Studies*, XL (1978), 361-73.

_____. "'A Schippe Behoues þe to Dight': Woven Arks of Noah in the Fourteenth Century", *Proceedings of the Sixth Annual Symposium of the Ottawa-Carleton Medieval-Renaissance Club*. Ottawa, 1978.

_____. "The London Thornton Manuscript: A New Collation", forthcoming in *Manuscripta*.

HÖRNING, Willy. *Die Schreibung der Hs. E des Cursor Mundi*. Diss. Friedrich-Wilhelms-Universität, Berlin, 1906.

HUPE, H. "*Cursor Mundi*", *Anglia Beiblatt*, I (1890-1), 133-6.

_____. "*Cursor Mundi*: Essay on the Manuscripts and Dialect" in Richard MORRIS, ed., *Cursor Mundi*. VII. 1893; rpt. London: Oxford University Press, 1962. EETS OS 101.

_____. "Zum Handschriftenverhältniss und zur Textkritik des *Cursor Mundi*", *Anglia*, XI (1889), 121-45.

JAMES, Montague Rhodes. *The Lost Apocrypha of the Old Testament*. London: SPCK, 1920.

JAUSS, Hans Robert, ed. *La Littérature didactique, allégorique et satirique*. Heidelberg: Carl Winter, 1970. *Grundriss der romanischen Literaturen des Mittelalters*, VI/1-2.

JONES, Gwyn. *A History of the Vikings*. London: Oxford University Press, 1968.

KAISER, Rolf. *Zur Geographie des mittelenglischen Wortschatzes*. 1937; rpt. New York: Johnson Reprint Corp., 1970. *Palaestra* 205.

KALUZA, Max. "Zu den Quellen und dem Handschriftenverhältniss des *Cursor Mundi*", *Englische Studien*, XII (1889), 451-8.

_____. "Zum Handschriftenverhältniss und zur Textkritik des *Cursor Mundi*", *Englische Studien*, XI (1888), 235-75.

KELLY, Henry Ansgar. "The Metamorphoses of the Eden Serpent during the Middle Ages and Renaissance", *Viator*, II (1971), 301-28.

KER, N. R. *Medieval Libraries of Great Britain*. 2nd ed. London: Royal Historical Society, 1964.

KING, R. W. "A Note on 'Sir Gawayn and the Green Knight' 2414ff", *Modern Language Review,* XXIX (1934), 435-6.

KIVIMAA, Kirsti. *"Bitwix and* in *Cursor Mundi",* in *Studies Presented to Tauno F. Mustanoja on the Occasion of his Sixtieth Birthday. Neuphilologische Mitteilungen,* LXXIII (1972), 134-42.

KOLVE, V. A. *The Play Called Corpus Christi.* Stanford: Stanford University Press, 1966.

KURATH, Hans, and Sherman M. KUHN, eds. *Middle English Dictionary.* Ann Arbor: University of Michigan Press, 1956-.

LAMBERTS, Jacob Justin. *The Dialect of Cursor Mundi (Cotton MS Vespasian A III).* Diss. Michigan, 1953.

————. "The Noah Story in *Cursor Mundi* (vv. 1625-1916)", *Mediaeval Studies,* XXIV (1962), 217-32.

LARSEN, Henning. *"Cursor Mundi* 1291" in *Philologica: The Malone Anniversary Studies.* Ed. Thomas A. Kirby and Henry Bosley Woolf. Baltimore: Johns Hopkins Press, 1949. Pp. 164-6.

————. "Origo Crucis" in *If by Your Art: Testament to Percival Hunt.* Lancaster, Pa.: University of Pittsburgh Press, 1948. Pp. 27-33.

LEGGE, M. Dominica. *Anglo-Norman in the Cloisters.* Edinburgh: Edinburgh University Press, 1950.

————. *Anglo-Norman Literature and its Background.* Oxford: Clarendon Press, 1963.

LETHABY, W. R. "The Painted Book of *Genesis* in the British Museum", *Archaeological Journal,* LXIX (1912), 88-111.

LEWIS, Jack P. *A Study of the Interpretation of Noah and the Flood in Jewish and Christian Literature.* Leiden: E. J. Brill, 1968.

LUBAC, Henri de. *Exégèse médiévale.* Paris: Aubier 1959-62. *Théologie,* 41, 42, 59.

McCOLLEY, Grant. "Milton's Battle in Heaven and Rupert of Saint Heribert", *Speculum,* XVI (1941), 230-5.

McINTOSH, Angus. "A New Approach to Middle English Dialectology", *English Studies,* XLIV (1963), 1-11.

McNALLY, Robert E. *The Bible in the Early Middle Ages.* Westminster, Md.: The Newman Press, 1959. *Woodstock Papers,* No. 4.

MAGOUN, Francis P., Jr. "Chaucer's Ancient and Biblical World", *Mediaeval Studies,* XV (1953), 107-36.

MARDON, Ernest G. *The Narrative Unity of the Cursor Mundi.* Glasgow: William MacLellan, 1970.

MELLINKOFF, Ruth. *The Horned Moses in Medieval Art and Thought.* Berkeley: University of California Press, 1970.

MENNER, Robert J. "Two Notes on Mediaeval Euhemerism", *Speculum,* III (1928), 246-8.

MILL, Anna Jean. "Noah's Wife Again", *PMLA,* LVI (1941), 613-26.

MOORE, Samuel, Sanford Brown MEECH and Harold WHITEHALL. "Middle English Dialect Characteristics and Dialect Boundaries" in *Essays and Studies in English and Comparative Literature.* Ann Arbor: University of Michigan Press, 1935.

MURDOCH, Brian. "An Early Irish Adam and Eve: *Saltair na Rann* and the Traditions of the Fall", *Mediaeval Studies,* XXXV (1973), 146-77.

MURRAY, James A. H., ed. *A New English Dictionary on Historical Principles.* Oxford: Clarendon Press, 1888-1928.

OHLANDER, Urban. "Old French Parallels to a Middle English Metrical Paraphrase of the Old Testament", in *Contributions to English Syntax and Philology, Gothenburg Studies in English,* XIV, pp. 203-24.

OWST, G. R. *Literature and Pulpit in Medieval England.* Cambridge: Cambridge University Press, 1933.

PARENT, J. M. *La Doctrine de la création dans l'École de Chartres.* Paris: J. Vrin, 1938. *Publications de l'Institut d'études médiévales d'Ottawa,* VIII.

PATCH, H. R. *The Other World According to Descriptions in Medieval Literature.* Cambridge, Mass.: Harvard University Press, 1950.

PICKERING, O. S. "The *Temporale* Narratives of the *South English Legendary*", *Anglia*, XCI (1973), 425-55.

QUINN, Esther Casier. *The Quest of Seth for the Oil of Life.* Chicago: University of Chicago Press, 1962.

RABY, F. J. E. *A History of Christian-Latin Poetry.* 2nd ed. Oxford: Clarendon Press, 1953.

ROBBINS, Frank Egleston. *The Hexaemeral Literature.* Chicago: University of Chicago Press, 1912.

ROBINSON, F. N. "A Note on the Sources of the Old Saxon Genesis", *Modern Philology*, IV (1906), 389-96.

ROWLAND, Beryl. *Blind Beasts.* [Kent, Ohio]: Kent State University Press, 1971.

SAJAVAARA, Kari. "The Use of Robert Grosseteste's *Château d'amour* as a Source of the *Cursor Mundi*", *Neuphilologische Mitteilungen*, LXVIII (1967), 184-93.

SALZMAN, L. F. *Building in England down to 1540.* 1952; rpt. Oxford: Clarendon Press, 1967.

SCHAPIRO, Meyer. "Cain's Jaw-Bone that Did the First Murder", *Art Bulletin*, XXIV (1942), 205-12.

SEVERS, J. Burke, ed. *A Manual of the Writings in Middle English 1050-1500.* Vols. I and II. Hamden, Conn.: Archon Books, 1967, 1970.

SHARP, D. E. *Franciscan Philosophy at Oxford in the Thirteenth Century.* London: Oxford University Press, 1930.

SHERWIN, Oscar. "Art's Spring-Birth: the Ballad of *Iacob and Ioseph*", *Studies in Philology*, XLII (1945), 1-18.

SKEAT, Walter W. "Cain's Jaw-Bone", *Notes and Queries*, 6th ser., II (Aug. 21, 1880), 143.

——. "Lucifer", *Notes and Queries*, 3rd ser., XII (Aug. 10, 1867), 110.

SKINNER, John. *A Critical and Exegetical Commentary on Genesis.* Edinburgh: T. & T. Clark, 1912.

SMALLEY, Beryl. *English Friars and Antiquity in the Early Fourteenth Century.* Oxford: Basil Blackwell, 1960.

——. *The Study of the Bible in the Middle Ages.* 2nd ed. Oxford: Basil Blackwell, 1952.

SNOUFFER, Eugene J. *Verbal Syntax of Cursor Mundi (Cotton MS Vespasian A III).* Diss. North Carolina, 1971.

SPICQ, P. C. *Esquisse d'une histoire de l'exégèse latine au moyen âge.* Paris: J. Vrin, 1944. *Bibliothèque Thomiste*, XXVI.

STERN, Karen. "The London 'Thornton' Miscellany", *Scriptorium*, XXX (1976), 26-37, 201-218.

STRANDBERG, Otto. *The Rime-Vowels of Cursor Mundi.* Uppsala: Almqvist & Wiksells Boktryckeri, 1919.

THOMPSON, James Westfall. *The Medieval Library.* 1939; rpt. New York: Hafner, 1967.

THRUPP, Sylvia L. *The Merchant Class of Medieval London.* Ann Arbor: University of Michigan Press, 1962.

TRAPP, J. B. "Iconography of the Fall of Man", in C. A. Patrides, ed., *Approaches to Paradise Lost.* Toronto: University of Toronto Press, 1968. Pp. 223-65.

UTLEY, Francis Lee. "The One Hundred and Three Names of Noah's Wife", *Speculum*, XVI (1941), 426-52.

VACANT, A. et al., eds. *Dictionnaire de théologie catholique.* Paris: Letouzey et Ané, 1909-51.

VISING, Johan. *Anglo-Norman Language and Literature.* London: Oxford University Press, 1923.

VON RAD, Gerhard. *Genesis: A Commentary.* Trans. John H. Marks. London: S.C.M. Press, 1961.

WALSH, C.M. *The Doctrine of Creation*. London: T. Fisher Unwin, 1910.

WALTHER, Hans. *Proverbia, Sententiaeque Latinitatis Medii Aevi*. Göttingen: Vandenhoeck & Ruprecht, 1963-9.

WARNER, George, ed. *Queen Mary's Psalter*. London: Longmans, 1912.

WELLS, Minnie E. "The Age of Isaac at the Time of the Sacrifice", *Modern Language Notes*, LIV (1939), 579-82.

————. "The Structural Development of the *South English Legendary*", *JEGP*, XLI (1942), 320-44.

WHITE, T. H. *The Book of Beasts*. London: Jonathan Cape, 1954.

WHITING, Bartlett Jere. "Notes on the Fragmentary Fairfax Version of the *Disticha Catonis*", *Mediaeval Studies*, X (1948), 209-15.

———— and Helen Wescott WHITING. *Proverbs, Sentences, and Proverbial Phrases from English Writings Mainly before 1500*. Cambridge, Mass.: Harvard University Press, 1968.

WILLIAMS, Norman Powell. *The Ideas of the Fall and of Original Sin*. London: Longmans, Green, 1927.

WOLFSON, H. A. "The Meaning of *Ex Nihilo* in the Church Fathers, Arabic and Hebrew Philosophy and St. Thomas", in *Mediaeval Studies in Honor of Urban T. Holmes, Jr. and Alex J. Denomy*. Cambridge, Mass.: Harvard University Press, 1948. Pp. 353-70.

WOOLF, Rosemary. *The English Mystery Plays*. Berkeley: University of California Press, 1972.

WORMALD, Francis and C. E. WRIGHT. *The English Library before 1700*. London: Athlone Press, 1958.

WRIGHT, C. E. *English Vernacular Hands from the Twelfth to the Fifteenth Centuries*. Oxford: Clarendon Press, 1960.

YOUNG, Wilfred. "Noah and his Wife: A Note on Three English Miracle Plays", *Hermathena*, XC (1957), 17-32.

ZINN, Grover. "Hugh of St. Victor and the Ark of Noah: A New Look", *Church History*, XL (1971), 261-72.

ZUPKO, Ronald Edward. *A Dictionary of English Weights and Measures*. Madison, Wisc.: University of Wisconsin Press, 1968.

————. *British Weights and Measures: A History from Antiquity to the Seventeenth Century*. Madison: University of Wisconsin Press, 1977.

Achevé d'imprimer par les travailleurs
des ateliers Marquis Ltée de Montmagny
le 30 novembre 1978